ENCYCLOPEDIA OF MAJOR LEAGUE BASEBALL

NATIONAL LEAGUE

Other Books by Peter C. Bjarkman ("Dr. Baseball")

The Baseball Scrapbook
Encyclopedia of Major League Baseball Team Histories:
American League **(Editor)**
Encyclopedia of Major League Baseball Team Histories:
National League **(Editor)**
Baseball & the Game of Life: Stories for the Thinking Fan
(Editor)
Baseball & the Game of Ideas: Essays for the Serious Fan
(Editor)
The History of the NBA
The Brooklyn Dodgers
Baseball's Great Dynasties: The Dodgers
Baseball's Great Dynasties: The Reds
The Toronto Blue Jays
Roberto Clemente (juvenile)
Duke Snider (juvenile)
Ernie Banks (juvenile)
Warren Spahn (juvenile)

ENCYCLOPEDIA OF MAJOR LEAGUE BASEBALL

NATIONAL LEAGUE

TEAM HISTORIES

Edited by
Peter C. Bjarkman, Dr. Baseball

Updated and Revised Edition

Carroll & Graf Publishers/Richard Gallen
New York

Copyright © 1991 by Meckler Publishing
Additional material copyright © 1993 by Peter C. Bjarkman

Published by arrangement with Meckler Publishing, a division of Meckler
Corporation.

First Carroll & Graf/Richard Gallen edition 1993

Carroll & Graf Publishers, Inc.
260 Fifth Avenue
New York, NY 10001

Library of Congress Cataloging-in-Publication Data

Encyclopedia of major league baseball : National League team histories
    / edited by Peter C. Bjarkman.
        p.   cm.
    Rev. ed. of: Encyclopedia of major league baseball team histories.
National League.
    Includes bibliographical references.
    ISBN 0-88184-975-8 : $14.95
    1. National League of Professional Baseball Clubs—History.
2. National League of Professional Baseball Clubs—Records.
I. Bjarkman, Peter C.   II. Title: Encyclopedia of major league
baseball team histories.   National League.
GV875.A3E53   1993
796.357'64'0973—dc20   93-19998
                                                                CIP

Manufactured in the United States of America

In loving memory of Robert Bjarkman (1911–1984),
who first showed me the National League, and thus started
this lifetime obsession.

Contents

Acknowledgments

This book (like its companion American League volume) would never have seen the reality of print without the assistance and support of numerous people, all of whom gave selflessly of their time and talents. Most important, this National League volume derives from the dedicated labor of its 10 contributing authors, whose individual chapters bear their personal bylines. If each had not been quite so knowledgeable in the field of baseball history, quite so receptive to editorial suggestion, and quite so dedicated to meeting strict deadlines, this volume would never have taken its present shape or achieved its planned dimensions.

But the book represented here is also equally indebted to baseball fan and publisher Alan Meckler, who is most responsible for its original conception, and to Meckler Corporation Vice President Anthony Abbott, whose continued editorial support and technical expertise kept the work properly on target and firmly on schedule. Others made significant contributions along the way and thus merit acknowledgment by name, even if their specific contributions cannot be fully detailed here. This list includes: Ronnie Wilbur, Barbara Gregorich, Phil Passen, William Friday, Lonnie Wheeler, John S. Bowman, Lloyd Johnson, Tony Formo, Allen Hye, Rob Plapinger, Bernard Titowsky, Jim Martin of Von's Bookstore in West Lafayette, and William Humber and Alan Arthurs in Toronto. A very special debt of gratitude is also owed by the project editor to Bruce L. Prentice of the Canadian Baseball Hall of Fame, and to Brent Shyer of the Los Angeles Dodgers, as well as to John Thorn and Richard Puff at *Baseball Ink.* To you all, then, may all your summer days be glorious doubleheaders!

Peter C. Bjarkman

Introduction
Breaking Traditions in
the Senior Circuit

PETER C. BJARKMAN

Hi, neighbor, have a Gansett . . . DOUBLE-X 9 GAMES
AHEAD OF BABE'S SWAT PACE . . . Oh God, Look,
Slaughter's going home! C'mon, Pesky, throw the ball . . .
YAWKEY VOWS PENNANT . . . but the lowly A's, rising
for three runs in the eighth, ripped the Hose in the second
game . . . Hi, neighbor . . . SPLINTER DEFIES SHIFT
. . . and now trail the Yanks by two in the all-important
loss column . . . He's better than his brother Joe, Dominic
DiMaggio . . . RADATZ IN NINETEENTH RELIEF
STINT . . . and if Pesky takes the ball over his right shoulder,
I'm telling you Enos is dead . . ."
Roger Angell, The Summer Game

The national game of baseball—with its intense historical fabric and relentless fan appeal—is essentially all memory and nostalgia. For some, it is an incomparable catch by Willie Mays of a towering Vic Wertz blast, in the deepest centerfield recesses of the now-phantom Polo Grounds; for others, perhaps, the home run trot which made Bobby Thomson a lasting legend; or the indelible images of Jackie Robinson stealing home or Roberto Clemente rifling an accurate throw from the outfield depths of ancient Forbes Field. It may be memories as time-worn as a faded daguerreotype of Honus Wagner at the end of the century's first decade; or as recent, yet nonetheless mythical, as Andy Hawkins' incredible no-hitter loss which opened its final decade, the latter performed on the exact afternoon in the summer of 1990 when Chicago's venerable Comiskey Park celebrated its unprecedented 80th anniversary of major league action. Baseball is also the favorite local big-league nine, with whom we live and die, and from whom we take our hopes and expectations and even shape our personalities and our ultimate outlook on life. Chicago Cubs fans seem always to be unassailably cheerful and resigned (the old bleacherite version of the Cubs fan from the Ernie Banks era, at least, if not the yuppiefied hordes which now find it fashionable to crowd a renovated Wrigley

Field). New York Yankee boosters have always appeared to take life's small victories as their personal and preordained due. By starkest of contrasts, the Red Sox and Tigers faithful are painfully worn and subdued; they seem resigned victims to daily life's most outrageous and unwarranted slings and arrows.

The team with which Roger Angell—our nation's poet laureate of baseball—lives and dies in the passage which serves as chapter epigram is his beloved Boston Red Sox, personal favorite of millions of American baseball fans captivated by the perennial underdog and the inevitable last-minute loser. Angell captures here an essential facet of baseball mythology as well as an undeniable fact of its history: that thousands (even millions) of New Englanders relive summer after endless summer of passion and pain with this regional and national institution which masquerades as a professional baseball team. The Boston rooter remains, in fact, the perfect archetype for the nation's millions of entranced baseball fans, a hopeless baseball addict with "the gleam of hope in his eyes as he pumps gas under the blighted elms of a New Hampshire village, listening all the while to the unceasing ribbon of bad news by radio from Fenway Park" (Angell, 1972, 175–176).

The Boston Red Sox (like the Chicago Cubs, the Brooklyn Dodgers, or almost any other major league team past or present) are such popular fan favorites precisely because they are such loveable losers. Baseball is, after all, a game of uncompromising failure and defeat. Its popularity lies in the fact that as sporting spectacle it has such uncanny ability to assume a deeper meaning; and much of that meaning has to do with failure and loss and with the lessons of life's multiple and persistent small daily defeats. Even the best teams over the years play little better than .500 baseball; the game's greatest hitters are successful at their trade only little better than three in ten times; and baseball's most loveable losers win almost as much as do its proud champions. Look at the daily baseball standings at any point in the summer over a morning cup of coffee and you will find but the scantiest margin of victory and defeat separating league contenders from hopeless also-rans. Or look at the changes in team fortunes from season to season (remembering that there have been twenty-four divisional champions since the dawning of expansion play in 1961) and the same message of life's shifting fortunes is driven home. Any championship major league baseball team is fortunate to win one hundred games; and any laughing-stock stumblebum is equally unlikely to lose as many as one hundred. This translates into the refreshing fact that baseball's best teams lose at least one third of their contests, while the league's most inept entries are almost assured of winning a third of the time as well. There is always another game tomorrow; and hardly ever is there such a thing as an upset in baseball—each new day's play brings reasonable if not equal hope of victory for fans of each and every big league team.

Baseball is also played each and every day throughout the summer months, and this very repetitiveness of the sport gives its fans refurbished hope and works to level every fan's expectations. It is this very daily repetition which mollifies defeats and sustains the dream of deferred glory. This explains, also, why baseball so wisely clings to its time-worn tradition of one winner per league (albeit the divisional play in effect since 1969 now produces four such seasonal winners rather than two), why it avoids like a hopeless plague the sham of "playoffs" (like those of football and basketball) where nearly all teams qualify for post-season play. In the NBA or NFL there is never any cry from the multitudes of "wait-till-next-year" since nearly all teams (and thus all fans) enjoy their cheapened playoff season at the end of each yearly round. Thus the professional football system exploits a rampant public need for instant gratification and for "having it all now" as we wind down each repeated season; we all (if we are football fans at least) want to be "number one" and all need to be nothing short of winners at each and every outing; gone forever under such a system of cheapened victories is the rugged perseverance found when the faithful stoic rooter faces repeated yearly disappointment at the hands of the local ballclub. But baseball appeals precisely to such delayed gratification soothed by instructive defeat. Managerial legend Earl Weaver perhaps best stated this case for baseball, which so clearly runs against the modern grain: "This ain't football . . . we do this every day!" once mused the sage Earl of Baltimore (quoted in Boswell, 1982, 5).

But individual human failure as well as team failure is at the very heart and soul of the old ballgame—baseball is a truly humbling experience. Yaz (the incomparably heroic Yastrzemski), as Angell describes him, is indeed the great hero of Boston and of all New England with its teeming millions of fans, and yet the matchless Yaz would also die quite ignobly—to the dismay of all those same millions—in the two most crucial games of his glorious career. In pivotal games in 1975 (the World Series seventh game) and 1978 (the single-game pennant playoff with New York), it would be Yaz who would be struck down for the final out, when he might have instead delivered victory; these two games would remain career landmarks in which a brilliant Hall-of-Fame legacy was tarnished by searing memories of the hometown hero's collapse, while long-sought victory was seemingly at hand. Yet Yaz is in supreme company with his failures. The archetypal baseball story is, of course, the story of the Mighty Casey of Mudville. Casey, as every fan knows, goes down swinging, the victim of *hubris* and an overpowering fastball from the enemy hurler. Bobby Thomson and Bill Mazeroski are baseball oddities with their dramatic final-inning season-saving home run blasts, and not at all baseball archetypes. More typical of the game's poignant and ever-present disasters are Ralph Branca and Ralph Terry, the men who delivered those dates with destiny to the triumphant Thomson and Mazeroski. The far more typical scenario than the instant stardom of Thomson and Mazeroski is the Casey-like fate of Hall-of-Fame batsman Nap Lajoie—a lifetime .339 hitter—striking out with the bases loaded in the final game of the 1908 campaign against hated rival Ed "Big Train" Walsh, thus losing a hotly contest summer-long pennant race when his vaunted Louisville slugger could have delivered a championship victory.[1] Such failure is repeated time and again, as the most successful batsman hits safely less than 30% of the time and a pennant-winning team may win only 20% more of its games than a cellar-dweller. And the nature of baseball play makes failure utterly visible and totally unforgettable; the game is completely visible to all who watch, its errors and flawed plays are lucid and thus understandable, its statistics record for posterity each hit and error and these relentless historical records make failure into infamy and thus also into legend. What fan does not remember Bonehead Merkle as well as Bobby Thomson, Fred Snodgrass or Mickey Owen as well as Bill Mazeroski or Carlton Fisk?

In the passage cited above Angell vividly portrays the Red Sox and their mythic past, as this past lives on—a vivid collage of games lost and pennants blown—in the collective memories of all true Boston fans. Angell himself holds a special love for the Red Sox, brought on by geography and personal memories that establish the preferences of any baseball fan. As scholar William Palmer notes (in perhaps the best critical assessment of Angell's baseball prose), Angell is able (as often our best baseball writers are) to "distill the mythic history of the Red Sox into an almost Joycean stream of consciousness passage, reminiscent of Molly Bloom's soliloquy in *Ulysses*" (Palmer, 1986, 20). Typical sights and sounds of the ballpark intermingle here with the most infamous moment of Boston baseball history, Pesky holding the ball while Slaughter dashes to the plate with a 1946 World Series victory. For me it has been the Dodgers of Brooklyn and Los Angeles, rather than the junior circuit Red Sox of Boston, who have time and again provided such moments of bittersweet nostalgia. First there was Dick Sisler of the Phillies striking the telling blow in 1950, a moment every bit as devastating to a nine-year-old Dodgers diehard as the failed throw by Pesky was in Boston a few short seasons earlier. Then, of course, there was that more painful moment still, Thomson's never-to-be-forgotten "shot heard round the world" in 1951. But there was seemingly a new heartache every few autumns for those who bled

Dodgers' Blue in the 1950s and 1960s—Don Larsen embarrassing the "Boys of Summer" with a first World Series no-hitter (and a perfect game at that!), mighty Gil Hodges completely whitewashed by Yankee pitching in the Fall Classic of 1952, and Stan Williams inexcusably walking home the winning run with a playoff pennant on the line against the hated Giants out on the West Coast in 1962.

As Professor Palmer deftly demonstrates, the achievement of Angell as our greatest chronicler of the game in large measure lies, as well, in his ability to eloquently explain these preferences for teams like the American League Bosox and the National League Dodgers, and then to turn them into evaluative commentary on the historical essence of the game of baseball itself. Angell's sympathies lie clearly with those teams and those individual baseball heroes that reflect best the historical traditions of the game. These are teams that, foremost, play in historical stadiums, ballparks that recapture and reestablish baseball's finest traditions and most lucid memories. Baseball takes perhaps its purest joy from the knowledge that Clemens is pitching from precisely the same mound (or at least from the same geographical spot) where Babe Ruth earlier toiled, and that Ryne Sandberg takes his cuts from the same batter's box once worn dusty by Ernie Banks and Hack Wilson a quarter and half-century earlier. Baseball thus links generations of spectators—it is a tightly woven fabric of shared traditions and shared memories. And the favorite teams are thus inevitably those like the Red Sox and the Tigers, or in the senior circuit the lowly yet lovable Chicago Cubs—those unchangeable teams with undeniable histories, perceptible traditions, legendary players, and historic ballparks.

If the Boston Red Sox and Detroit Tigers reflect baseball's truest traditions, by acknowledging and fostering historical connections, newer teams (those expansion franchises which have flooded the majors since 1962) have little appeal for Angell—as they do for most fans who don't happen to live in those specific cities. George Brett is not nearly the bold epical baseball hero that Yaz is, despite quite similar talents and parallel career moments. This is precisely because the latter toiled before hordes of history-drenched fanatics in Fenway Park for the beloved Sox, while the former has played out his career for the fans in the heartland's Royals Stadium. George Brett labors for the expansion-era Kansas City Royals, a team whose history does not reach back even to the early days of Vietnam or the first waves of the British pop music invasion. Brett is thus the unfortunate victim of a baseball legacy featuring a ballpark and ballclub of thin "tradition" and little historical appeal.

But expansion teams are not the only ones devoid of the historical trappings on which baseball's appeal thrives. Some of the sport's oldest franchises have ruthlessly cut the bonds with sacred tradition and thus lost something of their appeal for the purists among baseball fans. One example is the transplanted Dodgers, now resident in the foothills of Los Angeles, who traded in the intimacy and tradition of Brooklyn's Ebbets Field for the lustre and polished image of West Coast movieland. It is O'Malley's plush new ball park—dubbed by baseball's Wordsworth as "O'Malley's Safeway"—as well as the Dodger owner's obvious ploys to discard the sacred "Dem Bums" image of Brooklyn (cultivating in its place a new image of wholesome All-American innocence and virtue) which most galls Angell. The Dodgers of Garvey, Cey, Sutton, and Lopes hardly matched the charm of Babe Herman, Dixie Walker, Casey Stengel, and the precious "Boys of Summer" outfits anointed for saintdom by Roger Kahn. This Dodgers attitude is contrasted by Angell with a certain respect for tradition and baseball heritage still maintained (although perhaps only in a matter of degree) by those other transplanted West Coast tenants, the Giants of Horace Stoneham and his successors. The Giants' own pact with the past seemingly remains, despite the fact that Stoneham's franchise also uprooted decades of tradition and migrated across the continent as well. In one especially poignant Angell scene (Angell, 1977, 260–279, also 336–339) the author visits Stoneham's private box during the last days before the aging owner was to retire from a game that had slowly passed him by. Stoneham (who lovingly recalls great Giant moments from Mathewson to Hubbell to Willie Mays) is contrasted in stark outline with new Giants owner Bud Herseth (a baseball newcomer who appreciates nothing of the team's history and confuses Carl Hubbell with Freddie Fitzsimmons and Lefty Grove with George Earnshaw).

Baseball's sense of tradition lives on not only in ancient franchises born at the turn of the century—the Giants, Phillies, Cardinals, Braves or Dodgers. A team does not necessarily have to be old to have tradition or to possess a mythology that enriches its history. The best example in all of baseball is perhaps the National League's New York Mets. The ineptitude of the earliest Polo Ground years, the legendary heroes (Spahn, Snider, Ashburn, Mays) who became mere mortals and diamond failures in the twilights of their careers, the passionate relationships between dedicated fans and their all-too-human heroes—these were the building blocks of irrepressible baseball nostalgia. In the expansion Mets, over a short period of seven cellar-dwelling summers (1962–1968) something of the lively spirit of the erstwhile Brooklyn Dodgers was reborn (see Angell, 1972, 45–80). Perhaps of all baseball's expansion franchises, the Mets enjoyed the singular good fortune of inheriting a rich and ready-made New York National League tradition. Yet whatever the role of Providence and Polo Grounds charm, it was a stroke of good fortune which the Mets franchise quickly parlayed into America's greatest overnight sports success story.

Other older teams, however, have often reflected the Dodgers' disregard for sustaining tradition. The Reds and Cardinals are prime examples of such a disturbing break with a proud past, first by abandoning historical homes (ancient urban ballparks), then by mirroring (in their plush new downtown stadiums) the surrounding city's flight from urban blight and the consequent rebuilding of tradition through a new American myth. William Palmer cites the notion articulated by D. H. Lawrence of the myth of an America which starts out old and then sloughs off ancient skin to move toward new dreams and new traditions (Palmer, 1986, 23–24). It is, of course, the perfect myth for the National League, baseball's elder circuit born only a decade after the Civil War, yet pioneering in every innovation and game-changing development of the modern baseball era, sloughing off the traditional coat of daytime baseball in quaint green-grass parks and replacing it with domes, plastic grass, night baseball, and the age of television sport. As a baseball fan as well as a scholar of the game, Roger Angell's own favor is never with such revisionist developments; he prefers the image of a decaying and older, history-steeped European tradition, rather than a young and traditionless American dream. His sympathies are always with historic American League teams like the Red Sox and Tigers, not with those perennial National League innovators and transplants like the Dodgers, Cardinals, and Reds, with whom the back-looking Red Sox and Tigers have so many times done fruitless World Series battle.

There seems to be an unsavory irony, if not an actual historical distortion in all this. After all, isn't the National League the "Senior" Circuit? Did it not begin first—at the outset of the final quarter of the nineteenth century—and then work to maintain and even flaunt its nineteenth-century agrarian roots? Didn't John J. McGraw represent the very essence of hoary tradition when refusing to play that upstart American League team from Boston in the second World Championship match of 1904?[2] And in the modern era doesn't the Junior Circuit continue to fly in the face of vaunted traditions by adopting such baseball perversions as the much-debated designated hitter? Or cast aside all that is stable in baseball balance with its odd-numbered divisions and unwieldy seven-team divisional schedules?

True enough, and yet any serious historical study suggests that it has always been the pioneering radicals entrenched as National Leaguers who have brought about baseball's greatest innovations and its most dramatic breaks with tradition. The American League is, after all, the home of such purveyors of staunch tradition as Philadelphia's

Connie Mack and Boston's Tom Yawkey; the National League, by starkest contrast, has been home to innovative prodigies like Walter F. O'Malley, Larry MacPhail, and Branch Rickey. It was the Nationals, lest we forget, who broke the greatest (and most unfortunate) tradition of all—the noxious color barrier.[3] It is the National League again that brought West Coast continental expansion, that was home to the first domed stadium and consequent birth of indoor baseball, that first adopted the unobtrusive inside chest protectors for its umpires and thus revolutionized the strike zone and (in the process) both the art of pitching and the science of batting. In more recent days, the new age of superstation television coverage for the national pastime is almost exclusively a National League phenomenon, shared by the Braves in Atlanta (WTBS), the Cubs in Chicago (WGN), and the Mets in New York (WWOR). The National League was home to most of the earliest astroturf fields, to most of the anathema multipurpose stadiums shared with National Football League tenants (the Cubs are the sole Senior Circuit holdout, playing in the kind of antiquated ballpark which Roger Angell so loves). And it was the National League once more, through the genius of Larry MacPhail, that pioneered and fostered that other great development of the modern age, the most significant of all the game's changes—nighttime baseball.

The volume that follows captures this chronicle of pioneering change which constitutes the history of National League baseball. Each franchise is treated in depth, and with each unfolding chapter comes the fascinating tale of ceaseless change and evolution that has enlivened our national pastime, that has kept it abreast with (and even in the vanguard of) a century of expansion and flux that is 20th-century America. And yet familiar elements of staid baseball tradition are also captured here as well. In addition to the pioneering innovations of front office showmen Rickey, MacPhail, Perini, and O'Malley, there is also the ennobling saga of legendary—even mythical—on-field diamond heroes. Jackie Robinson, Willie Mays, Rogers Hornsby, Stan Musial, Carl Hubbell, Mel Ott, Hank Aaron, Honus Wagner, Warren Spahn, Grover Cleveland Alexander, the Dean Brothers and other Gas House Gangsters, Duke Snider and the "Boys of Summer" alongside Sandy Koufax, Ernie Banks, and Pete Rose—all their exploits come again vividly to life in the chapters and pages that follow.

The summer of 1989 witnessed a baseball season marked by the shockingly bizarre and elevated by the truly memorable. The headline-grabbing Pete Rose betting scandal; beloved Commissioner Bart Giamatti's sudden tragic death; Dave Dravecky's dramatic and emotional comeback from a bout with cancer and then sudden collapse at season's end; one-handed hurler Jim Abbott's courageous big league debut;

the spree of lost no-hitters (followed dramatically in 1990 by the even more remarkable spree of successful ones); Nolan Ryan's impossible pitching milestones (continued as well in 1990 with a record sixth no-hitter and landmark 300th career victory); the miraculous turnaround from the doldrums of 1988 by the fledgling Baltimore Orioles, and the equally miraculous turnaround from May and June by the oncharging Toronto Blue Jays; the grand formal opening of the space-age Toronto SkyDome; the renewed imaginary threat of a World Series played in Canada, and the very real threat of a World Series cancelled by natural disaster. This was also the 113th consecutive year of play in the National League—baseball's true Senior Circuit—and it was a season which saw the Senior Circuit flaunt some of its finest baseball traditions.

Birth of the National League came about most fittingly in the very centennial year of the nation itself, yet the organization of the most stable confederation yet known by the infant sport would mark neither the birth of organized leagues nor of the game itself. When Chicago businessman William Ambrose Hulbert (aided by successful pitching star and future sporting goods magnate Al Spalding) led an organized movement in early 1876 to scrap the existing loose-knit National Association, and to bring stability to a fledgling sport with his newly envisioned confederation of ballclubs, few could guess the impact of what Hulbert was launching. Hulbert and Spalding (themselves heading up a powerful Chicago franchise) first persuaded clubs from St. Louis, Cincinnati, and Louisville to join them during a secret January 1876 meeting in Louisville. Then on February 2, 1876, they signed on teams from Boston, Hartford, Philadelphia, and New York, as well, and the eight-team National League of Professional Base Ball Clubs was born. The National League would be the first professional league to survive and prosper, and it is now in the second decade of its second century. One of its proudest franchises (the Dodgers) in 1990 celebrated its centennial season—and National League clubs in St. Louis, Philadelphia, Boston, and Cincinnati trace their roots back still further yet (and unlike the Dodgers and Giants, without any changes in city playing venue). As baseball's oldest professional league, the National League has long adopted the mantle of baseball's haughty tradition. Resistance to the designated hitter rule has made this touted image of baseball conservatism seem most appropriate for the National League, but it is indeed one of baseball's many rich ironies that the conservative image transplanted to this league has never been all that consistent with documented historical fact. While the American League, in point of truth, remains more the bastion of changelessness and respect for historical precedent (see my "Introduction" to the American League

volume for still more details), the National League has been throughout the second half of the present century, at least, the pioneering
league of true innovation and precipitous change.

It was within the long-toothed National League that we were to
witness the first true break with baseball's half-century changeless
geographical face. For it was the often-lowly Braves from Boston (a
team that finished over .500 only five times between 1917 and 1945 and
never finished above fourth place) who were so suddenly transplanted
from New England coastal roots into a virgin midwest. This considerable gamble was masterminded by pioneering ballclub owner and
construction-industry magnate Lou Perini in what was, for 1953, a
development unparalleled throughout a half-century of previous major league play. Perini's gambling spirit was soon rewarded, both in
the league standings and at the marketplace. This inspired story of
baseball's first ambitious expansion westward is eloquently told here
by Morris Eckhouse, who recounts fully the optimism and unbridled
successes surrounding the unprecedented transplanting of Boston's
erstwhile Braves into the cornbelt village of Milwaukee—an event
which truly marks the launching of the modern baseball era.

Baseball's first expansion all the way to the West Coast was also to
come from the National League, through the bold vision of Walter
F. O'Malley and his immensely popular Brooklyn Dodgers. While
O'Malley is today often enough decried by nostalgic traditionalists—
especially those residing in the borough of Brooklyn—the move certainly made great sense at the time. (A recent scholarly treatment
of O'Malley's hotly debated franchise transfer, by Professor Neil J.
Sullivan, has placed responsibility more squarely where it seemingly
belongs: onto local government maneuvering which occurred on both
sides of the American continent.) Perhaps more revolutionary was the
sudden dismantling of baseball's unfortunate racial barriers, another
by-product of Senior Circuit baseball and the precedent-breaking
Brooklyn Dodgers. Black baseball historian John Holway (1975, 1988)
today contends with studied good reason that Branch Rickey did not
actually "liberate" blacks in baseball terms (the now-popular percep-
tion), but in truth merely "bought" them, staffing his own Brooklyn
ballclub in the process with a few prime players in order to race to the
top of the league standings. And one most unfortunate result within
black communities themselves was that the hidden world of black
baseball (the once-thriving Negro Leagues and the baseball business
they brought into the black communities of Pittsburgh, Kansas City
and other metropolitan venues) soon enough wilted and died in the
bright national glare of Rickey's experiment.[4] But whatever his motives, Branch Rickey opened the door to major league baseball for
not only thousands of North American black ballplayers, but for the

hundreds of Latin American athletes who have so impacted the game in the past four decades as well. Branch Rickey and Walter F. O'Malley—in the short span of a decade and with the same proud franchise—made baseball's two most dramatic and historical front office moves under the bold banner of National League play and in the process changed the shape of baseball forever.

Launching of the first true full-scale major league expansion also came within the Senior Circuit in 1962, with the addition of two new franchises, the New York Metropolitans (immediately shortened to Mets in the nation's press) and the Houston Colt 45's (now Houston Astros), a maneuver brought on in large part by a threatened interloper (viz., the still-born Continental League) of that old National League innovator, Branch Rickey himself. While the American League did add teams in Washington (with the old District of Columbia franchise being relocated in Minneapolis) and Los Angeles a full season earlier, in 1961, the National League had already approved its own inevitable expansion by that date and thus had already forced the American League hand in the matter.

It was again in the National League that major league baseball saw its first artificially lighted night game, a 2–1 Cincinnati victory over Philadelphia at Crosley Field (then called Redland Field) on May 24th, 1935. The brainchild of innovative Cincinnati general manager Larry MacPhail (who had earlier experimented with nighttime play while owner of the Columbus minor league ballclub in 1930), this pioneering arc light contest had actually been scheduled an evening earlier but was victimized by inclement weather. The event was surrounded with much hoopla, including a ceremonial throwing of the electronic switch by President Franklin D. Roosevelt (from his office in the nation's capital) which flooded the Cincinnati park with near daylight from the 632 specially installed arc light lamps. Larry MacPhail soon moved on to rustic Brooklyn, where he again pioneered nighttime play in the nation's baseball capital of New York City. Unexpectedly, at the first Brooklyn night game, played on June 15, 1938, the evening's festivities would belong entirely to a heretofore ignored journeyman pitcher who was about to achieve instant and lasting immortality. Cincinnati's Johnny Vander Meer had entered that first Brooklyn night contest fresh off a surprising no-hitter against the Boston Braves four days earlier; by evening's end the usually wild Vandy had crafted an even more shocking second consecutive masterpiece (perhaps aided by the eerie glow of the electronically illuminated field). Vander Meer thus became the only hurler before or since (though Cincinnati teammate Ewell Blackwell would fall only a whisker short a season later) to toss two consecutive no-hit games on a big league diamond. The advent of nighttime baseball and the moment of glory for southpaw hurler Johnny Vander Meer—inexplicably yoked by the hand of fate—remain one of the most delectable moments in the long saga which is National League baseball history.

The first indoor play was also a National League innovation, with the ceremonious construction of Houston's Astrodome—originally christened as the Harris County Domed Stadium yet widely touted from the beginning as Houston's own "Eighth Wonder of the World." From its much celebrated debut (on April 9, 1965, to a standing-room-only crowd of 47,876 fans, for a pre-season exhibition between the Astros and New York Yankees), the Houston dome was a true architectural wonder—nine and a half acres of ballpark, an overhead roof rising 208 feet from the floor and measuring 642 feet across, containing 4,596 seven-foot skylights. But the first games in the new space-age venue proved a glaring flaw in stadium construction: penetrating glare from the transparent dome roof during daylight play made it virtually impossible to track fly balls. Painting the huge suspended roof quickly solved one problem and as quickly created another—natural grass wilted and browned without sunlight. By the second season of play the Monsanto Chemical Company had provided the answer and reshaped the face of baseball forever with its serviceable synthetic grass appropriately named Astroturf. A mere quarter century later the remarkable Houston Astrodome is now itself something of an endangered baseball relic, perhaps soon to pass into extinction. Yet this first of the nation's domed ballparks has left an enduring legacy. The present-day preponderance of artificial turf fields which have so changed baseball play has arisen in largest measure within that bastion of baseball innovation, the National League. Four summers after Astroturf would debut in Houston, Cincinnati's Riverfront Stadium inaugurated the all-synthetic field, that baseball anomaly with an uninterrupted plastic carpet including an all-plastic infield, with only dirt sliding squares cut around the three bases. Similar models were soon to follow in St. Louis, Pittsburgh, Philadelphia, and Montreal as well.

It is in light of Larry MacPhail's experiments with arc light baseball and Houston's bold experiment with covered sky and chemical grass that arguments grow thin concerning the purported American League destruction of baseball tradition. It is the Senior Circuit from at least the final years before World War II that has most radically altered America's game. Today any player or manager will likely agree that night baseball and the astroturf field have together moved baseball eons farther from its traditional style and appearance than has the advent of such a minor tinkering with the batting order as represented by the American League's much-maligned designated-hitter rule.

Additional firsts registered by the National League can be touted as well. There were the farm systems, innovated by Branch Rickey in St. Louis and Brooklyn during the 1930s and 1940s (the first full-fledged and extensive minor league systems), yet actually launched by the always innovative Cincinnati Reds franchise as early as 1887 (when the American Association Reds team exercised a working agreement with the Emporia, Kansas, minor league ballclub). There were protective batting helmets, again a Brooklyn team innovation under Rickey in 1941 (although used experimentally by a few individual Senior Circuit players like Roger Bresnahan of the New York Giants in 1905) and later made standard playing equipment during Mr. Rickey's so-journ in Pittsburgh (being adopted permanently by the Pirates in 1953). There was the first major league franchise in Canada, coming with the birth of Montreal's Expos in the expansion year of 1969, and as a result of Canada's entry into the big leagues, there were also the first league championship playoff games (1981) and first All-Star Game (1982) to be played outside of United States terra firma. And the Cincinnati National League franchise alone, as baseball's oldest and most innovative, is itself responsible for more big league "firsts" than perhaps all other ballclubs combined. A short list of such pioneer-ing efforts by the Cincinnati franchise (though not all of them during their National League years) would include: the first professional ballclub (Cincinnati's 1869 Red Stockings), the first ladies day (launched on afternoons when "Apollo of the Mound" Tony Mullane pitched home games at the Queen City's League Park in 1886), the first optioning of a player to the minors (1887) and first farm club (the same year), the first team to try air travel (1934), the first uniformed manager (playing manager Harry Wright of the Red Stockings in 1869), the first fielder's glove (donned by Red Stockings catcher Doug-las Allison in 1869) and first catcher's mitt (employed by Buck Ewing in 1890), the first team trainer (M.A. Frey in 1898), the game's original season ticket plan (1934), big league nighttime play (1935), and in 1970 the first all-synthetic field at Riverfront Stadium (cf. Bjarkman, *Baseball's Great Dynasties: The Reds,* 1991; and Wheeler and Baskin, *The Cincinnati Game,* 1988). It was Cincinnati baseball that also provided the first recorded double play (1869), the seventh-inning stretch (1869), the first switch-hitter (Brooklyn's Bob Ferguson in an 1870 contest against the touring Red Stockings), beat writer (Harry Millar who accompanied the Red Stockings on their historic 1869 eastern tour), doubleheader (1876), and contract holdout (by Charles Sweasy of the original Red Stockings in 1870). And it was in Cincinnati as well that baseball saw its first southpaw hurler (Bobby Mitchell in 1877), National League home run (by Chicago's Ross Barnes against the

Queen City nine in 1876) and no-hitter (thrown at the Red Stockings by Boston's Joe Borden in 1876), stolen base by sliding (by Reds outfielder Bob Addy in 1877), and uniform numbers (1883), as well as the first brother battery (bespectacled hurler Will White and his younger brother Deacon in 1878), left-handed third baseman (Hick Carpenter in 1879), ambidextrous pitcher (Tony Mullane in 1886), and squatting catcher (Buck Ewing in 1880).

These radical changes—especially West Coast play, nighttime baseball, divisional play, enclosed domed stadiums, artificial turf—were to have a far greater impact on the game's outward appearances and hidden strategies than that tiresome rallying point—the American League's designated-hitter rule. It is not the fact that pitchers no longer bat in the American League that has changed the game nearly so much as the fact that outfield contours no longer are irregular, infields no longer give bad hops, and weather conditions are now neutralized by plastic carpets which can be sponged dry and domes which can shut out all threatening inclement weather. Of the nation's old-style pre-1950's ballyards, only one remains in the National League (Wrigley Field) while five exist in American League cities (Chicago, Detroit, New York, Boston, Cleveland).

In the end, the National League draws its lasting fame as home to baseball's most glorious franchises, both old (the east coast Dodgers and Giants, or immediate post-war Cardinals and Reds) and new (the pace-setting expansion New York Mets of the past quarter-century). While the American League indeed features the most storied individual stars of each new baseball age (Ruth, Gehrig, Williams, DiMaggio, Cobb, Mantle, Yaz, Reggie, and Clemens), the Senior Circuit can lay claim to the most colorful among teams—the Gas House Cardinals; McGraw's Polo Ground Giants; Brooklyn's "Boys of Summer" as well as their unforgettable predecessors, Wilbert Robinson's Daffiness Dodgers of the 1930s; the incomparable and seemingly invincible Big Red Machine of Pete Rose, Johnny Bench, and Sparky Anderson. It is home grounds as well to baseball franchises which represent the newer late-20th-century American myth of rebirth and regeneration. Abandoning their decaying inner-city ballpark at the end of the 1960s, Cincinnati's Big Red Machine followed the lead of the rival Cardinals, who also fled their ancient home in Sportsman's Park for a plush and uniform Busch Stadium, while at the same time trading in a colorful "Gas House" image for that of baseball's first passionless and consummately professional corporate team. With this sloughing off of an age-old traditional image of bold but daffy diamond play, the faceless Cardinals and equally uniform Reds of the sixties and seventies—with their symmetrical riverfront stadia and clean-shaven uniform image—were thus community tools in the desperate campaigns of their supporting cities to revive old and dying urban centers. And in large measure both (as the dominant National League teams of the 1970s and 1980s) were highly successful in this new role for baseball—as community rallying point and welcomed urban savior.

The National League is the undisputed nesting place of the game's most stable franchises. Stan W. Carlson portrays the Cardinals, from Hornsby and Dean down to the modern age of Musial, Gibson, and the light-hitting, swift-running teams of Whitey Herzog—a franchise somehow always able to assure its legions of fans a string of ballclubs which are nothing less than colorful, competitive, and exciting. Paul D. Adomites, in turn, recaps the 20th-century Pittsburgh Pirates, an ill-starred franchise laboring much of the century in the league cellar, yet boasting some of baseball's most worthy hitters in each of the game's evolving epochs: Honus Wagner, Lloyd and Paul Waner, Ralph Kiner, Roberto Clemente, and Willie "Pops" Stargell. Rich Westcott recounts the inspired saga ("often last, but never dull") of Philadelphia's Phillies, who take their special brand of baseball pride in being the oldest continuous one-name, one-city franchise in all of baseball. While this stability in name and image which marks the Phillies franchise provides one of the national pastime's longest-suffering traditions of victory drought, it offers some of the game's richest moments of nostalgia as well. Art Ahrens, in turn, captures the bittersweet flavor which surrounds the Chicago Cubs, baseball's most loveable losers throughout the post-World War II era, and a team that has now suffered longer than any other without a pennant thrill or World Series appearance. Fred Stein lovingly weaves the true "tale of two cities" that comprises the Giants' rich and storied baseball epic, from Coogan's Bluff to Candlestick Park, and from the stoic grace of the Great Matty down to the flamboyance of Willie Mays and the charismatic charm of Orlando Cepeda and Juan Marichal. Morris Eckhouse tracks the vagabond Braves as they trek across a full century and take up residence in three starkly contrasting surroundings—Boston's Old-World New England charm, Milwaukee's raw midwestern enthusiasm, and Atlanta's rich southern hospitality—the first offering one of baseball's most noble historical traditions, the second providing its most immediate over-night financial success story, and the last its most pointed expansion-age failure.

Spliced between these other nostalgia-filled histories of major league baseball's more venerable century-old franchises are found the accounts of two almost mythical ballclubs. First comes the enchanting tale of the history-rich Dodgers—complete from "Dem Bums" of the pre-World War II Daffiness Era, through the glorious "Boys of Summer" epoch of the final decade in Ebbets Field, on to the emerging Hollywood image of wholesome and laid-back Southern California which today still predominates. Then enfolds the saga of Cincinnati's hometown Reds—from the 19th-century pioneering days of baseball's first professional team, the 1869 Red Stockings, to the innovative exploits of Larry MacPhail in the 1930s, the Crosley Field sluggers of the post-war era, and the successful and glamorous "Big Red Machine" of Rose, Morgan, and Bench. These latter two ballclubs, above all the others perhaps, reflect best the special ability of National League franchises down through the decades to balance precariously the high points of tradition with the most significant elements of inventiveness. In the "down home" midwest town of Cincinnati, baseball's oldest franchise lives on through the spirit of the modern era's most colorful and controversial player—Pete Rose. Out on the sunbaked West Coast, its loveable "Brooklyn Bums" have miraculously transmogrified over the past three decades into the epitome of a cleancut Southern California corporate image which, for all its drawbacks, characterizes the late twentieth-century professional sports franchise.

Also found here is the intriguing story of brand-new ballclubs with their new baseball traditions. John M. Carroll chronicles the coming of baseball in Texas and the Deep South with the birth of the Houston Astros (neé Colt .45s), destined to be baseball's first indoor team and soon a perennial bridesmaid of National League play as well. While no major league club has been born and nurtured in more of a circus-like atmosphere than that which has surrounded the Astros in the Bayou City, San Diego's Padres (David L. Porter) provide us with still another amusing tale of "baseball's comic soap opera" only infrequently conjoined to well-tempered baseball success. For the San Diego club is a team short on pennants (enjoying but one quickly aborted miracle year in 1984) and yet long on colorful if inconsistent play, and boasting in recent seasons one of the game's most unpredictable owners of the 1970s (Ray Kroc) alongside one of its most reliable if unsung hitters of the past decade (Tony Gwynn). In recounting New York Mets history, Pete Cava, by contrast, inherits baseball's true expansion success story; the team he describes is the one which staked an early claim as heir-apparent to the Dodgers in New York, and a new colorful counterpart in the Big Apple to the staid and often bland Yankees of the post-Stengel era. Finally, there is the unfolding account of the improbable birth of big league baseball in the neighboring nation of Canada and the bizarre franchise which such international expansion was to foster—a ballclub featuring bilingual scoreboards and French-language yearbooks, boasting the game's most gaudy uniforms, and marching to the carnival-like beat of a French-language stadium public address system in the cavernous and usually half-empty Stade Olympique. From the Mets and Astros who pioneered expansion at the outset of the 1960s, to the Padres and Expos who soon reflected its greatest pitfalls a decade later, the story of National League expansion-era baseball is one of the true showcase features of the Senior Circuit's long-standing commitment to baseball innovation.

Detailed in the pages that follow is a full century of National League baseball history. Whether one is partial to a single favored hometown team, or simply thrills at the game's great stars and events down through the decades, or perhaps relishes reliving baseball's cherished lost moments, the dedicated fan will find it all here in this ambitious history of the diamond sport's venerable Senior Circuit. Each and every baseball fan savors his own private and lengthy list of near-mythical baseball heroes, events, and images: Wee Willie Keeler "hittin' them where they ain't" in the game's infant days; the bowlegged yet agile Honus Wagner gobbling up countless grounders in the Pittsburgh infield at the dawning of the present century; Tinker to Evers to Chance; John McGraw glowering from the Giants dugout; Grover Alexander, flaunting his ungainly and shambling walk and almost comical in his undersized cap and oversized baggy uniform, striking out fearsome Tony Lazzeri in a crucial game of the 1926 World Series; Pepper Martin running wild in the Gas House days of St. Louis; Daffiness Dodgers stumbling into memorable traffic jams along the basepaths; slight Carl Hubbell of the Giants mowing down an All-Star lineup in New York's Polo Grounds; barrel-chested Hack Wilson exploiting his blacksmith arms to drive home another Chicago run; the high-legged mound actions of Boston's Warren Spahn and San Francisco's Juan Marichal, and the falling away delivery of the Cardinals' Bob Gibson; Willie Mays, cap flying, catching up to Vic Wertz' towering drive; the Amazin' Mets molded by Gil Hodges and still more amazing Whiz Kids inspired by Eddie Sawyer; the last minute longball heroics of Bobby Thomson and Bill Mazeroski at the opening and close of baseball's true Golden Decade; Johnny Bench redefining the position of catcher and Hank Aaron redefining the standard for home run excellence; Pete Rose dropping hit number 4,192 into the Cincinnati outfield and then dropping the hopes and dreams of his millions of fans as well. It is just these images which are the heart and soul of our American National Pastime, and which breathe life into the National League team histories which follow. It is these indelible historical images as well which capture for casual and diehard fans alike the pioneering baseball spirit of that oldest yet most revolutionary of baseball confederations—the redoubtable yet always revolutionary National League.

Notes

1. The story of Nap Lajoie's life-like re-enactment of the Casey Saga is incisively and dramatically retold by J. M. Murphy in his penetrating biography of the great dead-ball-era batting star. It would be an injustice to recount it in any words but those of the author himself (Murphy, 1988, 29):

On Saturday, Oct. 3, the White Sox, still very much in the battle, were the opposition again. Cleveland fans were in a frenzy in the wake of Joss' masterpiece. [Cleveland's ace had vaulted the Indians into pennant aspirations with a perfect game, hurled against rival Big Ed Walsh one day earlier.—*Editor's note.*] 20,729 paid to see the clash. But the normally impeccable Lajoie disappointed them. He dropped a ball thrown by catcher Harry Bemis, and opened the gates to a pair of Sox runs. After six, the Naps [the team was named for their popular player-manager.— *Editor's note.*] trailed, 3–1. In the 7th, George Perring doubled off Frank Smith. Pinch-hitting for Glenn Liebhardt, Nig Clark struck out. Josh Clarke singled through Lee Tannehill at third, but Perring was held at third. Bradley walked, filling the bases. Though he had pitched the day before, Ed Walsh was called from the bullpen. Hinchman grounded to Tannehill, who threw home, forcing Perring.

Lajoie stepped in. Bases filled. Two out. He already had two doubles in the game. The count went to 3-and–2. Three times, Walsh shook off Sullivan, who was calling for a curve. Walsh would explain later he thought a fast ball down the middle would catch Lajoie by surprise. It did. Larry didn't take his bat off his shoulder. Umpire Silk O'Loughlin screeched, "You're out!" The Naps finally lost, 3–2.

Ernest L. Thayer could not have crafted a finer scenario, nor painted a more gripping pitch-by-pitch description. Once again the mythic world of true diamond action proves to be every bit the parallel and the match for the best of inventive diamond fiction.

2. John McGraw stated his haughty position with an uncompromising clarity at the time: "There is nothing in the constitution or the playing rules of the National League which requires the victorious club to submit its championship honors to a contest with a victorious club in *a minor league*" [emphasis added by editor]. (cf. Bowman and Zoss, 1986, 30)

3. While American League franchises in Cleveland (with Larry Doby appearing in 1947) and St. Louis (Hank Thompson and Willard Brown) integrated immediately upon the heels of Rickey's Brooklyn experiment, those more entrenched Junior Circuit bastions of tradition in Boston, New York, and Detroit resisted the acceptance of black players for much of the next decade, with Yawkey's heel-dragging Red Sox not integrating until the eventual lineup appearance of journeyman Pumpsie Green in July 1959, a full dozen summers after Jackie Robinson's Brooklyn debut.

4. Further (and heretofore unpublished) evidence for the depth of Branch Rickey's obsessions with "the internal disorder of the Negro Leagues" and his desires to undercut Negro League baseball has now been provided in an excellent and revealing article by John Thorn and Jules Tygiel (1990). In addition to underscoring Mr. Rickey's hostilities toward the Negro League structure, Thorn and Tygiel provide startling new evidence that Rickey's original plan for Negro League raiding in 1945 was far more extensive than previously thought, and that Rickey had, in fact, intended to announce the signing of several more black stars (simultaneously with Robinson) before fate and politics intervened to cast Jackie Robinson alone into the integration limelight.

References

Angell, Roger. *The Summer Game.* New York: The Viking Press, 1972 (New York: Ballantine Books, 1984).

Angell, Roger. *Five Seasons: A Baseball Companion.* New York: Simon and Schuster, 1977 (New York: Popular Library, 1978).

Bjarkman, Peter C. *Baseball's Great Dynasties: The Reds.* New York and London: W.H. Smith (Gallery Books), 1991.

Boswell, Thomas. *How Life Imitates the World Series.* Garden City, New York: Doubleday and Company, 1982.

Bowman, John S. and Joel Zoss. *The National League.* London, England: Bison Books, 1986.

Holway, John B. *Voices from the Great Black Baseball Leagues.* New York: Dodd, Mead and Company, 1975.

Holway, John B. *Blackball Stars: Negro League Pioneers.* Westport, Ct.: Meckler Books, 1988.

Murphy, J. M. *Napoleon Lajoie: Modern Baseball's First Superstar.* Special Issue of *The National Pastime* (Volume 7:1, Spring 1988). Kansas City, Missouri: Society for American Baseball Research, 1988.

Palmer, William. "History, Tradition, and Hubris: The Baseball Universe of Roger Angell," *Journal of Popular Culture* 20:2 (Fall 1986), 17–28.

Sullivan, Neil J. *The Dodgers Move West.* New York and London: Oxford University Press, 1987.

Thorn, John and Jules Tygiel. "Jackie Robinson's Signing: The Real, Untold Story" in: *The National Pastime: A Review of Baseball History* 10 (1990), 7–12 (Society for American Baseball Research).

Wheeler, Lonnie and John Baskin. *The Cincinnati Game.* Wilmington, Ohio: Orange Frazer Press, 1988.

1

Boston Braves-Milwaukee Braves-Atlanta Braves
More Woes Than Wahoos For Baseball's Wanderers

MORRIS ECKHOUSE

Baseball being a game of tradition, it seems risky and foolish for any major league club to take its tradition lightly. Take the Braves (please)! As the very first National League team, the Braves were a fixture in Boston for 75 years, even though lean years outweighed great ones, especially during the twentieth century. By 1953, facing microscopic attendance, club owner Lou Perini needed little persuasion to abandon Boston and head to the greener pastures of Milwaukee. For a time, the baseball gods smiled on the Milwaukee Braves, but soon, as it always does, the test of lean times came again. And again, under new ownership, the Braves did what now came naturally. They moved, again taking the major leagues to uncharted territory in the Southland. The Atlanta Braves have seemingly inherited the wrath of those baseball gods. There have been a couple ups, mostly downs, two divisional titles that only set up the club for one-sided defeats in Championship Series play, and no World Series play. Entering the 1990s, the Atlanta Braves are the only National League team (including expansion entries in Montreal and San Diego) never to win a League Championship Series game. Perhaps the only question that remains is, "Where can the Braves go now?"

Like their American League counterpart, the Athletics, the Braves are the wanderers of the National League, the only Senior Circuit club to occupy three different cities since World War II. Like the A's the Braves have a noble tradition blurred by time and movement. Like the A's the Braves have had some truly terrible years, and some memorable times among baseball's elite. And like the A's the Braves have come to rest in a town that can look like a baseball mecca or a baseball Siberia from one season to the next. Specifically, the Braves were an exceptionally good team during the nineteenth century, an amazingly bad one from 1901 until the end of World War II, with one glorious exception, the World Champions of 1914. Another pennant, in 1948, was the final hurrah in Boston. Dwindling attendance made the Braves the first club in decades to change location. The Milwaukee Braves were a baseball phenomenon during 13 tumultuous seasons (1953–65) in Wisconsin.

From the dizzying heights of record attendance and a World Championship in 1957, the Milwaukee Braves tumbled clear across country, a modern baseball tragedy hastened by absentee ownership and greed. Though the reception did not match Milwaukee's, Atlanta welcomed major league baseball with open arms. A cast of stars were a worthy attraction and brought a divisional title to the South in 1969. Only once since has the Atlanta Braves organization built a club similarly worthy of support, the 1982–84 squad mapped by Joe Torre. The 1982 divisional title was the watershed year of club ownership by controversial cable television pioneer Ted Turner. Beyond the 1982 pennant, Turner far overshadowed his declining club as the Braves finished out the 1980s with a floundering team reminiscent of the worst Boston days.

Though commonly known as the Braves, the Boston club did not engage that nickname until 1912. First they were the Red Stockings, then the Reds, Red Caps, the Beaneaters, the Nationals, the Doves, and the Rustlers. Beaneaters gradually replaced the Red derivations. Cincinnati had also joined the N.L. in 1876 and the name Reds seemed their birthright. Nationals was a natural when competition from the American League began in 1901. The next nickname honored new owners George and John Dovey. They bought out the Triumvers in 1906. John Russell purchased the franchise in 1910 to begat the Rustlers. Finally, Braves was the chosen nickname of James Gaffney who bought the club in 1912.

Boston's National League club predated the league by five seasons. From 1871 to 1875 the Red Stockings were the cream of the National Association. Harry Wright and brother George, both eventual Hall of Famers, left Cincinnati, birthplace of professional baseball in 1869, and set up shop in New England. After a slow start in 1871 Manager Harry led his club to first place in four straight seasons. In all, Boston's N.A. club was 277–60 (.791) and featured Hall-of-Famers Jim O'Rourke, Al Spalding, and the Wright brothers. The Red Stockings then moved into the newly formed National League. Boston began N.L. play on April 22, 1876 in the first N.L. game ever played. Harry Wright's club defeated Philadelphia 6–5, yet over the course of 1876 gave little evidence that they would be the dominant N.L. team of the nineteenth century. The 1876 Red Stockings finished fourth, well behind the Chicago club led by former Boston pitcher Al Spalding.

Members of Boston's nineteenth-century N.L. ballclub read like a who's who of baseball greats. Joining O'Rourke and the Wrights were Dan Brouthers, John Clarkson, Jimmy Collins, Hugh Duffy, Billy

Hamilton, Joe Kelley, "King" Kelly, Tom McCarthy, "Kid" Nichols, and "Hoss" Radbourne. Ownership was led by a group called The Triumvers: Arthur Soden, James Billings, and William Conant. Soden was club president from 1877 to 1906. The Red Stockings closed out the 1870s with first-place finishes in 1877 and 1878, then second, five games behind Providence, in 1879.

After two poor club performances in 1880 and 1881 Harry and George Wright left Boston for Providence. The Red Stockings quickly recovered, jumping back to lead the N.L. in 1883 and finish second, to Providence, in 1884. The addition of Clarkson in 1888 sparked a second-place finish for Boston in 1889. There were two more major additions in 1890. Kid Nichols joined the pitching staff and Frank Selee replaced Jim Hart as manager.

Even with many defections to the Players League, Selee guided the 1890 Beaneaters to a respectable 76 wins. With the return of second baseman Joe Quinn, third baseman Billy Nash, and the addition of outfielder Harry Stovey and pitcher Harry Staley, Boston shot to the N.L. titles of 1891–93. The 1894 team finished third despite perhaps the greatest offense ever seen. After a three-year title run by Ned Hanlon's Baltimore Orioles, Boston regained top honors in 1897 and 1898. The greatest decade in Boston baseball history ended with a second-place finish to Hanlon's Brooklyn club in 1899. Selee guided Boston into competition with the new American League in 1901, then left to finish his managerial career with Chicago's Senior Circuit club from 1902 to mid-1905 when tuberculosis forced his retirement.[1]

Selee's departure ushered in an era for the Boston club as bad as the 1890s were great. Not until the arrival of another distinguished manager in 1913 was the team able to recapture any of its nineteenth-century magic.

As important as the loss of Selee, the competition provided by the Boston Red Sox, beginning in 1901, ranks as the biggest blow to the Beantown N.L. club in the early days of the twentieth century. Of all the two-franchise major league cities, the Boston experience most closely parallels St. Louis. The Braves were rarely much better, often much worse than the Boston Red Sox from 1901 on, as were the Browns to the Cardinals. The Sox had a pair of American League pennants in 1903 and 1904, then quickly recaptured local baseball dominance from the Miracle Braves with three pennants from 1915 to 1918. They also gained an important advantage by building Fenway Park in 1912, three years before the N.L. club entered its new facility. Despite a World Championship banner and a brand new stadium for the Braves in 1915, the Red Sox drew over 150,000 more fans that year to Fenway Park. Even when the Red Sox floundered, they were, for the most part, better financed and had more glittering stars, especially from the time Tom Yawkey purchased them in 1933. The battle for baseball supremacy in Boston seems one that the Braves were destined to lose.

During the first decade of American and National League competition the new team consistently out-performed the old one both on the field and at the ticket window. Only in 1906 and 1907, when Boston's teams finished eighth and seventh, respectively, were they on par. Even then, the Junior Circuit squad, playing at the Huntington Avenue Baseball Grounds, attracted more than twice as many fans as the more established Braves.

In 1910 Clifton Curtis set a N.L. standard with 18 straight defeats in his final 18 decisions. He ran out of time to match the single-season record of 19 straight set by rookie Bob Groom of Washington in 1909.

Back-to-back last-place finishes brought the era of the Doves to an end in 1910. Local ownership returned to the Boston Nationals in the persons of publishers Louis and George Page, insurance man Frederic Murphy, along with New York lawyer William Hepburn Russell, head of the syndicate that purchased the club from John Harris. Russell then purchased Fred Tenney's stock to lure him back as manager.

The return and farewell of Cy Young was the most memorable contribution to baseball by the newly nicknamed Rustlers in 1911. The Boston favorite was brought back mostly for publicity. He was 4–5 before retiring after a loss on October 6 in Brooklyn, his 313th defeat in 906 games against 511 wins, all major league records (a handful of modern day relief pitchers surpassed Young's total games pitched record). Second baseman Bill Sweeney hit safely in 31 straight games, breaking Bill Dahlen's mark of 1894 with a standard that would hold up until Tommy Holmes' 37-game streak in 1945. (Note however, that this record is disputed by research reported in the 1979 *Baseball Research Journal*, pages 24–31.) Otherwise, the Braves set a club record for futility with a .291 winning percentage (44–107) that would stand until the horrendous 1935 season. Though Earned Run Averages were not tabulated in the N.L. until the following season, modern research shows that the 1911 club slaughtered any existing modern (since 1901) record for club ERA with a dismal 5.08 mark. By comparison, the N.L.'s next highest ERA was the Cardinals' 3.68. Clifton Brown picked up his 18-game losing streak of 1910 with another five straight defeats to open the 1911 season, a seemingly untouchable record of 23 consecutive defeats. Of the 43 different players to suit up for the 1911 Braves, only catcher Hank Gowdy, acquired from the Giants in a mid-season trade with Al Bridwell for Buck Herzog and pitcher Lefty Tyler, would enjoy the rise to glory in 1914. Buster Brown (8–18), the workhorse and big loser in 1911, would die before the 1914 campaign.

On- and off-field troubles proved too much for owner Russell who died on November 25, 1911. John Montgomery Ward, organizer of the Brotherhood and Players League of 1890, led a syndicate, along with New Yorkers James Gaffney and John Carroll, that purchased the Braves in 1911. Ward brought along baseball expertise. Gaffney, a contractor connected to the powerful New York political machine of Tammany Hall, brought along his millions. Gaffney's most pressing needs were a new field manager and a new field. For a new nickname, Gaffney pulled from his roots as a member of New York's political machine, and its symbol became the symbol of the Boston club, the Braves. The crumbling South End Grounds were improved, while veteran catcher Johnny Kling was tabbed as player-manager.

For all the peripheral changes, the Braves remained awful. On June 20 the Giants set a modern (since 1901) N.L. record with 11 stolen bases against Boston in a 23–12 rout. Such play drove Ward to resign as club president on July 31 and sell his stock to Gaffney, his replacement as chief Brave. Bill Sweeney was, again, a lone on-field hero, finishing third in the league batting race and also in runs batted in, second in hits, fourth in total bases, and setting a modern major league record with 459 putouts. Sweeney teamed with five shortstops in 1912, the fifth being 20-year-old Walter James Vincent "Rabbit" Maranville.

Maranville played in 26 games for the 1912 Braves, embarking on a 23-year major league career. A future Hall of Famer, Rabbit was one of the most colorful characters in big-league history. Famed for his basket catches of pop flies, the small-statured infielder eventually became one of baseball's all-time leaders in games and seasons played.

For the first time since Al Buckenberger inherited Frank Selee's declining champions for the 1902–04 seasons, the Braves hired a non-playing manager. Gaffney knew the work of George Stallings as manager of the Yankees in 1909 and 1910. That Gaffney also feuded with Stallings' former boss, Frank Farrell, made the selection that much easier.

George Tweedy Stallings of Augusta, Georgia, played in just seven major league games, three while managing Philadelphia's N.L. team from 1897 to 1898. As first manager of the Detroit Tigers, Stallings led the A.L. club to third place in 1901. Returning to the majors with the New York Yankees in 1909, George had that club running second after 145 games in 1910 when he was replaced by Hal Chase. At Boston Stallings inherited a team that had recently allowed more runs than any big-league nine and also sported the worst fielding percentage. From 1909 to 1912 the Boston club lost 416 games, finished last each year, never within 50 games of first place. Preaching strong fundamentals and a positive attitude, Stallings went to work on the worst team in baseball. Among position players, second baseman Bill Sweeney was the only holdover starter from 1912. Rabbit Maranville won the shortstop position. The new manager juggled players around the rest of the diamond. Pitchers Otto Hess, Lefty Tyler, and Hub Perdue were joined by righthanders Dick Rudolph and Bill James. These five, and Walt Dickson, gave Boston its best pitching rotation in years. For the first time since 1902 the Boston staff had a combined ERA (3.19) lower than the total N.L. ERA (3.20), allowing more than one run less per game than in 1912. Stallings had effected a remarkable turnaround with few dramatic changes beyond the pitching staff. Improvements aside, Boston finished 31½ games out of first place.

In 1913 second base was a problem for the Braves. Sweeney committed a league-high 45 errors and his offense did not approach the spectacular 1912 campaign. Meanwhile, the Chicago Cubs felt that their player-manager, second baseman Johnny Evers, was not a suitable skipper. Evers had replaced Frank Chance in 1913 and guided Chicago to a second straight third-place finish. In February 1914 the Braves dealt Sweeney and cash to the Cubs for Evers. Managing aside, Evers was a great field general and a key member of the great Cubs teams of 1906–08 as the middle man in the fabled (Joe) Tinker to Evers to (Frank) Chance double-play combination. Stallings immediately made Evers captain of the Braves. Maranville remained at shortstop. Boss Schmidt provided power at first base. Charlie Deal opened the season at third base, but Red Smith, acquired from Brooklyn at mid-season, matched Schmidt on offense. Hank Gowdy, a minor leaguer in 1913, was ready for full-time big-league duty after earlier trials with the Giants and Braves. In the outfield only Joe Connolly, the team leader with nine home runs and a .306 batting average, saw day-in day-out action. Stallings compensated for weakness elsewhere by platooning Possum Whitted and Larry Gilbert in center field and Leslie Mann, Herb Moran, and Josh Devore in right. Stallings became one of the earliest proponents of platooning.[2]

For all of Stallings' genius, the Braves stumbled into the 1914 season looking more like the teams of 1909–12 than a club on the rise. After 22 games the Braves were 4–18. Evers and Maranville were ailing, the pitchers were struggling. In June and July trades brought Devore, Whitted, Smith, and outfielder Ted Cather to bolster the troops. By the fourth of July the Braves were playing .500 baseball, 22–22 since the terrible start, but still last and 15 games behind the first-place Giants. Heading West to Chicago, the Braves stopped off for an exhibition game against Buffalo's International League team on July 7. Expecting an easy victory, the Braves suffered an embarrassing 10–2 loss to the minor leaguers. Evers, for one, would later call that defeat in Buffalo the turning point in Boston's season.[3]

On July 19 Boston finally shook last place for good by sweeping a doubleheader from the Reds, giving the Braves nine wins in 12 games since the exhibition. The big-three pitchers, Rudolph, James, and Tyler, then pitched four shutouts in five games against the Pirates. Thanks to a nine-game winning streak, the Braves climbed into second place of the tightly bunched N.L. on August 10, setting the stage for three games with the Giants. Wins by Rudolph, against Rube Marguard, and James, against Jeff Tesreau, set the stage for a big third game between Tyler and Christy Mathewson. Both hurlers were masterful, posting goose-eggs for nine innings. Gowdy broke the 0–0 tie with a run-scoring triple, then scored himself. Though New York loaded the bases in the 10th, Tyler escaped with the shutout win. The three-game sweep left Boston 3½ games behind the Giants, now believers in "The Miracle Man" (Stallings) and his club after earlier laughing off Boston boasts that they would challenge for the pennant.

Before New York could recover, John McGraw's men had lost nine of 10 games. Still relying on great defense, timely hitting, and the pitching of James, Rudolph, and Tyler, the Braves moved into a tie for first place on August 23. When the Miracle Men opened a home stand on September 7, they took the field of Fenway Park. At the invitation of Red Sox owner Joe Lannin, the Braves would finish the season at the new park with a seating capacity about three times the size of South End Grounds. A Labor Day morning-afternoon doubleheader against the Giants brought over 70,000 fans out to the park. In the early game Mathewson took a 4–3 lead to the ninth inning. A single by Devore and a double by Herb Moran set the stage for Evers. "The Crab" delivered a looping single that scored both runners for another dramatic Boston victory. New York won the second game, but James' three-hitter the next day sent the Giants away in second place.

In a season of unexpected events, one of the most unexpected occurred on September 9. After an unsurprising first game, as Grover Cleveland Alexander defeated the Braves, George Davis took the hill for Boston against Philadelphia's Ben Tincup. Davis, who started just six games in 1914, baffled the Phillies with his spitball. Aside from three walks in the fifth inning, Davis was never threatened. The Williams College graduate and Harvard Law School student pitched a no-hitter. Now unstoppable, the Braves coasted through the remainder of September, clinching their amazing pennant on September 29 and finishing 10½ games ahead of the Giants. Since the fourth of July, Boston had gone 68–19 (.782) for the greatest finish in baseball history.

Having disposed of one of baseball's greatest teams, the Giants, the Braves were faced with a collection of Hall of Famers in Connie Mack's A.L. champion Philadelphia Athletics. Mack's club had prevented an all-Boston series, outdistancing the second-place Red Sox by 8½ games. The 1914 World Series began on October 9 at Shibe Park in Philadelphia, matching 27-game winner Rudolph against 17-game winner Chief Bender. The game was as mismatched as the records. Rudolph scattered five hits, Gowdy went three-for-three, and Maranville drove in three runs as the Braves surprised the A's with a 7–1 win. James, 26–7 during the regular season, topped Rudolph with a two-hitter in Game 2, but Eddie Plank of the A's matched up with eight shutout innings. In the Boston ninth, Deal reached second with a double when center fielder Amos Strunk lost his line drive in the sun. Deal stole third and scored on a two-out single by Mann. James finished with eight strikeouts and a 1–0 victory. Back in Boston 35,520 fans packed Fenway Park to see Tyler face Joe Bush for Game 3. Like the second game, the third was close, tied 2–2 after nine innings. In the 10th "Home Run" Frank Baker's bases-loaded single gave Philadelphia a 4–2 lead. Gowdy, fast becoming the offensive hero of the Series, belted a home run over center fielder Jimmy Walsh. Moran walked, took third on Evers' single, and scored the tying run on Connolly's fly out. James relieved Tyler and preserved the tie with two hitless innings. Bush continued on for the A's. In the 12th Gowdy led off again and doubled to left. Mann replaced Gowdy as a pinch runner and Larry Gilbert, batting for James, drew an intentional pass. When Moran bunted to the mound, Bush threw wildly past third baseman Baker. Mann scored, giving Boston a 5–4 win. The miracle was no longer in doubt.

The crowning moment in Boston Braves history came on October 13, 1914. The A's scratched out one run on seven hits against Rudolph. Boston broke a 1–1 tie in the fifth with two out. Rudolph singled, Moran doubled, and Evers singled home both runners with a drive off loser Bob Shawkey. With two out in the ninth, Stuffy McInnis grounded to third. Deal threw to Schmidt and the Boston Braves were World Champions of baseball.

In the first half-century of modern major league baseball (1901–1950) only two teams, the Braves and the Washington Senators, could boast of a sole World Championship season (the St. Louis Browns, Brooklyn Dodgers, and Philadelphia Phillies could boast of none). That, coupled with the miraculous way in which the Braves captured the brass ring, might explain the hold 1914 had over the Boston franchise. For the next three decades, seemingly every element of Braves baseball was viewed in terms of 1914. Even today the 1914

Braves remain one of the most discussed and written about of baseball clubs. As the Braves slipped back into the nether regions of the National League, there was little else for their fans to cling to but memories of 1914.

The 1914 World Champions entered a new home on August 18, 1915. Braves Field, home of the Braves from 1915 to 1952, must be considered one of the primary troublespots in the battle of Boston for local baseball fandom. When Gaffney purchased the club in 1912 it was playing in rundown South End Grounds, rebuilt in 1894 after a fire, during a game between the Beaneaters and Orioles on May 15, destroyed the initial, larger facility. Gaffney fixed up the old grounds while searching out a new home for the Braves. In 1914 Gaffney purchased Allston Golf Course on Commonwealth Avenue. Leaving the front of the lot for retail businesses, he began construction of a large, modern ballpark on the banks of the Charles River. His vision for the park was a traditional baseball fan's dream, so large that inside-the-park home runs could be hit to any field. Conversely, an over-the-fence home run would be near impossible. When Ty Cobb first saw Braves Field he said, "Nobody is ever going to hit a ball over those fences." As a pitchers' park, Braves Field de-emphasized the home run just as the circuit clout was about to become the biggest offensive weapon in baseball. Worse, the Braves never seemed as able to take advantage of the spacious park as well as their opponents. Finally, the size and location of Braves Field made for increasing problems in tough times. As baseball's biggest park when first built, the facility would appear empty and dank when small crowds turned out, which was often. Like any park built on a waterfront, Braves Field was susceptible to chilling winds off the Charles. Although Braves Field is fondly remembered by many still-loyal Boston Braves fans, it will never capture the imagination of baseball fans in the same way as Fenway Park.

In contrast to its nineteenth-century ballclub, the modern Boston Braves acquired many Hall of Famers, but almost all of them on the verge of retirement. As the Braves usually came to rest at or near the bottom of the N.L. standings, an inordinate number of baseball greats laid their careers to rest with the Boston Braves. Of the 22 Hall of Famers to play for the Boston Braves from 1902 to 1953, 14 of them played two seasons or less with the club, all but Bill McKechnie at the tail ends of their career. Unfortunately, with the exception of Maranville, who spent a decade with other clubs, the modern Boston Braves simply cannot claim any great superstar as truly their own. Warren Spahn had his greatest success in Milwaukee and Eddie Mathews played just one season for Boston.

The transient Hall of Famers were of little help to a franchise that suffered one of baseball's greatest dryspells for three decades beginning in 1917. Four times last, 11 times seventh, and never higher than fourth, the Braves gave their fans little to cheer about. Jim Tobin provided a single bright moment with a no-hitter against Brooklyn on April 27, 1944.

One of baseball's most captivating beauties is its symmetry. A correct baseball scorecard is perfectly balanced at the end of a game. Perfect balance is not always found in the histories of all major league clubs. In the case of the Braves, unparalleled success in the 1890s is balanced by unequalled failure in the twentieth century. The miracle season of 1914 is balanced by the unreasonably inept 1935 club. The genius of a Frank Selee is matched by the mismanagement of a Judge Fuchs. Even though the equation was broken up with two franchise shifts, the predominant success of the Milwaukee Braves is balanced with the primarily second-rate nature of the Atlanta Braves.

After fielding competitive clubs in 1915 and 1916, the bottom dropped out of the Braves in 1917. A shoulder injury finished James in 1915. Rudolph and Tyler were joined by Tom Hughes, 22-year-old lefty Art Nehf and Pat Ragan, purchased from Brooklyn in May. Hughes pitched a no-hitter against Pittsburgh on June 16, 1916. Evers, the oldest player on the club, suffered a severe ankle injury in 1915, an arm injury in 1916. Last on July 15, the 1915 Braves had another big finish, but still finished second to Philadelphia. The 1916 club finished a close third, despite the premature and unexpected retirement of first baseman Butch Schmidt. Better than average pitching could not compensate for poor hitting as it had in 1914. Jim Gaffney's tenure as owner of the Braves ended on January 8, 1916. Gaffney sold out to a syndicate of Boston bankers at a huge profit. On July 12, 1917 the playing sparkplug of the 1914 Braves was waived to the Phillies. Evers' departure officially ended a bright era in Braves history. For the next 30 years (1917–1946) the Braves finished no closer than within 12 games of first place, with the exception of 1933, going through 11 managers in the process.

Boston was hit hard by World War I. Gowdy was the first major league player to sign up for military service on June 2, 1917. Gowdy and Maranville were both sidelined by military duty in 1918. Even the addition of the amazing athlete Jim Thorpe, in 1919, could not create another miracle. Boston's most memorable game of 1919 took place on August 1. Nehf pitched all 21 innings of a marathon, 2–0 loss against Pittsburgh. The Braves were sold again, after three seasons of local ownership, to a New York group led by George Washington Grant. Rumors of the day had Grant a pawn of Giants manager John McGraw. Those rumors were accelerated by a deal that sent Nehf to New York for four players and cash. Nehf helped the Giants win four consecutive pennants from 1921 to 1924.

During the 1920s, when most of baseball was rejoicing at the advent of the lively ball, the Braves suffered what might be the worst single decade for any big-league team. In those 10 years the Braves lost 928 games and managed a miserable .394 winning percentage, even worse than the 1900–1909 period (877 losses and a .401 winning percentage). Cavernous Braves Field was not the place to be when the home run took hold. The scattered highlights of the decade included an unforgettable contest on May 1, 1920. Joe Oeschger, one of the pitchers acquired for Nehf, squared off against Brooklyn's Leon Cadore. These strong, young righthanders battled for 26 innings to a 1–1 stalemate in the longest major league game (by innings) ever played. On May 3 Boston and Brooklyn again struggled through 19 innings before the Braves prevailed 2–1. In between, Brooklyn suffered a 13-inning home loss to the Phils.

Aware that Boston's new management did not have the financial resources to build a winner, Stallings resigned in November. His former coach, Fred Mitchell, became the new skipper. While one veteran of the 1914 champions returned, another left. Rabbit Maranville was traded to the Pirates for outfielders Billy Southworth and Fred Nicholson, shortstop Walt Barbare, and cash. All three additions batted over .300 and helped Boston score almost 200 more runs than in 1920. With Oeschger winning 20 games in 1921, Mitchell's Braves finished fourth. In 1922 Southworth was hurt, Barbare and Nicholson slumped dramatically. Oeschger lost 21 games, and the Braves slid to last place. Grant had had his fill of the Braves and the club went through another ownership change in 1923.

A colorful, if unsuccessful, era in Braves baseball began February 11, 1923, with the sale of the team. Heading up the new ownership was Judge Emil Fuchs, attorney for the Giants, and former New York pitching ace Christy Mathewson. Fuchs was basically a fan and agreed to the purchase only on the condition that Matty would run the club. "Big Six" had been undergoing medical treatment since being gassed during World War I. Mathewson assured Fuchs he was ready and able to guide the Braves. With Mathewson to provide the baseball expertise, Fuchs could concentrate on promotions. He initiated Ladies' Day and a Knot Hole Gang for young fans. He gained approval for Sunday baseball and initiated radio broadcasts. Attendance fluctuated, but basically remained terrible. The 1923 Braves barely moved up a notch to seventh place. Shortstop Ernie Padgett provided a highlight with the first unassisted triple play in N.L. history on October 6.

Boston acquired its next manager in a trade with the Giants on November 12. New York sent World Series hero Casey Stengel, Bill Cunningham, and Dave Bancroft to the Braves for Southworth and Oeschger. Shortstop Bancroft became player-manager. The luck of the 1920s Braves is evidenced by a tragic accident in February 1924. Tony Boeckel, popular and successful third baseman of the Braves, was involved in an automobile accident. Boeckel emerged from the wreck unhurt. While dusting himself off in the street, Boeckel was hit and killed by another vehicle. Bancroft was ill much of 1924 and the Braves finished last again. With a healthy Bancroft batting .319 and new first baseman Dick Burrus, a one-year wonder, batting .340, the 1925 Braves jumped to fifth place. Catcher Frank Snyder made a liar of Ty Cobb by hitting a home run out of Braves Field, over the left-field fence on May 28. Stengel played 12 games for Boston, then was sent to manage a farm club at Worcester. Fuchs, however, made the mistake of naming Stengel club president as well as player-manager. In 1926 Casey released himself as player-manager so he could become player-manager of the Toledo Mud Hens.

Boston suffered another blow on October 7, 1925 when Mathewson died. Matty's contribution was limited by his frequent medical visits, but his death left no one in Boston's front office with baseball expertise. Outfielder Ed Brown, acquired in a trade from Brooklyn, led the N.L. with 201 hits in 1926 and set a league record by playing in his 534th consecutive game in 1927. Only the Phillies kept the 1926 and 1927 Braves out of last place. Dick Rudolph ended 15 years with the club and Bancroft sold himself to the Dodgers.

No sooner was Jack Slattery named manager for the 1928 Braves than competition arrived on January 10, 1928. Boston obtained the peerless hitter Rogers Hornsby from the Giants for Shanty Hogan and Jimmy Welsh. Hornsby's attitude was as volatile as his bat and probably the biggest reason New York traded him. He had been manager of the 1926 World Champion St. Louis Cardinals, then traded to the Giants for Frank Frisch and Jimmy Ring. Rumors that "the Rajah" wanted to succeed McGraw as New York manager were also cited as a reason for the trade. Friction between Slattery and Hornsby began with the start of spring training. Just 31 games into the regular season, Slattery, a former college coach, turned in his resignation. Captain Hornsby became Manager Hornsby. Concentrating on hitting, not managing, Hornsby became Boston's first N.L. batting champ since Hugh Duffy hit .440 in 1894. Rogers' .387 batting average was 60 points higher than Boston's winning percentage. Another great hitter, George Sisler, batted .340 after being purchased from Washington in May, but Philadelphia was again the only club between the Braves and last place.

Going from the sublime to the absurd, Judge Fuchs replaced Hornsby with himself as manager of the 1929 Braves. Hornsby was traded to the Cubs for five players and a much needed $200,000. Despite the aid of coach Johnny Evers, Fuchs was a disaster as a manager. Not even the return of Rabbit Maranville and Hawk Gowdy, evoking memories of 1914, could keep the Braves out of the basement.

The debacle of 1929 may have spurred Fuchs to his best decision as president of the Braves. The Braves went from one extreme to another as Fuchs replaced himself with two-time pennant-winning manager Bill McKechnie. A former Brave himself, McKechnie had guided the Pirates to a World Championship in 1925 and the Cardinals to the 1928 N.L. flag. Exiled to the minors after St. Louis was buried by the Yankees in the 1928 World Series, Deacon Bill was brought back to replace Billy Southworth before the 1929 season ended. Where the Cards would offer no manager more than a one-year contract, Boston was glad to sign McKechnie to a three-year deal. Bill thus became the first of two Hall of Fame managers that would guide the Boston club over 14 consecutive seasons without coming remotely close to a championship. McKechnie did bring improvement and re-spectability, including first-division finishes in 1933 and 1934 with the most competitive Braves clubs since the days of George Stallings.

Improved pitching and fielding helped, as did the first bonafide star in years that could legitimately be called a Boston Brave. In a transaction loosely connected to the deal sending Hornsby to the Cubs, Boston acquired a power-hitting outfielder from Chicago's farm club at Los Angeles. In Wally Berger, the Braves finally had a slugger around which to build an offense. Lopping some 13 feet off the distance from home plate to the left-field fence at Braves Field helped the club hit a record 66 home runs, still fewest in the N.L., in 1930. Berger hit 38 homers himself, setting a major league record for most four-baggers by a rookie. The 24-year-old Berger was an exception on one of the older teams in baseball, led by 37-year-old Sisler and 38-year-old Maranville, McKechnie, Berger, and company led the 1930 Braves to an improvement of 14 wins and two positions up to sixth place, plus a club record attendance of 464,835 fans at Braves Field. Boston slumped back to seventh in 1931, then regained fifth in 1932. Maranville moved to second base, but improved pitching was the big difference. Only the Cubs had a better team ERA than Boston in 1932. Ed Brandt, Bob Brown, Ben Cantwell, Huck Betts, and Tom Zachary gave Boston five hurlers with 10 or more wins and a break-even record (77–77) for the first time since 1921. At 13 games behind the N.L. champion Cubs, the Braves were closer to first than at any time since 1916. On Sunday, May 22 a Braves Field record crowd of 47,123 fans saw a twin-bill against the Phillies. On July 4 the Braves were second, but soon returned to the second division.

They continued to improve in 1933. The Braves held second place in August and had Boston fans in a frenzy unseen since 1914. By 1933 the Braves were clearly, if briefly, Boston's favorite baseball team. The biggest surge toward a new home attendance record came in a showdown series against the Giants at the end of August. Over 150,000 fans came out for five games. Boston won the first as Berger homered and Cantwell pitched, but New York won the next three. The series concluded with a 4–4 tie, leaving the Braves eight games out of first. By the end of a long Western road trip, Boston was fifth. On the final day of the season Berger was sick and in street clothes as Boston faced Philadelphia, but got into uniform hoping for one chance to pinch hit. The chance came in the seventh with the bases loaded. On a two-strike pitch Wally drove a grand slam into the left-field bleachers. A 4–1 win put Boston into fourth place, its only first-division finish since 1921. The homer was number 27 for Berger, Boston's representative in the first All-Star Game. Cantwell won 20 games, Brandt added 18 wins, Frankhouse 16.

That Boston finished fourth again in 1934 is a tribute to McKechnie. The 42-year-old Maranville, the Peter Pan of baseball, suffered a broken leg during spring training, ending his playing career. Cantwell won just five games, as Frankhouse, Brandt, and 37-year-old Huck Betts led the pitching staff. Even without the help of Maranville and Betts, Boston won five more games than they lost.

From 1930 to 1934 the Braves had struggled back to respectability. Attendance was up and the club, while still several players away from pennant contention, was competitive. Then two events again turned the tide of Boston baseball. First, in February 1933, 30-year-old Tom Yawkey bought the Red Sox from Bob Quinn. Almost two years to the day later, in February 1935, the Braves corrected a Boston error made by the Red Sox 15 years earlier that many feel has haunted that franchise ever since.

The biggest change in the makeup of the Braves from 1934 to 1935 was the addition of the greatest player and drawing card in the history of the game. The 1935 addition of one George Herman "Babe" Ruth, however, was actually neither a boon to attendance nor an on-field baseball success. A bloated shell of one-time greatness at age 40, Ruth came to Boston with the idea of becoming a manager or executive. His Boston contract titled Ruth as assistant manager and vice president, though the Braves had no thought of making Ruth manager or an active member of the front office, but simply wanted to use Ruth as a promotional tool. Perhaps the baseball gods were irked into turning a run-of-the-mill team into the worst in modern, pre-expansion, baseball history. Ruth hit a home run in his first game with the Braves and a climatic three on May 25 at Pittsburgh, including the 714th of his career over the right-field stands at Forbes Field. On June 2, however, an embittered Ruth, aware he was a sideshow attraction for the Braves, angrily announced his retirement. The 1935 Braves could scrape up just 38 wins and lost 115 times, more than 75 percent of their games. Since 1900, no N.L. team has won a smaller percentage of its games than the 1935 Braves.[4]

The Babe Ruth fiasco was the last gasp of the colorful Fuchs era of Braves baseball. The Judge had tried everything, even trying to get baseball's permission to run dog races at night at Braves Field. The rental income from the races might have kept the Judge in business, but the other Judge, baseball commissioner Kennesaw Landis, ruled against dog racing. The disaster of 1935 left Fuchs with no choice but to completely surrender ownership of the Braves. Actually, Fuchs owned less and less of the club over the years, selling off club interest for operating capital. He was also leasing Braves Field. The National League had bailed out Fuchs by taking over the ballpark lease, then subletting the property back to Fuchs. While taking over the lease, the league had demanded that Fuchs find a buyer for the club.

Boston businessman Charles F. Adams, owner of the Boston Bruins of the National Hockey League, took control of the Braves on August 1, 1935. Adams certainly had the business acumen to make the Braves a success. Unfortunately a conflict of interest, one which would later keep other sportsmen out of baseball, necessitated different ownership. Adams was part of the syndicate that owned the successful Suffolk Downs race track. Just as Judge Landis would not hear of dog racing connected with major league baseball, he absolutely refused to have a race track owner running a major league club. Rather than gamble on the Braves, Adams decided to get out of baseball. Following the 1935 season, Bob Quinn thus became owner of the Braves.

Just as the Braves seemed to be taking charge of the baseball situation in Boston, Yawkey's purchase of the Red Sox and the disastrous Braves' season of 1935 dealt a double blow to the N.L. club's fortunes. From 1930 to 1933 the Braves had significantly outplayed and outdrawn their crosstown rivals. Then Yawkey began pouring his money into the Red Sox and Fuchs simply did not have the resources to keep up. The Red Sox began drawing two to three times as many fans to Fenway Park and returned to pennant contention for the first time since they traded Ruth. Enter Bob Quinn, a fabled name in baseball history, associated with the game since the turn of the century as a successful minor league administrator. He was business manager of the St. Louis Browns from 1917 to 1922, president of the Red Sox from 1923 to 1932, head of the Sox' Reading farm club in 1933 after selling the big-league club to Yawkey and Eddie Collins. Since 1934 Quinn had been business manager of the Dodgers. Unfortunately, at the big-league level, Honest Bob Quinn was associated with losing baseball. Aside from a second-place finish by the 1922 Browns, one game behind the Yankees, none of Quinn's major league clubs came remotely close to championship laurels. His Red Sox were even worse than the Braves. In his 10 years with the franchise the Red Sox were 544–988 (.355) with eight last-place finishes and were crippled by the same lack of finances that plagued the Braves. Coming back to Boston represented a chance for Quinn to reverse his destiny and make up for his embarrassing failure across town. Disregarding the Braves' increasingly distant proud past, Quinn sought to start with a clean slate. Among his first moves, Quinn initiated a fan poll to choose a new name for the Braves.

Quinn reasoned that whatever glory rested in Braves' history was overshadowed by the recent and consistent failures of the franchise and so justified changing the club nickname. Actually, he was correct in associating the nickname "Braves" with a losing tradition. Since the club did not become known as the Braves until 1912, the 1914 championship was the only true bright spot in "Braves" history. After pouring over hundreds of suggestions, Quinn chose to call his club the Boston Bees. In retrospect, Bees was about the worst choice possible for the Boston club. Not only did the change incur the wrath of the old-timers and traditionalists, it did nothing to spark the imagination of others. As the Bees, the club could not very well play in Braves Field. The park was renamed National League Field. In all, the name change and subsequent six years of the Boston Bees rank as another embarrassing episode in franchise history. Quinn made a smarter and more popular decision by retaining McKechnie as manager.

National League Field was again altered and hosted the 1936 All-Star Game. The N.L. won its first mid-summer classic in four tries, but a record-low 25,556 fans attended the contest.

Minus the tribulations of 1935, Boston rose back to its 1934 level with a sixth-place finish. The addition of catcher Al Lopez was a help. With a pair of 20-game winners, Jim Turner and Lou Fette, in 1937, the Bees finished fifth. A fading Wally Berger was traded to the Giants in June. So little was thought of the talent on the club that McKechnie was given Manager of the Year honors for keeping the Bees competitive. Bill ended an eight-year stint in Boston and moved on to Cincinnati where he would win N.L. pennants in 1939 and 1940.

Boston hired its second straight future Hall of Fame manager when Casey Stengel returned to the N.L. club in 1938. Bob Quinn also made Stengel, out of baseball in 1937, a part owner. Other than being Hall of Famers, there were few similarities between McKechnie and Stengel. Casey enhanced his image as baseball's greatest clown, but the underfinanced Bees sank back to the depths of the Senior Circuit. The progress made by McKechnie was undone by the tandem of Stengel and Quinn. Fette and Turner combined for just 25 wins in 1938 though Boston ranked fifth again. On June 11 Boston suffered the first of Johnny Vander Meer's back-to-back no-hitters. Max West, a rookie in 1938, provided some precious offense. His home run won the 1940 All-Star Game for the N.L., but his career was curtailed by World War II.

Stengel displayed none of the genius that would lead the New York Yankees to 10 pennants in 12 seasons from 1949 to 1960. Casey's Bees/Braves were almost the complete opposite of his Yankees, finishing below .500 in all but the first of his six terms as manager of the Boston club. From 1939 to 1945 the Braves could not come within 30 games of first place. Ernie Lombardi, one of those Hall of Famers finishing up in Boston, took a batting title with a .330 mark in 1942 and then got traded to the Giants after being a holdout in 1943. Pitcher Jim Tobin, who would hurl a no-hitter in 1944, hit three home runs against the Cubs on May 13. Tobin hit six homers in 1942, tying the record for pitchers. Paul Waner, another fading star headed to the Hall of Fame, also got his 3,000th hit in a Boston uniform. After four straight seventh-place finishes, the Braves made a slight climb to sixth in 1943, despite losing their manager for two months. Just before Opening Day, Casey was hit by a car and suffered a broken leg. Attendance was terrible and the club seemed even worse off than the one purchased by Quinn in 1935. Enter the "Three Little Steam Shovels."

Lou Perini, Guido Rugo, and Joseph Maney, all minority stockholders in the Braves, were tired of constant cash calls to keep the club afloat. In January 1944 the three Boston contractors purchased the club. Thanks to wartime construction, Perini, Rugo, and Maney were the best financed owners of the Braves in years. They also had the good sense to stick to the business end of the operation and find baseball men to run the team. As the search began, Stengel was fired, replaced by coach Bob Coleman. Coleman could fashion no improvement and was replaced by coach Del Bissonette during the 1945 campaign. Tommy Holmes, swiped from the Yankees farm system in 1942, had a brilliant season (28, 117, .352), leading the league in home runs, hits, doubles, and earning Most Valuable Player honors from *The Sporting News*. Holmes' heroics aside, Boston finished sixth again. Bob Quinn was shoved over into player development while his son, John, was made general manager.

John Quinn believed Billy Southworth was the best manager available. Since taking over the Cardinals during the 1940 season, the former Brave had finished first three times and second twice. When Perini opened his checkbook, Southworth came to Boston.

For the first of two times in two cities, Perini and company were in the right place. Baseball was about to enjoy a post-war boom with record attendance throughout both leagues. The Braves were ready to capitalize. Though only the Cubs waited longer for home night games among N.L. clubs than Boston, the Braves beat the Red Sox to night baseball by over a year. Braves Field hosted its first night game on May 11, 1946. By season's end, Braves attendance had more than doubled to almost 970,000. And, led by public relations chief Billy Sullivan (later owner of the New England Patriots of the National Football League), the Braves were at the forefront of promotional advances. Boston led the way with a sketch book (forerunner of the yearbooks published by most teams) and a promotional film about the team, in addition to a wide variety of game promotions at Braves Field.

Billy Southworth was a radical departure from Stengel, a throwback to Bill McKechnie. The fun-loving Braves might be a little more disciplined, but they would start providing more fun for their long-suffering fans. The 1946 Braves not only added Southworth, but also the two pitchers forever linked in baseball lore. Johnny Sain and Warren Spahn had both pitched briefly for Boston in 1942, then spent three full years in military service. Sain had a brilliant 1946 season (20–14, 2.21 ERA). Spahn, spending part of the year in the service, finished with a 8–5 record. Helped by veterans Mort Cooper and Bill Lee, Boston improved by 14 games and returned to fourth place.

John Quinn made his best trade on September 30, 1946. Aging star Billy Herman was shipped to Pittsburgh with three other players for third baseman Bob Elliott and catcher Hank Camelli. Pittsburgh's mistake (they wanted Herman as player-manager) was Boston's break. The 30-year-old Elliott was a first-rate run producer. Across the diamond, rookie first baseman Earl Torgeson complemented Elliott. Spahn and Sain both won 21 games; Red Barrett, purchased from the Cardinals, added 11 wins; and Bill Voiselle, added in a trade for Mort Cooper in June, rounded out the starting staff. The 1947 Braves finished third, eight games from first, their best effort in either column in 31 years. Elliott was voted N.L. Most Valuable Player and led the club to the top of the league batting average standings for the first time since 1877.[5]

Trader John Quinn, with Perini's money, kept dealing after the 1947 season. First, outfielder Jim Russell, catcher Bill Salkeld, and pitcher Al Lyons were acquired from Pittsburgh. Outfielder Jeff Heath was purchased from the Browns. Second baseman Bobby Sturgeon was obtained from the Cubs. The biggest trade came on March 6, 1948. Quinn sent second baseman Bama Rowell and first baseman Ray Sanders (whom he re-purchased in April) to the Dodgers for second baseman Eddie Stanky. Stanky, usually referred to as a player who could do nothing but beat you, teamed with rookie Alvin Dark to give Boston its best keystone combination since Evers and Maranville.

Using the poetic formula, "Spahn and Sain and pray for rain" whenever possible, the Braves charged to their first pennant in 34 years. Sain was brilliant (24–15, 2.60) as Boston led all N.L. teams in ERA. Spahn won 15 games, Voiselle 13, and rookie Vern Bickford 11. Barrett, rookie Bobby Hogue, and midseason pick-up Nels Potter headed a strong bullpen. Boston also led the N.L. in team batting for the second straight season. Dark earned Rookie of the Year honors and Holmes finished third in the batting race. Stanky suffered a broken ankle on July 8 and played just 66 games, but Sibby Sisti (the greatest name in baseball history) filled in adequately. Heath also suffered a broken ankle, but only after batting .319 with 20 homers and 79 RBIs, second only to Elliott in the power figures. After a slow start, Boston surged into first place in early June, fought off threats by the Cardinals and Dodgers in August, and finished 6½ games ahead of second-place St. Louis. Braves fans responded with a record home attendance of 1,455,439. Baseball was never better in Boston. Almost 100,000 more fans packed Fenway Park as well during the tight A.L. pennant race. Hopes of an all-Boston World Series were dashed when the "Braves" of the A.L., the Cleveland Indians, beat the Red Sox in a one-game playoff at Fenway Park.

Braves Field played host to its first World Series as the N.L. park (the Red Sox had used the field during the 1915 and 1916 World Series) on October 6. Sain faced Cleveland's dominant fastballing pitcher Bob Feller and held his own through seven scoreless innings. In the Boston eighth Salkeld walked, Mike McCormick sacrificed, and Stanky was given a free pass. In one of the most controversial plays in World Series history, pinch-runner Phil Masi was called safe when the Indians tried a pick-off play. Photographs later showed seemingly conclusive evidence that Masi had been tagged out by Cleveland short-stop and MVP Lou Boudreau. One out later, Holmes slashed a single to left, scoring Masi. Boston managed just two hits, but Sain handcuffed Cleveland and the Braves won 1–0.

Visions of another miracle were soon dimmed, however, by brilliant Cleveland pitching and timely hitting. The Braves scored just two runs in the next three games, losing them all, despite fine pitching efforts by Spahn in Game Two, Bickford, Voiselle, and Barrett in Game Three, and Sain in Game Four. With a staggering 86,288 fans packing Cleveland Municipal Stadium for the fifth game, Boston tagged Feller for seven runs. Elliott hit two homers, Salkeld one, and Boston brought the Series home to Boston with an 11–5 win. Cleveland took a 4–1 lead in the sixth game, then braced for Boston's final challenge. A sacrifice fly by pinch-hitter Clint Conaster and Masi's pinch-hit, RBI double made the score 4–3 in the eighth. With runners on second and third Mike McCormick bounced out to relief pitcher

Gene Bearden to end the threat. In the ninth Stanky opened with a walk, but pinch-hitter Sisti, trying to bunt, popped into a double play. Holmes' fly to left fielder Bob Kennedy ended the game and the season.

Big winners in 1948, the Braves were the big losers of 1949. Boston's 16-game turnaround (from 91 wins to 75) was the biggest drop of any team. The offense slipped, but not as much as the pitching staff. As is often the case, troubles kept in control by on-field success later surface with a decline in the standings. A major problem for the 1949 Braves was a thinly veiled feud between Southworth and Stanky. Southworth fell into a well-populated category of managers adept at guiding a strong club to a pennant. A disciplinarian, but willing to let his players play, Southworth did not get in the way of the 1948 Braves. When things went sour in 1949, the discipline was harder to take. The lack of strategy was more apparent, especially in the eyes of Stanky.[6] There were rumors of increased drinking by the manager. Citing "ill-health," Perini sent Southworth home on a leave of absence that lasted the remainder of the season. Coach Johnny Cooney took the helm and Boston won nine of its next 12 games, but staggered through September en route to fourth place. Injuries to first basemen Ray Sanders and Earl Torgeson and an off season from Johnny Sain accelerated the slide. The full extent of ill feelings between Southworth and his players became evident when the skipper was voted only a half-share of Boston's fourth-place cut of World Series money.

After the 1949 season there was little doubt that Stanky and Southworth could not co-exist. The Braves opted to sacrifice the keystone combination of Stanky and Dark to improve its offense for 1950. The deal, one of the worst in club history, brought third baseman Sid Gordon, outfielder Willard Marshall, shortstop Buddy Kerr, and pitcher Red Webb from the Giants for Dark and Stanky. Adding two sluggers may have figured to help on paper, especially with attendance, but moving Gordon and Marshall out of the Polo Grounds with its cozy left- and right-field dimensions to spacious Braves Field failed to make an expected impact. The deal must be given substantial credit for New York pennants in 1951 and 1954.

Perhaps the Braves would have continued to struggle even with Dark and Stanky. Without them, however, the Braves vanished from contention during their remaining days in Beantown. Gordon, shifted to left field, held up his end with a fine offensive season and helped the Braves hit a club-record 148 home runs, but Marshall faltered in limited action. None of the acquired players could make up for the fall off up the middle. Kerr batted just .227 and second baseman Roy Hartsfield led the N.L. with 26 errors. One bright spot was Rookie of the Year Sam Jethroe, the first black player in Boston's modern major league history—an erratic fielder, but an exciting baserunner and offensive threat. Playing center field, Jethroe led the N.L. in errors, but also defensive double plays and stolen bases. In addition to Spahn and Sain, Bickford came within one win of giving the Braves three 20-win hurlers. The big three combined for 60 of Boston's 83 wins in 1950.

Wins were up in 1950, but attendance was down again by almost 140,000 fans. The Billy Southworth era in Boston ended after 59 games in 1951. In a move that was popular, convenient, and cost effective all at once, fan favorite Tommy Holmes was named to replace Southworth. At age 58 with four pennants, two World Championships, and one of the highest winning percentages ever compiled (.593), Billy Southworth was done as a big-league manager. The contract from Boston's last managerial change, when no expense was spared to hire the best man available, is indicative of a struggling franchise. Yet Holmes guided his mates to a winning record (48–47) and a fourth-place finish in the final 95 games.

The 1951 Braves featured a more balanced pitching staff in winning 76 games. Spahn reached the 20-win circle for the third straight year, but Sain managed just five wins and Bickford added only 11 for the fourth-place club. Disappointed and disappointing were local Braves fans. Less than 500,000 came to Braves Field in 1951, a drop of almost 50 percent from 1950 and barely more than a third of the record total of 1948. Since the Red Sox maintained solid attendance with a third-place club, a logical conclusion could be drawn that Boston could/would support two teams in only the very best of circumstances.

If attendance was a problem in 1951, it became a crisis in 1952. Then again, Braves' owners could not have asked for a better excuse for considering a move out of Boston. Holmes, an unskilled skipper, had no chance with the rebuilding Braves. He was replaced by Charlie Grimm after 35 games and just 13 victories. A brand new infield included second baseman Jack Dittmer, shortstop Johnny Logan, and third baseman Ed Mathews, Boston's second star rookie of the decade. Mathews tied Gordon for fourth in the N.L. in home runs, but earned just one vote for Rookie of the Year honors. The slugging tandem provided the only power in an offense that ranked second-to-last in runs, batting average, and slugging percentage. Spahn could manage just 14 wins despite a 2.98 E.R.A.

With a youth movement in place, the Braves looked every bit the Boston Braves early in 1953. Indeed, it seemed at the time that the first migratory major league team of the live-ball era would be Bill Veeck's St. Louis Browns. Veeck wanted to return to the site of his initial baseball triumphs, Milwaukee. Since Lou Perini owned the Milwaukee Brewers of the American Association, he could, and did, help foil Veeck's plans. Perini could also draw no other conclusion from Veeck's interest than that Milwaukee was ripe for major league baseball. Rather than chance another season in Boston and tempt the anger of a Milwaukee community denied big league ball, Perini suddenly looked West. Backed up by the poor recent support from Boston fans, Perini won quick and easy approval to move the Braves from Boston to Milwaukee for the 1953 season. Ford Frick, commissioner of baseball during the Braves' move to Milwaukee and during the early maneuvers of the move to Atlanta, showed little sympathy for Boston N.L. fans. In his book *Games, Asterisks and People,* Frick writes:

> There was some grumbling on the part of partisan fans. (Boston fans have ever been articulate, and though they were notoriously short on financial support, they were long on pride and tradition.) But the move was generally accepted in good spirit and with a modicum of opposition. The Braves, in effect, were trading an antiquated, down-at-the-heel ball park, and a sizable annual deficit for a modern new park and a million-and-a-half attendance bonanza. They were happy, and Boston fans still had baseball, and their favorite Red Sox.

Milwaukee: From Beantown to Beertown

Milwaukee, Wisconsin was thrilled to get major league baseball, never mind the quality. Little did Milwaukee fans know they were getting a Braves team so close to pennant contention. The Braves that quickly changed course from Boston to Milwaukee, and changed schedules with Pittsburgh, featured an ace pitcher in Warren Spahn and a budding slugger in Eddie Mathews, cornerstones of the 1953–60 Braves. If treated as a separate entity from the Boston and Atlanta clubs, the Milwaukee Braves can lay claim to being the only club in professional history (in existence any substantial length of time) that never suffered a losing season. In essence, it could be argued, the Braves took three seasons to recover from the Dark-Stanky trade and replace some worn parts with younger talent.

The core of the initial Milwaukee Braves (1953) included four holdover position players (Mathews, Logan, Gordon, and Dittmer) and a pitching staff led by Spahn, Lew Burdette, and Max Surkont. The addition of first baseman Joe Adcock, catcher Del Crandall, and outfielder Billy Bruton helped elevate the Braves by 28 victories and from seventh place to second. The re-emphasis that the new ownership had placed on player development was paying quick dividends. The prize addition to the Braves came in 1954 by way of a young second baseman turned outfielder named Henry Aaron. The combination of Aaron and Mathews became the most feared one-two punch in the National League. From 1955 to 1965 the Braves finished first or second in club home runs nine times. Adcock, Aaron, and Mathews all took turns among the N.L. home run leaders during the first decade in Milwaukee. While the offense provided excitement, improved pitching was of equal or greater importance in the rise of the Braves. From 1953 to 1959 the Braves finished first or second in fewest runs allowed six times. The Braves were, indeed, the top dog. From an outdated facility in a city with divided baseball loyalties, the Braves were now the favorites not only of Milwaukee, but of baseball fans throughout Wisconsin and in Iowa, Minnesota, and even parts of Illinois. Any fears that Milwaukee would maintain its minor league image in support of the Braves was squashed as 1,826,297 fans herded into County Stadium in 1953, the increase in attendance from 1952 most likely the greatest in major league history. For the next four years, more than two million fans attended Braves games in Milwaukee each year. Only the Yankees, in the great metropolis of New York, had drawn more than two million fans a season in as many consecutive years as the Braves (1946–50).

Led by Mathews' league-high 47 homers and Spahn's circuit-best 23 wins, the Braves were the surprise team of 1953. Surkont became a fan favorite and won nine of his first 10 decisions. An inability to control his weight would be Surkont's downfall. Burdette, another great pick-up from the Yankees (coming with $50,000 for John Sain in 1951), Johnny Antonelli, and Bob Buhl gave the Braves a championship caliber pitching staff, a league-high 14 shutouts, and the lowest ERA (3.30) in the N.L. Mathews, Gordon, and Adcock led the Braves to a club-record 156 homers, eight more than the 1950 squad. Adcock and outfielder Jim Pendleton were obtained as part of a four-team deal with the Dodgers, Reds, and Phillies. Veteran outfielder Andy Pafko, obtained from the Dodgers for Hartsfield and $50,000, provided championship experience and 17 home runs while becoming a fan favorite. Actually, each member of the Braves seemed to have a core of devoted fans. Despite fading after a fast start, the Braves rewarded their new fans with a second-place finish, 13 games behind the Dodgers.

With a new following and new power, the Braves were suddenly back among the elite ballclubs of baseball. One nagging problem remained, however—the second base position, a sore spot since Eddie Stanky had been traded. The problem was compounded after the 1953 season when Gordon, Jethroe, pitchers Surkont, Curt Raydon, Fred Walters, Larry Lasalle, and $100,000 were shipped to the Pirates for second baseman Danny O'Connell. One hole was supposedly filled, but another opened as the departure of Gordon left a vacancy in left field. General Manager John Quinn then turned back to the Giants. Sending another $50,000 and pitchers Johnny Antonelli, Don Liddle, catcher Ebba St. Claire, and infielder Billy Klaus to New York, Milwau-

kee received outfielder Bobby Thomson and catcher Sammy Calder-
one. Thomson was nearing the end of his career, while Antonelli
would win 21 games in 1954 for the World Champion Giants and 108
games in seven seasons with the Giants.

Antonelli, not Thomson and O'Connell, might have been the
missing cog needed to put the Braves back in the World Series. Replace
number-four starter, 23-year-old lefty Chet Nichols, and his nine wins,
with Antonelli's 21 and the Braves win 102 games, five more than the
Giants. O'Connell was, at best, slightly better than Jack Dittmer.

The O'Connell and Thomson trades might have been as big a
setback as the Stanky-Dark deal if not for the big break of March 13,
1954. The break was to Bobby Thomson's ankle while sliding into third
base during an exhibition game. The highly touted Aaron jumped into
the lineup and began one of baseball's most memorable careers. A
variety of other injuries set back the 1954 Braves. Never hitting their
1953 stride they finished third, though only eight games from first,
and uncovered new pitching depth in Boston holdovers Gene Conley
(14–9), also a pro basketball player, Ernie Johnson (5–2), Jim Wilson
(8–2), and sophomore relief pitcher Dave Jolly (11–6). Aaron gave a
slight glimpse of his future by hitting .280 with 13 homers and 69
RBIs before fracturing his right ankle on September 5.

With a big investment at stake, the Braves gave O'Connell two
more seasons as starting second baseman, all the while looking to shore
up the remaining weak link in an otherwise awesome attack. The
1955–56 Braves were a virtual all-star team, with only left-fielder
Bobby Thomson, first basemen Joe Adcock and George Crowe, and
O'Connell out of the running. Pitchers Spahn, Burdette, Buhl, Conley,
and Ray Crone anchored a strong pitching staff, though a weak bullpen was a hindrance. For all this talent, however, 1955 was the year
of the Dodgers, not the Braves. Their combination of power, speed,
and experience, all brought together by sophomore manager Walt
Alston, was too much for the rest of the league to match. The Dodgers'
starting pitchers did not rank with Milwaukee's, but a strong bullpen
made the difference. A slow start and Joe Adcock's broken arm also
contributed. Aaron (.314, 27, 106) paced the N.L. with 37 doubles.
He also played 27 games at the troublesome second base spot.

So confident were the 1956 Braves that the club made not one
transaction after the 1955 campaign. They were still slow footed (second to last in stolen bases), and still weak at second base and in
relief pitching. On the plus side Joe Adcock was healthy and Bobby
Thomson was ready for one more solid season. The Dodgers were a
year older, at that tenuous stage between experienced and over the
hill. The power-laden Cincinnati Reds would also be a threat in the
best N.L. pennant race since 1951. Milwaukee took the league lead on

May 3 and held the top spot for a month. A June swoon brought the end of the Grimm regime. After a 3–2 loss to Brooklyn on June 16, the 12th in 15 games for Milwaukee, Jolly Cholly resigned. On June 17 Joe Adcock, recently returned to the Braves starting lineup, belted three home runs and Milwaukee beat Brooklyn to launch an 11-game winning streak, quickly climbing from fifth place back to first before the end of the month. Following the All-Star break the first-place Braves swept a four-game set with the Dodgers before delighted home crowds at County Stadium in the process of building a 5½-game lead by late July. With 20 wins in August Brooklyn closed the gap, while Milwaukee began to struggle.

In contrast to the frenzy in Milwaukee, attendance was poor in Brooklyn. As 33,384 fans filled Ebbets Field on September 11 (Brooklyn's second biggest home crowd of the year), Sal Maglie beat the Braves, pulling the Dodgers into a first-place tie. Milwaukee beat Don Newcombe the next night to regain a lead that would change from day to day. On September 25 Maglie pitched a no-hitter against the Phils, but Spahn won his 20th to keep the Braves up by a half game. A Brooklyn loss put Milwaukee within two wins of the pennant entering the final weekend of the season. At St. Louis, the pressure showed on the young Braves. Buhl's poor performance and a rare throwing error by Crandall enabled the Cards to withstand a rally and win 5–4. Saturday afternoon the Dodgers swept a twinbill from the Pirates. That night Spahn pitched brilliantly; only Al Dark's RBI double blemished his pitching line. Milwaukee could also manage but one run, thanks to two miraculous, ninth-inning catches by Bobby Del Greco. In the 12th, Musial's double and Rip Repulski's bad-hop grounder off Mathews' knee gave St. Louis a 2–1 win and the Dodgers a one-game lead. Burdette won on Sunday, but Brooklyn defeated Pittsburgh again to clinch the pennant.

The second-place finish overshadowed some exceptional performances. Aaron led all batters with a .328 average and finished third, behind Newcombe and Maglie, in the MVP voting. Burdette led the N.L. in ERA and shutouts, Spahn was second in wins and ERA. Buhl won a career-high 18 games. The Braves had the best team ERA, the third highest scoring offense, and the second best slugging percentage in the N.L., but no pennant.

The missing piece to Milwaukee's pennant puzzle was added June 15, 1957, and involved the two principles of the back-to-back 1953–54 trades that were supposed to complete the puzzle. O'Connell, Thompson, and pitcher Ray Crone were traded to the Giants for second baseman Red Schoendienst. The 34-year-old redhead had spent 11 full seasons with the Cardinals before being traded to the Giants in 1956. An all-star performer both at bat and in the field,

Schoendienst gave the Braves an unbeatable lineup. Red hit in 25 straight games, batted .309, and tied for the N.L. lead in fielding percentage for second basemen. Even injuries to Adcock and Billy Bruton could not deter the 1957 Braves. Wes Covington, called up from the minors immediately after the big trade, stepped into Thomson's position without a hitch. Aaron (.322, 44, 132) had one of many career seasons, hitting the game-winning home run in the pennant clincher on September 23 and earning Most Valuable Player honors. Cy Young Award winner Spahn had 21 victories, Buhl 18, Burdette 17. Hard-throwing righthander Don McMahon joined Ernie Johnson and Dave Jolly to give the Braves a respectable bullpen. With a 35–18 record in August–September, Milwaukee outlasted challengers Brooklyn, Cincinnati, Philadelphia, and St. Louis to win by eight games. Milwaukee's faithful responded with an N.L. record home attendance of 2,215,404.

Not since 1946 had a team West of New York represented the N.L. in the World Series. Fittingly, the Braves went to New York for the first game of the Fall Classic. Whitey Ford outpitched Spahn for a 3–1 win in the opener, but Burdette evened things with a seven-hitter in Game Two. Covington's spectacular catch and RBI single, Aaron's RBI triple, and Logan's home run sparked Milwaukee's 4–2 victory. With 45,804 fans at the first World Series game in Milwaukee, local native Tony Kubek, shortstop of the Yankees, hit two homers as New York routed Buhl 12–3. Aaron's three-run homer and Frank Torre's solo shot staked Spahn to a 4–1 lead in the fourth contest. With two runners on and two men out in the ninth, Elston Howard hit Spahn's 3–2 pitch into the left-field stands to tie the game. New York broke the tie when Hank Bauer's triple scored Kubek in the tenth.

Milwaukee then began a final rally with one of baseball's most memorable plays. A seemingly harmless pitch to Nippy Jones sent the pinch hitter to first base when umpire Augie Donatelli found shoe polish on the ball, proving Jones had been hit on the foot. After Schoendienst sacrificed against reliever Bob Grim, Logan doubled home pinch-runner Felix Mantilla with the tying run. Mathews followed with a dramatic, two-run game-winning homer. Milwaukee took the series lead the next day when Burdette beat his former mates again with a seven-hit shutout. Covington made another unbelievable catch and consecutive singles by Mathews, Aaron, and Adcock produced the only run off Ford. In the sixth game A.L. Cy Young Award winner Bob Turley bested Buhl, 3–2, to set up a seventh game showdown between Burdette and Don Larsen. A sudden, four-run Milwaukee third, featuring Mathews' two-run double and Aaron's RBI single, was all Series MVP Burdette needed. On just two days rest (Spahn was sidelined with the flu), Lew pitched his third seven-hitter and second straight shutout. When Bill Skowron hit a two-out, bases loaded smash to Mathews in the ninth, Eddie made a backhanded grab and stepped on third to give the Milwaukee Braves their first and only World Championship.

Making most pre-season prognosticators look good, the Braves duplicated their 1957 regular season and took the 1958 N.L. flag by another comfortable margin of eight games. They survived Schoendienst's illness, diagnosed as tuberculosis after the season, and knee injuries to Bruton and Covington. The Braves scored almost 100 fewer runs in 1958, but compensated with the best pitching in baseball. Spahn (22–11) and Burdette (20–10) tied for the N.L. lead in winning percentage, but Buhl and Conley were both derailed by injuries. Taking up the slack were youngsters Joey Jay, Juan Pizarro, rookie Carl Wiley, and veteran newcomer Bob Rush. Wiley led the N.L. with four shutouts, and the four hurlers were a combined 32–22. Once again the Braves held their own in the early season, then pulled away with a 38–20 record during August–September.

Milwaukee's overall dominance was evident in the first four games of the 1958 World Series. In the first Spahn survived two home runs and won in 10 innings on singles by Adcock, Crandall, and Bruton. The second game was decided by a seven-run Milwaukee first inning featuring homers by Bruton and Burdette. Lew pitched his fourth straight seven-hitter against the Yankees for his fourth straight win against the A.L. champs. Don Larsen and Ryne Duren combined to shut out the Braves in the third contest, but Spahn returned the favor with a two-hitter in Game Four.

The Braves were one win away from becoming the first N.L. team to win consecutive World Series since the 1921–22 Giants. Turley kept faint Yankee hopes alive with a shutout in the fifth game, sending the series back to Milwaukee. RBI hits by Aaron and Spahn gave the Braves a 2–1 lead, but New York forged a tie in the sixth inning. In the 10th Gil McDougald homered and Skowron delivered an insurance run off McMahon. With two out in the Milwaukee 10th Aaron singled home Logan and Adcock singled Henry to third. Pinch-hitter Frank Torre hit a soft liner to McDougald to end the game. Once again Burdette was called on with two days rest. He surrendered two runs in the second, but Crandall's solo homer tied the game in the sixth. The Bronx Bombers completed their comeback and sank the Braves with two out in the eighth. Yogi Berra doubled, just missing a home run, Elston Howard singled to break the tie, Andy Carey singled, and Skowron hit a three-run homer. Series MVP Bob Turley, making his third straight appearance, allowed just two hits in six and two-thirds innings to deny Milwaukee a second straight title.

After the Series a number of changes in the Milwaukee front office occurred. Former Cincinnati manager Birdie Tebbetts was appointed executive vice president. Although Haney was signed to an extension as manager, Tebbetts was seen by some as a potential new skipper. In January John Quinn resigned as general manager to take the same position with the Phillies. John McHale was lured from the Tigers to replace Quinn.

With basically the same team for the fourth straight year, the Braves were heavy favorites for a third straight pennant. Challenging the champs were the young and powerful San Francisco Giants and an improved Los Angeles Dodgers club. The biggest absence on the 1959 Braves was that of Red Schoendienst, sidelined all but three games by his bout with tuberculosis. Seven different second basemen could not fill the void. The departure of Gene Conley also hurt. Traded to Philadelphia, Conley won 12 games while the players that came to the Braves were of little help. Still, with Aaron and Mathews battling for the home run lead, the Braves started fast. After 28 wins in the first 44 games, Milwaukee floundered through the summer, playing .500 ball until September 5. A seven-game winning streak put the Braves back in the hunt. When Burdette shut out the Giants on September 16 the Braves were a game from first, but Spahn was bombed the following day. The Dodgers then swept the Giants to keep the race close. On September 21 Spahn's 20th win gave the Braves a share of first place for the first time since August 5. Milwaukee's win-one-lose-one syndrome continued to the finish. Squandering chance after chance to pull away, the Braves finally landed in a tie with Los Angeles when Buhl beat Philadelphia on September 27 to force the third tie-breaking playoff in N.L. history.

Just 18,297 fans came to County Stadium on Monday, September 28 as Danny McDevitt and rookie Larry Sherry beat the Braves 3–2. At the Los Angeles Memorial Coliseum the next day, the Braves were set to tie the series, leading 5–2 in the ninth. As in the seventh game of the 1958 World Series, Burdette tired quickly. Three singles loaded the bases. McMahon came in and gave up a two-run single to Norm Larker. Spahn relieved McMahon and allowed Carl Furillo's game-tying sacrifice fly. Only Aaron's brilliant catch of Junior Gilliam's drive preserved the tie. Stan Williams blanked Milwaukee the next three innings. With two out in the 12th Rush gave up a walk to Gil Hodges and a single to Joe Pignatano. Furillo hit a tough bouncer to Felix Mantilla, playing short because Logan had been hurt earlier in the game. Mantilla's off-balance throw to first was wild and sent Hodges home and the Dodgers to the World Series.

As in 1956, the near miss took away from some great individual performances. Aaron won his second batting title, Mathews his second home run crown. Spahn and Burdette, both 21–15, tied for the N.L. win lead, but Warren was 0–5 against the Dodgers. Buhl won 15 games, despite a sore arm, but the pitching depth of 1958 was missing. Pizarro, Jay, Rush, and Wiley were a combined 22–28.

The frustrating finish had many fans and some players calling for Fred Haney's head. Like Billy Southworth, Haney was viewed as a disciplinarian who used little baseball strategy and relied too much on his veterans, especially ace hurlers Spahn and Burdette. Five days after losing to the Dodgers, Haney, leader of two pennant winners and a second-place club in three seasons, resigned. Taking Haney's place was former Dodgers skipper Charlie Dressen. Dressen assumed the reins of the oldest club in the N.L., slumping, if only slightly, on the field and at the gate. The 1959 Braves had the worst winning percentage (.551) and worst attendance (1,749,112, second best in the majors) of their seven seasons in Wisconsin. Still, if not for the surprising Pirates, Milwaukee might have returned to the World Series in 1960. Spahn won 21 games, Burdette 19, Buhl 16; Aaron (.292, 40, 126) and Mathews (.277, 39, 124) paced the offense. Spahn and Burdette both pitched no-hitters. Only Pittsburgh and Los Angeles had more wins than losses against the 1960 Braves, but that left Milwaukee second again, eight games behind the Bucs.

Following the 1960 campaign the Braves were undone by a new quest to repair their keystone situation. First Bruton, pitcher Terry Fox, catcher Dick Brown, and second baseman Chuck Cottier were shipped to Detroit for second baseman Frank Bolling and outfielder Neil Chrisley. Then pitchers Joey Jay and Juan Pizarro (and the 1961 N.L. pennant) were tossed to the Reds for 30-year-old shortstop Roy McMillan. Neither Bolling nor McMillan were long-term solutions. Worse, Jay and Pizarro, groomed to replace Spahn and Burdette, would win a combined 136 games the next five years (Pizarro's with the White Sox). The 40-year-old Spahn (21–13) and 34-year-old Burdette (18–11) got some help from 20-year-old Tony Cloninger (7–2). Warren's memorable year included his second no-hitter, April 28 against the Giants, and his 300th victory on August 11 against the Cubs. Del Crandall's arm injury opened the door for rookie Joe Torre, Frank's younger brother. Lee Maye moved into the outfield and outfielder Mack Jones made his debut. The addition of slugger Frank Thomas in May gave the Braves four players with 25 or more home runs. A 10-game winning streak in August raised hopes. Yet on September 2 Dressen was fired as manager of the third-place Braves. Tebbetts took over an uninspired club. Even a league-high 188 homers could not keep the Braves from falling to fourth place, nor home attendance to just over 1.1 million.

Faced with the need for a youth movement McHale, Tebbetts, and company made few strides in that direction. They also received nothing but cash for two productive players, Thomas and McMahon. McMahon, frustrated by lack of work, would last another decade as a top relief pitcher. They got 29-year-old pitcher Bob Shaw from the Athletics, but gave up three prospects in the deal. In 1962 Spahn pitched his third no-hitter but slipped to 18 wins. Shaw won 15, but Burdette only 10. Even Aaron and Mathews could not prevent a slide to fifth place in the expanded 10-team N.L.

The Lou Perini era of Braves baseball ended on November 16, 1962. During his ownership the Braves had won three pennants and finished with a losing record just five times in 19 seasons, compiling an overall record of 1,576–1,355. For better or worse, Perini ushered in the expansion era by moving the Braves West to Milwaukee. He sold the majority of Braves stock to a group including McHale and six former minority owners of the Chicago White Sox; William Bartholomay, Thomas Reynolds, Jr., James McCahey, Delbert Coleman, John Louis, Jr., and Daniel Searle. Bartholomay became Chairman of the Board, Reynolds and Louis vice presidents, Searle treasurer. McHale remained President and General Manager. Thus, the seeds were planted for the demise of the Milwaukee Braves.

The remaining three seasons of the Milwaukee ballclub were overshadowed by the machinations of absentee owners that would eventually take the club South. Although Braves' cumulative attendance since arriving in Milwaukee was second only to the Dodgers, a dramatic decline had occurred since 1957. In 1962 only the Cubs and Phillies ranked lower in N.L. home attendance than the Braves. Fans had turned off on a middle-of-the-road club whose owners did not seem to have the best interests of the community at heart. Just as the city of Milwaukee aggressively pursued a dying Boston Braves franchise, so did civic leaders in Atlanta court the Milwaukee Braves. Actually, Charlie Finley's Kansas City Athletics were the first likely choice to go South, but, like Bill Veeck, the maverick Finley was blocked by A.L. owners. In April 1964 Atlanta representatives announced that a club had committed to moving there. The city began construction of a multi-million-dollar stadium to open in April 1965. Finally, after the 1964 season. Braves owners admitted negotiations were under way to move the team. They also purchased Atlanta's International League franchise and set up an office there. As legal action began on both sides, the Braves' bid to relocate in 1965 was denied by the N.L. One year remained on the lease at County Stadium, so the league forced the Braves to stay in Milwaukee until 1966. From the sixth-best home attendance in the N.L. in 1964 (910,911), angered Milwaukee fans and a complete lack of promotion resulted in an N.L. low gate of 555,584 in 1965 (only Finley's A's drew fewer fans). The primarily adversarial attitude of the local Milwaukee government did not help matters, but the new Braves owners seemed set on moving regardless.

On the field the 1963–65 Braves finished sixth, fifth, and fifth under new manager Bobby Bragan. Spahn had his last brilliant season (23–7, 2.60) in 1963 before his amazing left arm lost its magic. Burdette was traded in 1963, Spahn in November 1964. With a little better pitching, the 1964 Braves might have seriously challenged in one of the most hectic N.L. races ever. They finished five games back with a team ERA (4.11) highest of any N.L. club except Casey Stengel's Mets. N.L. highs in runs scored (a club record since 1900 with 803), doubles, batting average, and slugging average (plus five players with 20 or more homers) could not offset the poor pitching. The 1965 Braves got 24 wins from Tony Cloninger and had six players with 20 or more homers, but scored almost 100 fewer runs. Aaron, Mathews, Joe Torre, and 1964 rookie Rico Carty would make up the offensive nucleus of the new Atlanta Braves.

On September 22, 1965, 12,577 fans came to County Stadium for the final home game of the Milwaukee Braves and saw the Dodgers win 7–6. Legal battles would continue throughout the first season in Atlanta, until December 13, 1966, when the United States Supreme Court voted 4–3 against hearing the case and letting stand the decision of the Wisconsin Supreme Court that allowed the move to Atlanta. Throughout 1965 Ed Fitzgerald and Bud Selig had been prime movers in efforts to secure a new team for Milwaukee. Their efforts would be rewarded in 1970 when the A.L. expansion Seattle Pilots became the Milwaukee Brewers. The Brewers would return Milwaukee to the World Series in 1982, while Atlanta was still waiting.

Atlanta: From North to South

From a geographic standpoint the shift from Milwaukee to Atlanta makes sense. Instead of being the northernmost N.L. club, closest to Chicago, the Braves strengthened the Senior Circuit in the South with teams in Atlanta, Houston, and St. Louis. The similarities between the departures from Boston and Milwaukee are striking. In each case fans had turned their backs on non-contending teams. In each case the departing team was just a player or two from contention. But while the divorce from Boston was quick and relatively uncomplicated, the shift out of Milwaukee was one of the ugliest affairs in baseball history.[7] Attendance had fallen off, but so had Braves wins. Milwaukee had no American League team, like the Red Sox, to keep major league baseball in its community. The abandonment of Milwaukee by absentee owners after just 13 seasons, smacked of carpetbaggery matched only by the

A.L. Athletics. Legal haggling kept the Braves in Milwaukee in 1965, prolonging the distasteful exchanges between the club, the city, and major league baseball itself. Finally, in 1966, the Braves forced their way out of Milwaukee and brought major league baseball to Georgia.[8]

Approaching nearly a quarter-century of Southern exposure, Atlanta Braves history can, for convenience sake, be broken up into two periods defined by both on- and off-field leadership. The Atlanta Braves were first defined by owner Bill Bartholomay and Hall of Famer Henry Aaron, then owner Ted Turner and two-time Most Valuable Player Dale Murphy. Each era included one club that reached post-season play. The Bartholomay/Aaron era (1966–1975) combined veteran players from the Milwaukee days with newcomers that began establishing an Atlanta identity. The Turner/Murphy era (1976–present) began with the task of picking up the pieces of a broken franchise characterized by its absentee (literal and figurative) ownership. Turner-led efforts built the Braves back into a contender, but his later commitment came into question during the waning years of the 1980s.

Like the Milwaukee clubs the 1966 Braves had plenty of power, setting a franchise record with 207 home runs. The myth of the "launching pad" (aka: Atlanta Fulton-County Stadium) was soon born.[9] When Braves owners made their secret agreement with the city of Atlanta in 1964, Mayor Ivan Allen, Jr., led efforts to build the 18 million dollar facility. Atlanta's AAA farm club played there in 1965. The new jewel of the Peach State helped attract 1,539,801 fans to Atlanta home games in 1966, almost three times the 1965 Milwaukee total, but less than the miraculous 600 percent increase from Boston Braves attendance in 1952 to Milwaukee Braves attendance in 1953. Also, the 1953 Braves led the N.L. in attendance; the 1966 Braves were sixth. Of course, they were also a lackluster fifth, not a rising second, in the 1966 N.L. standings. Despite big years by Aaron, Felipe Alou, who finished second in the N.L. batting race to brother Matty, and tubby Joe Torre, and an N.L. high 782 runs scored, the Braves struggled with poor pitching and defense. On June 25 longtime baseball manager and executive Paul Richards was hired as vice president in charge of baseball operations. The addition of Richards brought about the exit of John Mullin, head of the Braves minor league department since 1953, and General Manager John McHale. Mullin went to the Houston Astros, McHale to the commissioner's office. Jim Fanning, assisted by Bill Lucas, replaced Mullin. Manager Bobby Bragan was fired on August 9. Coach Billy Hitchcock took over and reinstated veteran Eddie Mathews at third base. A hot 33–18 finish bought Hitchcock a managerial contract for 1967.

Pitching and defense, not power, ruled baseball as offense declined in the 1960s. The Braves were ill-equipped for such competition. Developing the common loser's formula of improving in weak areas while slipping in strengths, Atlanta was slightly better on the mound and in the field, but scored 151 fewer runs, despite a league-high 158 homers. Atlanta also remained one of the slowest teams in baseball. These weaknesses and injuries to Cloninger, Torre, Alou, Carty, and others resulted in a distant seventh-place finish and Hitchcock's firing on September 29. Plusses were Phil Niekro's conversion from relief pitcher to starter and third baseman Clete Boyer's acquisition from the Yankees. Niekro won the ERA title and Boyer, a brilliant fielder, had his best offensive season ever. Getting Boyer marked the end of Eddie Mathews' 15 seasons with the Braves. He was traded to Houston. Richards brought in his pal Lum Harris as new manager. In 1968 speed was added with the new keystone combination of second baseman Felix Milan and shortstop Sonny Jackson. Aaron stole 28 bases and the Braves finished third in the N.L. in thefts. Injuries were again a problem, most notably Rico Carty's season-long battle with tuberculosis. The addition of Milt Pappas gave Atlanta above-average starting pitching and Cecil Upshaw proved to be a dependable reliever. Still, the Braves were an improved, but distant, fifth and attendance declined for the second straight year.

With rules changes and the beginning of divisional play in 1969, the Braves were back in contention. They became stronger, in several ways, on March 17 when Torre was traded to the Cardinals for first baseman Orlando Cepeda, the N.L. MVP in 1967. Cepeda brought great enthusiasm and recent pennant experience to Atlanta. With Torre gone 20-year-old Bob Didier and veteran Bob Tillman took over catching chores. Unlike Torre, Didier was adept at handling Phil Niekro's knuckleball. Niekro blossomed, at age 30, with a 23–13 season. Outfielder Tony Gonzalez, acquired in June from the new San Diego Padres, was a big offensive plus. Carty returned to hit .342 with 16 homers in just 304 at-bats. Aaron hit 44 homers and moved into third place on the all-time home run list. In September Richards acquired another old friend, Hall of Fame relief pitcher Hoyt Wilhelm. Wilhelm's knuckleball accounted for two wins and four saves down the stretch to augment Upshaw and his 27 saves. Behind Niekro, former pro basketball player Ron Reed (18–10), young lefty George Stone (13–10), and Pat Jarvis (13–11) offset a poor season from Pappas (6–10). On August 19 the Braves suffered a no-hitter at the hands of Chicago's Ken Holtzman, then won 27 of their next 37 games. On September 30 Niekro won his 23rd game and 44,000 fans at Fulton-County Stadium celebrated a pennant-clinching win against the Reds.

Expectations for the first-ever National League Championship Series were for a battle between Atlanta's offense and New York's pitching. In three games the Braves scored 15 runs and hit five homers, three by Hank Aaron. The Mets scored 27 runs, hit six homers, batted .327, and continued to shock baseball by sweeping the series. Atlanta seemingly never recovered from New York's five-run game-winning rally in the eighth inning of Game One in Atlanta.

Unfortunately the 1969 Braves were an aberration, as pitching and defensive woes returned in 1970. Problems seemingly solved at catcher, shortstop, and center field arose anew. Niekro had a terrible season and Upshaw missed the entire summer when he severed arteries in his ring finger while showing off his ability to dunk a basketball. Reed was also hurt. Pappas, sold to the Cubs in June, had more wins than any Atlanta pitcher in each of the next two seasons. Atlanta's team ERA jumped almost a full run from 3.53 to 4.33. Carty led the N.L. with a .366 batting average and helped the Braves lead the league in batting. Carty, Aaron, and Cepeda all drove in over 100 runs, but the Braves sank to fifth place and attendance dropped to a new Atlanta low.

With an interesting mix of age, youth, and power, plus some weak competition, the Braves improved again in 1971, though attendance fell at the same time. Youth was represented by Rookie-of-the-Year Earl Williams, speedy outfielder Ralph Garr, shortstop Marty Perez, and third baseman Darrell Evans. Williams was the man without a position, playing behind Boyer and Cepeda until settling behind the plate. His defense was suspect, but 33 homers helped compensate. Aaron responded to increased play at first base, after Cepeda was hurt, with a single-season-high 47 home runs, including his 600th, and a .327 batting average. Carty missed the entire season with a knee injury and Cepeda was sidelined with the same problem. Comebacks by Niekro and Upshaw fortified a shaky pitching staff. Boyer became the center of controversy after verbally blasting Richards in May. Clete bought his release from the club, though Commissioner Kuhn later ordered the check returned. Kuhn also fined Boyer for betting on college and professional football games. Whether because of the gambling, his defiance of the system, or a secret "blacklist," Boyer never played another major league game. With Cincinnati's Big Red Machine suffering a team slump, Atlanta slipped into third place behind the Giants and Dodgers. When the new and improved Reds rebounded in 1972, the rest of the N.L. West suffered.

The Paul Richards era in Atlanta ended in 1972 as the Braves finished a distant fourth. Eddie Robinson, head of Atlanta's minor league system, replaced Richards and Bill Lucas filled Robinson's vacancy. Robinson's first deal was the marquee trade of the year, sending Cepeda to the A's for problem child Denny McLain, a deal that helped neither club. Harris, generally recognized as Richards' puppet, was fired and popular Eddie Mathews was elevated from the coaching staff, though there was no noticeable improvement. Aaron took over permanently at first base and Dusty Baker, who first played for the Braves as a teenager in 1968, became a starting outfielder and batted .321, third in the N.L. The Braves were about as bad as their new uniforms. Many observers thought the new threads were appropriate for a softball team, especially the road outfits with a solid blue top and white pants.

Record setting home run heroics and a revamped pitching staff made no noticeable difference in the overall performance of the 1973 Braves. Following the 1972 season Robinson had traded Williams and infielder Taylor Duncan to Baltimore for catcher Johnny Oates, second baseman Dave Johnson, and pitchers Pat Dobson and Roric Harrison. The trade figured to help pressing needs for pitching and defense. Instead, Johnson hit 43 home runs (25 more than he had, or would, hit in any other season) teaming with Aaron and Evans to make the Braves the first club in history with three 40-homer players in one season. Atlanta led the N.L. in hits, runs, home runs, batting average, and slugging average, but finished last in team ERA (4.25) and fifth in the N.L. West. Dobson was given up on early and traded in June to the New York Yankees (where he won 19 games in 1974) for four nobodies. Because of injuries Oates was not a big help, nor was flashy veteran Joe Pepitone, acquired from the Cubs in May for a young first baseman named Andre Thornton. Another deal, sending Milan and Stone to the Mets for pitchers Gary Gentry and Danny Frisella, back-fired when both new hurlers suffered injuries. Carl Morton, acquired from the Expos for Pat Jarvis, was a surprise with a club-high 15 wins and Phil Niekro pitched a no-hitter against the Padres.

When the Braves arrived in Atlanta in 1966, their new fans may have envisioned pennants and World Series games and other great baseball events, but probably none imagined a front row seat to one of the most indelible moments in baseball history. On Opening Day 1966, 32-year-old Hank Aaron had hit 398 major league home runs. With over 500 circuit blasts, Willie Mays, not Aaron, was perceived as the chief threat to the most hallowed baseball record, the 714 career home runs of Babe Ruth. Even back-to-back home run titles by Aaron in 1966 and 1967 left Aaron well behind Mays and Ruth. Consistent to a fault, Henry kept Hammerin'. Home run number 500 came in 1968, number 600 in 1971, and number 700 on July 21, 1973. Defying time, Hank hit more home runs from 1966 to 1971 than in any other six-year period in his career. Not so suddenly, Aaron was a serious threat to Ruth. On September 29 Aaron hit his 40th and final home run of 1973. With his own eighth 40-homer season, Aaron had 713 career homers, one short of the record. He was still at 713 when the 1973 season ended, leaving six months of speculation and controversy surrounding the now-certain eclipsing of Ruth's record. There were the racial slurs, even threats of violence, that seemingly must accompany any major event involving a black person and a white person (even if the white person had been dead over 30 years). There was controversy over whether Aaron would play the opening series in Cincinnati.

Financially, the Braves wanted the record broken in Atlanta, and if Aaron took awhile, so much the better. The Braves were virtually assured of a sellout for every home game until the record fell. When, in February, Bartholomay announced Hank would be kept out of the lineup for the Cincinnati series, baseball traditionalist were livid. They cried that the Braves would not be fielding their best lineup, damaging the integrity of the game. Others argued that the Braves, paying Aaron $200,000 a season, had every right to try and capitalize on his achievement. Commissioner Kuhn announced that, barring injury, he expected Aaron to play in the Cincinnati series. Rather than defy the commissioner, the Braves had Aaron in their Opening Day lineup at Cincinnati on April 4, 1974. Before 52,154 fans, Aaron faced Jack Billingham in the first inning. On a 3–1 pitch Aaron blasted home run 714, pulling even with the Babe. Atlanta officials no doubt held their breath the rest of the weekend, during which Hank went hitless. On April 8, a standing-room-only crowd of 52,870 fans filled Atlanta Fulton-County Stadium to see the Braves face the Dodgers. At 9:07 Eastern Daylight Time, Aaron connected with a 1–0 pitch from lefty Al Downing. The ball went sailing over the left-field fence into the glove of relief pitcher Tom House in the Atlanta bullpen. Bedlam broke loose upon the event later selected the single greatest moment in baseball history. Aaron was greeted at home plate by the entire Atlanta team, then escorted to a microphone for comments. Commissioner Kuhn was embarrassingly absent, holding to an engagement in Cleveland. Monte Irvin represented the commissioner's office. Aaron simply, and honestly, said he was happy the chase was over.

The great spectacle over, the Braves could concentrate on playing some improved baseball. Only the division champs of 1969 and 1982 could claim a better won-lost percentage than the 1974 Braves. The improvement, though, did not come fast enough to save Manager Eddie Mathews, fired during the All-Star break with the Braves a game above .500. The firing became a hot topic when Aaron, previously uninterested in managing, suddenly announced that he wanted the job. Aaron had always maintained an interest in a front-office job only, but apparently thought his appointment as manager would boost the hiring of blacks to baseball's management positions. Bartholomay had already chosen his special assistant and former big league manager Clyde King to replace Mathews and stuck with the decision. Finishing strong under King, the Braves rose to third place. Leading the way were N.L. batting champ Ralph "The Roadrunner" Garr and ERA champ Buzz Capra. Among N.L. clubs only the Dodgers had a better team ERA than the Braves, even though Reed, Gentry, and Harrison were all hurt. After his early heroics, Aaron fell far short of his 1973 performance. Now 40 years old, Henry seemed better suited to the American League and its new designated hitter position. On November 2, after 21 seasons with the Braves, Aaron was returned to Milwaukee for outfielder Dave May and pitcher Roger Alexander. Soon after one home run king was sent packing, another was acquired, at least on paper. On December 3 the Braves gained the rights to 1974 A.L. homer champ Dick Allen for cash and a player to be named. Actually, Aaron's successor as the next dominant force of the Braves came into the organization just two months after the historic 715th home run. Catcher Dale Bryan Murphy was the first selection of the Braves, the fifth player taken overall, in the free-agent draft of June 5, 1974. While Murphy would develop slowly in the minors, King was rewarded with a multi-year contract through 1976 to continue improving the big-league club.

The 1975 season in Atlanta was similar to 1935 in Boston. The '75 Braves won 21 games fewer than the previous year as injuries took their toll and one-year wonders did not produce. Allen never did play for the Braves and his rights were traded to the Phillies in May. Capra was ruined by a shoulder injury. Reed, traded to the Cardinals, would move to the Philadelphia bullpen in 1976 and have nine successful seasons as a relief pitcher. King's managerial duties were suddenly yanked away on August 30. Clyde returned to the front office and Connie Ryan became interim skipper. Dave Bristol replaced Ryan after the season. The biggest news of the season came with the announcement that yachtsman and television magnate Ted Turner was prepared to purchase the ballclub.

The Ted Turner era of Braves baseball began on January 14, 1976, when Turner Communications bought the club from Bill Bartholomay's group. Bartholomay remained chairman of the board.[10] Turner was a much-needed breath of fresh air for the Braves, providing local ownership, enthusiasm, and a bright imagination. He would also become a trend setter in the turbulent and radically changing system of major league baseball.

Free agency, baseball's biggest change, is largely due to the efforts of pitchers Dave McNally and Andy Messersmith to escape the reserve clause. Turner wasted no time in signing Messersmith to a three-year, $1 million contract on April 10, 1976. (Turner did not learn his lesson when Messersmith, winner of 39 games the previous two seasons, went

11–11.) The new hurler was given uniform number 17, the channel number of Turner's television station WTCG, the UHF flagship station of the Braves, soon to become "Superstation" WTBS (for Turner Broadcasting System). With federal approval to beam his programming across the country by satellite, WTCG/WTBS was competing with local baseball broadcasts throughout the nation. The Braves became the biggest source of programming for the cable station. Often, in the early days of the Superstation, Braves games were shown twice, once live and again, via tape-delay, during late-night hours for insomniacs, shift workers, and true fanatics. With such vast exposure the Braves became known as "America's Team."

Another foray into free agency cost Turner a one-year suspension, a fine, and the loss of some draft choices. His target was Gary Matthews, star outfielder of the Giants. Turner again got his man, but only after tampering with Matthews by making known his intentions before Gary had fulfilled his obligation to the Giants.

While trades such as the deal that brought former A.L. MVP Jeff Burroughs resulted in some temporary success, two moves provided a long-term setback. Following the 1975 season Dusty Baker was traded to the Dodgers. Atlanta gained a valuable role player in Jerry Royster, but Jim Wynn, Baker's replacement, spent just one season in Atlanta. Dusty, by contrast, was a dependable run producer in LA for several seasons. During the 1976 season Evans and Perez were traded to the Giants for three players, including Willie Montanez. Montanez, the ultimate hot dog, hit well in his one-and-a-half seasons with the Braves, but Evans hit another 283 homers before returning to Atlanta in 1989.

Off the field Turner made two moves both popular and historic. Well-liked and well-respected Bill Lucas became director of player personnel, replacing Eddie Robinson. Lucas became the highest ranking black in any major league organization. To replace Lucas, Turner brought the newly retired Henry Aaron back to Atlanta as director of player development. Another significant addition was former Braves star pitcher, turned pitching guru, Johnny Sain, as pitching coach.

Turner pulled a Fuchs-like move in 1977, a season that could easily be mistaken for one of those suffered by Fuchs' Boston Braves. While appealing his suspension, Turner figured he would attempt to end a 16-game club losing streak by replacing Dave Bristol as manager. Manager Ted Turner lasted one game, a loss to the Pirates, before being banished from the dugout by Commissioner Kunn and baseball law. Bristol returned to preside over the Braves' worst season since 1935 (61–101). Injuries to pitchers Dick Ruthven and Messersmith, Montanez, and Matthews, crippled an already poor club. Niekro lost

20 games and the team 4.85 ERA was the worst in the majors. A single consolation for Turner was his victory as captain of the "Couragous" in the America's Cup yacht race.

Another setback for the 1977 Braves was a curious development regarding star prospect Dale Murphy. Billed as the next Johnny Bench, especially because of his strong throwing arm, Murphy suddenly found himself unable to throw accurately. Even the taken-for-granted toss back to the pitcher was an adventure. After a series of embarrassing exhibition games Murphy was reassigned to the minor league camp. With encouragement from Turner, Lucas, Aaron, and minor league manager Tommy Aaron, Murphy delivered an outstanding offensive season at Richmond (AAA), despite recurring throwing trouble, and regained his future-star status.

Joining Murphy with the 1978 Braves was a 20-year-old third baseman who would give Atlanta a one-two punch that, when healthy, was reminiscent of Aaron-Mathews. Bob Horner jumped straight from Arizona State University to the Braves after signing for a bonus reported at $175,000. Horner hit a home run in his first major league game, one of 23 in just 323 at-bats, and earned N.L. Rookie-of-the-Year honors. Relief specialist Gene Garber arrived via trade and attendance improved for the third straight season despite a third straight last-place finish.

Slowly, from without and within, the Braves were building back toward respectability. Then the organization was jolted when Lucas, prime architect of the rebuilding program, died of a brain hemorrhage and cardiac arrest on May 5, 1979. John Mullin returned to the Braves as Lucas' replacement. Even before Lucas' death the Braves had been disrupted by Horner's holdout. Though Horner (33), Mathews (27), and Murphy (21), converted from catcher to first base, topped 20 homers, the Braves finished last again and attendance dipped sharply. Niekro won 21 games, but lost 20 and was the only Atlanta hurler with more than eight wins as the Braves closed out their first decade since the 1930s without a post-season appearance.

Three more new faces that would propel the Braves upward arrived in 1980. With the addition of first baseman Chris Chambliss, in a deal that sent outfielder Barry Bonnell to Toronto, Atlanta obtained a championship player with proven run-producing ability. His acquisition also enabled Murphy to move to center field. Home-grown Bruce Benedict emerged as a capable catcher. Second baseman Glenn Hubbard and shortstop Rafael Ramirez locked up starting assignments as the Braves added strength up the middle. Another farm product, Rick Camp, proved to be a reliable closer in relief. Camp, Garber, and free agent acquisition Al "The Mad Hungarian" Hrabosky gave

Atlanta its best bullpen in years. Horner (35 homers) and Murphy (33) powered the offense. Rising to fourth place, the Braves had a winning record (81–80) for the first time since 1974.

Dipping back into the free-agent pool, Turner's money bought two-time Cy Young Award winner Gaylord Perry and outfielder Claudell Washington. An ill-advised trade sent hurler Doyle Alexander to San Francisco for pitcher John Montefusco. Regardless, the Braves did not challenge in either half of the strike-torn 1981 season, after which Cox was replaced as manager.

Joe Torre, who hit the first major league home run in Atlanta Fulton-County Stadium, returned to become manager of the Braves in 1982 after finishing no higher than fifth in five seasons as skipper with the Mets. Just as his former club was on the verge of great success, so was his new squad. Going beyond success, the Braves were "unconscious" opening the 1982 season. With one improbable win after another, Atlanta went 13 games without a defeat, the best start in N.L. history. In fact, those 13 games were the difference in the N.L. West race and each of those wins proved vital at season's end. With the highest scoring offense in the N.L., Torre's team raced to a 61–37 record and a nine-game lead on July 29. Then it went into a tailspin to match the record start. Losing in equally amazing ways, the Braves lost 19 of 21 games, falling four games out of first place. Pascual Perez, a minor league acquisition from the Pittsburgh farm system, was scheduled to try and stem the tide on August 19. The Dominican Republic native, having just learned to drive, set out on the beltway (I-285) that surrounds Atlanta, en route to the ballpark. Around and around he went, three times, before running out of gas, completely unable to find the stadium. Perez finally arrived 10 minutes late, with Phil Niekro having been rushed into an emergency start.

The misadventure of Pascual Perez seemed to be the comic relief the young, uptight Braves needed to rebound. With 13 wins in 15 games, starting with Niekro's win on the 19th, the Braves bounced back into first place. Steve Bedrosian joined Garber to further fortify the Atlanta bullpen. Murphy earned MVP honors with a league-high 109 RBIs, 36 homers, 113 runs scored, and a Gold Glove for outfield play. Hubbard, Ramirez, Benedict, and Royster all peaked and veteran Bob Watson, acquired from the Yankees in April, provided bench strength and leadership. Led by Washington and Ramirez, the Braves topped 150 steals for the first time since the days of George Stallings. Another slump dropped the Braves three games from first place with 10 games to play. Atlanta, Los Angeles, and San Francisco played "no, you take it" until the final day. The Braves lost their finale, but the Giants beat the Dodgers to give Atlanta a one-game edge in the N.L.

West final standings. A wild locker-room celebration would be the last for the 1982 Braves. Atlanta was soundly defeated in three games by the St. Louis Cardinals.

For much of 1983 the Braves were an improvement on the 1982 edition. They were 71–46 on August 13 with a 6½-game lead in the N.L. West when Horner suffered a broken wrist. Pitcher Len Barker, acquired on August 29, was hoped to be the addition that would put the Braves over the top. Instead, Barker struggled. So did Niekro. Perez and Craig McMurtry won 15 games each; Bedrosian and new-comer Terry Forster kept the bullpen strong. The offense, again the biggest scorer in the N.L., was paced by Murphy's second straight MVP year and his first 30-steal, 30-homer campaign. For the first time in modern Braves history (since 1901), three club members topped 30 thefts (Murphy, Washington, and Brett Butler). Positives (including an Atlanta record attendance [2,119,935]) aside, the Braves were a disappointing second in 1983. After the season Butler and promising third baseman Brook Jacoby were lost to Cleveland, the payoff for Barker. In perhaps Ted Turner's most unpopular move, Phil Niekro was released.

Another injury to Horner was the most significant of several problems for the 1984 Braves. Age was creeping up on some players and rumors accused Torre of being unable to work with younger players. Atlanta's most successful manager was fired on October 1, the day after Torre's Braves edged into a tie for second place with an unacceptable 80–82 record.

Focusing on young farm talent, the elevation of minor league manager Eddie Haas to the Braves seemed to make sense. Instead, the move backfired when highly touted prospects Gerald Perry and Brad Komminsk flopped. Turner's latest big bucks free-agent purchase, relief great Bruce Sutter, also backfired when the ace split-finger fastball hurler struggled throughout the season with a sore shoulder. Even a healthy Horner could not prevent across-the-board declines on offense. Haas, berated by many as a misplaced minor leaguer, was relieved as big-league skipper after a 50–71 start. The troubles of 1985 seemed to confirm worst fears that the front-office tandem of Mullin and Aaron were not producing players necessary to keep the club in contention.

If the claim of being "America's Team"—so often trumpeted on owner Ted Turner's cable network—often proved hollow and absurd to the rest of the nation, it could hardly be denied by 1992 that the Atlanta Braves were already the National League team of the 1990s. A multitude of young talent horded in the late 1980s began to bear rich fruit in the new decade. The result was a first place finish in 1991 which allowed the Braves to share a distinction with Minnesota's Twins as baseball's first teams to vault from last to first in a single season. And the Braves new-found success was met by a landslide turnout of "fair weather" Atlanta fans who now packed Fulton County Stadium in record numbers. In addition to jumping on the Braves bandwagon, Atlanta's patrons created a new baseball phenomena in 1991 with their "tomahawk chop chant" which created a post-season ballpark environment seemingly more appropriate for football than baseball.

But the great chop soon turned into the great flop for the hordes of "Johnny-Come-Lately" Atlanta fans. One of the most exciting World Series in history took a turn for the worse in Atlanta when a baserunning error by Lonnie Smith allowed the Minnesota Twins to steal a thrilling seventh-game extra-inning world championship in 1991. And then after rushing to an expected second NL divisional title in 1992, the Braves would again raise title hopes of the locals with a comeback ninth-inning deciding playoff victory against the Pittsburgh Pirates in perhaps the wildest NLCS seventh game ever. Yet once again the Braves proved busts in the World Series, this time allowing Toronto's Blue Jays to bring a first world title onto Canadian soil. Somehow it seemed ironically fitting that the self-proclaimed "America's Team" itself had allowed the World Series banner to escape from American soil for the first time ever in baseball's century and a half history.

Notes

1. An important *National Pastime* (Winter 1985) essay on Boston's Frank Selee by A.D. Suehsdorf is one of the most insightful articles yet written on a truly great and largely forgotten baseball manager.

2. *The Bill James Historical Baseball Abstract* provides an insightful article on "platooning" which gives Stallings significant credit for his early use of the tactic.

3. Joe Overfield's useful article in *Baseball Digest* (May 1961) details the events of the exhibition loss and its subsequent effect on the Braves' famous pennant run.

4. The 1935 Braves are one of baseball's most remarkable phenomena. Don Nelson provides an intelligent look at the '35 Braves within his 1982 *National Pastime* article. Nelson offers a valuable perspective in the context of the 1934 and 1936 teams, with some possible explanations offered for the abomination that was Boston's worst baseball club ever.

5. Evidence for the upsurge in Braves' interest was the publication of two histories of the club, a definitive work by Harold Kaese and an informal retrospective by Al Hirshberg. Hirshberg's book reviews the club only from 1914 through the 1947 season.

6. Alvin Dark discusses the Stanky-Southworth feud in his biography, *When in Doubt, Fire the Manager*, perhaps the best single treatment of the controversy available.

7. *The Sporting News Baseball Guides* of 1965 and 1966 are detailed in the events leading up to the Braves departure from Milwaukee. Also, Bowie Kuhn's biography, *Hardball*, gives an insider's look at the legal actions surrounding one of baseball's most controversial of all franchise moves.

8. For an Atlanta perspective on the Braves' move south, see the book *Miracle in Atlanta: The Atlanta Braves Story*, by Furman Bisher.

9. Research-minded publications like SABR's *Baseball Research Journal, The Elias Baseball Analyst,* and *The Bill James Baseball Abstract* have all carried articles about the apparent proliferation of home runs in Atlanta's big-league park. Giving some credit to an emphasis on home run hitting in the 1970s, and to the prevalence of southern humidity in Fulton-County Stadium, the consensus seems to be that Atlanta's reputation as a home run haven is mostly unsubstantiated.

10. Aside from leading the Braves from Milwaukee to Atlanta, Bill Bartholomay's most significant (and universally popular) move came when he signed Hall of Famer Satchel Paige to a contract in 1968. Paige was days short of qualifying for the major league pension. Though he never pitched in a game for the Braves, Satch was able to qualify for his well-deserved pension payments.

References

Bisher, Furman. 1966. *Miracle in Atlanta: The Atlanta Braves Story.* New York: World Publishing Company.

Dark, Alvin, and John Underwood. 1980. *When in Doubt, Fire the Manager.* New York: E.P. Dutton Publishers.

Frick, Ford. 1973. *Games, Asterisks and People: Memories of a Lucky Fan.* New York: Crown Publishers.

Hirshberg, Al. 1948. *Braves, the Pick and Shovel.* Boston: Waverly House.

James, Bill. 1986. "A History of Platooning." In *The Bill James Historical Baseball Abstract,* 112–123. New York: Villard Books.

Kaese, Harold. 1948. *The Boston Braves.* New York: G.P. Putnam.

Kuhn, Bowie. 1987. *Hardball.* New York: Times Books.

Liebman, Ronald. 1979. "Consecutive Game Hitting Streaks." *Baseball Research Journal* 8: 24–31. Cooperstown, N.Y.: The Society for American Baseball Research.

Nelson, Don. 1982. "The Hapless Braves of 1935." *The National Pastime* 2:1 (Fall): 10–13. Cooperstown, N.Y.: The Society for American Baseball Research.

Overfield, Joe. 1961. "How Losing an Exhibition Sparked Miracle Braves." *Baseball Digest* (May): 83–85.

Suehsdorf, A.D. 1985. "Frank Selee, Dynasty Builder." *The National Pastime* 4:2 (Winter). 35–41. Cooperstown, N.Y.: The Society for American Baseball Research.

Annotated Bibliography

Aaron, Henry, with Furman Bisher. *Aaron.* New York: Thomas Y. Crowell Company, 1974. 236 pp.

A revised version of *Aaron, r.f.,* Hammerin' Hank's first autobiography, covers his career through the 1973 season and his first 713 major league home runs. A chart listing all 713 homers is included, plus spaces to add numbers 714 and 715.

Bisher, Furman. *Miracle in Atlanta: The Atlanta Braves Story.* Cleveland, Ohio: World Publishing Company, 1966. 180 pp.

As a leading sportswriter in Atlanta, Bisher gives an insider's look at efforts to bring major league baseball to Georgia culminating with the arrival of the Braves. Along with a detailed account of the move from Milwaukee and the quick construction of Atlanta Fulton-County Stadium, Bisher provides a look at the rich tradition of minor league baseball in Atlanta.

Buege, Bob. *The Milwaukee Braves, A Baseball Eulogy.* Milwaukee, Wisc.: Douglass American Sports Publications, 1988. 415 pp.

The definitive history of the Braves from 1953 to 1965 is lovingly and thoroughly recounted in one of the best baseball books to come off a small press. Buege includes "Time Capsules" highlighting extra special events, a chief "nemesis" for each season, an ignoble moment ("Feat of Clay"), "Swan Songs" of departing players, and an in-depth review of each season of the Milwaukee Braves.

Creamer, Robert. *Stengel: His Life and Times.* New York: Dell Publishing Company, 1984. 349 pp.

As a player and manager for the Boston Braves, Stengel is both an integral and interesting part of club history. Like his epic work on Babe Ruth, Creamer's biography of Casey is well researched and entertaining.

Davidson, Donald, with Jesse Outlar. *Caught Short.* New York: Atheneum, 1972. 177 pp.

Born in Boston in 1925, Davidson became a clubhouse boy/bat boy/mascot for the Braves in 1936 and remained with the organization until 1976, rising to positions as public relations director, traveling secretary, and special assistant. Few individuals have seen as much Braves baseball as the 48-inch-tall Davidson. His anecdotes cover a broad spectrum of club history.

Frick, Ford. *Games, Asterisks and People: Memories of a Lucky Fan.* New York: Crown Publishers, 1973. 244 pp.

Frick presided as commissioner of baseball during both the Braves' move to Milwaukee and most of the departure to Atlanta. The move from Boston was the first shift of a major league franchise (American or National League) since the early 1900s. Surprisingly little is said about the two moves, but a disdain for the loss of Boston Braves fans is revealed.

Hirshberg, Al. *Braves, the Pick and the Shovel.* Boston: Waverly House, 1948. 224 pp.

An anecdotal history that picks up Boston Braves history in 1914, Hirshberg's book is quite readable and provides a suitable overview to modern (1914–47) Boston Braves history.

Kaese, Harold. *The Boston Braves.* New York: G.P. Putnam, 1948. 269 pp.

As with most of the Putnam series, Kaese's book is the definitive study of its selected team from inception to publication date. Especially useful is the detailed account of Boston's American Association club and the N.L. clubs of the nineteenth century. Like the Hirshberg book, the biggest disappointment here is that the 1948 season is not included.

Kuhn, Bowie. *Hardball.* New York: Times Books, 1987. 453 pp.

As the ranking attorney for the National League during the tug-of-war for the Braves between Milwaukee and Atlanta, Kuhn provides unique insight into the second shift in the history of the franchise. Unlike Ford Frick, Kuhn shows an appreciation of the historical ramifications of the Milwaukee to Atlanta move and a sense of loss for the fans of Wisconsin.

Meany, Thomas. *Milwaukee's Miracle Braves.* New York: A.S. Barnes, 1957.

Similar to his books *The Artful Dodgers* and *The Magnificent Yankees,* Meany offers brief sketches of the players that brought major league baseball to Milwaukee.

Murphy, Dale, with Brad Rock and Lee Warnick. *Murph.* Salt Lake City, Utah: Bookcraft, 1986. 168 pp.

    Focusing on Murphy's religious beliefs and conversion to The Church of Jesus Christ of Latter-day Saints, his biography also details the trials and tribulations in becoming the biggest Braves star since Hank Aaron. In the course of profiling Murphy, this story also covers much of the more recent history of the Atlanta Braves.

Onigman, Mark. *This Date in Braves History.* New York: Stein and Day, 1982. 288 pp.

    A standard volume in the "This Date" series, Onigman provides a variety of daily highlights from Boston, Milwaukee, and Atlanta, along with the usual statistical information.

Year-by-Year Standings and Season Summaries

Year	Pos.	Record	Pct.	GB	Manager	Player	BA	Player	HR	Player	W-L	ERA
1876	4th	39–31	.557	15	Wright	O'Rourke	.327	Murane Manning O'Rourke Brown	2	Manning	18–5	2.14
1877	1st	42–18	.700	—	Wright	White	.387	White	2	Bond	40–17	2.11
1878	1st	41–18	.683	—	Wright	O'Rourke	.278	O'Rourke Sutton	1	Bond	40–19	2.06
1879	2nd	54–30	.643	5	Wright	O'Rourke	.341	Jones	9	Bond	43–19	1.96
1880	6th	40–44	.476	27	Wright	Jones	.300	O'Rourke	6	Bond	26–29	2.67
1881	6th	38–45	.458	17.5	Wright	Sutton	.291	Hornung	2	Whitney	31–33	2.48
1882	3rd	45–39	.536	10	Morrill	Whitney	.323	Whitney	5	Whitney	24–21	2.64
1883	1st	63–35	.643	—	Burdock Morrill	Burdock	.330	Hornung	8	Whitney	37–21	2.24
1884	2nd	73–38	.658	10.5	Morrill	Sutton	.346	Hornung	7	Ruffinton	48–16	2.15
1885	5th	46–66	.411	41	Morrill	Sutton	.313	Morrill Wise Sutton	4	Ruffinton	22–27	2.88
1886	5th	56–61	.479	30.5	Morrill	Wise	.289	Morrill	7	Radbourn	27–31	3.00
1887	5th	61–60	.504	16.5	Morrill	Wise	.334	Morrill	12	Radbourn	24–23	4.55
1888	4th	70–64	.522	15.5	Morrill	Kelly	.318	Johnston	12	Clarkson	33–20	2.76
1889	2nd	83–45	.648	1	Hart	Brouthers	.373	Kelly	9	Clarkson	49–19	2.73
1890	5th	76–57	.571	12	Selee	Brodie	.296	Long	8	Nichols	27–19	2.21
1891	1st	87–51	.630	—	Selee	Long	.288	Stovey	16	Clarkson	33–19	2.79
1892	1st	102–48	.680	—	Selee	Duffy	.301	Long	6	Nichols	35–16	2.83
1893	1st	86–43	.667	—	Selee	Duffy	.363	Lowe	13	Nichols	34–14	3.52
1894	3rd	83–49	.629	8	Selee	Duffy	.438	Duffy	18	Nichols	32–13	4.75
1895	4th	71–60	.542	16.5	Selee	Duffy	.352	Nash	10	Nichols	26–16	3.41
1896	4th	74–57	.565	17	Selee	Hamilton	.365	Long	6	Nichols	30–14	2.83
1897	1st	93–39	.705	—	Selee	Stahl	.358	Duffy	11	Nichols	31–11	2.64

Year	Pos.	Record	Pct.	GB	Manager	Player	BA	Player	HR	Player	W-L	ERA
1898	1st	102–47	.685	—	Selee	Hamilton	.369	Collins	15	Nichols	32–12	2.13
1899	2nd	95–57	.625	8	Selee	Stahl	.351	Stahl	8	Willis	27–8	2.50
1900	4th	66–72	.478	17	Selee	Hamilton	.333	Long	12	Dinneen	20–14	3.12
1901	5th	69–69	.500	20.5	Selee	DeMontreville	.304	DeMontreville	5	Willis	20–17	2.36
1902	3rd	73–64	.533	29	Buckenberger	Tenney	.315	Tenney	2	Willis	27–20	2.20
								Long				
								Carney				
								Lush				
								Kittredge				
1903	6th	58–80	.420	32	Buckenberger	Tenney	.313	Moran	7	Pitinger	19–23	3.48
1904	7th	55–98	.359	51	Buckenberger	Delahanty	.285	Cooley	5	Willis	18–25	2.85
1905	7th	51–103	.331	54.5	Tenney	Tenney	.288	Delahanty	5	Young	20–21	2.90
1906	8th	49–102	.325	66.5	Tenney	Tenney	.283	Bates	6	Young	16–25	2.94
1907	7th	58–90	.420	32	Tenney	Beaumont	.322	Brain	10	Flaherty	12–15	2.70
1908	6th	63–91	.409	36	Kelly	Ritchey	.273	Dahlen	3	Lindaman	12–15	2.36
1909	8th	45–108	.295	65.5	Bowerman	Beaumont	.263	Becker	6	Mattern	16–20	2.85
					Smith							
1910	8th	53–100	.346	50.5	Lake	Miller	.386	Beck	10	Mattern	15–19	2.98
1911	8th	44–107	.291	54	Tenney	Miller	.333	Miller	7	Brown	7–18	4.29
1912	8th	52–101	.340	52	King	Sweeney	.344	Houser	8	Perdue	13–16	3.80
1913	5th	69–82	.457	31.5	Stallings	Titus	.297	Lord	6	Tyler	16–17	2.79
1914	1st	94–59	.614	+10.5	Stallings	Connolly	.306	Conolly	9	Rudolph	27–10	2.35
1915	2nd	83–69	.546	7	Stallings	Connolly	.298	Schmidt	2	Rudolph	21–19	2.37
								Gowdy				
								Maranville				
								Smith				
								Magee				
1916	3rd	89–63	.586	4	Stallings	Konetchy	.260	Maranville	4	Rudolph	19–12	2.16
1917	6th	72–81	.471	25.5	Stallings	Smith	.295	Powell	4	Nehf	16–8	2.16
1918	7th	53–71	.427	28.5	Stallings	Smith	.298	Wickland	4	Nehf	15–15	2.69
1919	6th	57–82	.410	38.5	Stallings	Holke	.292	Maranville	5	Rudolph	13–18	2.17

Year	Pos.	Record	Pct.	GB	Manager	Player	BA	Player	HR	Player	W-L	ERA
1920	7th	62-90	.408	30	Stallings	Holke	.294	Powell	6	Oeschger	15-13	3.46
1921	4th	79-74	.516	15	Mitchell	Cruise	.346	Powell	12	Oeschger	20-14	3.52
1922	8th	53-100	.346	39.5	Mitchell	Powell	.296	Powell / Boeckel	6	Miller	11-13	3.51
1923	7th	54-100	.351	41.5	Mitchell	Southworth	.319	Boeckel	7	Genewich	13-14	3.72
1924	8th	53-100	.346	40	Bancroft	McInnis	.291	Tierney	6	Barnes	15-20	3.23
1925	5th	70-83	.458	25	Bancroft	Burrus	.340	Welsh	7	Benton	14-7	3.09
1926	7th	66-86	.434	22	Bancroft	Brown	.328	Burrus / Welsh	3	Benton	14-14	3.85
1927	7th	60-94	.390	34	Bancroft	Richbourg	.309	Fournier	10	Genewich	11-8	3.87
1928	7th	50-103	.372	44.5	Slattery / Hornsby	Hornsby	.387	Hornsby	21	Smith	13-17	3.83
1929	8th	56-98	.364	43	Fuchs	Sisler	.326	Harper	10	Siebold	12-17	4.73
1930	6th	70-84	.455	22	McKechnie	Spohrer	.317	Berger	38	Siebold	15-16	4.12
1931	7th	64-90	.416	37	McKechnie	Berger	.323	Berger	19	Brandt	18-11	2.92
1932	5th	77-77	.500	13	McKechnie	Berger	.307	Berger	17	Brandt	16-16	3.97
1933	4th	83-71	.539	9	McKechnie	Berger	.313	Berger	27	Cantwell	20-10	2.62
1934	4th	78-73	.517	16	McKechnie	Jordan	.311	Berger	34	Frankhouse	17-9	3.20
1935	8th	38-115	.248	61.5	McKechnie	Lee	.303	Berger	34	Frankhouse	11-15	4.76
1936	6th	71-83	.461	21	McKechnie	Jordan	.323	Berger	25	MacFayden	17-13	2.87
1937	5th	79-73	.520	16	McKechnie	English	.290	Moore	16	Turner	20-11	2.38
1938	5th	77-75	.507	12	Stengel	Garms	.315	DiMaggio	14	MacFayden	14-9	2.95
1939	7th	63-88	.417	32.5	Stengel	Hassett	.308	West	19	Posedel	15-13	3.92
1940	7th	65-87	.428	34.5	Stengel	Cooney	.318	Ross	17	Erickson	12-13	3.16
1941	7th	62-92	.403	38	Stengel	Cooney	.319	West	12	Tobin	12-12	3.10
1942	7th	59-89	.399	44	Stengel	Lombardi	.330	West	16	Javery	12-16	3.03
1943	6th	68-85	.444	36.5	Stengel*	McCarthy	.314	Workman	10	Javery	17-16	3.21
1944	6th	65-89	.422	40	Coleman	Holmes	.309	Nieman	16	Tobin	18-19	3.01
1945	6th	67-85	.441	30	Coleman / Bissonette	Holmes	.352	Holmes	28	Tobin	9-14	3.84
1946	4th	81-72	.529	15.5	Southworth	Hopp	.333	Litwhiler	8	Sain	20-14	2.21

Year	Pos.	Record	Pct.	GB	Manager	Player	BA	Player	HR	Player	W-L	ERA
1947	3rd	86–68	.558	8	Southworth	Elliott	.317	Elliott	22	Spahn	21–10	2.33
1948	1st	91–62	.595	+ 6.5	Southworth	Holmes	.325	Elliott	23	Sain	24–15	2.60
1949	4th	75–79	.487	22	Southworth	Rickert	.292	Elliott	17	Spahn	21–14	3.07
1950	4th	83–71	.539	8	Southworth	Cooper	.329	Gordon	27	Spahn	21–17	3.16
1951	4th	76–78	.494	20.5	Southworth Holmes	Cooper	.313	Gordon	29	Spahn	22–14	2.98
1952	7th	64–89	.418	32	Holmes Grimm	Gordon	.289	Mathews Gordon	25	Spahn	14–19	2.98
1953	2nd	92–62	.597	13	Grimm	Mathews	.302	Mathews	47	Spahn	23–7	2.10
1954	3rd	89–65	.578	8	Grimm	Adcock	.308	Mathews	40	Spahn	21–12	3.14
1955	2nd	85–69	.552	13.5	Grimm	Aaron	.314	Mathews	41	Spahn	17–14	3.26
1956	2nd	92–62	.597	1	Grimm Haney	Aaron	.328	Adcock	38	Spahn	20–11	2.78
1957	1st	95–59	.617	+ 8	Haney	Aaron	.322	Aaron	44	Spahn	21–11	2.69
1958	1st	92–62	.597	+ 8	Haney	Covington	.330	Mathews	31	Spahn	22–11	3.07
1959	2nd	86–70	.551	2	Haney	Aaron	.355	Mathews	46	Spahn	21–15	2.96
1960	2nd	88–66	.571	7	Dressen	Adcock	.298	Aaron	40	Spahn	21–10	3.50
1961	4th	83–71	.539	10	Dressen Tebbetts	Aaron	.327	Adcock	35	Spahn	21–13	3.02
1962	5th	86–76	.531	15.5	Tebbetts	Aaron	.323	Aaron	45	Spahn	18–14	3.04
1963	6th	84–78	.519	15	Bragan	Aaron	.319	Aaron	44	Spahn	23–7	2.60
1964	5th	88–74	.543	5	Bragan	Carty	.330	Aaron	24	Cloninger	19–14	3.56
1965	5th	86–76	.531	11	Bragan	Aaron	.318	Aaron Mathews	24	Cloninger	24–11	3.29
1966	5th	85–77	.525	10	Bragan Hitchcock	Alou	.327	Aaron	44	Johnson	14–8	3.30
1967	7th	77–85	.475	24.5	Hitchcock Silvestri	Aaron	.307	Aaron	39	Jarvis	15–10	3.66
1968	5th	81–81	.500	16	Harris	Alou	.317	Aaron	29	Jarvis	16–12	2.60
1969	1st	93–69	.574	+ 3	Harris	Carty	.342	Aaron	44	Niekro	23–13	2.57
1970	5th	76–86	.469	26	Harris	Carty	.366	Aaron	38	Jarvis	16–16	3.61

Year	Pos.	Record	Pct.	GB	Manager	Player	BA	Player	HR	Player	W-L	ERA
1971	3rd	82–80	.506	8	Harris	Garr	.343	Aaron	47	Niekro	15–14	2.99
1972	4th	70–84	.455	25	Harris Matthews	Garr	.325	Aaron	34	Niekro	16–12	3.06
1973	5th	76–85	.472	22.5	Matthews	Aaron	.301	Johnson	43	Morton	15–10	3.41
1974	3rd	88–74	.543	14	Matthews King	Garr	.353	Evans	25	Niekro	20–13	2.38
1975	5th	67–94	.416	40.5	King Ryan	Office	.290	Evans	22	Morton	17–16	3.50
1976	6th	70–92	.432	32	Bristol	Montanez	.321	Wynn	17	Niekro	17–11	3.29
1977	6th	61–101	.371	37	Bristol Turner	Bonnell	.300	Burroughs	41	Niekro	16–20	4.04
1978	6th	69–93	.426	26	Cox	Burroughs	.301	Burroughs Murphy Horner	23	Niekro	19–18	.288
1979	6th	66–94	.413	23.5	Cox	Horner	.314	Horner	33	Niekro	21–20	3.39
1980	4th	81–80	.503	11	Cox	Chambliss	.282	Horner	35	Niekro	15–18	3.63
1981	4th	25–29	.462	9.5	Cox	Washington	.291	Horner	15	Camp	9–3	1.78
	5th	25–27	.481	7.5								
1981*	5th	50–56	.472									
1982	1st	89–73	.549	+1	Torre	Royster	.295	Murphy	36	Niekro	17–4	3.61
1983	2nd	88–74	.543	3	Torre	Horner	.303	Murphy	36	McMurtry	15–9	3.08
1984	2nd	80–82	.494	12	Torre	Murphy	.290	Murphy	36	Perez	14–8	3.74
1985	5th	66–96	.407	29.5	Haas Wine	Murphy	.300	Murphy	37	Mahler	17–15	3.48
1986	6th	72–89	.447	23.5	Tanner	Griffey	.308	Murphy	29	Mahler	14–18	4.88
1987	5th	69–72	.426	20.5	Tanner	James	.312	Murphy	44	Smith	15–10	4.09
1988	6th	54–106	.338	39.5	Tanner Nixon	Perry	.300	Murphy	24	Mahler	9–16	3.69
1989	6th	63–97	.394	28	Nixon	Smith	.315	Smith	21	Glavine	14–8	3.68
1990	6th	65–97	.401	26	Nixon/Cox	Gant	.303	Gant	32	Smoltz	14–11	3.85
1991	1st	94–68	.580	+1	Cox	Pendleton	.319	Gant	32	Glavine	20–11	2.55
1992	1st	98–64	.605	+8	Cox	Pendleton	.311	Pendleton Justice	21 21	Glavine	20–8	2.76

*Split Season Totals (Players' Union Strike).

All-Time Braves Career and Season Records

Career Batting Leaders (1876–1992)

Games Played	Hank Aaron	3,076
At Bats	Hank Aaron	11,628
Runs Scored	Hank Aaron	2,107
Hits	Hank Aaron	3,600
Batting Average	Billy Hamilton	.338
Home Runs	Hank Aaron	733
Stolen Bases	Hank Aaron	240

Career Pitching Leaders (1876–1992)

Innings Pitched	Warren Spahn	5,046
Wins	Warren Spahn	356
Strikeouts	Phil Niekro	2,912
Games	Warren Spahn	714
Shutouts	Warren Spahn	63
Saves	Gene Garber	141
Games Started	Warren Spahn	635
Complete Games	Warren Spahn	374
Wild Pitches	Phil Niekro	199

Single-Season Batting Records (1900–1992)

Batting Average (502 ABs)	Rogers Hornsby	.387	1928
Home Runs	Hank Aaron	47	1971
Home Runs (left handed)	Eddie Mathews	47	1953
Runs Batted In	Eddie Mathews	135	1953
Hits	Tommy Holmes	224	1945
Singles	Ralph Garr	180	1971
Doubles	Tommy Holmes	47	1945
Triples	Ray Powell	18	1921
Slugging Percentage	Hank Aaron	.669	1971
Extra Base Hits	Hank Aaron	92	1959
Game-Winning Hits	Dale Murphy	14	1982
	Claudell Washington	14	1982
	Dale Murphy	14	1983
	Dale Murphy	14	1985
Sacrifices	Fred Maguire	31	1931
	Johnny Logan	31	1956
Stolen Bases	Ralph Meyer	57	1913
Strikeouts	Dale Murphy	145	1978
Total Bases	Hank Aaron	400	1959
Hitting Streak	Tommy Holmes	37	1945
Grand Slam Home Runs	Sid Gordon	4	1950
Hit by Pitch	Felipe Alou	12	1966

All-Time Braves Career and Season Records *(continued)*

Single-Season Pitching Records (1900–1992)

ERA	Phil Niekro	1.87	1967
Wins	Vic Willis	27	1902
	Charles Pittinger	27	1902
	Dick Rudolph	27	1914
Losses	Vic Willis	29	1905
Winning Pct. (10 decisions)	Tom Hughes	.842	1916
Strikeouts	Phil Niekro	262	1977
Walks	Phil Niekro	164	1977
Saves	Gene Garber	30	1982
Games	Rick Camp	77	1980
Complete Games	Vic Willis	45	1902
Games Started	Vic Willis	45	1902
Shutouts	Charles Pittinger	7	1902
	Irv Young	7	1905
	Warren Spahn	7	1947
			1951
			1963
Innings Pitched	Vic Willis	402	1902
Home Runs Allowed	Phil Niekro	41	1979
Consecutive Games Won (season)	Dick Rudolph	12	1914
Consecutive Games Lost (season)	Clifton Curtis	18	1910
Wild Pitches	Tony Cloninger	27	1966

2
Brooklyn Dodgers-Los Angeles Dodgers
From Daffiness Dodgers to the Boys of Summer and the Myth of America's Team
PETER C. BJARKMAN

The Brooklyn Dodgers, who ceased to exist as a team in 1957, and their shrine, Ebbets Field, which was levelled in 1960 to make way for an apartment block, have in some ways gained strength in their demise as a kind of metaphor for the belief that baseball teams are ultimately public property . . . The Brooklyn Dodgers are the first team owned solely by their fans.
William Humber, Let's Play Ball! Inside the Perfect Game

First came the notorious Daffiness Dodgers of the 1920s and the 1930s, bungling big-league pretenders stumbling into memorable traffic jams along the basepaths. Later arose the glorious "Boys of Summer" Dodgers immortalized for all manner of true baseball fans by the lively prose and nostalgic portraits of authors Roger Kahn and Donald Honig. More recent seasons have witnessed the efficient and distressingly businesslike Los Angeles ballclub of the much-maligned Walter O'Malley and his family heirs—transplanted California Dodgers boasting a wholesome new image and asserting relentless domination over National League baseball wars for the past three decades. While many present-day ballclubs have dared to commandeer the hollow title of "America's Team," no franchise in baseball history has so persistently captured the imagination and had the rabid following of so many of the nation's zealous baseball fans.

The story of the Dodgers is essentially the dramatic saga of evolution from one of baseball's most lamentable if beloved mid-century teams to one of its most potent dynasties during the decades under Larry MacPhail, Branch Rickey, and Walter O'Malley. It is also the saga of two of professional baseball's most daring front-office experiments—Branch Rickey's bold challenge to baseball's loathsome color barriers at the close of World War II, and Walter O'Malley's shocking break with baseball's rigid geographical boundaries a brief decade later. Rickey opened up the game to a new generation of talented black and Hispanic athletes who provide the very lifeblood of today's professional game. Although he broke the hearts of millions of Brooklyn faithful by accelerating baseball's coast-to-coast expansion, O'Malley in turn brought eyewitness baseball fandom into markets from Houston to Anaheim to Seattle, providing hometown teams for millions of fans who had heretofore known nothing but a lifetime of radio baseball.

Those Daffy Dodgers of Not So Long Ago

Few professional baseball clubs have displayed such distinctive personalities in the different eras of their history as have the Dodgers in Brooklyn and Los Angeles. The present-day Los Angeles ballclub of Walter F. O'Malley and his immediate successors provides today's idealized portrait of the impersonally efficient modern-day pro sports franchise: unchallenged at the box office as baseball's premier drawing card, and a consistent National League powerhouse which has brought five World Championships, nine league pennants, and seven divisional titles to the City of Angels during three storied decades of California major league play (see Bjarkman, *Baseball's Great Dynasties: The Dodgers,* 1990). For skeptical baseball fans around the nation, however, the O'Malley-Alston-Lasorda Dodgers of the past three decades suggest the very epitome of the streamlined winning baseball organization, and of the professional on-field conduct and impersonal businesslike demeanor expected of today's high-salaried modern ballplayers.

This is a far different public image from the one paraded before the baseball world by the Daffy Dodgers of the 1920s and 1930s under colorful field managers like Wilbert Robinson and Casey Stengel, or the lovable yet exasperating 1940s Brooklyn Bums inspired by the controversial Leo Durocher and the daring dark-skinned Jackie Robinson. Even the glorious "Boys of Summer" Dodgers—masters of the National League throughout the early and mid-1950s—remain one of baseball's most colorful and memorable teams, famed for daring and pugnacious play and for the intense fanaticism of their Ebbets Field faithful. While the Dodgers of O'Malley have become entrenched in the popular imagination of most baseball fans across the country as complacently efficient winners, the earlier stumblebums of Brooklyn have withstood the decades as storied progenitors of baseball's most famous plaintive loser's lament—"Wait until next year!"

Through seven decades of residence in the sprawing borough of Brooklyn, the Flatbush Dodgers were anything but the proficient and businesslike tinsel-town ballclub which later methodically conquered all upstart National League rivals from its new West Coast home. The Dodgers of an earlier era were relentlessly dogged by a far different set of ballpark images—those of madcap clowns and buffoons in baggy baseball flannels, catastrophic traffic jams cluttering the basepaths, insanely zealous fans rooting vainly for hopeless chronic losers. Perhaps in no age of baseball history has a team been more passionately beloved and revered by the locals, more intensely followed, more intimately taken to heart as the very spirit and soul of the community that housed them. Such was the fate of Dodgers teams calling Brooklyn home from the earliest National League years to the middle of the present century. Yet no team was also more reviled for their failures and blunders than these same Dodgers, and perhaps only the "Gas House Gang" Cardinals of the 1930s provided as many excuses for unbridled derision or more legitimate disheartening blows to the local baseball faithful.

The origin of professional baseball in the borough of Brooklyn predates the National League Dodgers by little more than a full decade. Amateur teams with such exotic monikers as Excelsiors, Atlantics, Putnams, and Eckfords had of course played there as far back as 1849, and a loosely knit 24-team federation of East Coast teams which launched play in 1857 numbered no fewer than nine ballclubs representing Brooklyn borough neighborhoods. And these clubs were not without historical baseball distinction. It was the Eckfords who first paid an athlete (Al Reach) for his baseball services; the Excelsiors embarked on baseball's maiden extended road trip; the Brooklyn Stars featured hurler Candy Cummings who boasted the game's first curveball; and the Atlantics earned early baseball notoriety with an 1870 victory over Cincinnati's Red Stockings—baseball's first all-professional club, shattering the latter team's remarkable two-season 78-game unbeaten streak. The score was an undistinguished 8–7 in 10 innings, yet the result was perhaps the most famous ever recorded in the annals of amateur league play.

But it was not until 1883 that the embryonic Dodgers emerged. That occurred when real estate executive and practicing attorney Charles H. Byrne—purportedly at the urging of New York *Herald* editor George Taylor—decided to invest capital in this promising new sport that was so rapidly becoming the craze of a booming industrial nation. Byrne, with financial backing from known gamblers Joe Doyle and Gus Abell, entered his new team in the short-lived Interstate League that year, having hurriedly constructed a makeshift ballpark on the very site where the nation's forefather, George Washington, had once fought a key Revolutionary War battle against the British. Entrenched in their new park (often credited as the nation's first enclosed ball yard), Brooklyn's original "Dodgers" walked away with a pennant in that first and only season of Interstate League play.

Buoyed by such immediate success, Byrne then transferred his team to the more established American Association for the following season, an overly ambitious move which saw his club dashed from championship caliber to a ninth-place finish in the older 12-team circuit. While a lasting tradition of winning baseball was not born from these earliest seasons, a proud fixture of team identity was. It was in these first American Association years that the nickname "Dodgers" first came to common currency. It seems that horse-drawn trolley cars were a backbone of the early transportation network linking the numerous Dutch villages of which Brooklyn was composed. In an age of pedestrians, however, neighboring Manhattan residents had found this maze of carriages to be both confusing and even life-threatening upon occasion. Thus the disparaging appellation "Trolley Dodgers" was a derisive gibe which these Manhattanites often flung at residents from the borough across the East River. The nickname quickly stuck to common citizens of Brooklyn, as well as to the professional ballclub which now represented borough pride. It continued for some time to share equal currency with more standard baseball nicknames such as Bridegrooms, Brooklyns, Brooklyners, or simply Brooks.

Proud performances by the Brooklyn entry in the Interstate League of the early 1880s, and then in the much stronger American Association at the end of that decade, prompted Charles Byrne once again to transfer his Washington Park franchise to the even better situated National League in time for the 1890 spring season. And in one of the earliest ironic episodes surrounding the star-crossed Brooklyn team, the upstart Trolley Dodgers, managed by handsome mustachioed William McGunnigle and paced by strapping righthanded hurler Bill "Adonis" Terry, romped to an easy pennant victory by six and a half lengths in their very first National League campaign. McGunnigle had also manufactured an earlier pennant for the Brooklyns during the final year of American Association play, but such successes were to matter little when front-office upheaval shook the Brooklyn ballclub a scant season later and McGunnigle was dismissed after only three seasons at the helm.

The 1890 season—the first in Brooklyn's full-fledged major league history—also witnessed less noble baseball endeavors. Formation of the abortive Players' League, along with the inevitable ensuing bidding war for established baseball talent, left Brooklyn with teams in all three professional leagues that year (National League, Players' League, and American Association), as well as stripping Byrne's

Dodgers of some of their best talent and driving the two lesser leagues entirely out of business in the process. An ensuing shakeup of Brooklyn baseball personnel which left Bill McGunnigle on the sidelines as Brooklyn manager ushered in John Montgomery Ward, drafted from the borough's Players' League entry as McGunnigle's replacement. Ward was a colorful enough character—a longtime National League star shortstop and pitcher, eventual Hall-of-Famer, off-season distinguished lawyer who battled baseball's early reserve clause and was instrumental in the Players' League movement of 1890. Yet Ward proved far less successful as a big-league field boss. A sparseness of Brooklyn talent in the wake of the Players' League fiasco soon meant a succession of managerial replacements—Dave Foutz, William Barnie, Mike Griffin—all of whom did little to assuage sagging Brooklyn baseball fortunes throughout the remainder of the century's last decade.

Baseball progress is not measured by wins and losses alone, and the final decade of the nineteenth century was altogether significant in Brooklyn annals for matters transcending the team's dearth of on-field successes. The gay 1890s also witnessed the rise to power of the borough's first remarkable baseball personality. Charles Hercules Ebbets, an intelligent, affable, and ambitious young businessman who came into the employment of Charles Byrne and his partners in 1894, was shortly to leave his indelible mark on the fortunes and vicissitudes of Brooklyn baseball history. But Ebbets' even-keeled rise to power with the Dodgers was often slow and painstaking during his earliest years with the ballclub.

One of the more memorable events from the early tenure of Charles Ebbets with the Brooklyn team was a business transaction now somewhat hard to fathom in the frame of modern-day baseball management. Ebbets had already been a loyal employee with Brooklyn for six seasons by the time the Trolley Dodgers joined the National League; he sold scorecards and tickets, cleaned the grandstands and the club offices, and kept most of the financial ledgers as well. He even took over as field manager for the hapless ballclub for part of the 1898 season, when the 10th-place Bridegrooms (as they were now known) reached rock bottom in their tailspin of the late 1890s.

While making himself indispensable in the front office, Ebbets also shrewdly purchased whatever available club stock his limited resources would allow. In 1897, though owning only 10 percent of the club at the time, Charles Ebbets was elected team president, being acknowledged by his fellow owners (Byrne and his various shady associates) as the only knowledgeable baseball man in the organization. And it was in the following season that his baseball acumen and business guile conspired to pull off a first blockbuster deal designed to transform

Brooklyn baseball fortunes radically. Although his Baltimore Orioles were the unrivaled league champion of the period (pennant winners in 1894–96), owner Harry Von der Horst (a Baltimore brewer with little real baseball interest) had enjoyed little success with his club at the gate. The crafty Ebbets, aware of Von der Horst's flagging interest, conspired to transfer majority ownership of the financially successful Brooklyn team to Von der Horst as well. League rules did not prevent multiple team ownership in those days. To the delight of Brooklyn rooters (and the immense satisfaction of the devious Ebbets), Von der Horst was then persuaded to enhance his new investment by shipping a cartload of his best Baltimore players over to Brooklyn, along with crack manager Ned Hanlon to boot. Paced by ex-Orioles Wee Willie Keeler, Hughie Jennings, Joe Kelley, Joe "Iron Man" McGinnity, and Jimmy Sheckard, the transformed Hanlon-led Brooklyn team predictably swept to easy pennants in both 1899 and 1900.

Hanlon's Baltimore-flavored Brooklyn team was like a momentary supernova, launched at the end of the National League's own brief monopoly on professional baseball. In 1901 a rival American League was put in place and the new eight-club circuit immediately set to work raiding rosters of the established National League rivals, precisely as the Players' League had done a decade earlier. No club was more damaged by the bidding crossfire than Brooklyn (which had suffered in similar fashion during the Players' League Wars a decade earlier), with outfield standouts Keeler and Kelley and pitching stars McGinnity and Wild Bill Donovan immediately jumping to the new high-paying league. Ned Hanlon's teams soon tumbled to fifth (1903), sixth (1904), and eighth (1905), losing 105 games in his final season of 1905 and finishing 56½ games behind the pace-setting World Champion Giants. That the rival New Yorkers had emerged as baseball's newest power-house under John J. McGraw, while Ned Hanlon's renamed Superbas (formerly the Bridegrooms) stumbled to the league's basement, was particularly galling to the hoards of Brooklyn faithful.

Yet Charles Ebbets himself had little reason to grieve excessively. Ebbets had finally bought out Von der Horst with borrowed funds in 1904 and now was virtually sole owner of the ballclub. He had immediately re-elected himself club president, simultaneously raising his own salary from $4,000 to $10,000 and cutting that of his field manager from $11,500 to $7,500. By the conclusion of the disastrous 1905 campaign the disgruntled Hanlon had already departed and N.L. standout Wild Bill Donovan's brother, Patsy Donovan, was quickly appointed the new Brooklyn skipper for the 1906 league season.

Brooklyn's rollercoaster baseball fortunes continued to dip precipitously during the post-Hanion years; two fifth-place finishes and a seventh-place season under Donovan; a single sixth-place campaign with Harry Lumley at the helm in 1909; two sixth-place years and two seventh-place finishes under ex-shortstop Bill Dahlen between 1910 and 1913. A National League MVP season by first baseman Jack Daubert, who hit at a .350 clip in 1913, provided a rare uplift to the sagging Brooklyn fortunes. Yet Ebbets was well occupied at this time, about to hatch his grandest scheme yet—the one which would leave his most enduring mark on the Brooklyn baseball franchise that had become his personal foster child. Having moved his club by 1898 into a fresh new 12,000-seat wooden stadium, renamed Washington Park and located in south Brooklyn (they had played at Eastern Park since abandoning the original Washington Park in 1891), Ebbets had for some time longed for a still larger ballpark with more seats and better control over paying customers. As the natural rivalry with McGraw's cross-town Giants heated up, regularly drawing huge crowds after the turn of the century, Ebbets was acutely aware of the financial boon represented by a new stadium. Especially one that would prevent further freeloading by the Washington Park fans who—disgruntled with the team's diminished talents—preferred free vantage points atop the surrounding tenements to paid admissions (at a mere fifty cents a ticket) in the increasingly empty ballpark bleachers.

Again borrowing heavily in order to purchase a desired parcel of land near the outskirts of Flatbush—smack within the murky shanty-town area known quaintly to locals as "Pigtown"—Ebbets successfully constructed his colossus of a ballpark in the nick of time for the opening of the 1913 season. The cost was steep—a quite considerable sum of $750,000 was invested in the new ballpark. It was an impressive edifice indeed—arguably the finest in the major leagues—solid brick construction with great arched ornamental windows and basilica-like rotunda entrance. Seating was available for 18,000 and a total capacity of 21,000 was possible with standees. On April 9, 1913 Ebbets Field first opened with a rain-diminished crowd of 12,000 in attendance to witness an inaugural loss of 1–0 to the Philadelphia Phillies. Unsung hero of this first Ebbets Field game was none other than Brooklyn's Casey Stengel. The young outfielder provided the Flatbush faithful with one genuine thrill for the otherwise dreary afternoon—a spectacular first-inning left-field catch which nearly saved the day for hard-luck Brooklyn southpaw hurler Nap Rucker.

The financial arrangement which made possible the glorious new ballpark in Flatbush was, however, to have severe consequences for the next several generations of Brooklyn baseball management. Its fallout was still being felt, right down to the days of Branch Rickey at the dawn of the Jackie Robinson era. Ebbets had actually located his preferred site for the new ballpark as early as 1908, yet it took four years to obtain title to the entire four and a half acre tract, and when construction of the ballpark began in 1912 the scheming Brooklyn owner was again strapped for cash. To finance construction of his new baseball home Ebbets was forced to relinquish a full 50 percent of his holdings in the club to Brooklyn contractors Edward J. and Stephen W. McKeever. In return, the affluent brothers infused the project with a much-needed $100,000 cash investment.

The new partnership resulted in two makeshift corporations, Brooklyn Baseball Club, Inc., with Ebbets as president and Ed McKeever as vice president, and the Ebbets-McKeever Exhibition Company (owner and operator of the ballpark facility), with the senior McKeever installed as president and Ebbets holding down the vice presidential post. Steve McKeever served as treasurer of both companies, and while the ballpark operation ran smoothly enough under this arrangement, operation of the team was quite another matter. With the sudden death of Charlie Ebbets in the spring of 1925, followed almost immediately by that of Ed McKeever (who contracted pneumonia at Ebbets' funeral and succumbed himself a mere week later) the younger McKeever was soon to make his own grab for the privilege of ownership, ushering in a period of front-office stalemate and a decade and a half of constant bickering and factionalism between the McKeever and Ebbets' interests in the faltering ballclub.

If Ebbets Field had been the foremost legacy of Charles Ebbets' nearly 30 years at the helm of the Dodgers, the event of second greatest impact was his selection of the jovial Wilbert Robinson to direct the team's on-field fortunes. Robinson, who had once starred for Baltimore's Orioles of the 1890s and still holds a century-old big-league record for stroking seven hits in seven at-bats during a single game, became the new Brooklyn manager at the outset of the second season of play in Ebbets Field. Wilbert Robinson and Charles Ebbets were almost an ideal complementary pair to guide Brooklyn baseball fortunes in the period between the two world wars. The stuffy Squire of Brooklyn, as Ebbets was widely known, was time and again offset by the rotund mild-mannered 51-year-old ex-catcher and longtime friend of ex-Baltimore sidekick John Muggsy McGraw. Robinson's well-established baseball image was, in fact, that of the consummate peacemaker, a role he had played while teammate to the irascible McGraw in Baltimore and then again as McGraw's trusty coach and advisor with the Giants. Only an irreparable split between Robinson and McGraw brought on by a bitter quarrel during the 1913 World Series gave Ebbets the opportunity to seize the talented and immensely popular Robinson for his own, and to inflict a small wound upon the hated McGraw and his Giants in the process. Robinson, in turn, managed to bring the Brooklyn team two pennants in his first seven seasons under Ebbets, a much welcomed improvement for a franchise which had not enjoyed victory since the 1900 campaign.

By the time the excessively good-natured Robinson was forced out of his managerial post almost two full decades later, Ebbets Field would be a venerable National League fixture more than twice the size of its original structure, the Daffiness Dodgers of the 1930s would be in full flower, and baseball would be standing on the doorstep of the modern radio and television age. Robinson's early years were promising enough. The 1916 club, buoyed by a third-place 1915 finish and the acquisition of pitchers Jack Coombs from the Athletics (for whom he had won 30 games a few seasons earlier), spitballing Larry Cheney from the Cubs, and lefthander Rube Marquard from the Giants, held on through the summer for a scant 2½-game pennant margin over the Phillies, who were paced by Grover Cleveland Alexander's spectacular 33 victories. While the 1916 team was quickly dispatched four games to one by the Red Sox and Babe Ruth in Brooklyn's first World Series appearance, the 1920 club under Uncle Robbie rebounded from three disastrous wartime years (seventh in 1917 and fifth the following two campaigns) and raced to a comfortable seven-game final margin over runner-up New York.

This time around the Brooklyns (now called Robins after their colorful manager) were confident of World Series victory against the opposition, which happened to be a heavy-hitting Cleveland club, led by playing-manager Tris Speaker with his robust .388 batting average and league-leading 50 doubles. Yet the 1920 Series, this time played under the experimental five-of-nine format instituted at the outset of World War I, again proved disheartening for Brooklyn, the final tally being five-games-to-two in favor of the Indians. Ace spitballer Stan Coveleski shut out Brooklyn three times, only Zack Wheat (.333) and shortstop Ivy Olsen (.320) hit with any consistency for Uncle Robbie's men, and Burleigh Grimes provided the solitary bright spot for Brooklyn by shutting down Cleveland without a run in the second game:

The real story of the 1920 World Series, however, was the remarkable fifth game, played in Cleveland's League Park on October 10, and won handily 8–1 by the American League Indians. This single game—one of the most unforgettable in Series history—saw two unprecedented "firsts" and one spectacular "only" which more than spiced the day's play. In inning one Elmer Smith of Cleveland connected against Brooklyn ace Burleigh Grimes for the first-ever World Series grand slam homer. Not to be outdone, Cleveland hurler Jim Bagby (31–12 that season) touched Grimes as well for a three-run shot in inning three, the first homer by a pitcher in World Series play. But both hits were obscured for future generations by what transpired during the following inning. With Robins runners hugging each base, pitcher Clarence Mitchell was allowed by Uncle Robbie to bat for himself and promptly answered his skipper's faith by lining a screamer toward center field. What happened next stunned all in attendance, as Mitchell's apparent hit was miraculously speared by Indians second baseman Bill Wambsganss. Wamby achieved instant immortality by converting Mitchell's smash into the only unassisted triple play in World Series annals. It is only an amusing footnote to this memorable moment that in Mitchell's next at-bat that day the Brooklyn spitballer also lined into a double play, thus becoming perhaps the only man in baseball history to account for five outs with just two swings of his impotent bat.

The final years of Uncle Robbie's reign ushered in unprecedented front-office bickering, accompanied by new low points in the on-field fortunes of the struggling Brooklyn ballclub. A close second-place finish behind McGraw's Giants in 1924 was the only bright spot in a decade which brought six sixth-place finishes during seven futile seasons. This was the era of the Daffy Dodgers, when the only highlights were unmatched zany on-field escapades and the low-points were definitely the ongoing series of hopeless front-office stalemates.

With the sudden deaths of Ebbets and McKeever, the two factions controlling the ballclub were each left holding exactly 50 percent of the stock and corresponding voting rights. While 70-year-old Steve McKeever coveted the team presidency for himself, the only acceptable compromise seemed to be the popular and harmless Uncle Robbie. Robinson was always a "team man" and thus he reluctantly assumed the president's role alongside his managerial duties during the 1925 season. But deteriorating relations with Steve McKeever—who was further aggravated by Robinson's indelicate handling of the Brooklyn press—soon forced the disillusioned Wilbert Robinson to shun his executive office at Ebbets Field altogether and conduct what little business got done from his lonely clubhouse desk. The bitter standoff continued right up until Robinson's removal as president in 1929 and his subsequent dismissal as manager in 1931. John Heydler, president of the National League, had grown tired of rapid deteriorations in Brooklyn's team management and intervened at long last with a series of compromise actions which spelled Uncle Robbie's eventual demise. Foremost of these was appointment of league representative Walter "Dutch" Carter as new Brooklyn board member, since it was Carter who eventually broke the deadlock and voted for Robinson's ouster. It was Carter as well who dictated that his own personal choice, Max Carey, was to be brought in as the new Brooklyn skipper in 1932.

The Robinson Years did witness some of the most colorful and talented ballplayers ever to wear the Brooklyn uniform, as well as some of the most storied events of Brooklyn baseball lore. Zack Wheat amassed Brooklyn's longest playing career, hitting over .300 in 13 different seasons and enjoying two consecutive .375 seasons in 1923 and 1924. While toiling for weak-hitting Brooklyn teams between 1907 and 1916 and compiling an unimpressive lifetime mark of 134–134, Nap Rucker is today considered perhaps the finest natural lefthander ever to pitch for Brooklyn. The hard-luck Rucker once won 22 games for a 1911 Brooklyn ballclub which amassed only 64 total season victories. Babe Herman was, for all his defensive shortcomings, perhaps the finest natural hitter ever to put on the Brooklyn colors, enjoying a remarkable 1930 campaign in which he batted .393 (an all-time franchise standard) and drove home 130 runs. Dazzy Vance and Burleigh Grimes provided Brooklyn with the league's most intimidating pitching duo of the 1920s, with Vance leading the league twice in games won and Grimes winning 20 on four different occasions.

It was ultimately the colorful exploits of the 1920s Dodgers as bumbling baseball showmen that most distinguished the Wilbert Robinson chapter of Brooklyn baseball history, however. It seems Robinson was a man always dogged by unusual events. Most legendary perhaps is the 1926 debacle in Ebbets Field when headstrong Babe Herman ran a certain double into an unpredictable double play, a matchless and often retold moment which found three confused Dodgers simultaneously hugging third base. Equally bizarre was the parallel happenstance in which catcher Zack Taylor (the incident is often erroneously reported as involving Herman) legged out a triple and then stepped off the bag to receive the back-slapping congratulations of his bemused manager—then coaching third—only to be tagged out in the process. Even visiting teams brought such zaniness to Ebbets Field during Robinson's long tenure, and Casey Stengel punctuated his famous 1918 return to Brooklyn in a Pittsburgh uniform by doffing his cap to the jeering crowd and releasing a captive sparrow tucked under his headgear. But Uncle Robbie himself had set the tone for such highjinks among his Brooklyn charges, attempting to catch a baseball dropped from a circling biplane during spring training of 1916. This particular incident ended with appropriate embarrassment for the proud manager when the falling sphere turned out to be a grapefruit (supplied by the puckish Stengel) which splattered over the panicked ex-catcher, convincing him momentarily that his own head had been split open in the process.

The remaining years of the 1930s saw three talented yet star-crossed managers try vainly to lift the entertaining but ultimately hapless Dodgers out of a decade of second-division play. Max Carey (1932–1933), Casey Stengel (1934–1936), and Burleigh Grimes (1937–1938) took turns at righting the Brooklyn fortunes, yet each met with similar failures. Carey enjoyed the most productive campaign, a third-place finish in 1932; neither Stengel nor Grimes posted a single winning mark nor a finish higher than fifth. But the standard for daffy play which reached its height in the final seasons under Wilbert Robinson maintained its course under his three successors as well. Stengel, in particular, was blessed with a continuation of Dodger daffiness to which Casey himself contributed in ample measure, assisted by memorable characters like outfielder Frenchy Bordagaray, streaky hitter Len Koenecke, and intemperate slugger Hack Wilson. Bordagaray reputedly once gave up on a fly ball against the Cubs to chase his wind-blown cap instead. Another famous incident involves Hack Wilson suffering through a gigantic hangover on a sunny afternoon in Philadelphia's Baker Bowl. Dodgers hurler Walter "Boom Boom" Beck, distraught about being removed from the mound that day by Manager Stengel, refused to hand Casey the ball and instead whirled and threw the offending sphere high against the tin right-field fence. Wilson, at that moment lost in private thought while squinting at the grass before him during his momentary respite, whirled suddenly, seized the baseball, and threw a perfect strike to third base, well ahead of the phantom runner.

The expected departure of Manager Burleigh Grimes after the 1938 season ironically opened the door for the long-awaited first decade of sustained baseball success in Brooklyn franchise history. And the primary authors of that success were a rampaging innovative general manager and the fireplug field manager who was to be his first and most remarkable front-office acquisition. Under pioneering general manager Larry MacPhail and dugout general Leo "The Lip" Durocher, the Dodgers wasted little time launching a decade of baseball triumphs that would end forever Brooklyn's long-standing image of impossible losers and incorrigible baseball clowns.

The long-awaited transition in Brooklyn baseball fortunes did not come, however, without considerable pressure from outside forces. Nearly a decade and a half of feuding for control of the organization, precipitated by Charles Ebbets' sudden death in 1925, had left the Brooklyn organization on the brink of destruction. By the close of the 1937 season National League President Ford Frick—fearing the possible demise of one of the circuit's oldest and once most stable ballclubs—intervened and urged that Brooklyn ownership employ fresh blood in the front office. Frick's nominee for such a role was Leland Stanford MacPhail, a Branch Rickey protege who had most recently run the Cincinnati club for Powel Crosley. MacPhail had already established his phenomenal front-office skills while in Cincinnati, turning around an almost moribund ballclub in a few short seasons and pioneering with such firsts as the advent of major league night baseball and the commercial radio broadcasting of Cincinnati home ballgames.

MacPhail was quick to bring these same innovations to Brooklyn, employing his honey-voiced Cincinnati broadcaster, Walter (Red) Barber, to broadcast the first games from Ebbets Field, and scheduling as well the first New York City night game of Ebbets Field in June 1938. MacPhail—a genius for crowd-promoting gimmicks—also hired Babe Ruth as his Dodgers first-base coach and batting instructor. While Ruth lasted only one season and was bitterly disappointed at not being considered for a managerial slot at the conclusion of 1938, his brief appearance in Brooklyn did bring hordes of fans out to the grandstand to watch the Babe take batting practice and crush line drives onto nearby Bedford Avenue. MacPhail also spent his first season in Brooklyn acquiring hitting talent that would change the course of Dodgers history within a few short seasons: batting star Dolph Camilli was purchased from the Phillies for $50,000; future fan-favorite Fred "Dixie" Walker was obtained on waivers from the Tigers in July 1939; a young jewel from the St. Louis Cardinals' farm system, promising outfielder "Pistol Pete" Reiser, was plucked from free agency (imposed by Commissioner Ford Frick) for an almost laughable $100 bonus; Harold "Pee Wee" Reese was similarly stolen from the Boston Red Sox organization early in 1940; and slugging star Joe Medwick was acquired from the Cardinals as well in 1940. Medwick, however, was injured severely when beaned by St. Louis hurler Bob Bowman a mere week after the trade and never proved the valuable outfield addition the Dodgers and MacPhail had hoped for.

MacPhail was a considerable breath of fresh air for Brooklyn and New York baseball. The new Dodgers boss spent several thousand dollars renovating Ebbets Field, painting and repairing the well-worn grandstand and refurbishing restroom and clubhouse facilities. His decision to send home games out over the radio airwaves in 1938 was a stroke of commercial genius. The move broke a longstanding gentleman's agreement between the three New York clubs not to provide free radio access to locally played games and thus launched the age of regular radio baseball broadcasts in the nation's largest city. MacPhail's dismissal of Grimes as manager and his simultaneous promotion of shortstop Leo Durocher to the bench for the opening of the 1939 campaign began a new era of Dodger success at the outset of the 1940s. That success was quickly realized with a near-pennant in 1940 and the team's first league title in 21 seasons the following year.

But it was MacPhail's introduction of night baseball which provided the final highlight moment of the 1930s and gave witness to one of the most remarkable events in all Dodger history. Fan response to the first Ebbets Field night game on June 15, 1938—played against MacPhail's former club, the Cincinnati Reds—was so overwhelming that fire marshalls had to close the gates to further admissions several hours before actual game time. MacPhail's circus-like pre-game events were highlighted by an exhibition footrace featuring recent Olympic hero Jesse Owens. Enhancing the special atmosphere of the evening was the fact that the Reds' starting hurler, fastballing young lefthander Johnny Vander Meer, was fresh off a masterful no-hit performance against the Boston Braves only four nights earlier. History was on MacPhail's side that night, as under the influence of Brooklyn's new archlights Vander Meer became the first and only pitcher in baseball's entire history to pitch a second consecutive no-hit game. A new era of nighttime baseball had opened under master entrepreneur MacPhail with perhaps the most famous game ever played in the 44-year history of storied and ill-fated Ebbets Field.

Wartime Dodgers—From Hurricane Larry to Rickey and Robinson

The 1940s was a decade in which the face of professional baseball was changed forever by events both internal and external to the nation's favorite pastime. The outbreak of World War II in December 1941 meant the loss of the bulk of hearty major leaguers to military conscription, as well as wartime travel restrictions and material shortages which had a huge impact upon the game as well. Baseball also faced further manpower problems while war raged on across Pacific and European theaters: a newly formed Mexican League made severe player-raiding forays into both the American and National Leagues in 1946; big-league ownership soon faced a nearly successful organization of the much-feared players' union; and by the close of the decade the game had opened up to both blacks and Hispanics for the first time in the present century. Air travel began to replace train travel and increased radio coverage of big-league games was followed at war's end with the first glimmers of televised baseball. And night baseball had become an established practice by the demise of the decade as well.

In National League ballparks two great ballclubs were also busy establishing their domination over the sport in this new age of rapid technological change and social upheaval. The St. Louis Cardinals, reaping a bounteous harvest from their elaborate farm system cultivated by Branch Rickey throughout the 1930s, captured four pennants and three World Series, while also finishing second five times between 1941 and 1949. And in Brooklyn, the newly constructed Dodgers, put in place by Larry MacPhail at the close of the previous decade, also emerged as a potent force, winning three pennants and grabbing three second-place finishes as well. Only 1945 (Cubs) and 1948 (Braves) saw anything but Cardinal and Dodger domination of the Senior Circuit during the remainder of the war-torn decade.

Foundations for the great Brooklyn Dodgers teams of the 1940s and early 1950s were carefully laid in place by Hurricane Larry Mac-Phail well before the outbreak of the war years in December 1941. Pee Wee Reese (plucked from the Red Sox farm system), Pete Reiser (similarly stolen out of the Cardinal organization), Dolph Camilli (purchased from the Phillies for $50,000), and the popular Fred "Dixie" Walker, universally known to the Brooklyn fans (in quaint Brooklynese) as "The Peepul's Cherce," were among the major Mac-Phail acquisitions of 1939 and 1940. Camilli socked 34 homers and drove home 120 runs, both league-leading totals, in 1941. Walker hit .308 and .311 in his first two Brooklyn seasons, while Reiser paced the National League in batting (.343 in 1941) and stolen bases (twice, with 20 in 1942 and 34 in 1946) before injuries halted his promising career. Reese was to become a mainstay of pennant-contending Dodger teams through most of the next two decades.

One such deal, however, went quickly sour for the usually crafty franchise builder who had taken over the Dodgers' front office only months before the death of club president Steve McKeever. On June 12, 1940 MacPhail announced his most startling trade of all, the purchase of slugging St. Louis outfielder Joe "Ducky" Medwick, along with side-arming pitcher Curt Davis, for four players and the then huge sum of $125,000 cash. Medwick was a true superstar, having led the league in RBI totals thrice (1936–1938) as well as in homers (31 in 1937) during immediately preceding seasons. At age 28 the slugging future Hall-of-Famer was certainly anything but washed up. But Medwick's star was ill-fated in Brooklyn right from the start and his rapid downward spiral began his very first game in Brooklyn flannels. With the Cardinals in town only a week after the Medwick deal was announced, St. Louis hurler Bob Bowman viciously struck down the new Dodger slugger with a dangerous beanball, triggering a bench-clearing brawl between the two heated rivals. Howls of protests arose from Dodger manager Durocher, who had reason enough to believe the incident was premeditated. Bad blood had long stood between Bowman and ex-Cardinal Durocher, and a pre-game incident reportedly witnessed Medwick and Durocher needling Bowman in a hotel elevator only hours before the ill-fated encounter. Medwick, at any rate, was hospitalized for a week and upon his return to the Brooklyn lineup had seemingly lost forever the aggressive posture which had made him one of the league's outstanding batters. Medwick did hit slightly over .300 for most of the next three seasons before the Dodgers finally dispatched him to the Giants in 1944, yet he produced less than 30

Brooklyn home runs and never did justify MacPhail's hefty investment. Durocher and MacPhail, meanwhile, protested vehemently to League President Ford Frick, demanding a lifetime ban for Bowman. The protest fell on deaf ears, however, as did MacPhail's subsequent attempts to have the villainous Cardinal hurler indicted by civil authorities on a charge of attempted murder.

Of all MacPhail's astute moves in rebuilding the Dodgers ballclub, none was more unanticipated than his surprise announcement at the close of the 1938 World Series that fireplug veteran shortstop Leo Durocher would replace longtime Dodger favorite Burleigh Grimes as field general for the 1939 campaign. It was not that the demise of Grimes was entirely unexpected (his teams lost over 80 games both years he managed), but rather that the colorful Durocher would be deemed worthy as his replacement. Leo was already a household baseball figure of considerable reputation, especially as a more-than-competent shortstop for Branch Rickey's St. Louis Gas House Gang of the 1930s. Durocher had been reluctantly dealt away to the second-division Dodgers by Rickey in 1937 only after the growing conflicts between Durocher and equally volatile Cardinal manager Frankie Frisch became too much for the St. Louis clubhouse to bear.

A first noticeable milestone for the resurrected Dodgers under Larry MacPhail was the season of 1940. That first summer of the new decade saw a more competitive Brooklyn team, but one still somewhat green in the heat of the final stretch drive by a powerful Cincinnati Reds team. This was the same Cincinnati ballclub, of course, which MacPhail had built before quarrelling with Reds owner Powel Crosley. Cincinnati had raced to a 4½ game season-final lead over Rickey's Cardinals in 1939, and paced by 20-game winners Bucky Walters and Paul Derringer, the Reds were again easy winners (by a full 12 games) this time around over the upstart Dodgers. Yet Brooklyn astonished everyone by winning 88 games under Durocher in 1940. Medwick and Camilli paced the hitting attack, ranking third and fourth in the league in total bases. Veteran pitcher Witlow Wyatt was league runner-up in strikeouts and tied for the lead in shutouts, while also winning 15 games. Although never seriously challenging the powerful Cincinnati ballclub after mid-summer, Brooklyn's second-place finish nonetheless rejuvenated most ardent Dodgers supporters, this being the best showing the team had mustered since the remote campaign of 1924.

The 1941 pennant race allowed the first glimpse of full-blown Dodger successes to come. For the summer of 1941 demonstrated surprising maturity in young players like Reese and Reiser and the joyous result was an unexpected pennant for Brooklyn under third-year manager Leo Durocher. Reiser (the league's youngest batting champion ever at age 22) and Camilli (home run king and RBI champion, as well as league MVP) were the offensive stalwarts, while Mac-Phail's latest acquisition, fastballer Kirbe Higbe from the Phillies, tied Witlow Wyatt with a league-leading 22 victories. Reiser and Wyatt trailed Camilli by only a handful of votes for National League MVP honors. The pennant race was a nailbiter right down to the wire, with Brooklyn edging out the rival Cardinals by 2½ games in what was a strictly two-team race almost from the opening bell. On September 25, with but three games to play, Wyatt shut down the Braves in Boston and the Dodgers had claimed their first pennant after an incredible dryspell of 21 years.

If the summer of 1941 was a glorious time to sit in the bleachers of Ebbets Field and root for the triumphant Dodgers, the autumn of that same season was a time of diminished joy, bringing with it perhaps the darkest single moment in the long rollercoaster saga of Brooklyn baseball. For it is the 1941 World Series which will always be remembered for one inexcusable play, a single bonehead moment which revived ghosts of hapless Brooklyn seasons past. Even Wambsganss's triple play in 1920 pales beside the World Series disaster which befell the Dodgers on October 5, 1941—the only game in Series history to be won and lost after a batter actually struck out with two men already retired and his team trailing in the top of the ninth. The events of that nightmarish afternoon would also serve to set the tone for a string of Brooklyn World Series disasters to be played out several times over the next decade and a half. It was Game Four in Ebbets Field when veteran catcher Mickey Owen unwittingly grabbed hold of baseball infamy by failing to maintain his grasp on one of reliever Hugh Çasey's patented fastballs. With the Dodgers leading 4–3 in the top of the ninth and two men already retired, Casey blazed strike three past Yankee mainstay Tommy Henrich; unfortunately the pitch also eluded Owen and opened the floodgates for a four-run uprising which provided the New Yorkers with an insurmountable 3–1 Series lead. This moment was to live on for a decade as the darkest hour in Dodgers history—that is, until Thomson's wallop against Branca at the Polo Grounds almost exactly 10 years later to the day.

Although the outbreak of war against Japan and Germany in late 1941 robbed the Dodgers of one key veteran player—infielder Cookie Lavagetto being the first Brooklyn player to join the war effort—the remainder of the squad stayed intact and the Dodgers appeared to be runaway repeat winners as they built up a 10-game lead over St. Louis by August of 1942. But the Cardinals were the supreme National League team throughout most of the decade, with sluggers Stan Musial, Enos Slaughter, and Walter Cooper pacing their potent attack, and in the final months of 1942 St. Louis pulled off one of baseball's greatest finishes. League MVP Mort Cooper, with 22 victories and an incredible 1.77 ERA, was the pitching hero as St. Louis took 21 of 26 September games, 106 for the season, and bested the Dodgers in the end by a scant two games. Brooklyn's 104 victories in 1942 set a club record, and yet they were insufficient to overcome a devastating injury which kayoed Pete Reiser in St. Louis during mid-July. Batting nearly .390 at the time, Reiser crashed into the outfield wall in hopeless pursuit of an Enos Slaughter home run ball, an episode which caused the brilliant Dodger outfielder to suffer dizzy spells, headaches, and double vision throughout much of the remaining summer. Reiser played erratically after July and slipped to a .310 average by season's end. This tragic event—coupled with Durocher's refusal to rest his star player later in the season—brought a premature end to Reiser's short career and robbed him of almost certain Hall-of-Fame credentials as well.

Larry MacPhail's own short but highly successful reign with the Dodgers also came to a sudden end at the conclusion of the 1942 campaign. It was in December of that year that MacPhail, stirred by the action overseas, resigned to accept a commission in the U.S. Army's Office of Service and Supply and thus became the first ranking baseball executive to cast his lot with the steamrolling military effort. MacPhail was not done on the New York baseball scene of course; his return as Yankee General Manager after the war was destined to embroil Yankees and Dodgers managements in a series of bitter confrontations before the end of the 1947 season. But MacPhail's legacy and contribution in Brooklyn was already beyond measure by the time of his unexpected 1942 departure. Ebbets Field had been refurbished and renovated for night baseball; adroit dealing had brought a bevy of new players—Camili, Medwick, Reiser, Wyatt, Higbie, Arky Vaughan, Billy Herman—who had finally lifted Brooklyn to the pinnacle of National League prominence; young talent like Reese, Lavagetto, and Dixie Walker seemingly also promised future Brooklyn successes for the remainder of the decade.

Yet for all the upswing in baseball fortunes during MacPhail's Brooklyn reign, the McKeever and Ebbets heirs still in control of the club were not entirely happy with financial matters. While $600,000 of debt to the Brooklyn Trust Company had been paid off and existing mortgages on the ballpark had been reduced considerably, most of the team's soaring profits had been poured back into player purchases and into a farm system resembling Mr. Rickey's model in St. Louis. MacPhail himself was drawing a princely salary, but ownership saw little likelihood of their own investments turning an appreciable business profit. Thus when MacPhail made known his plans for army enlistment the Board of Directors did little to dissuade him. Steve McKeever's son-in-law, Jim Mulvey, and Ebbets spokesman Joe Gilleaudeau were also acutely aware at the time that Branch Rickey, architect of those Cardinals teams which had proved such a Dodgers nemesis, had recently come to a bitter parting with St. Louis owner Sam Beardon. Rickey was promptly hired by the Dodgers' governing board and given a five-year deal almost identical to the one under which MacPhail had operated for the previous half-decade. "The Mahatma"—as New York sportswriter Tom Meany had affectionately tabbed him—had now arrived in Brooklyn, and baseball and the Dodgers would never be quite the same again.

Rickey is justifiably remembered today almost exclusively for Jackie Robinson and baseball's noble integration experiment. But more significant to Brooklyn baseball fortunes, in reality, was the concept of an expansive farm system which he imported from his years in St. Louis. Rickey's style was to recruit virtually every promising teenager spotted by his extensive scouting organization, to sign eager youngsters for nothing but a pittance and the slim hope of someday making the big time, and then to select out the most exceptional talent through one of baseball's most exacting winnowing processes. The backbone of a Dodger team that was to win five pennants in the late 1940s and early 1950s was soon put carefully in place with the Old Mahatma's time-tested methods: young Edwin "Duke" Snider, spotted as a California prep star; Gil Hodges, signed as a shortstop and later converted to a catcher before eventually assuming his destined spot at first base; Carl Furillo, Carl Erskine, and an eventual host of black prospects as well, headlined by Robinson, Campanella, and pitchers Joe Black and Dan Bankhead.

World War II temporarily derailed the Dodgers, as it did most other major league teams of the early and mid-1940s. More than 60 percent of major league personnel was to be found in military uniform by the 1944 and 1945 seasons, and big-league play was staffed largely by 4-F's (one-armed Pete Gray appeared with the Browns and two epileptics held down infield spots with Cincinnati), overaged veterans (Pepper Martin returned to the Cardinals at age 40 after a four-year retirement), unprepared youngsters (Joe Nuxhall took the mound for one game with the Reds at age 15 and amassed a 67.50 season ERA), and the first tentative wave of Latin American players as well. With few bonafide major leaguers themselves, the Dodgers slipped to seventh in 1944, while maintaining the third slot in 1943 and 1945. Durocher was still on the scene, having miraculously escaped the draft with a punctured eardrum, as well as Dixie Walker, who personally salvaged something of 1944 with a National League batting title. Such undistinguished names as Alex Campanis (later Dodgers player personnel director), Gene Mauch (long-time big-league manager), Ed Basinski (an off-season concert violinist), and Tommy Brown (a 16-year-old interim shortstop) attempted vainly to fill in for the departed Reese, Camilli, Lavagetto, Higbie, Reiser, Hugh Casey, Billy Herman, and other departed regulars lost temporarily to the war effort.

The first full post-war year of 1946 saw the Dodgers back on track. With peacetime optimism and a full complement of players returned to the big-league scene, a torrid pennant race unfolded in the National League that summer, one which found longtime rivals Brooklyn and St. Louis again locked in a dead heat on closing day. The unwanted result was the first post-season pennant playoff series in the history of the national pastime, a two-game affair promptly swept by the hot Cardinals in two straight.

Greatness was clearly on the horizon for the Dodgers, and 1946 was a season that seemed to vindicate Rickey's slow rebuilding process, so hampered by four previous seasons of wartime baseball. But this was also a season notable on several further counts. Jackie Robinson began his organized baseball career that summer for the Dodgers' top International League affiliate in Montreal. Promising 24-year-old outfielder Carl Furillo was promoted to the parent club in Brooklyn and hit .284 his rookie campaign. Mexican millionaire Jorge Pasquel launched his abortive plan aimed at enticing major league talent to sign on for Mexican League play, plucking outfielder Luis Olmo and catcher Mickey Owen from the Dodgers and such stars as Sal Maglie (Giants) and Max Lanier (Cardinals) from other big-league rosters. A short-lived player's union movement failed to get off the ground but did set the stage for the full unionization of players that was eventually realized the following decade. And before a July 5 game at the Polo Grounds, Leo Durocher reportedly uttered his famous aphorism that "Nice guys finish last," in response to a reporter's request for Leo's commentary on rival manager Mel Ott of the Giants.

The crown jewel of Rickey's all-too-brief tenure in Brooklyn was the championship 1947 season. That second post-war year has been immortalized in the hindsight of history, of course, as "The year all hell broke loose in baseball" (Barber, *1947—When All Hell Broke Loose in Baseball,* 1982). Rickey launched his successful plan to tear apart baseball's long-standing policies of unjust racial prejudice. This season was without doubt dominated from start to finish by the story of Jackie Robinson's dramatic rookie season and baseball's hard-won campaign for true integration. But in Brooklyn this was also the dawn of the "Boys of Summer" Dodgers team that was destined to rule the National League for the next full decade.

Led by Robinson, baseball's first Rookie-of-the-Year selection, Brooklyn surged to its first pennant under the tempestuous partnership of Branch Rickey and Leo Durocher, a five-game bulge over the still-pesky Cardinals that was never quite as close as the final margin would suggest. But the season was filled with drama enough—some of it transpiring even before spring training had ended and Robinson had appeared in his first tension-filled National League game. Brooklyn's season had started with a bang during spring training in Havana when skipper Durocher received a stunning suspension from Commissioner Happy Chandler. The charge was consorting with known gamblers and suspected criminal types. Baseball's extreme sanction of Durocher was to last for a full season and was brought on in large part by an ongoing feud between the Dodgers manager and a familiar enough foe, his ex-boss Larry MacPhail. Now president and part owner of the Yankees, MacPhail was galled by earlier published barbs from Durocher and took the opportunity to protest successfully to the commissioner's office about the Brooklyn manager's longstanding and widely publicized underworld contacts.

The 1947 World Series was one of the most dramatic and inspired of modern baseball's first half-century. That the crosstown Yankees again prevailed in seven hard-fought games is but the barest outline of the story. Game Four was the centerpiece, an "almost" first World Series no-hitter by journeyman New York pitcher Bill Bevens. But the ill-fated Bevens saw his dream of immortality shattered when a two-out ninth-inning double off the bat of pinch-hitter Cookie Lavagetto brought home two crucial runs. Bevens, who had already walked 10 and given up an earlier run, had lost not only his masterpiece but the game itself (by the count of 3–2) in the process. Almost anti-climactic in the face of Game Four was Al Gionfriddo's incredible left-field grab the next day of DiMaggio's sinking line drive, a play which saved the day for Brooklyn and sent the Series to another seventh-game finish. Henrich was the batting hero and Joe Page shut down Brooklyn with five innings of sterling relief as the Yankees emerged victorious in Game Seven. This 1947 Series seemingly opened the door on what was soon to prove a long string of frustrating October losses to the apparently invincible New York Yankees.

In 1948 the heat of racial tensions dulled somewhat on big-league diamonds throughout the land, once Roy Campanella joined Robinson in Brooklyn and Larry Doby played his first full season for Cleveland in the American League, alongside ageless veteran Negro League star Satchel Paige. That summer also saw a temporary lull in Dodgers fortunes as Boston surged to the top of the Senior Circuit and St. Louis again sat entrenched in second. Durocher's men tumbled to third, 7½ games behind the Boston pacesetters. The irrepressible Durocher had returned from his one-year suspension by Opening Day of 1948, but that earlier incident had brought as its predictable fallout an irrevocable rift between Rickey and his controversial manager. Durocher was out again by mid-season, this time signing on—in a highly improbable move—as the new manager for Brooklyn's long-hated rivals, the crosstown Giants.

By 1949 the full complement of needed players was finally in place for Rickey and his new manager Burt Shotton, and not surprisingly the Dodgers charged to their third pennant of the decade. Robinson enjoyed his best career season as league batting champion (.342) and MVP, and a brilliant relief outing by Jack Banta during a 10 inning season finale at Philadelphia allowed Brooklyn to hang on this time for a one-game victory over the always contending Cardinals. A rather unspectacular 1949 World Series brought more of the same expected mixture of drama and heart-breaking defeat which was becoming standard fare in head-to-head inter-city combat with the Yankees. This time it was a 4–1 New York advantage, in what was to be the first of five consecutive world titles for the Bronx Bombers under former Daffy Dodger Casey Stengel. This final year of the decade was also the first full season for three stars about to emerge in the decade to come. Duke Snider, Gil Hodges, and Don Newcombe all contributed heavily to the Dodgers' pennant chase throughout the summer of 1949, Newcombe winning Rookie-of-the-Year honors, while Snider and Hodges cracked 23 home runs apiece.

Rickey's Brooklyn Dodgers of the late 1940s will always be remembered as modern baseball's first racially integrated team. It is increasingly difficult—more so with each passing decade—to recapture in print the contemporary impact of Branch Rickey's bold move in signing Robinson. Nor can we quite appreciate the full daring of young players like Robinson, Bankhead, Campanella, Newcombe, and Joe Black, who were the first in their race to tackle a sport populated by white players throughout three quarters of a century. The Robinson story has been told and retold many times over and the best accounts are perhaps those of journalist Harvey Frommer, historian Julies Tygiel, and Dodgers' broadcaster Red Barber (see the annotated bibliography section at the end of this chapter). Yet books alone can never do complete justice to the fevered tensions disrupting that first integrated baseball season of 1947. Robinson's rookie summer was witness to an outpouring of racial hatred and endless incidents of bigotry and harassment, both on the field of play and within the grandstands and hotels around the league. Rickey's own former team, the Cardinals, threatened to strike rather than play against blacks. St. Louis took to the field at Brooklyn only after League President Frick vowed to suspend the charter of any such uncooperative franchise. An early-season contest at Ebbets Field with Philadelphia brought merciless racial taunts from the Phillies' bench and from manager Ben Chapman. Even Robinson's teammates were less than accepting at first. Southerner Dixie Walker demanded to be traded rather than play alongside the first black, and Reese and Hodges were reportedly the only Dodgers who struck up genuine clubhouse friendships with Robinson during that first dramatic season.

Remembering Kahn's Glorious Boys of Summer

The Dodgers occupying Ebbets Field from the end of World War II until the dawn of California baseball in 1958 are perhaps the most famous and nostalgia-laden team in all baseball history. Author Roger Kahn's best-selling classic, *The Boys of Summer,* has provided this team with its lasting niche and permanent identity for a generation of the nation's most literate baseball fans. *The Boys of Summer* memorably portrays a dozen teammates from the 1953–1956 Dodgers. These were men who bravely faced the collective pain of diamond defeats throughout their brief baseball careers. They were also men who gallantly struggled with life's larger tragedies once baseball glory was only a proud memory for the likes of Carl Erskine, Duke Snider, Carl Furillo, and Billy Cox. It was, of course, one of baseball's true ironies—in a sport which derives its very life blood from the unexpected moment and the ironic circumstances—that the New York Yankees of Stengel and Mantle and Yogi Berra won World Series upon World Series throughout the 1950s, yet remained for most fans the universally hated symbol of cold corporate efficiency. Yet these Dodgers of Campanella and Hodges and Reese—who suffered heart-breaking defeat upon gut-wrenching late-season calamity—still somehow managed to win lasting devotion from a generation of the nation's baseball fans.

The Dodgers of the 1950s were above all else a true "common man's" team. For all their prowess, all their National League pennants, and October near-glories, this was a team fated by history to be branded as hopeless losers. In October, when the World Series rolled around, it was always the Bronx Bombers of Gotham who somehow prevailed; it was the Yankees who appeared in every Series between 1949 and 1962 but two, winning an unprecedented five World Titles in succession. This Dodgers team was not only the second-best team in baseball, then, it was only the second-best team in the City of New York!

But history and time have conspired to blur our picture of the Dodgers franchise in the final years of Branch Rickey and the initial years of Walter O'Malley. Kahn and other writers have sentimentalized the tough defeats and sudden calamities: Bobby Thomson's crushing home run at the Polo Grounds; Dick Sisler's traumatic season-ending blow a year earlier in Ebbets Field; five bitter World Series defeats at the hands of the indomitable Yankees between 1941 and 1953. Baseball historians John Bowman and Joel Zoss suggest a far different picture, however—one more in line with the hard facts of baseball's statistical realities (Bowman and Zoss, *The National League: A History,* 1986, 90ff). This was one of the National League's best teams ever, a team so dominating in their own league for over a decade that their achievements fall only a whisker below those of the vaunted American League Yankees themselves.

Between 1946 and 1956 six pennants were won by tenants at Ebbets Field, with three more barely lost by the narrowest of margins. A five-game deficit to the Giants during the second-place finish of 1954 represents one of two seasons in this entire stretch of marvelous summers where a pennant was neither won nor lost on the season's final day. A third-place 1948 campaign (7½ games behind Boston) represents the only summer in 11 that the Dodgers were not serious contenders until the season's final week. Victories on the final day of the campaign in 1946, 1950, and 1951 would, in fact, have given Brooklyn an unprecedented nine of 11 pennants, and only 19 more victories (less than two a year between 1946 and 1956 would have resulted in an unimaginable 11 consecutive National League flags). Even the Yankees never accomplished that kind of domination.

Offense was of course the Dodgers' strongest suit. The slugging trio of Snider, Campanella, and Hodges enjoyed five consecutive seasons during which they hit an aggregate 100 or more home runs; Reese and Robinson were base stealers without parallel in an era which unfortunately placed altogether little emphasis on daring base running; and Dodger hitters accounted for two batting titles (Robinson in 1949; Furillo in 1953), one home run crown (Snider in 1956), two RBI standards (Campanella in 1953; Snider in 1955), and four stolen base champions (Reiser in 1946; Robinson in 1947 and 1949; Reese in 1952) during the 1946–56 era. Pitching and defense did not lag very far behind, though some would contend that a shortage of dominant pitching was always the Dodger nemesis in late-season pennant drives and World Series play. Don Newcombe did win over 17 games on five separate occasions, and the relief pitching of Labine, Maglie, Loes, and Bessent was perhaps the best of the era in the Senior Circuit. Only starting pitching seemed a sustained weakness, with steady Carl Erskine (11 or more victories for six consecutive seasons) the single reliable starter year-in and year-out behind the tireless Newcombe.

Although not every Brooklynite of the early 1950s was a passionate Dodgers fan—or even a baseball fan—those who were witnessed some of the most exciting baseball of the modern era. The 1950 National League flag was ultimately captured on the season's final day by the upstart Philadelphia Phillies team that has been known to the ages as simply "The Whiz Kids." In a single-season burst of glory, a young Philadelphia team (the average age of such stars as Richie

Ashburn, Dick Sisler, ace hurlers Curt Simmons and Robin Roberts, and MVP fireballer Jim Konstanty was a mere 26), hung on until season's end to capture their first title in 35 long seasons. Robin Roberts paced a strong Philadelphia staff with 20 victories and Konstanty became the first relief pitcher ever to cop MVP honors.

But the Phillies' glorious pennant year did not come easy and late season Dodgers heroics almost saved the day for rabid Ebbets Field rooters. Holding a seven-game margin over the Dodgers with but 11 contests remaining, the Phils of Manager Eddie Sawyer saw their vaunted pitching staff decimated by injury at season's-end and their pennant dreams reduced to a final season's game against Brooklyn on October 1. That final crucial Ebbets Field contest was not only one of the most ill-fated and memorable of Dodgers history, but perhaps ranks second only to the 1951 Polo Grounds finale in the annals of historic National League pennant contests. Newcombe and Roberts battled 1–1 until the ninth, when the Dodgers opened their last at bat with men at first and second and none out. The Dodgers enjoyed a moment of euphoric hope when Duke Snider singled to center, but Richie Ashburn scooped up Snider's liner and gunned down Dodgers runner Cal Abrams at the plate. This set the stage for a dramatic 10th inning in which journeyman outfielder Dick Sisler (son of Hall-of-Famer George Sisler) smashed a three-run homer to end the valiant Dodgers' late season surge.

The 1950 season had brought with it, however, numerous signs of the bright Dodgers future which lay ahead. In late August Gil Hodges belted four homers in a single Ebbets Field game—a 19–3 pasting of the Boston Braves—to become only the fourth National Leaguer and sixth big-leaguer to accomplish such a slugging feat. Snider led the senior circuit in total bases and Brooklyn as a team paced the league by a wide margin in both batting and slugging averages. Jackie Robinson (.328 B.A.) enjoyed one of his finest seasons in 1950, as well, finishing second to Stan Musial (.346 B.A.) for the league batting crown, while teammate Snider (.321) followed in third position among the league's best hitters.

With the arrival of spring training at Vero Beach, Florida, in 1951, it looked at long last to the faithful in Flatbush that the long-anticipated "next year" had finally arrived. This seemed destined to be the season in which the Bums would at long last shed their well-worn image as annual losers; the Phillies seemed an overnight flash, devastated in the 1950 World Series by the proud Yankees, and Brooklyn again returned a lineup that was arguably the strongest in either league. The season itself, spiced with the sudden return to prominence by the Giants of Leo Durocher and the exciting rookie play of electrifying Willie Mays, was again a bitter race which stretched till the final days of September. Sparked by the arrival of Mays in late May, New York roared down the stretch in August of 1951 with the most torrid finish since the "Miracle Braves" of 1914. Winning 16 straight between August 12 and September 9 (while the Dodgers were playing .500 ball over the same stretch), Durocher's men then copped 16 of their final 20 to close a 5½-game Dodgers lead and force the National League's second-ever post-season playoff series. It was only Jackie Robinson's own heroics on the final afternoon in Philadelphia that prevented New York from sweeping past the Dodgers at regular season's end. Repaying the Phils for damage inflicted in the finale of 1950, Robinson first saved the Dodgers with a miraculous catch of an Eddie Waitkus liner in the 12th with the bases loaded; Robbie then proceeded to produce the game winner with perhaps the most dramatic Dodgers home run ever in the top of the 14th. The 1951 season was thus destined to end with a thunderous bang—two of the most dramatic moments in all Dodgers history—one of them bringing euphoria, the other lined with the darkest tragedy.

Events of the final Dodgers-Giants playoff game of October 1951 have been told over and over again down through the years. The "Miracle at Coogan's Bluff"—as it is now known—is perhaps the most widely discussed single moment of baseball history. It is estimated that three million or more family television sets were tuned to the National League Championship game that day, and Bobby Thomson's dramatic game-ending ninth-inning homer was perhaps the nation's first major sporting moment viewed simultaneously by a live national audience. For generations of fans the vivid image has remained of Thomson rounding third and heading for a mob of teammates waiting at the plate, Manager Durocher leaping in hot pursuit from the third-base coaching box, dejected Dodgers' hurler Ralph Branca (with the ominous number 13 in full view on his uniform back) strolling forlornly to the distant Brooklyn clubhouse in deep center field. The 1951 Dodgers had seemed an invincible team at the outset. Hodges hit 40 homers that year; Robinson batted .338; Preacher Roe compiled an incredible 22–3 mark on the hill; the Brooklyn juggernaut paced the league in almost all offensive categories—homers, RBIs, hits, doubles, stolen bases, batting average, slugging percentage, and even double plays. But it was not enough, as Thomson's timely three-run homer brought a pennant-clinching 5–4 victory for the Giants and an improbable last-minute triumph in the rare best-of-three tie-breaking overtime series. Again the frustrated Brooklyns would have to look helplessly toward the promise of another "next year."

The pennant races of 1952 and 1953 were never much in doubt as the strengthened Brooklyn team glided home 4½ ahead of the Giants in 1952 and then raced to a 13-game advantage over the upstart transplanted Milwaukee Braves in 1953. The Giants had threatened to rival the Dodgers again in 1952, but the early season loss of sophomore-sensation Willie Mays to Army induction ended any serious hopes for another "Miracle at Coogan's Bluff" and left the New Yorkers in strong but hopeless pursuit of powerful Brooklyn. The Dodgers' own loss of ace Don Newcombe to the military was largely offset by the sensational rookie season of pitcher Joe Black (15–4, 15 saves, 2.15 ERA). Although taking Rookie-of-the-Year honors, Black did not post sufficient innings pitched to earn the league's ERA crown, that title going to another outstanding rookie, future Hall-of-Famer Hoyt Wilhelm of the Giants (2.43).

Much of the story of the 1953 campaign was the Braves—newly settled in Milwaukee as a result of the first major league franchise shift of the century and compiling a subsequent National League home attendance mark of 1,826,397. Yet the on-field play of the Braves was no match for the powerful Dodgers; paced by Erskine's pitching (20–6) and the league-leading .344 BA of Carl Furillo, Brooklyn amassed 105 victories under third-year manager Charlie Dressen, most in franchise history. The Braves and Dodgers teams of 1953 were perhaps the two most potent lineups ever to take the field in the same National League season. Milwaukee boasted the league's best staff, paced by veteran Warren Spahn who led the league in both victories (23–7) and ERA (2.10), and the powerful hitting of third sacker Eddie Mathews, tops in the league in homers (47) and second in RBIs (135). But Brooklyn had even more hitting, with five regulars (Furillo, Hodges, Snider, Robinson, Campanella) hitting over .300, Snider and Campanella both surpassing 40 homers, and Campanella leading in RBIs (142) and achieving the coveted league MVP award for the second time in three seasons. To add to the luster of this most powerful of all Dodgers teams, second baseman Jim Gilliam won Rookie-of-the-Year honors and the Brooklyn team BA (.285) was a full 20 points better than the second-place Braves.

World Series play in both 1952 and 1953 seemed near carbon-copies of the 1947 and 1949 Dodgers-Yankees Subway Series staged at the end of the previous decade. The 1952 Series is perhaps best remembered for the failures of slugging first baseman Gil Hodges who, despite 32 homers and 102 RBIs in regular season play, could not muster a single hit in 21 Series at-bats. While the Dodgers won the first, third, and fifth games, including two of the three games played in Yankee Stadium, the Yankees roared back with two final victories at Ebbets Field, sending the ill-fated Dodgers to their sixth consecutive World Series defeat. The 1953 Series saw only more of the same, this time a four-games-to-two margin for the Bronx Bombers, despite the rebound of Hodges with a .364 average and a Brooklyn team BA of

.300 for the series. The true highlight of the 1953 Series, however—the Dodgers' seventh consecutive without victory—was Erskine's record 14 strikeouts (four against Mantle) in Game Three, a 3–2 Dodgers win in Ebbets Field. Erskine's masterpiece game, along with his first no-hitter against the Cubs in June of 1952, had established the Indiana righthander by season's end as the new ace of a Brooklyn staff weakened by Newcombe's military tour and apparently an insufficient match for the Yankees' awesome starting rotation consisting of Allie Reynolds, Vic Raschi, Eddie Lopat, and Hall-of-Famer Whitey Ford.

The 1954 campaign was something of a surprise off-year in Brooklyn, as the Giants again rebounded under the inspired play of Willie Mays and the managerial skills of ex-Dodger skipper Durocher. Fresh from military service, Mays batted a league-leading .345 and stroked 41 homers. Not that the Dodgers played badly, but 92 victories were not enough to make for a close pennant race throughout most of the summer of 1954. Erskine again won 18, but the newly returned Don Newcombe was off-form (9–8, 4.55 ERA) and the Dodgers limped home second, five games out. But all this was only a quiet prelude for the long-awaited heroics and considerable fireworks of the 1955 campaign. For 1954 had brought an important change to the Dodgers franchise, one that was to pay incalculable dividends for the course of the next two decades. When skipper Charlie Dressen had demanded a long-term contract after the 1953 World Series loss, Walter O'Malley wasted little time in dispatching Dressen and replacing him with little-known organization man, Walter Emmons Alston, a failed player with only one big-league at-bat, yet a successful minor-league manager long groomed by Branch Rickey as the future big-league skipper of the Dodgers. Alston's soft-spoken ways and hands-off clubhouse policies were the final catalyst necessary to turn these power-hitting Dodgers into the unbeatable champions that the Brooklyn faithful had long expected to emerge.

There was little serious challenge for the 1955 edition of the Dodgers, the second under Alston, as they pulled away early with 22 victories in their first 24 games, building a 9½ game lead by the end of April and never looking back at the trailing Braves (13½ games) and Giants (18½ games). Again a Dodgers-Yankees Subway Series was the familiar venue for the fall of 1955. Yet this was fated to be a year in which it would all be different somehow. Just when it seemed like the Dodgers would never quite manage to win the big games in October, baseball fate smiled fondly on the long-suffering Dodger fans and intervened in the form of some much needed pitching help. Don Newcombe had returned to earlier form with a 20–5 1955 record and durable Clem Labine had led the Senior Circuit that season with 60 game appearances. Yet it was a young third-year pitcher with a lifetime

29–21 mark who unexpectedly emerged as the most robust of all Dodgers World Series heroes. Under the spectacular hurling of lefty Johnny Podres (2–0, 1.00 ERA) the Dodgers finally were to shut down the powerful Yankees and accomplish what no Brooklyn team ever had before.

When the dust settled on 1955 World Series play, the Dodgers had at long last emerged with a 4–3 Series triumph, keyed by Podres' brilliant seventh-game shutout pitching, Hodges' two RBIs in that final dramatic 2-0 game, and the memorable defensive gem of journeyman outfielder. Sandy Amoros in the sixth inning of that most treasured game in Dodgers baseball history. With two men aboard and Berra at bat, Amoros had raced deep to the left-field corner to rob Berra of a certain hit and the game-tying RBIs. Finally the bridesmaids were bridesmaids no more and the entire borough of Brooklyn was overcome with celebration of its first and only baseball World Championship. It was Podres' brilliant pitching on October 4 that was most responsible for cementing the championship season of 1955, yet Snider's four homers and .320 BA, as well as timely relief pitching by Clem Labine in Game Four (in which he earned the victory) and Game Five (in which he was credited with the save) contributed greatly as well.

The summer of 1956 brought new challenges to the first Dodgers team ever to defend a World Title in Ebbets Field. A torrid season found the Dodgers nipping out Milwaukee by one game and the power-laden Cincinnati team by a mere two, in one of the tightest pennant races of the decade. The old order was now finally passing away and new faces were appearing all too slowly to plug the increasing gaps in Manager Alston's veteran team. The 1956 year would be Jackie Robinson's last; Billy Cox was gone as a fixture in the infield, as was Preacher Roe from the mound. Joe Black had faded as rapidly as he had appeared and was toiling again in the minors by 1954, before being traded off to Cincinnati in 1955. But the lineup which Alston fielded in 1956 was still awesome and experienced and another pennant was the inevitable result. It didn't come easy this time around though, and the Dodgers needed a final-day victory over the Pirates— Don Newcombe's 27th win of the campaign—to assure a pennant victory. Newcombe, enjoying the finest season of his career, was fittingly honored for his effort with the league's first-ever Cy Young Award.

The 1956 World Series was perhaps the most anti-climactic in Dodgers history, another tight seven-game Series lost in almost predictable fashion to the crosstown rival Yankees. Yet this Series was always to be remembered for a single dramatic game—perhaps the best-remembered of any single game in the eight decades of World Series play. As had happened with Podres and Amoros the season before, or with Bill Bevens and Cookie Lavagetto in 1947, World Series play often selects the most unlikely of heroes to capture the nation's imagination for one brief day of immeasurable glory. On October 8, 1956, in Series Game Five, Yankee Don Larsen achieved baseball immortality with the first and only no-hitter (a perfect game at that) in the annals of the nation's Fall Classic. Larsen's perfect game was ironically the singular career highlight of a pitcher who was to win but 81 big-league games and lose 91, while pitching with eight different teams over 14 mediocre seasons. Don Larsen's single day of glory also provided the death-knell for another frustrating Dodgers summer in aging Ebbets Field, as the Yankees took the second of the final two games at Ebbets Field to register their sixth Series title in seven tries against Brooklyn. While few could perhaps sense it at the time, that final Series game of October 10, 1956 was also the last ever to be played by a team wearing the Brooklyn uniform.

Summer 1957 was destined to be the final season in Brooklyn, though hardly anyone realized this when the Dodgers broke spring training camp in Vero Beach that April. The signs of impending divorce between Walter O'Malley and the community which had so long sustained the Dodgers' rich baseball tradition were already in the air, of course. Brooklyn had scheduled seven "home games" in Jersey City Stadium in 1956—one against each other National League rival—and again in 1957. O'Malley clearly chafed under the knowledge that Milwaukee's Braves, with their new showcase stadium, continued to draw over two million spectators each season between 1954 and 1957.

The 1957 baseball season itself was downbeat and quiet for Brooklyn. The ever-improving Braves won 95 ball games and finished eight lengths in front of the second-place Cardinals, 11 full games above the fading Dodgers, who limped home 14 games over .500. While Snider hit 40 homers again and Furillo batted a fraction over .300, for the first time in almost a decade the Dodgers failed to lead the National League in a single offensive category. This was an altogether anti-climactic and unfitting end for the glorious tradition of Dodger baseball in the borough of Brooklyn—a tradition which had provided so many thrills and heroes during the glorious dozen seasons that had followed World War II. Yet as the end came for Brooklyn baseball in autumn 1957, most fans—for all the obvious signs of the past two seasons—still didn't realize that the demise of their beloved team was quite so near at hand.

Pennants to Poverty in the Decade of Koufax and Drysdale

The 1950s were a difficult act to follow for the men still wearing the blue flannels of the team called Dodgers, despite their new home 3,000-plus miles west of Flatbush and Bedford Avenue. There had been five new Dodger pennants in a span of 10 years topped off by two World Championships, three additional second-place finishes, and a total of nine years in third place or better. The "Boys of Summer" Dodgers of Ebbets Field had arguably been the most talented team in a half-century of modern National League play. Against the backdrop of such unparalleled franchise success, the 1960 Dodgers roster—crammed as it was with fading Brooklyn veterans and unproven youngsters—was hardly an optimistic sign for continued glory or measured improvement.

The metropolis of Los Angeles greeted the Dodgers and Mr. O'Malley with open arms during the anticipatory winter and the exciting new baseball season of 1958. After shivering through an opening series in tiny Seals Stadium in San Francisco, where the Dodgers lost their first West Coast game 8–0 to the transplanted Giants, the new Los Angeles team arrived with the Giants for their hometown opener on April 18, with a 2–3 record and little of the luster of the World Championship outfit that had graced Brooklyn several seasons earlier. Yet the new Dodgers were greeted like returning heroes. L.A. Coliseum was overflowing with 78,000-plus fans who turned out for a slapstick 6–5 triumph against the superior San Francisco club featuring sluggers Willie Mays, Orlando Cepeda, Felipe Alou, and Willie Kirkland. The opening home series drew 167,204 (55,000 per game), nearly 16 percent of the entire 1957 Ebbets Field turnout. Besides a thrill-packed major league ball game, Opening Day 1958 in Los Angeles included a huge motorcade of the type usually reserved for World Series celebrations alone, an on-field celebrity-studded pre-game ceremony featuring Hollywood comedian Joe E. Brown, and an enormous Coliseum throng constituting the largest turnout ever to witness a National League game. Such crowds did not cease as the summer progressed, despite increasingly ragged Dodgers play, and by All-Star break the Dodgers had already exceeded the entire-season 1957 Brooklyn attendance, while at that very moment they continued to languish in last place.

Baseball opened on the West Coast under bizarre playing conditions, to say the least. For starters, the cavernous Los Angeles Coliseum was perhaps the strangest and most inhospitable professional ballpark of all time. L.A.'s Coliseum had been constructed for the 1932 Olympics and subsequently utilized as a college and professional football stadium; to prepare it for baseball, a steel wire fence had been erected from the right-field corner across the open stretches to center field, leaving sufficient dimensions of 300 feet at the foul line and 440 feet to the center-field corner. But the close left-field stands (250 feet at the foul line) could only be shielded by a ridiculous 40-foot-high screen. "The Chinese Screen," as it was known, seemed like little true protection against a potent slugger like strapping first baseman Gil

Hodges, who was anticipated to pound out perhaps 60 or 70 round trippers in the ill-shaped home ballpark. The strange configuration of the Los Angeles park spurred writers and fans to comment that this was a stadium built to accommodate 90,000 fans but only two outfielders. Yet while home runs did not come as easy as anticipated (193 in 1958), which was less than in Ebbets Field in the several preceding seasons), huge paying crowds of spectators did. The Dodgers drew 1.8 million in the summer of 1958 (up 800,000 over the previous year in Brooklyn); an all-time record Opening Day crowd of 78,672 witnessed the first-ever home victory over San Francisco on April 18; an identical number attended an August 30 game with the Giants as well. Yet the slide of Dodger veterans which had begun in 1957 continued in 1958: Snider alone hit .300; Hodges and Neal were the home run leaders with a mere 22 each; Podres led the pitching staff with only 13 victories; and Koufax (11-11) was the only Dodger starter to pitch at .500

The 1958 season, for all the hoopla it generated among baseball-starved West Coast fans, was clearly a rebuilding season for the Dodgers contingent that O'Malley and Alston had brought to the City of Angels. Alston's first Los Angeles team featured a tattered collage of fading Brooklyn Dodger heroes resurrected in a strange West Coast setting and presenting a mere shadow of their former National League prominence. The 1958 and 1959 editions of the Dodgers were a strange mixture of grizzled veterans and raw youngsters as well. Snider, Gilliam, Furillo, and Erskine were on their way out. Carl Erskine would win only four games in 1958 and none in 1959; Furillo appeared in as many as 100 games for the final time during the 1958 season, and Snider hit .300 and connected for over 20 homers for the last time in 1959 as well. Drysdale, Koufax, Howard, Roseboro, and Sherry were the Dodgers stars of the future, and established pitcher Johnny Podres still had his best seasons before him (he would be 18–5 and lead the league in winning percentage in 1961). Yet the old order had passed and only Snider, Hodges, and Junior Gilliam would repeat 1955 World Series starts in 1959.

Baseball fortunes reversed themselves quite dramatically and drastically on the West Coast in the summer of 1959. The Dodgers wasted no time in re-emerging as a league power on the heels of their disappointing seventh-place finish of 1958, which saw the team which Rickey had originally built finish under .500 (71–83) for the first time since before the end of World War II. And the rival Giants in San Francisco were not lagging far behind, completing a second consecutive strong third-place ledger and improving from 12 to only four games off the league-leading pace. The Giants actually led the close 1959 pennant race into the final two weeks of the season, but as San Francisco slipped down the stretch the Dodgers and Braves closed fast to finish in a dead heat and create the third tie-breaking playoff in National League history—and the third such playoff for the Dodgers franchise as well. Yet unlike the disappointments of 1946 against the Cardinals and 1951 against the Giants, the 1959 overtime series was one in which the Dodgers were not to be denied. The opening game was a squeaker, 3–2, in Milwaukee; Game Two a dramatic double come-from-behind 6–5 marathon in 12 innings at the L.A. Coliseum. The Dodgers' dramatic playoff victory did not come without a steep price, however, as Game Two was played with little rest after an all-night flight by both teams from Milwaukee to Los Angeles. The exhausting contest lasted four hours and six minutes and involved 20 Dodgers players, six of the 11-man pitching staff. And World Series play was scheduled to open for the drained National League Champions only a day later back in Chicago, against a refreshed White Sox team which had won 94 games and breezed to an easy pennant over the Indians and Yankees, sparked themselves by a dominant pitching trio of Early Wynn, Bob Shaw, and crafty veteran Billy Pierce.

The 1959 World Series, like the playoffs which preceded it, was again all Los Angeles, however, bringing the Dodgers their second World Championship and the West Coast its very first. It also brought fans in unheard-of numbers to three Series games played in the over-sized Coliseum. Crowds of 92,394, 92,650, and finally 92,796 crammed the oval amphitheater for Games Three, Four, and Five, each breaking the previous single-game mark of 86,288 established by Cleveland in 1948. And what had taken nearly 75 years in Brooklyn was accomplished in only two short seasons in the Dodgers' glamorous new Pacific home. Two victories and two saves by Series MVP hero Larry Sherry sparked a 4–2 triumph over Chicago's White Sox, a team with its own storied history of endless baseball poverty. Not since the infamous Black Sox season of 1919 had the Chicago American League franchise made a World Series appearance. Nor would the White Sox be destined to appear again in the Fall Classic after the 1959 season. And in the autumn of 1959 the "Go-Go-Sox" of Manager Al Lopez, with their blazing speed but lackluster hitting, offered surprisingly little challenge to the hot Dodgers, who won two of three contests in both cities to claim their second world title flag in club history and the first ever to be flown in a West Coast city. Each Dodgers player took home a record $11,231 paycheck from the first West Coast Series, and when the final game ended with a 9–3 victory in Chicago's Comiskey Park on October 8, a jubilant Walter O'Malley (who turned 56 that very day) threw a gala party of champagne and caviar to celebrate with Hollywood flair his team's surprise victory and his own final vindication as well.

By the outset of the 1960 season the Dodgers' lineup was dotted with new young faces and sustained with only a smattering of the old guard. Heavy-hitting Charlie Neal had forced Junior Gilliam off second base before the 1958 and 1959 seasons and remained a regular at that position only until the end of the 1961 campaign, when he was swooped up by the New York Mets in the league's first expansion draft. Wally Moon came over from the Cardinals in 1959 and took an instant liking (despite being a lefthanded batter) to the Coliseum's famed left-field Chinese Wall. Moon slugged 19 homers in 1959 while leading the circuit in triples; yet his finest Dodger summer was in 1961 when he paced the team in batting at .328. Mammoth Frank Howard, an All-American basketball player out of Ohio State University, became a starting outfielder in 1960 and copped National League Rookie-of-the-Year honors that same season. Howard would crush 121 home runs in his five seasons as a Dodgers regular. Norm Larker (also to be lost in the 1962 expansion draft to Houston) had replaced Furillo as the right fielder by the end of 1959 and led the Dodgers in hitting the very next season with a proud .323 average. Speedster Maury Wills broke in at shortstop in 1959 as well and was a fixture there by the following season. Johnny Roseboro was the new catcher after Roy Campanella's crippling automobile accident in January 1958 and would catch the bulk of Dodgers games through the end of the 1967 season. Roseboro would hit with moderate power and deftly handle a wealth of promising young pitchers. Gil Hodges still anchored down first on Opening Day of 1960, and Snider still patrolled center, yet the former was 37 and slipped to only eight homers in 1960 and 1961 before departing to the Mets, while the latter never again hit .300 or displayed his familiar power after his last hurrah of 1959. Reese had retired in 1958 and Carl Furillo was unceremoniously released after feuding with management at the outset of the 1960 campaign.

While the great "Boys of Summer" teams had consistently triumphed with awesome longball power and the lofty batting averages of Furillo, Snider, Robinson, and Hodges, the California Dodgers of the early 1960s seemed destined to be a team meant to survive on the talents of an impressive stable of young pitching thoroughbreds. While Sandy Koufax toiled in relative obscurity his first six big-league seasons, winning in double figures only once (11) in 1958, his strikeout totals had climbed to 173 and 197 by the 1959 and 1960 seasons. Koufax also displayed flashes of true brilliance, as on the night in July of 1959 when he had established a club record by striking out 16 Phillies, and again a month later when he fanned 18 Giants to tie Bob Feller's 1938 major league mark. Lefty Johnny Podres had built on his sterling 1955 World Series performance to become a true mainstay of the Dodgers staff by 1958, winning 13 games or more the first six seasons in Los Angeles. But the mainstay of the revamped Dodgers mound corps was the young Don Drysdale (only 22 in 1958), ace of the 1959 pennant-winning Dodgers with a 17–13 mark and the Opening Day starter for Walter Alston in all four inaugural games in the L.A. Coliseum. Another youngster, Stan Williams, became a starter in 1960 and won 14 games twice and 15 once in his three full-time seasons (1960–1962). A highlight for this young Dodgers staff came in the three-day span of June 22–24, 1960, when Drysdale, Williams, and Roger Craig combined to hurl three consecutive shutouts at the opposition.

The Dodgers never contended during 1960 for the pennant they had won a season earlier. Led by Dodger refugee Roberto Clemente, the Pittsburgh Pirates pulled steadily away from the Braves and Cardinals throughout the summer while the Dodgers, finishing at 10 games above .500, limped home a distant fourth, 13 games behind the pace-setters and only three ahead of the fifth-place Giants and the woeful second division. Bright spots of the 1960 season, however, were the emergence of Maury Wills as a dazzling base thief (he led the National league with 50 steals), the Rookie-of-the Year honors garnered by oversized Frank Howard, and the arrival of two additional young farmhands by the identical name of Davis. Tommy Davis became the regular left fielder that summer and Willie Davis arrived from Spokane before season's end to lay claim to the center-field position of Duke Snider as well.

Most of the furor surrounding the Dodgers' 1961 season involved Walter Alston's coaching staff, at least in the early going before the pennant race heated up. Leo Durocher had returned to the Dodgers after almost 15 seasons, this time in the capacity of Alston's third-base coach, and speculation was quickly fueled that O'Malley had signed on the still-colorful Durocher as eventual replacement for Alston himself. The manager and his illustrious boss both vehemently denied any such scenario and the issue quickly wilted when Los Angeles won 18 of their first 31 ball games and shared first place with Cincinnati by June 1. By late June, though, the Reds with such sluggers as Frank Robinson and Vada Pinson and superb pitching from Joey Jay, Jim O'Toole, Bob Purkey, and Jim Brosnan, had pulled ahead of the field and were able to hold off the spunky but overmatched Dodgers by four games at the wire. The Dodgers had thus managed to escape another ill-fated World Series date with one of the most explosive New York Yankees teams of all-time, one featuring Roger Maris and Mickey Mantle fresh off their incredible fence-busting performances of 61 and 54 home runs, respectively.

Spring of 1962 brought the long-awaited new stadium to Los Angeles and with it the final fulfillment of Walter O'Malley's bold dream for West Coast Dodgers baseball. Dodger Stadium—dubbed Taj O'Malley by local wags and sportswriters—opened to appropriate hoopla and ceremony on April 10, 1962, before a sellout crowd of 52,564. The afternoon's only disappointment was a 6–3 loss to the visiting Cincinnati Reds on the strength of Wally Post's late-inning three-run homer. The new ballpark itself was a state-of-the-art multi-tiered structure arising from the dusty hills of Chavez Ravine, 10 minutes outside downtown Los Angeles. The 300-acre plot, once littered with dry empty gulches and squatters' shacks, had been fully transferred to O'Malley as part of the original deal which relocated the Dodgers franchise, and the city had spent several million dollars to grade and develop the site and several million more to build appropriate roads and freeways leading to the huge concrete and steel ballpark.

The Dodgers' successful 1962 season also signalled one of the most exciting pennant races in franchise history. Koufax had finally overcome the control problems that had plagued his first six seasons and had posted 18 victories in 1961; Stan Williams joined Koufax with 14 victories apiece in 1962, while Podres added 15 and Drysdale led the league with a 25–9 mark. Pitching carried the Dodgers to a lead as large as four games over the Giants in late July; Tommy Davis was batting .350 and Maury Wills was stealing bases at a pace which threatened the once untouchable record of immortal Ty Cobb. The Dodgers Express was nearly derailed on July 17, however, when Sandy Koufax developed a numbness in his pitching hand which was later diagnosed as Reynaud's Phenomenon and which had the practical result of sidelining the young lefty for almost two months of the remaining season. The Dodgers faded badly in late September and Koufax's return in the final weeks of the campaign proved ineffectual and of little help. By closing day the Giants had caught up to the sagging Dodgers who had still held a two-game advantage with only four to play. A final-day loss by Los Angeles to lowly St. Louis had forced the fourth tie-breaking playoff in National League history, to begin at Candlestick Park the succeeding afternoon. Ironically, this was also the fourth league playoff for the Dodgers themselves, and only once (in 1959) had they been able to win such an unscheduled post-season series. Here again the Dodgers were to falter under playoff pressure when a complete collapse of the L.A. bullpen in the top of the ninth (Stan Williams walked home the winning run) of the decisive third game gave the Giants a 6–4 victory and the 1962 pennant.

What was perhaps most remarkable about the 1962 season was the degree of statistical dominance in the National League by the

Dodgers. Wills had indeed shattered Cobb's legendary record of 96 with 104 stolen bases. Koufax, despite his injuries, had struck out 18 in a single game for the second time and hurled his first no-hit game. Third-year-man Tommy Davis had led the entire majors in batting at .346, as well as in total hits (230) and RBIs (153). Frank Howard smacked 31 round trippers and drove home 119 runs. Don Drysdale had enjoyed his best season ever with league-leading efforts in wins (25), strikeouts (232), and innings pitched (314). With 20 saves Ron Perranoski trailed only Elroy Face of Pittsburgh in that department. Drysdale was the Cy Young winner and Wills had captured the MVP. Collective memory of the 1962 season almost two and a half decades later recalls an awesome San Francisco team propelled by the bats of Mays, McCovey, and Cepeda and the pitching arms of Marichal, Billy Pierce, and Jack Sanford. But a closer look at the record reveals that the Dodgers in fact dominated as much or more throughout all but the final days of that memorable campaign.

And it was not long before the Dodgers were back on top as one of the most dominating teams in baseball. With Koufax returning to form and enjoying the first of his three remarkable seasons in a four-year stretch (25–5, 1.88 ERA), and Drysdale posting another sterling year (19–17), 2.63 ERA), Los Angeles battled throughout the 1963 summer in a three-team race with St. Louis and San Francisco. A three-game sweep of the Cards in mid-September was the turning point as the Dodgers edged ahead for a final margin of six games over the Cardinals and 11 over the Giants.

For the second time in six years on the Pacific Coast the Dodgers were in the World Series and the opponent was again their longtime nemesis, the Yankees of New York. Ralph Houk's aging Yankees had waltzed through the American League and possessed pitching and hitting enough of their own. Whitey Ford and Jim Bouton were 20-game winners that summer and Roger Maris, Elston Howard, Joe Pepitone, and Tom Tresh had all hit 20 homers or more. Yet the Yankee bats never got untracked against the strong Dodger arms and after four games the Dodgers enjoyed only their second World Series victory over the New Yorkers in eight tries. For the third time the Dodgers were World Champions and for the first time they had swept a World Series in the minimal four games. Koufax went the distance in the first and fourth games, posted a 1.50 ERA, and earned the first of his two Series MVP honors. In Game One he had struck out 15 to surpass Erskine's 1953 single-game record. The hitting stars were Tommy Davis who batted .400 and Bill (Moose) Skowron (playing his lone season with the Dodgers) who pounded the ball at a .385 clip.

The 1963 season had been the first step in establishing Sandy Koufax as the truly dominant pitcher of his decade. Koufax had started slowly, hampered by an inability to get the ball over the plate and a desire to overthrow on almost every pitch. But eventually the Brooklyn-born southpaw rewarded the patience of Alex Campanis, who had vetoed every effort to trade or option the struggling young fastballer. Once Koufax caught fire in 1961 he was the most unhittable lefthander National League hitters had ever seen, and his four-year span between 1963 and 1966 is perhaps the most remarkable extended stretch any major league hurler has ever enjoyed. With the lively left and right arms of Koufax and Drysdale, and plenty of adequate pitching help from lefthander Claude Osteen (15 wins in 1965 and 17 in 1966) and from newcomer Don Sutton (12–12 in his 1966 rookie season), 1965 and 1966 were the true glory years of the Koufax-Drysdale Dodgers. An early-season loss of hitting star Tommy Davis to a broken ankle in May of 1965 slowed Los Angeles at mid-season and a hot pennant race involving L.A., San Francisco, Cincinnati, and Milwaukee simmered into the final weeks of September. But Koufax's fourth no-hitter in as many years, this time against the Cubs in early September, along with Don Drysdale's 20th victory in the midst of a late-season 13-game winning streak carried the Dodgers past San Francisco in the final weeks en route to a narrow 11th-hour pennant victory and World Series date with Minnesota's Twins.

The Twins boasted an awesome hitting attack, paced by American League batting champion Tony Oliva and MVP Zoilo Versalles, who had led the Junior Circuit in triples, doubles, and runs scored. Early on it seemed that Minnesota's bats would, in fact, carry the day in the 1965 Series, but after lopsided 5–2 and 8–1 victories in Minneapolis the Twins' bats cooled. Three Dodger shutouts over the final five games (one by Osteen and two by Koufax, the Series MVP) settled the matter in favor of the National Leaguers, and once again pitching had proven to be the deciding factor between two well-balanced ballclubs.

The World Series of 1966 was by contrast one of the most one-sided affairs ever involving a Brooklyn or Los Angeles team. The matchup between the Dodgers and Baltimore promised a Series again based upon a classical baseball confrontation of potent American League hitting and overpowering Los Angeles pitching. Youngster Jim Palmer was the leading Baltimore hurler with only 15 victories and Baltimore had no moundsmen among the American League leaders in any statistical category. Offense was Baltimore's strongest suit: Frank Robinson had just become the first American League triple crown winner in a decade and was amply supported by Boog Powell (third in homers and RBIs and fourth in BA), as well as the 23 homers and 100 RBIs of third baseman Brooks Robinson. But the World Series rarely follows form, and after Drysdale was knocked from the box early in the opening game—won 5–2 by Baltimore on the superb relief pitching of veteran Moe Drabowski—the young and untouted Orioles staff completely shut down the Dodgers bats and ran off three consecutive shutout victories. The three complete-game shutouts were provided by Palmer, Wally Bunker, and Dave McNally, and while Koufax, Claude Osteen, and Drysdale pitched admirably enough in the final three contests, they were consistently overmatched by the surprising fledgling Oriole staff which spun a string of 33 consecutive scoreless innings and compiled an unheard-of 0.50 ERA at the expense of the punchless Dodgers. The legacy of the 1966 World Series in the end was a litany of new World Series records for futility, all set by the undermanned Dodgers: most consecutive World Series shutouts suffered (3); most consecutive scoreless innings (33); fewest runs (2), fewest hits (17), fewest total bases (23), and lowest team batting average (.142).

No player has ever gone out on top quite like Koufax did in the season of 1966. He posted 27 victories and only nine defeats; an incredible 1.73 ERA; 317 strikeouts in a league-leading 323 innings pitched. He was the league pace-setter in shutouts and complete games; a Cy Young Award winner and second (behind Roberto Clemente) in the race for league MVP. No player in baseball history has walked away from the game at age 31 on the heels of quite such a season. Add to the 1966 totals the following achievements of 1965–1966: two consecutive years as major league strikeout leader; back-to-back Cy Young awards (three in four years); 1965 league leader in winning percentage (26–8, .765); 1965 World Series MVP; an unparalleled five consecutive seasons as National League ERA king. It is little wonder that Sandy Koufax would be elected by the Baseball Writers of America as the game's "player of the decade" at the close of the 1960s. One writer has suggested that it was as if a pole vaulter had soared above the world record and then simply failed to return to earth! But the pain in Koufax's pitching arm had become unbearable and doctors warned that permanent disability was a probable consequence of continuing to throw a baseball at upwards of 100 miles an hour. His elbow was constantly encased in ice packs throughout the latter stages of the 1966 season and Koufax knew he was finished long before fans or teammates or front-office management dared to face that possibility. Six brilliant summers (129 victories against 47 defeats between 1961 and 1966), piled on top of six mediocre early-career seasons (36 wins and 40 losses), and the greatest left-hander in Dodgers history was suddenly gone. It was a fittingly strange end to one of the strangest careers in Dodgers history.

Drysdale's greatest single achievement ironically came in the Dodgers' most disappointing 1968 campaign, his own last successful season in a 12-year span in which he garnered all but 10 of his 209 big-league victories. In June of that year Drysdale was at his flame-throwing best as he reeled off an incredible record string of 58⅔ scoreless innings over a seven-game span, including a record six consecutive complete-game shutouts. One of baseball's greatest single pitching performances toppled a major-league standard established by the immortal Walter Johnson a full half-century earlier in 1913. The six consecutive shutouts during this string bested a 1904 record of five by Doc White of the Chicago White Sox. A little less than two months later Drysdale would top off his final blazing summer by pitching three scoreless All-Star Game innings and recording his second consecutive All-Star Game victory for the National League.

The end of the turbulent decade of the 1960s was more of a whimper than a bang for the Los Angeles National League baseball franchise. While the nation as a whole saw political assassinations, race riots in its southern cities, and violent anti-war demonstrations in the large metropolitan centers of its industrial north, baseball on the West Coast was a time of disillusionment as well for the faithful patrons of Dodger Stadium. The real unraveling had begun in January 1967, only weeks after the Dodgers' crushing defeat in the 1966 World Series at the hands of Baltimore. Unable to stand the pain of his arthritic elbow for another season, Sandy Koufax stunned his teammates and legions of fans with an announcement of his premature retirement at age 31. While many of the Dodgers traveled on a barnstorming tour through the Far East in the fall of 1966, team captain Maury Wills balked at the post-season activities in Japan and made an unauthorized early return to the United States in mid-tour. Infuriated team officials promptly dealt Wills off to the Pittsburgh Pirates, a brief exile from which he would later return for three final mediocre seasons in the early 1970s.

Other stars of the decade fell by the wayside as well, as Tommy Davis, slowed by a severe ankle injury, was peddled to the Mets during spring training of 1967 and veteran Junior Gilliam ended his 14-year career with retirement that same spring. The on-field results were equally depressing, as the Dodgers fell to 16 games under .500 in 1967 and 13 below for 1968. The inevitable results were an eighth-place finish—the first season at that subterranean level since back in 1905—followed by a tie for the seventh spot a year later. Never before in National League play had a pennant winner fallen quite so low in the standings in the span of a single year.

Off-season trades during the winter of 1968 for such battle-worn veterans as shortstop Zoilo Versalles of the Twins and former sluggers Rocco Colavito and Ken Boyer from the White Sox did little to bolster the still sagging 1968 and 1969 Dodgers teams. When Drysdale was also forced into early retirement in 1969 by nagging shoulder problems, one of baseball's most potent teams of the recent modern period had been completely dismantled in the span of little more than four seasons. The fans in Los Angeles were predictably restless as the curtain fell on the 1960s, and the period between 1967 and 1970 witnessed the four lowest season attendance marks in the club's 30 years of California play—the all-time low of 1,581,093 coming in 1968. With an aging 1968 pitching staff on which the now-departed Drysdale had been the only winner at 14–12, there seemed little reason to imagine the Dodgers could rebound from this slide at the end of the 1960s in quite the same dramatic fashion with which they had rebounded from similar slides exactly a decade earlier.

The Kids of Summer—Exit Walter Alston, Enter Tommy Lasorda

Hurricane Larry MacPhail and the Old Mahatma, Branch Rickey, left their impact on the Dodgers organization with a seemingly endless string of matchless player personnel decisions. Walter O'Malley's legacy to Dodgers baseball and the national pastime was indisputably the inauguration of West Coast baseball and the building of Taj O'Malley. The massive stadium at Chavez Ravine remains, a full quarter century later, one of baseball's most luxurious and yet fan-friendly ballparks and a true mecca for California baseball fans of all persuasions. But one personnel decision of Walter O'Malley's was also destined to shape the direction of the franchise for the coming three decades. When Walter Alston signed the first of his 23 single-year renewable contracts to manage the Dodgers in 1954, no one could imagine that he would still be there and thriving a quarter of a century and seven World Series appearances later.

The summer that Alston began his 15th year at the Dodger helm, 1969, had been an historic year for baseball on the whole and for the Dodgers in particular. This was baseball's centennial year and the year when Branch Rickey's scheme for the new Continental League almost got off the ground. On the baseball map, the greatest expansion in big-league history also came about in 1969, a fact not unrelated to Rickey's loud efforts, earlier in the decade, to launch a new professional league outside of baseball's traditional establishment. Four new ballclubs were added, with Montreal and San Diego joining the fold in the Senior Circuit, the Kansas City Royals and Seattle Pilots in the Junior Circuit. Two 10-team leagues were revamped as four six-team divisions and the annual playoff derby known as the League Championship Series was born as a boon to televised baseball if something of a boondoggle to baseball traditionalists. In Los Angeles Walter O'Malley finally relinquished control of his team, passing the reins of power after 19 years to his talented son, Peter O'Malley. The junior O'Malley became club vice president and chief operating officer in 1969, stepping up to president in 1970, while the senior O'Malley withdrew to the semi-retirement of board chairmanship. Major league baseball now reached all the way into Canada, yet the man who had first stretched the nation's pastime from coast to coast had silently passed from the active scene.

Amidst all the changes swirling around him, Walter Alston was still there for a 15th season and his revamped team was a fixture in the first division throughout the first half of the new decade featuring divisional play. The year 1970 was, in fact, Alston's 30th consecutive season as manager of a professional baseball team, putting him in the longevity department with men like Connie Mack, Wilbert Robinson, and Casey Stengel. But Alston at 60 was as spry as ever as the new decade opened, and two second-place finishes in 1970 and 1971 were followed by a third-place year in 1972, and then another second place in 1973. This was, of course, within the new divisional-play alignment which featured a Western Division consisting of Atlanta (where the Braves had relocated in 1966), Cincinnati, Houston, San Diego, and San Francisco.

Of the first four summers of the new decade, only the 1971 season was a truly close pennant race for the Dodgers. In that summer they finished a tantalizingly close second to the Cincinnati Reds, losing out ultimately by only a single game. The 1971 Dodgers team featured a newly revamped roster that was the outgrowth of extensive rebuilding efforts after the dismal twin seasons of the late 1960s. Bill Russell had appeared on the scene in 1969 as a slugging young outfield prospect who had risen rapidly through the Dodgers lower farm system. By 1971 Russell was making his first scattered appearances at shortstop, the position he would soon man regularly until the mid-1980s. Two other promising youngsters also emerged from the minors in 1969 and enjoyed their first full flowering during the 1971 campaign: Steve Garvey played regularly at third base for the first time in 1971 (he did not move permanently to first base until 1973) and Bill Buckner became an outfield regular in 1971 as well.

The Dodgers entered 1971 with a renewed spirit, youth, speed, and a new infusion of power. The most important arrivals in spring training that year were Ron Cey and Davey Lopes. Cey would become the all-time L.A. home run leader early in the next decade and Lopes would lead the National League in stolen bases in 1975–76 while manning second base for a full decade. Neither would make the big club until 1973, but their presence that spring was part of a bold youth movement also featuring Steve Yeager, who became a regular catcher by 1974.

Trades had also improved the Dodgers by 1971, with power-hitting catcher Duke Sims coming aboard from Cleveland and slugger

Richie Allen being acquired in a blockbuster deal with the Cardinals. This youth was balanced with a few remaining veterans from the immediate post-Koufax era. Bill Singer had moved into the regular pitching rotation in 1967 and had won 20 games in the fourth-place season of 1969. Wes Parker was a fixture at first base where he won six consecutive Gold Glove Awards (1967–72) and established himself as one of the game's greatest defensive first sackers ever. Maury Wills had returned from short sojourns in Pittsburgh and Montreal to reclaim the shortstop position and was now the unchallenged patriarch of the team. Jim Brewer was still saving games (20 in 1969, 24 in 1970, 22 in 1971) as the best reliever in club history.

For the 1971 season the Dodgers had to square off with a revamped Giants team as well as with the powerful Big Red Machine of Sparky Anderson in Cincinnati. L.A. played well early and moved into second place by June, 9½ games behind the pace-setting Giants. Still only three games out as late as September, the Dodgers had surprised the skeptics and perhaps Alston himself by staying in the thick of the race right down to the final week. The last weekend of the season brought a crucial series with Houston—the Dodgers needing a sweep to stay even with the pace-setting Giants—but it was the Giants this time who held on to capture the Western Division flag.

The next serious run at the pennant came in 1974 when L.A. fielded its best team in a decade or more. A runaway 102 victories that season were the most by a Dodgers outfit since 1962, and the most for a Dodger pennant winner since the franchise-record 105 achieved way back in 1953 at Ebbets Field. The 1973 campaign had already provided indications of this renewed strength that was to come to the Dodgers by mid-decade. But 1973 will be remembered as one of the more disappointing summers in Dodgers annals. While Nolan Ryan was tearing up the A.L. a few miles away in Anaheim—pitching two no-hitters and outstripping the memory and standards of Koufax by striking out a big-league record 383 batters—the Dodgers were doing a September swan dive and allowing the Reds to come on strong for their second straight Western Division flag.

The 1974 season was a truly historic one in sunny California, bringing with it the first all-California World Series ever played. And the Dodgers were the bulk of the West Coast baseball story that summer of Watergate and Richard Nixon. The club was strengthened by key trades that brought relief-specialist Mike Marshall from the Expos for 34-year-old Willie Davis and slugger Jim "Toy Cannon" Wynn from Houston in exchange for veteran hurler Claude Osteen. Los Angeles started fast, losing only their first game in Atlanta on the very April night when Aaron equalled Ruth's legendary record by reaching the 715 homer mark off the serving of Al Downing in Fulton-County

Stadium. Andy Messersmith (20–6) and Don Sutton (19–9) led the mound corps throughout 1974. Garvey (.312, 21 HRs) and Buckner (.314 BA) swung the big bats for most of the summer, and Wynn immediately proved his value with 32 roundtrippers and 108 RBIs. Unlike 1973 the Dodgers didn't fold in the stretch, though they faltered a bit in mid-September when Cincinnati cut the lead to 1½. Alston exhorted his men to remember 1973 and the Dodgers responded by hanging on for a four-game margin at the close. When individual honors were handed out that fall, Garvey capped his fine season by becoming the first Dodgers MVP since Sandy Koufax in 1966.

The 1974 World Series was a dream come true for California baseball fans. The opponent for Los Angeles this time around was the turmoil-ridden Oakland Athletics of flamboyant owner Charlie Finley. This was a team that featured such superstars as Reggie Jackson, Cy Young winner Catfish Hunter, and Vida Blue, and supplied enough off-field fireworks to rival the 1930s Daffiness Dodgers or the Gashouse Gang era of Dizzy Dean and Frankie Frisch in St. Louis. Charlie Finley's boys were all business in October of 1974, however, and breezed to their third consecutive World Title, aided amply along the way by six crucial Dodgers errors over the short five-game Series.

By 1975 the Cincinnati Reds' powerful hitting machine of Joe Morgan, Johnny Bench, Tony Perez, George Foster, and Pete Rose had matured fully and left the rest of the Western Division far behind. The Dodgers were second in both 1975 and 1976, yet fell far behind Sparky Anderson's Reds (20 games in 1975 and half that many the following season). Individual achievements were all that could be boasted for Los Angeles, but these were by no means insignificant. Steve Garvey became the first Dodger ever to collect 200 hits in three consecutive seasons, also earning three Gold Gloves at first base over the same span. Don Sutton moved into third place on the all-time Dodgers victory list by the end of 1976 and also recorded his 2,000th career strikeout, again good for third place. The end of an era was also at hand as 1976 closed. The 1976 baseball season would be the last for durable Walter Alston and fittingly Alston achieved his 2,000th career victory on July 17. Only five other managers in the game's storied history had won that many: Connie Mack, John McGraw, Bucky Harris, Joe McCarthy, and Larry MacPhail's old nemesis, Leo Durocher.

After a first, five second-place finishes, and a third, it seemed that little room had been left for an encore, but 1977 saw Los Angeles again dominating the National League West. The Dodgers coasted that year to a 10-game final margin over Cincinnati, winning 98 games and hitting more home runs (191) than any major league team except

Boston (213) and the White Sox (192). But the big news was a new manager at the helm. With but four games remaining in 1975, Walter Alston had finally stepped down, at age 65 and after 23 seasons on the bench with his beloved Dodgers. Assistant Tommy Lasorda had been immediately named the new permanent Dodgers skipper. And for the 49-year-old Lasorda it was also the consummation of a love affair; the ex-Dodger farm hand and longtime coach had reputedly turned down at least three firm offers to manage other big-league clubs in order to wait his expected turn at the Dodgers bench command.

The team Lasorda inherited was one well worth waiting for. Trades had again altered and improved the Dodger lineup: catcher Johnny Oates had been acquired from the Phillies and talented out-fielder Rick Monday arrived from the Cubs in exchange for Bill Buck-ner and reserve infielder Ivan DeJesus. Restocked with power-hitting and fine defense, and paced by the 20-win season of veteran lefthander Tommy John (four other pitchers also won 12 or more), the Dodgers streaked to a first-place finish and an easy playoff victory over the Philadelphia Phillies.

Autumn 1977 would also witness another thrilling Dodgers World Series, the sixth in 18 seasons of Los Angeles residence. But there would again be disappointment in the end, as for the third consecutive World Series matchup the Dodgers would come away without a World Championship banner to hang above Dodger Stadium. This was to be a Series dominated by the offensive exploits of a single superstar as perhaps no Series had ever been dominated before. It was all Reggie Jackson, as the Yankees slugger crushed a total of five homers (with 10 RBIs), three consecutive in the final game (on three pitches off three different hurlers). "Mr. October" wrote his name alongside Ruth and Mantle with one of the purest World Series hitting exhibitions ever witnessed. In the end the New Yorkers took two of three contests in each city. For those who were still keeping track, it was the seventh Dodger loss in World Series competition with the Yankees, compiled over a stretch of nine matchups since their first meeting in 1941.

The 1978 edition of Lasorda's Dodgers showed little sign of falter-ing, however. Competition in the division was more intense, as Cincin-nati (92 wins) and San Francisco (89 wins) hung around until almost the final week of the season. But with a thrilling pennant race at hand between the Western Division's three longtime rivals the turnstiles clicked as never before and the Dodgers franchise set two marvelous attendance marks, becoming the first club ever to draw three million at their home park and drawing a record 5.5 million total spectators with road attendance added on. For the second season in a row the Phillies provided little N.L.C.S. opposition and a 10th-inning single by veteran Bill Russell in the fourth playoff game provided the winning margin and put the Dodgers into their third World Series of the decade.

The 1978 World Series would bring still another defeat at the hands of the hated Yankees. Reggie Jackson was back to inflict more damage, hitting at a .391 clip and stroking two more homers, in the first and final games. The Dodger bats had been the most potent in the N.L. throughout the 1978 campaign, as the team paced the Senior Circuit in slugging (.402), home runs (149), RBIs (686), and runs (727), but against the Yankees they were outhit .306 to .261 in the six-game series and were swept four games in a row after two opening Dodger Stadium victories. The vaunted L.A. pitching staff with its 3.12 ERA (best in the majors) also collapsed (5.46 Series ERA) against the active Yankee bats. Shortstop Bucky Dent (Series MVP, .417 B.A.) and second baseman Brian Doyle (.438 B.A.) were unlikely Yankee Series heroes, and each stroked three hits in the 7–2 New York victory that wrapped up the Yankees' 22nd fall title and eighth (in 10 tries) over the Dodgers themselves.

Optimism was buoyed, both by two straight World Series appearances and some old familiar faces around the Dodgers' Vero Beach camp in the spring of 1979. Sandy Koufax had returned to the fold as a pitching coach, and another trusty arm, Andy Messersmith, was also back with the Dodgers organization for a final shot at recapturing the glory which had brought him 20 victories in 1974 and 19 in 1975. The 34-year-old free-agent hurler had been released by the Yankees due to his chronic shoulder problems and not unsurprisingly saw only sparse action (2–4, 4.94 ERA) in his final comeback attempt with the Dodgers. Some more substantial pitching help also arrived via the trade route in the form of Pittsburgh ace Jerry Reuss, as well as from the minors in the person of highly touted prospect Rick Sutcliffe. Reuss did not produce anticipated results until 1980, when he compiled an impressive 18–6 mark, but Rick Sutcliffe paid more immediate dividends. The big right hander was 17–10 and voted the league's top rookie in the process.

The hitting was there in 1979, as Steve Garvey remained among the league leaders in most offensive categories and the Dodgers paced the N.L. in homers (Garvey, Lopes, and Cey each had 28). But with little pitching beyond Sutcliffe (Sutton won 12 and Hooton 11) and porous defense, L.A. was not much of a force in the Western Division during this last season of the decade. The 1979 team slumped badly in the first half, falling 18 games behind the Houston Astros by early July, and then came back slowly at season's end for a less-than-respectable third-place finish and sub-.500 record. More important, Walter O'Malley died in late August at the age of 75, and another era had solemnly ended for the storied Dodgers franchise.

If Koufax and Drysdale were the dominant Dodgers stars of the 1960s, that laurel falls upon Steve Garvey and Don Sutton in the decade of the 1970s. A cornerstone of the remarkable infield of Ron Cey, Bill Russell, and Davey Lopes—the Kids of Summer—Garvey played in every Dodgers game for seven seasons, his remarkable streak ending in 1983 at 1,207 games, fourth longest in major league history. His 211 career homers as a Dodger placed him fifth on the all-time club list, and in 1977 the 11-time league all-star became the first National Leaguer ever to garner over four million votes in a single year's All-Star balloting. Sutton proved every bit as durable, perhaps more surprising still for a pitcher. In a Dodger career that stretched from 1966 to 1980, the handsome curly headed righthander amassed numbers that put him atop eight different pitching categories among all-time Dodgers hurlers: wins (233), losses (181), games started (553), games appeared (558), strikeouts, (2,696), innings pitched (3,815), hits allowed (3,291), and career shutouts (52).

From Fernando to "The Natural"—Baseball Finally Goes Hollywood

Dodger historian Richard Wittingham has called Tommy Lasorda "a unique amalgam of Casey Stengel, Knute Rockne, Toots Shor, and Billy Sunday" and the unlikely composite caricature in this instance seems fittingly appropriate. It was clear when Tommy Lasorda took command of the Dodger dugout in late 1976, after five summers as key coaching assistant to Walter Alston, that Lasorda's qualifications for the job consisted of far more than his welcomed and shrewd sense of baseball strategy. For Lasorda was also built somewhat in the Alston mode, despite the many stark contrasts in personality type. First and foremost the new Dodgers skipper was a fiercely loyal organization man, one who bled Dodgers blue and who always spoke of "we" and "the team" as Alston had done before him. Lasorda was also passionately loyal to his players and exerted a calming influence in the clubhouse with his youthful "Kids of Summer" ballclubs of the late 1970s.

Much like Alston before him, Lasorda had been a journeyman player with the briefest possible big-league career. While Walt Alston had enjoyed but a single big-league plate appearance against the Cubs in Sportsman's Park in 1936, Lasorda pitched 13 innings with the Dodgers and 45 with Kansas City between 1954 and 1956, suffering four defeats and never winning a major league contest. He then became a career organization man whose dedication to serving the Dodgers was eventually rewarded when his own time fell due. And not without justification, for in seven seasons as a minor league pilot in the Dodgers organization, Lasorda had won five pennants and once even been honored as minor league manager of the year.

Lasorda was not the only colorful character to emerge from the L.A. clubhouse at the outset of the 1980s. A cherubic roly-poly pitcher with a herky-jerky windup and unhittable screwball also appeared out of nowhere from the refuge of the Mexican League and the Dodgers overnight had their first colorful character in the mold of Dizzy Dean and Pepper Martin since perhaps Babe Herman or Pete Reiser in the late 1940s.

Fernando Valenzuela was also every bit as much a pitching star as he was a media sensation and darling of the fans. The strike-interrupted 1981 season was the one in which Valenzuela burst on the scene with a 13–7 mark, and over the course of the summer ruled the National League. It surprised no one who saw him pitch that year that Valenzuela was a runaway choice as Cy Young Award winner and an equally obvious selection as the National League's Rookie of the Year. In copping the latter prize he became the 10th Dodger so honored and the third of four in succession. Sutcliffe had taken the honor in 1979, lefthanded pitcher Steve Howe won in 1980, and infielder Steve Sax would follow suit in 1982 as well.

Valenzuela's first outings actually came in late 1980 when he appeared in 10 games, tossed 18 innings, and won two decisions without allowing a single earned run. The 1980 season had seen the Dodgers return to respectability with a second-place finish, 92 victories, and a near pennant which was lost on the final day of the season. This was quite a rebound from the first losing season in 11 years which had unfolded only a summer earlier. The 1980 campaign saw several new young stars in addition to Valenzuela, most notably relief hurler Steve Howe. Howe carved out a Dodger rookie record with 17 saves (Joe Black had 15 in 1952) on his way to freshman-of-the-year honors. A milestone event as well was Jerry Reuss's no-hitter at San Francisco, only the second by L.A. pitchers other than Koufax.

And 1980 also marked the end of the line for one of the greatest Dodger hurlers of all time. When Don Sutton tested the free-agent market that year, signing on with Houston, he had already won 11 or more games for a remarkable 15 consecutive years while in Los Angeles uniform, rewriting the bulk of franchise pitching records. Sutton was not quite finished, of course, and he would go on pitching with Milwaukee, Oakland, and California through 1987, compiling an astronomical 321 career wins against 250 defeats. In wins Sutton today ranks 12th on the all-time list, seventh among pitchers of the modern age.

The strike-torn 1981 baseball season was one of the most bizarre in the century of major league play. On June 12 the Players' Union walkout left ballparks emptied across the nation until August 9, and when play did resume the owners had adopted a plan to restore the rest of the season—a plan which seemed to have been conceived by men with the baseball sensitivity of a Martian. Action would resume with all teams at 0–0; those four teams in first place on June 12 were simply declared division winners by retroaction, and another layer of playoffs would be held before the L.C.S. games, this time to settle the score between first-half and second-half division winners. This was a stroke of incredible good fortune for the Dodgers who held a mere ½ game lead over the Reds when the ballparks had been shut down. It all seemed good stuff for television, but it wasn't much for the fan who believed that the long course of the summer's 162-game season always provided something in the way of victory by attrition, which was the very distinctiveness which baseball enjoyed over all other sports.

For the Dodgers this was a year of mitigated success and tempered good fortune. This was a strong Dodgers team but not a dominant one, and only the quirk of strike-interrupted play allowed yet another pennant to fly in L.A. Cincinnati, with the best record in baseball, did not qualify for post-season action, nipped by the Dodgers in the first half and falling 1½ games behind Houston in the second makeshift session. Regular composite standings would have left the Reds three games up on the Dodgers and a full five above the Astros, but this was not to be a summer in which either logic or good form applied. Given a window of opportunity, the Dodgers seized it and squeaked by both the Astros and Expos in the bizarre set of twin ad hoc playoff series. The ultimate thriller came with outfielder Rick Monday's solo home run, stroked in the top of the ninth inning of Game Five at Montreal, clinching another Dodgers pennant by a tight 2–1 score and frustrating the Expos, so close to being Canada's first World Series entry ever.

Some sense of normalcy returned to baseball by October. The World Series was after all the World Series, and again it was a clash of traditional rivals. The 1981 Series meant another shot at the omnipresent New York Yankees, and in this year of extraordinary Dodgers karma, luck would finally rest with Los Angeles for a change and thus against the hated New Yorkers. National League Manager of the Year Tom Lasorda saved his rookie ace Valenzuela for Game Three on the Coast, and the Dodgers posted their first Series triumph as Fernando staggered to a complete-game 5–4 victory, despite allowing nine hits and issuing seven walks. From there it was three straight wins for Lasorda's men, with Steve Howe picking up one win and one save down the stretch and Burt Hooton hurling a complete-game five-hitter in Game Five. Pete Guerrero was the batting star in the final contest, driving in five runs as the Dodgers pounded six Yankee pitchers for 13 hits and a commanding 9–2 win. Guerrero shared World Series

MVP honors with Ron Cey (.350 B.A.) and catcher Steve Yeager (.286, 2HRs), and the Dodgers were World Champions for the first time in the new decade and the fourth time since O'Malley had taken them West more than two decades earlier.

The Dodger teams of the early 1980s were again teams in transition, and mixtures of old stars and new hopefuls. Steve Garvey moved on to San Diego for the 1983 campaign, a casualty of the free-agent market which was now dominating baseball's business transactions; Ron Cey was dealt to the Chicago Cubs in January of 1983 for two unheralded minor leaguers; and Steve Howe lost a battle with alcohol which rendered him ineffectual long before his departure in 1985. Hurler Bob Welch, also battling through substance abuse problems, became a mainstay of the mound corps with 115 victories between 1978 and 1987. Fernando Valenzuela proved to be no mere rookie flash, continuing to dominate N.L. hitters for several seasons to come and posting 19 victories in 1982 and 21 in 1986 (his only 20-game winning season). Before being dealt to the St. Louis Cardinals in 1988 Pedro Guerrero, heavy-hitting Dominican outfielder and third baseman, emerged as the new Dodgers slugging star. Guerrero smashed 32 homers in 1982 and 1983, and a career-high 33 in 1985, a total of 166 over an 11-year span.

Two more division crowns would fall to the Los Angeles Dodgers in the mid-1980s. After a defeat at the wire in 1982, falling by one game to Atlanta, the Dodgers hung on against the same Braves for a three-game margin in 1983. But the League Championship Series was swept in three of four by the hot Phillies of Philadelphia, paced by three homers from Gary Matthews and the stellar pitching of aging veteran Steve Carlton. In 1985 the Dodgers won 95 and waltzed home comfortably in late September with a 5½ game lead over Cincinnati. But again the playoffs were dominated by an Eastern Division rival, this time the Cardinals of St. Louis, 4–2, in the new seven-game L.C.S. format. The middle years of the 1980s were a time of individual achievements for the Dodgers, however. Alejandro Peña took the league ERA title in 1984 (12–6, 2.48). Emerging pitching hero Orel Hershiser (19–3, .864) paced the N.L. in winning percentage in 1985, the first Dodger to do so since Rick Rhoden (12–3, .800) had accomplished the feat in 1976. And Ron Cey finally became the all-time Dodgers home run leader in Los Angeles by 1982, stroking his 228th and also moving into fourth place (behind Snider, Hodges, and Campanella) on the combined all-time Dodgers list.

The 1988 campaign was perhaps the most Cinderella-like year in all of Dodgers history, as the L.A. entry charged from the gate and maintained the pace over the summer for a final seven-game margin on Cincinnati, now managed by all-time career-hits leader Pete Rose.

A young Dodgers team was given little attention in pre-season polls yet took the lead in the first weeks of the season and never looked back at the trailing Reds and Padres. This was an emotional team, inspired by new acquisition Kirk Gibson who had joined Lasorda's men as an expensive free-agent refugee from the Detroit Tigers. Gibson added his name to the lengthy tradition of colorful Dodgers characters early on, storming from the Dodgers spring training camp when his team-mates subjected the high-priced outfielder to some welcoming boyish clubhouse pranks. Gibson promptly returned, but not before admon-ishing his new mates that he had come to win and that such tomfoolery had little place in a winning organization. His spring training emo-tional antics established Gibson's flair for color and controversy, but it also inspired his Dodgers teammates. Gibson was a fitting MVP for the National League in 1988, one who demonstrated the true meaning of the award and contributed as much with his hustle and clubhouse spirit as with his impressive statistics (.290 B.A., 25 HRs, 76 RBIs) and clutch hitting throughout the campaign.

The 1988 Dodgers season was also the incredible success story of pitcher Orel Hershiser, who enjoyed as honor-filled and accomplished a summer as any known by a long list of Dodger pitching greats. The supreme highlight of Hershiser's campaign was his remarkable season-ending streak of 59 consecutive scoreless innings, bettering Don Drys-dale's 20-year-old mark. Ironically, Drysdale had recently returned to the Dodgers as a TV commentator, and was fittingly on hand to witness and describe Hershiser's prodigious feat. There was also a Cy Young Award for the Dodgers righthander when the campaign ended, as well as league-leading totals in victories (23) and innings pitched (267).

The 1988 League Championship Series between the heavily fa-vored Eastern Division New York Mets and the upstart Dodgers was one of the most hard-fought, surprising, and bizarre in the 20-year history of L.C.S. play. The most memorable moment was the doctored-ball incident and suspension of Dodgers hurler Jay Howell. Howell had been ejected from Game Two when protests from Mets skipper Davey Johnson brought an umpire's inspection of Howell's glove and discovery of illegal pine tar. The Dodgers reliever later avowed that he had utilized the foreign substance to improve his grip on baseballs during cold weather and that the tar had negligible impact on the flight of a thrown pitch. National League Commissioner A. Bartlett Giamatti disagreed and suspended the Dodgers ace reliever for three full games, effectively eliminating him from the remainder of the championship series. But again adversity only inspired the men of Tommy Lasorda who responded with a thrilling seven-game triumph, highlighted by Hershiser's stellar 6–0 final-game masterpiece.

The 1988 World Series was also a time of further heroics and constant fireworks. A rematch with the slugging Oakland Athletics was a fitting venue in the second-ever all-West-Coast Series, and the men of Oakland were the heavy favorites once more, seemingly invincible behind the home run power of Mark McGwire and Jose Canseco and the dominating staff of Dave Stewart (21–12, 3.23 ERA), Dennis Eckersley (45 saves), and former Dodger Bob Welch (17–9, 3.64 ERA). The Dodgers lavished in their familiar underdog role, however, and it proved to be Orel Hershiser and Kirk Gibson who would steal the latent thunder from Stewart, Eckersley, McGwire, and Canseco. Hershiser was as dominant on the mound as he had been all season (a shutout three-hitter in Game Two), and Howell (with a save in crucial Game Four) combined with Tim Belcher, Tim Leary, and Alejandro Peña to completely shut down the potent Oakland bats in a surprisingly short five-game Series.

The most memorable single moment of this or any other Dodgers World Series may have occurred in the ninth inning of the very first game and was witnessed by millions around the country. If the L.A. Dodgers under Lasorda had become the team of Hollywood style and connection, then what happened that night within Dodger Stadium was ironically fitting. Kirk Gibson, hampered with knee problems and unavailable for outfield play, strode to the plate in an uncharacteristic pinch-hitting role and delivered a dramatic ninth-inning circuit blow from which the stunned Athletics never fully recovered.

Success in baseball like anything else is the toughest act to follow, and 1989 could never match the excitement generated in L.A. by the pennant race of 1988. Thus, the Cinderella 1988 campaign quickly turned to a pumpkin in the spring and summer of 1989. Gibson was hurt and played little after mid-season. Hershiser pitched well—perhaps better than could be hoped—but he did not dominate as in previous seasons, and with a career-high six consecutive defeats even dropped to 14–14 in the season's final week. Veteran second baseman Steve Sax had departed to free agency and the New York Yankees and his free-agent replacement, Willie Randolph, did not carry an equal load. Heralded newcomer Eddie Murray, who brought 333 career homers from his 12 seasons in Baltimore, had predictable difficulty in adjusting to National League pitching. Only Jay Howell lived up to expectations of 1988, carrying a phenomenal 0.67 ERA into the final weeks of the season. Dodger pitching was superb, but there was little offense with the departure of Sax and Guerrero, the injuries to Gibson, and the slumping of Eddie Murray. The hot Giants ran away early from the rest of the pack while the Dodgers languished in fifth place, ahead only of the hapless Atlanta Braves. For Tommy Lasorda, now already in his 13th year, it was back to the drawing board for another rebuilding year in 1990 and beyond.

But at decade's close the Dodgers were still a proud franchise with proud baseball tradition on full display. Fans continued to flock into Dodger Stadium to the tune of over three million each season. The summers of 1987 and 1988 witnessed the only years after the unprecedented 3.6 million major league attendance mark was established in 1982 that the ballclub did not draw more than three million, and in 1988 they had fallen only 20,000 short. And a host of young prospects and established veterans with many good seasons ahead were ample indication that some of the best chapters in the history of this storied franchise were still to be written in the years somewhere just around the corner.

References

All scholars working on historical accounts of the Dodger franchise which has called both Brooklyn and Los Angeles home are indebted to the useful bibliography (cited below) by Myron Smith, an exhaustive compendium of references and materials on this team unlike anything available on any other major league franchise. Smith's scholarship has proven invaluable throughout the writing of this particular team history.

Barber, Red, 1982. *1947—When All Hell Broke Loose in Baseball.* Garden City, N.Y.: Doubleday and Company (New York: Da Capo Press, 1982).

Bjarkman, Peter C. 1990. *Baseball's Great Dynasties: The Dodgers.* New York: W.H. Smith Publishers (Gallery Books).

Bowman, John S., and Joel Zoss. 1986. *The National League: A History.* New York: W.H. Smith Publishers (Gallery Books).

Honig, Donald. 1981. *The Brooklyn Dodgers: An Illustrated Tribute.* New York: St. Martin's Press.

Humber, William. 1989. *Let's Play Ball! Inside the Perfect Game.* Toronto, Ont.: Lester, and Orpen Dennys Publishers.

Kahn, Roger. 1972. *The Boys of Summer.* New York: Harper and Row Publishers.

Smith, Myron, J. 1988. *The Dodgers Bibliography: From Brooklyn to Los Angeles.* Westport, Conn.: Meckler Books.

Annotated Bibliography

No ballclub has been so celebrated in baseball's extensive literature as Brooklyn's Daffy Dodgers, especially Roger Kahn's "Boys of Summer" Dodgers of the final melodramatic Flatbush decade in the 1950s. Inspired by Kahn's *The Boys of Summer,* dozens of volumes have chronicled the frenetic and often bizarre history of baseball's most fabled franchise. Of these sizable archives devoted to Dodger lore and legend, the following selective list comprises an essential library for all true Dodgers fans and historians.

Allen, Lee. *The Giants and Dodgers: The Fabulous Story of Baseball's Fiercest Feud.* New York: G.P. Putnam's Sons, 1964.

No competition in all of American sports history can compare in sheer ferocity with that between the Dodgers and Giants. Allen unfolds the full account of this famed rivalry, from the turn of the century in the boroughs of New York through the early 1960s in Southern California. Amusing, nostalgic, packed with zany episodes and magical moments of diamond heroism, this is an unsurpassed narrative portrait of our two most notorious baseball franchises.

Allen, Maury, *Jackie Robinson: A Life Remembered.* New York and Toronto: Franklin Watts Publishers, 1987.

The most complete and balanced portrait of Jackie Robinson, both during his pioneering baseball playing days and throughout his ceaseless post-retirement crusades for civil rights during the late 1960s. Numerous teammates—alongside dozens of National League rivals—provide unassailable testimony to Robinson's impact upon a generation of Americans. The Jackie Robinson emerging from Allen's deft portrait stands for the reader as a uniquely sensitive and articulate human being, as well as a supremely gifted pro ballplayer.

Barber, Red. *The Rhubarb Patch: The Story of the Modern Brooklyn Dodgers.* New York: Simon and Schuster, 1954.

Rare collection of Barney Stein's official Dodgers photos from the 1938–1953 era, accompanied by Red Barber's nostalgic and often witty text. An unsurpassed portrait album of the Brooklyn teams which Barber and Stein covered, just before the glorious mid-1950s epoch of Snider, Hodges, and Campanella, presented here as a series of rare vignettes capturing Barber's memories of important moments and priceless events.

———. *1947—When All Hell Broke Loose in Baseball.* Garden City, N.Y.: Doubleday and Company, 1982 (New York: Da Capo Press, 1982).

Famous Dodgers broadcaster provides rare behind-the-scenes stories about Jackie Robinson's historical debut appearance with the Dodgers in 1947, plus the unraveling background saga of Branch Rickey's bold plan to bring long-awaited integration to America's pastime. Perhaps the most thorough insider's story of Robinson's struggle to break down baseball's long-standing racial barriers.

Bjarkman, Peter C. *Baseball's Great Dynasties: The Dodgers.* New York: W.H. Smith Publishers (Gallery Books), 1990.

The most recent and one of the most colorful among a long chain of coffee-table histories on the Dodgers' two-city franchise. Released to correspond with the ballclub's 100th Anniversary summer of 1990, this oversized glossy volume contains 110 photographs (some rarely seen in earlier Dodgers histories), as well as decade-by-decade summaries of the most hotly contested pennant races, the heartbreaking defeats, and the dozens of colorful Dodgers heroes of yesteryear.

Campanella, Roy. *It's Good to Be Alive.* Boston: Little, Brown and Company, 1959 (New York: Signet New American Library, 1959).

An inspirational autobiographical account of Campy's brilliant big-league career, cut short by that sudden paralyzing automobile accident in January of 1958. Insights on Campanella's role in baseball integration are abundant, as are portraits of his "Boys of Summer" Dodger teammates—Snider, Robinson, Reese, Furillo, Erskine, Roe, Labine, and the other "Boys of Summer."

Fitzgerald, Ed, ed., Foreword by Red Barber. *The Story of the Brooklyn Dodgers.* New York: Bantam Books, 1949.

A concise history of the pre-1950s Dodgers, with 14 individual chapters by such notable baseball writers as Tom Meany, Dick Young, Red Barber, Ed Fitzgerald, and Jack Sher. Many inspired first-hand accounts of the unbridled excitement surrounding the 1930s–1940s-vintage Dodgers, with two outstanding chapters on Stengel (Quentin Reynolds) and Hugh Casey (Tom Meany). All entries except those by the editor are reprints of earlier magazine articles of the late 1930s and 1940s.

Frommer, Harvey. *Rickey and Robinson: The Men Who Broke Baseball's Color Barrier.* New York: Macmillan Publishing Company, 1982.

Perhaps the most readable popular account of baseball integration and the history-making role of both Rickey and Robinson in those unforgettable baseball events of 1947, unfolding in Brooklyn and across the National League. Rickey's motivations in carrying out baseball's integration are well documented here, as is Robinson's short but dramatic major league career. Only Jules Tygiel's academic study (see below) is more enlightening and more insightful on this topic.

Golenbock, Peter. *Bums: An Oral History of the Brooklyn Dodgers.* New York: G.P. Putnam's Sons, 1984.

The most exhaustive scholarly history of the old Dodgers, featuring extensive interviews with most living Dodgers personalities from the 1940s and 1950s. Enthralling oral history of what it was like to be deeply involved with those Dodger ballclubs of the Jackie Robinson and Duke Snider era—what the players thought of Durocher's antics, of Branch Rickey's integration experiment, of Jackie Robinson's enormous impact on baseball and so much more.

Holmes, Tommy. *The Dodgers.* New York: Collier-Macmillan Publishing Company ("Baseball's Great Teams" Series), 1975.

Daffy moments from Dodgers history, great players and immortal managers, unforgettable seasons and games that live on in bittersweet infamy, Brooklyn and Los Angeles baseball milestones, early team history, statistical summaries, and club records—all are found in abundance within this most complete (though now considerably outdated) of the Dodger team histories.

Honig, Donald. *The Brooklyn Dodgers: An Illustrated Tribute.* New York: St. Martin's Press, 1981.

Black-and-white photograph album of the Brooklyn Dodgers, enriched with lively accompanying historical text on each memorable Dodgers epoch. While more thorough in its pictorial record than in its narrative content, this is perhaps still the single best coffee-table-format volume devoted to the original Dodgers. Many player portraits appear here which are found in no other source, and Honig's historical text is always gripping if sometimes regrettably brief.

———. *Dodgers: The Complete Record of Dodgers Baseball.* New York: Collier-Macmillan Publishing Company, 1986.

Extensive statistical records, compiled through 1985, and featuring detailed player career statistics for all past and present (1984) Dodgers; lifetime pitching, batting and fielding leaders; all-time Dodger player rosters; new Dodger graphics which track yearly pennant races and both offensive and defensive play; World Series summaries as well as post-season boxscores.

Kahn, Roger. *The Boys of Summer.* New York: Harper and Row Publishers, 1972 (New York: Harper Perennial Library, 1987).

Perhaps baseball's best loved and most widely read single book—part autobiography of Roger Kahn, part story of the glorious 1950s Ebbets

Field Dodgers, and part inspirational account of how 13 beloved ex-ballplayers have dealt with life's vicissitudes since the sunset of their own personal playing careers a decade or more earlier. No other work has better captured those special features of the Jackie Robinson decade which have made Brooklyn's long love affair with the 1950s Dodgers an unprecedented and unique baseball phenomenon.

Robinson, Jackie, as told to Alfred Duckett. *I Never Had It Made*. New York: G.P. Putnam's Sons, 1972 (Greenwich, Conn.: Fawcett Crest Books, 1974).
Robinson's own gripping and often highly opinionated account of his early Brooklyn playing days, his pioneering role in integrating baseball, his relationships with old teammates in Montreal and Brooklyn, his painful experience as a black man stuck within the hostile all-white world of amateur and professional sport, and his post-baseball struggles on behalf of the 1960s civil rights movement in a nation divided by racial ferment. Aggressive in tone, this personal statement is our best measure of Jackie Robinson—"the private man."

Shapiro Milton J. *Jackie Robinson of the Brooklyn Dodgers*. New York: Julian Messner, 1966 (New York: Washington Square Press, 1967).
The earliest detailed account of Robinson's pioneering big-league career and barnstorming campaigns for civil rights during his immediate post-baseball years. Covers in detail the story of Robinson's collegiate athletic career, his brief Negro League baseball experience, his historic first meetings with Branch Rickey, his first season in organized baseball at Montreal, and his pioneering 1947 season campaign (as Rookie of the Year) with the Dodgers—yet all delivered without the invaluable historical perspective usually found in most subsequent studies.

Snider, Duke, with Bill Gilbert. *The Duke of Flatbush*. New York: Kensington Publishing Corporation (Zebra Books), 1988.
The most revered and yet most distant and mysterious of the "Boys of Summer" reveals his own account of those glory years of the 1950s Brooklyn Dodgers, as well as the pioneer seasons of West Coast baseball with Walter O'Malley's newborn Los Angeles Dodgers. Snider provides close personal (and not always entirely complimentary) portraits of his teammates (Reese, Furillo, Erskine, Durocher, Campanella, Hodges, etc.) from that most unforgettable of all Dodgers teams. Sixteen pages of excellent black-and-white photographs enhance a fine personal memoir and valuable testimonial to the chemistry that solidified one of baseball's most remarkable teams.

Sullivan, Neil J. *The Dodgers Move West*. New York: Oxford University Press, 1987.
Scholarly treatment (by a professional historian and university professor) which probes details of O'Malley's historic move of the Brooklyn franchise to Los Angeles. This book balances the stilted popular conception (that O'Malley cold-heartedly abandoned the devoted Brooklyn fans for the easy-money harvest of Los Angeles) with more accurate assessment (that O'Malley was in fact stymied and driven away by an uncooperative New York City administration which blocked his use of an ideal Atlantic Avenue site for his much-desired new Brooklyn stadium). More than a baseball history, this special study offers new insight into the bizarre workings of political power in the nation's two largest cities, uncovering the hidden business side of O'Malley's story.

Tygiel, Jules. *Baseball's Great Experiment: Jackie Robinson and His Legacy*. New York: Oxford University Press, 1983 (New York: Random House Vintage Books, 1984).

A seminal review of Jackie Robinson's and Branch Rickey's noble experiment to integrate professional baseball at the close of World War II. A scholarly work requiring attentive reading and featuring careful documentation of historical records, extensive personal interviews with baseball men of the era, and meticulous analysis of the background and events surrounding Robinson's appearance in the big leagues. Tygiel provides the proper social context within which to assess the true significance of Robinson's and Rickey's dramatic contributions to the welcomed destruction of racial barriers within American sport.

Wittingham, Richard. *An Illustrated History of the Los Angeles Dodgers.* New York: Harper and Row Publishers, 1982.

The finest coffee-table-format book yet done on the Los Angeles version of the Dodgers, with a balanced historical text, hundreds of quality black-and-white photographs, and extensive statistical summaries and team records. Valuable photos and historical episodes on the old-time Dodgers, as well as detailed summary of remarkable pennant races and individual mileposts in the 1960s and 1970s. Season-by-season Opening Day lineups spice the 17-chapter narrative of the Los Angeles Dodgers era, as do "trivia insets" and candid player interviews.

Bjarkman, Peter C. *The Brooklyn Dodgers.* New York: Chartwell Books (Books Sales), 1992.

A true collector's item which was glowingly reviewed in *The New York Review of Books* by renowned biologist-evolutionist and childhood Yankee fanatic Stephen Jay Gould as "a loving portrait, filled with superb images, of a team I hated with a purity that can only be called hidden love." This oversized 80-page coffee table volume is crammed with rarely seen action shots and posed portraits from all seven decades of Flatbush diamond lore. Many of these photos are rarely published color images of the "Boys of Summer" favorites—Snider, Reese, Hodges, Furillo, Robinson, Roe, Podres, Branca, Erskine, Newcombe, Campanella, and others. The accompanying text is stocked with historical detail and designed to bring vividly to life the quirkiness that was from beginning to end the very essence of Brooklyn National League baseball.

Cohen, Stanley. *Dodgers: The First 100 Years.* New York: Birch Lane Press, 1990.

A worldwind tour through the first hundred years of baseball's most storied ballclub, sometimes fascinating but too often sketchy in its rapid-paced treatment of franchise "glory moments" in both Brooklyn and Los Angeles. The highlight here is perhaps the well-researched chapter devoted to the often-told Rickey-Robinson integration story. Throughout the first half of the book, however, very little is captured in print of the unique aura that surrounded both the "Daffiness Boys" Dodgers of the 1930s and the "Boys of Summer" Dodgers of the 1950s—two of baseball's most engaging success stories. A scattering of familiar black and white photographs also do little to entice readers or enhance the eleven-chapter narrative, and there is almost nothing in this volume that long-time Dodgers fans have not already read about (often in more gripping detail) in dozens of other historical tomes devoted to this colorful ballclub.

Year-by-Year Standings and Season Summaries

Brooklyn Dodgers, 1890–1957

Year	Pos.	Record	Pct.	GB	Manager	Player	BA	Player	HR	Player	W-L	ERA
1890	1st	86–43	.667	+6.0	McGunnigle	O'Brien	.314	Burns	13	Lovett	30–11	2.78
1891	6th	61–76	.445	25.5	Ward	Burns	.285	O'Brien	5	Lovett	23–19	3.69
1892	3rd	95–59	.617	9.0	Ward	Brouthers	.335*	Joyce	6	Haddock	29–15	3.14
1893	6th	65–63	.508	20.5	Foutz	Brouthers	.337	Daly	8	Kennedy	26–20	3.72
1894	5th	70–61	.534	20.5	Foutz	Griffin	.365	Daly	8	Stein	27–14	4.54
1895	5th	71–60	.542	16.5	Foutz	Griffin	.335	Anderson	9	Kennedy	18–13	5.12
1896	9th	58–73	.443	33.0	Foutz	Jones	.353	LaChance	7	Daub	12–11	3.60
1897	6th	61–71	.462	30.0	Barnie	Anderson	.325	LaChance	4	Kennedy	19–22	3.91
								Anderson	4			
1898	10th	54–91	.372	46.0	Barnie Griffin-Ebbets	Jones	.302	LaChance	5	Kennedy	16–20	3.37
1899	1st	101–47	.682	+8.0	Hanlon	Keeler	.377	Kelley	6	Hughes	28*–6	2.68
1900	1st	82–54	.603	+4.5	Hanlon	Keeler	.368	Kelley	6	McGinnity	29*–9	2.90
1901	3rd	79–57	.581	9.5	Hanlon	Keeler	.355	Sheckard	11	Donovan	25*–15	2.77
1902	2nd	75–63	.543	27.5	Hanlon	Keeler	.338	McCreer	4	Kilson	19–12	2.84
								Sheckard	4			
1903	5th	70–66	.515	19.0	Hanlon	Sheckard	.332	Sheckard	9*	Jones	20–16	2.94
1904	6th	56–97	.366	50.0	Hanlon	Gessler	.290	Jones	9*	Jones	17–25*	2.75
1905	8th	48–104	.316	56.5	Hanlon	Lumley	.293	Scanlan	7	Scanlan	14–12	2.92
1906	5th	66–86	.434	50.0	Donovan	Lumley	.324	Jordan	12*	Scanlan	18–13	3.19
1907	5th	65–83	.439	40.0	Donovan	Jordan	.274	Lumley	9	Rucker	15–13	2.06
1908	7th	53–101	.344	46.0	Donovan	Jordan	.247	Rucker	12*	Rucker	17–19	2.08
1909	6th	55–98	.395	55.5	Lumley	Hummel	.280	Hummel	4	Bell	16–15	2.71

Year	Pos.	Record	Pct.	GB	Manager	Player	BA	Player	HR	Player	W-L	ERA
1910	6th	64–90	.416	40.0	Dahlen	Wheat	.284	Daubert	8	Rucker	17–18	2.58
1911	7th	64–86	.427	33.5	Dahlen	Daubert	.307	Erwin	7	Rucker	22–18	2.71
1912	7th	58–95	.379	46.0	Dahlen	Daubert	.308	Wheat	8	Rucker	18–21	2.21
1913	6th	65–84	.436	34.5	Dahlen	Daubert	.350*	Wheat	7	Rucker	14–15	2.87
								Stengel	7			
								Cutshaw	7			
1914	5th	75–79	.487	19.5	Robinson	Daubert	.329*	Wheat	9	Pfeffer	23–12	1.97
1915	3rd	80–72	.526	10.0	Robinson	Daubert	.301	Wheat	5	Pfeffer	19–14	2.10
1916	1st	94–60	.610	+2.5	Robinson	Daubert	.316	Wheat	9	Pfeffer	25–11	1.92
1917	7th	70–81	.464	26.5	Robinson	Wheat	.312	Sengel	6	Marquard	19–12	2.55
								Hickman	6			
1918	5th	57–69	.452	25.5	Robinson	Wheat	.335*	Myers	4	Grimes	19–9	2.14
1919	5th	69–71	.493	27.0	Robinson	Myers	.307	Griffith	6	Pfeffer	17–13	2.66
1920	1st	93–61	.604	+7.0	Robinson	Wheat	.328	Wheat	9	Grimes	23–11	2.22
1921	5th	77–75	.507	16.5	Robinson	Wheat	.320	Wheat	14	Grimes	22*–13	2.83
1922	6th	76–78	.494	17.0	Robinson	Wheat	.335	Wheat	16	Ruether	21–12	3.53
1923	6th	76–78	.494	19.5	Robinson	Fournier	.351	Fournier	22	Grimes	21–18	3.58
1924	2nd	92–62	.597	1.5	Robinson	Wheat	.375	Fournier	27*	Vance	28*–6	2.16*
1925	6th	68–85	.444	27.0	Robinson	Wheat	.359	Fournier	22*	Vance	22*–9	3.53
1926	6th	71–82	.464	17.5	Robinson	Herman	.319	Herman	11	Petty	17–17*	2.84
1927	6th	65–88	.425	28.5	Robinson	Statz	.274	Herman	14	Vance	16–15	2.70
1928	6th	77–76	.503	17.5	Robinson	Herman	.340	Bissonette	25	Vance	22–10	2.09*
1929	6th	70–83	.458	28.5	Robinson	Herman	.381	Frederick	24	Clark	16–19*	3.74
1930	4th	86–68	.558	6.0	Robinson	Herman	.393	Herman	35	Vance	17–15	2.61*
1931	4th	79–73	.520	21.0	Robinson	O'Doul	.336	Herman	18	Clark	14–10	3.20
1932	3rd	81–73	.526	9.0	Carey	O'Doul	.368*	Wilson	23	Clark	20–12	3.49
1933	6th	65–88	.425	26.5	Carey	Frederick	.308	Cuccinello	9	Mungo	16–15	2.72
								Taylor	9			
								Wilson	9			
1934	6th	71–81	.467	23.5	Stengel	Leslie	.332	Cuccinello	14	Mungo	18–16	3.37
								Koenecke	14			

Year	Pos.	Record	Pct.	GB	Manager	Player	BA	Player	HR	Player	W-L	ERA
1935	5th	70–83	.458	29.5	Stengel	Leslie	.308	Frey	11	Mungo	16–10	3.65
1936	7th	67–87	.435	25.0	Stengel	Hassett	.310	Phelps	5	Mungo	18–19	3.35
1937	6th	62–91	.405	33.5	Grimes	Manush	.333	Lavagetto	8	Mungo	9–11	2.91
1938	7th	69–80	.463	18.5	Grimes	Koy	.299	Camilli	24	Tamulis	12–6	3.83
1939	3rd	84–69	.549	12.5	Durocher	Lavagetto	.300	Camilli	26	Hamlin	20–13	3.64
1940	2nd	88–65	.575	12.0	Durocher	Walker	.308	Camilli	23	Wyatt	15–14	3.46
1941	1st	100–54	.649	+2.5	Durocher	Reiser	.343*	Camilli	34*	Wyatt	22*–10	2.34
										Higbe	22*–9	3.14
1942	2nd	104–50	.675	2.0	Durocher	Reiser	.310	Camilli	26	Wyatt	19–17	2.73
1943	3rd	81–72	.529	23.5	Durocher	Herman	.330	Galan	9	Wyatt	14–5	2.49
1944	7th	63–91	.409	42.0	Durocher	Walker	.357*	Davis	13	Davis	10–11	3.34
1945	3rd	87–67	.565	11.0	Durocher	Rosen	.325	Rosen	12	Gregg	18–13	3.47
1946	2nd**	96–60	.615	2.0	Durocher	Walker	.319	Reiser	11	Higbe	17–8	3.03
1947	1st	94–60	.610	+5.0	Shotton	Walker	.306	Robinson	12	Branca	21–12	2.67
						Reese		Branca	12			
1948	3rd	84–70	.545	7.5	Durocher / Shotton	Robinson	.296	Hermanski	15	Barney	15–13	3.10
1949	1st	97–57	.630	+1.0	Shotton	Robinson	.342*	Hodges	23	Newcombe	17–8	3.17
								Snider	23			
1950	2nd	89–65	.578	2.0	Shotton	Robinson	.328	Hodges	32	Roe	19–11	3.30
										Newcombe	19–11	3.70
1951	2nd**	97–60	.618	1.0	Dressen	Robinson	.338	Hodges	40	Roe	22–3	3.04
1952	1st	96–57	.627	+4.5	Dressen	Robinson	.308	Hodges	32	Black	15–4	2.15
1953	1st	105–49	.682	+13.0	Dressen	Furillo	.344*	Snider	42	Erskine	20–6	3.54
1954	2nd	92–62	.597	5.0	Alston	Snider	.341	Hodges	42	Erskine	18–15	4.15
1955	1st	98–55	.641	+13.5	Alston	Furillo	.314	Snider	42	Newcombe	20–5	3.20
1956	1st	93–61	.604	+1.0	Alston	Gilliam	.300	Snider	43*	Newcombe***	27*–7	3.06
1957	3rd	84–70	.545	11.0	Alston	Furillo	.306	Snider	40	Podres	12–9	2.66*
										Drysdale	17–9	2.69

131

Los Angeles Dodgers 1958–1992

Year	Pos.	Record	Pct.	GB	Manager	Player	BA	Player	HR	Player	W-L	ERA
1958	7th	71–83	.461	21.0	Alston	Snider	.312	Hodges	22	Podres	13–15	3.72
								Neal	22			
1959	1st	88–68	.564	+2.0	Alston	Snider	.305	Hodges	25	Drysdale	17–13	3.46
1960	4th	82–72	.532	13.0	Alston	Larker	.323	Howard	23	Drysdale	15–14	2.84
1961	2nd	89–65	.578	4.0	Alston	Moon	.328	Roseboro	18	Koufax	18–13	3.52
										Podres	18–5	3.74
1962	2nd**	102–63	.618	1.0	Alston	T. Davis	.346*	Howard	31	Drysdale***	25*–9	2.83
										Koufax	14–7	2.54*
1963	1st	99–63	.611	+6.0	Alston	T. Davis	.326*	Howard	28	Koufax***	25*–5	1.88*
1964	6th	80–82	.494	13.0	Alston	W. Davis	.294	Howard	24	Koufax	19–5	1.74*
1965	1st	97–65	.599	+2.0	Alston	Wills	.286	Lefebvre	12	Koufax***	26*–8	2.04*
								Johnson	12			
1966	1st	95–67	.586	+1.5	Alston	T. Davis	.313	Lefebvre	24	Koufax***	27*–9	1.73*
1967	8th	73–89	.451	28.5	Alston	Roseboro	.272	Ferrara	16	Osteen	17–17	3.22
1968	7th	76–86	.469	21.0	Alston	Haller	.285	Gabrielson	10	Drysdale	14–12	2.15
1969	4th†	85–77	.525	8.0	Alston	W. Davis	.311	Kosco	19	Singer	20–12	2.34
										Osteen	20–15	2.66
1970	2nd	87–74	.540	14.5	Alston	Parker	.319	Grabarkewitz	17	Osteen	16–14	3.82
1971	2nd	89–73	.549	1.0	Alston	W. Davis	.309	Allen	23	Downing	20–9	2.68
1972	3rd	85–70	.548	10.5	Alston	Mota	.323	F. Robinson	19	Sutton	19–9	2.08
								W. Davis	19	Osteen	20–11	2.64
1973	2nd	95–65	.590	3.5	Alston	Mota	.314	Ferguson	25	Sutton	18–10	2.42
1974	1st	102–60	.630	+4.0	Alston	Buckner	.314	Wynn	32	Marshall***	15–12	2.42
										Messersmith	20*–6	2.59
1975	2nd	88–74	.543	20.0	Alston	Garvey	.319	Cey	25	Messersmith	19–14	2.29
1976	2nd	92–70	.568	10.0	Alston	Garvey	.317	Cey	23	Sutton	21–10	3.06
1977	1st	98–64	.605	+10.0	Lasorda	R. Smith	.307	Garvey	33	John	20–7	2.78
1978	1st	95–67	.586	+2.5	Lasorda	Garvey	.316	R. Smith	29	Hooton	19–10	2.71

Year	Pos.	Record	Pct.	GB	Manager	Player	BA	Player	HR	Player	W-L	ERA
1979	3rd	79–83	.488	11.5	Lasorda	Garvey	.315	Garvey	28	Sutcliffe	17–10	3.46
								Lopes	28			
								Cey	28			
1980	2nd**	92–71	.564	1.0	Lasorda	R. Smith	.322	Baker	29	Reuss	18–6	2.52
1981	1st	36–21	.632	+0.5	Lasorda	Baker	.320	Cey	13	Valenzuela***	13–7	2.48
	4th	27–26	.509	6.0								
1981‡	2nd	63–47	.573	4.0								
1982	2nd	88–74	.543	1.0	Lasorda	Guerrero	.304	Guerrero	32	Valenzuela	19–13	2.87
1983	1st	91–71	.562	+2.0	Lasorda	Guerrero	.298	Guerrero	32	Welch	15–12	2.65
1984	4th	79–83	.488	13.0	Lasorda	Guerrero	.303	Marshall	21	Peña	12–6	2.48*
1985	1st	95–67	.586	+5.5	Lasorda	Guerrero	.320	Guerrero	33	Hershiser	19–3	2.03
1986	5th	73–89	.451	23.0	Lasorda	Sax	.332	Stubbs	23	Valenzuela	21*–11	3.14
1987	4th	73–89	.451	17.0	Lasorda	Guerrero	.338	Guerrero	27	Hershiser	16–16	3.06
1988	1st	94–67	.584	+7.0	Lasorda	Gibson	.290	Gibson	25	Hershiser***	23*–8	2.26
1989	4th	77–83	.481	14.0	Lasorda	Randolph	.282	Murray	20	Belcher	15–12	2.82
										Hershiser	15–15	2.31
1990	2nd	86–76	.531	5.0	Lasorda	Murray	.330	Daniels	27	R. Martinez	20–6	2.92
1991	2nd	93–69	.574	1.0	Lasorda	Butler	.296	Strawberry	28	R. Martinez	17–13	3.27
1992	6th	63–99	.389	35.0	Lasorda	Butler	.309	Karros	20	Candiotti	11–15	3.00

*Led the National League
**Tied for 1st but lost pennant in playoff
***Cy Young Award Winner
†Western Division (first season of divisional play)
‡Split Season Totals (Players' Union Strike)

All-Time Dodgers Career and Season Records

Brooklyn Dodgers Career Batting Leaders (1901–1957)

Games Played	Zack Wheat	2,318
At Bats	Zack Wheat	8,859
Runs Scored	Pee Wee Reese	1,338
Hits	Zack Wheat	2,804
Batting Average (1,800 ABs)	Willie Keeler	.360
Home Runs	Duke Snider	389
Runs Batted In	Duke Snider	1,271
Extra Base Hits	Duke Snider	814
Stolen Bases	Mike Griffin	264
Doubles	Zack Wheat	464
Triples	Zack Wheat	171
Total Bases	Zack Wheat	4,003

Los Angeles Dodgers Career Batting Leaders (1958–1992)

Games Played	Bill Russell	2,181
At Bats	Willie Davis	7,495
Runs Scored	Willie Davis	1,004
Hits	Willie Davis	2,091
Batting Average (1,800 ABs)	Manny Mota	.315
Home Runs	Ron Cey	228
Runs Batted In	Steve Garvey	992
Extra Base Hits	Willie Davis	585
Stolen Bases	Maury Wills	490
Doubles	Steve Garvey	333
Triples	Willie Davis	110
Total Bases	Willie Davis	3,094

Brooklyn Dodgers Career Pitching Leaders (1901–1957)

Innings Pitched	Brickyard Kennedy	2,857
Earned Run Average (1,100+ Inns.)	Jeff Pfeffer	2.31
Wins	Dazzy Vance	190
Losses	Brickyard Kennedy	149
Strikeouts	Dazzy Vance	1,918
Walks	Brickyard Kennedy	1,128
Games	Clem Labine	425
Shutouts	Nap Rucker	38
Games Started	Brickyard Kennedy	332

Los Angeles Dodgers Career Pitching Leaders (1958–1992)

Innings Pitched	Don Sutton	3,815
Earned Run Average (1,100+ Inns.)	Sandy Koufax	2.76
Wins	Don Sutton	233
Losses	Don Sutton	181
Strikeouts	Don Sutton	2,696
Walks	Don Sutton	996
Games	Don Sutton	550

All-Time Dodgers Career and Season Records *(continued)*

Shutouts	Don Sutton	52	
Saves	Jim Brewer	125	
Games Started	Don Sutton	533	

Brooklyn Dodgers Single-Season Batting Records (1901–1957)

Batting Average	Babe Herman	.393	1930
Home Runs (lefthanded)	Duke Snider	43	1956
Home Runs (righthanded)	Gil Hodges	42	1954
Runs Batted In	Roy Campanella	142	1953
Runs Scored	Babe Herman	143	1930
Hits	Babe Herman	241	1930
Singles	Willie Keeler	179	1900
Doubles	John Frederick	52	1929
Triples	Henry Myers	22	1920
Slugging Percentage	Babe Herman	.678	1930
Extra Base Hits	Babe Herman	94	1930
Sacrifices	Jim Casey	32	1907
Walks	Eddie Stanky	148*	1945
Strikeouts	Dolph Camilli	115	1941
Fewest Strikeouts (150 Games)	Jim Johnston	15	1923
Total Bases	Babe Herman	416	1930

Los Angeles Dodgers Single-Season Batting Records (1958–1992)

Batting Average	Tommy Davis	.346	1962
Home Runs	Steve Garvey	33	1977
	Pedro Guerrero	33	1985
Runs Batted In	Tommy Davis	153	1962
Runs Scored	Maury Wills	130	1962
Hits	Tommy Davis	230	1962
Singles	Maury Wills	179	1962
Doubles	Wes Parker	47	1970
Triples	Willie Davis	16	1970
Slugging Percentage	Pedro Guerrero	.577	1985
Extra Base Hits	Steve Garvey	66	1978
	Pedro Guerrero	66	1983
Sacrifices	Charlie Neal	21	1959
Walks	Jim Wynn	110	1975
Strikeouts	Bill Grabarkewitz	149	1970
Fewest Strikeouts (150 games)	Jim Gilliam	28	1960
Total Bases	Tommy Davis	561	1962
Grand Slam Home Runs	Frank Howard	2	1970
	Ron Cey	2	1977
	Steve Garvey	2	1977
	Greg Brock	2	1985
	Mike Marshall	2	1985
Games	Maury Wills	165**	1962

All-Time Dodgers Career and Season Records *(continued)*

Brooklyn Dodgers Single-Season Pitching Records (1901–1957)

ERA	Rube Marquard	1.58	1916
Wins	Joe McGinnity	29	1900
Losses	George Bell	27	1910
Winning Percentage	Fred Fitzsimmons	.889 (16–2)	1940
Strikeouts	Dazzy Vance	262	1924
Games	Clem Labine	62	1956
Games Started	Oscar Jones	41	1904
Shutouts	Burleigh Grimes	7	1918
	Whitlow Wyatt	7	1941
Innings Pitched	Oscar Jones	378	1904
Home Runs Allowed	Don Newcombe	35	1955
Hit Batsmen	Joe McGinnity	41**	1900
Wild Pitches	Lawrence Cheney	15	1916

Los Angeles Dodgers Single-Season pitching Records (1958–1992)

ERA	Sandy Koufax	1.73	1966
Wins (lefthander)	Sandy Koufax	27*	1966
Wins (righthander)	Don Drysdale	25	1962
Winning Percentage	Phil Regan	.933 (14–1)	1966
Strikeouts (lefthander)	Sandy Koufax	382**	1965
Strikeouts (righthander)	Don Drysdale	251	1963
Saves	Jim Brewer	24	1970
Games	Mike Marshall	106**	1974
Games Started	Don Drysdale	42	1963
			1965
Shutouts (lefthander)	Sandy Koufax	11	1963
Shutouts (righthander)	Don Sutton	9	1972
Innings Pitched	Sandy Koufax	336	1965
Home Runs Allowed	Don Sutton	38	1970
Hit Batsmen	Don Drysdale	20	1961
Wild Pitches	Sandy Koufax	17	1958

*National League Record
**Major League Record

3

Chicago Cubs
Sic Transit Gloria Mundi
ART AHRENS

One of the time-honored mottoes of the Roman Catholic Church is "sic transit gloria mundi" which, in so many words, means that the glories of the world are fleeting. If this venerable axiom can be applied to the history of any baseball team, it is that of the Chicago Cubs. Between 1876 and 1945 the Cubs flew 16 pennants; since then, only two divisional titles. A legacy that was once among the proudest in baseball has changed to one more akin to that of the late St. Louis Browns. Not to mention the notorious endings of 1969 and 1984, as well as the Cubbies eventually running out of gas in 1989. And even in their halcyon days, the Cubs displayed an embarrassing penchant for falling apart in the World Series.

Although the team's official history dates back to 1876, the foundations extend even a few years earlier. And they were not always known as the Cubs. Following the example set by the Cincinnati Red Stockings in 1869, a professional baseball team was organized in Chicago. Since the team's uniforms included white hose, they were appropriately called the White Stockings.

The National Association of Professional Baseball Players—known popularly as the National Association—was formed in 1871. The White Stockings entered the league and contended for the championship until the Chicago fire destroyed their ballpark. Forced to play their last three games on the road, they lost the championship (Federal Writers Project, 1939, 26).

As Chicago resurrected itself from the ashes, the White Stockings lapsed into semipro status. When the team reentered the Association in 1874 it was a mediocre entity; all the best players had been signed by Eastern teams. It was a this point that William Hulbert entered the picture.

A local businessman, Hulbert purchased controlling interest in the club in June of 1875. Determined to build a winner, he secretly signed Boston pitching ace Albert Spalding for the next season. Spalding, in turn, recruited Ross Barnes, Deacon White, and Cal McVey from Boston, and Adrian Anson and Ezra Sutton from Philadelphia, although the last mentioned backed out (Spalding, 1911, 208). When the news hit the press the Association threatened all five "seceders" with expulsion, but Hulbert reassured them that they were bigger than the league itself.

To be sure, the National Association had fallen on hard times. Scheduling was piecemeal, contract jumping rampant, betting was openly flaunted at the ballparks, and rowdiness abounded. Largely through Hulbert's efforts the Association was dissolved and replaced by the National League on February 2, 1876 (Spalding, 1911, 210–14).

Cubs baseball officially began on April 25, 1876, as Spalding hurled the White Stockings to a 4–0 victory at Louisville. Playing their home games at 23rd and State Streets on Chicago's South Side, the rejuvenated White Stockings captured the new league's first pennant. Between July 20th and 27th they scored 88 runs in four games, to set a major league record which still stands.

Although Spalding (47 wins) and Barnes (.403 BA) were the main heroes of the initial season, it was Anson who became baseball's first genuine superstar. The nineteenth-century equivalent of "Mister Cub," Anson played through 1897, collecting 3,041 hits and a .333 lifetime average. He is still the lifetime club leader in hits, doubles, runs scored, and runs batted in. Sadly, he was also responsible in the 1880s (with some assistance, however) for the exclusion of blacks from professional ball.

Success, though sweet, was short-lived. In 1877 the White Stockings plummeted to fifth place in a still struggling league that had shrunk from eight teams to six because New York and Philadelphia had been expelled. As Spalding joined Hulbert in the front office, things were only marginally better the following year (fourth out of six), when the team relocated to Lakefront Park at Michigan and Randolph Streets in Downtown Chicago. The only remaining player from 1876 was Anson. Already, the Cub tradition of "paradise lost" was taking root.

The turning point came in 1879 when Anson was moved to first base and named manager; hence, his nickname "Cap." (At that time, the terms captain and manager were synonymous.) The trio of Anson, Hulbert, and Spalding quickly began assembling the team that would soon dominate the league. Important arrivals that season included second baseman Joe Quest, third baseman Ed Williamson, catcher Frank Flint, and outfielders George Gore and Abner Dalrymple. With Anson leading the batting charge as well as the strategies, the White Stockings finished a strong fourth in a revamped eight-team circuit.

In 1880 they were joined by shortstop Tommy Burns, catcher-outfielder Mike Kelly, and pitchers Larry Corcoran and Fred Goldsmith. Moreover, the adoption of the much-maligned reserve clause enabled owners to retain the permanent services of their players until they decided to trade, sell, or release them.

The result was an unbeatable combination that brought three straight pennants to Chicago in 1880, 1881, and 1882, the year Spalding assumed the club ownership upon Hulbert's death. The 1880 team won 21 consecutive games to set a club record (tied in 1935), and finished at 67–17 for a .798 percentage, still highest in National League annals. Although it is questionable whether they could have maintained that torrid a pace with a longer schedule, they were nonetheless an outstanding team. In his memoir *A Ballplayer's Career,* Anson recalled that "they were the cracks of that time, and perhaps as strong a team as the league had seen up to that date" (Anson, 1900, 109). On August 19, 1880 Larry Corcoran pitched the first no-hit game in Cub history, a 6–0 gem over Boston.

Although Anson has been given the bulk of the credit—and not without reason—for the team's success in the early 1880s, it should be remembered that he had a fine supporting cast as well. Gore and Kelly (the latter, like Anson, an eventual Hall of Fame member) were lifetime .300 hitters, while Dalrymple, a one-time batting champion, finished reasonably close. Fred Goldsmith is sometimes credited with inventing the curveball; in any case, he had made the first publicly recorded demonstration in 1870. Larry Corcoran, who recorded two more no-hitters, won 175 games for Chicago in a period of slightly more than five years before his arm went lame early in 1885. Even conceding that the pitching distance was only 50 feet prior to 1893 (and 45 feet before 1881), it was a remarkable achievement.

By 1883 the White Stockings were again in a period of transition, finishing a close second that season and a disappointing fourth the next campaign, thanks largely to a mediocre first half. On September 6, 1883 they set a major league record by scoring 18 runs in the seventh inning of a 26–6 victory over Detroit. The German-speaking Fred Pfeffer, an outstanding fielder, had already replaced Joe Quest at second base. By September of 1884 the fading Goldsmith was being phased out in favor of the youthful John Clarkson, an eventual 300-game winner.

Having moved to West Side Park at Congress and Loomis Streets, the White Stockings bounced back with pennants in 1885 and 1886. These were probably Chicago's finest teams of the nineteenth century, and possibly the best in the National League during the 1880s. Aside from the fabled "Stonewall Infield" of Anson, Pfeffer, Burns, and Williamson, the outfield of Gore, Kelly, and Dalrymple continued to excel also. Late in the 1885 season Chicago signed rookie Jimmy Ryan, who would gather 2,531 hits with a .310 lifetime batting average by the time he retired from the majors in 1903.

Pitching every game throughout much of the season, Clarkson won an incredible 53 games in 1885 (including 10 shutouts and a no-hitter), second highest in major league history. Anson regarded him as "the best that Chicago ever had" (Anson, 1900, 130). Later in the year the White Stockings obtained Jim McCormick, who relieved some of Clarkson's pitching burden by winning 20 himself. The following year the staff was expanded to a three-man operation with the addition of rookie John Flynn, who proved to be only a one-year wonder. With a league schedule that had been gradually expanded to 124 games, the 1886 White Stockings became the first team to win 90 games. Anson considered the 1885–86 aggregation as "the strongest team that I ever had under my management but, taken all in all, one of the strongest teams that has ever been gotten together in the history of the league . . ." (Anson, 1900, 128).

Nevertheless, they met their match in the World Series both seasons when they played the St. Louis Brown Stockings of the American Association, the first rival major league, which lasted from 1882 through 1891. This franchise is not to be confused with the latter-day St. Louis Browns of the American League.

In 1885, after an eventful seven games that included contests in Pittsburgh and Cincinnati, violence on and off the field, and frequent disputes over the umpiring, a committee declared the Series over with the teams tied with three wins apiece and one tie, that game having been called because of darkness. Not surprisingly, each side claimed victory. The next season, with the Series played on a winner-take-all basis, the White Stockings won two of the first three contests played in Chicago, then dropped three straight in St. Louis for a shocking letdown. Spalding was reportedly so incensed that he refused to pay his team's train fare home (Levine, 1985, 36).

Blaming the post-season failure on the drinking habits of his players, Spalding sold rights to the "worst" offenders—Kelly, McCormick, and Gore—even though all three were at the peak of their playing abilities. The declining Dalrymple was also dealt away. Kelly's sale price, an unprecedented $10,000, created headlines. The departure of these veterans and their replacement with callow youngsters led to a new team nickname, Colts, which did not catch on immediately.

While he doubtlessly could not have realized it at the time, Spalding's pious gesture for the virtues of temperance led to a pennant drought that would plague the club for 20 years. Anson's glory days as a manager were already behind him.

Although greatly weakened, the White Stockings remained a contender for five more seasons, finishing third in 1887, second in 1888, third in 1889, and second in 1890 and 1891. The late 1880s witnessed the emergence of Jimmy Ryan as a genuine star with home run power and an outstanding throwing arm, the sale of John Clarkson to Boston, and the arrival of pitcher Bill Hutchison, who became the staff workhorse. During the winter of 1888–89 the White Stockings and a team of "All Americas" conducted baseball's first world tour. While the jaunt was not a financial success—Spalding lost roughly $5,000 on it—it brought the sport to such faraway cities as Sydney, Melbourne, Cairo, Naples, Rome, Paris, and London (Levine, 1985, 109). In Egypt the players were photographed atop the Sphinx and used one of the Pyramids for a backstop.

When nearly the entire team defected to the short-lived Players League in 1890, the club quickly recruited a team of youngsters, as Colts became the dominant nickname. The following season, with the nascent Players League crushed, only three of the deserters—Pfeffer, Ryan, and Ad Gumbert—were returned to Chicago. The Colts led for most of the year but finished second when the Boston Beaneaters, the eventual winners, won four straight from the New York Giants under suspicious circumstances during the final week. Anson openly accused the Giants of throwing the games (Anson, 1900, 295–97). Although an inquiry was conducted, nothing conclusive was proven.

During the winter the American Association went bankrupt, with four of its clubs being absorbed by the National League, bloating the circuit to 12 teams. It was at this point that Chicago's decline as a league power became serious.

Part of the reason was Spalding's appointment of James Hart to the club presidency in 1892. Never on good terms, Hart and Anson grew increasingly antagonistic toward each other as the years went on. Hart regarded Anson as a relic of the past who was unwilling to change with the times. Anson countered by calling Hart a usurper who undermined his authority by encouraging rebellion among the players.

Regardless of who was right or wrong, the remainder of the nineteenth century was marked more by individual achievement than team effort. The once-proud Colts sank to seventh in 1892, ninth in 1893, and eighth in 1894. Aside from Anson and Ryan, what little excitement there was came from such upcoming stars as shortstop Bill Dahlen, pitcher Clark Griffith (a 20-game winner for six consecutive years beginning in 1894), and center fielder Bill Lange, who batted .330 in seven seasons before retiring prematurely after the 1899 campaign.

In 1893—the year the team moved to the fabled West Side Grounds at Taylor and Wood Streets—the pitching distance was lengthened to its present-day 60 feet, six inches, while the pitcher's box was replaced by the mound and slab. The effect on pitchers was devastating for the next several years, as batting averages reached all-time highs while pitching duels dwindled to their lowest ebb. The 1894 Colts batted .314 as a team, as Bill Dahlen put together back-to-back hitting streaks of 42 and 28 games. At the other end of the spectrum Chicago's pitching staff had an ERA of 5.16 while suffering the embarrassment of not posting a single shutout the entire season, both club records in futility.

Anson's Colts enjoyed a mini-revival in 1895 and 1896, finishing fourth and fifth with records that were practically identical. In 1895 rookie third baseman Bill Everett batted .358, still the club record for a freshman. However, catching, second base, and pitching, with the exception of Griffith, were chronic sore spots.

Following two strong finishes Anson felt confident that he could produce a pennant winner in 1897. Such was not the case, however, as injuries to key players and dissension within the ranks toppled the team back to ninth place. Highlights in an otherwise disappointing season included a record 36–7 romp over Louisville on June 29, and Anson's 3,000th career hit, a fourth-inning single in a 6–3 victory over Baltimore on July 18 (Ahrens and Gold, 1982, 47).

By now relations between Anson and Hart had deteriorated to the point of no return. Spalding, forced to make a decision, announced on February 1, 1898 that Anson's contract would not be renewed. Following Anson's dismissal the Colts were rechristened the Orphans for the next four summers.

With former infielder Tommy Burns as their new manager, the Orphans were a pleasant surprise in 1898, finishing a solid fourth. As Jimmy Callahan joined Griffith as a 20-game winner, Chicago found itself with the best pitching in the league, including 13 shutouts and a 2.83 ERA. Ryan and Lange continued to excel, as home attendance climbed to an unprecedented 424,352. The most significant event of the year, although hardly noticeable at the time, was the arrival of Frank Chance, a second-string rookie catcher.

Again the resurgence was only temporary, as the Orphans dropped to eighth in 1899. With Tom Loftus replacing Burns as manager, they finished in a tie for fifth in 1900, when the National League was cut back to eight teams. At the end of the 1900 season the venerable Ryan was released as Chicago concluded its 25th major league year.

The new century brought new problems. The youthful American League—originally formed as the Western League, a minor circuit—had placed a franchise called the White Stockings (soon to be shortened to White Sox) on Chicago's South Side. In 1901 the American League defied the National Agreement, declaring itself a major league. When the National League refused to recognize its new competitor, the young confederation retaliated by raiding the older league's clubs, luring away established stars with lush contracts.

The Chicago National League team was hard hit by the raids. No less than seven players on the 1900 squad, most of them regulars, defected to the American League in 1901. To make matters worse three former stars—Griffith, Callahan, and outfielder Sam Mertes— were playing for the crosstown, pennant-bound White Sox. Their ranks decimated, the Orphans (frequently called the Remnants) fell to sixth place with a 53–86 record, the worst showing yet by a Chicago team. They escaped last place by only one game.

The American League raids continued in 1902 as Danny Green, Rube Waddell, Barry McCormick, and Tully Hartsell jumped to the fledgling circuit. Frank Selee, the team's new manager, emphasized youth in his rebuilding program; hence a new nickname, Cubs. The name first appeared in the *Chicago Daily News* of March 27, 1902, but it took several years for it to be fully accepted, as the name Colts also enjoyed a comeback for awhile.

A veteran manager who had led the Boston Beaneaters to five pennants during the 1890s, Selee wasted no time in putting the shattered team back together during a year of experimentation and transition. From Boston he grabbed outfielder Jimmy Slagle. Rookie Joe Tinker won the shortstop's job while sophomore Johnny Kling became the regular catcher. After four inconsistent years pitcher Jack Taylor matured into a 22-game winner. Pitcher Carl Lundgren, who would later play an important role, joined the team in June. At this time Spalding sold his final holdings in the club to Hart (Levin, 1985, 123).

Late in the season Selee moved Frank Chance to first base despite the latter's insistence that he could not play the position. Concurrently, the 21-year-old Johnny Evers began to appear occasionally at second base. When the first Tinker-to-Evers-to-Chance double play was recorded on September 15, 1902, it symbolized the dawning of a new era (Ahrens and Gold, 1982, 66). For the year the team finished fifth at almost .500.

With a regular lineup now solidified, Selee's Colts jumped to third place in 1903, their best showing in 12 years. Jake Weimer and Bob Wicker helped beef up the pitching staff, while Chance batted .327 and stole 67 bases. However, when Jack Taylor was suspected of throwing games to the hated White Sox in the post-season City Series, he was traded to the Cardinals for Mordecai "Three Finger" Brown and Jack O'Neill.

The addition of Brown further strengthened an already formidable mound corps, as the Colts inched up to second in 1904. By now, thanks to trick pitches and the foul strike rule, pitching had become the dominant factor in baseball once again and low-scoring games the rule. Near the end of the year outfielder Frank Schulte joined the club.

In 1905 Chicago slipped to third as freshman Ed Reulbach became an immediate mainstay on the mound. His body ravaged by tuberculosis, Frank Selee resigned as manager on August 1 in favor of his hand-picked successor, Chance. The latter, who came to be known as the "Peerless Leader," went on to a Cub managerial record of 778–396 for a .649 percentage. Chance also preferred the nickname Cubs, and his preference led to increased usage of the new name. Sadly, Selee's contributions in rebuilding the team have largely been forgotten by historians, since he had already departed by the time his efforts bore fruit.

In the meantime Charles A. Murphy had purchased the club from Hart. Over the off-season, the team that would soon dominate the league took on its definitive form. Third baseman Harry Steinfeldt was acquired from the Reds, and outfielder Jimmy Sheckard from the Brooklyn Superbas. Pat Moran became a dependable backup catcher to Kling. Pitching was given yet another boost with the addition of a much-needed lefthander, Jack Pfiester. In mid-1906 it was fortified still more by the acquisition of Orval Overall from the Reds and the reacquisition of Taylor from St. Louis.

The result was an unstoppable juggernaut that laid all opposition to waste. More frequently than not called Murphy's Spuds, the 1906 Cubs won a record 116 games to finish 20 notches ahead of the runner-up Giants.

Yet there were no bona fide superstars on the 1906 team, with the possible exception of pitcher Brown, who won 26 games. They were simply a collection of good, journeyman ballplayers who jelled as a unit. Understandably, many of the accolades went to Chance, whose relentless aggressiveness on the field set a powerful example. He played with the zeal of a fanatic, even to the point of not getting out of the way of beanballs in order to reach first base. Like Anson, he was a stern disciplinarian as a manager, not averse to using his fists in bringing home a message to an unruly player.

His infield partners, Tinker and Evers, were light batsmen (dangerous in the clutch, however), but easily compensated in their defensive and baserunning skills. Although their greatness was decidedly exaggerated by Franklin P. Adams' poem, "Baseball's Sad Lexicon," the trio was the cement of the Cubs' turn-of-the-century defense.

On the city's South Side the White Sox were surprise pennant winners in the American League, primarily on the impetus of a 19-game winning streak in August. Dubbed the "Hitless Wonders," they posted a team batting average of .230, worst in either league. The Cubs were three-to-one favorites with the oddsmakers, especially since they had won the 1905 City Series in five games.

In Chicago's only crosstown World Series the Sox humbled the mighty Cubs in six games, for the first upset in modern Series play. Cub highlights in a losing cause included a one-hit game by Reulbach and a two-hitter by Brown. Frank Chance admitted defeat only with reluctance:

> The Sox played grand, game baseball and outclassed us in this series . . . But there is one thing that I will never believe and that is that the White Sox are better than the Cubs.

Although obviously biased on his team's behalf, Chance was probably correct. While the White Sox did not repeat as winners until 1917, the Cubs were on the verge of a dynasty.

Undaunted, Chance's men rebounded with 107 victories and another easy pennant in 1907. Pitching was better than ever as the staff hurled 30 shutouts with an ERA of 1.73, still the all-time low.

This time the Cubs met the Detroit Tigers of Ty Cobb and Sam Crawford in the World Series. After the first game was called as a 3–3 tie because of darkness at the end of 12 innings, the Cubs went on to skin the Bengals in four straight. Cub pitching held Cobb to a .200 average while Chicago stole 18 bases, a record for a five-game set. Nevertheless, the most exciting heroics of the "Tinker-to-Evers-to-Chance" era were to be enacted the following year.

Unlike the previous two seasons the 1908 pennant race was a three-way struggle between the Cubs, Giants, and Pirates. Long smoldering, the Chicago-New York enmity reached its zenith.

On the road to the year's exciting finish, Brown and Reulbach enjoyed their greatest seasons, posting respective records of 29–9 and 24–7. In addition, both pitchers assembled streaks of four consecutive shutouts, which remained the league record until Don Drysdale exceeded it 60 years later. Included in Reulbach's streak was a shutout doubleheader victory over Brooklyn on September 26, the only such occurrence in major league history.

In a crucial game at the Polo Grounds on September 23, Moose McCormick of the Giants crossed home plate on Al Bridwell's single in the bottom of the ninth, in what appeared to be the winning run in a 2–1 victory. As fans poured onto the field Johnny Evers got ahold of the ball (or one just as good) and stepped on second base, claiming a force. Fred Merkle, who had been on first when Bridwell singled, had failed to touch second base but instead headed for the clubhouse. Umpire Hank O'Day ruled Merkle out, and the game was declared a tie because it was impossible to resume play. League officials upheld O'Day's decision, ordering the game to be replayed if it were a factor in the championship.

Predictably, after the Pirates were eliminated, the Cubs and Giants stood neck and neck. In the replay, on October 8, the Cubs bested Christy Mathewson, 4–2, to capture the pennant—and left the Polo Grounds under a police escort. Hungry for a scapegoat, sportswriters labeled Merkle, a competent player, "Bonehead," which hung on him like an albatross for the rest of his career. Ironically, Merkle later became the Cubs' regular first baseman (1917–20).

Evers' quick thinking was not the only factor in the season's outcome. Harry Coveleski, a rookie Phillies pitcher, had beaten the Giants three times between September 29 and October 3. Had New York won even one of these contests, there would have been no need to replay the September 23 game. The "Merkle boner" would have been no more than a footnote to history, while Merkle would have been minus a demeaning sobriquet. And the Cubs would have been minus a pennant.

Once again, the Cubs pulverized the Tigers in a five-game World Series, with Detroit salvaging one victory this time. The Cubs thus had become the first team to win consecutive World Titles.

Following that dramatic season catcher Johnny Kling retired because he had won the pocket billiard championship. In his absence the catching was divided between Pat Moran and Dublin-born Jimmy Archer, as the Cubs finished second in 1909. Although Kling returned the following year, the ownership never forgave his "desertion," blaming that for the Cubs' failure to repeat again. The real reason was that the Pirates simply outdid them, winning 110 games to the Cubs' 104.

However, the Cubs came back to win their fourth pennant in five years in 1910, with a repeat 104 wins and a 13-game lead over the Giants. Rookie pitcher Len "King" Cole stole the show with a 20–4 record, while Archer and the young Heinie Zimmerman began shaping into major leaguers.

The Cubs entered the 1910 World Series as distinct favorites, but a younger and faster Philadelphia Athletics squad demolished them in five games. Chicago committed a record 23 errors, and it took the Cubs 13 innings to gain their only victory. It was the first sign that Chance's machine was starting to gather rust.

By 1911 the Cubs were clearly an aging team as they finished a distant second, Frank Schulte's 21 home runs notwithstanding. Vic Saier was supplanting Chance at first base, while Evers missed most of the season with a nervous breakdown. Overall retired and Kling was dealt to the Braves, as Archer became the regular catcher.

The graceful decline continued the following year as the Cubs slipped to third, despite Zimmerman's league-leading .372 average and rookie Larry Cheney's 26 wins. Chance appeared in only two games while Brown, after six consecutive 20-win seasons, won only five times.

Age was not the only thing catching up to the team. Not happy with their performance, owner Murphy called the Cubs a gang of drunkards and carousers who were not putting forth their best effort. Chance, who was having contract difficulties, countered by calling Murphy a cheapskate who was only milking the team. On September 28, 1912 the Peerless Leader was given his release. Like Anson before him Chance left the scene of his former glory in bitterness and recrimination. During the off-season Tinker and Brown were traded to the Reds.

Over the next several years the decline of the once-mighty Cubs accelerated as managers went in and out on a revolving door basis—Evers in 1913, Hank O'Day in 1914, Roger Bresnahan in 1915, and Tinker in 1916. The team finished third in 1913, fourth the next two seasons, and fifth in 1916, with a shrinking victory total each year. Batting averages were low, pitching inconsistent, and the once-impenetrable Cub infield had turned into a veritable sieve. One of the few exciting features of a generally mediocre period was the pitching of lefty Jim "Hippo" Vaughn, who won 20 or more games five times in six years between 1914 and 1919.

There were changes in the upper echelon also. After the 1913 season a group headed by Charles Thomas and Charles Taft bought out Murphy. This absentee ownership lasted roughly two years.

On January 16, 1916 chewing gum magnate William Wrigley, Jr. became a minority shareholder ($50,000) when Charles Weeghman purchased the team. Within two years Wrigley had become the majority holder, and by 1921, the sole owner (Angle, 1975, 57).

It was also in 1916 that the Cubs relocated to the North Side ballpark at Clark and Addison Streets, which had been built two years earlier for the Chicago Whales of the short-lived Federal League. Then called Weeghman Park (Weeghman had been the Whales' owner), it was later called Cubs Park, and later Weeghman Park, before being rechristened Wrigley Field in 1926.

Fred Mitchell, hired as manager in 1917, finally broke the one-year pattern by hanging on for four full seasons. His reign did not begin with any great fanfare as Chicago again finished fifth. But on May 2, 1917 Weeghman Park was the scene of the greatest pitching duel in baseball history, and one not likely to be ever duplicated. Jim Vaughn locked horns with Fred Toney of the Reds in a double no-hitter for nine innings before Cincinnati eked out two safeties in the tenth to win, 1–0. Vaughn, who took the loss lightly, went on to the winningest year of his career.

During the winter of 1917–18 some important deals gave the Cubs a much-needed shot in the arm. They obtained pitchers Grover Alexander (and batterymate Bill Killefer) from the Phillies, and George "Lefty" Tyler from the Braves. In another trade outfielder George Paskert was also acquired from Philadelphia, while Charlie Hollocher was brought up from the minors to play shortstop.

Thanks to the hitting of Hollocher and the pitching of Vaughn, Tyler, and Claude Hendrix, the Cubs won the 1918 pennant in a season that was curtailed after Labor Day by the federal government's "work or fight" order. Ironically, Alexander was not a significant factor in the championship, since he was drafted into the army early in the season.

In the World Series the Boston Red Sox beat the Cubs in six games, in a Series that featured strong pitching on both sides. Babe Ruth, then still mainly a pitcher, beat the Cubs twice. Interestingly, the Cubs outscored Boston, 10–9, for the Series. For another oddity, the Chicago contests were played at Comiskey Park because of its larger seating capacity. With America's mind on World War I, baseball attendance everywhere had suffered.

Success was fleeting as the Cubs skidded to third in 1919, fifth in 1920, and seventh in 1921. Back from the service, Grover Alexander became the ace of the staff. Although he could not carry the team by himself, he certainly gave it a noble try in 1920 with 27 wins.

Johnny Evers, rehired to manage the Cubs in 1921, did not get along with the players and was gone by midseason, being replaced by Bill Killefer. This was also the first season in which the Cubs held spring training on Wrigley's Catalina Island.

Under Killefer's reign the Cubs enjoyed moderate success for several years, finishing fifth in 1922, fourth in 1923, and fifth in 1924, with a winning record each season. With the new lively ball now in vogue, baseball in the 1920s was notable for blistering batting averages and unprecedented home run production. Baseball's greatest slugfest took place at Cubs Park on August 25, 1922, as the Cubs outlasted the Phillies, 26–23, almost blowing a one-time 25–6 lead. The Phillies left the bases loaded in the top of the ninth. Ever since, the ballpark has had the reputation of being a pitcher's graveyard.

During this era Alexander and Hollocher continued to set the pace. Bob O'Farrell, a veteran of the 1918 champions, turned into a first-class receiver under Killefer's tutelage. Other front liners included first baseman Ray Grimes, muscular outfielder Lawrence "Hack" Miller, infielder Sparky Adams, outfielder Arnold Statz, pitcher Vic Aldridge, and third baseman Barney Friberg.

It was a time of brief, meteoric careers. Grimes was a consistent .300 hitter until he suffered a slipped disc, which hastened the end of his playing days. Miller would hold fans and teammates breathless with feats of strength, such as uprooting trees at Catalina Island, bending iron bars with his bare hands, and pounding spikes through auto gates at Cubs Park with his fist (Grimm, 1968, 26). Hack batted .352 as a 1922 rookie but was a defensive liability because he was so muscle bound. He played his last major league game in May of 1925. By that time, the once-stellar Hollocher was gone also, an early retirement from a stomach ailment that many thought to be imaginary.

This pleasant but unexceptional period came to an abrupt halt in 1925, when the Cubs tumbled to last place for the first time in their history. In this tumultuous season there were three managers—Killefer, shortstop Rabbit Maranville, and finally George "Moon" Gibson. Maranville, whose leadership generally guided the players into speakeasies, was arrested for beating up a cab driver in Brooklyn. On another occasion, he dropped a bag of water on the head of traveling secretary John O. Seys. Still later, he ran through a Pullman car, anointing passengers from a spittoon. Shortly thereafter, he was relieved of the managerial duties he probably never wanted to begin with (Grimm, 1968, 42–43). By that time the season was a lost cause. Other than the Rabbit's antics, the only developments of note were the emergence of catcher Charles "Gabby" Hartnett as a full-fledged star, and the arrival of first baseman Charlie Grimm via a trade with Pittsburgh. Grimm would remain with the organization more or less for the rest of his life, becoming one of the most beloved figures in Chicago baseball history.

Following the embarrassment of 1925, major changes were in the wind. Hired as the new Cub manager, Joseph "Marse Joe" McCarthy met his challenge head on. In so doing, he helped usher in a time replete with powerful teams and colorful performers.

Mac's first move was to tip off club president William Veeck, Sr., on Lewis "Hack" Wilson, whom the Giants had left unprotected in their farm system. A blue-collar equivalent of Babe Ruth, Wilson set Chicago afire with his powerful hitting and nocturnal escapades. He smashed home runs off the Wrigley Field scoreboard (then situated at ground level), was arrested in "beer flats," climbed into the grandstand to punch out a heckler, and had to be pried loose after he tried to squeeze out through the men's room window to escape a speakeasy raid (Grimm, 1968, 57). More than anyone else, he epitomized "Roaring Twenties" Cubs baseball.

Other newcomers who paid immediate dividends were pitcher Charlie Root and outfielder Riggs Stephenson. Guy Bush, who had joined the team in 1923, began reaching his potential, while second baseman Sparky Adams had rounded into the best leadoff man in the league.

In addition, McCarthy embarked on a strict disciplinary program, quickly coming into conflict with alcoholic pitching ace Alexander.

Marse Joe laid down the rules, Alex defied them, and was waived to the Cardinals in June of 1926. From that point on, everyone knew who was in charge. More important, the Cubs rebounded to a strong fourth as the 1920s finally began to roar in earnest.

Bolstered by Root's 26 wins and Wilson's 30 home runs, the Cubs pulled in fourth again in 1927, although with an improved record. On May 30 shortstop Jimmy Cooney—whose father had been a Cub from 1890 through 1892—turned the only unassisted triple play in Cub history, and the last in the National League to date, during the morning game of a doubleheader at Pittsburgh.

In the bottom of the fourth inning the Pirates had Lloyd Waner on second base and Clyde Barnhart on first. Lloyd's brother Paul was at the plate. With the hit-and-run on, Cooney snagged the elder Waner's line drive, stepped on second to double Lloyd, then tagged Barnhart coming down the line. The Cubs went on to win, 7–6, in 10 innings (Ahrens and Gold, 1982, 29).

Only eight days after his heroic moment, Cooney was traded to the Phillies for pitcher Hal Carlson, as the youthful Woody English assumed the shortstop duties. By the time the year was over, the Cubs had become the first team in the National League to draw a million in home attendance, as 1,163,347 paid their way into the recently double-decked Wrigley Field.

In 1928 outfielder Kiki Cuyler and pitcher Pat Malone joined the Cubs to help boost them to a close third, four games behind the champion Cardinals. The Cubs appeared to be only one player away from a pennant.

William Wrigley then unloosened his purse strings, delivering $200,000 and five run-of-the-mill players to the Braves for second baseman and seven-time batting champion Rogers Hornsby. Although the "Rajah" had already left his best years behind him with the Cardinals, he still maintained a potent bat. Furthermore, the poverty stricken Braves could not afford Hornsby's lucrative contract beyond one season.

The addition of Hornsby proved to be the final piece in the jigsaw puzzle, making the 1929 team possibly the greatest in Cub history. Buttressed by a .303 team batting average and 140 home runs, Chicago won the pennant by a 10½-game margin over Pittsburgh. Four players—Hornsby, Wilson, Cuyler, and Stephenson—drove in more than 100 runs. The Rajah batted .380 for a twentieth-century Cub high while Kiki pilfered 43 bases to lead the league. Malone won 22 games, Root 19, and Bush 18. Charlie Grimm considered this team the best he ever played on (Grimm, 1968, 236).

In the World Series the Cubs met the Philadelphia Athletics, featuring such notables as Lefty Grove, Jimmy Foxx, Al Simmons,

Mickey Cochrane, and Jimmy Dykes. Although the teams appeared to be evenly matched, Connie Mack's machine steamrolled the Cubs in five games.

Surprise starter Howard Ehmke, 37 years old, fanned a then-record 13 Cubs in Game One, making them jumpy the rest of the Series. Chicago's worst humiliation came in Game Four, when the A's rallied for 10 runs in the bottom of the seventh to destroy an 8–0 Cub lead, and went on to win, 10–8. The following afternoon the Series was history. For the Cubs, the habit of folding up in the World Series was beginning to become an unpleasant tradition.

It was also a signal that Joe McCarthy's days as manager would be numbered if the Cubs did not rebound in 1930. Despite Hack Wilson's National League record 56 home runs and major league record 190 RBIs, plus career years by Cuyler and Hartnett, the Cubs slipped to second. Hornsby spent most of the season on the bench with an ankle injury, and a healthy Rajah would probably have meant another pennant. But Wrigley had already made up his mind that McCarthy had outlasted his usefulness and fired him during the final week of the season, a case of poor judgment that would haunt the Cubs for years to come.

Hornsby, who was Marse Joe's successor, was not the man for the job. Unlike McCarthy, who had a firm hand but knew when to lay off, the taciturn Hornsby continually berated the players, causing an undercurrent of resentment. This was especially so with Hack Wilson, whose output plummeted along with the stock market as the Cubs finished a disappointing third in 1931. On the positive side, the year witnessed the permanent arrival of pitcher Lon Warneke, shortstop Billy Jurges, and second baseman Billy Herman.

In December of 1931 the redoubtable Wilson was traded to the Cardinals, signifying the end of the flapper era. The following January William Wrigley died, leaving the club to his son, Phillip K. Wrigley.

By mid-1932 the Cubs were a distant second and going nowhere, as resentment against Hornsby's Cromwellian rule began to boil over. Relations between the Rajah and President Veeck had deteriorated also. Rumors, and finally an investigation, of Hornsby's racetrack habits did not help either (Grimm, 1968, 80–86).

On August 2 Hornsby was fired and replaced by the congenial Grimm. Rallying after the change in leadership, the Cubs won 37 of their last 57 games to capture the pennant. Warneke, Jurges, and Herman blossomed into stars, while Cuyler and the recently obtained Mark Koenig provided awesome hitting in the stretch run.

In the American League the Yankees of Babe Ruth, Lou Gehrig, and company had nailed down an easy pennant. For Joe McCarthy, now the Yankee skipper, it was sweet revenge as his powerful New

Yorkers swept the Cubs in four straight. The Cubs could take solace only in the fact that few expected them to triumph.

The highlight of the Series was Babe Ruth's legendary "called shot" off Charlie Root at Wrigley Field on October 1. Whether or not Ruth actually pointed to center field and/or announced that he would put the ball there will likely be argued as long as baseball remains our national pastime. Ruth's teammates tended to be adamant that he did indeed point, while Cub players were equally insistent that he did not. Obviously, both sides had an axe to grind.

In his definitive biography of Ruth, *Babe,* Robert W. Creamer does not take sides in the matter. Nevertheless, he presents strong evidence to indicate that Ruth *probably* did not point, but that to have done so would have been consistent with his character. Only the Babe himself knew for sure, and he frequently changed his story or equivocated (Creamer, 1974, 357–68).

The next two years were a period of retrenchment as the Cubs finished third in 1933 and again the following year. Ex-Brooklyn slugger Floyd "Babe" Herman was obtained in 1933 for pennant insurance, but he was not the answer, nor was Chuck Klein, who was purchased from the Phillies in 1934.

Meanwhile, a massive changing of the guard was taking place. After seeing only limited action the previous two seasons, Stan Hack secured the regular third baseman's job in 1934 and held on to it for the next 12 years. Outfielder Frank Demaree, who also debuted in 1932, was back up for good by 1935. Pitcher Bill Lee and outfielder Augie Galan came up in 1934, both proving themselves quickly. Late in that season young Phil Cavarretta arrived as Grimm's replacement at first base.

During the winter of 1934–35, veteran hurlers Bush and Malone were dealt away, while Stephenson was released. Larry French and Tex Carleton replaced Bush and Malone, and veteran Freddie Lindstrom was picked up to help in the outfield. By July of 1935, Cuyler was gone also.

When the face-lifted Cubs won the 1935 pennant, thanks to a 21-game winning streak in September, the only holdovers left from the 1929 Murderer's Row were Root, Hartnett, Grimm, and English, with the latter two seeing only occasional action. Gabby Hartnett became the first Cub to win the baseball writers' Most Valuable Player Award as the Cubs won 100 games, their most in 25 years. Grimm considered it the finest team he managed during his career (Grimm, 1968, 236).

Regardless, the World Series jinx reared its ugly head again, as the Tigers took the Cubs in six games. Of the normally formidable Chicago staff, only Warneke was able to hurl a victory.

Despite a 15-game winning streak early in the season, the Cubs had to settle for a tie for second in 1936, and a close second the following campaign as well. Between seasons Warneke had been traded to the Cardinals for first baseman Rip Collins in a questionable deal. During 1937 and 1938 the Wrigley Field bleachers were rebuilt, and the familiar vines installed.

If 1951 was the year of the "Miracle Giants," then 1938 was the time of the "Miracle Cubs." Off to their slowest start in several years, they were on a third-place treadmill when Grimm voluntarily relinquished the managerial reins to Gabby Hartnett on July 26.

Changing horses in midstream worked again. As the Cubs gathered steam, Lee won 22 games (including four straight shutouts), and a sore-armed Dizzy Dean, purchased from the Cardinals as a gate attraction, came through with several clutch victories. The Cubs charged to the top with a 10-game winning streak during the last week and a half of the season, highlighted by Gabby Hartnett's famed "Homer in the Gloamin' " off Mace Brown of the Pirates on September 28. A two-out blast in the bottom of the ninth as darkness enveloped Wrigley Field, it could not have come under more dramatic circumstances, giving the Cubs a 6–5 victory.

Contrary to popular belief, however, the Hartnett home run did not clinch the pennant for the Cubs; it only gave them a half-game lead over Pittsburgh. The flag was not nailed down until October 1, when the Cubs beat the Cardinals, 10–3, at St. Louis. Even so, Gabby's homer was the catalyst that led to championship, because it destroyed the Pirates psychologically.

The Cubs were quickly brought back down to earth. The World Series turned out to be a replay of 1932, as McCarthy's Yankees demolished the Cubs in four straight, again to no one's great surprise. Babe Ruth was gone, but Joe DiMaggio filled his shoes without much trouble. The only Cub pitcher who even came close to checkmating New York was Dean, who lasted until the eighth inning in the second game.

Hartnett's Irish luck waned quickly as the Cubs sank to fourth in 1939, a season notable for the arrival of outfielder Bill Nicholson and pitcher Claude Passeau, who would be the mainstays of the power and pitching departments in the near future. In 1940 the Cubs finished fifth, in their first losing season and second-division finish in 15 years. After Hartnett was released that November, only Charlie Root remained as a last link to the 1920s, and he would soon retire himself.

By 1941 serious weaknesses were increasingly evident, as springtime found the Cubs with their first general manager, former sportswriter James Gallagher, and a new field overseer, Jimmy Wilson.

Together, they embarked upon a series of deals that made the Cubs look like a farm club for the Dodgers.

Billy Herman was traded to Brooklyn for infielder Johnny Hudson, outfielder Larry Gilbert, and $25,000. Lou Stringer, Herman's replacement at second base, could not hold a candle to Billy, either as a hitter or a fielder. Late in the year, Larry French and Augie Galan were handed to Brooklyn on a silver platter. While the Dodgers won their first pennant in 21 years, the Cubs skidded to sixth.

When Pearl Harbor came the big leagues heard the call from the armed forces. Although the 1942 season was almost up to pre-war standards, the playing quality plummeted thereafter. With most of the real talent being vacuumed up by the military, rosters brimmed with fuzzy-faced teenagers, minor league journeymen, and has-beens who were too old to be drafted.

For the Cubs it was a time when such legendary characters as shortstop Lennie Merullo, outfielders Lou Novikoff and Dom Dallessandro, pitcher Hiram Bithorn, and infielder Heinz Becker flourished. And while it is true that Merullo once committed four errors in one inning, the story about the fly ball bouncing off Novikoff's head is purely apocryphal. He did, however, think that the Wrigley Field vines were poison ivy (Grimm, 1968, 151).

Weak up the middle and with few quality pitchers, the Cubs repeated their sixth-place showing in 1942. Fans could look with pride only to the steady work of Stan Hack, the slugging of Bill Nicholson, the pitching of Claude Passeau, the catching of Clyde McCullough, and the hustling of Phil Cavarretta, who had been recycled at first base after several years as a utility outfielder. Outfielder Harry "Peanuts" Lowrey and pitcher Hank Wyse were given brief trials.

The next season the Cubs moved up to fifth, as Cavaretta and Nicholson approached their peaks. Lowrey looked good in the outfield, Wyse worked his way into the rotation, Novikoff staged a holdout, and Eddie Stanky showed promise at second base. However, when Don Johnson was brought up at the end of the season, the Cubs soured on Stanky prematurely. The following June he was traded to Brooklyn.

In 1944 the Cubs got off to the worst start in their history, losing 13 straight after winning the opener. The unpopular Jimmy Wilson was fired, and in his place returned Charlie Grimm, after coach Roy Johnson served as interim manager for one day.

The Cubs slowly recuperated, eventually finishing fourth. Don Johnson, although pushing 33, was a pleasant surprise, as was rookie Andy Pafko in center field.

During the spring of 1945 most writers picked the Cubs to finish second or third behind the Cardinals, who had won three straight flags and two World Series. When the team started off sluggishly, it looked as if the scribes would be right.

Nevertheless, Chicago gathered momentum, capturing the lead on July 8, in the midst of an 11-game winning streak. St. Louis provided stiff competition, and perhaps an added incentive.

On July 27 GM Gallagher pulled a genuine steal by obtaining pitcher Hank Borowy from the Yankees on waivers. In spite of recurrent blisters, Borowy proved to be the right tonic for the stretch drive. Winning 11 of 13 decisions, he was their only pitcher who was effective against the Cardinals, who took 15 of 22 contests with the Cubs.

The Cubs clinched their "most recent" pennant with a 4–3 victory at Pittsburgh on September 29, with the Cardinals only three games behind. Winning the MVP award, Cavarretta batted a league-leading .355, highest ever by a lefthanded Cub batter. Pafko, Lowrey, Hack, and Johnson also enjoyed excellent seasons at the plate. Wyse won 22 games, and Passeau 17. Two aging hurlers, Paul Derringer and Ray Prim, provided unexpected heroics.

Cynics claimed—and still do—that the Cubs won the 1945 pennant because they had more 4-F's than any other team in the league. Although somewhat magnified, this criticism is not entirely without foundation. While the Cubs had a good lineup by wartime standards, these standards were not nearly as good as in peacetime. The Cardinals, for example, had just lost Stan Musial to the Navy, and he likely would have made the difference. Even so, the pennant was still a welcome treat to war-weary Cub fans.

In the World Series the Cubs met the Tigers for the fourth time. This time, the Series went the full seven games before the Cubs finally succumbed, their best showing since 1908. Cub highlights included Passeau's one-hit shutout in Game Three and Stan Hack's clutch double in the bottom of the 12th inning to win the sixth game.

The Cubs' joy would soon pass. The Cubs had not been hurt by the draft as badly as most other teams, but in 1946 this temporary advantage vanished. Furthermore, many of their stars were aging players for whom 1945 had been essentially their "last hurrah." In this category were Hack, Johnson, Derringer, Passeau, Prim, and infielder Roy Hughes. Of the entire roster, the only one who maintained his 1945 productivity after the war was Pafko. Unable to compete against the stiffer competition, the defending champions tumbled to a distant third.

Cub players back from military duty included Johnny Schmitz, Bob Scheffing, Eddie Waitkus, Clyde McCullough, Emil Kush, and a number of lesser names. Waitkus was an immediate hit at first base, pushing Cavarretta back into the outfield. Schmitz was a hard luck lefthander whose statistics belied the quality of his pitching. Kush became the Cubs' first bona fide relief specialist, while Scheffing, a catcher, had a couple of good seasons ahead of him.

Regardless, these players were insufficient to keep the Cubs in contention, as other clubs had superior talent rejoining them after their military hiatus. The fissures in the Cub dyke became gaping holes in 1947. With the old men a year older, the team sank to sixth place.

The following year the Cubs went for youth, bringing up rookie after rookie from their largely fruitless farm system. Unfortunately, only a handful of them had noteworthy careers, and some of those could best be regarded as anti-heroes. By June of 1948 only Cavarretta, Pafko, Nicholson, Lowrey, Borowy, and Bob Chipman remained from the champions of three years earlier.

Roy Smalley, the new shortstop, had fine range and frequently made spectacular stops—only to fire the ball over the first baseman's head. Often booed, he became the symbol of Cub frustration in the post-war era. Bob Rush, like Schmitz, was a talented pitcher who was usually betrayed by poor support. Outfielder Hal Jeffcoat had an outstanding throwing arm but was a weak hitter. He was eventually converted to a pitcher. Meanwhile, the Cubs finished dead last for the first time in 23 years. At the close of the season GM Gallagher commented, "The 1948 Chicago Cubs were the best team ever to finish last in the National League." But if they were such a good team, why did they finish last? (Chieger, 1987, 279).

On June 12, 1949 Frankie Frisch replaced the beleaguered Charlie Grimm as Cub manager. Three days later the Bruins traded Peanuts Lowrey and Harry Walker to the Reds for Hank Sauer and Frankie Baumholtz, one of the few deals of that era that worked in the Cubs' favor. Popularly called "the Mayor of Wrigley Field," Sauer replaced the departed Nicholson as the Cubs' new home run hero, while Baumholtz was a dependable singles hitter. Even so, they could not prevent another eighth-place finish. After seven decades of generally being part of the upper crust, the Cubs were now in the lower echelon of the National League.

Over the winter Jim Gallagher was kicked upstairs and given the title of business manager, while Wid Matthews was hired as director of player personnel. A blind optimist, Matthews was forever discovering the next Babe Ruth or Cy Young, but in name only.

In 1950 the Cubs went on their biggest home run binge in 20 years, kissing 161 baseballs good-bye. However, everything else continued dismally. The Cubs escaped the cellar by one notch only because the Pirates were even worse. All the while, Chicago's porous infield of Preston Ward at first, Wayne Terwilliger at second, Smalley at short, and Bill Serena at third set new lows in blundering.

By the next season the Cubs were back in the dungeon, in a year that featured future movie star Chuck Connors as a part-time first baseman, and Phil Cavarretta replacing Frisch as manager. On June 15, 1951 the Cubs traded Andy Pafko, Johnny Schmitz, Rube Walker, and Wayne Terwilliger to the Dodgers for Eddie Miksis, Bruce Edwards, Gene Hermanski, and Joe Hatten. This trade was the ultimate in Cub front office ineptitude up to that point in time. It was obvious from the outset that all four ex-Dodgers combined were not worth Pafko, easily the best player the Cubs had. To add insult upon injury, Matthews came out with his inane statement, "Miksis will fix us." Despite it all, there were signs of hope in rookie first baseman Dee Fondy and sophomore third baseman Ransom Jackson, both of whom became solid performers.

In 1952 the Cubs vacated Catalina Island in favor of Mesa, Arizona, for spring training. Cavarretta's team was the surprise of the league, climbing to fifth place with a .500 record. Leading the league in RBIs and tied for the lead in home runs, Hank Sauer was voted MVP, while Frankie Baumholtz challenged Stan Musial's monopoly on the batting title. Fine pitching came from Rush, Warren Hacker, Paul Minner, and bullpen ace Dutch Leonard. Compared to what the team had been through, it was a satisfying year.

Just as the Cubs were beginning to look respectable again, they slid into reverse gear, finishing seventh in 1953. It was the year that slugger Ralph Kiner was obtained from the Pirates, completing the hallowed outfield troika of Kiner in left, Baumholtz in center, and Sauer in right. The common joke was that Baumholtz played all three positions because the other two were so slow. Although obviously an exaggeration, it symbolized Cub anti-heroics of the period.

During the final two weeks of the season the Cubs brought up their first black players, shortstop Ernie Banks and second baseman Gene Baker. Although Banks went on to become the most revered player in Cub annals, it was Baker whom they were grooming for stardom at that time. Banks' contract was purchased from the Kansas City Monarchs of the Negro American League so that Baker would have a roommate (Chieger, 1987, 280).

The spring of 1954 opened on a sour note when Phil Cavarretta was fired as manager after he gave owner P.K. Wrigley an honest appraisal of the team's chances. His accuracy was borne out by another seventh-place showing under his successor, Stan Hack. On a positive note, Banks and Baker gave the Cubs their best infield duet since Jurges and Herman.

The next season the Cubs got off to a fast start but faded in July, finishing sixth. Ernie Banks established himself as a superstar, and outfielder Bob Speake as a would-be Babe Ruth. He hit 10 home runs in May but only two for the rest of the season. On May 12, 1955 history was again made at Wrigley Field when Cub pitcher Sam Jones became the first black to hurl a no-hitter in the majors, blanking Pittsburgh, 4–0, despite walking the bases loaded with nobody out in the ninth inning. It was the park's first no-hit game in 38 years.

During the off-season the Cubs pulled what looked like yet another Brooklyn-inspired boner when they dealt Ransom Jackson to the Dodgers for two unknowns, Don Hoak and Walt "Moose" Moryn. Although Hoak lasted only one season as a Cub, Moryn became a dependable clutch hitter and the hero of the blue-collar fans.

The Cubs packed a good one-two punch with Banks and Moryn, but the team still had a soft underbelly. In 1956 they "celebrated" their 10th consecutive season in the second division by dropping to last place. Clyde McCullough, the lone veteran of 1945, played his last game in mid-season. After the seventh year of Wid Matthews' five year plan, the heads of Matthews, Gallagher, and Hack rolled. The somber-faced John Holland became the team's new general manager, while Bob Scheffing replaced Hack as the field boss.

The team fared little better in Scheffing's first year, as the Cubs finished in a tie for seventh with Pittsburgh. Lee Walls joined Moryn in the outfield while Dale Long, another home run threat, became the new first baseman. Pitchers Dick Drott and Moe Drabowsky enjoyed splendid rookie seasons, but their accomplishments were sparse thereafter.

For the Cubs the 1950s were a period of massive home run power but little else. This was never more evident than in 1958, when they smashed a league-leading 182 home runs, setting a club record which lasted 29 years. A record five Cubs belted 20 or more home runs— Banks 47, Moryn 26, Walls 24, Bobby Thomson 21, and Long 20. Nevertheless, the Cubs could move up only to a tie for fifth place with the Cardinals. Considering the near total lack of reliable starters (rookie Glen Hobbie was the "ace" of the staff with 10 wins), Scheffing had done a creditable job with what he had.

The Cubs performed an encore in 1959, again finishing in a tie for fifth as Banks won his second straight MVP award. Hobbie won 16 games but pitching continued to be a problem, as firemen Don Elston and Billy Henry were worn out by year's end. A ray of hope could also be seen in rookie outfielder George Altman, who displayed an uncanny penchant for murdering the Giants. But after giving the Cubs their best record (74–80) in seven years, Bob Scheffing was fired.

An aging Charlie Grimm was resurrected to manage the Cubs in 1960, but this time he found it to be too many headaches. After only 17 games, he switched places with radio color man Lou Boudreau for the remainder of the season.

The Cubs began poorly and played consistently so for the entire year, escaping the cellar by only one game. Moreover, they were again in the throes of an agonizing change. Most of their well-liked regulars of the late 1950s—Moryn, Walls, Thomson, Long, Henry, Al Dark, and Tony Taylor—were gone by midseason, some felled by advancing age, others removed by bad trades. Don Cardwell, a pitcher obtained from the Phillies in exchange for Taylor, hurled a no-hitter in his first start as a Cub, on May 15, 1960. Unfortunately, he had a poor year otherwise.

On December 21, 1960 the enigmatic Wrigley announced that henceforth the Cubs would no longer have a field manager but would be run by a system of eight rotating coaches. The original eight were Grimm, Rip Collins, Elvin Tappe, Goldie Holt, Vidie Himsl, Harry Craft, Bobby Adams, and Rube Walker. Others who floated in and out before the system was junked were Bob Kennedy, Buck O'Neill, Lou Klein, Charlie Metro, Al Dark, Freddie Martin, Mel Wright, and Mel Harder.

As anyone outside of the Cub brass could have predicted, the result was utter chaos. One head coach would tell a player to play his position one way, the next would have him learn it in a different manner. The same applied to hitting and pitching.

Not unexpectedly, the Cubs again finished seventh in 1961, as the head coach position drifted from Himsl to Craft to Tappe. Outfielder Billy Williams was voted Rookie of the Year, and third baseman Ron Santo Sophomore of the Year. George Altman played like a coming superstar. Ernie Banks began to slow down at shortstop and was first moved to left field, with little success, and then to first base, where he remained for the rest of his career.

In 1962 the National League expanded to 10 teams, locating fledgling franchises in New York and Houston. For the Cubs, it was especially embarrassing as the infant Colt 45s (now Astros) beat them out for eighth place. It was the worst record yet by a Cub team as they lost 103 games. The ultimate in futility came on June 6, when shortstop Andre Rodgers had a chance for an unassisted triple play—and muffed it. Among the few redeeming features were rookies Lou Brock and Ken Hubbs, the latter winning the Rookie of the Year award for his outstanding defense at second base. Again, the head coach job revolved three times, from Tappe to Lou Klein to Charlie Metro.

That winter former White Sox infielder Bob Kennedy was named head coach while Robert Whitlow, a retired air force colonel, was hired as Athletic Director. Larry Jackson and Lindy McDaniel were obtained from St. Louis for Altman, Cardwell, and Moe Thacker, to help shore up an abominable pitching staff.

The coaches stopped spinning as, for all practical purposes, Kennedy was manager in all but title. The 1963 Cubs also stopped staggering around in a daze, thanks to strong pitching both in the frontline and in the bullpen. They held second place until mid-July and although they eventually sank to seventh, their 82–80 record was the best by a Cub team in 17 years. Dick Ellsworth, at 22–10, was the first Cub lefty to win 20 games since Jim Vaughn in 1919, while McDaniel won 13 and saved 22.

The revival was given a tragic setback when Ken Hubbs was killed in a plane crash in February of 1964, leaving a pall of gloom on the team and rendering them weak at second base. The pitching reverted to its previous form as only Jackson and, to a lesser extent, Bob Buhl, displayed consistent effectiveness. Santo and Williams enjoyed their first .300 seasons but could not prevent the Cubs from dropping to eighth in the standings.

One of the reasons was the deal that was unquestionably the worst in Cub history. On June 15, 1964 the Cubs traded Lou Brock and pitchers Paul Toth and Jack Spring to the Cardinals for pitchers Ernie Broglio and Bobby Shantz, and outfielder Doug Clemens, the principals being Brock and Broglio. At the time, the trade appeared to be highway robbery by the Cubs. Some writers predicted everything short of a Cub dynasty, as Broglio had won 21 games in 1960 and 18 in 1963. Apparently, the Cubs' front office neglected to consider the possibility of buying damaged goods. While the sore-armed Broglio won a total of seven games in three Cub seasons, Brock blossomed as soon as he left Chicago, helping the Cardinals win three pennants and two World Series en route to a niche in Cooperstown.

In January of 1965 Whitlow was dismissed, and by mid-June, so was Kennedy. His replacement, Lou Klein, fared no better. Banks, Santo, and Williams remained a triple threat, but beyond that the Cub offense was roughly equivalent to that of a cub scout pack. Submariner Ted Abernathy was a one-man bullpen, but little could be said for the starters. There was a glimmer of sunshine in the arrival of second baseman Glenn Beckert and shortstop Don Kessinger, but once again the Cubs could beat out only the Astros and the Mets.

On October 25, 1965 the predictably unpredictable P. K. Wrigley released another bolt of lightning when he announced that Leo Durocher—the antithesis of the staid Cub image—would be the new field manager. A *Sporting News* editorial called it "a revival meeting in the Windy City."

Still as outspoken as ever, the fiery Durocher vowed to get rid of the country club atmosphere in the Cubs' dugout, and lay down the law to "safety first" players. Declaring that the Cubs had the nucleus of a good team, Leo said, "The Cubs are not an eighth-place ball club and I'm here to find out why they are where they are" (Chieger, 1987, 281). He was more than correct in his assertion about the Cubs not being an eighth-place team. They finished 10th in 1966, tying the club record with 103 losses.

But there was hope in spite of it all. Thanks to Durocher's insistence, catcher Randy Hundley and pitcher Bill Hands were obtained from the Giants, and pitcher Fergie Jenkins from the Phillies. Under the guidance of coach Pete Reiser, Beckert and Kessinger became respectable at the plate while improving defensively. Rookie pitcher Ken Holtzman displayed potential, and by the last month of the year, the Cubs were playing competitive ball.

By 1967 most of the dead wood from the 1965 club had been chopped away, leaving only the reliables and some unproven youngsters. Even so, virtually no one saw the Cubs improving beyond eighth place. But the Cubs proved their critics wrong, soaring all the way to third place for their first upper-berth finish since 1946. Led by Jenkins' tireless arm, the pitching improved vastly, while the tightened infield gave the Cubs the league lead in defense. Signs reading "Durocher for Mayor" began popping up in Wrigley Field, as fans savored their most robust cheers in more than two decades.

The Cubs were at last being touted as a factor in the pennant race by someone other than Ernie Banks or television sportscaster Jack Brickhouse, their video voice since 1948. However, it looked like business as usual when the team began poorly in 1968, at one point being shut out for 48 consecutive innings. Fortunately, the Cubs put their act together in the second half, again capturing third place. Additional strength came from the rising of Bill Hands as an effective starter, and the acquisition of outfielder Jim Hickman and fireman Phil Regan from the Dodgers. Home attendance crossed the million mark for the first time since 1952.

Then came the unforgettable but ultimately false euphoria. In 1969 both major leagues expanded to 12 teams, dividing each circuit into an Eastern and Western division. For most of the year it was a dream season, with the Cubs as the flagship team of the National League East. The year was characterized by power, clutch hitting, spectacular defense, and the most shutouts (22) by a Cub pitching staff since 1918. It was the year of Willie Smith's game-winning home run on opening day, Ron Santo clicking his heels after every home victory, pitcher Dick Selma leading the yellow-helmeted "Bleacher Bums" in cheers, Leo Durocher's television commercials for Schlitz beer, the free Cub photos in Chicago supermarkets, Ken Holtzman's first no-hitter, and a then-record attendance of 1,674,993.

The 1969 Cubs were number one from the beginning, building up an 8½ game lead by mid-August. Then the Mets, whom literally no one took seriously, charged to the Eastern Division title (and then the pennant and the World Series) while the Cubs collapsed in September, finishing in second, eight games behind New York. Some blamed Durocher for not resting his regulars, and for being a strict disciplinarian. Others felt that the players had become so overconfident from early success that they panicked under pressure. Either way, the dream had turned into a nightmare.

Although everyone denied it, psychological scars had been left also. The Cubs of 1970 belted 179 home runs—including the beloved Banks' career 500th—but could do no better than a tie for second place, in spite of Hickman and Williams enjoying their greatest seasons. The Cubs procured such seasoned veterans as Johnny Callison, Joe Pepitone, and Milt Pappas in hopes of finding the finishing touch, but to no avail.

An 11-game winning streak early in the season was obliterated by a 12-game losing spree a short time later. The infield was slowing down at the corners, while the bullpen had fallen apart completely. Some writers began suggesting that Durocher should retire. More ominously, the camaraderie and unity which had constituted Leo's early years was rapidly disintegrating.

By 1971 relations between Durocher and the players had so deteriorated that the coaches served as intermediaries. The season of Jenkins' Cy Young award, Holtzman's second no-hitter, and Banks' farewell was also the year of the clubhouse rebellion. By demanding everything short of sending him to the guillotine, Durocher's numerous enemies in the press only succeeded in pouring gasoline into the flames. On September 3 P. K. Wrigley took out a paid advertisement in the Chicago papers, stating that "the dump Durocher clique might as well give up" (Angle, 1975, 169). Apparently, the notice neither inspired nor struck fear into the hearts of the players, who lost nine of their last 11 games, finishing in a tie for third with the Mets.

In hopes of capturing that elusive championship, the Cubs fielded two-thirds of a new outfield in 1972, obtaining Rick Monday from the Athletics and Jose Cardenal from the Brewers. Wonderful feats were expected from rookie pitchers Rick Reuschel and Burt Hooton, the latter no-hitting the Phillies on April 15.

Whatever the reason, the team languished. Yielding to the pressure, Durocher resigned on July 24 with the team two games above .500. A few years later he wrote in his autobiography, *Nice Guys Finish Last,* that "the greatest disappointment of my career is that I wasn't able to win a pennant for him (Wrigley)" (Durocher, 1975, 352).

With Whitey Lockman taking over as manager, the Cubs climbed to second place by the year's end. Jenkins won 20 games for the sixth consecutive year, while Pappas came within a hair's breadth of a perfect game against the Padres on September 2. After retiring the first 26 batters, he walked Larry Stahl on a three-two count, then retired Garry Jestadt to preserve the no-hitter.

Following the Cubs' strong finish, hopes were high. This was especially so with the anti-Durocher forces, who had finally gotten rid of their scapegoat.

At the outset of the 1973 season, it looked as if Durocher's detractors were vindicated. By early July the Cubs were 46–31, with an eight-game lead. Thereafter came a collapse that dwarfed 1969 as the club nosedived to fifth place, seven games below .500. The front line was simply worn out from advancing age.

P. K. Wrigley promised to "back up the truck," and did so. By the following spring Santo, Jenkins, Beckert, Hundley, Pappas, and Hickman had all been dispatched by one means or another. As could have been easily predicted, the Cubs of 1974 finished last in their division.

Two years to the day after he had replaced Durocher, Lockman was himself ousted in favor of Jim Marshall. Bill Madlock, the new third baseman, was the only youngster of any promise. Over the winter, stalwart Billy Williams was dealt to the Athletics. By that time 1969 seemed long ago and far away.

In 1975 the Cubs started off like a rocket but fizzled in June, sinking to fifth place. They could boast a dependable second baseman in Manny Trillo, while Madlock's league-leading .354 average was the highest by a Cub in 30 years. As had been the case so many times in the past, lack of pitching was the team's downfall. Reuschel continued to lose the heart-breakers, while Bill Bonham and Ray Burris were inconsistent at best. Shortstop Don Kessinger, the sole survivor of 1969, was traded after the season.

The Cubs marked their 100th anniversary in 1976 by dragging themselves up to fourth, but with an identical record to the year before. The season was basically an instant replay of 1975—Madlock won the batting crown, Cardenal was the top Cub base stealer, and Monday the only home run threat.

The off-season brought more of what critics dismissed as "cosmetic changes." Bob Kennedy was named general manager, and Herman Franks, who had had impressive but limited success as the Giants' mentor, was hired to run the dugout. With the era of free agency about to begin, Madlock and Monday demanded substantial raises and were sent packing. Bobby Murcer, obtained from the Giants for Madlock, was given a meatier contract than the lugging third baseman had asked for. On April 12, 1977 the 82-year-old P. K. Wrigley died, leaving the club to his son, William.

Although the Madlock deal was more than questionable, the Monday trade turned out to be a winner. Shortstop Ivan DeJesus combined with Trillo to form a popular "Latin connection" in the infield. Bill Buckner, who came from Los Angeles with DeJesus, became the Cubs' best overall hitter, as well as an outstanding hustler, during his fruitful stay.

Suddenly, the Cubs were winning again, zooming to first place with a 47–22 record at one point. The primary reason was Bruce Sutter. Virtually unnoticed the previous year, the young fireman emerged as the terror of the league with his "split-fingered" fastball, a pitch that defied definition as well as batters.

But as Sutter went, so went the team. After he was sidelined in August with a knot in his shoulder, the team sputtered, then fell apart totally in September, finishing fourth with an 81–81 mark. At least Reuschel, after years of poor support, finally won 20 games.

In 1978 the Cubs edged up to third, but it was a Pyrrhic victory, as they fell back below .500. Despite the acquisition of slugger Dave Kingman, their home run count of 72 was their lowest since 1947.

The 1970s pattern of false hopes and idle dreams continued in 1979, a season dominated by Kingman and Sutter. Enjoying the most productive campaign of his checkered career, "Kong" thrilled fans and won numerous games with his 48 prodigious blasts. Sutter, for his part, won the Cy Young Award with 37 saves and six relief wins. Although the Cubs played exciting ball for much of the year, peaking at 67–54, their patented September swoon dropped them to the familiar environs of fifth place. Berating some of the players, Herman Franks resigned with a week left in the season, as Joey Amalfitano took the thankless job of interim manager.

In 1980 the Cubs hired Preston Gomez as manager, but he was hardly the answer. Lacking both leadership and morale, the Cubs were listless all season, finishing dead last despite a Buckner batting title and another fine year from Sutter. Dave Kingman, by a combination of erratic behavior and injuries which many thought to be a heavy case of malingering, went from hero to goat. Gomez, meanwhile, did not even last the season, being replaced by Amalfitano after 90 games.

By this time, fans were becoming increasingly critical of the Wrigley regime, especially when Sutter was traded to the Cardinals for Leon Durham, Ken Reitz, and Ty Waller after he had won an arbitration suit. It appeared that the ownership was only interested in running a bargain basement operation.

The 1981 season opened with the aura of a wake. The Players Union was threatening a strike, and the Cubs, minus Sutter, looked weaker than ever. From Day One, the 1981 Cubs played as if they were whipped before they even took the field. Fans groaned even more when their only reliable starter, Reuschel, was dealt to the Yankees for practically nothing. On June 12 the players of both leagues walked out over the issue of free agency. This turned out to be a mercy killing for the Cubs, who were already buried hopelessly in the bottom of the National League East.

Then came bigger news: on June 16 William Wrigley announced the sale of the franchise to the *Chicago Tribune* Corporation, thereby ending 65 years of Wrigley family affiliation. When the season resumed on August 10 following the strike settlement, the Cubs continued on their path to oblivion, after which Joey Amalfitano was relieved of his managerial duties.

In October Dallas Green was lured away from the Phillies to become the Cubs' new general manager. Vowing to "build new traditions," he appeared merely to be on an ego trip when his picture was plastered over the team program the following year. When he announced that the Cubs needed night home games in order to be competitive, he alienated a minority of residents near the ballpark, but brought a chorus of cheers from many others. Regardless of what one thought of Green personally, there could be no doubt of his desire to win, a trait that was evidently lacking during some of the previous regimes. And in his early years at least, most of his trades worked out to the Cubs' advantage.

With Lee Elia as field manager, it looked like a continuation of the old tradition in early 1982, as the Cubs wallowed in the National League mudhole. During the final third of the season, however, came a surprising turnabout as they won 33 of their final 55 to finish fifth. The bullpen of Lee Smith, Mike Proly, and Bill Campbell came forth as one of the best in baseball, while youngsters Ryne Sandberg, Jody Davis, and Leon "Bull" Durham were rapidly blossoming. After August 1 the Cubs had the second best record in the league.

In the spring of 1983 Elia proudly announced that the Cubs were capable of playing .500 ball. But when the team started in a sputtering fashion, he vented his frustration upon the Wrigley Field fans, calling them unemployable unmentionables—although in less diplomatic terms.

Although Elia made a public apology, a sour tone was set for the rest of the season. Once again the lack of dependable starters was the team's Achilles Heel. At one point, the Cubs were up to 38–39, but the bullpen soon began to crumble from overwork. Administrative Assistant Charlie Fox took over for Elia, but it was too late to reverse the downward trend. The Cubs again finished fifth but with two fewer wins. The ".500 ball club" was 20 games under.

At the close of the season, Fox was moved back upstairs and replaced by Jim Frey, who had a winning record in his brief tenure as manager of the Kansas City Royals, capturing a pennant in the process in 1980.

Nevertheless, there was no cause for optimism when the 1984 season unfolded. The team's 7–20 spring training record was the worst in the majors. It looked like another long, sorrowful year in the making.

This time Chicago was in for a welcome shock. GM Green literally swindled the Phillies out of outfielders Bobby Dernier and Gary "Sarge" Matthews. On May 25 Green traded Bill Buckner to the Red Sox for pitcher Dennis Eckersley. He then made his coup de grace, obtaining pitcher Rick Sutcliffe in a seven-player deal with the Indians. Sutcliffe became the Hank Borowy of 1984, winning 14 straight in a dream season.

Although the Cubs had played well since the start of the season, the general consensus was that it was too good to be true. Possibly the turning point came on June 23 when Ryne Sandberg slammed game-tying home runs in both the ninth and tenth innings. The Cubs edged the Cardinals, 12–11, in 11 innings and were rolling. Their main obstacle was the Mets, whose rise paralleled that of the Cubs. Eventually, Chicago surged past New York, winning 11 of the last 14 games with the Mets to exorcise the spectre of 1969.

By mid-September the Mets had all but conceded defeat. When Sutcliffe slammed the door on the Pirates, 4–1, on September 24 at Pittsburgh, the champagne flowed. The Cubs had won the Eastern Division Championship. For the first time, more than two million fans passed through the portals of Wrigley Field. Six Cubs—Durham, Davis, Sandberg, Matthews, Keith Moreland, and Ron Cey—drove in at least 80 runs. Dernier's 45 stolen bases were the most by a Cub player since Johnny Evers had 46 in 1907. On a more ominous note, the aging Larry Bowa was a weak link at shortstop, while the staff ERA of 3.75 was 10th out of 12 in the league.

Another miracle team, the San Diego Padres, had won the National League Western Division title. When the Cubs won the first two playoff games at Wrigley Field, long suffering fans could almost taste the first pennant in 39 years. But such was not to be as the Padres won the next three on their own turf to take it all. The Cubs had the enemy by the throat but had failed to deliver the killing blow. Even Sandberg's MVP award, Sutcliffe's Cy Young honors, and Frey's Manager of the Year citation could not erase the fact that the Cubs had again fallen short.

Skeptics claimed that the primary, if not the only, reason for the Cubs' success in 1984 was that most of their key players were having career years simultaneously. Subsequent history has tended to bear this criticism out. The glory of 1984 turned out to be even more transient than that of 1945.

In early 1985 it looked as if the Cubs would continue in their championship ways, winning 34 of 53 games. But as an inconceivable number of injuries hit the team, these soon took their toll. When the team lost 13 straight to tie the club record for futility, the Cubs were out of the race that quickly. It was all downhill thereafter, as Dernier,

Matthews, Sutcliffe, Eckersley, Steve Trout, Scott Sanderson, and Dick Ruthven all spent time on the disabled list, while Davis missed considerable action because of a virus.

With the entire starting staff sidelined, Green had to reach into his barren farm system for pitching help, and with disastrous results. The Cubs skidded to fifth but regained fourth when the Phillies went into a late-season tailspin. The only players who equaled or exceeded their 1984 performances were Sandberg and Moreland, and the latter was a liability defensively. As Bowa was being phased out, Shawon Dunston began taking over the shortstop duties. He displayed fine potential, but a lack of consistency which would plague him for several seasons to come.

The club that was supposed to have a great future continued to decline in 1986, as Dallas Green's public utterances began to take on the appearance of impotent rage. Jim Frey's head rolled, as Gene Michael became Cub manager after John Vukovich served as interim leader for two days.

With the Cubs on their way to fifth place, the half-crippled pitching staff went from bad to worse. For the first time in their history, the Cubs suffered the ignominy of not having a single pitcher who was able to win 10 games. Sutcliffe, the ace of 1984, had fallen to 5–14. Even the previously dependable reliever, Lee Smith, was beginning to display a disturbing tendency to get shelled in pressure situations. Dunston, however, in his first full season, led all National League shortstops in putouts, assists, and double plays, but also in errors.

Shortly before the start of the 1987 season, the Cubs bolstered their withering offense with the signing of veteran outfielder Andre Dawson via free agency—and for a bargain price by today's standards.

It was to be Dallas Green's last major accomplishment. With Dawson topping the league in home runs (49) and RBIs (137), the Cubs were again an exciting team, if not a winning one. Led by Dawson, the Chicago wrecking crew smashed 209 home runs, to pace the league and shatter the old Cub record. However, the fact that the majors in general witnessed a sharp increase in home runs gave credence to the belief that the ball had been tampered with, denials to the contrary.

Even Dawson's heroics and a comeback season from Sutcliffe could not prevent the same old story at bottom line, as the Cubs fell to last in their division. They were also last in the league in stolen bases, and next to last in team ERA. For the third time in five years, the Cub manager did not make it through the season. With 25 games left Green fired Michael, naming Frank Lucchesi as yet another interim manager.

Green was soon history himself. Shortly after the end of the campaign, he announced his resignation from the Cub organization, although many suspected that he was forced out. Ironically, he was replaced by one of the men he had fired, as Jim Frey was named general manager. Frey, in turn, named his old comrade Don Zimmer, a former Cub second baseman and coach, as field manager.

On December 8, 1987 Frey traded Lee Smith to the Red Sox for pitchers Al Nipper and Calvin Schiraldi, leaving only Davis, Durham, Sandberg, Sanderson, and Sutcliffe from 1984. Although many felt that Smith's best years were behind him, it was equally apparent that the Cubs could have received more in return had they driven a harder bargain.

For the Cubs the 1988 season was one of promise, disappointment, and even history-making. With their copyrighted good first half, the Cubs placed six players on the All-Star team, their most since 1936. Thereafter, the team declined to finish fourth, eight games below .500. The primary reasons for the Cubs' demise were a lack of clutch hitting and a totally ineffective bullpen led by Rich "Goose" Gossage, who was literally booed out of the North Side after one season. Home run production plummeted to 113, barely half of the 1987 total.

There were positive developments also. Rookie Mark Grace caught on immediately at first base, sending Durham packing to Cincinnati. He was given the *Sporting News* Rookie of the Year Award for his efforts. Damon Berryhill, another rookie, began to supplant Davis behind the plate and did so well that by September, Davis was gone also. Sophomore Greg Maddux won 18 games, but only three after the All-Star break. Outfielder Rafael Palmeiro, while hitting for an impressive average, was disappointing with runners in scoring position.

After months of negotiations with the Chicago City Council, the Illinois State Legislature, and neighborhood pressure groups, night baseball finally became a reality at Wrigley Field on August 8, 1988. However, with the Cubs leading the Phillies, 3–1, in the bottom of the fourth inning, a torrential downpour and a two-hour delay caused the much-ballyhooed affair to be cancelled because of the rain. Somehow, it figured. The following evening, in the first night game that counted, the Cubs took the Mets, 6–4.

Finally, on September 30, 1988, President Ronald Reagan became the first chief executive to attend a Cubs home game while in office since William Howard Taft in 1909. A former sportscaster himself, the president joined Harry Caray in the radio booth to briefly help with the broadcast. Unfortunately, the Pirates put a damper on the affair by edging the Cubs, 10–9, in 10 innings. The Cubs had lost one for the Gipper.

Over the off-season the Cubs began preparing for the new year by pulling another controversial trade, swapping Rafael Palmeiro and pitchers Jamie Moyer and Drew Hall to Texas for pitchers Mitch Williams, Paul Kilgus, and Steve Wilson, infielders Curt Wilkerson and Luis Benetiz, and outfielder Pablo Delgado. By trading a batter who had just hit .307 (Palmeiro) and a promising young pitcher (Moyer) for an assemblage of unknown quantities, the Cubs appeared to be duped, as usual.

That was the way it still looked at the close of a miserable spring training. The prevailing prognosis was that the Cubs would finish fifth. Said Steve Wulf of *Sports Illustrated.* "The Cubs, who haven't won a world championship since 1908, have had only one winning season since 1972. You can be certain this will not be their second." Frey and Zimmer would later concede that they were only hoping that the team would be good enough to break even.

Once the season started, the Cubs defied the experts by pulling off one miracle after another. Lefty Mitch Williams gave fans cardiac arrest with his terrible control and unorthodox delivery, but got the job done, registering 36 saves. Mike Bielecki, who heretofore had won only 12 games in his entire career, came through with 18 wins. Outfielders Jerome Walton and Dwight Smith, neither of whom had played beyond Class AA ball, responded with outstanding rookie seasons. The former, who batted safely in 30 consecutive games to set a twentieth-century team record, was voted league Rookie of the Year by the baseball writers.

After four seasons of inconsistent promise, Shawon Dunston finally became a genuine major leaguer at the plate as well as in the field. Maddux, following a 1–5 start, rallied to finish at 19–12, while Sutcliffe won 16. Sandberg enjoyed his most productive season in four years, while Grace did not fall victim to the sophomore jinx. Journeyman outfielder Lloyd McClendon provided added bench strength while Luis Salazar, obtained from San Diego late in the year to help the slumping Vance Law at third base, put forth a hot bat as well.

Although the 1989 Cubs flirted with first place during the early months of the season, there was still a sense of impending doom among their fans, who waited for the inevitable August or September collapse. But this time the swoon did not come as the "Boys of Zimmer" never relinquished the lead once they regained it on August 7. When the Cubs rallied to defeat the Astros, 10–9, on August 29 after spotting them a 9–0 lead, many a non-believer was converted. Dwight Smith remarked, "It's a message this club is for real."

The Cubs finally clinched the National League East crown on September 26 with a 3–2 victory over the Expos at Montreal. Appropriately, Mitch Williams fanned Mike Fitzgerald with the tying run on third base to preserve the win for Maddux. The Cubs had won their division despite sub-par years from Dawson and Law, losing Berryhill to the disabled list, not having a dependable fourth starter, and not having at least one player with 80 or more RBIs. A city record 2,491,942 paid their way into ancient Wrigley Field in its 75th anniversary season.

In the meantime, the Giants had outlasted the Padres in the West, with home run power that the Cubs could not match. The Cubs entered the N.L. playoffs as distinct underdogs and came out the same way, falling to San Francisco in five games. The power punch of Will Clark, Kevin Mitchell, and Matt Williams utterly demolished the Cub pitching staff. Although the Cubs batted .303 as a team during the playoffs, they stranded 43 men on base, an indication that they had run out of miracles. Once again, their glory was not lasting. Nevertheless, their demise was hardly like the trauma of 1984, because this time around the Giants clearly had a superior team.

There was little pennant challenge for the Chicago northsiders throughout the early campaigns of the 1990s, with three identical fourth-slot finishes and nearly identical season's records. Perhaps the only bright spots were Andre Dawson's approach to 400 career homers, Ryne Sandberg's continued slugging (40 homers in 1990), and Greg Maddux on the hill, with a rare Cy Young plaque in 1992.

References

Ahrens, Art, and Eddie Gold, eds. *Day by Day in Chicago Cubs History.* West Point, N.Y.: Leisure Press, 1982.

Angle, Paul, M. *Phillip K. Wrigley: Memoir of a Modest Man.* Chicago: Rand McNally and Company, 1975.

Anson, Adrian C. *A Ballplayer's Career.* Chicago. Era Publishing Company, 1900.

Chieger, Bob, ed. *The Cubbies.* New York: Atheneum Press, 1987.

Creamer, Robert W. *Babe: The Legend Comes to Life.* New York: Simon and Schuster Publishers, 1975.

Durocher, Leo. *Nice Guys Finish Last.* New York: Simon and Schuster Publishers, 1975.

Grimm, Charlie, with Edward Prell. *Baseball I Love You: Jolly Cholly's Story.* Chicago: Regnery Publishing Company, 1968.

Federal Writers Project, WPA. *Baseball in Old Chicago.* Chicago: A.C. McClurg and Company, 1939.

Langford, Jim. *The Game is Never Over: An Appreciative History of the Chicago Cubs, 1948–1980.* South Bend, Ind.: Icarus Press, 1980.

Levine, Peter. *A.G. Spalding and the Rise of Baseball.* New York: Oxford University Press, 1985.

Spalding, A.G. *America's National Game.* New York: American Sports Publishing Company, 1911.

Annotated Bibliography

Anson, Adrian C. *A Ballplayer's Career.* Chicago: Era Publishing Company, 1900. 339 pp.

    As old as it is, Cap Anson's autobiography remains the most thorough, and most enjoyable, narrative about Cubs baseball in the nineteenth century. His lengthy chapters on the world tour of 1888–89, constituting nearly one third of the book, make the reader wish he were there. This is the original source of the famed photograph of the ballplayers posing on the Sphinx. Anson was also extremely opinionated, and many of his remarks concerning various individuals would likely result in lawsuits today.

Banks, Ernie, with Jim Enright. *Mr. Cub.* Chicago: Follett Books, 1971. 240 pp.
    Probably mostly ghostwritten, this story of Ernie Banks and his great career is pleasant reading, but somewhat superficial, and very Pollyanna-ish in tone. It has the appearance of having been assembled in a very short period of time. Even so, it is valuable to the historian if for no other reason than it is, at present, the only biography of the Cubs' greatest hero of modern times (excluding a children's-oriented book by Bill Libby).

Boone, Robert S., and Gerald Grunska. *Hack.* Highland Park, Ill.: Highland Press, 1978. 149 pp.
    Possibly the most larger-than-life figure ever to play for the Cubs, Lewis "Hack" Wilson dominated Chicago baseball as the Cubs' first modern home run hero from 1926 through 1930. The story of Wilson's meteoric life, from his less-than-humble beginnings, through his glory days in baseball, to his sad finale as a glorified derelict in Baltimore, is well chronicled in this informative volume.

Chieger, Bob. *The Cubbies.* New York: Atheneum Press, 1987. 307 pp.
    Chieger's contribution to Cub lore is this extensive anthology of quotations by and about the Cubs, their fans, and their city, going back to the beginning. His effort contains many familiar quotes, as well as many that are not so well known. From cover to cover, it is captivating, and frequently hilarious, reading.

Enright, Jim. *Chicago Cubs.* New York: MacMillan Publishing Company, 1975. 192 pp.
    Rather than a chronological narrative, this Cub history is oriented toward outstanding performers, great teams, historic moments, and oddball characters. Like most newspaper sportswriters, the late Enright treated the nineteenth century as if it did not exist, save for a token piece on Cap Anson. On the positive side, it is profusely illustrated with excellent photographs, and includes box scores of memorable games, as well as a complete roster of Cub players up to that time.

Gold, Eddie, and Art Ahrens. *The Golden Era Cubs, 1876–1940,* and *The New Era Cubs, 1941–1985.* Chicago: Bonus Books, 1985. 180 pp. and 274 pp.
    These companion volumes present biographical sketches of nearly every historically significant Cub player, as well as a general outline of the team's history from the beginning. Unfortunately, the second book also includes stories about several forgettable (and, by now, largely forgotten) players from the Dallas Green era, which the authors were pressured into including, ostensibly to help book sales.

Grimm, Charlie, with Ed Prell. *Jolly Cholly's Story: Baseball I Love You.* Chicago: Henry Regnery Company, 1968. 242 pp.
    Although not nearly as extensive as Cap Anson's memoirs, Charlie Grimm's autobiography is to Cubs baseball in the 1920s, 1930s, and 1940s what Anson's book is to the nineteenth century. Pleasantly nostalgic without being sappy, the Grimm tale is replete with the warmth and humor that made Charlie one of the most popular figures in the saga of Chicago baseball. The illustrations are good, but not exceptional.

Langford, Jim. *The Game Is Never Over.* South Bend, Ind.: Icarus Press, 1980. 252 pp.

For readers who enjoy cheerleading publications, Langford's is the ultimate volume. A Cub rooter and historian, the author presents a fan's-
eye-view of the team's fortunes, such as they were, from 1948 to 1980.
Although unashamedly optimistic, he does not neglect the fact that the
Cubs fielded some of the worst teams in baseball during the period in
question. An especially pleasing touch is the Opening Day lineup for each
season covered.

Levine, Peter. *A. G. Spalding and the Rise of Baseball.* New York: Oxford University Press, 1985. 184 pp.

In his study of professional baseball's foremost pioneer, author Levine
packs considerable fascinating material into a relatively short volume.
Scholarly yet readable, the work is thoroughly researched and footnoted.
Of particular interest is his presentation of the financial aspects of the
Chicago club's operations in its early days, an area hitherto largely ignored. For the historical student of Cub baseball, this volume is highly
recommended.

Murphy, James M. *The Gabby Hartnett Story.* Smithtown, N.Y.: Exposition Press,
1983. 78 pp.

Since Hartnett's death in 1972, relatively little has been written about the
perky Irishman who was easily the greatest catcher in Cub history, and
one of the key men on their talented rosters of the late 1920s and 1930s.
Although much too short to do justice to Hartnett's career, Murphy's
biography is well written, and provides a good base which can be expanded
upon in the future. For a brief book it is exceptionally well illustrated,
featuring many previously unpublished photographs.

Schwab, Rick. *Stuck on the Cubs.* Evanston, Ill.: Sassafras Press, 1977. 192 pp.

Geared more for humor than history, this witty vignette reflects a fan's
look at the Cubs' institutionalized incompetence from the "Aw, nuts"
rather than "Gee whiz" school of writing. It has been dismissed as mindless
reading by critics who obviously lack a sense of humor; however, the book
is not intended to be an intellectual analysis of the team's founderings.
For those who grew up in Chicago as Cub fans during the 1950s and
1960s, it is a grand slam home run full of laughs and nostalgia.

Spalding, Albert G. *Base Ball.* New York: American Sports Publishing Company, 1911. 542 pp.

Spalding's lengthy, semi-autobiographical work traces the history of baseball back to the days of its predecessors. Due to Spalding's long association
with the Chicago team, his reflections cover much of the same territory
as Anson's, but contain many stories and anecdotes not found in the
former book. Like Anson's memoir, Spalding's is a fine sample of Victori-
an-era values and attitudes. It also helped create the myth that baseball
was invented by Abner Doubleday at Cooperstown, New York, in 1839.

Williams, Billy, with Irv Haag. *Billy; The Classic Hitter.* Chicago: Rand McNally
and Company, 1974. 206 pp.

Like Williams himself, this excellent autobiography has been generally
unnoticed and underrated, possibly because Billy spent most of his career
in the shadow of Ernie Banks. Compiled from extensive tape recorded
interviews, Billy's words jump out at the reader in italicized print, while
co-author Haag (now deceased) puts together a thorough team history
from the late 1950s to the early 1970s. In telling his life story, Williams
is candid without being self-serving.

Year-by-Year Standings and Season Summaries

Year	Pos.	Record	Pct.	GB	Manager	Player	BA	Player	HR	Player	W-L	ERA
1876	1st	52–14	.788	—	Spalding	Barnes	.403	Hines	2	Spalding	47–13	1.75
1877	5th	26–33	.441	15.5	Spalding	McVey	.368	None		Bradley	18–23	3.31
1878	4th	30–30	.500	11	Ferguson	Ferguson	.351	Start	1	Larkin	29–26	2.24
						Start	.351	Remsen	1			
								Hankinson	1			
1879	4th	46–33	.579	10.5	Anson	Anson	.396	Peters	1	Larkin	31–23	2.44
								Williamson	1			
								Flint	1			
1880	1st	67–17	.798	—	Anson	Gore	.360	Gore	2	Corcoran	43–14	1.95
1881	1st	56–28	.667	—	Anson	Anson	.399	Burns	4	Corcoran	31–14	2.31
1882	1st	55–29	.655	—	Anson	Anson	.362	Flint	4	Goldsmith	28–16	2.42
1883	2nd	59–39	.602	4	Anson	Gore	.334	Kelly	3	Corcoran	34–20	2.49
1884	T4th	62–50	.554	22	Anson	Kelly	.354	Williamson	27	Corcoran	35–23	2.40
1885	1st	87–25	.777	—	Anson	Gore	.313	Dalrymple	11	Clarkson	53–16	1.85
1886	1st	90–34	.726	—	Anson	Kelly	.388	Anson	10	Clarkson	35–17	2.41
1887	3rd	71–50	.587	6.5	Anson	Anson	.421*	Pfeffer	16	Clarkson	38–21	3.08
1888	2nd	77–58	.578	9	Anson	Anson	.344	Ryan	16	Krock	24–14	2.44
1889	3rd	67–65	.508	19	Anson	Anson	.342	Ryan	17	Dwyer	16–13	3.59
										Gumbert	16–13	3.62
										Hutchison	16–17	3.54
1890	2nd	84–53	.613	6	Anson	Anson	.312	Wilmot	14	Hutchison	42–25	2.70
1891	2nd	82–53	.607	3.5	Anson	Anson	.294	Wilmot	11	Hutchison	43–19	2.81
1892	7th	70–76	.479	30	Anson	Dahlen	.295	Ryan	10	Hutchison	37–34	2.74
1893	9th	56–71	.441	29	Anson	Anson	.314	Lange	8	McGill	17–18	4.61
1894	8th	57–75	.432	34	Anson	Anson	.395	Dahlen	15	Griffith	21–11	4.92
1895	4th	72–58	.554	15	Anson	Lange	.389	Lange	10	Griffith	25–13	3.93
1896	5th	71–57	.555	18.5	Anson	Dahlen	.361	Dahlen	9	Griffith	22–13	3.54
1897	9th	59–73	.447	34	Anson	Lange	.340	Dahlen	6	Griffith	21–19	3.72

*Includes bases on balls as hits.

Year	Pos.	Record	Pct.	GB	Manager	Player	BA	Player	HR	Player	W-L	ERA
1898	4th	85–65	.567	17.5	Burns	Ryan	.323	Lange	6	Griffith	26–10	1.88
1899	8th	75–73	.507	26	Burns	Lange	.325	Mertes	9	Griffith	22–13	2.79
1900	T5th	65–75	.464	19	Loftus	Green	.298	Mertes	7	Griffith	14–13	3.05
1901	6th	53–86	.383	37	Loftus	Hartsell	.335	Hartsell	7	Waddel	13–15	2.81
1902	5th	68–69	.496	34	Selee	Slagle	.315	Tinker	2	Taylor	22–11	1.33
1903	3rd	82–56	.594	8	Selee	Chance	.327	Kling	2	Weimer	21–9	2.30
										Taylor	21–14	2.45
1904	2nd	93–60	.608	13	Selee	Chance	.310	Chance	6	Weimer	20–14	1.91
1905	3rd	92–61	.601	13	Selee	Chance	.316	Chance	2	Brown	18–12	2.17
					Chance			Tinker	2	Weimer	18–12	2.27
								Maloney	2	Reulbach	18–13	1.42
1906	1st	116–36	.763	—	Chance	Steinfeldt	.327	Schulte	7	Brown	26–6	1.04
1907	1st	107–45	.704	—	Chance	Chance	.293	Schulte	2	Overall	23–8	1.70
								Evers	2			
1908	1st	99–55	.643	—	Chance	Evers	.300	Tinker	6	Brown	29–9	1.47
1909	2nd	104–49	.680	6.5	Chance	Hofman	.285	Tinker	4	Brown	27–9	1.31
								Schulte	4			
1910	1st	104–50	.675	—	Chance	Hofman	.325	Schulte	10	Brown	25–13	1.86
1911	2nd	92–62	.597	7.5	Chance	Zimmerman	.307	Schulte	21	Brown	21–11	2.80
1912	3rd	91–59	.607	11.5	Chance	Zimmerman	.372	Zimmerman	14	Cheney	26–10	2.85
1913	3rd	88–65	.575	13.5	Evers	Zimmerman	.313	Saier	14	Cheney	21–14	2.57
1914	4th	78–76	.506	16.5	O'Day	Zimmerman	.296	Saier	18	Vaughn	21–13	2.05
1915	4th	73–80	.477	17.5	Bresnahan	Fisher	.287	Williams	13	Vaughn	20–12	2.87
1916	5th	67–86	.438	26.5	Tinker	Zimmerman	.286	Williams	12	Vaughn	17–14	2.20
1917	5th	74–80	.481	24	Mitchell	Mann	.273	Doyle	6	Vaughn	23–13	2.01
1918	1st	84–45	.651	—	Mitchell	Hollocher	.316	Flack	4	Vaughn	22–10	1.74
1919	3rd	75–65	.536	21	Mitchell	Flack	.294	Flack	6	Vaughn	21–14	1.79
1920	T5th	75–79	.487	18	Mitchell	Flack	.302	Robertson	10	Alexander	27–14	1.91
1921	7th	64–89	.418	30	Evers	Grimes	.321	Grimes	6	Alexander	15–13	3.39
					Killefer			Flach	6			

174

Year	Pos.	Record	Pct.	GB	Manager	Player	BA	Player	HR	Player	W-L	ERA
1922	5th	80–74	.519	13	Killefer	Grimes	.354	Grimes	14	Alexander Aldridge	16–13 16–15	3.63 3.52
1923	4th	83–71	.539	12.5	Killefer	Statz O'Farrell	.319 .319	Miller	20	Alexander	22–12	3.19
1924	5th	81–72	.529	12	Killefer	Grantham	.316	Hartnett	16	Kaufmann	16–11	4.02
1925	8th	68–86	.442	27.5	Killefer Maranville Gibson	Grimm	.306	Hartnett	24	Alexander	15–11	3.39
1926	4th	82–72	.532	7	McCarthy	Wilson	.321	Wilson	21	Root	18–17	2.82
1927	4th	85–68	.556	8.5	McCarthy	Stephenson	.344	Wilson	30	Root	26–15	3.76
1928	3rd	91–63	.591	4	McCarthy	Stephenson	.324	Wilson	31	Malone	18–13	2.84
1929	1st	98–54	.645	—	McCarthy	Hornsby	.380	Wilson Hornsby	39 39	Malone	22–10	3.57
1930	2nd	90–64	.584	2	McCarthy Hornsby	Stephenson	.367	Wilson	56	Malone	20–9	3.94
1931	3rd	84–70	.545	17	Hornsby	Grimm Hornsby	.331 .331	Hornsby	16	Root	17–14	3.48
1932	1st	90–64	.584	—	Hornsby Grimm	Stephenson	.324	Moore	13	Warneke	22–6	2.37
1933	3rd	86–68	.558	6	Grimm	Stephenson	.329	Hartnett Herman	16 16	Bush	20–12	2.75
1934	3rd	86–65	.570	8	Grimm	Cuyler	.338	Hartnett	22	Warneke	22–10	3.21
1935	1st	100–54	.654	—	Grimm	Hartnett	.344	Klein	21	Lee Warneke	20–6 20–13	2.96 3.06
1936	T2nd	87–67	.565	5	Grimm	Demaree	.350	Demaree	16	Lee French	18–11 18–9	3.31 3.39
1937	2nd	93–61	.604	3	Grimm	Hartnett	.354	Galan	18	Carleton French	16–8 16–10	3.15 3.98
1938	1st	89–63	.586	—	Grimm Hartnett	Hack	.320	Collins	13	Lee	22–9	2.66

Year	Pos.	Record	Pct.	GB	Manager	Player	BA	Player	HR	Player	W-L	ERA
1939	4th	84–70	.545	13	Hartnett	Leiber	.310	Leiber	24	Lee	19–15	3.44
1940	5th	75–79	.487	25.5	Hartnett	Hack	.317	Nicholson	25	Passeau	20–13	2.50
1941	6th	70–84	.455	30	Wilson	Hack	.317	Nicholson	26	Passeau	14–14	3.35
1942	6th	68–86	.442	38	Wilson	Hack	.300	Nicholson	21	Passeau	19–14	2.68
						Novikoff	.300					
1943	5th	74–79	.484	30.5	Wilson	Nicholson	.309	Nicholson	29	Bithorn	18–12	2.60
1944	4th	75–79	.487	30	Wilson / Johnson / Grimm	Cavarretta	.321	Nicholson	33	Wyse	16–15	3.15
1945	1st	98–56	.636	—	Grimm	Cavarretta	.355	Nicholson	13	Wyse	22–10	2.68
1946	3rd	82–71	.536	14.5	Grimm	Waitkus	.304	Nicholson	8	Wyse	14–12	2.69
								Cavarretta	8			
1947	6th	69–85	.448	25	Grimm	Cavarretta	.314	Nicholson	26	Schmitz	13–18	3.22
1948	8th	64–90	.416	27.5	Grimm	Pafko	.312	Pafko	26	Schmitz	18–13	2.64
1949	8th	61–93	.396	36	Grimm / Frisch	Cavarretta	.294	Sauer	27	Schmitz	11–13	4.35
1950	7th	64–89	.418	26.5	Frisch	Pafko	.304	Pafko	36	Rush	13–20	3.71
1951	8th	62–92	.403	34.5	Frisch / Cavarretta	Baumholtz	.284	Sauer	30	Rush	11–12	3.83
1952	5th	77–77	.500	19.5	Cavarretta	Baumholtz	.325	Sauer	37	Rush	17–13	2.70
1953	7th	65–89	.422	40	Cavarretta	Fondy	.309	Kiner	28	Minner	12–15	4.21
										Hacker	12–19	4.38
1954	7th	64–90	.416	33	Hack	Sauer	.288	Sauer	41	Rush	13–15	3.77
1955	6th	72–81	.471	26	Hack	Banks	.295	Banks	44	Jones	14–20	4.10
1956	8th	60–94	.390	33	Hack	Banks	.297	Banks	28	Rush	13–10	3.19
1957	T7th	62–92	.403	33	Scheffing	Long	.298	Banks	43	Drott	15–11	3.58
1958	T5th	72–82	.468	20	Scheffing	Banks	.313	Banks	47	Hobbie	10–6	3.74
1959	T5th	74–80	.481	13	Scheffing	Banks	.304	Banks	45	Hobbie	16–13	3.69
1960	7th	60–94	.390	35	Grimm / Boudreau	Ashburn	.291	Banks	41	Hobbie	16–20	3.96

Year	Pos.	Record	Pct.	GB	Manager	Player	BA	Player	HR	Player	W-L	ERA
1961	7th	64–90	.416	29	None	Altman	.303	Banks	29	Cardwell	15–14	3.82
1962	9th	59–103	.364	42.5	None	Altman	.318	Banks	37	Buhl	12–13	3.69
1963	7th	82–80	.506	17	None	Santo	.297	Santo	25	Ellsworth	22–10	2.11
								Williams	25			
1964	8th	76–86	.469	17	None	Santo	.313	Williams	33	Jackson	24–11	3.14
1965	8th	72–90	.444	25	None	Williams	.315	Williams	34	Ellsworth	14–15	3.81
1966	10th	59–103	.364	36	Durocher	Santo	.312	Santo	30	Holtzman	11–16	4.07
1967	3rd	87–74	.540	14	Durocher	Santo	.300	Santo	31	Jenkins	20–13	2.80
1968	3rd	84–78	.519	13	Durocher	Beckert	.294	Banks	32	Jenkins	20–15	2.63
1969	2nd	92–70	.568	8	Durocher	Williams	.293	Santo	29	Jenkins	21–15	3.21
1970	2nd	84–78	.519	5	Durocher	Williams	.322	Williams	42	Jenkins	22–16	3.39
1971	T3rd	83–79	.512	14	Durocher	Beckert	.342	Williams	28	Jenkins	24–13	2.77
1972	2nd	85–70	.548	11	Durocher Lockman	Williams	.333	Williams	37	Jenkins	20–12	3.21
1973	5th	77–84	.478	5	Lockman	Cardenal	.303	Monday	26	Jenkins	14–16	3.89
										Reuschel	14–15	3.00
										Hooton	14–17	3.68
1974	6th	66–96	.407	22	Lockman Marshall	Madlock	.313	Monday	20	Reuschel	13–12	4.29
1975	T5th	75–87	.463	17.5	Marshall	Madlock	.354	Thornton	18	Burris	15–10	4.12
1976	4th	75–87	.463	26	Marshall	Madlock	.339	Monday	32	Burris	15–13	3.11
1977	4th	81–81	.500	20	Franks	Ontiveros	.299	Murcer	27	Reuschel	20–10	2.79
1978	3rd	79–83	.488	11	Franks	Buckner	.323	Kingman	28	Reuschel	14–15	3.41
1979	5th	80–82	.494	18	Franks Amalfitano	Kingman	.288	Kingman	48	Reuschel	18–12	3.62
1980	6th	64–98	.395	27	Gomez Amalfitano	Buckner	.324	Martin	23	Reuschell	11–13	3.40

Year	Pos.	Record	Pct.	GB	Manager	Player	BA	Player	HR	Player	W-L	ERA
1981	6th	15–37	.288	17.5	Amalfitano	Buckner	.311	Buckner	10	Krukow	9–9	3.69
								Durham	10			
1981**	5th	23–28	.452	6								
	6th	38–65	.369	21								
1982	5th	73–89	.451	19	Elia	Durham	.312	Durham	22	Jenkins	14–15	3.15
1983	5th	71–91	.438	19	Elia	Moreland	.302	Cey	24	Rainey	14–13	4.48
					Fox			Davis	24			
1984	1st	96–65	.596	—	Frey	Sandberg	.314	Cey	25	Sutcliffe	16–1	2.69
1985	4th	77–84	.478	23.5	Frey	Moreland	.307	Sandberg	26	Eckersley	11–7	3.08
1986	5th	70–90	.438	37	Frey	Sandberg	.284	Davis	21	Smith	9–9	3.09
					Vukovich			Matthews	21	Sanderson	9–11	4.19
					Michael							
1987	6th	76–85	.472	18.5	Michael	Sandberg	.294	Dawson	49	Sutcliffe	18–12	3.68
					Lucchesi							
1988	4th	77–85	.475	24	Zimmer	Palmeiro	.307	Dawson	24	Maddux	18–8	3.18
1989	1st	93–69	.574	—	Zimmer	Grace	.314	Sandberg	30	Maddux	19–12	2.95
1990	4th(T)	77–85	.475	18	Zimmer	Dawson	.310	Sandberg	40	Maddux	15–15	3.46
1991	4th	77–83	.481	20	Essian	Sandberg	.291	Dawson	31	Maddux	15–11	3.35
1992	4th	78–84	.481	18	Lefebvre	Grace	.307	Sandberg	26	Maddux	20–11	2.18

**Split Season Totals (Players' Union Strike).

All-Time Cubs Career and Season Records

Career Batting Leaders (1876–1992)

Games Played	Ernie Banks	2,528
At Bats	Ernie Banks	9,421
Runs Scored	Cap Anson	1,719
Runs Scored, since 1903	Billy Williams	1,306
Hits	Cap Anson	3,041
Hits, since 1903	Ernie Banks	2,583
Batting Average	Riggs Stephenson	.336
Home Runs	Ernie Banks	512
Runs Batted In	Cap Anson	1,715
Runs Batted In, since 1903	Ernie Banks	1,636
Stolen Bases	Frank Chance	404
Strikeouts	Ron Santo	1,271

Career Pitching Leaders (1876–1992)

Innings Pitched	Charlie Root	3,138
Earned Run Average	Mordecai Brown	1.80
Wins	Charlie Root	201
Losses	Charlie Root	156
Winning Percentage	John Clarkson	.705
Winning Pct., since 1903	Mordecai Brown	.689
Strikeouts	Fergie Jenkins	2,038
Walks	Bill Hutchison	1,106
Walks, since 1903	Charlie Root	871
Games	Charlie Root	605
Shutouts	Mordecai Brown	50
Saves	Lee Smith	180
Complete Games	Bill Hutchison	317
Complete Games, since 1903	Mordecai Brown	206
Games Started	Fergie Jenkins	347

Single-Season Batting Records (1876–1992)

Batting Average (502 AB)	Rogers Hornsby	.380	1929
Batting Average (100 games)	Bill Lange	.389	1895
Batting Avg. (100 games, since 1903)	Rogers Hornsby	.380	1929
Home Runs	Hack Wilson	56	1930
Home Runs (lefthanded)	Billy Williams	42	1970
Runs Batted In	Hack Wilson	190	1930
Hits	Rogers Hornsby	229	1929
Singles	Sparky Adams	165	1927
Doubles	Billy Herman	57	1935 1936
Triples	Frank Schulte	21	1911
	Vic Saier	21	1913
Slugging Percentage	Hack Wilson	.723	1930
Extra Base Hits	Hack Wilson	97	1930
Game-Winning RBIs	Gary Matthews	19	1984

All-Time Cubs Career and Season Records *(continued)*

Sacrifices	Jimmy Sheckard	40	1906
Stolen Bases	Frank Chance	67	1903
Pinch Hits	Thad Bosley	20	1985
Strikeouts	Byron Browne	143	1966
Total Bases	Hack Wilson	423	1930
Hitting Streak	Bill Dahlen	42	1894
Hitting Streak, since 1903	Jerome Walton	30	1989
Grand Slam Home Runs	Ernie Banks	5	1955
On-Base Percentage	Mike Kelly	.483	1886
On-Base Pct., since 1903	Rogers Hornsby	.459	1929
Hit by Pitch	Adolfo Phillips	12	1966

Single-Season Pitching Records (1876–1992)

ERA (150 innings)	Mordecai Brown	1.04	1906
ERA (100 innings)	Mordecai Brown	1.04	1906
Wins	John Clarkson	53	1885
Wins, since 1903	Mordecai Brown	29	1908
Losses	Bill Hutchison	34	1892
Losses, since 1903	Dick Ellsworth	22	1966
	Bill Bonham	22	1974
Winning Pct. (10 decisions)	Rick Sutcliffe	.947	1984
Strikeouts	John Clarkson	340	1886
Strikeouts, since 1903	Fergie Jenkins	274	1970
Walks	Bill Hutchison	199	1890
Walks, since 1903	Sam Jones	185	1955
Saves	Bruce Sutter	37	1979
Games	Ted Abernathy	84	1965
	Dick Tidrow	84	1980
Complete Games	John Clarkson	68	1885
Complete Games, since 1903	Jack Taylor	33	1903
	Grover Alexander	33	1920
Games Started	Bill Hutchison	71	1892
Games Started, since 1903	Fergie Jenkins	42	1969
Shutouts	John Clarkson	10	1885
Shutouts, since 1903	Mordecai Brown	10	1906
Innings Pitched	Bill Hutchison	627	1892
Innings Pitched, since 1903	Grover Alexander	363	1920
Home Runs Allowed	Warren Hacker	38	1955
Consecutive Games Won	Jack Luby	17	1890
Consecutive Games Won, since 1903	Ed Reulbach	14	1909
	Rick Sutcliffe	14	1984
Consecutive Games Lost	Bob McCall	13	1948

4

Cincinnati Reds

Cincinnati's Hometown Game, from the Red Stockings to the Big Red Machine

PETER C. BJARKMAN

Pete Rose would have liked managing the original Red Stockings; they were his kind of men.
Lonnie Wheeler and John Baskin, The Cincinnati Game

Above all else, Cincinnati's beloved hometown Reds are baseball's unsurpassed champions of innovation and invention. Infrequently has a ballclub representing the city of Cincinnati stood first in the National League; only three pennants were won there in over a century of play that preceded the glorious Big Red Machine teams of the mid-1970s. Cincinnati baseball, however, has witnessed such pioneering moments as the nation's first professional team (1869); baseball's first rainout (ironically in the first official Red Stockings game scheduled against the Antioch nine on May 31, 1869); the first uniformed manager (Harry Wright in 1869); the first fielder's glove (donned by Red Stockings catcher Douglas Allison in 1869) and catcher's mitt (devised by Harry Decker in 1890); even the initial double play (unassisted by Fred Waterman in 1869 against the New York Mutuals). When fresh ground has been broken in the game of baseball, one can almost always look to the "River City" of Cincinnati.

Cincinnati's special penchant for baseball pioneering has ranged over the years from the truly momentous to the downright trivial: the first-ever seventh-inning stretch (1869) and baseball's first beat writer (Harry Millar in 1869); the advent of Spring Training (1870); the sport's first switch-hitter (Bob Ferguson in the famous 1870 game against the Brooklyn Atlantics when the invincible Cincinnati nine tasted their first defeat in 130 incredible outings), doubleheader (1876), and no-hit game (1876, against the Red Stockings by Boston's Joe Borden). The first home run in National League history involved the Cincy ballclub (slugged by Chicago's Ross Barnes on May 2, 1876, to be followed with one by Cincinnati's Charley Jones in the same contest), as did the league's inaugural lefthanded pitcher (Bobby Mitchell in 1877). The invention of the catcher's squat (Buck Ewing in 1880) and the debut of uniform numbers (briefly in 1883) were also long-lost Cincinnati baseball credits. In addition, Cincinnati was initial home to an unprecedented ambidextrous pitcher (Tony Mullane in 1886) and a lefthanded third baseman (Hick Carpenter in 1879); the advent of ladies day at the ballpark (1886); the first farm system (1887, with a working agreement between the Cincinnati American Association ballclub and a minor league team in Emporia, Kansas) and the sale of season tickets (1934); the first-time-ever posting of "errors" upon the Crosley Field scoreboard (1934); the first air travel by a big-league ballclub (1934); inauguration of big-league night baseball (at Crosley Field on May 24, 1935), and the first televised league games three seasons later (the first involving Cincinnati at Brooklyn on August 26, 1939); and the very first all-synthetic playing surface in present-day Riverfront Stadium (1970).

Blended with this spirit of radical innovation—rare in a sport known for its conservatism—is the Cincinnati ballclub's longstanding sense of baseball tradition. Cincinnati is, after all, the city where professional baseball first began in 1869, and it remains today's proud home to the annual spring rite of Opening Day. Throughout the past century and a quarter this venerable baseball franchise, which fittingly debuted in the National League in 1876 as a charter member of baseball's Senior Circuit, has also been home to some of the game's greatest moments and some of its most colorful players. In fact, no two single players in the game's entire history have ever been as unbendingly revered by the adoring hometown fans as lead-footed yet free-swinging catcher Ernie Lombardi, who enlivened the lackluster 1930s prewar Reds, and homegrown hero Pete Rose ("Charlie Hustle"), the fire and spirit behind the modern-day Big Red Machine, baseball's dominant team in National League play of the early and mid-1970s.

The factors which link baseball tradition and innovation in the Queen City are all-pervasive. Cincinnati baseball historians Lonnie Wheeler and John Baskin have even suggested (in their unsurpassed 1988 coffee-table history, *The Cincinnati Game*) that the city's modern-day baseball folk hero, Pete Rose, would have been altogether at home managing that original Red Stockings outfit of Harry Wright, which pioneered organized baseball during the immediate post–Civil War Years.[1] The thought of Pete Rose—baseball's true prodigal son of the 1990s—linked together with the pantalooned cricket players that were the Cincinnati Red Stockings of 1869—America's first professional barnstorming baseball team—at first seems to defy both common sense and the most fertile of imaginations. Yet there is something quite alluring about the prospect. As Wheeler and Baskin suggest, Rose and the Red Stockings of Harry Wright would have been a more comfortable match than one might expect from individuals of two distinct centuries. For there is a seemingly inevitable and unbroken link between the knicker-clad pioneers who first brought sporting fame to the Queen City (especially given their "rough-and-tumble" style of play and business-like approach to winning) and the hard-nosed tradition-breaker who a full century and a quarter later would become baseball's much-glorified all-time hitting champion and its most embarrassing "bad boy" outcast, virtually simultaneously. "They were his kind of men," observe Wheeler and Baskin, commenting on Rose's assumed attitudes about the hard-playing , fast-living (and certainly free-wagering) men of Wright's original pioneering Cincinnati nine.

Baseball in Cincinnati is an irrepressible link to the game's well-established nineteenth-century heritage. This strictly blue-collar city on the shores of the Ohio River has taken its identity from its professional ballclub perhaps more exclusively than any other metropolis in history. Opening Day of the new baseball season remains the major civic event on Cincinnati's annual social calendar, a fact which remains as true in the seemingly traditionless 1990s as it was in the pre-television age of radio baseball. The "Pete Rose Affair" which so troubled the baseball world throughout the late summer of 1989 was this entire city's exclusive and ubiquitous political and social passion. An issue of endless radio talk-show debate and heated public emotions, it dragged on seemingly for months and inevitably grew to be wearisome "old news" in other cities across the land. Nowhere is baseball tradition more alive and fermenting than in the city which gave the nation its first taste of night baseball, daily radio baseball, commercial televised baseball, the prototype contemporary artificial playing field, and almost every other important diamond innovation. Cincinnati's Reds reign today without doubt or dispute as the ballclub infused with the most tradition. They stand unrivaled as the oldest, proudest, and most storied national franchise in all of American sports history.

Part of Cincinnati's special link with baseball's past rests in its status as the first baseball city. But it has been home to some of the game's greatest moments and most colorful players as well. There is the still vivid sight of ungainly Ewell Blackwell in the immediate post-war years, mowing down hitters with his whiplash sidewinder delivery and crafting a memorable no-hitter against the Boston Braves. There is the lasting image of Bill McKechnie, the team's greatest manager, carrying on his own wartime tactics in the 1940s against the league's embattled umpires. There is also the unforgettable portrait of Jimmy

Ripple racing across home plate with the winning run of the 1940s World Series against Detroit, of Paul Derringer staggering to a pennant-clinching victory against the Cardinals at the eleventh hour of the 1939 campaign; of Ernie Lombardi pawing the dirt behind home plate and terrorizing the league's pitchers during baseball's Golden Decade of the 1930s. Above all else, there is the undying memory of that young and unheralded New Jersey strongboy, Johnny Vander Meer, weaving baseball legend with his yet unparalleled feat of two consecutive no-hit performances. And there is the heavy artillery fleet of longball sluggers led by musclebound Ted Kluszewski blasting out a league-record onslaught of prodigious homers in the mid-1950s. Daydreams of an earlier era still conjure up the immortal portrait of incomparable center-fielder Edd Roush lashing out countless hits and lunging for countless spear-like catches in the deep recesses of Crosley Field's outfield pastures; of Fred Toney matching up with Chicago's Hippo Vaughn during the memorable summer of 1917 to craft baseball's only double no-hit game ever witnessed during the sport's full century of modern play; of immortal Christy Mathewson making his single memorable pitching appearance in Reds colors during a classic matchup with his arch foe, Three Finger Brown; and of Cy Seymour splashing base hits across National League fields during his team-record .377 batting season of 1905. And at the game's dawn in the previous century there is the rare memory of Bid McPhee ending his hold-out in 1896 as the last big-league fielder without a glove; of Tony Mullane pitching to befuddled batters with either arm in the 1886 through 1893 seasons (the only hurler to be listed in the *Baseball Encyclopedia* with the odd distinction of "BB" and "TB" indicating switch-pitching as well as switch-hitting!). And finally, there are dusty ferrotype images of the original Red Stockings under Harry and George Wright, barnstorming their way cross-country to 130 consecutive victories against all comers in two summers of incomparable skilled play.

Storied players have, in fact, worn the Cincinnati flannels in every generation and throughout every decade of baseball play. Buck Ewing and Bid McPhee were incomparable stars of the nineteenth century: the former revolutionized play as a catcher, batsman, and manager; the latter was hailed in pioneer diamond days as the "king bee of second basemen" and held the franchise record for career hits (2,249) until Pete Rose came along. Wahoo Sam Crawford and Edd Roush had few peers as both hitters and fielders in the National League outfields of the current century's first two decades. Bucky Walters and Paul Derringer were as fearsome a pitching duo (jointly winning 52 games in the first pennant year of 1939 and 42 the next) as National League hitters would see in the immediate pre–World War II years.

The "Big Sticks" hitters of the 1950s—Kluszewski, Post, Bell, Bailey, and Robinson—rewrote ancient baseball records and formed lasting baseball legends; and even if they were to bring altogether few victories and no pennants to tiny Crosley Field, they were nonetheless to brutalize the league's pitchers in tandem onslaught for five glorious summers, when Elvis Presley was still a novelty and rock and roll the newest national craze. Finally, the original Big Red Machine of the early 1970s—Bench, Morgan, Perez, and Rose—was arguably the most dominant single team in National League history, save only the Boys of Summer Dodgers of the Jackie Robinson-Branch Rickey era.

Cincinnati has also remained home to unusual and nostalgic diamond events, often of the strangest and most unprecedented order. Most memorable was the remarkable "double no-hitter" of 1917, the only game of its kind ever to occur in big-league play. Cincinnati's Fred Toney won this unique matchup with 10 innings of hitless magic, while his ill-starred mound opponent, the Cub's Jim Vaughn, wove nine hitless innings before surrendering two hits and victory in the fateful 10th frame. While this greatest pitching duel in baseball history was actually staged at Chicago's Weeghman Park, it was a Cincinnati stalwart who served as central player in what remains baseball's most unusual pitching moment. There were the back-to-back no-hitters of Cincinnati's Johnny Vander Meer, this time transpiring in June of 1938 at Crosley Field and four days later at Brooklyn's Ebbets Field, the latter record-shattering affair ironically being the first night game in New York baseball history. And since history-making no-hit performance seems to be a special Cincinnati entertainment, there was the April 1964 game in Houston in which Astros hurler Ken Johnson became the first moundsman (the only one until Andy Hawkins of the Yankees joined this select club in 1990) to toss a nine-inning no-hitter and actually *lose*, being victimized 1–0 by the opportunistic Redlegs. And if this were not all enough, the Reds' own Jim Maloney would, the very next season, become the only pitcher in all of baseball history to toss two extra-inning no-hitters (one of which he managed to lose), opportunistically cramming his two masterpieces together into the same action-packed summer.

In the modern age, the Reds have maintained their longstanding franchise penchant for both uncompromising baseball tradition and unparalleled baseball innovation. Over the course of the past two decades the Cincinnati ballclub has represented better than any present-day club, save perhaps the Cardinals in St. Louis, the vital link between baseball's evolution and the proud revitalization of America's downtown urban centers. A shift in 1970 from neighborhood-friendly yet decaying Crosley Field to sterile waterside Riverfront Stadium was admittedly a calculated showpiece in the city's onslaught against urban blight and its game plan for downtown civic rejuvenation and inner-city renaissance. At the same time, the Cincinnati ballclub has repeatedly touted deep-rooted formal connections with baseball tradition, especially during the era of the Big Red Machine Reds under the administration of General Manager Bob Howsam. Clean-shaven ballplayers, white flannels (with uniform black shoes and old-style high socks), and absolute uniformity of team appearance demanded by Howsam were not only a rejection of the gaudy uniforms, unkempt appearance, and showy displays of individual uniform variation which were the trademark of such other modern-day teams as the Oakland Athletics of Charlie O. Finley. They were also part of a carefully orchestrated corporate master plan to market longstanding commitments by the Cincinnati National League franchise to baseball's most cherished and sustaining old-time traditions.

And Cincinnati's modern-era Reds, down to the present hour, have maintained a trademark local tradition of colorful and controversial players as well. No single athlete fits this bill in the present decade more than Pete Rose, baseball's prototypical modern-day bad boy and for baseball fans everywhere the very epitome of ceaseless hustle and win-at-all-costs play. But there have been other colorful Queen City diamond characters down through the lean years and the glory years. Dolf Luque, baseball's first Latin American star, charged from the mound in the heat of play to flatten heckling Casey Stengel on the Giants bench in an infamous 1922 incident, while fashioning the single finest Reds mound performance in history (27–8, 1.93 ERA in 1923), and pioneering as the first Latin pitcher in post-season play during the celebrated 1919 Black Sox Series. Ted Kluszewski, rippling his huge biceps under the sleeveless jerseys he inspired for the 1950s Redlegs, crushed mammoth Crosley Field home runs, yet also surprisingly led National League first basemen in fielding a major-league-record five consecutive seasons. "Dummy" Hoy was baseball's greatest deaf player who reputedly inspired the umpire's hand signals and indisputably banged out enough base hits (2,054) and demonstrated sufficient baserunning and fielding skills in four different leagues at the turn of the century to stand as a legitimate Hall-of-Fame candidate in his own right. Ewell Blackwell possessed baseball's most celebrated and unusual pitching delivery, and gigantic Ernie Lombardi owned the game's slowest pair of feet and yet one of its most fearsome and heavy bats. Noodles Hahn, an incomparable fastballer of the "dead ball era," outranked such contemporary Hall-of-Fame moundsmen as Jack Chesboro, Cy Young, Rube Waddell, and Christy Mathewson for six years (1899–1904). Each of these rare and colorful Cincinnati baseball legends (along with dozens more chronicled in the following pages) has contributed in unique ways to what is now an indelible part of American sports history: the story of Cincinnati's special hometown hardball game.

Birth of National League Tradition in the Queen City

From the outset Cincinnati worked hard to carve out its well-earned reputation as the national pastime's most persistent pioneer. In the earliest years, however, triumphs were often only temporary and a permanent place in baseball history was never very solidly assured. In fact, Cincinnati's brief spectacular impact on the founding of the professional game had been of only the most fleeting duration. Harry Wright's barnstorming Red Stockings of 1869–70 were hastily disbanded after only a second season of play, once hoopla surrounding the club's fabulous unbeaten streak sagged (along with attendance at the games) on the heels of four defeats at the tail end of a second campaign. Wright's experiment had launched such burgeoning popularity for the game, however, that a full-fledged league was almost immediately formed under the name of the National Association in 1871. Harry Wright himself simply moved his baseball operation lock-stock-and-barrel into Boston, where he took over operation of a regrouped Red Stockings ballclub (forefather of the modern Red Sox) in this newly minted professional league. Cincinnati, on the other hand, would have to wait five more summers for the rival National League to come along before it was once more back in the baseball business.

When the time-honored National League was christened, some 115 summers back, baseball's original pioneer city was, of course, there to be tallied as a respected charter member. The first decade of National League play was far from glorious, however, for the midwestern team still wearing red stockings and already boasting a distinguished if short-lived baseball heritage. The opening campaign, in fact, saw the Red Stockings post a record for futility which has not even been approximated in the long century-plus history of big-league action which has followed. Cincinnati's first baseball owner, Jósiah Keck, seemingly displayed impeccable judgment in hiring as his first manager the only homegrown Cincinnatian to have played with the original roving Red Stockings under Harry Wright. But local hero Charlie Gould proved anything but up to the task, as his inaugural club achieved infamy by becoming the only professional team ever to win fewer than double-digits for an entire season. With but nine wins and a season's .138 victory percentage, Gould's single managerial season set a record of ineptitude matched perhaps only by the 1899 Cleveland Spiders who rang up an immortal 20–134 league mark. Things didn't get much better in very much of a hurry in the nation's leading beer town either, as only the second-place 1878 team under

Manager Cal McVey made anything like a respectable run at the league championship trophy. If there was a single bright spot in the opening decade of National League play in Cincinnati, it was the iron-man performance of bespectacled hurler Will White, who singlehandedly pitched an entirely unimaginable 1,148 innings in 1878–79, hurling in an astonishing 76 of his team's 78 league games (75 as a starter) in the latter of those two years.

When the new rival league, the American Association, opened its doors for formal business in 1882, baseball's true pioneer franchise was once again there at the very head of the line. It seems that when a group of disenchanted midwestern baseball promoters, all of whom resented the National League's steadfast ban on the sordid practices of Sunday baseball and beer sales at the league's ballparks, got together under the leadership of St. Louis brewing magnate Chris von der Ahe to form their own rival league without such business-tainting policies, popular Cincinnati baseball writer Oliver P. Caylor was counted in their number. Cincinnati had just suffered through the 1881 campaign without any league affiliation or even any team at all, after the Reds had been suspended from National League play for their continued defiant policies of ballpark beer vending and leasing their vacant baseball grounds to amateur teams for Sunday play. The real reason for the expulsion, however, seems to have been that the crusading Caylor had convinced Reds' president William C. Kennett to petition the league bosses to drop the circuit's reserve-clause policies, contending that such contracts which restricted a player's commitment endlessly to a single franchise were both illegal and immoral. The league fathers' predictable response was to consider the upstart Cincinnati management to be filled with dangerous radicals and to promptly boot the club out of the league.

Once Cincinnatian Caylor joined with Von der Ahe and renowned St. Louis writer Al Spink to form the new freewheeling league—which immediately announced popular beer and alcohol sales at its parks and dropped admission prices to 25 cents, half that of the established National League—Cincinnati baseball was back in business and the revived franchise marked its new beginning most visibly by shortening its adopted club name from Red Stockings to simply Reds. With Kennett still in the front office, this revival of the old hometown ballclub, with a new league to play in, also sported a startling new look. Retaining only two players from the 1880 team (pitcher Will White and third baseman Hick Carpenter), the Reds took the field under new skipper Pop Snyder with a stunning appearance that would have made Charles Finley proud. Each player was brightly clad in a different color uniform: White wore blue, Snyder scarlet, barehanded rookie second sacker Bid McPhee orange and black, and so on. Whether they stunned their opponents with these visual effects or simply with too much pitching prowess on the part of Will White (40–12), too much defense (where they led the league with a .907 pct. in an age not known for adept fielding play), or too much hitting by Hick Carpenter (league leader with 120 hits), the Cincinnatians ran off to a 55–25 record for their best winning percentage of the decade. The result was an unchallenged 11½-game final margin over runner up Philadelphia. This was indeed an auspicious new start, but not one to be maintained very long as the club tumbled quickly to third the following summer, despite White's second straight 40-win outing (and perhaps because of a return to more traditional baseball garb).

Eight American Association seasons were hardly successful for the Cincinnati nine, despite a surprising start in 1882 and a solid if not invincible club on three other occasions. There were respectable second-place finishes in 1885 and 1887 (though 16 games off the pace in one of those campaigns and a full 14 the other), to go with one third (1883) and a single inaugural-year league pennant in the surprising season of 1882. Yet if the team won only one championship flag, it also suffered but one sub-.500 campaign, that in 1886. And what was often little more than average league play was spiced up by the performances of several slightly spectacular pitchers who wore the Cincinnati colors in those forgotten pioneer years. One Cincinnati hurler in particular, William Henry "Will" White, sported both a proud family heritage in the new hardball sport and a record of diamond accomplishment that today seems more the stuff of legend than the fallout of history.

In a brief 10-year career now all but buried in the musty archives of nineteenth-century baseball lore, Will White accomplished the now unimaginable feat of posting back-to-back 40-win seasons in the first two summers of American Association play, a yeomanly but not unparalleled summer's work at the time. Respected baseball historian Lee Allen refers to White as "one of the game's true greats who has never received his due" from a baseball establishment which largely ignores the game's pre-turn-of-the-century roots. The first player to wear eyeglasses on the field of play, Will White is as well known today for being the brother of Deacon White (member of both Harry Wright's first Red Stockings lineup and Cap Anson's White Stockings outfit which took the first-ever National League crown) as he is for what should be his lasting fame—American Association standards in ERA (2.09 in 1883) and winning percentage (40–12, .769, in 1882). Author of a 40-victory season in the National League as well in 1879, White was more often than not a victim of hapless support from his inept Cincinnati teammates, witnessed by his 18–42 mark (in which he personally accounted for 42 percent of his ballclub's defeats) for the last place Queen City team during the 1880 National League campaign. Ambidextrous Tony Mullane (31 victories in both 1886 and 1887), southpaw Elmer Smith (33–18, with a league-best 2.94 ERA in 1887), and righthander Jesse Duryea (32–19 in his rookie 1889 season) were also 30-game winners for Cincinnati during this decade of the soon-to-disappear rubber-armed nineteenth-century hurler.

The "Gay Nineties" joyfully saw the Cincinnati ballclub back in the National League fold where it seemingly belonged all along, though the largest cheers at the time probably went up in rival cities around the league, thrilled at the prospect of beating up again on the doormat Reds team. The American Association had made quick peace with the rival National League and was eventually exploited as something of a helpless pawn of the more established and wealthier circuit, whose crafty owners attempted to ward off the latest challenge to the reserve clause in the form of a divisive Players' League revolt by convincing American Association owners to expand to a dozen teams for 1890. The move had its calculated results for the National League owners, of course, as the Players' League lasted but one strife-torn season and the financially over-extended American Association was absorbed back into the National League after the 1891 season.

Rejoining the Senior Circuit wars in 1890 (thus making the present year something of a centennial in the Queen City) the Reds amassed a decade-long mark of 729–639 (.534). This was certainly short of disastrous, yet it brought only two finishes (1896 and 1898) as high as third place and no single season within 10 games or less of the circuit leader. The best club of the decade was undoubtedly the 1896 team, one which benefitted from the first blockbuster trade in franchise history, a pioneering deal that brought hurler Red Ehret (18–14 that year) and catcher Heinie Peitz (.299 BA) over from St. Louis. Finishing a strong third behind Baltimore (led by the booming bats of Willie Keeler and Hugh Jennings) and Cleveland (featuring batting champ Jesse Burkett hitting a lofty .410), this 1896 Cincinnati nine boasted a first-rate outfield of Dummy Hoy, Eddie Burke, and Dusty Miller, a trio who batted a composite .314 and pilfered an astounding 179 bases.

The final decade of the outgoing century did witness some remarkable individual stars for the hometown Cincinnati ballclub, despite the endlessly mediocre team finishes spread throughout the era. It was during this decade and the one that preceded it that tiny Bid McPhee established himself as a hometown baseball institution, playing longer at second base (18 seasons) than any man for any other team before or since. An even more spritely Hugh Nicol arrived in Cincinnati from the St. Louis team in time for the 1887 American Association season and amassed 138 stolen bases, a record never to be matched in the modern age of big-league play. Hick Carpenter was undoubtedly the game's greatest lefty-throwing third sacker (if admittedly the competition has remained almost nil for such an honor), though he batted above .300 only once in his dozen big-league seasons. And showing a special penchant for pint-sized diamond heroes, Cincinnati was also home to a 5-foot-7-inch slugger named Bug Holliday who belted out the then-extraordinary league-leading home run totals of 19 and 13 in 1889 and 1892 respectively. Exploiting a squatty stance and the quickest swing of his era, Holliday seems from today's perspective to have been something of a rare nineteenth-century equivalent to such popular "toy cannons" of later ages as Hack Wilson, Mel Ott, Jim Wynn, and Kirby Puckett.

An unparalleled all-around star (he played and excelled at virtually every position) and future Hall-of-Famer graced the Cincinnati baseball scene before decade's end as well. Cincinnati-native Buck Ewing returned home from his successful years with the Giants in the 1880s to replace Charles Comiskey as Reds manager in the summer of 1895. Over the final five seasons of the century the versatile Ewing became one of the most successful managers in team history, amassing 394 career wins and a lifetime .570 victory pace. Such was the stature of Buck Ewing in his own primitive baseball era that at the time of a premature death caused by Bright's Disease in 1906 the local headlines mourned the passing of one of the game's true giants: "Great catcher dead at his East End home . . . Best all-around player in history."

Something extraordinary happened along the downtown banks of the Ohio River on the afternoon of April 16, 1990. The venerable baseball club known for nearly a century and a quarter as the Cincinnati Reds opened up the home portion of the first National League baseball season in a new decade before a large but non-sellout throng of 38,000, downing the San Diego Padres 2–1 for the club's fifth consecutive win to start the young campaign. But it was not the winning streak (which reached a club-record 10 straight before it was halted) that was the real story. The home opener was being played after a week on the road, an ordinary enough occurrence for about half the league's ballclubs each year. Only in this case it was indeed extraordinary, for it put an end to a nearly century-long tradition.

Over the years Opening Day of the baseball season had become a full-scale national tradition in Cincinnati. As one wag has put it, it is the single honor bestowed upon America's first baseball city by the Lords of Baseball, that it should have the consolation of the season's first game, a fitting compensation for being as often found at the bottom of the league standings as on the top of the innovators' list. Another humorist once noted that Cincinnati was the city where everyone flocked to the ballpark on Opening Day and then stayed home throughout the remainder of the summer. But however misguided the humor, it is indeed true that Opening Day has long been Cincinnati's proudest baseball badge.

This time-honored tradition of league home openers dates back to the tireless effort and considerable vision of early team executive Frank C. Bancroft, one-time theatrical agent and Reds business manager from the early National League days of 1891 until his death 30 years later. Relying on his expertise in theatrical promotion and his raw enthusiasm for his newfound baseball passion, Bancroft annually stirred such wintertime enthusiasm for the forthcoming edition of the Reds each new season that he regularly sold out first-game tickets months before the crack of the first bat. What began as purely profit-motive ticket promotion soon was established as festive civic occasion, and by the time of Banny's death in 1921 the Opening Day phenomenon had reached epidemic proportion. Schools were closed for the occasion, offices shut down, electricity filled the air, and citizens marched through the streets in a special celebration of baseball's rites of spring unmatched in any other league city. And so it remained up to the World War II years, when league officials began formally recognizing baseball's oldest city with a ceremonial first league game—and so it has remained down to the present.

The first two decades of the new century brought an all-too-familiar story—season after dull season buried in the middle of the National League pack for the talent-thin Cincinnati team of popular owner Garry Herrmann. Seventeen of these 19 seasons would count finishes in fourth place or below. Two remarkable pitchers, however, enlivened Cincinnati baseball throughout these otherwise barren years. The first was Frank "Noodles" Hahn, a slight but ferocious moundsman who won 22 games for three successive seasons in 1901–03, all for teams which badly floundered almost any time Hahn himself was not upon the hill. Noodles Hahn tossed a 1900 no-hitter, then struck out 16 batters for a single-game club record which would stand until bested by Jim Maloney as late as 1965. He had already won 121 league games before turning 26; but before turning 27, Hahn had also injured his arm and was tragically out of baseball altogether less than a year later.

The second remarkable pitcher of this era was the hard-throwing Fred Toney, a mammoth 245-pound righthander who won 24 games for the 1917 Reds and established a reputation over his 12-year career as one of the best-hitting pitchers gracing the game. Yet Fred Toney will live on in baseball's collective memory for one remarkable outing still unique to sporting history. That matchup with the Cubs' Jim "Hippo" Vaughn (another colossal pitching heavyweight) was played in old Weeghman Park—forerunner to Chicago's venerable Wrigley

Field—on January 11, 1917, and was indeed one of the two or three most memorable and bizarre games in baseball history. Perhaps only the losing 12-inning perfect-game effort of Harvey Haddix in 1957, or the remarkable 4–0 no-hitter loss of Andy Hawkins in 1990, can match it for exceptional occurrence. For on that day, for the only time in big-league history, two pitchers conspired to throw a double no-hitter against each other for a full nine innings. And in a final irony of the kind with which baseball is so replete, the batter who eventually delivered the game-deciding blow was one of the nation's most storied athletes from a bygone era, one whose role in this game and in baseball as a whole is almost entirely forgotten. Olympic hero and full-blooded Indian Jim Thorpe, a reserve Reds outfielder for only part of that single season, stroked the second hit of the Reds' 10th-inning uprising, a slow roller along the third-base line which sent home shortstop Larry Kopf with the game's only and deciding run.

Considerable changes in the now tedious baseball fortunes experienced yearly by the River City soon coincided rather fortuitously with the long-coveted arrival of an established big-league hero, in this case the incomparable Christy Mathewson of the New York Giants. Mathewson ironically had been lost to Cincinnati at the very outset of the Hall-of-Fame career which would bring him 373 big-league victories while laboring for McGraw in the Polo Grounds. Owning the original draft rights to Matty, Cincinnati peddled him to the Giants in the club's worst trade ever, receiving in exchange a sore-armed Amos Rusie who had not been able to pitch for over a year. (It seems that Reds' outgoing owner John T. Brush was about to close a deal to purchase the Giants and was looking to stock his new team with enough talent to assure victory when he himself got there.) Yet if Mathewson figured in possibly the worst trade of franchise history, he also stood prominently in the middle of one of the very best as well. Sixteen seasons and 372 victories after his unfortunate departure from the Cincinnati fold, Matty was now brought back in July 1916, as part of the only deal ever to land a ballclub three future Hall-of-Famers in the course of a single transaction (Edd Roush and Bill McKechnie were the other principals.) Mathewson had been brought to Cincinnati to take over as manager, and he would make only one final mound appearance in Reds colors, a staged affair against his old rival Three Finger Brown at Weeghman Park in September 1916.

By 1918 the team of Roush, Groh, and company which outgoing manager Mathewson had put together over a few short summers began to show some measureable improvement, edging its way above .500 (68–60) and solidifying a third-place finish. Roush batted .333 and teammate Groh hit .320, good enough for second and third among league batsmen, behind Brooklyn's own hitting machine Zack Wheat.

With Roush (the league leader at .321) and Groh (.310) continuing to pound the league's pitchers in 1919, and with Hod Eller (20–9), Slim Sallee (21–7), and Dutch Ruether (19–6) now forming the best starting trio around, rookie manager Pat Moran was able to lead his charges home nine full games ahead of the runner-up John McGraw team. Mathewson would be gone, amidst controversy and personal disillusionment, before the end of his third Cincinnati season. Yet the proud Matty certainly deserves a lion's share of credit for the team triumphs that lay hidden only around the next bend.

The National League campaign of 1919 was indeed a remarkable one for the perennial doormat ballclub that had regularly resided in the Queen City. The season's winning percentage of .686 (96–44) would stand as the best in franchise history even after the Big Red Machine years of the 1970s. While considered no match in the upcoming World Series for a Chicago White Sox team considered one of the best in all baseball history, the Reds had actually won nine more regular season games than the Chicago ballclub. And perhaps most noteworthy of all, the final missing cog in the first pennant-winning Cincinnati machine of the modern era had been only hastily inserted the previous off-season when likable owner Garry Herrmann had swung deals for first baseman Jake Daubert, second sacker Morrie Rath, and shortstop Larry Kopf, building an entire new infield around talented third sacker Heinie Groh. And if this were not enough, the astute Herrmann had earlier rescued seemingly washed up hurler Slim Sallee—about to enjoy his career season—plucking the grateful lefty off the waiver list from none other than his closest pennant contenders, John McGraw's New York Giants.

Over time the World Series of 1919 has received as much press as any Fall Classic in baseball's earliest decades, and perhaps more than all but a handful of dramatic Series clashes—the Giants and Indians in 1954, the Yankees and Dodgers the following autumn, the Cardinals and Tigers in 1968, or the Reds and Red Sox in 1975. What is seemingly forgotten in all the hoopla surrounding eight infamous Chicago turncoats, however, is the fine Series play of a talented and inspired Cincinnati nine. The bare facts of that Series have now been rehearsed in novels, films, and even serious scholarly tomes. While the underdog Reds managed to pull an upset of major proportions by besting the powerhouse White Sox team of tight-pocketed Chicago owner Charles Comiskey five games to three, the baseball world had smelled a rotting fishpile from early on in Series play. A year later it would be determined by newly installed Commissioner Judge Kenesaw Mountain Landis that eight Sox stars had conspired with gamblers to throw the Series; the revelation, which shook the baseball world to its very foundations, would mean a lifetime ban from the sport for all eight, including certain Hall-of-Famer Joe Jackson. No matter that a Chicago grand jury had already acquitted the banished eight of all such charges. Despite the controversy, the facts remain that the un-daunted and unintimidated Reds bolted from the gate to a 4–1 Series lead behind the brilliant pitching of Eller, Ruether, Sallee, and Jimmy Ring (a previously unheralded spot pitcher with a Series 0.64 ERA over 14 innings). Taking full advantage of a nine-game Series format utilized briefly in 1919–21, the Cincinnati club then held on doggedly to win on Hod Eller's second complete-game victory in Game Eight.

Another long overshadowed feature of the 1919 World Series was the historic role of skilled Cincinnati relief pitcher Adolfo Luque, the first Cuban to taste the thrill of World Series play. One of a small handful of non-black Cubans who were able to boast big-league experi-ence in the early decades of the century, Luque began as a spot starter with the Reds at the end of the World War, appearing in a dozen games in 1918, then shifting to relief chores in 1919 and posting a 9–3 season's mark, winning three games in relief and saving three more. In the ill-starred 1919 Series Luque would relieve brilliantly for five innings spread over two games, allowing but one hit and striking out eight. By the following season he was an established starter, posting a 13–9 record, and for the next nine summers Luque would regularly post double-digit victory seasons on the hill for the Reds. Now that baseball abounds with Latin American talent, and since the Hall-of-Fame careers of the likes of Marichal, Clemente, and Luis Aparicio, it is easy to forget that the Reds' Adolfo Luque was the first of his Spanish-speaking countrymen to set foot in baseball's World Series play (see Bjarkman 1990).

Cincinnati's Game in the Big-Stick Era

The greatest ironies surrounding the tainted Fall Classic of 1919 were yet to unfold, of course. While the Reds were winners on the field of battle in October of 1919, a certain longstanding pall—almost a curse—was soon to fall over both once-proud franchises which partic-ipated in that tainted Fall Classic. As though it were somehow their due as accidental co-conspirators, the innocent and victorious Reds would not again taste pennant fever for two full decades; the sinful Chicago Pale Hose would not again know the joy of hoisting a champi-onship flag for exactly 40 summers. The Pale Hose, then, seem to have had the clear edge on futility, if one tallies up only the number of pennants won as a measure of baseball penance. Yet as the next three decades unfolded it is indeed hard to say which club had seemingly been more cursed. In the 19 full seasons before their next pennant triumph the Cincinnatians and their stoic fans would experience 13 second-division seasons, 11 of them in a row falling after 1927. The

White Sox would count 16 such seasons over the same stretch. The Reds would actually play at over a .500 clip for most of the 1920s (a last "deadball decade" when pitching was still in vogue) and not plummet to the depths of despair until the 1930s rolled in (the era of the modern slugger when "big bats" took over the national game). But enough misfortune lay immediately around the corner for the proud Cincinnati ballclub which seemed to be coming off such a remarkable World Series high as the "roaring twenties" burst forth upon an optimistic and prosperous post-war nation.

One of the true tragedies in those seasons immediately surrounding 1919 is the saga of the final years of the immortal Christy Mathewson. Matty was the greatest pitcher of an age replete with pitching greats. Featuring a "magic pitch" which was the precursor to today's screwball, Mathewson today still ranks behind only Cy Young and Walter Johnson in career victories, yet more remarkably, perhaps, breezed through most games throwing only 75 or 80 pitches and walked an average of only 1.6 batters for nine innings throughout his 17-year career. As important to his legend were his striking good looks and college education, which in an age of ruffians made Matty the first national baseball idol. Mathewson was never destined for success in the Queen City, however, and only a few short seasons after his arrival he was to depart in a cloud of intrigue and bitter personal disappointment. The true culprit here seemed to be the heavy hitting yet highly unsavory Hal Chase, Cincinnati first baseman for three seasons after 1916. While Chase's first season with the Reds was the most productive of his career and featured a league batting title (.339 in 1916), questions constantly surrounded the integrity of his play and rumors linked him to efforts by gamblers to fix games. So strong were these charges that Mathewson in his new capacity as manager suspended Chase for the balance of the season in August 1918. When Chase filed a civil suit against his manager and subsequently was tried by the league itself, he was found innocent of any charge or implication of impropriety (an acquittal which had more to do with League President Heydler's unwillingness to admit dishonesty within the game than with Chase's own freedom from guilt). Matty was disheartened enough by the affair to retire 10 games from season's end and enlist promptly for military service, a move that led to an accident involving poison gas, tuberculosis, and premature death at age 47. Mathewson's final year in Reds flannels did not shed kind light upon the contemporary world of baseball, nor did off-field events that same year make the Cincinnati franchise shine. If the Reds were beneficiaries of crooked play in the World Series of 1919, they had experienced their own sordid brush with gambling elements in the game little more than a season earlier.

But if the trade which brought Christy Mathewson to Cincinnati set in motion the wheels of personal pain and disillusionment for the fabled Matty, it had also opened one of the brightest chapters in the story of Cincinnati baseball. Another important addition to the growing Cincinnati arsenal in that memorable July 1916 deal with the Giants was the stellar outfielder Edd Roush, perhaps the best all-around flychaser in Cincinnati big-league history. But despite his numbers, few would claim that Roush was the best Cincinnati hitter before Rose: like Rose he was a singles-hitter who became one of the best paid players of his era. Lonnie Wheeler and John Baskin sum up Roush's remarkable style of play as "a fierce integrity that fell somewhere between Ty Cobb's indiscriminate wickedness and Rose's inexhaustible vigor" (*The Cincinnati Game*). Roush was to be the first legitimate franchise Hall-of-Famer years down the road, when the Hall of Fame itself became an institution as noble and nostalgia-driven as the Reds baseball club itself. Yet a decade before baseball's permanent memorial in Cooperstown was conceived, Edd Roush was reeling off 10 straight seasons in which he batted no lower than .321, five times above .340, and copped two National League batting crowns (1917, 1919) in the process.

Of course there had been some great hitters in Cincinnati before Edd Roush. Wahoo Sam Crawford (a Hall-of-Famer, after his brilliant 15-year residence with Detroit) stayed only briefly (1899–1902), yet left a considerable mark by leading the league in home runs one season (16 in 1901) and triples (23) the next. Cy Seymour enjoyed a burst of Cincinnati stardom even briefer (1903–05) than that of Crawford, but hardly less spectacular, as he batted .342, .313, and a remarkable .377, the latter still a club record for single-season excellence. Hal Chase, for all his infamy, was a hitter of considerable renown and a second league batting champion for the Reds during this era, when his heady 1916 campaign also produced a league-best in hits with 184. But any such list of accomplished batsmen of early franchise history must include the famed Heinie Groh, also acquired from the cooperative Giants in a 1913 deal involving five players and cash. Groh is best known today for his unusual "bottle bat" with its thin handle and nontapered barrel. Groh was an outstanding leadoff man whose peculiar wide-open stance and deft batting eye enhanced his offensive specialties—drawing the base-on-balls and dropping down the deadly successful bunt. Though his best years were to come after he returned to the Giants in 1922, for eight seasons Groh was one of the finest hitters ever to perform on Redlands Field.

With Roush and Groh and a supporting cast slugging the ball throughout the 1920s there was enough firepower to entertain the fans, but hardly enough for a significant move up in the league's standings. Only the 1923 team—riding the surprising pitching arm of Dolph Luque—and the 1926 squad—with another fine one-year mound wonder in Pete Donohue—challenged seriously for league titles. Luque would enjoy the finest single season of his career in 1923, and arguably the best single campaign ever contributed by a Cincinnati moundsman. Twenty-seven victories (enhanced by a league-best 1.93 ERA) not only paced all Senior Circuit hurlers that summer, but also established a Cincinnati team standard matched only by Bucky Walters' superlative effort 16 summers down the road. Righty Donohue also enjoyed a career plateau three seasons later by pasting together 20-win efforts in both 1925 and 1926. A third sensational moundsman, Eppa Rixey, pitched brilliantly at times in the 1920s, with a league-best 25–13 mark in 1922 and two additional 20-win performances over the next three summers, yet Rixey's best years unfortunately corresponded with remarkably uninspired team play. The lackluster Reds ballclubs for which he hurled for 13 summers played a significant role in making Eppa Rixey a pitcher of remarkable contrast—the winningest lefthander in baseball history (266) before Warren Spahn, yet also the seventh-biggest loser (251) ever to stride upon a major league rubber. And there were plenty of individual hitting honors to go around in that decade. Bubbles Hargrave won a single batting title (.353 in 1926) and thus became the first catcher ever to turn such a feat. Roush won two titles in his first three Cincinnati summers, while Jake Daubert brought his considerable defensive skills at first base over from Brooklyn in time for the 1919 championship run and then carried some heavy lumber for the Redlegs of Manager Pat Moran.

The worst Reds team of the "Roaring Twenties" was the 1929 version, a fact that did not bode well for the new decade. Age had overtaken the ballclub which Jack Hendricks inherited from Moran after 1923, and the departure of Roush to the Giants in 1927 signaled the final stages of a doleful decline. When bats boomed around the rest of the league during the incredible hitting year of 1930, those in Cincinnati were strangely silent. The entire National League hit at an astounding .303 pace that unforgettable year, yet the Cincinnatians came in with a league-worst .281, an altogether unexpected turn for a team whose bats had been so potent across the deadball era only a few seasons earlier.

Things would pick up later in the decade, but only after a string of four last-place finishes which made the seasons of 1931–34 a low-water mark for Cincinnati rooters everywhere. Plucked off the Brooklyn roster in 1932 (along with Babe Herman, in exchange for second baseman Tony Cuccinello and receiver Clyde Sukeforth), strapping Ernie Lombardi slowly improved as the decade wore on and by 1935 the much-loved "Schnozz" was to begin a string of four remarkable hitting years which saw his batting average range between .333 and .343 and place him among the league's best. Lombardi was famed around the circuit for his lack of speed and his relentless bat, yet he was far more than a one-dimensional hitter. He was one of the league's most durable and dependable receivers and would soon catch Johnny Vander Meer's two remarkable no-hitters at decade's end. His hitting was his forte, however, and with infielders playing him so deep as to leave almost no outfield grass exposed, Lombardi was forced to rely solely on powerful line smashes which streamed from his over-sized 44-ounce bat. But above all else Lombardi was a remarkable baseball rarity, a catcher who could hit well enough to win not one but two batting titles, an accomplishment still not duplicated.

The pitching was also improving under short-term managers Dan Howley (1930–32) and Donie Bush (1933), thanks in large part to the arrival of franchise-builder Paul Derringer. Derringer, who today ranks third on the club's all-time winning list, had already helped the Cardinals to a 1931 league flag with a rookie 18–8 mark (garnering the league's best winning percentage) before coming to Cincinnati in a surprise 1933 trade for popular shortstop Leo Durocher. While Derringer's first summer in a Cincinnati uniform was less than spectacular (7–27, 3.30 ERA), he was a remarkable pressure pitcher whose best years would come as the Reds moved into pennant races late in the decade. Paul Derringer would start and win the first major league night game in Cincinnati in 1935, would string together three consecutive 20-win seasons in 1938–40, and would enjoy a remarkable 25–7 1939 campaign which would finally lead Cincinnati out of its long pennant drought.

Another remarkable pitching legend was "Dutch Master" Johnny Vander Meer, baseball's all-time exemplar of the single brief moment of diamond glory. Vander Meer's considerable legend was somewhat like that of Fred Toney's two decades earlier, resting on one spectacular achievement and not on the years of consistent toil which earned recognition for stable hurlers like Rixey and Derringer. For Vander Meer it was two incredible games and not one (as was the case with Toney) that would give him instant baseball immortality. It was a stellar yet not particularly remarkable moment when the erratic fastballing lefty no-hit the Boston Bees on June 11, 1938, in Cincinnati's Crosley Field. Four days latter, however—in a ball game that should have drawn its significance from its stature as the first Ebbets Field night game—Vander Meer proved unhittable once again, setting down the

Dodgers 6–0 with the aid of dim arch-lights and untouchable "heat" from his flaming delivery. Never before or since (though another remarkable Cincinnati hurler would later come tantalizingly close) has a big-league pitcher thrown two no-hitters in consecutive trips to the mound. A lifetime loser (119–121) who often struggled with control of his lively fastball, Vander Meer had nonetheless made himself into a lasting baseball legend with two unmatched outings in the mid-summer of his second big-league season.

The pitching improvement that had been built around Derringer and Vander Meer was solidifed in another great Reds trade when Bucky Walters was acquired from the Phillies in a seemingly inconse-quential deal of June 1938. Walters almost immediately gave the Reds the kind of tandem they had not seen since Eller and Sallee in the legendary 1919 season. Converted from third base to the mound by the Phillies in 1934, Walters led the league in victories his first two seasons in Redsland (27–11 in 1939 and 22–10 in 1940), and the results of this new tandem of Derringer and Walters surpassed anything seen in Crosley Field since Eller and Sallee. With new manager Bill McKechnie now at the helm, the Reds jumped into the 1939 pennant race as a surprise entry. The acquisition of third sacker Bill Werber (from the Athletics for cash in March 1939) had provided a missing link in an otherwise now-solid ballclub, and the Reds surged through early and midseason, inching ahead of the favored Cardinals and the strong Dodgers now piloted by ex-Red shortstop Leo Durocher. In late September it was Derringer who clinched the long awaited pen-nant with a hard-fought 5–3 victory over the challenging Cardinals in the finale of a crucial three-game series at Crosley Field.

The World Series of 1939 would prove something of an embar-rassment—four straight losses to the powerful New York Yankees, a team batting average of only .203 (Lombardi hit but .214), and only an opening game that was at all close. The Yankees were an awesome outfit featuring an outfield of DiMaggio, Keller, and Selkirk and a middle infield of Frankie Crosetti and Joe Gordon, and the Reds were outclassed from the first. But a corner had been turned. The pieces now seemed in place for several years of success. Of course, it should not be forgotten that the last time the Reds had won a pennant, disaster in the form of a World Series fix would strike the national game at the very height of their victory dance. In the post-pennant euphoria of winter 1939, events were again transpiring—this time far beyond baseball's grandstands and fences—which would soon enough throw the national pastime into a tailspin which would again threaten its very existence. Given the global and diamond events which followed the Reds' only two pennant triumphs of 1919 and 1939, the cynic might secretly speculate that it was indeed a good thing the Cincinnatians did not win more league flags than they did!

Innovative Wartime Baseball in Crosley Field

No single decade of baseball play—at least none since the shaping of the modern game during the 1880s—so changed the face of our national sport as the war-ridden decade of the 1940s. The five years of global fighting which broke out across Europe and the Pacific theater would eventually reach into every phase of American life. And baseball was shaken to its very roots as a result. While some might argue that only four brief inconsequential seasons—1942–45—experienced such major inconveniences as dismantled rosters, disappearing box office throngs, slapstick play, restricted travel, and shortened schedules, none can dispute that individual player careers were frequently disrupted, occasionally launched unpredictably and sometimes tragically halted. Players joined the war effort in droves while wet-eared youngsters (the Reds' Joe Nuxhall at 15) and over-achieving handicapped people (the Browns' one-year and one-armed outfielder Pete Gray) stayed home to man the major league infields and outfields. Spring Training was radically altered as well by wartime travel restrictions, with disgruntled ballplayers working out their inevitable winter kinks in such frigid venues as West Lafayette, Indiana, and Medford, Massachusetts. Benefitting from a league-wide neutralization of talent that had descended like a pall by 1944, the stumblebum St. Louis Browns would make their only post-season appearance in a laugh-filled half-century of American League existence. The fans' baseball passions turned elsewhere as the war effort heated up and patriotic causes supplanted pennant races. And yet through it all baseball was kept very much afloat; its daily appearance in the ballparks and on the sports pages was seemingly vital to morale back home and the patriotic national war effort on the distant battlefield.

Radical change storming across the face of baseball had, of course, already made an appearance long before the rude jolt of Pearl Harbor. And a focal point for that change was once more the innovative baseball franchise belonging to Cincinnati. But while so many other innovations fostered by Cincinnati baseball down through the years—the seventh-inning stretch, the catcher's squat, a league-first switch hitter or unprecedented double play—had "just sort of happened casually" as a byproduct more of circumstance than forethought, what came to National League baseball via the Queen City in the immediate pre-war years were the carefully orchestrated strategies of one of baseball's greatest entrepreneurial innovators. The motivating force behind this latest change, which soon swept across the national pastime, was the noisy tinkerer and flamboyant hothead Larry MacPhail, an innovative genius usually not talked about today in the same breath with Bill Veeck or Charlie Finley or Branch Rickey. Yet MacPhail was every bit as much a revolutionary giant as Veeck or Finley in his lasting influences upon the game. First there came radio baseball in Cincinnati in the mid-1930s with the debut of honey-throated southerner Red Barber (who would eventually follow MacPhail to Brooklyn in 1938). Then there was the experiment of night baseball in 1935, with the Reds and Paul Derringer defeating Philadelphia 2–1 before more than 20,000 curious patrons on May 24 in major league baseball's first arch-light game. Soon there was a team travelling by air, as MacPhail chartered two American Airlines planes to motor his charges to Chicago in 1934, then flew the team from the Dominican Republic to Miami after a springtime exhibition two seasons later. The progressive management of MacPhail would introduce the season ticket plan and the flashing "E" on the Crosley Field scoreboard to inform fans of scoring decisions during the 1934 season as well. And in the midst of all this tinkering with tradition, Larry MacPhail would also demonstrate his considerable baseball savvy by pasting together a Cincinnati team that would be a solid pennant winner by the time he himself was ensconced in Brooklyn at decade's end.

If the winds of change and upheaval were blowing strong before this new decade progressed beyond its earliest months, this change seemed but a temporary distraction for the solid ballclub daily taking the field in Cincinnati. For the Reds were now engaged in the surprising business of defending a pennant, a fact which in itself was quite a radical departure from the usual bleak saga of Cincinnati baseball fortunes. Flush from their pennant success of 1939, the 1940 Reds rumbled home with the second best season in franchise annals (32 percentage points short of the World Champion 1919 outfit). At long last a club representing Cincinnati won 100 games, dispatching the Dodgers by 12 games behind the league's best fielding and the booming bat of first baseman Frank McCormick, the league's MVP and leader in both hits (191) and doubles (44) while runnerup in RBIs (127) and total bases (298) as well. The pennant race was over early as McKechnie's men showed a rare talent for winning the close contests, besting the opponent by a single run in 43 of the team's 100 victories. Bucky Walters dominated the league's pitchers with highwater marks in victories (22) and ERA (2.48) and Derringer was again but a shade behind (20–12, 3.06). While McCormick was the hitting and fielding star (topping his position in putouts, double plays, and fielding percentage), Lombardi enjoyed one more fine season as well, hitting .300 for the final time in a Reds' uniform. The tragedy of reserve catcher Willard Hershberger—who took his own life midseason in a Boston hotel—was therefore but a momentary sour note to an otherwise sterling Cincinnati campaign.

The 1940 Reds entered World Series play as a team with a clearcut mission. This time there would be no embarrassment like the hitting (.203 Series BA) and pitching (4.33 ERA) collapse which witnessed a four-game shellacking at the hands of the powerful Yankees a year earlier. The Series this time around would be as dramatic and exciting as its 1939 counterpart was lopsided and uninteresting. Play would stretch the full seven games to the wire against the Hank Greenberg-led Detroit Tigers, and in the end the heroes wearing red and grey flannels were Bucky Walters and reliable third sacker Billy Werber. Walters authored two complete-game victories, the second a brilliant shutout effort woven in Game Six with the Reds on the verge of elimination and spiced by Walters' own eighth-inning homer. Werber batted .370 and tied Greenberg with a Series-high 10 base hits. These Reds were indeed one of history's most underrated champions, and when World Series heroics ended with Jimmy Ripple racing across home plate carrying the lead run in the seventh-inning of the Crosley Field finale, McKechnie's men had provided the National League with its first World Series winner since the 1934 Gas House Gang Cardinals had struck down these same Detroiters a half-dozen autumns earlier.

The champions which Manager Bill McKechnie had painstakingly pulled together and then inspired down the stretch in 1939–40 did not unravel immediately, despite the subsequent outbreak of European war and the widespread raiding of club rosters that affected virtually all teams after 1942. By the zenith of the war effort, however, the Reds were already "the worst of the worst" among war-ravaged ballclubs of the National and American Leagues. A third-place finish in 1944 would mark the last first-division effort until 1956. The 1945 team, in turn, was an all-time low: with only McCormick and shortstop Eddie Miller and a much diminished Bucky Walters on hand as experienced and talented holdovers, the Reds slumped to the worst record of the McKecknie era—93 losses and a distant seventh-place finish, 37 games behind the champion Cubs. Against this bleak backdrop, one of the few interesting wartime stories in Cincinnati was the 1944 appearance of baseball's youngest-ever pitcher of the twentieth century, future Reds mound star and longtime broadcaster Joe Nuxhall. With a depleted wartime roster in hand and his team already hopelessly out of contention, McKechnie sent Nuxhall to the mound on June 10 for a brief ninth-inning stint against the potent league-leading Cardinals. The nervous 15-year-old Nuxhall (signed by the Reds only with permission of his high school principal) allowed five runs on two hits and five walks while retiring but two St. Louis batters. It would take seven long years of minor league toil before Nuxhall would have a second less pressure-packed chance to pitch for his hometown ballclub in 1952.

In a decade of surprising phenoms, one-year wonders, and brief-flashing diamond dreams, Cincinnati would have its own Horatio Alger as well as its overmatched Baby Wags. When established players drifted back slowly from the war, one gangly returning veteran in particular literally exploded on the Cincinnati baseball scene in the first months after VE Day and VJ Day. Six-foot six-inch beanpole Ewell Blackwell was the most exciting newcomer in a Cincinnati uniform since Ernie Lombardi had debuted with a .303 rookie batting average in the "Big Stick" era of the thirties. In his remarkable sophomore season of 1947 Blackwell won 16 in a row, the longest league victory skein since Rube Marquard's 1912 string of 19. During this remarkable hot stretch the unorthodox sidewinding hurler even more surprisingly nearly duplicated Vander Meer's unheard of and still unmatched double no-hit feat of 1938; having goose-egged the Braves in a rare night game on June 18, he next came within one sparse inning of dual perfection in his subsequent outing against Brooklyn, only to have Eddie Stanky ruin the bid with a one-out heart-wrenching single. But it was a brilliant season for Blackwell—a true career season—in which "The Whip" paced the Senior Circuit in wins (22–8), complete games (23), and strikeouts (193) for the otherwise lackluster fifth-place Reds.

Ewell Blackwell was the final glorious story of the wartime baseball years in Redsland. Arm miseries took all the snap out of "The Whip" after that one brilliant summer of 1947, and brief comeback seasons in 1950 (17–15, 2.97 ERA) and 1951 (16–15, 3.45 ERA) never reached the dizzying heights of that first dream season, when National League hitters fell like flies before the exploding sidearm delivery of baseball's most famous stringbean hurler. Before and after Blackwell's brief post-war fling, Cincinnati baseball seemed little more than a painful saga of overachieving journeymen and underachieving prospects. Eddie Miller, who manned the center of the infield from 1942 through 1947, was a fine defensive shortstop with occasional power (19 homers and a league-leading 38 doubles in 1947) who some called the finest at his position in a Reds uniform until the flashy Roy McMillan came along. Stonefaced Hank Sauer brought some needed boom to the ballpark with 35 roundtrippers (surpassing Ival Goodman's club mark of 30) before taking his questionable talents over to the even more lackluster Cubs. Grady Hatton was the league's best-fielding third sacker in 1949 and one of its least offensive-minded hotcorner heroes as well. By the last years of the decade the Reds were from top to bottom a distinctly seventh-place club. Only the hapless Chicago Cubs (a mere half game in arrears of the Crosley Field campers in 1948 and but a single full game in 1949) kept them from being something less, and then only by the slimmest of margins.

Muscle-Bound Redlegs of Baseball's Golden Era

Five imposing baseball figures dominate the epoch of Reds baseball history which stretches from the outbreak of the Korean War through man's first miraculous landing upon the surface of the moon. It was an age of unprecedented social and scientific change across the nation, and a time of staggering change within the nation's ballparks as well. In Cincinnati these were the final two memorable decades of exciting diamond action at the venerable old Crosley Field site on Findlay and Western, a setting in which baseball had been played continuously and without interruption every season since 1884.

Two of these figures—Ted Kluszewski and Frank Robinson—were power-hitting outfielders flush in the mainstream tradition of heavy-hitting Cincinnati ballclubs of the past. A third—Jim Maloney—was a remarkable but ill-starred pitcher already in danger a mere two decades later of being overlooked by the ebb and flow of unkind baseball fortune. Still another—stoic and genial Fred Hutchinson—remains the most popular manager and perhaps the most tragic figure in all Reds history, an immensely popular bench leader who guided the usually humdrum Redlegs to their single sojourn atop the National League heap during the three decades which stretch from Pearl Harbor to the close of the Vietnam era. The last though by no means least—young Pete Rose—was still a wet-behind-the-ears favorite son and neophyte baseball legend, first tentatively stretching his wings and testing his muscles in the final lame years before the pennant juggernaut that would soon be known as the Big Red Machine. Cincinnati Reds history of the 1950s and 1960s unavoidably hangs on the careers of these five memorable men; and any attempt to retell that history takes its shape and direction in large part from their individual stories as well as their collective stories.

A sixth baseball relic, old Crosley Field itself, was to play a prominent role in this chapter of Reds history as well. Once a haven for pitchers, the compact steel and concrete ballpark had become a paradise for sluggers by the post-World War II years, and in 1948 slow-footed outfielder Hank Sauer rewrote the local recordbooks by clouting 35 roundtrippers for Johnny Neun's seventh-place Reds. But Hank Sauer was quickly enough forgotten in Cincinnati (he was subsequently traded away to Chicago in 1949) when muscular lefthanded first baseman Ted Kluszewski began smashing the ball with such regularity in the early 1950s. Big Klu was an imposing physical specimen who had been signed directly off the Indiana University campus where he had been enrolled as a promising football star, and where the Reds had been forced to hold temporary Spring Training headquarters under wartime conditions in the late winter of 1944. Kluszewski started slowly enough in a big-league uniform, utilizing his massive frame to launch only 74 homers in his first five full seasons. But by 1952 the strapping young slugger's batting average had soared to .320, and then for four remarkable seasons between 1953 and 1956 Big Klu went on a relentless tear, smashing 40, 49, 47, and 35 homers and amassing over 100 RBIs each of those four campaigns.

Buoyed by Kluszewski's personal power outburst, a surge of Reds power hitting was soon launched which would witness 166 team homers in 1953, 147 in 1954, 181 in 1955, and then a league-record 221 circuit blasts in 1956. This new contingent of Crosley Field fence busters was a team the fans could love and the 1956 lineup boasted an awesome display of raw muscle from top to bottom of the batting order: first sacker Kluszewski (35 HRs), third baseman Ray Jablonski (15), right-fielder Wally Post (36), center-fielder Gus Bell (29), left-fielder Frank Robinson (38), backstop Ed Bailey (28), and reserves George Crowe (10) and Smokey Burgess (12). So enthralled with their hometown heroes were the Queen City fans, in fact, that at the outset of the following season the Cincinnati faithful would stuff the ballot boxes in the annual league All-Star Game fan voting, an unprecedented development which led to Redleg starters being selected for all eight field positions with the exception of first base (where Stan Musial and Gil Hodges outpolled Cincy's George Crowe). Commissioner Ford Frick predictably intervened to remove two fortuitous beneficiaries of such misguided fan enthusiasm (Roy McMillan and Don Hoak), yet left five Reds (Robinson, Bell, Post, Bailey, and second sacker Johnny Temple) in the game's starting lineup.

There was certainly plenty to cheer about in Crosley Field besides the explosion of longballs and proliferation of league all-stars as the decade of the fifties entered its second half. The 1956 season saw the power-laden if pitching-short Cincinnati team surge from 11 straight seasons in either fifth, sixth, or seventh place to a surprising third-place finish, a mere two games off the pace set by Brooklyn and a single game behind the resurgent Braves now relocated in Milwaukee. The charges of third-year skipper Birdie Tebbets surged to more than 90 victories for the first time since the pennant seasons of 1939 and 1940, and Cincinnati was not eliminated from the hot pennant race by Brooklyn until the season's final day. It was a banner year for Reds faithful and the onslaught of home run excitement, coupled with the rare presence of a true pennant race, was enough to push Crosley Field attendance well over the million mark for the first time ever. To add sweet icing to the cake, exciting Reds rookie outfielder Frank Robinson tied Wally Berger's 1930 mark for first-year homers and became the first-ever unanimous choice in the league's barely 10-year-old Rookie-of-the-Year balloting.

Kluszewski indisputably represented the most visible and lasting image of the heavy-hitting Reds team of the mid-1950s. The hulking first baseman's bulging biceps were even responsible for a revolutionary sleeveless uniform design well-suited to a bevy of big-armed sluggers. But Big Klu was more than a lumbering Bunyanesque slugger; he was also a fine all-around hitter who not only led the majors in longballs and RBIs in 1954 but paced the Senior Circuit as well in total hits the following summer, and batted above .300 in each of his five productive years between 1952 and 1956. Kluszewski was also one of the finest fielding first sackers of his era, pacing his position in fielding a record five straight summers. Injuries drastically cut the big man's effectiveness after 1956, however, and when GM Gabe Paul and field boss Tebbetts decided somewhat unwisely after a fourth-place season of 1957 to exchange slugging for pitching, Klu was unceremoniously dealt off to Pittsburgh before the outset of the 1958 season. The exchange, of course, was not a very good one (despite Kluszewski's obvious declining effectiveness) and the Reds themselves continued to slump, dipping back below .500 in 1958 and tumbling once more into the league's second division the following summer. Skipper Tebbetts himself was gone from the helm before the 1958 campaign was played out and a brief if glorious era of legendary Redleg power had effectively come to an end after five short seasons.

Kluszewski's assault on National League fences in the mid-1950s received plenty of hometown support from a contingent of heavy-hitting teammates who supplied a heavy-lumbered lineup even surpassing that fielded by the league's strongboys—the Boys of Summer Dodgers and the Aaron-Mathews-led Milwaukee Braves. Outfielder Wally Post smashed 40 homers of his own in 1955 (with 109 RBIs) and 36 in 1956, yet led the league in strikeouts as well both summers. Smooth-fielding Gus Bell also chipped in 30 homers in 1953 and 27 and 29 during the power years of 1955–56, while enjoying three consecutive 100 RBI years (1953–55) and patrolling center field with great distinction. Catcher Ed Bailey pounded out 28 homers as well during the record-setting roundtripper onslaught of 1956. And George Crowe, Kluszewski's alternate at first base during his final injury-plagued year of 1957, also provided 31 circuit blasts of his own in a mere 494 at-bats.

Yet the heaviest artillery of the homer-crazy season of 1956 belonged to a second imposing figure who fortified Reds baseball in the decade of the fifties, richly talented outfielder Frank Robinson. Robinson burst on the National League scene in 1956 with a then-rookie-record 38 homers (second in the league to Duke Snider), league leadership in runs scored, and a fourth-place league standing in slugging percentage (.558) and total bases (319). A runaway choice as Rookie of the Year in 1956, Robbie would continue to slug homers at an awesome pace in Cincinnati over the entire next decade, amassing 324 in that period, though somehow never once managing to lead the league in this most visible offensive category. Robinson slugged away throughout the remainder of the 1950s and the first half of the 1960s, hitting over .300 on five occasions and winning the league slugging crown three separate times.

A third crucial actor in the Reds' colorful saga of the late-1950s era came on board in 1959 when Fred Hutchinson inherited the manager's post from interim skipper Mayo Smith, a full 80 games into the 1959 campaign. A talented pitcher with the Tigers in the late 1940s (95–71, 3.73 ERA), Hutch had already enjoyed short managerial stints with the Tigers and Cardinals before being hired on by new Cincinnati GM Frank "Trader" Lane. The new bench boss quickly proved extremely popular with his players and would waste little time in converting undying player loyalty into a desperately needed formula for winning baseball. Hutchinson inherited a 1959 team struggling in seventh place which was able to right itself only enough by season's end to rise to a fifth-place tie, despite leading the league in runs scored, batting average, and slugging percentage. The still-potent Reds attack was now led by second-year center-fielder Vada Pinson, who paced the league in doubles and runs scored while batting .316, as well as by a rapidly maturing Frank Robinson (.311, 36 homers, 125 RBIs) and by veteran second sacker Johnny Temple, sporting a career-high .311 BA. The weakness in this first edition of Hutchinson-led Reds was clearly in the pitching, where staff leader Bob Purkey (with 13 victories) lost 18 and compiled an unimpressive 4.25 ERA, which was still best among the club starters. Quickly assessing the vital need for front-line pitching, Hutchinson (himself an ex-pitcher) engineered a trade by season's end which brought on board Cleveland hurler Cal McLish, a 19-game winner, in exchange for the veteran Temple. The trade had been a somewhat hasty one, however, as McLish would prove altogether ineffective in the tiny Crosley Field confines and would slump to but four victories in the disastrous sixth-place 1960 season which was to follow.

Hutchinson's second full season in command also offered little of real promise, as the 1960 edition of the Reds fell 20 games below .500 and 28 games off the pennant pace. Robinson and Pinson both slumped below .300 and the team, so recently an offensive power-house, couldn't offer a single .300 hitter. The pitching showed some improvement, with the turnaround of 17-game winner Bob Purkey and the surprise showing of young fastballer Jim O'Toole (12–12,

3.80 ERA). Undaunted by his failed first effort to exchange veteran infielders for much-needed pitching, Hutchinson struck again in December of 1960, shipping veteran stellar defensive shortstop Roy McMillan to the Braves for promising bonus baby hurler Joey Jay, then acquiring a hard-hitting third baseman, Gene Freese, from the White Sox to take over the hot corner while rapidly improving Eddie Kasko was moved into the vacant shortstop slot. The pieces suddenly seemed to be falling into place for the risk-driven Hutchinson, if only Pinson and Robinson could improve from off-seasons in 1960, and youngsters O'Toole and Jay could deliver on their untold pitching promise.

Unsettling change surrounded the Reds in the front office as well as on the diamond when the 1961 season opened its Spring Training camps. General Manager Gabe Paul had left to oversee a planned expansion franchise in Houston after the 1960 season. Longtime owner Powel Crosley died suddenly before the ballclub even broke Spring Training camp. Bill DeWitt was now on board as a new GM, faced immediately with sagging attendance brought on by several seasons of mediocre Crosley Field play. When season's play began there was little if anything to foreshadow the upsurge that was now lurking just around the corner, as the ballclub won but six of the first 24 games. A late April deal which sent veteran catcher Ed Bailey to the Giants for infielder Don Blasingame seemed insignificant enough at the time. The pieces had all fallen silently into place, however, and the revamped Reds slowly closed in on the Dodgers and Giants as midseason progressed. Robinson (.323) and Pinson (.343) again slugged with authority, the latter barely missing out to Pittsburgh's Bob Clemente for the hotly contested league batting crown. Jay sparkled with a league-best 21 victories and O'Toole added 19, while Purkey chipped in 16 and Jim Brosnan added 10 more from the bullpen. The Dodgers lost 10 straight in mid-August and the Reds soon slipped in front to stay. By the season's final day it was a four-game margin over Los Angeles and the city unleashed its first wild pennant celebration in 21 full seasons. Frank Robinson was league MVP and the gate had predictably doubled over the 1960 season to 1.1 million paying fans. An unexpected World Series slump by Cincinnati bats which would bring a quick five-game victory to a powerful New York Yankees team paced by the slugging duo of Mantle and Maris was only a small tarnish on what had been a delightful surprise season for the long-suffering Cincinnati baseball faithful.

Hutchinson's teams of the next three campaigns could never match their sterling 1961 play, and even an improvement to 98 victories in 1962 could not prevent a fall off to third slot behind the runaway Giants and Dodgers. The 1963 ballclub showed improved pitching, as youngster Jim Maloney won 23 (with six shutouts and a 2.77 ERA) and O'Toole contributed 17; but Purkey and Jay were plagued with persistent arm troubles and won only 13 ballgames between them. It was the hitting which broke down altogether, however, as only Pinson remained above .300 (.313 with 22 homers), Robinson slumped to a career-worst .259 (hitting one less homer than Pinson), and the team as a whole logged a .246 mark, only sixth-best in the entire league. The result was a fifth-place finish, still 10 games above .500 but 13 games off the league-leading pace of high-riding Los Angeles.

Two final bright spots appeared in this lackluster 1963 campaign, however. Jim Maloney had emerged—from virtually nowhere—as a new and much-needed strong-armed pitching hope. And a brash homegrown rookie second baseman named Pete Rose—logging more plate appearances than anyone wearing the Reds' colors that summer, save tireless veteran Vada Pinson— hit a respectable .273 and (with 170 base knocks) moved to within a mere 4,021 career hits of immortal Ty Cobb on the first leg of his three-decade chase after the all-time major league hits leader.

Quite by contrast, the 1964 baseball season in Cincinnati was perhaps the saddest in club history, certainly the one most tinged with human suffering. Now almost forgotten is the fact that the Reds lost yet another pennant that year, this time by dropping four of the final five games after a stirring stretch drive which saw 11 victories in 12 games and which had put them in first place as late as September 27. Better remembered than the final week's slump is the sad fact that popular manager Fred Hutchinson—beloved by fans and players alike—had been diagnosed the previous winter as suffering from terminal cancer. Hutch managed bravely throughout the early season until entering the hospital for needed treatment in late July. The wan and emaciated skipper returned for several brief stints in August but was finally forced to hand over daily club operations to his assistant Dick Sisler for the fateful September pennant stretch drive. The ballclub gamely battled in an all-out effort to win the flag for their popular skipper, but a Cinderella ending was simply not to be. The pennant was lost in the final weeks as a wild finish saw the Phillies enact their own tragic ending with a final two-week tailspin which turned a 6½-game Philadelphia league-lead into a one game pennant victory for the on-charging St. Louis Cardinals. The Redlegs bravely kept pace, finishing in a second-place dead-heat with Gene Mauch's collapsing Phillies. The biggest loser, however, was Fred Hutchinson, who silently passed away in Bradenton, Florida, on November 12th, at the young age of 45, wasted and disfigured by the disease against which he had so valiantly battled.

Although hitting was the forte of Cincinnati teams throughout the 1950s and 1960s, one hurler from that era surprisingly became— at least for brief flashes throughout the latter decade—one of the most dominant moundsmen ever to don a Cincinnati uniform. Jim Maloney featured a blazing fastball that was once timed at 99.5 mph in 1965, and he was able to use it effectively enough to win in double figures each year between 1963 and 1969. Maloney enjoyed his finest season ever at 23–7 in his first full-time campaign of 1963, and once again won 20 in 1965. Yet it was rare moments of superb brilliance rather than long-haul consistency that marked Jim Maloney's schizophrenic career. During this period he became the only Reds hurler ever to throw as many as three no-hitters. In 1965 he enjoyed the rarest of distinctions, tossing two 10-inning no-hitters in the same season. The first of these two rare gems, authored against the New York Mets in June, saw 10 innings of perfection and 18 strikeouts squandered as an 11th-inning homer by New Yorker Johnny Lewis resulted in a 1– 0 loss. In August of the same summer the strapping righthander again tossed 10 hitless innings, this time with more positive results as he bested the Cubs, 1–0. Maloney's career also featured five one-hitters and a then-league-record performance in which he would strike out eight Braves in a row on May 21, 1963. A damaged Achilles tendon and painful shoulder injury were to cut Maloney's brilliant career off by decade's end, however, and his respectable 134–84 lifetime mark was to remain as only a thin shadowy reminder of what might well have been.

The second half of the 1960s was marked by the departure of slugging hero Frank Robinson, the emergence of Pete Rose as a promi- nent hitting star, and the return of a string of lackluster second- division finishes which the 1950s had featured and the earliest years of the 1960s had so far succeeded in reversing. The total collapse of Redlegs pitching in 1965 had prompted GM Bill DeWitt to peddle the popular Robinson to Baltimore for established righthanded starter Milt Pappas, yet the deal—one of the worst in club history—quickly fizzled as Pappas pitched at .500 for two seasons in Cincinnati while Robinson promptly won an American League triple crown during his very first year with the high-flying Baltimore Orioles. Pete Rose soon filled the void in the batting average department if not the power department, as he led the club in hitting all five seasons of the decade's second half, capturing two of his three career league batting titles (1968, 1969) during this otherwise barren stretch. Rose would bang out 200 or more hits in 1965, 1966, and 1968, and pace the league in runs scored in 1969 as well. Well before the opening of Riverfront Stadium and the first faint rumbles of the Big Red Machine, the legend of hometown hero Pete Rose was already alive and swinging in the old ballpark down on Findlay Avenue.

Big Red Machine and "Charlie Hustle"

The National League—baseball's oldest and most stable—has known only a handful of truly dominant teams in its glorious century-plus history. Quite unlike the upstart Junior Circuit—which has chafed under the domination of such juggernauts as Connie Mack's Athletics of 1929–31, New York's Yankees under Miller Huggins in the twenties and Joe McCarthy in the thirties, Casey Stengel's Bronx Bombers throughout the fifties and early sixties, and the Oakland A's of the early seventies and late eighties—the Senior Circuit has been by-and-large a truly balanced league over the course of its 113-year history. There were, of course, the Honus Wagner Pirates at the turn of the century, followed by McGraw's Giants of the Mathewson era. And there were the short-lived Gas House Gang Cardinals of the late 1930s and their heavy-hitting wartime heirs paced by Mize, Musial, and Slaughter in the 1940s. Standing a full head and shoulders above all other legendary teams to terrorize baseball's older league for an extended period were Roger Kahn's "Boys of Summer Dodgers" of the 1950s. Although winning only one World Championship in that decade, that Brooklyn team of Jackie Robinson, Duke Snider, Roy Campanella, and Pee Wee Reese holds legitimate title to the honor of the most dominant team of National League history over a full decade's play. But for a few key missing wins (for example, final day victories in 1946, 1950, and 1951), the ballclub which Branch Rickey built would have boasted nine championship flags in 11 summers; had they won only 19 more games over this 11-year stretch (1946–56), the Bums of Flatbush would have garnered an unheard of 11 straight pennants, a record not even approached by the Casey Stengel Yankees of the same era within the less-balanced American League.

When it comes to dominant Senior Circuit teams, however, due consideration must also be given to the Big Red Machine outfits which paraded their wares in the brand spanking new Riverfront Stadium during baseball's revival decade of the 1970s. From 1970, when the hastily rebuilt team guided by new skipper George "Sparky" Anderson won its first Western Division title in only the second year of divisional play, through 1979, when largely the same outfit walked off with its sixth divisional race of the decade, the Reds won more total games and took more league titles than any other single major league ballclub. Cincinnati, in fact, piled up 953 regular season victories in this stretch (a remarkable 95 per year), thus amassing a cool .593 winning percentage (162-game schedule) for the entire decade-long era. The "Boys of Summer" Dodgers, by way of comparison, had reeled off 949 victories over the course of their own decade of domination, playing at a .614 percentage (154-game schedule) over a comparable 10-year period. No other National League franchise can boast similar marks over an equal stretch of play. Consistency of winning-style play, it can be safely said, was an honorable badge which had now finally arrived at the Queen City under the tutelage of Sparky Anderson and his exciting charges, as it had in no previous Cincinnati baseball decade.

It was indeed a fresh new era facing Reds fans when baseball play began in the 1970s. And in Riverfront Stadium there was to be a fitting new venue which would appropriately match the team's drastically revised onfield image. Reds fans had said formal goodbye to crumbling Crosley Field on June 24, 1970, and opened modern-era Riverfront Stadium only six days later. The old ballpark, under its several guises as Redland Field and Crosley Field, had been the site for a total of 4,543 big-league games since its own proud dedication day on April 11, 1912. The glitzy new ballpark destined as its replacement would be the undisputed epitome of baseball change and would usher in an entirely new era of multipurpose stadia and radically altered baseball play. The Reds and their fans, therefore, were saying goodbye to the first century of baseball's oldest professional team in more than a symbolic fashion. At the outset of the 1970s there was more to the Reds' altered appearance than their spiffy new carpeted stadium. For Bob Howsam's administration was ushering in a modernized baseball era with a clever game plan for marketing a radically new baseball identity. And much of this new identity was credited by Howsam himself to the man selected to guide the revamped Redlegs on the field of play. George "Sparky" Anderson took over as field skipper in 1970 and remained in that post virtually the entire decade, guiding the onfield baseball strategy as well as enforcing Howsam's new clubhouse philosophies regarding the New Era clean-cut Reds.

General Manager Howsam's novel conception was a "Team of the 70s" that would earn the nickname "Big Red Machine" for its relentless winning-style of play. This was a team that would excite fans all across the nation in the "global village era" of televised baseball.[2] And in addition to building an anticipated national following, a rekindled hometown appeal soon lured 21 million fans into the new Riverfront Stadium over the course of the decade as well. Despite all the protestations heard from Howsam's front office about rebuilding the popularity of Reds baseball on the linchpins of Cincinnati's touted baseball traditionalism, this was a franchise prepared to abandon the most sacred elements of the sport's sustaining traditions. Plush and carpeted Riverfront Stadium was a certain victory for downtown urban revitalization in the Queen City and boasted a seating capacity that promised to fill the club coffers with exploding revenue; yet its circular design and plastic playing surface was clearly designed for the city's promised N.F.L. franchise and offered little resemblance to the quaint urban ballparks that were baseball's richest heritage. Bob Howsam's pronouncement that all Reds players would appear clean-shaven and short-haired, don uniformly black baseball shoes, and sport their uniform pantlegs at a prescribed height, was reportedly a franchise reaction to the unkempt appearance and non-traditional uniform style of certain big-league teams like Charlie Finley's renegade Oakland ballclub. It was more properly assessed, however, as a clever front-office tactic to sell a popular Reds image of "old-style baseball professionalism" to a regional midwestern audience of fans calculated to hold middle-American working class values and to seek leisure-time escape at the ballpark from the social upheaval of the shiftless 1970s.

If Howsam's marketing strategies might be questioned, however, there could be no challenging his baseball game plan. The onfield record of the 1970s Cincinnati Reds is an unchallenged legacy of baseball perfection. Hometown fans were soon to be thrilled by 12 championships in all, six Western Division titles (1970–72–73–75–76–79), four National League flags (1970–72–75–76), and back-to-back World Championships in 1975 and 1976. The Reds so dominated National League play during this span that they walked off with league MVP honors six times in an eight-year span. Johnny Bench won the coveted award first, in 1970, and then again in 1972, when he led the N.L. in both homers and RBIs. Pete Rose copped the honor as well in 1973, when he paced the league in hitting for the third time. Joe Morgan became only the second Senior Circuit player to take back-to-back MVP honors when he turned the trick in the two World Championship seasons. George Foster added a final MVP star to the Cincinnati bandwagon when he blasted a club-record 52 homers and added 149 RBIs. Since that time only Cecil Fielder, in 1990, has come close to Foster's home run total, with 51 round-trippers for the Detroit Tigers. And while a fifth Cincinnati star, Tony Perez, failed to match his stellar teammates with league MVP honors, Perez nonetheless earned an unequalled reputation for clutch hitting and superb infield play across the entire decade. Bench and Perez, in fact, ranked one-two in the majors in RBIs throughout the decade of the heady 1970s.

One key to the chemistry of this impressive championship team was the fact that the four luminous stars at its center—Johnny Bench, Joe Morgan, Tony Perez, and Pete Rose—were men of totally different emotional makeups, personal styles, and off-field personalities; yet together they maintained a relentless drive toward victory after victory and championship after championship—as well as toward eventual Cooperstown enshrinement. In unique tandem, they provided a perfect balance of batting power, basepath speed, defense, clutch hitting, and iron-willed stability under championship pressure. Bench was the defensive leader and ranks perhaps as the game's greatest catcher. His 1989 enshrinement in Cooperstown was a foregone conclusion almost from his sensational rookie season of 1968 (15 HRs, 82 RBIs, .275 BA); if not for his all-time record home run performance as a catcher (325, a record since broken by Carlton Fisk during the 1990 season), then certainly for his stature as the man whose flashy one-handed style of receiving revolutionized the modern art of catching. The infield cornerstone was Joe Morgan, who would fittingly follow Bench into Cooperstown in 1990. Morgan had been literally stolen from the Houston Astros in a blockbuster 1971 deal which ranks as the best in franchise history, and which brought Red Machine stars Jack Billingham and Cesar Geronimo on board as well.[3] Throughout the seventies, Little Joe was the greatest power-hitting second baseman since Rogers Hornsby, extracting a remarkable 268 lifetime roundtrippers from his diminutive 5'7" and 150-pound frame. Rose—baseball's all-time hit leader—and Perez—the all-time home run champion among Latin American big leaguers—will themselves find Cooperstown induction only a matter of marching time, though one is now plagued by his mounting off-field problems and a lifetime ban from the sport, the other by stereotypes which still haunt Latin American ballplayers seeking full acceptance into America's national game.

Surrounding the four superstars who were the heart and soul of the Big Red Machine stood a full contingent of role players and supporting lesser stars who enjoyed outstanding performances year-in and year-out throughout the 1970s. Dave Concepcion was unrivaled by all other league shortstops of the period and teamed with Morgan to form a double-play combination which won four Gold Gloves and which some consider the best of the past three decades. Ken Griffey batted .307 in nine years during his first tenure with the Reds, and patrolled the outfield with unmatched skill and speed. George Foster carried a much-deserved reputation for lackluster outfielder play, yet in his halcyon period he was a true offensive giant who averaged 32 homers and 107 RBIs over a seven-year period. Cesar Geronimo anchored the other outfield spot and won four Gold Gloves across the brilliant decade.

The highlight seasons of this vanguard period in Reds history were the runaway pennant summers of 1975 and 1976. The 1975 team marched to a club-record 108 victories (only the 1940 and 1970 squads had previously cracked the century mark) and an unprecedented 20-game divisional lead by season's end. Anderson's men were the only ballclub in either league to score in excess of 800 runs, and they led the circuit in fielding as well. Yet they did not dominate the league's team offensive statistics this time around, as would their successors of the following summer. Nor did they boast a single league individual hitting or pitching leader, Bench coming closest as runnerup in the league's RBI race. Great teams are often far more than the sum of their individual parts, however, and Pittsburgh's Pirates (the league's overall pacesetter in both slugging average and home run totals) could provide little challenge for Sparky Anderson's juggernaut in the N.L.C.S. series which climaxed the National League pennant chase of 1975. It was the Reds in three straight, with only the final contest dragging on to the final inning as a hotly contested tie game.

The World Series of 1975 has been called by many the most dramatic and well-played affair of post-season baseball history. Few would dispute that the seven-game toe-to-toe slugfest which featured five one-run decisions was far more entertaining than the 13-game difference between the opponents' regular season records might have forecast. The opposition was a strong Red Sox team which had outdistanced Baltimore in the A.L. East and then swept defending World Champion Oakland in a one-sided A.L.C.S. The Series which unfolded between these first-time rivals was crammed with nail-biting excitement and numerous individual heroes. The evenly matched teams (despite their uneven season records) split the first four games and then the next two as well. Game One featured a masterful performance by Sox starter Luis Tiant, the fiery Cuban veteran sporting a fine 18–14 season's mark, who shut out the slugging Reds with the first Series complete game effort in four years. Games Three and Six were both extra-inning affairs, the first falling to the Reds 6–5 in one extra bataround and the latter to the Bosox 7–6 in 12 frames. The dramatic sixth game will live forever in baseball history through the indelible televised image of Sox catcher Carlton Fisk frantically waving fair his dramatic game-winning and Series-tying shot—barely inches fair— into the left-field screen at Fenway Park. And the final game went to the wire once again, as Joe Morgan's clutch bloop hit eventually decided it with two Reds already retired in the ninth. When reliever Will McEnaney set down the Boston side in order in the bottom of the ninth the Reds and the long-suffering city of Cincinnati were finally able to celebrate their very first world title in 35 long and seemingly ill-starred pennant-barren years.

The following season saw the invincible Big Red Machine resist resting on its laurels as the unmatched Cincinnati powerhouse again rolled over all National League competition. This year the men of Sparky Anderson headed the Senior Circuit in virtually every offensive category (Philadelphia was the only team to post a batting average within 10 points of the Reds' .280 mark) and in fielding percentage as well. The final margin this time was 10 games over the Dodgers and

22 over third-place Houston in a pennant race that was virtually over before late spring planting had begun in the nation's Midwest. The Phillies (with a comparable regular season ledger of 101–61, against the Reds' 102–60) provided N.L.C.S. opposition, yet were no more obstacle than the Pirates the previous year, falling in three straight games despite outhitting the Ohioans in two of the three N.L.C.S. contests. Timely clutch hitting, especially by Foster and Bench with back-to-back game-tying homers in the third contest, brought the Redlegs back from the brink of defeat in all three games, and it was Ken Griffey's dramatic bouncing chopper off first baseman Bobby Tolan's glove which keyed a third-game three-run ninth-inning rally, bringing the Big Red Machine a delirious second pennant celebration in the late evening hours of October 12. If there were still any lonely doubters left, Griffey's charmed hit had not only dispatched Pirate hopes, but had made it altogether clear once again that these middle years of the 1970s belonged exclusively to the clean-shaven and business-like Cincinnati Reds.

The World Series of 1976 was one of the more lopsided in Series history, a four-game whitewashing in which the Reds simultaneously became the first National League repeat World Champion since McGraw's 1921–22 Giants 54 years earlier, as well as the first ballclub since the advent of divisional play to sweep both a League Championship set and a World Series. In a Series devoted to firsts, this was also the Fall Classic which introduced the newfangled American League designated hitter, and in the full spirit of the one-sided affair the Reds' assigned D.H. Dan Driessen pounded the ball at .357 clip, while his three Yankee counterparts (Lou Piniella, Carlos May, and Elliot Maddox) were as totally ineffective at the plate as their position-playing mates. Johnny Bench emerged as the Series batting star with eight hits (four for extra bases), a lofty .533 BA and stratospheric 1.133 slugging average, and two mammoth home runs in the Game Four clincher. Three different Reds starters (Don Gullett, Pat Zachry and Gary Nolen) claimed victories, and the Reds' under-employed bullpen was hardly tested during the lopsided Series encounter in which the New Yorkers garnered only eight runs and held the lead but once, during the first three innings of Game Four.

The Reds remained competitive for the final three years of the decade, even taking another divisional title in 1979, after second-place finishes in the two intervening years. But the 1979 playoff series went easily to the Pirates who had emerged as a new National League power by the end of the decade. The 1979 Western Division pennant chase had seen a close race with Houston that went right down to the season's final days. Yet despite solid seasons from some old stalwarts like George Foster (.302 BA, 30 HRs) and Johnny Bench (22 HRs, 80

RBIs), this was no longer the same Red Machine that had thrilled Riverfront Stadium fans for so long. The winds of change were blowing in Cincinnati as they were throughout the land, and the surprise departures of both Rose (as a free agent to the Phillies) and Anderson (unceremoniously dumped by an ungrateful Reds management after two pennant-less years) seemed to signal the end of the Cincinnati National League dynasty. If the depletion of the Reds' former strength was not altogether apparent during 1979 regular season play under new skipper John McNamara, it had become more tangible during the N.L.C.S. in which the eventual World Champion Pirates swept by scores of 5–2, 3–2, and 7–1, and in which Cincinnati bats languished at only a .215 clip.

There were a few additional highlights of this most glorious decade of Reds history. Future Hall-of-Fame pitcher Tom Seaver was acquired in a blockbuster deal in 1977 and performed consistently in his Cincinnati years at the end of the decade, even if he did not match his heralded mound performances earlier in the decade with the New York Mets. Seaver tossed a Riverfront Stadium no-hitter versus St. Louis on June 16, 1978, the only hitless masterpiece of the entire 1970s for Cincinnati. And as the decade wore down in 1978, Pete Rose provided one final memorable highlight before taking his free-agent act to Philadelphia, amassing an exciting 44-game hitting streak to establish a modern-day National League milepost which has never seriously been approached since. Rose's streak, which gripped the nation throughout June and July, surpassed the twentieth-century league standard of Tommy Holmes (37 in 1945) and equaled the nineteenth-century mark established by Cooperstown immortal Wee Willie ("Hit'em Where They Ain't") Keeler way back in 1897. As though Rose's extended hitting string were not a memorable enough farewell gift for the Cincinnati faithful who had cheered him lustily for 15 summers, the colorful Rose also stroked an historic Riverfront Stadium base hit on May 5 which made him only the 13th player in major league history to reach the lofty milestone of 3,000 career safeties.

Decade of Disappointment at Riverfront

Even the most casual ball fan knows that no player has banged out more base hits over the course of baseball's last century than Peter Edward Rose, the firebrand "Charlie Hustle" so permanently linked in baseball memory to the Cincinnati franchise for which he played all but a fraction of his tempestuous career. It is equally obvious, if somewhat less quantifiable, that no player has earned more press coverage in the past decade than this same Peter Edward Rose. The 1980s, after all, were the decade in which ballooning contracts and labor disputes often drove base hits and pennant races from the front pages of even the daily sports sections, and if Rose was indisputably the silent heart of Cincinnati baseball in the 1970s, he was the acknowledged front-and-center media attraction upon his return engagement in the Queen City during the 1980s. At each turn the Cincinnati baseball story was seemingly another momentous Rose achievement or another cataclysmic Rose revelation. And while the news was always front-page stuff, it wasn't always good and it wasn't always about baseball achievements. Rose's failures as a field manager first disappointed the faithful throughout the decade's middle years. His revealed failures as a role model and baseball idol then crushed the hometown Reds fans and the nation as a whole throughout 1989. What had begun with the glorious celebration of Rose chasing Cobb at decade's dawning had dwindled to the sad image of Rose chasing his own lost stature as baseball hero by decade's dreary close.

It didn't begin this way at the outset of the 1980s, however, as the Pete Rose story was still strictly baseball milestones at that time. The early years of the eighties were, in fact, the years that Pete Rose was strangely absent from Riverfront Stadium, though hardly absent as headline grabber from the larger baseball scene. Pete was now chasing down Ty Cobb in the rival city of Philadelphia. Having mounted the last serious threat to DiMaggio's legendary hit-streak and also becoming the youngest player ever to reach the 3,000-hit milestone at the outset of the 1978 campaign, Rose turned to the lure of the free-agent market once the Reds allowed his contract to lapse at the conclusion of that same season. In the fierce bidding war that followed, Rose signed on for a then-staggering four-year $3.2 million contract with the rebuilding Phillies. And the events that surrounded his departure from his hometown were only the first painful episode in the reckless dismantling of the team that had so dominated the previous baseball decade. Rose only justifiably grabbed a piece of the free-agent bonanza which now awaited high-profile superstars and which was apparently not to be offered by the frugal Reds who had exploited his talents for 15 summers. And Rose was not the only past star who was now cast aside or allowed to drift away by the front-office regime of new club president Dick Wagner. Tony Perez was first unloaded to Montreal on the heels of the 1976 World Series triumph for mainstream pitchers Woodie Fryman and Dale Murray. When Joe Morgan's own free-agent status arrived in January 1980 the incomparable second sacker was allowed to drift unchallenged back to Houston where his career had started. So too went George Foster, dealt to the Mets for two journeyman pitchers and undistinguished catcher Alex Treviño before the opening of the 1982 season. Even such lesser figures as Ken Griffey (sent to the Yankees for minor league hurlers Fred Toliver and Bryan Ryder in November 1981) and Cesar Geronimo (peddled to Kansas City in January 1981) were allowed to escape to greener pastures in more free-spending baseball organizations.

But if the 1980s were to be a period of decline and disappointment at Riverfront Stadium, this was not yet evident to the local partisans at the outset of the 1981 season, no matter how many new and untried faces (like Ron Oester at second, Ray Knight at third, Dan Driessen at first, and Dave Collins in right) had replaced the popular old guard of Morgan, Rose, Perez, and Griffey. Few big-name stars still donned Cincinnati uniforms: Dave Collins (.303) was the only regular to hit at .300; Foster (25) and Bench (24) provided the home run power but were far in arrears of the league leaders. The Reds battled valiantly for a pennant in 1980 but didn't quite make it down the stretch, finishing three games behind Houston and L.A. in a tightly contested league race which saw the issue between Los Angeles and Houston decided in a dramatic playoff contest, forced by the Dodgers' sweep of the Astros in the season's final three games. Most frustrating for Cincinnati fans, meanwhile, was the fact that while the locals came up with just too little hitting to stay glued to the Dodgers and Astros, Pete Rose was leading Philadelphia to a pennant and world title with his consistent bat and stellar first base play.

Yet the makings of a good team were still there, and the 1981 season seemed to be the proof that the Big Red Machine had sputtered but was hardly dead in the water. The 1981 season, however—arguably the most bizarre in all of baseball history—was to prove perhaps the most frustrating in Cincinnati's long history. It was certainly the most unfair! Unable to reach agreement with ownership over the issue of free-agent compensation, the Players' Association called a halt to the season's action on June 12, launching a 50-day labor action which proved the longest strike in the history of organized sport and wiped out 714 big-league games. Cincinnati had boasted baseball's best record (66–42, .611 pct.) that year, from opening gun to final bell. Yet the unpopular players' strike did what the rest of the league could not, altogether derailing the Reds' cherished pennant plans. A makeshift and illogical jerry-built playoff system, driven by the owners' and players' apparent joint greed for television dollars, dictated that once play resumed on August 1 the season would (after the fact) be divided into two independent segments. Half-season winners would meet in an additional set of lucrative revenue-producing playoffs. The result was that the team with baseball's best record would not participate, while one team (the New York Yankees) that finished in sixth place during the post-strike segment would somehow be a playoff guest. The Reds—who were one-half game behind the Dodgers when Strike Day abruptly concluded "Season One" and then trailed Houston by a game-and-a-half at the close of the makeshift "Season Two"—found little satisfaction and reaped little fan promotional payoff by hoisting their own flag (proclaiming their ownership of baseball's best record) at season's end on the final weekend of play in Riverfront Stadium.

There were some bright stories in 1981, though, and the brightest was perhaps Tom Seaver. Seaver in this senseless season became only the fifth hurler in history to reach the milestone of 3,000 career strikeouts, surpassing that number in an April 18 game with St. Louis, ironically only 11 days before veteran Steve Carlton of Philadelphia's Phillies also reached the charmed 3,000 circle. For Seaver, who led the strike-shortened campaign in victories (14) and winning percentage (.875), 1981 was a final milestone season preceding a less fortunate sub-.500 swansong in Cincinnati the following summer.

Things were soon to get worse before they got much better, and the three summers following the bizarre 1981 campaign were a period of change, turmoil, and plummeting league standings throughout Redsland. The altogether forgettable 1982 campaign brought with it the only Reds ballclub ever to lose as many as 100 league contests. And there were three consecutive embarrassing seasons in the second division during this stretch, a period of decline which saw the front office test first Russ Nixon and then Vern Rapp as possible successors to ousted skipper John McNamara. Meanwhile, Rose had been joined in Philadelphia by Morgan and Perez, and the aged Red Machine was now grinding out yet another pennant in the City of Brotherly Love, sweeping to a 1983 National League flag and World Series date with Baltimore which was Philly's second in four summers.

In the midst of this dramatic and dispiriting downturn some familiar faces unexpectedly returned to Riverfront Stadium and thus temporarily buoyed sagging hometown spirits. The first was Bob Howsam, back on board as club president after the dismissal of unpopular Dick Wagner, Howsam's replacement in 1978 and target of fan ire for his role in dismantling the fabled Big Red Machine. And Howsam's first and most popular act was to bring Rose back home to Cincinnati. Saddled with a burdensome salary, aging legs, and an expired Philadelphia contract, Pete had moved on to Montreal in spring 1984, where he promptly stroked his 4,000th career hit, a day before his 44th birthday and exactly 21 years from the date of his first big-league hit. In August—one of the most glorious stretches of Reds history—Rose was traded back to his hometown Reds, installed as player-manager, and responded with a .365 BA down the final 26-game stretch of the season. While Pete Rose was again the major news on the field in 1984, the front office underwent another significant change, as new owner Marge Schott came on board with the reputation of a hard-nosed business lady who let her heart rule in baseball matters but her pocketbook rule all else. The baseball marriage of Pete Rose and Marge Schott was to be a rocky one from the beginning, as was the marriage of the unpredictable auto dealer and the bulk of Cincinnati's fans. Reds supporters soon ran the gamut of emotions with their new owner: excited by her free-spending acquisition of expensive ballplayers like Buddy Bell, Bo Diaz, and Bill Gullickson but exasperated by her ubiquitous Saint Bernard Schottzie, her meddling with baseball matters best left to the baseball people in the organization, and most of all her dismantling of the Reds farm system under the direction of Branch Rickey III.

The season of 1985 was indisputably the "Year of Pete Rose" as the nation's summer seemingly revolved around Rose's unwinding chase after the ghost of Ty Cobb. Tension mounted as Rose approached the vaunted record in a September weekend series in Chicago. Playing-manager Rose had intended to sit out the September 8 game at Wrigley Field—still two hits shy of Cobb—and assure the record-setting moment for the home crowds in Cincinnati. But a last-minute Cubs pitching change (righty Reggie Patterson for the announced lefty Steve Trout) had the win-at-all-costs Rose back in the lineup and owner Marge Schott scurrying to the Windy City in a hastily chartered jet to be on hand just in case. A Rose single in the first inning brought Chicago pandemonium and another in the fifth brought not only a tie with the immortal Cobb but horror in the Reds front office back at Cincinnati. Reds management breathed a gasp of relief, however, when the record-shattering hit did not materialize during Rose's final two at-bats in Chicago, then braced for both a gate bonanza and an inevitable joyous celebration in the hometown park the following week. After almost two seasons of nonstop media glare, the dramatic chase of Cobb came to its fitting emotional conclusion in Riverfront Stadium on the night of September 11, as the irrepressible Rose lined a single to left off Padres starter Eric Show to pass Cobb in the official record books, if not also in the game's unofficial yet immortal halls of legend.

With the coveted hit record finally in his pocket, Rose turned to full-time managing after a final summer of part-time play in 1986. The next several seasons would bring repeated disappointments, however, as Rose's teams always seemed predestined to be bridesmaids rather than brides. Picked as the divisional shoo-in in March of 1987 and 1988, two more somewhat lackluster second-place finishes made it four straight runnerup slots for Rose since assuming full-time control in 1985. None of these races actually went down to the wire—the closest finish was the 5½-game debit to the Dodgers in 1985—and the local faithful were beginning to wonder aloud if the management-ownership team of Rose-Schott had the wherewithal to return winning baseball to the ballpark which had enjoyed such unbroken success during its maiden decade.

There were some limited individual heroics in this stretch, to be sure. Tom Browning's rain-delayed perfect game (1–0 versus Los Angeles) at Riverfront on September 16, 1988, was the first "perfect ace" in Reds history and the first as well in 23 years of National League play. Slender yet powerful Eric Davis emerged by 1987 (37 homers, National League All-Star selection, Gold Glove winner) as a new superstar and one of the finest young slugging outfielders of the decade. But there was also a distinctly bitter taste after each runnerup campaign when so much had been forecast and so little had been won. As the Reds headed into the portentous 1989 season, with another divisional crown already on the lips of many pre-season pundits, Pete Rose's managerial skills—especially his ability to effectively use his overtaxed bullpen and properly shuffle his starting mound rotation—was subject for lengthy serious debate among casual fans and "baseball experts" alike.

But all this was lost with the dramatic events of 1989, one of baseball's worst public relations seasons since the devastating Black Sox summer of 1919, which ironically had also involved Cincinnati. News of a commissioner's investigation of Rose for possibly wagering on baseball games first surfaced during Spring Training. From the moment the story dramatically broke, the Reds and their popular manager were the focus of a relentless media glare. Little chance remained for a successful National League season with Rose at the helm, as attention was too distracted from the total team concentration necessary for winning a league pennant. Rose refused to step down, however, and maintained his innocence of all charges and freedom as well from rumored gambling addiction. Marge Schott steadfastly refused to remove her beleaguered manager, obviously aware of his remaining untarnished local popularity. The season, quite predictably, drifted away in the process as the Reds fell far off the pace early and maintained a season's edge on only the hapless Braves from Atlanta. Finally, the dramatic mid-summer announcement was made by Commissioner A. Bartlett Giamatti that Rose had agreed to a lifetime suspension from the national pastime. Days later Rose shocked the remaining faithful by admitting his longstanding gambling addiction. Coach Tommy Helms was named interim manager and the season was played out under the darkest of palls. If the events of the tragic 1989 season were not shocking enough, popular Commissioner Giamatti suffered a fatal heart attack only one week after issuing his landmark edict against Rose. The Hall-of-Fame was now no longer a certainty for Pete Rose. Yet this seemed a small enough matter as deep personal problems mounted for baseball's tarnished hero, who faced income tax evasion charges stemming from hidden track winnings and unreported dealings in baseball memorabilia. Meanwhile the nation's fans continued to debate whether or not Rose—baseball's greatest hero of the post-Vietnam era but also now a convicted felon—still merited their nod for Hall of Fame enshrinement in Cooperstown.

The summer of 1990 seemed to bring winds of fresh hope, with the Rose scandal largely behind the Reds beleaguered organization and a new management team now on board. Ex-Yankee skipper Lou Piniella had taken over the reins from interim skipper Helms, and Piniella's charges started remarkably fast, sprinting to a double-digit lead over the Dodgers and Giants in the season's first six weeks and maintaining a 5-game edge and a .562 winning percentage by season's end. The Reds were barely a .500 club after June 1, but the men of Lou Piniella never folded completely when a National League crown was on the line in the month of September, something that couldn't be said of Cincinnati teams during the half-dozen previous campaigns. Heroes on the young club were many, but most media attention went to the "Nasty Boys" bullpen (31 saves for Randy Myers and 11 for Rob Dibble). And the starting pitching of Danny Jackson and Jose Rijo soon proved the difference in a 4–2 pennant waltz over the Eastern Division Pirates, setting the stage for Cincinnati's first World Series appearance since the era of the Big Red Machine. Piniella's charges would indeed find post-season play almost as easy as it had been for those legendary teams of Bench, Morgan, and Rose. Oakland's highly touted Athletics never got into the fall classic spirit as the Reds raced to a surprisingly effortless four-game championship sweep. Thus as the decade of the 1990s set in across the Queen City, Redlegs fans were once again dreaming the most pleasant of dreams—about a new Cincinnati baseball dynasty.

Notes

1. No single volume devoted to the history of the Cincinnati Reds baseball club—or the larger spectrum of baseball in Cincinnati from the Red Stockings to Pete Rose—can match the fine coffee-table history/encyclopedia produced by Lonnie Wheeler and John Baskin. This colorful and unique volume (available in hardcover and paperback) is a delightful collage of historical record, narrative summary, graphic illustrations, and encyclopedic compendium of every aspect of Cincinnati's rich baseball history and is both an intellectual and visual delight from cover to cover. No other major league team enjoys an anthology quite like this one and this author found it an immense help in preparing the present chapter. I am indebted as well to all the following pinch hitters and bullpen aces: Bill Friday, Ronnie Wilbur, Tony Formo, Chester Waits, Bill Deane, and Allen Hye.

2. Professor Walker (in both his article and book) argues that the Reds' marketing plan under Howsam was clearly a smashingly successful effort to link the 1970s Reds to their glorious century-long baseball past. To this observer, the strategy was neither very convincing, nor motivated by any sincere sense of baseball tradition. The conformity that marked the Reds under Howsam and Sparky Anderson was the epitome of a corporate mentality in tune with the 1970s and with the game of football, much more so than baseball—i.e., the stress on conformity to the team game plan, mechanistic superiority implied by the "Big Red Machine" nickname, clean-pressed and simplistic white home uniforms. The old-time baseball ambiance was one marked by individualism, not by the length of hair, cut of beard, or style of uniform. Ironically, the Red Stockings days themselves were fraught with facial hair and shabby manicure. In this sense it was the Oakland team of Finley that was far more in tune with the baseball individualism of the nineteenth century than was the team marketed by Bob Howsam.

3. Wheeler and Baskin (*The Cincinnati Game,* 180–83) ranked Cincinnati Reds trades down through the franchise history as follows:

Best

1. **Joe Morgan** (IF), Jack Billingham (P), Denis Menke (IF), Cesar Geronimo (OF), and Ed Armbrister (OF), acquired from Houston for Lee May (1B), Tommy Helms (F), and Jimmy Stewart (IF) (November 1971, by Bob Howsam).

2. **Edd Roush** (OF), Christy Mathewson (P), and Bill McKechnie (3B), acquired from the New York Giants for shortstop-manager Buck Herzog and Red Killefer (OF) (July 1916, by Garry Herrmann).

3. **Bucky Walters** (P), acquired from Philadelphia Phillies for Spud Davis (C), Al Hollingsworth (P), and $50,000 (June 1938, by Warren Giles).

Worst

1. **Christy Mathewson** (P), traded to New York Giants for Amos Rusie (P) (December 1900, by John Brush).

2. **Frank Robinson** (OF), traded to Baltimore Orioles for Milt Pappas (P), Jack Baldschun (P), and Dick Simpson (OF) (December 1965, by Bill DeWitt).

3. **Smokey Burgess** (C), Harvey Haddix (P), and Don Hoak (3B), traded to Pittsburgh Pirates for Whammy Douglas (C), Jim Pendleton (OF), Frank Thomas (OF), and Johnny Powers (OF) (January 1959, by Gabe Paul).

References

Bjarkman, Peter C. "First Hispanic Star? Dolf Luque, of Course" in: *The Baseball Research Journal* 19 (1990), 28–32. Cleveland, OH: The Society for American Baseball Research.

Walker, Robert Harris. 1988. "The Reds: Inventing the Midwest." In *The Antioch Review* 46:3 (Summer): 284–302.

———. 1988. *Cincinnati and the Big Red Machine.* Bloomington, Ind.: Indiana University Press. 158 pp.

Wheeler, Lonnie, and John Baskin. 1988. *The Cincinnati Game.* Wilmington, Ohio: Orange Frazer Press. 272 pp.

Annotated Bibliography

Allen, Lee. *The Cincinnati Reds.* New York: G.P. Putnam Publishing Company, 1948. 302 pp.

The most detailed and authoritative history of the Reds ballclub through the end of the World War II era, written by one of baseball's truly legendary scribes. Written with the colorful prose and flair that was Allen's trademark, this is one of the more entertaining volumes in the classic series of Putnam team histories, with its focus on the bizarre, unprecedented, and pioneering events which made the Reds of the first half-century baseball's most colorful and innovative franchise, if far from its most successful or pennant-rich ballclub.

————. "Cincinnati Reds." In *The National League.* New rev. ed., edited by Ed Fitzgerald, 212–46. New York: Grosset and Dunlap Publishers, 1966.

The compact and updated single-chapter version of Allen's more spacious Putnam team history is every bit as lively and entertaining, if somewhat less rich in its historical detail. An excellent catalogue of early-century Cincinnati baseball memories and pioneering franchise innovations— ladies day, farm system, air travel, televised games, night play—is provided, alongside considerable detail about the club's nineteenth-century roots in National League and American Association play. Allen's fascination is with the colorful if often cellar-dwelling Crosley Field teams of the century's first several decades, and while this revised history runs through the 1965 season, only six of 35 pages are devoted to the post-1950 seasons, while 15 are expended upon the decades between the turn of the century and the outbreak of the second great war.

————. "Cincinnati Reds." In *The Book of Major League Baseball Clubs: The National League,* edited by Ed Fitzgerald, 187–216. New York: A.S. Barnes and Company, 1952.

The earliest version of Allen's chapter-length version of his Reds history, here complete only through the 1951 season, and thus detailing the first 75 seasons of franchise history. There are only minor wording differences between this version and the one cited above, and therefore no reader would be interested in searching for the 1952 original if the 1966 republication, updated and revised, is available. (One small advantage of the earlier edition of the Fitzgerald team histories volume, however, is a useful name and subject index, which has been eliminated from subsequent reprintings.)

Asinoff, Eliot. *Eight Men Out: The Black Sox and the 1919 World Series.* New York: Henry Holt and Company, 1987 (New York: Holt, Rinehart and Winston, 1963).

One of baseball's small handful of five or six truly classic historical books, capturing the details of the national sport's most earthshaking and nearly ruinous moment, as well as the bizarre aftermath of this infamous hour. The focus throughout is clearly on the White Sox ballclub of penurious owner Charles Comiskey, yet there is much as well on the Reds and the circumstances surrounding the most forgotten glory moment in the long annals of team play. Asinoff leaves no stone unturned in ferreting out the true story behind the original fix, the actual legitimacy of Series play, the exposure and trial of the now legendary eight White Sox stars who allegedly took part in the only known fix of a major American sports championship competition, and the aftermath and impact of the scandalous Series for both the players involved and the stunned nation of disbelieving and saddened baseball fans.

Bjarkman, Peter C. *Baseball's Great Dynasties: The Reds.* New York: W.H. Smith (Gallery Books), 1991. 80 pp.

The most recent and most heavily illustrated coffee-table format history of the Cincinnati ballclub, featuring seven chapters, brief composite statistical summaries, lively prose treatment, and 110 black-and-white and full-color photos from all eras of Reds history. Following the standardized format of the "Great Dynasties" Series, this fast-paced volume traces Reds history from the touring 1869 Red Stockings of Harry Wright through the glory years of the Big Red Machine and on to the disappointing years of defeat, controversy, and scandal that have marked Riverfront Stadium baseball of the 1980s.

Brannon, Jody. *Cincinnati Reds*. Major League Baseball Team History Series. Mankato, Minn.: Creative Education Publishing Company, 1982. 48pp.

Written as a juvenile history (part of a series covering all 26 big-league franchises), this small volume offers little to adult readers and fans beyond its two-dozen full-page black-and-white action and portrait photographs, and its capsule overview of team history. Not as error-riddled as a number of other poorly researched books in this same series (such as the horrendous volume on the Texas Rangers which incorrectly links that ballclub with the original Washington Senators franchise of Walter Johnson days), this is the best available young-adult history of the Cincinnati club and must reading for all youthful Cincinnati Reds fans.

Brosnan, Jim. *Pennant Race*. New York: Harper and Row Publishers, 1962 (New York: Dell Publishing Company, 1962). 250 pp.

Following up on the best-selling journalistic narrative of his 1959 season with the St. Louis Cardinals, baseball's best pitcher-turned-writer chronicles the 1961 championship campaign at Crosley Field. Brosnan, the pitcher, was a major element in the pennant victory of that particular season—the team's top relief ace with 10 victories, 16 saves, and an ERA of 3.04—and Brosnan, the writer, proves also to be an unmatched observer of the inside workings of a major league summer, detailing without sentimentality or false enthusiasm the seemingly endless ordeal of winning and losing streaks, tragedies and comedies, cliff-hangers and "laughers" which make up the adventures of any six-month baseball summer.

Collett, Ritter. *The Cincinnati Reds: A Pictorial History of Professional Baseball's Oldest Team*. Virginia Beach, Va.: Jordan-Powers Corporation, 1976. 192 pp.

At the time of its release, this was clearly the best pictorial history of Cincinnati big-league baseball. Collett's text is now 15 years out of date, but is still the best source for rare photographs of Reds' players, executives, and ballparks of the pre-World War II epochs. The historical text here is skimpy and choppy throughout and one-sentence paragraphs abound, yet the photographs are the book's showpiece and stand by themselves throughout. Coverage of the 1919, 1939, and 1940 championship teams is particularly memorable, as is the treatment of the four outstanding pitchers—Bucky Walters, Paul Derringer, Ewell Blackwell, and Johnny Vander Meer—of the World War II years.

Connor, Floyd, and John Snyder. *Day-by-Day in Cincinnati Reds History*. West Point, N.Y.: Leisure Press, 1984. 336 pp.

A standard volume in the Leisure Press team chronologies, this work like the others features all of the following: date-by-date chronology of significant events in team history; team and manager won-loss records; year-by-year and composite summaries of team batting and pitching leaders; individual club batting and pitching records in all categories; features on post-season play, awards, nicknames, and club Hall-of-Famers; all-time club rosters and chronological index; plus a small but adequate sampling of historical photographs and individual player portraits. This standard reference work provides the best overall team statistical record on the ballclub, outside of yearly team media guides and press guides.

Frommer, Harvey. "Big Red Machine: The Reds." In *A Baseball Century: The First 100 Years of the National League*, edited by Jeanne McClow, 190–203. New York: Rutledge Books, 1976.

A standard brief overview single-chapter history, complete through the 1975 World Championship season and touching upon major highlights of team history. Eighteen large-sized photographs cramp the limited text and only the most sketchy (if lively) historical summary is possible within such limited framework. A unique sidebar here provides dates, scores, and attendance for inaugural games in all five Cincinnati major league ballparks—a special feature of each of the team histories of this volume. Yet the reader should not anticipate anything else here that is not available in all previous historical summaries of the Cincinnati National League franchise.

Hertzel, Bob. *The Big Red Machine: The Inside Story of Baseball's Best Team.* Englewood Cliffs, N.J.: Prentice-Hall Publishers, 1976. 198 pp.

Fast-paced and entertaining portrait of the Big Red Machine Reds of the Rose-Bench-Morgan-Perez dynasty years, written at the conclusion of the dramatic 1975 World Championship season and focused on details of the 1975 campaign, from Spring Training through the final innings and post-Series celebration climaxing one of the most unforgettable World Series ever played. Three four-page inserts of candid black-and-white photographs, detailed reports of front-office intrigue, and numerous locker room and dugout anecdotes make this a highly predictable yet entertaining portrait of the most unforgettable season of Cincinnati Reds history.

Meany, Thomas. "A Cloud in the Sky: The 1919 Reds." In *Baseball's Greatest Teams,* 151–63. New York: A.S. Barnes, 1949.

One of baseball's immortal writers provides behind-the-scene and long-forgotten details on one of baseball's most overlooked powerhouse champions, a remarkable heavy-hitting club which won 96 games, featured the National League's best hitter in Edd Roush and two of its finest pitchers in Hod Eller and Slim Sallee, boasted baseball's first true Latin American star in Dolf Luque, and waltzed to an easy league pennant, yet is remembered by history only as the "other club" that was handed an embarrassing 1919 World Championship by the infamous Black Sox team of Happy Felsch, Buck Weaver, and Shoeless Joe Jackson. One highlight of this piece is its insightful and fact-filled discussion of the events surrounding the Black Sox World Series itself, an account which predates Elliot Asinoff's scholarly study of the Black Sox by over a decade.

Rathgeber, Bob. *Cincinnati Reds Scrapbook.* Virginia Beach, Va.: Jordan-Powers Corporation, 1982. 151 pp.

One-page personal prose portraits and facing full-page black-and-white photographs for 63 personalities and memorable moments down through the decades of Reds history, compiled here by a one-time Cincinnati Reds publications director and later sports copy editor for the Cincinnati *Enquirer.* Each portrait offers personal anecdote or lively reminiscence to supplement rich historical baseball detail, and all is presented in an attractive oversized coffee-table format. Early and often forgotten stars such as Buck Ewing, Noodles Hahn, Hod Eller, Cy Seymour, Bob Bescher, Adolfo Luque, and the remarkable pinch-hitting pitcher Red Lucas receive especially fine treatment here.

Rose, Pete, and Roger Kahn. *Pete Rose: My Story.* New York: Macmillan Publishing Company, 1989. 300 pp.

One of the best-selling baseball books of the late 1980s due to the hoopla surrounding the controversial lifetime baseball suspension of Rose and the magnetic link of Rose's name with that of Roger Kahn, author of one of baseball's most beloved books in *The Boys of Summer* (1971). Yet this volume fails as thoroughly to live up to its promise as the authoritative

Rose story as Rose failed to live up to his once unassailable image as baseball's true pop culture hero. Rose states worn-out platitudes about his freedom from gambling addiction and innocence on the damning charges of baseball betting, Kahn rambles endlessly about his own life's preoccupations, and the reader knows nothing of value upon closing the book that he didn't already know before opening it.

Vaughn, Jim, as told to Hal Totten. "1917: Cincinnati Reds 1, Chicago Cubs 0." In *The Fireside Book of Baseball,* edited by Charles Einstein. 356–57. New York: Simon and Schuster, 1956.

The colorful inside story of one of baseball's most unusual games—the 1917 "double no-hitter" which matched the Reds' Fred Toney versus the Cubs' Jim "Hippo" Vaughn—as recalled four decades later by the game's losing pitcher. Toney's no-hitter remained intact in extra frames, while Vaughn surrendered a hit and a run to lose his masterpiece in the 10th. Vaughn here provides the long-forgotten and often misconstrued bizarre details surrounding the game-winning play, which itself featured earlier football and Olympic great, Indian Jim Thorpe, at the time an unheralded Reds utility outfielder. Vaughn clears up the bungled fielding play involving catcher Art Wilson that allowed Cincinnati's Larry Kopf to scamper home with the winning tally.

Walker, Robert Harris. "The Reds: Inventing the Midwest." In *The Antioch Review* 46:3 (Summer 1988): 284–302.

An overblown and largely unsuccessful argument that Reds General Manager Robert L. Howsam merits almost complete responsibility for the widespread national and regional appeal of the 1970s Big Red Machine. The thesis here is that Howsam "invented the Midwest in baseball terms" by designing a ballclub and its associated image that would appeal perfectly to regional midwest tastes and attitudes—those glorifying traditional values, clean-living, hard work, and perfect balance of individual freedom within the confines of group responsibility. The argument that the 1970s Reds were the standard carriers of old-time baseball tradition (since they shunned facial hair and multi-color uniforms) is blind to the stark fact that the Cincinnati ballclub of the Howsam era—with its football-appropriate nickname (Big Red Machine), flying-saucer multipurpose stadium, nylon-pajama uniforms, and blue-tinged astroturf playing field—was the image of everything in the decade which flew directly in the face of traditional baseball flavor.

———. *Cincinnati and the Big Red Machine.* Bloomington, Ind.: Indiana University Press, 1988. 158 pp.

The most recent and one of the most readable of the half-dozen books on baseball's "team of the seventies" and the colorful baseball antics of Pete Rose, Joe Morgan, Johnny Bench, Tony Perez, Sparky Anderson, and company. Focus is again on the clean image, careful marketing, and narrow regional appeal of the Cincinnati ballclub of this period, and on the Reds' successes in capturing national following through careful orchestration of baseball's perceived traditional roots and imagery (clean-shaven faces, business-like work ethic, sanitary white uniforms, etc.). Interview format is featured over historical narrative, and off-field personnel receive as much focus as game-action details.

Wheeler, Lonnie, and John Baskin. *The Cincinnati Game.* Wilmington, Ohio: Orange Frazer Press, 1988. 272 pp.

A delightful pictorial history of Cincinnati baseball, with focus on the hometown Redlegs ballclub from the pioneering Red Stockings team of Harry Wright down through the disappointing Pete Rose Reds of the mid-1980s, with space as well for features on the Queen City's rich and lengthy baseball connections and on its numerous native sons who have played, managed, or directed other major league clubs. Coffee-table format in design and unique in its format, this volume features numerous rare black-and-white photographs, eye-catching graphic layouts, and unusual sidebar spreads which make it one of the most colorful and rewarding pictorial baseball histories of all time.

Honig, Donald. *The Cincinnati Reds: An Illustrated History.* New York: Simon and Schuster, 1992. 256 pp.

Overflowing with hundreds of familiar and also less familiar (even rare) black and white photos from more than a century of Reds history, this is one of the finest available scrapbook histories on this ballclub, at least from a purely visual perspective. The narrative text itself adds little if anything not found in earlier club portraits, and Honig's patented chatty style is often just as colorless as the black and white snapshots that fill the volume. All-in-all, however, this is a tome which any avid Reds fanatic will certainly want to have in his or her collection. A brief and unusual appendix provides a listing of all Reds league leaders in major hitting and pitching categories.

Year-by-Year Standings and Season Summaries

Year	Pos.	Record	Pct.	GB	Manager	Player	BA	Player	HR	Player	W-L	ERA
National League												
1876	8th	9–56	.138	42.5	Gould	Jones	.286	Jones	4	Dean	4–26	3.73
1877	6th	15–42	.253	25.5	Pike	Manning	.317	Pike	4*	Cummings	5–14	4.34
					Addy							
1878	2nd	37–23	.617	4.0	McVey	Pike	.324	Jones	3	White	30–21	1.79
1879	5th	38–36	.514	14.0	McVey	Kelly	.348	Kelly	2	White	43–31	1.99
					White			Dickerson	2			
1880	8th	21–59	.263	44.0	Clapp	Purcell	.292	Manning	2	White	18–42*	2.14
								Mansell	2			
1881	No Team											
American Association												
1882	1st	55–25	.688	+11.5	Snyder	Carpenter	.341	five with 1 each		White	40*–12	1.54
1883	3rd	61–37	.622	5.0	Snyder	Reilly	.311	Jones	11	White	43*–22	2.09
1884	5th	68–41	.624	8.0	Snyder	Reilly	.339	Reilly	11	White	34–18	3.32
					White							
1885	2nd	63–49	.563	16.0	Caylor	Jones	.322	Fennelly	10	McKeon	20–13	2.86
1886	5th	65–73	.471	27.5	Caylor	Lewis	.318	McPhee	7*	Mullane	31–27	3.70
1887	2nd	81–54	.600	14.0	Schmelz	Corkhill	.311	Reilly	10	Smith	33–18	2.94
1888	4th	80–54	.597	11.5	Schmelz	Reilly	.321	Reilly	13*	Viau	27–14	2.65
1889	4th	76–63	.547	18.0	Schmelz	Holliday	.343	Holliday	19*	Duryea	32–19	2.56
National League												
1890	4th	78–55	.586	10.5	Loftus	Knight	.312	Reilly	6	Rhines	28–17	1.95
1891	7th	56–81	.409	30.5	Loftus	Browning	.343	Holliday	9	Mullane	24–25	3.23
1892	5th	82–68	.547	20.0	Comiskey	Browning	.303	Holliday	13*	Mullane	21–10	2.59
1893	6th	65–63	.508	20.5	Comiskey	Holliday	.310	Holliday	5	Dwyer	18–15	4.13
								Canavan	5			

Year	Pos.	Record	Pct.	GB	Manager	Player	BA	Player	HR	Player	W-L	ERA
1894	10th	54–75	.419	35.0	Comiskey	Holliday	.383	Holliday	13	Dwyer	19–22	5.07
								Canavan	13			
1895	8th	66–64	.508	21.0	Ewing	Miller	.335	Miller	8	Rhines	19–10	4.81
1896	3rd	77–50	.606	12.0	Ewing	Burke	.340	Miller	4	Dwyer	24–11	3.15
								Hoy	4			
1897	4th	76–56	.576	17.0	Ewing	Beckley	.345	Beckley	7	Breitenstein	23–12	3.62
1898	3rd	92–60	.605	11.5	Ewing	Smith	.342	Beckley	4	Hawley	27–11	3.37
1899	6th	83–67	.553	19.0	Ewing	Beckley	.333	Beckley	3	Hahn	23–7	2.68
								Selbach	3			
1900	7th	62–77	.446	21.5	Allen	Beckley	.341	Crawford	7	Scott	17–21	3.82
1901	8th	52–87	.374	38.0	McPhee	Crawford	.330	Crawford	16*	Hahn	22–19	2.71
1902	4th	70–70	.500	33.5	McPhee	Crawford	.333	Beckley	5	Hahn	22–12	1.76
					Bancroft							
					Kelley							
1903	4th	74–65	.532	16.5	Kelley	Donlin	.351	Seymour	7	Hahn	22–12	2.52
								Donlin	7			
1904	3rd	88–65	.575	18.0	Kelley	Seymour	.313	Dolan	6	Harper	23–9	2.37
1905	5th	79–74	.516	26.0	Kelley	Seymour	.377*	Odwell	9*	Ewing	20–11	2.51
1906	6th	64–87	.424	51.5	Hanlon	Huggins	.292	Seymour	4	Weimer	20–14	2.22
								Schlei	4			
1907	6th	66–87	.431	41.5	Hanlon	Mitchell	.292	Mitchell	3	Ewing	17–19	1.73
								Kane	3			
1908	5th	73–81	.474	26.0	Ganzel	Lobert	.293	Lobert	4	Ewing	17–15	2.21
1909	4th	77–76	.503	33.5	Griffith	Mitchell	.310	Mitchell	4*	Fromme	19–13	1.90
								Lobert	4			
								Hoblitzell	4			
1910	5th	75–79	.487	29.0	Griffith	Lobert	.309	Mitchell	5	Suggs	19–11	2.40
1911	6th	70–83	.458	29.0	Griffith	Bates	.292	Hoblitzell	11	Suggs	15–13	3.00

Year	Pos.	Record	Pct.	GB	Manager	Player	BA	Player	HR	Player	W-L	ERA
1912	4th	75–78	.490	29.0	O'Day	Marsans	.317	Mitchell Bescher	4	Suggs	19–16	2.94
1913	7th	64–89	.418	37.5	Tinker	Tinker	.317	Bates	6	Johnson	14–16	3.01
1914	8th	60–94	.390	34.5	Herzog	Groh	.288	Niehoff	4	Benton	17–18	2.96
1915	7th	71–83	.461	20.0	Herzog	Griffith	.307	Griffith	4	Toney	15–6	1.58
1916	7th	60–93	.392	33.5	Herzog Mathewson	Chase	.339*	Chase	4	Toney	14–17	2.28
1917	4th	78–76	.506	20.0	Mathewson	Roush	.341*	Chase Roush Thorpe	4 4 4	Toney	24–16	2.20
1918	3rd	68–60	.531	15.5	Mathewson Groh	Roush	.333	Roush	5	Eller	16–12	2.36
1919	1st	96–44	.686	+9.0	Moran	Roush	.321*	Groh	5	Sallee	21–7	2.06
1920	3rd	82–71	.536	10.5	Moran	Roush	.339	Roush Daubert	4 4	Ring	17–16	3.23
1921	6th	70–83	.458	24.0	Moran	Roush	.352	Roush	4	Rixey	19–18	2.78
1922	2nd	86–68	.558	7.0	Moran	Harper	.340	Daubert	12	Rixey	25*–13	3.53
1923	2nd	91–63	.591	4.5	Moran	Roush	.351	Hargrave	10	Luque	27*–8	1.93*
1924	4th	83–70	.542	10.0	Hendricks	Roush	.348	four with 4 each	8	Mays	20–9	3.15
1925	3rd	80–73	.523	15.0	Hendricks	Roush	.339	Roush Smith	8	Rixey	21–11	2.88
1926	2nd	87–67	.565	2.0	Hendricks	Hargrave	.353*	Roush	7	Donohue	20*–14	3.37
1927	5th	75–78	.490	18.5	Hendricks	Hargrave	.308	Walker	6	Lucas	18–11	3.38
1928	5th	78–74	.513	16.0	Hendricks	Allen	.305	Picinich	7	Rixey	19–18	3.43
1929	7th	66–88	.429	33.0	Hendricks	Walker	.313	Walker	7	Lucas	19–12	3.60
1930	7th	59–95	.383	33.0	Howley	Heilmann	.333	Heilmann	19	Lucas	14–16	5.38
1931	8th	58–96	.377	43.0	Howley	Stripp	.324	Cullop	8	Lucas	14–13	3.59
1932	8th	60–94	.390	30.0	Howley	Herman	.326	Herman	16	Lucas	13–17	2.94
1933	8th	58–94	.382	33.0	Bush	Hafey	.303	Bottomley	13	Lucas	10–16	3.40
1934	8th	52–99	.344	42.0	O'Farrell Shotton Dressen	Pool	.327	Hafey	18	Derringer	15–21	3.59

Year	Pos.	Record	Pct.	GB	Manager	Player	BA	Player	HR	Player	W-L	ERA
1935	6th	68–85	.444	31.5	Dressen	Lombardi	.343	Goodman	12	Derringer	22–13	3.51
1936	5th	74–80	.481	18.0	Dressen	Lombardi	.333	Goodman	17	Derringer	19–19	4.02
1937	8th	56–98	.364	40.0	Dressen	Lombardi	.334	Kampouris	17	Grissom	12–17	3.26
					Wallace							
1938	4th	82–68	.547	6.0	McKechnie	Lombardi	.342*	Goodman	30	Derringer	21–14	2.93
1939	1st	97–57	.630	+4.5	McKechnie	McCormick	.332	Lombardi	20	Walters	27*–11	2.29*
1940	1st	100–53	.654	+12.0	McKechnie	Lombardi	.319	McCormick	19	Walters	22*–10	2.48*
1941	3rd	88–66	.571	12.0	McKechnie	McCormick	.269	McCormick	17	Riddle	19–4	2.24*
1942	4th	76–76	.500	29.0	McKechnie	McCormick	.277	McCormick	13	Walters	15–14	2.66
										Starr	15–13	2.67
1943	2nd	87–67	.565	18.0	McKechnie	McCormick	.303	Tipton	9	Riddle	21–11	2.63
1944	3rd	89–65	.578	16.0	McKechnie	McCormick	.305	McCormick	20	Walters	23*–8	2.40
1945	7th	61–93	.396	37.0	McKechnie	Libke	.283	Miller	13	Walters	10–10	2.68
1946	6th	67–87	.435	30.0	McKechnie	Hatton	.271	Hatton	14	Beggs	12–10	2.32
1947	5th	73–81	.474	21.0	Neun	Galan	.314	Miller	19	Blackwell	22*–8	2.47
1948	7th	64–89	.418	27.0	Neun	Adams	.298	Sauer	35	Vander Meer	17–14	3.41
1949	7th	62–92	.403	35.0	Walters	Kluszewski	.309	Cooper	16	Raffensberger	18–17	3.39
1950	6th	66–87	.431	24.5	Sewell	Kluszewski	.307	Kluszewski	25	Blackwell	17–15	2.97
1951	6th	68–86	.442	28.5	Sewell	Wyrostek	.311	Ryan	16	Blackwell	16–15	3.45
1952	6th	69–85	.448	27.5	Sewell	Kluszewski	.320	Kluszewski	16	Raffensberger	17–13	2.81
					Brucker							
					Hornsby							
1953	6th	68–86	.442	37.0	Hornsby	Kluszewski	.316	Kluszewski	40	Baczewski	11–4	3.45
					Mills							
1954	5th	74–80	.481	23.0	Tebbetts	Kluszewski	.326	Kluszewski	49*	Nuxhall	12–5	3.89
1955	5th	75–79	.487	23.5	Tebbetts	Kluszewski	.314	Kluszewski	47	Nuxhall	17–12	3.47
1956	3rd	91–63	.591	2.0	Tebbetts	Kluszewski	.302	Robinson	38	Lawrence	19–10	3.99
1957	4th	80–74	.519	15.0	Tebbetts	Robinson	.322	Crowe	31	Lawrence	16–13	3.52

Year	Pos.	Record	Pct.	GB	Manager	Player	BA	Player	HR	Player	W-L	ERA
1958	4th	76–78	.494	16.0	Tebbetts Dykes	Temple	.306	Robinson	31	Purkey	17–11	3.60
1959	5th	74–80	.481	13.0	Smith Hutchinson	Pinson	.316	Robinson	36	Newcombe	13–8	3.16
1960	6th	67–87	.435	28.0	Hutchinson	Robinson	.297	Robinson	31	Purkey	17–11	3.60
1961	1st	93–61	.604	+4.0	Hutchinson	Pinson	.343	Robinson	37	Jay	21*–10	3.53
1962	3rd	98–64	.605	3.5	Hutchinson	Robinson	.342	Robinson	39	Purkey	23–5	2.81
1963	5th	86–76	.531	13.0	Hutchinson	Pinson	.313	Pinson	22	Maloney	23–7	2.77
1964	2nd	92–70	.568	1.0	Hutchinson	Robinson	.306	Robinson	29	O'Toole	17–7	2.66
1965	4th	89–73	.549	8.0	Sisler	Rose	.312	Robinson	33	Ellis	22–10	3.79
1966	7th	76–84	.475	18.0	Heffner Bristol	Rose	.313	Johnson	24	Maloney	16–8	2.80
1967	4th	87–75	.537	14.5	Bristol	Rose	.301	Perez	26	Pappas	16–13	3.35
1968	4th	83–79	.512	14.0	Bristol	Rose	.335*	May	22	Maloney	16–10	3.61
1969	3rd**	89–73	.549	4.0	Bristol	Rose	.348*	May	38	Merritt	17–9	4.37
1970	1st	102–60	.628	+14.5	Anderson	Perez	.317	Bench	45*	Merritt	20–12	4.08
1971	4th	79–83	.488	11.0	Anderson	Rose	.304	May	39	Gullett	16–6	2.64
1972	1st	95–59	.617	+10.5	Anderson	Rose	.307	Bench	40*	Nolan	15–5	1.99
1973	1st	99–63	.611	+3.5	Anderson	Rose	.338*	Perez	27	Billingham	19–10	3.04
1974	2nd	98–64	.605	4.0	Anderson	Morgan	.293	Bench	33	Billingham	19–11	3.95
1975	1st	108–54	.667	+20.0	Anderson	Morgan	.327	Bench	28	Gullett	15–4	2.42
1976	1st	102–60	.630	+10.0	Anderson	Griffey	.336	Foster	29	Nolan	15–9	3.46
1977	2nd	88–74	.543	10.0	Anderson	Foster	.320	Foster	52*	Seaver	14–3	2.34
1978	2nd	92–69	.571	2.5	Anderson	Rose	.302	Foster	40*	Seaver	16–14	2.87
1979	1st	90–71	.559	+1.5	McNamara	Knight	.318	Foster	30	Seaver	16–6	3.14
1980	3rd	89–73	.549	3.5	McNamara	Collins	.303	Foster	25	Pastore	13–7	3.26
1981	2nd	35–21	.625	0.5	McNamara	Griffey	.311	Foster	22	Seaver	14*–2	2.55
	2nd	31–21	.596	1.5								
1981**1st+		66–42	.611	+4.0								

Year	Pos.	Record	Pct.	GB	Manager	Player	BA	Player	HR	Player	W-L	ERA
1982	6th	61–101	.377	28.0	McNamara Nixon	Cedeño	.289	Driessen	17	Soto	14–13	2.79
1983	6th	74–88	.457	17.0	Nixon	Oester	.264	Redus	17	Soto	17–13	2.70
1984	5th	70–92	.432	22.0	Rapp Rose	Parker	.285	Parker	16	Soto	18–7	3.53
1985	2nd	89–72	.553	5.5	Rose	Parker	.312	Parker	34	Browning	20–9	3.55
1986	2nd	86–76	.531	10.0	Rose	Bell	.278	Parker	31	Gullickson	15–12	3.38
1987	2nd	84–78	.519	6.0	Rose	Davis	.293	Davis	37	Gullickson	10–11	4.85
1988	2nd	87–74	.540	7.0	Rose	Larkin	.296	Davis	26	Jackson	23–8	2.73
1989	5th	75–87	.463	17.0	Rose Helms	Davis	.281	Davis	34	Browning	15–12	3.39
1990	1st	91–71	.562	+5.0	Piniella	Larkin	.301	Sabo	25	Browning	15–9	3.80
1991	5th	74–88	.457	20.0	Piniella	Morris	.318	O'Neill	28	Rijo	15–6	2.51
1992	2nd	90–72	.556	8.0	Piniella	Roberts	.323	O'Neill	14	Rijo	15–10	2.56

*Led National League
**National League West (first season of divisional play).
***Split Season Totals (Players' Union Strike).
+Did not qualify for League Championship Series under split-season playoff format.

All-Time Reds Career and Season Records

Career Batting Leaders (1901–1992)

Games Played	Pete Rose	2,722
At Bats	Pete Rose	10,934
Runs Scored	Pete Rose	1,741
Hits	Pete Rose	3,358
Batting Average (300 or more games)	Cy Seymour	.333
Doubles	Pete Rose	601
Triples	Edd Roush	153
Home Runs	Johnny Bench	389
Extra Base Hits	Pete Rose	868
Runs Batted In	Johnny Bench	1,376
Stolen Bases	Joe Morgan	406
Total Bases	Pete Rose	4,645

Career Pitching Leaders (1901–1992)

Innings Pitched	Eppa Rixey	2,890
Earned Run Average (1000-plus innings)	Bob Ewing	2.37
Wins	Eppa Rixey	179
Strikeouts	Jim Maloney	1,592
Walks	Johnny Vander Meer	1,072
Games	Pedro Borbon	531
Shutouts	Bucky Walters	32
Saves	John Franco	148
Games Started	Eppa Rixey	356
Complete Games	Noodles Hahn	207

Single-Season Batting Records (1901–1992)

Batting Average (350 ABs)	Cy Seymour	.377	1905
At Bats	Pete Rose	680	1973
Home Runs	George Foster	52	1977
Runs Batted In	George Foster	149	1977
Hits	Pete Rose	230	1973
Runs	Frank Robinson	134	1962
Singles	Pete Rose	181	1973
Doubles	Frank Robinson	51	1962
	Pete Rose	51	1978
Triples	Sam Crawford	23	1902
Slugging Percentage	Ted Kluszewski	.642	1954
Extra Base Hits	Frank Robinson	92	1962
Stolen Bases	Bob Bescher	81	1911
Pinch Hits	Jerry Lynch	19	1960, 1961
Strikeouts	Lee May	142	1969
Walks	Joe Morgan	132	1975
Total Bases	George Foster	388	1977
Hitting Streak	Pete Rose	44	1978
Hit By Pitch	Frank Robinson	20	1956
Sacrifice Bunts	Roy McMillan	31	1954
Sacrifice Flies	Johnny Temple	13	1959

All-Time Reds Career and Season Records *(continued)*

Single-Season Pitching Records (1901–1992)

ERA (150 Innings)	Fred Toney	1.75	1915
Wins	Dolf Luque	27	1923
	Bucky Walters	27	1939
Losses	Paul Derringer	25	1933
Winning Pct. (10 decisions)	Tom Seaver	.875	1981
		(14–2)	
Winning Pct. (20 victories)	Bob Purkey	.821	1962
		(23–5)	
Strikeouts	Mario Soto	274	1982
Walks	Johnny Vander Meer	162	1943
Saves	John Franco	39	1988
Games	Wayne Granger	90	1969
Complete Games	Noodles Hahn	41	1901
Games Started	Noodles Hahn	42	1901
Shutouts	Jack Billingham	7	1973
	Rod Eller	7	1919
	Fred Toney	7	1917
	Jake Weimer	7	1906
Innings Pitched	Noodles Hahn	375	1901
Home Runs Allowed	Tom Browning	36	1988
Consecutive Games Won	Ewell Blackwell	16	1947
Consecutive Games Lost	Si Johnson	12	1933
	Peter Schneider	12	1914
	Henry Thielman	12	1902
Hit Batsmen	Jake Weimer	23	1907
Wild Pitches	Jim Maloney	19	1963, 1965

5
Houston Colt .45s-
Houston Astros
From Showbiz to Serious
Baseball Business
JOHN M. CARROLL

On the afternoon of April 10, 1962 more than 25,000 Houston fans witnessed the first official major league baseball game played in the Bayou City. The following day Houston *Post* sportswriter Clark Nealon wrote that "Little Bobby Shantz and Ramon Mejias etched their names deep into a monument for Houston baseball Tuesday afternoon at Colt Stadium . . . Shantz, the last classic ballplayer to be developed by legendary Connie Mack, pitched a masterful five-hitter and Mejias, a compact Cuban, blasted a pair of three-run home runs as the Colts beat the Chicago Cubs, 11–2, before 25,271 paying fans." Nealon went on to note that "Thus did the Colts at least for a day match the tremendous effort that finally brought major league ball to Houston, Texas, and the South for the first time" (Ray, 1980, 283). After the Colt .45s completed a three-game sweep of the Cubs, Houston *Post* columnist Morris Frank "could be heard in the press box chanting: 'Break up the Colts' " (Nealon, et al., 1985, 43)!

Few Houston sportswriters noted during that opening series that major league baseball in the Bayou City of Houston began amid a circus-like atmosphere which would be part and parcel of the Colt .45/Astros baseball franchise for much of its history. The man responsible for this was Judge Roy Hofheinz, who by the early 1960s had gained control of the Houston Sports Association (HSA) which was largely responsible for bringing a major league team to Houston. Hofheinz decked out Colt Stadium, a temporary structure to be used while awaiting the building of a domed stadium, in a fabulous manner. Patrons were met in the parking lot by "car directors," dressed in gaudy 10-gallon hats, blue handkerchiefs, and white overalls, who guided them to sections of the asphalt designated "Wyatt Earp Territory" and "Matt Dillon Territory." Inside the park fans saw pennants of every color and heard recorded pre-game music. Turnstile attendants wore 1880-type baseball caps, blue and white blazers, and bright orange trousers. The seats, rather than baseball's traditional dull green, were divided into four price ranges by color: chartreuse, turquoise, burnt orange, and flamingo. A corps of 150 usherettes, known as the Triggerettes and selected for their looks, wore baseball-style outfits in gaudy colors. In addition to the recorded music, fans could enjoy a Dixieland band which paraded through the aisles. Upstairs, wealthier patrons who belonged to the Fast Draw Club, roughly patterned on *Gunsmoke's* Long Branch Saloon, could sample the cuisine which included son-of-a-gun stew, bragging beans, and Fast Draw salad. The New York *Daily News* reported that Colt Stadium "is the damndest you ever saw," proclaiming "its atmosphere is a blend of Disneyland and the old wild west that made the Houston Park the talk of the majors" (Ray, 1980, 283–84).

Despite all the glitter and showbiz which Hofheinz provided for fans in 1962, Houstonians were no strangers to solid and more traditional baseball. The Bayou City had had a team in the more-than-respectable Texas League from its founding in 1888 until the Houston Buffs, as they were most frequently called, moved to the American Association in 1959. Old-time local fans had seen Tris Speaker win a batting title for Houston in 1907, and had witnessed the play of future major league standouts Dizzy Dean, Howie Pollet, Ducky Medwick, and Pepper Martin after the Buffs became associated with the St. Louis Cardinals in the 1920s. Houston's Buffalo Stadium, erected in 1928, was considered at the time the "finest minor league plant" in the United States (O'Neal, 1987, 260). Despite winning 16 Texas League pennants over the years, fan interest in minor league baseball in Houston, as in many other cities, began to wane by the late 1950s.

The first sustained campaign to bring a major league baseball franchise to Houston began with George Kirksey, a public relations man and sports enthusiast. After failing to entice St. Louis Cardinal owner, Fred Saigh, to sell his franchise to a Houston group in 1952, Kirksey joined forces with William A. Kirkland, a banker, and Craig Cullinan, the son of a prominent Texas oil man, in 1957 to establish what would be called the Houston Sports Association. Over the next several years the three businessmen met frequently with major league owners making their case for a big-league franchise for Houston and its 2.1 million residents. Like other promoters, the Houston trio was informed by the owners to "get a stadium and we will talk to you about a team" (Nealon, et al., 1985, 13). In 1958 the Houston businessmen were delighted when Harris County approved a bond issue for $20,000,000 to construct a stadium at a site yet to be determined. With the move of the Brooklyn and New York National League franchises to the West Coast in 1957, the HSA was optimistic about obtaining a franchise for Houston in the near future.

But despite the major league franchise shifts and the encouraging events in Houston, members of the HSA were frustrated in their efforts to either purchase or transfer a big-league team to Houston. In 1959 the HSA joined forces with other frustrated promoters in non-major league cities to organize a third major league, the Continental League. Led by New York attorney William Shea, Continental League representatives mounted a political attack in Congress against the existing major league's reserve clause and its immunity from antitrust statutes. Shaken by the assault on their privileged status, National and American League owners began to seriously consider expansion in order to short circuit the fledgling Continental League. Meanwhile, Cullinan, who was anticipating Houston's entrance into the new league, began looking for a "clean-up hitter" within HSA who could "commit substantial sums of money when and if the new league gained official sanction to begin play" (Nealon, et al., 1985, 23).

R. E. "Bob" Short, a wealthy oil man, emerged as a leading financial force behind HSA's efforts to bring a major league team to Houston. It was through Short that Judge Roy Hofheinz, a flamboyant and controversial former Harris County judge and mayor of Houston, began to play a large role in the affairs of the HSA. Short and Hofheinz were business partners, and the judge was extremely knowledgeable about public land use and the building of municipal facilities. Kirksey and Cullinan willingly accepted the judge's assistance, and Hofheinz took charge of matters pertaining to the building of a stadium. Hofheinz entered the campaign to bring a major league franchise to Houston late, but he would quickly emerge as a dominant force.

As the Houston Sports Association organized its resources in preparation for fielding a team in the Continental League, political events in Washington dramatically changed the focus of HSA's strategy. On June 28, 1960 Senate Bill 3483, the Kefauver bill, which provided that major league baseball be subject to existing antitrust laws, barely failed to gain passage in the upper chamber by a margin of four votes. Alarmed by the slim margin of defeat and the obvious threat posed by the Continental League, major league owners scheduled a meeting of their expansion committee with Continental League representatives set for early August 1960 in Chicago. After some posturing by both sides, the expansion committee agreed to add two new teams to each major league by 1962 with Continental League cities given preference. On the eve of the final game of the 1960 World Series in which Bill Mazeroski's ninth-inning home run gave the Pittsburgh Pirates a dramatic victory over the New York Yankees, the

National League announced the awarding of expansion franchises to both Houston and New York. The Continental League was quickly dissolved, and it was disclosed that the two new teams would begin championship play starting with the 1962 season.

The HSA cleared the way for its control of the Houston franchise when it purchased the Houston Buffs in early 1961. Veteran baseball man Gabe Paul was brought in as general manager of the team, and he brought with him from Cincinnati an able group of assistants. Paul hired Harry Craft to pilot the Buffs in their final minor league season, and Craft would be retained as manager of the Colt .45s when that name was selected for the Houston big-league team. With the new franchise safely under the control of the HSA, attention turned to the building of a new permanent stadium. Judge Hofheinz took the lead in selling the idea of a domed, air conditioned stadium to the National League and to Houston voters because additional public money would be needed for its construction. He also became an active force in running the baseball operations of Houston's two minor league teams which competed in 1961. Paul and Hofheinz apparently clashed because Paul abruptly resigned as general manager in late April 1961. He was replaced by another baseball veteran, Paul Richards, who managed Baltimore in 1961, and joined the Colts after the season.

In what Richards described as "the biggest fraud since the Black Sox!" Houston picked 23 players of questionable talent from other National League clubs for $1,750,000 (Nealon, et al., 1985, 42–43). Richards selected a blend of young and veteran players, and supplemented that talent with some skillful trades and free agent signings, including "bonus babies" Rusty Staub and Dave Giusti. Playing at hastily constructed Colt Stadium on the site where the domed stadium was to be constructed, the 1962 Colt .45s surprised the National League by finishing eighth, ahead of the expansion Mets and the Cubs. Partly due to Hofheinz's elaborate decor and promotions, the team drew more than 924,000 fans to the small park. The ballclub was weak hitting, but boasted two 10-game winners during its first season, Dick Farrell and Bob Bruce. Roman Mejias was the only consistent hitter, leading the Colts in 10 offensive categories. Right from that first season relatively weak hitting and stronger pitching became trademarks of the Houston franchise.

During the next two seasons the Colts failed to make much progress, and dropped in the standings to ninth place with identical records of 66–96 in 1963 and 1964, a notch ahead of the hapless Mets. Dick Farrell managed 14 wins in 1963 and Bob Bruce won 15 the following year, in which Hal Woodeshick recorded 22 saves. The highlights of the two seasons, however, were no-hitters by Don Nottebart in 1963 and Ken Johnson in 1964. Johnson was the victim of a sluggish Colt offense and lost his game, 1–0. Despite Richards' acquisition of some veteran name players (Nellie Fox, Bob Turley, and Don Larsen) to bolster interest in the team, attendance fell off perceptively in 1963–64 to just over 700,000 for each season. The main problem was Colt Stadium, nicknamed "Mosquito Heaven." According to Philip J. Lowry, it was home of the largest and peskiest mosquitoes in major league history. The park was regularly sprayed by the grounds crew between the innings (Lowry, 1986, 53). Toward the end of the 1964 season Richards fired Craft as manager and replaced him with Luman Harris as the team looked forward to its move to the new domed stadium being built adjacent to Colt Stadium. The relocation to the new facility in 1965 soon to be nicknamed the Astrodome, a new name for the team, the Astros, and the arrival of some promising new talent—Rusty Staub, Joe Morgan, and Jimmy Wynn—made Richards and Hofheinz optimistic about the future.

The idea of a domed, air conditioned stadium may not have originated with Judge Hofheinz, but once he was smitten with the idea he made it his own and relentlessly guided the project until the Harris County Domed Stadium or Astrodome was a reality. According to Texas folklore the idea for the Astrodome was based on a "valarium" or awning-type cooling device used at the Roman Colosseum and operated by slaves to protect emperors and patricians from the hot sun. Judge Hofheinz was supposedly impressed with the idea and determined to bring such comfort to Houston baseball fans on a grander scale. After numerous delays caused by inadequate funding, architectural problems, and labor disputes, which the judge and his associates ably surmounted, the domed stadium was completed on a 260 acre site on South Main Street in early 1965. As the stadium neared completion, Hofheinz maintained that "it will antiquate every other structure of this type in the world. It will be an Eiffel Tower in its field." When the Astrodome opened in the spring, Houstonians boasted that it was the "Eighth Wonder of the World" (Reidenbaugh, 1986, 250–53).

Spectacular in every conceivable way, the Houston Astrodome occupied nine and a half acres and rose 208 feet above the playing surface. It had the largest dugouts in the major leagues (120 feet), the longest and largest scoreboard with a half-acre of information surface, and an air conditioned system capable of producing 6,600 tons of cooling. In addition, the Astrodome had the brightest lighting in the majors, a closed-circuit television system, the first cushioned seating decked out in extravagant colors, and "bomb sight" pictures of the playing field made possible by a retractable gondola stationed over the center of the field. Affluent patrons, as was the custom in ancient Rome, could view the game from choice seating high above the field in 53 specially built skyboxes. But Hofheinz was also concerned about the comfort of all fans. He provided 53 spaces for wheelchairs on the mezzanine, 30 for the blind who could hear the game on radio, and a completely equipped first aid area with a doctor and registered nurses.

When the first intersquad games were played in the Astrodome in April 1965, it became apparent that the glare of the sun coming through the Plexiglas roof would make normal daytime play difficult for fielders attempting to track fly balls. Hofheinz had the roof painted to solve that problem, but soon discovered that the natural grass would not grow because of insufficient sunlight. In 1966 the Monsanto Company developed an artificial surface, AstroTurf, which was laid down during the course of the year. The first exhibition game was played in the Astrodome on April 9, 1965. Houston defeated the Yankees 2–1 on that gala evening which attracted 47,876 fans, including President and Mrs. Johnson. Yankee slugger Mickey Mantle registered the first hit in the Astrodome and later in the game recorded the first home run. During a five-game exhibition series the Astros drew 188,000 fans and netted over $500,000 in revenue. A few days later the Astros opposed Philadelphia in the first official game. Richie Allen spoiled Opening Day for the Astros with a two-run third-inning homer, the first, official round-tripper in the Dome, which gave the Phillies a 2–0 victory.

The 1965 season was a financial success with 2,151,470 fans turning out to see the Astros and the Dome, but there was little improvement in the team. Despite a solid season from Joe Morgan (163 hits and 100 runs scored) and encouraging performances from Staub and Wynn, the Astros finished in ninth place, one game behind their 1964 pace. At the end of the season Hofheinz fired Luman Harris and Paul Richards, and made Grady Hatton field manager. The next three seasons brought little improvement before Hatton gave way to Harry Walker in June 1968. Houston finished ninth twice and 10th during 1966–68. Jimmy Wynn emerged as an offensive star with 37 home runs and 107 RBIs in 1967 and Rusty Staub managed 182 hits and a .333 average the same year, but the team lacked consistent offense and solid all-around pitching. Don Wilson threw another Astro no-hitter in 1967 and struck out 18 batters in one game the following season. The Astros' largest crowd, 50,908, watched Sandy Koufax pitch in the Dome in 1966 while a smaller gathering saw Houston defeat the Mets 1–0 in a 24-inning contest in 1968. But, all in all, the quality of play was distinctly inferior to the carnival-like atmosphere of the Astrodome.

Always the showman and promoter, Hofheinz tried to provide the entertainment that his teams failed to deliver. After AstroTurf was installed, a space-suited grounds crew vacuumed the infield at mid-game. A ragtime band played between innings and the huge scoreboard became the center of attention for many fans. As Paul Burka recalled, "Houston fans docilely became conditioned to respond not to the game but to the scoreboard's message center. When it showed a pair of applauding hands, they clapped rhythmically. When it tooted a bugle call they yelled, 'Charge!' When it flashed the word 'noise' they screamed in tongues." For Burka, the low point came with a promotion known as a "foamer," which was designed to draw fans who had become less numerous after the 1965 season. When an Astro hit a home run while an orange light on the scoreboard was lit, patrons were entitled to a free beer. According to Burka, "It was a safe offer" (Burka, 1980, 160). The diversions were usually welcomed because play on the field was often erratic and bizarre. In 1965 Hal Woodeshick had a runner picked off first base, but his first baseman was napping and let the throw bounce off his stomach. Undaunted, Woodeshick tried the same maneuver on the next play with the same result. Jim Bouton recalled that when he joined the Astros in 1969 "they had a very weird outfield, a demented pitching staff and a totally insane third baseman." Utility infielder Julio Gotay, Bouton remembered, had his cheese sandwich fall out of his back pocket while sliding into second base (Bouton, 1989, 15). A few years later Astro pitcher Joaquin Andujar took himself out of a game in which he was leading because of jock itch. Aghast by such antics, some Houston fans seemed to prefer the scoreboard and other manifestations of Hofheinz's hucksterism.

During the National League's first season of divisional play in 1969, Manager Harry "The Hat" Walker kept the Astros in contention for most of the season, and recorded Houston's best-ever record of 81–81. As late as September 10 the Astros were only two games behind the division leader, but managed only six wins in their last 22 games. Still, the season provided some encouragement for the future. Larry Dierker posted a 20–11 record to become Houston's first 20-game winner. Don Wilson won 16 games including a no-hitter, and posted a club record 235 strikeouts. Reliever Fred Gladding saved 22 games for a strong Houston pitching staff. The offense was weaker, but Wynn, Denis Menke, and Doug Rader provided some occasional muscle. Joe Morgan added speed by tying a club record of 49 stolen bases. In their first respectable season, the Astros finished at .500, 12 games behind in the hotly contested Western Division race.

During the next two seasons the Astros showed considerable promise, but failed to play winning baseball as they slipped to four games below .500 in both 1970 and 1971. The arrival of rookie Cesar Cedeño in 1970, however, lifted the spirits of Astro fans as the Dominican native showed speed and some power as he batted .310 during his first campaign. Wynn, Rader, Menke, and Jesus Alou (acquired from

Montreal) provided more offense than usual for the Astros, and Joe Morgan continued to play a steady second base. The pitching staff struggled in 1970–71 with only Dierker, Wilson, and Jack Billingham (acquired from Montreal) showing any consistency. But with young and promising arms on the staff, such as Ken Forsch and Tom Griffin, and the development of Cedeño, who some experts were touting as a future all-star center fielder, many Astro fans expected a brighter future.

After the 1971 season Hofheinz and his general manager, H. B. "Spec" Richardson, cast about for a deal that might bring the right additional player personnel to Houston in order to win a divisional championship. Richardson had long been the judge's right-hand man in running the franchise and was known by HSA employees as the "hatchet man" (Ray, 1980, 520). From the early days of the Houston franchise, Richardson made a number of trades and deals which had weakened the team. The authors of *The Baseball Hall of Shame 2* have concluded that "nearly every major deal Richardson made backfired. He traded away enough talent to fill an All-Star lineup in return for stumblebums who didn't even belong on the farm team" (Nash and Zullo, 1986, 97). While this might be a slight exaggeration, by 1971 Richardson had managed to deal away future all-stars Mike Cuellar, Dave Giusti, Rusty Staub, Mike Marshall, and John Mayberry for players of considerably lesser ability. He traded John Mayberry to Kansas City, for example, in exchange for Jim York and Lance Clemons. A month before the Mayberry trade, in November 1971, Richardson made a blockbuster deal with Cincinnati which Houston fans will not soon forget. He swapped future Hall-of-Famer Joe Morgan, Denis Menke, Jack Billingham, Cesar Geronimo, and Ed Armbrister for Lee May, Tommy Helms, and Jimmy Stewart. The former players proved to be the missing ingredients which Cincinnati Manager Sparky Anderson needed to put together the "Big Red Machine" of the 1970s.

The long-range implications of this disastrous trade were not immediately apparent to Houston fans as the Astros got off to the best start in franchise history in 1972. Almost halfway through the campaign, Houston stood 13 games above .500 and tied for first place in the National League Western Division. From that point on the Astros could not keep pace with the powerful Cincinnati nine and finished in second place, 10½ games behind the Reds. Still, Houston posted a record of 84–69, which was by far its best-ever slate. Cesar Cedeño led an uncharacteristically potent offense which paced the league in scoring. The 21-year-old Astro center fielder batted .320, with 39 doubles, eight triples, and stole a club record 55 bases, and appeared to be emerging as one of the game's top players. He was ably assisted by Lee May, who contributed 29 home runs and 98 RBIs, and Jimmy Wynn, Doug Rader, and Bob Watson, all of whom batted in more than 85 runners. The Houston pitching staff hurled 14 shutouts and was once again paced by Larry Dierker and Don Wilson who both posted 15 victories. In August, after the Reds opened a sizable lead on Houston, Richardson fired Harry Walker and replaced him with veteran National League field boss, Leo Durocher, who finished the season with a 16–15 mark.

Under the once fiery but now sometimes somnolent Durocher, the Astros remained in the 1973 Western Division race until early July before they slipped well behind the eventual champion Reds. Cedeño had another fine year with a .320 batting average, 25 home runs, and 56 stolen bases. Bob Watson and Lee May also contributed power and consistency to another potent Astro offensive attack. The pitching staff was not up to 1972 standards, however, mainly because Larry Dierker spent most of the season on the disabled list with a sore shoulder and Don Wilson suffered through a hard luck 11–16 campaign. Dave Roberts, acquired from San Diego in 1971 in one of Richardson's better deals, kept Houston competitive with a 17–11 record and a 2.86 earned run average. The Astros finished fourth with a respectable 82–80 record, but trailed league-leading Cincinnati by 17 games. At the end of the season Durocher retired and Richardson hired Preston Gomez to replace him.

During the off-season Richardson made two more trades which were unpopular with the fans and proved to further weaken the team. He dealt Jimmy Wynn, the celebrated "Toy Cannon" and Houston's all-time home run leader, to Los Angeles for pitcher Claude Osteen. The Toy Cannon's best years were behind him, but he was a veritable institution in Houston and sorely missed by the fans. When Osteen failed to live up to expectations and was dealt to St. Louis during the summer, the Astro faithful became increasingly annoyed with Trader Spec. Richardson also peddled Jerry Reuss to Pittsburgh for much-needed catching help in Milt May. May had a respectable season in 1974, but never proved as valuable as Reuss would have been in building Houston into a contender. The steady Astro catcher was dealt to Detroit in 1975.

On the field Gomez could keep the Astros in contention only until mid-May when the team slipped badly. Houston managed to finish with a .500 record, but trailed the league champion Dodgers by 21 games. Cedeño had another outstanding season as did right fielder Greg Gross, who posted a .314 batting average in his rookie season. The Houston pitching staff struggled once more, however, as Don Wilson and Dave Roberts finished with losing records. Larry Dierker made a modest comeback with a 11–10 record and Tom Griffin led the staff with 14 victories. One of the highlights in an otherwise dreary campaign was Phillie Mike Schmidt's mammoth blast in the Astrodome which hit an overhead speaker in fair territory and dropped into short left field for a single. Where the blast might have landed had it not hit the obstruction (which was later removed) is anybody's guess. The discontent with the team's play and Richardson's wheeling and dealing was registered by the fans, as only a little over a million paid their way into the Astrodome, the fewest since the club had moved to the new stadium.

The 1975 season was preceded by a tragedy which proved to be a portent. Astro pitcher Don Wilson, who had been one of the anchors of the Houston staff for many years, was asphyxiated in his garage by carbon monoxide fumes. Stunned by the tragic event, the Astros never got out of the starting blocks. By the end of April Houston was in sixth place and already seven and a half games behind the leader. As the season progressed the Astros' troubles mounted and they finished the season with a 64–97 slate, and a colossal 43½ games behind the eventual world champion Cincinnati Reds. It was the Astros' worst performance in franchise history. What grated on some Houston fans as much as the losing season was that Joe Morgan, who Richardson had shipped off to Cincinnati, tore up the National League on his way to the first of two consecutive MVP seasons. Meanwhile in Houston, his replacement, Tommy Helms, batted .207 during 132 games in 1975. Astro fans expressed their displeasure with the team and its management by staying away from the Astrodome in droves. For the first time since 1964 Houston drew under one million customers. The only bright spot in an otherwise dismal campaign was the emergence of James Rodney "J. R." Richard, a six-foot-eight, raw-boned Louisiana right-hander, as one of the most feared pitchers in the National League. Although he recorded only a 12–10 record, mainly because of his league-leading 138 walks, Richard managed to strike out 176 batters with a near 100 miles-per-hour fastball and a sharp breaking slider which he threw at only a slightly slower speed.

In early August 1975, with the team more than 30 games under .500, Judge Hofheinz fired his longtime friend and general manager, Spec Richardson, and replaced him with Talbot M. "Tal" Smith. Smith was originally brought to Houston by Gabe Paul and had worked as his administrative assistant. When Paul left, Smith continued to work under Richardson for 13 years before joining the New York Yankee organization in 1973. Within two weeks of being named general manager, Smith began his rebuilding effort by firing Gomez, and hiring Bill Virdon, who had previously served as field boss for the Yankees and Pirates. Virdon was able to put a stop to the bleeding as he piloted the team to a 23–17 record during the remainder of the season.

Although Tal Smith is generally given credit for the revival of the Astros from the depths of despair in 1975 to the emergence of a pennant-contending team by the end of the decade, some of the pieces for the resurgence were already in place when he took the reins as general manager in 1975. Bob Forsch, J. R. Richard, and Joe Niekro (whom Richardson had purchased from Atlanta before he left) would form the basis of a strong pitching staff. Cedeño, Jose Cruz, Bob Watson, and Enos Cabell provided the nucleus of a more-than-respectable offensive attack. Smith, however, seemed to understand more fully than Richardson that for the Astros to contend in the powerful N.L. Western Division the team had to be built around pitching, defense, and speed. For reasons that nobody fully understood, the ball did not carry well in the Astrodome. Time and again, sluggers saw their drives die in the spacious power alleys and fall into outfielders' mitts. Smith was determined to take advantage of this situation by emphasizing strong pitching and defense. He also had the wisdom to appoint Virdon as manager. As one of the former premier defensive outfielders in the National League, Virdon shared Smith's belief in constructing a team around pitching and defense, and was patient enough to slowly assemble and nurture the right blend of talent.

Before the 1976 season began Joaquin Andujar and Joe Sambito were brought up from the Astro farm system to bolster the pitching staff, and Smith acquired utility infielder Art Howe from Pittsburgh in exchange for Tommy Helms. The Astros rebounded during the bicentennial year and finished just two games under .500. Although the team did not seriously contend after the beginning of June, there were a number of encouraging developments. J. R. Richard finished strongly and managed to post 20 wins against 15 losses, making him Houston's second 20-game winner. In the process, he logged 291 innings and struck out 214 batters. Rookie Joaquin Andujar, although often erratic, pitched four shutout games. On offense Cedeño, Watson, and Cruz turned in strong performances. On July 16 a record of sorts was established at the Astrodome when a game was cancelled because of rain. After 10 inches of rain fell in Houston, a game with the Cubs was postponed because umpires, fans, and stadium personnel were unable to get to the Astrodome. Despite the impressive improvement over 1975, Astro fans were still skeptical about the rebuilding effort as fewer than 900,000 turned out for 82 home games.

During the next two seasons it was not clear that Tal Smith was in the process of putting together a pennant-contending team. The 1977 Astros improved their record over the previous year by one game and notched Houston's first .500 season since 1974. The arrival of speedy rookie outfielder Terry Puhl, who batted .301 in 60 games, was a definite plus, as was the emergence of Jose Cruz as a solid all-around player. The pitching staff was still anchored by Richard, Niekro, and Andujar, who posted impressive if not spectacular seasons. Smith and Virdon, however, had still not found the missing links to make the Astros into a contender. The 1978 season appeared to be a step backward instead of forward for the Astros as the team struggled to a fifth-place finish, 14 games under the .500 mark. The only bright spots in an otherwise disappointing season were J. R. Richard's 18–11 mark with 303 strikeouts, a National League record for a righthanded pitcher, and Enos Cabell's solid offensive performance. But during the season and through the winter, Smith began to make a series of deals which would transform the club into a winner.

Before the 1978 campaign began Smith had acquired Vern Ruhle, a sore-arm pitcher of some promise, who had been released by Detroit. During the season Houston also traded catcher Joe Ferguson to the Dodgers in exchange for Rafael Landestoy and Jeff Leonard. Smith bolstered the catching position in the fall when he got Alan Ashby from Toronto for three expendable players. The following month Smith filled a weakness at shortstop by trading a former Astro number one draft pick, pitcher Floyd Bannister, to Seattle for Craig Reynolds. It was not apparent at the time that the combination of these moves had substantially improved the team, but the performance of the Astros the following season would show that Smith had, indeed, made some very shrewd maneuvers.

By the beginning of the 1979 season Judge Hofheinz relinquished control of the HSA, and the Ford Credit Corporation acquired a majority interest in the HSA and the Astros. The Astros broke out of the gate in April as though they were being pursued by a pack of creditors. Relying mainly on strong pitching, defense, and speed, Houston led the National League West by four games at the end of April. With Richard, Niekro, and Andujar providing sound starting pitching and Joe Sambito closing many tight games, the Astros clung to a one-game lead at the end of May. Then using team speed (five Astros stole more than 20 bases) to come from behind in close contests, Houston opened a 10-game lead over the Cincinnati Reds on the Fourth of July. The powerful Cincinnati team whittled away the Astro lead during July and August as Andujar went into a tailspin and Richard pitched inconsistently. On September 9, the Astros still maintained a half-game lead as they opened a crucial two-game series at Cincinnati's Riverfront Stadium. In two closely contested contests, the Reds bested the Astros and held on to a slim lead to the end. When Houston beat Los Angeles on the final day of the season (Niekro's 21st victory), the Astros trailed the Western Division Champion Reds by a game and a half.

Despite the mid-season slump, Smith and Virdon were well pleased with the Astros' performance in 1979. The team drew just short of one million fans and had played exciting baseball all season long. Smith, however, was not content to sit tight with the pennant contender he had assembled. In November he signed free-agent strikeout artist Nolan Ryan and several months later reacquired second baseman Joe Morgan in the same manner. The Astros seemed primed to capture their first league championship in franchise history. During the early months of the 1980 season the Astros edged in and out of first place in the hotly contested Western Division race. Houston's strong pitching staff was bolstered not only by Ryan, but Vern Ruhle, who had recovered from nagging arm problems, and rookie Dave Smith, who aided Sambito with sparkling relief work. Jose Cruz and Cesar Cedeño provided some much-needed offense and were assisted by the consistent hitting of Art Howe and Terry Puhl. Veteran Joe Morgan assumed the role of the team's inspirational leader. When the Astros reeled off 14 wins in 16 games in early June to take a three-game lead, Houston fans rejoiced.

The Astros entered the All-Star break in a first-place tie with the Los Angeles Dodgers, but the team already appeared to be in trouble. J. R. Richard, who had compiled a 10–4 record, complained of a dead arm and an assortment of other ailments and went to the sidelines. Some sportswriters and players accused Richard of malingering, and suggested that "his ailments could be miraculously cured by a contract equal to Nolan Ryan's" (Burka, 1980, 264). Many would regret such statements when Richard suffered a stroke while working out at the Astrodome on July 30. At the time, the Astros were in first place, a game and a half in front of the Dodgers. The team went into a brief slump and fell a game behind Los Angeles in mid-August, but J. R.'s absence seemed to take the pressure off the Astros, who were no longer considered the favorite in the race. Sparked by the pitching of Nolan Ryan, the Astros won 10 straight games during the dog days of August. For the next month Houston slipped in and out of first place. On October 2 the Astros completed a three-game sweep of Atlanta which put Houston three games ahead of the Dodgers with but three games to be played against Los Angeles on the West Coast. Houston's first divisional championship seemed within grasp.

Fighting tooth and nail, the Dodgers' experienced lineup managed to frustrate Houston's hopes. In a series of one-run games, dramatic Dodger home runs left the Astros stunned and desperate after the series ended. Joe Ferguson's 10th inning blast won the first game, and homers by Steve Garvey and Ron Cey on the following days found the Astros and Dodgers in a dead heat after the final regular season game was completed. Many Astro fans expected the worst as the two teams prepared for a one-game playoff on October 6. To the delight of the Bayou City faithful, Joe Niekro pitched a masterful game (his 20th victory) and Astro bats came alive as Houston dominated the Dodgers, 7–1. Houston, at last, had a division-winning team.

The Astros entered the best-of-five National League Championship Series against the powerful Philadelphia Phillies. In Game One in Philadelphia, Steve Carlton mowed down the Astros and got a late-inning home run from Greg Luzinski to preserve the victory. For the first six innings in Game Two, the Astros played like a team waiting to get beat as they trailed, 2–1. In the seventh, Bill Virdon inexplicably allowed starting pitcher Nolan Ryan to lead off the inning. Ryan managed a walk and later came plodding home on a double by Terry Puhl to tie the score. From that point on the series became one of the most memorable in N.L. history, featuring four straight extra-inning games. The Astros evened the series by pushing across four 10-inning runs, and held off a Phillie comeback for a 7–4 victory. When the series moved to Houston, Joe Niekro baffled Phillie batters with his flutter balls for 10 innings, and Dave Smith preserved the shutout into the 11th. In the bottom of that frame, Joe Morgan led off with a blast to right-center and ran gimpy-legged to third base. Several batters later Rafael Landestoy, Morgan's replacement, raced home with the winning run on a sacrifice fly.

The fourth game had enough drama and controversy for an entire season. In the third inning, the game was held up for 20 minutes as umpires tried to decide if Astro pitcher Vern Ruhle had trapped or caught a low line drive by a Phillie batter. If he had done the former it was one out, while a catch would result in a triple play. The umpires somehow decided to split the difference, awarding the Astros two putouts. By the sixth inning Houston led 2–0 when outfielder Gary Woods appeared to widen the lead by one as he tagged up and scored on a fly ball. Having noted the umpires' emphasis on legalisms, the Phillies appealed the play and Woods was declared guilty of leaving third too soon. The run would be sorely missed as Philadelphia rallied for three runs in the eighth to take a 3–2 lead. When the Astros pushed across a run in the bottom of the ninth, the score was only tied and the game moved into an extra frame. Two Phillie runs in the 10th were enough to even the series.

The final game of the series had all the ups and downs of the previous four. In the sixth inning the Astros managed to tie the game at two, and hoped that their superior pitching would prevail. When the Astros scored two runs in the bottom of the seventh, Houston fans were jubilant as they realized that only six outs separated their team from a first-ever World Series appearance. Nolan Ryan was on the mound in the eighth and all seemed well. But Ryan was wild and

Virdon went to his seasoned bullpen. The relievers were not up to the task as Philadelphia scored five runs in the frame. In keeping with the series motif, Houston responded with two runs of its own in the bottom of the inning, sending the fourth straight contest into overtime. But in the 10th, the Astro magic ended as the Phillies pushed across an easy run and the Astros failed to respond. Despite the disappointment, Houston took pride in the team's great achievement and looked forward to a bright future.

Two weeks after the season Houston fans and sportswriters were shocked when John McMullen, the leading partner of a syndicate which had gained control of the HSA, fired Astro General Manager Tal Smith and replaced him with Al Rosen. As Smith was generally regarded as one of the shrewdest front-office men in baseball, Houstonians were bewildered by the move. Rosen, however, quickly pacified some of the Astro faithful by signing free agent Don Sutton to bolster an already strong Houston pitching staff. The 1981 strike-shortened season began badly for the Astros as they struggled with a 28–29 record at the end of the first half of the truncated season. In the second half Houston rebounded brilliantly by posting a 33–20 division-leading record. Sutton, Ryan, and Bob Knepper, acquired from San Francisco for Enos Cabell, paced the pitching staff. Art Howe put together a club-record 23-game hitting streak, and Jose Cruz provided a much-needed spark on offense. On September 26 in Los Angeles, Ryan pitched his record-breaking fifth no-hitter to go along with a league-leading 1.69 earned run average. As a result of the mid-season strike, the Astros would face Los Angeles (winner of the first half) in a best-of-five series to determine who would represent the Western Division in the N.L. Championship Series.

In Game One at the Astrodome, Nolan Ryan and Fernando Valenzuela had locked up in a classic pitching duel before Alan Ashby smashed Dodger reliever Dave Stewart's fastball for a two-run ninth-inning homer and a 3–1 victory for the Astros. Joe Niekro and Jerry Reuss hooked up in another pitchers' duel in the second contest, which was scoreless at the end of regulation play. The Astros scored a run in the 11th on Denny Walling's pinch-hit single to give Houston a 1–0 win and a commanding lead in the series. When the series moved to Los Angeles, however, Astro bats went silent. Houston managed just 12 hits and two runs in 27 innings while dropping three straight games, 6–1, 2–1, and 4–0. It rankled some Houston fans that former Astro, Jerry Reuss, another who Spec Richardson had sent packing, notched the closing shutout which ended Houston's post-season play.

The Astros slumped badly in 1982. Bob Knepper and Vern Ruhle suffered through losing seasons, and veteran pitchers Sutton, Ryan, and Niekro could not take up the slack. Ray Knight, whom Rosen had acquired by trading Cesar Cedeño to Cincinnati, had a strong offensive year, but the batting slump which started in Los Angeles the previous fall continued for many Astro batters. In early August, with the Astros 13½ games out of first place, Rosen fired Virdon and replaced him with Bob Lillis. At the end of the month Rosen sent Don Sutton to Milwaukee in exchange for Kevin Bass, Frank DiPino, and Mike Madden. Despite the shuffling, Houston finished in fifth place with a 77–85 record. The team rebounded the following season under Lillis with a late-season rally which put them in third place, six games behind Los Angeles at the wire. The Astros were never in the pennant chase, however, and fans showed their displeasure with McMullen and the team by staying away from the Astrodome. Jose Cruz and Ray Knight hit consistently and Dickie Thon, whom Rosen had acquired from California, appeared to be emerging as a premier N.L. shortstop before a serious beaning late in the season threatened his career.

The 1984 Astros were a respectable, but uninspiring team. The trio of Ryan, Niekro, and Knepper delivered adequate pitching, but the Astros had little offense except for the bat of Jose Cruz. Houston players hit only 79 home runs for the season, with only 18 being hit in the Astrodome. The Astros managed to finish in a tie for second place, but were two games under .500 and 12 games behind league-leading San Diego. Concerned about the lack of offense and dwindling gate receipts, Astro management moved the fences in at the Astrodome at the end of the season in the hope of sparking fan interest. The Astros did no better in the standing or at the gate in 1985, but did hit a few more home runs. Glenn Davis clouted 20 round-trippers in his rookie year, and two young players, Kevin Bass and Bill Doran, showed signs of making a substantial contribution. Although the pitching staff had an off year, one big surprise was Mike Scott, whom Rosen had acquired from the Mets in 1982. The powerful righthander, who featured a split-fingered fastball, put together an 18–8 record.

John McMullen was not pleased with the team's performance or the dwindling attendance which had slipped to under 1.2 million in 1985. Before the 1985 campaign was over, he replaced Rosen with Dick Wagner as general manager. Wagner fired Lillis at the end of the season and installed Hal Lanier as his field boss. Still, there was much discontent in Houston as the 1986 season began. McMullen announced that if attendance did not pick up he was considering moving the team to Washington, D.C. Some disgruntled Houston sportswriters were predicting as many as 100 losses for the Astros. But, surprisingly, 1986 was one of those storybook years in the end that every franchise dreams about. The Astros broke out of the gate fast and never slowed down. By late July they had established a three-game lead, and increased it to an eventual 10-game bulge over second-place Cincinnati. Mike Scott, who would win the N.L. Most Valuable Player award with 18 victories, 306 strikeouts, and a 2.22 earned run average, clinched the division title with a no-hitter against San Francisco on September 25. Glenn Davis, who finished second in the MVP voting, smashed 31 home runs and drove in 101 runs. Kevin Bass joined the 20/20 club with 20 home runs and 22 stolen bases. In all, the Astros finished 30 games over .500 for the best year in franchise history.

The Astros opposed the heavily favored New York Mets in a best of seven 1986 Championship Series which began in Houston. More than 44,000 watched as Mike Scott outdueled Dwight Gooden in Game One, and shut down the powerful Mets. Fittingly, Glenn Davis's second-inning homer provided the 1–0 margin of victory. New York evened the series the next day when Bob Ojeda beat Nolan Ryan, 5–1. Houston suffered a heartbreaking defeat at Shea Stadium in Game Three as Lenny Dykstra hit a two-run home run in the last of the ninth which made the Mets 6–5 winners. But the Astros bounced back on the strength of Scott's three-hitter to even the series. Before the Mets scored a run off Scott in the eighth inning of Game Four, the former Met pitcher had shut out New York for 16 consecutive innings. Mets Manager Davey Johnson complained to umpires that Scott was doctoring the ball, but all to no avail. If the Astros could win one of the next two games, the Mets would have to face Scott in Game Seven in Houston.

Houston appeared ready to do that in Game Five as Ryan struck out 12 Mets in nine innings and allowed only two hits. Unfortunately, one of those hits was a Darryl Strawberry home run. Houston, however, could manage to push across only one run on nine hits against Gooden. Astro fans will not soon forget an apparent miscall by umpire Fred Brocklander in the second inning which deprived Houston of a run, and possibly a victory in regulation play. The game was finally decided in favor of the Mets in the 12th on a Gary Carter single. That set up the memorable sixth game in Houston, which one New York sportswriter has called "the greatest game ever played" (Izenberg, 1987).

The Astros broke on top early with three first inning runs, and appeared to have the game sewed up as Bob Knepper carried a shutout into the ninth. But the Mets scored three times to tie the contest and send it into extra innings. The teams remained tied at three until the 14th when New York pushed across a run. Houston got even again in the bottom of the frame as Billy Hatcher homered off the foul pole in left field. Two innings later, the Mets exploded for three runs to take a seemingly safe 7–4 lead. But the Astros rallied for two of their own before Jesse Orosco retired the final Houston batter. Astro fans were drained and exhausted after the nearly five-hour contest. Most believed that if Houston had won Game Six, Mike Scott would have clinched the Astros' first National League pennant the next day. The Houston faithful were confident, however, that the Astros would contend for years to come.

The Astros have contended in the N.L. Western Division for the past three years, but have experienced a collapse in mid-to-late August during each campaign. In 1987 the Astros' August/September breakdown left them 10 games under .500 and 14 games behind the front-running Giants. The following year Houston remained in the thick of the pennant race until late August before the team slumped in the final month of the campaign with an 11–18 record and a fifth-place finish. After the 1988 season General Manager Bill Wood, who had replaced Wagner, fired Hal Lanier and hired the popular former Astro infielder Art Howe as field manager. John McMullen came under heavy criticism from Houston fans again in 1988 when he refused to meet contract demands set by Nolan Ryan. Soon after his talks broke down with Astro officials, Ryan, one of the most popular players in Houston history, signed a lucrative contract with the Texas Rangers. Astro fans were in a surly mood when the 1989 campaign began, and became even more critical of McMullen when he released well-liked catcher Alan Ashby. Houston team officials further stirred controversy when they banned signs blatantly critical of McMullen from the Astrodome. Some of the hostile feelings abated when the Astros put together a 10-game winning streak in late May and early June which put them back in the thick of the pennant chase. Under the even-handed guidance of skipper Art Howe, the Astros challenged the league-leading Giants until late August before another late-season slump put them out of serious contention.

And serious pennant contention was not something that Art Howe's Astros were likely to taste again for awhile once the digits on the calendar turned from 80's to 90's and his youth-filled ballclub as quickly transformed from budding contenders into predictable tailenders. The primary weaknesses were familiar ones in Astroland, a scarcity of both dependable pitching and any semblance of power hitting. No Houston hurler would win more than 11 games in the first three seasons of the new decade; no one in the lineup would smack 25 homers or hit .300. Yet Howe's men did make some news in 1992 by playing sound baseball over the second half of the campaign, despite a rare four-week roadtrip necessitated by a national political convention scheduled into the Astrodome. And the lowly Astros did launch a pennant rush in early September that brought them all the way back to .500 for the first time in the new decade and left them but a single game shy of a surprising third-place finish.

References

Bouton, Jim. 1989. "Revisiting the 'Ball Four' Astros." *The Sporting News* (August 21): 15.

Burka, Paul. 1980. "Houston Astros." *Texas Monthly* (December): 156–61, 264–71.

Izenberg, Jerry. 1987. *The Greatest Game Ever Played*. New York: Henry Holt and Company.

Lowry, Philip J. 1987. *Green Cathedrals*. Cooperstown, N.Y.: Society for American Baseball Research.

Nash, Bruce, and Allen Zullo, 1986. *The Baseball Hall of Shame 2*. New York: Pocket Books.

Nealon, Clark, Robert Nottebart, Stanley Siegel, and James Tinsley. 1985. "The Campaign for Major League Baseball in Houston." *The Houston Review: History and Culture of the Gulf Coast* (7): 2–46.

O'Neal, Bill, 1987. *The Texas League, 1888–1987: A Century of Baseball*. Austin, Tex.: Eakin Press.

Ray, Edgar W. 1980. *The Grand Huckster: Houston's Judge Roy Hofheinz, Genius of the Astrodome*. Memphis: Memphis State University Press.

Reidenbaugh, Lowell. 1986. *The Sporting News Selects Baseball's 50 Greatest Games*. St. Louis: The Sporting News Publishing Company.

Annotated Bibliography

Burka, Paul. "Houston Astros." *Texas Monthly* (December 1980): 156–61, 264–71.

A lively account of the 1980 Astros' drive for the N.L. Western Division pennant. Burka gives some good insight into the history of the team, and how he and other Houston fans suffered through the early years. The article praises General Manager Tal Smith and criticizes John McMullen for firing Smith after the 1980 season. Burka recalls some of Judge Hofheinz's early promotions and gives an excellent account of the Astros-Phillies championship series.

Izenberg, Jerry. *The Greatest Game Ever Played*. New York: Henry Holt and Company, 1987. 163 pp.

Nationally syndicated sportswriter Izenberg gives a detailed account of the 1986 National League Championship Series. One might question his assertion that Game Six between the Mets and Astros was "the greatest game ever played," but he does justice to one of the most dramatic post-season clashes. The book is weighed toward the Mets in terms of coverage.

Nealon, Clark, Robert Nottebart, Stanley Siegel, and James Tinsley. "The Campaign for Major League Baseball in Houston." *The Houston Review: History and Culture of the Gulf Coast* 7 (1985): 2–46.

A comprehensive and scholarly examination of the struggle to bring major league baseball to Houston. The authors undertook painstaking research to produce an accurate and even-handed account. In their interpretation, Judge Hofheinz receives less credit than a number of lesser-known figures who were instrumental in making Houston a big-league city.

Ray, Edgar W. *The Grand Huckster: Houston's Judge Roy Hofheinz, Genius of the Astrodome.* Memphis: Memphis State University Press, 1980. 530 pp.

Ray's biography of Hofheinz is mainly based on interviews and newspaper sources. It is not particularly strong on coverage of the Colt .45s/Astros. The author is overly sympathetic to the judge, and gives him too much credit for bringing major league baseball to Houston. Ray is mainly uncritical of Hofheinz's interference with Astro baseball operations. The sections on the beginning of the Colt .45s and the opening of the Astrodome contain good portraits of Hofheinz as the grand huckster.

Ryan, Nolan, and Harvey Frommer. *Throwing Heat: The Autobiography of Nolan Ryan.* New York: Doubleday, 1988. 236 pp.

An "as told to" account of Ryan's memorable career including five no-hit games. The book contains about 80 pages on Ryan's years in Houston. *Throwing Heat* is a rather bland narrative, based on numerous interviews, and Ryan seldom mentions a discouraging word about anyone.

Year-by-Year Standings and Season Summaries

Year	Pos.	Record	Pct.	GB	Manager	Player	BA	Player	HR	Player	W-L	ERA
1962	8th	64–96	.400	36.5	Craft	Mejias	.286	Mejias	24	Bruce	10–9	4.06
1963	9th	66–96	.407	33.0	Craft	Spangler	.281	Bateman	10	Farrell	14–13	3.02
1964	9th	66–96	.407	27.0	Craft / Harris	Aspromonte	.280	Bond	20	Bruce	15–9	2.76
1965	9th	65–97	.401	32.0	Harris	Wynn	.275	Wynn	22	Farrell	11–11	2.60
1966	8th	72–90	.444	23.0	Hatton	Jackson	.292	Wynn	18	Giusti	15–14	4.20
1967	9th	69–93	.426	32.5	Hatton	Staub	.333	Wynn	37	Cuellar	16–11	3.03
1968	10th	72–90	.444	25.0	Hatton / Walker	Staub	.291	Wynn	26	Wilson	13–16	3.28
1969*	5th	81–81	.500	12.0	Walker	Menke	.269	Wynn	33	Dierker	20–13	2.33
1970	T4th	79–83	.488	23.0	Walker	Menke	.304	Wynn	27	Dierker	16–12	3.87
1971	T4th	79–83	.488	11.0	Walker	Cedeño	.264	Morgan	13	Wilson	16–10	2.45
1972	2nd	84–69	.549	10.5	Walker / Durocher	Cedeño	.320	L. May	29	Dierker	15–8	3.40
1973	4th	82–80	.506	17.0	Durocher	Cedeño	.320	L. May	28	Roberts	17–11	2.85
1974	4th	81–81	.500	21.0	Gomez	Gross	.314	Cedeño	26	Griffin	14–10	3.54
1975	6th	64–97	.398	43.5	Gomez / Virdon	Watson	.324	Johnson	20	Dierker	14–16	4.00
1976	3rd	80–82	.494	22.0	Virdon	Watson	.313	Cedeño	18	Richard	20–15	2.75
1977	3rd	81–81	.500	17.0	Virdon	Cruz	.299	Watson	22	Richard	18–12	2.97
1978	5th	74–88	.457	21.0	Virdon	Cruz	.315	Watson	14	Richard	18–11	3.11
1979	2nd	89–73	.549	1.5	Virdon	Cruz	.289	Cruz	9	Niekro	21–11	3.00
1980	1st	93–70	.571	+1.0	Virdon	Cedeño	.309	Puhl	13	Niekro	20–12	3.55

Year	Pos.	Record	Pct.	GB	Manager	Player	BA	Plyer	HR	Player	W-L	ERA
1981	3rd	28–29	.491	8.0	Virdon	Howe	.296	Cruz	13	Ryan	11–5	1.69
	1st	33–20	.623	+1.5								
1981**	3rd	61–49	.555	6.0								
1982	5th	77–85	.475	12.0	Virdon Lillis	Knight	.294	Garner	13	Niekro	17–12	2.47
1983	3rd	85–77	.525	6.0	Lillis	Cruz	.318	Thon	20	Niekro	15–14	3.48
1984	T2nd	80–82	.494	12.0	Lillis	Cruz	.312	Cruz	12	Niekro	16–12	3.04
1985	T3rd	83–79	.512	12.0	Lillis	Cruz	.300	Davis	20	Scott	18–8	3.29
1986	1st	96–66	.593	+10.0	Lanier	Bass	.311	Davis	31	Scott	18–10	2.22
1987	3rd	76–86	.469	14.0	Lanier	Hatcher	.296	Davis	27	Scott	16–13	3.23
1988	5th	82–80	.513	12.5	Lanier	Ramirez	.276	Davis	30	Scott	14–8	2.92
1989	3rd	86–76	.531	6.0	Howe	Davis	.269	Davis	34	Scott	20–10	3.10
1990	4th(T)	75–87	.463	16.0	Howe	Biggio	.276	Stubbs	23	Darwin	11–4	2.21
1991	6th	65–97	.401	29.0	Howe	Biggio	.295	Bagwell	15	Portugal	10–12	4.49
1992	4th	81–81	.500	17.0	Howe	Caminiti	.294	Anthony	19	D. Jones	11–8	1.85

*Denotes beginning of divisional play.
**Split Season Totals (Players' Union Strike).

All-Time Houston Career and Season Records

Career Batting Leaders (1962–1992)

Games Played	Jose Cruz	1,870
At Bats	Jose Cruz	6,629
Runs Scored	Cesar Cedeño	890
Hits	Jose Cruz	1,937
Batting Average	Bob Watson	.297
Home Runs	Jimmy Wynn	223
Runs Batted In	Jose Cruz	942
Stolen Bases	Cesar Cedeño	487
Strikeouts	Jimmy Wynn	1,088

Career Pitching Leaders (1962–1992)

Innings Pitched	Larry Dierker	2,295
Earned Run Average	Joe Sambito	2.42
Wins	Joe Niekro	144
Losses	Larry Dierker	117
Strikeouts	Nolan Ryan	1,866
Walks	Joe Niekro	818
Games	Dave Smith	514
Shutouts	Larry Dierker	25
Saves	Dave Smith	176
Games Started	Larry Dierker	320
Complete Games	Larry Dierker	106
Hit Batsmen	Jack Billingham	31
Wild Pitches	Joe Niekro	118

Single-Season Batting Records (1962–1992)

Batting Average (502 ABs)	Rusty Staub	.333	1967
Home Runs	Jimmy Wynn	37	1967
Home Runs (lefthanded)	Jose Cruz	17	1977
Runs Batted In	Bob Watson	110	1977
Hits	Enos Cabell	195	1978
Singles	Sonny Jackson	160	1966
Doubles	Rusty Staub	44	1967
Triples	Roger Metzger	14	1973
Slugging Percentage	Cesar Cedeño	.537	1972
Extra Base Hits	Jimmy Wynn	69	1967
	Cesar Cedeño	69	1972
Sacrifices	Craig Reynolds	34	1979
Stolen Bases	Gerald Young	65	1988
Pinch Hits	Ken Boswell	20	1976
Strikeouts	Lee May	145	1972
Total Bases	Cesar Cedeño	300	1972
Hitting Streak	Art Howe	23	1981

All-Time Houston Career and Season Records *(continued*

Grand Slam Home Runs	Bob Aspromonte	2	1963
			1964
			1966
	Bob Watson	2	1970
	Lee May	2	1973
	Mark Bailey	2	1985
Hit by Pitch	Cesar Cedeño	11	1977
	Glenn Davis	11	1988

Single-Season Pitching Records (1962–1992)

ERA (150 innings)	Mike Cuellar	2.22	1966
	Mike Scott	2.22	1986
ERA (100 innings)	Nolan Ryan	1.69	1981
Wins	Joe Niekro	21	1979
Losses	Dick Farrell	20	1962
Winning Pct. (10 decisions)	Juan Agosto	.833	1988
Strikeouts	J. R. Richard	313	1979
Walks	J. R. Richard	151	1976
Saves	Doug Jones	36	1992
Games	Juan Agosto	82	1990
Complete Games	Larry Dierker	20	1969
Games Started	Jerry Reuss	40	1973
Shutouts	Dave Roberts	6	1973
Innings Pitched	Larry Dierker	305	1969
Home Runs Allowed	Larry Dierker	31	1970
Consecutive Games Won	Juan Agosto	10	1988
Wild Pitches	Larry Dierker	20	1968
	J. R. Richard	20	1975

(Photo courtesy National Baseball Library, Cooperstown, NY)

Jackie Robinson, Brooklyn Dodgers (1947–1956)

The Dodgers are the Daffiness Boys who bungled the basepaths of the 1930s; they are the glorious "Boys of Summer" who dominated the National League for a decade; they are the powerful swing of Duke Snider and the unmatched fastballing duo of Koufax and Drysdale; they are the flamboyant managerial style of Durocher and Lasorda and the stoic bench silence of Alston and Dressen.But above all else the Dodgers are the brave pioneering of Jackie Robinson and Branch Rickey, who together broke the noxious racial barriers of sport and made baseball a truly democratic All-Amerian national pastime.

(Photo courtesy National Baseball Library, Cooperstown, NY)

Ernie Banks, Chicago Cubs (1953–1971)

"Okay, Ernie, its a beautiful day for baseball . . . let's play two in the Friendly Confines!" For nearly twenty years the original "Mr. Cub" was Chicago baseball—season after season of colorful and exciting afternoon play without the bothersome distraction of a single pennant race, World Series, or anachronistic league championship series. For Cubs fans of the old school, Ernie Banks was the alpha and zeta of Cubs' baseball—before synthetic turf, artificial lighting in Wrigley Field, softball-style road jerseys, or the raspy hucksterism of Johnny-Come-Lately Harry Caray.

(Photo courtesy National Baseball Library, Cooperstown, NY)

Pete Rose, Cincinnati Reds (1963–1978, 1984–1986)
Somehow the thought of Pete Rose linked together with the 19th-century Red Stockings of Harry and George Wright seems to defy common sense logic and even fertile imagination, and yet there is something alluring about this wild prospect. Certainly there remains an unquestioned link between the rough-house knicker-clad pioneers who first launched baseball and the hard-nosed tradition-breaker of the 1990s who first imitated Cobb's rare hitting prowess, then also unwittingly replayed the sad saga of Shoeless Joe Jackson.

(Photo courtesy National Baseball Library, Cooperstown, NY)

Willie Mays, New York Giants-San Francisco Giants (1951–1972)

First it was Willie, then it was Mickey and the Duke. They ranked on the field as they did in the popular song title, for Mays was without peer among the game's center fielders. While only Aaron and Ruth hit more homers, neither played in a spacious and wind-blown park. No other star has received more ardent support as the game's most complete player. Mays had no match in hitting for average and power; he ran the bases with speed and intelligence; and he possessed one of baseball's greatest arms. No one ever donning spikes was a greater fan pleaser.

(Photo courtesy National Baseball Library, Cooperstown, NY)

Tom Seaver, New York Mets (1967–1977)

"Tom Terrific" was also labelled "The Franchise" by Mets fanatics on the late 1960s, and that he was in the summers that stretched between the Metropolitans' miracle pennants of 1969 and 1974. No statistic justifies this label more than the fact that during his ten years in the Big Apple he won a full 25% of the New Yorkers' total victories for that era. Seventeenth man to join the magic circle of 300-game winners, Seaver established a major league mark by striking out 200 or more hitters across ten seasons (since bettered by ageless Nolan Ryan), nine consecutively over a tenure with the upstart Miracle Mets.

(Photo courtesy National Baseball Library, Cooperstown, NY)

Robin Roberts, Philadelphia Phillies (1948–1961)

As much as any franchise, the Phillies are almost synonymous with second-division play. They have toiled through the decades in the anonymity of the league's basement. And for a decade on the heels of a rare 1950 Whiz Kid pennant, Robin Roberts himself toiled in obscurity as perhaps the best unknown righthander in baseball history—a six-straight-year 20-game winner with an anemic lineup behind him, a rare elastic-armed hurler who won over 200 games and lost that many as well, a Hall-of-Famer who paced the league in total innings-pitched five times.

(Photo courtesy National Baseball Library, Cooperstown, NY)

Roberto Clemente, Pittsburgh Pirates (1955–1972)

Simply put, he may have been the most exciting ballplayer who ever lived; the very sight of him tearing around the base paths, legging out extra base hits, was as thrilling an image as any moment culled from baseball's exciting history. His cannon-like throwing arm was unmatched anywhere in the game's long history. Only Jackie Robinson ran the bases this way, and perhaps only Willie Mays played outfield with quite the same flare. Latin America's first Hall-of-Famer was also its most dramatic and exciting diamond star.

(Photo courtesy National Baseball Library, Cooperstown, NY)

Dizzy Dean, St. Louis Cardinals (1930–1937)

For any fan who remembers real grass and daytime baseball, the Cardinals conjure up memories of reckless old-time baseball, gas-house daffiness, and baseball humor and color in unmatched abundance. The beginning and ending of such imagery was on Jerome "Dizzy" Dean, who just happened as well to be one of the finest natural pitchers and fiercest competitors of the early modern era. Here was the very archetype for baseball's legendary country-boy hurler of unlimited poteniial and unfilled promise.

6

Montreal Expos
Bizarre New Diamond Traditions
North of the Border

PETER C. BJARKMAN

The subject is baseball in French—or more properly, baseball in a French atmosphere. My first reaction was that it is revolting. But first reactions, conditioned to shock, are likely to be extreme . . . Irritating is what it is. Irritating as hell!
Art Hill, I Don't Care If I Never Come Back

The American League has the Texas Rangers to offer for down-right baseball silliness; the National League in turn has its own version of comic relief in the guise of the Montreal Expos.[1] From the beginning there has been something altogether outlandish and humorous at the very core of this first ballclub to represent the national pastime as it is played by our northern neighbor. It could be the uniforms; the red, white, and blue color scheme is certainly traditional enough, but the inexplicable script logo and tricolored beanie of a hat seem more appropriate to a TV episode of "The Bad News Bears" than to the staid business of ball playing in the big leagues.[2] Or perhaps it was the idea of roly-poly Rusty Staub being taken as a serious big-league slugging hero, demanding the same kind of reverence as Ernie Banks, Willie Mays, or Jimmie Foxx. Then again it may simply be Youppi—easily baseball's silliest mascot—a seeming refugee from Sesame Street and the only club mascot in modern memory to actually be ejected from the premises by a league umpire during the playing of a major league game.

Perhaps the colorful name and the associated image of Jose Alberto "Coco" Laboy contributed to the Expos' comic image; his unforgettable moniker coupled with his totally forgettable third base play made him a baseball monument etched in the style of such inexplicable immortals as Pumpsie Green, Ding-a-Ling Clay, Goober Zuber, Noodles Zupo, and Skeeter Scalzi. The Expos' two unprecedented ballparks have not helped their image either: one featured a swimming pool target within easy home run reach of right-field pull hitters, and the other was perhaps best described as something appropriate "to transport thousands of earth colonists to Alpha Centauri" (Hill, 1980, 145). Whatever the cause, the fact remains that it has been difficult to take the Montreal Expos very seriously, at least outside of Quebec.

This is not to say that National League baseball in Canada has been played without its share of exciting moments or memorable diamond heroes. For one thing, the Expos' single brief appearance in post-season play provided one of the most exciting climaxes in Senior Circuit history, at least since the introduction of that disturbing appendage to regular season play known as the National League Championship Series. No team has had a no-hitter thrown by a favored hometown hurler any earlier in its franchise history, or has had a pitcher throw two no-hitters any sooner than did Bill Stoneman in Montreal. And bizarre no-hit action seems to be a Montreal Expos specialty: an Expos pitcher (Stoneman again) provided the first big-league no-hitter ever tossed outside of the United States;[3] and Expos pitchers Dave Palmer and Pascual Perez hurled two of the last three rare truncated no-hit efforts lasting for less than a full nine-inning game. And no big-league game of recent memory has been more unusual or controversial than the Expos' 22-inning 1–0 loss to the Dodgers in Olympic Stadium on August 23, 1989—a single six-hour game filled with enough bizarre events (described later in the chapter) to fill an entire chapter of any franchise history.

The overall silliness which has surrounded the Montreal organization has not, however, overshadowed the careers of several Expos who rank among the game's most colorful and exciting players of the past two decades. Great hitters have included Al Oliver, a seven-time league all-star and Senior Circuit pacesetter in four batting departments (BA, hits, RBIs, doubles) during his one Montreal season in 1982, and Andre Dawson, an awesome slugger for a decade north of the border and still club record holder in seven career offensive categories (games, at-bats, hits, homers, doubles, RBIs, total bases). For blazing basepath speed and all-around fine play there is Tim Raines, owner of 585 career swipes and four-time National League stolen base champion. And several fine pitchers have also toiled in the tricolors of the Expos over the past two decades. Righthander Steve Rogers was one of the league's most durable starters of the early 1980s, most fortunately aggravating the league's hitters for 13 Expos seasons (with 158 wins plus a league ERA crown in 1982), if less fortunately alienating a large corps of his own teammates along the way with his haughty self-opinion and pompous self-designated nickname "Cy" (as in Young). New York Mets castoff Jeff Reardon also set new standards for relief pitchers with a major-league-best 41 saves in 1985 and a team-record 152 saves over five Montreal seasons. And Dennis Martinez, since coming to the Expos from Baltimore in 1987, has continued his climb up the ladder as one of the game's all-time great Latin American hurlers, now standing sixth among his Latino countrymen with 153 lifetime victories.

It is also true that for a brief few years at the outset of the present decade the Expos emerged as one of the most formidable ballclubs in the National League. Not only did Dick Williams' talented charges surprise by coming from seemingly "out of nowhere" to register 95 wins in 1979 and 90 more in 1980 (good for two second-place finishes and two straight seasons within two games or less of the division winner at the wire), but 1981 brought a first league playoff appearance and 1982–83 two additional strong campaigns in the league's third slot. By the outset of the 1982 baseball campaign the nation's pre-season baseball publications were unrestrained in their most lavish prognostications for the veteran Montreal ballclub painstakingly built by Dick Williams and his replacement Jim Fanning. "The Expos' starting lineup may be the strongest in baseball," intoned *Baseball Digest*. "Our neighbors to the north of the border will be in the post-season classic," projected *Ken Collier's Baseball Book*. "Nothing stands between Montreal and greatness," suggested popular *Washington Post* baseball analyst Thomas Boswell. And for those who doubted that a new National League dynasty was about to bud in baseball's only French-speaking capital, no lesser an authority than statistics guru Bill James pronounced a final glowing verdict: "The Expos are without a doubt the best team in baseball today" (all quotes from Turner, 1983, 34–35). That such enthusiasm about the Montreal Expos at decade's dawning proved to be a bit premature and more than a bit off the mark was, in retrospect, hardly enough to dull the enthusiasm of Expos fans little more than six seasons back.

The most exasperating aspect of the Expos throughout much of their first two decades—especially after such a promising emergence from the doldrums of typical expansion play only a few short seasons back—may be the unfriendly and inappropriate baseball surroundings in which they have been forced to perform for the past 13 seasons. Of course, it was not always this way, since for a few short summers Jarry Park provided one of the most pleasant ballparks in all North America. Parc Jarry was a single-decked structure with grandstands extending almost to the foul lines and several thousand inexpensive bleacher seats providing economical close-up views of the field of play. There wasn't an obstructed view (no poles) or distant corner anywhere in this most intimate of major league parks. Olympic Stadium, on the other hand, can best be described with the words of astute ballpark observer Art Hill as "awesome, gigantic and futuristic . . ." and filled up with "come-to-the-fair, greatest-show-on-earth, tell-ya-what-I'm-gonna-do hype and hoopla" hardly attuned to the traditional fan's enjoyment of big-league baseball (Hill, 1980, 146). While fans in cities like Cincinnati, St. Louis, or Pittsburgh have to put up with stadiums built almost exclusively with NFL football franchises in mind, Montreal ball fans suffer from a far different curse—the multi-purpose arena syndrome. Theirs is a structure built originally for track and field events at the 1976 Olympics; if a preferred seat in 1976 gave an excellent view of a baton handoff in the 400-meter relay, Expos fans are hardly ever in a position in 1990 for a close call at second or third base. And while front-row seats might have been right on top of the high-jump pit, they are now seemingly miles from the pitchers mound or from home plate.

And then there is the matter of the very appearance of this team, decked out in blue flannel road duds featuring a red-white-and-blue beanie that looks something like those tiny wearable umbrellas mounted on a leather headband. Charlie Finley's multi-colored softball-style uniforms never quite matched the Expos traditional uniforms for pure garishness, nor did some of the silly costumes the White Sox donned in recent years (not even the nineteenth-century knickers and flap collars which Bill Veeck tried in 1977, or the striped polyester of the 1982–86 ChiSox which rotund slugging outfielder Greg Luzinski once accurately described as looking most like a cereal box). It takes more than a professional look to perform like a respectable big-league team, but one has to wonder if it wouldn't help the Expos.

But ultimately the fault with the Montreal Expos is seemingly the same fault that has characterized a disturbingly lackluster Texas Rangers franchise residing in such ignominy in the Junior Circuit during these same two decades: the inability of a few expansion teams to break out of an early inept expansion era of franchise history, when victories and star performers are expected by fans and management alike to be altogether few, and thus colorful if sometimes inept play has to substitute regularly for the inherent thrill of a serious pennant race. It is the continued inability (somehow not found in Toronto or Kansas City but apparently endemic to Montreal and Arlington) to build up a young pool of talent down on the farms, make a few astute (perhaps even lucky) trades and free-agent acquisitions, obtain a talented manager or two or three, and thus become a legitimate league contender. And as with the Rangers, the truly exasperating thing about the Expos is that they seem to have had so many chances of late.

Canada Joins the Big Leagues with a Big Bang!

> *To be honest, the glacier hadn't completely receded. There were still five-foot snow banks behind the outfield fence, but they provided a fine vantage point from which to watch the action.*
>
> Dan Turner, The Expos Inside Out

The team that first represented Canadian interests in the world of major league baseball was remarkable enough simply for the long and seemingly unprecedented string of "firsts" it chalked up. This was the first big-league team to set foot on a field in Canada and thus the first to set up camp outside of the United States, a fact which would launch a whole string of "firsts" during the team's maiden game and in its first weeks. Yet this penchant for "firsts" stretches back well before the first pitch was actually thrown in Jarry Park in April 1969. On expansion draft day in October 1968, for example, the Expos would become the first team ever to select a native Latin American as their very first rostered player, naming Pittsburgh outfielder Manny Mota to the initial Canadian roster spot.[4] And what team can boast a no-hitter in its first month of existence? Or the first big-league homer on foreign soil? Or an inaugural road uniform that looked more like a barber pole than the sharp flannels of a professional baseball nine? Or, for that matter, the first rotund .280 hitter in baseball's long and glorious history to be lionized as a true national hero and even to be compared favorably in the hometown imagination with Ty Cobb and the immortal Babe Ruth?

But the most spectacular "first" in the eyes of veteran baseball watchers had to be the altogether unanticipated maiden franchise no-hit effort which occurred only three days after the history-making debut of major league play on Canadian soil. Some ballclubs have waited decades for such an event. (Canadian rival Toronto reached its 14th season before experiencing a hitless masterpiece by a member of the hometown mound staff.) Yet three-year veteran Bill Stoneman's no-hit effort of April 17, 1969, came in only his fifth big-league start— and in the ballclub's ninth outing ever, a mark for no-hit promptness most likely to stand forever in the annals of expansion baseball wonders. In baffling the Phillies 7–0 at Connie Mack Stadium before a sparse early-season turnout of 6,494 fans (many of whom had come to witness the return of ex-Phillies skipper Gene Mauch), Stoneman became the first and only hurler ever to toss a no-hitter for an expansion outfit during its debut season of play—in this case in its second week out of the gate. A further irony surrounding Stoneman's rare outing was the fact that the 25-year-old righthander was not even a scheduled game starter on the day of his brush with immortality, but had been substituted for veteran Jim "Mudcat" Grant who had fallen victim to a sore knee and had to be scratched at the last moment from Gene Mauch's pitching rotation. Thus Stoneman, who had never before thrown a complete game in the majors and had only once accomplished the feat in the minors, unexpectedly provided a rare masterpiece which remains one of the true highlight moments of Expos franchise history.

The Expos story of course begins months before Stoneman shocked the baseball world with his no-hit mastery. It begins with the business deals and back-room intrigues that were instrumental in landing a new major league franchise for a tradition-rich expansion city at the conclusion of baseball's unpredictable and unsettled decade of the sixties. Montreal had long sported a rich minor league heritage as home to a Brooklyn Dodgers' showcase farm team of the 1940s and 1950s; the Montreal Royals had once drawn 600,000 fans to Delorimier Downs (later known as Montreal Stadium and Hector Racine Stadium) and turned a profit of $332,000 in the 1949 International League season alone. And what baseball fan doesn't know that Jackie Robinson first broke modern baseball's odious color barrier while wearing the 1946 uniform of Montreal's proud Royals? Thus what may have been a rude shock to expansion hopefuls in cities like Buffalo, Dallas, and Milwaukee was anything but a surprise to Quebec partisans when National League President Warren Giles announced that dark horse Montreal would join San Diego as a new league franchise when league play opened for the 1969 season.

In reality, however, the joy which first greeted Giles' spring 1968 announcement almost proved to be as hollow and disappointing as the raw north winds blasting across the Canadian frontier during much of the period that the rest of the continent takes for gentle summer. Between the May announcement and the league's imposed August deadline, an initial $1.1 million payment had to be made on the $10 million franchise initiation fee; ownership had to be solidified; and a ballpark had to be found suitable for big-league play. Prospects were not bright for any of this to happen when multi-millionaire backer Jean Luis Levesque abandoned the effort and Seagram's magnate Charles Bronfman was left seemingly alone to work an overnight miracle. Mayor Jean Drapeau had often talked boldly of landing the 1976 Olympics and of building a state-of-the-art domed stadium, but such talk had never been translated into reality and the matter of an acceptable playing facility loomed as the greatest obstacle to Montreal's fulfillment of its big-league dreams. Tiny Parc Jarry—an amateur baseball facility with seating for only 2,000—seemed the only possibility for temporary quarters, and league president Giles was ultimately brought to Montreal in the company of Baseball Commissioner Bowie Kuhn in a last-ditch effort to convince baseball's top brass that Montreal could indeed provide an adequate playing site. A local amateur league game was in progress at the very hour of Giles' historic visit, and the apocryphal story has circulated for 20 years that the impressionable National League boss was immediately sold on Montreal when the sparse crowd on hand fortuitously recognized his presence with cries of "Le gran patron!" (Frommer, 1976, 169).

Possessing a new major league franchise in the late autumn of 1968 and having received league sanction to play in a revamped Jarry Park, the city fathers of Montreal now had to hastily adapt an outmoded arena into a site suitable for temporary major league play. At a formidable expense of slightly more than $4 million (Canadian), a nearly miraculous transformation was indeed wrought in a period of little more than four months, as 26,000 makeshift seats and 5,000 parking spaces were added to a facility which at mid-summer had looked more like a local sandlot field than a future showcase stadium for a parade of big-league stars. And once the work was well under way on a refurbished Jarry Park, veteran baseball executive John McHale was hired to run the baseball operation itself, with Jim Fanning installed at his side as club vice president. Racing against the fast-approaching deadline of the 1969 spring season, McHale took his first giant step by hiring Gene Mauch (late of the Philadelphia Phillies) as first team manager, and his second in hastily compiling scouting reports which would soon result in the first makeshift Expos roster during the fall expansion draft scheduled for October 14. It was that memorable draft day—as with any newborn expansion franchise—that would first provide flesh-and-blood names and faces of real big-league ballplayers for a once seemingly hopeless Montreal expansion baseball dream.[5]

The celebrated franchise opening game was one that would bring almost more than its justified share of anticipation for the sparse thrills and often-repeated disappointments to be laid before Canadian fans throughout the first season of expansion baseball in Montreal. The fitting opening day competition was to be the erstwhile laughing-stock New York Mets, who only seven summers earlier had lost an incredible 120 games, and yet who were now about to turn from pumpkins into royal coaches with their sudden transformation into "Miracle Mets" only a few short months down the road. Having won seven of their 13 spring contests, however, the yet-to-be-christened Montrealers were anything but awed by a New York team which had finished the previous campaign in ninth place (of ten National League teams) and only a single game up on the cellar-dwelling Astros. And just for that single glorious Opening Day contest of April 8, 1969, played in New York's Shea Stadium, it was the expansion Expos and not the veteran Metropolitans who looked like the true miracle team of the decade's last baseball season.

The final score would read 11–10, as the Montrealers battled back from a shaky start by Mudcat Grant to launch five doubles and three homers en route to a 12-hit attack that would dispatch Mets' starter Tom Seaver after five frames, then rudely greet relievers Cal Koonce and Al Jackson with six more markers in innings six, seven, and eight.

Rusty Staub belted the first circuit blow, rookie Coco Laboy surprised with the second, and—most incredible of all—relief hurler Dan McGinn contributed the third—the only such power display of McGinn's five-year big-league stay. Journeyman southpaw Don Shaw (a lifetime 13-game winner) was destined to achieve a special place in Canadian baseball history with the first recorded Expos pitching victory, yet only after an ample final-out assist from equally unheralded Carroll Sembera (winner of but three lifetime contests) who recorded the history-making save. "IT AIN'T FAIR!" shouted banner headlines in the next day's New York *Daily Mirror*, as the now-grizzled Mets fans tasted bitter defeat at the hands of baseball's newest expansion stepchild.

If the team's inaugural game was fittingly dramatic, it was no more so than the long-awaited home opener which unfolded six days later. The opponents this time were the St. Louis Cardinals, and unlike their Canadian archrivals in Toronto who would launch Canadian American League play with a wintry blizzard eight seasons later, the Expos were blessed on the afternoon of their home debut with balmy 65-degree weather to buoy the spirits of the first-day throng of 29,000 patrons. Yet if the weatherman was seemingly prepared for the first appearance of baseball in the nation better known for April ice and snow, the crew charged with hasty renovations to Jarry Park almost weren't. With scheduled ballpark improvements still far from complete, frenzied last minute preparations (including the installation of 6,000 folding chairs where box seats should have been) would delay the anticipated cry of "Play Ball!" for more than 15 minutes. Yet when baseball finally came, it was a glorious action-packed day indeed. The Expos would display a true expansion identity by making five errors and giving up seven runs within a single inning; later they would demonstrate rookie fearlessness as well by battling back to a hard-won 8–7 victory which was keyed by the offense of Mack Jones (who hit both a homer and a triple and drove home five runs) and Coco Laboy (who doubled and scored the winning marker). Displaying a special penchant for opening-game heroics, Dan McGinn was again a key figure as the winning hurler; and Rusty Staub and center-fielder Don Bosch joined Jones with noteworthy two-hit batting performances.

Yet for all these opening-day heroics, the first season of National League baseball in Montreal, once fully under way, was destined to provide a typical saga of painful expansion baseball blues. Using 42 players in all, the Expos won barely 50 games, lost well over 100—at one point dropping 20 ball games in a row—and finished at a distant 48 lengths behind the league pace-setters. And when the book was finally closed on the first season of revamped divisional play, the fledgling Expos had duplicated the record of their expansion partner, the San Diego Padres; yet the Montrealers could boast having out-drawn their new California rivals by better than two to one, with a credible home attendance of more than 1.2 million in baseball's tiniest park. The month-long losing streak was itself typical of first-year expansion play and even included an embarrassing (if unofficial) 5–3 exhibition pasting at the hands of their top farm club in Vancouver, two days before the taxing losing streak would end in Los Angeles. By the time the folly of a near-month of continuous losing was finally over on June 8 the fast-opening Montreal ballclub had dropped from just a notch below .500 to a coffin-slamming 13–37 ledger. It was indeed the true stuff of expansion baseball, a nightmare of futility already experienced in the venerable Polo Grounds (New York Mets) less than a decade earlier, and soon to be played out yet again in ancient Griffith Stadium (Washington Senators) and spanking new Arlington Stadium (Texas Rangers) in seasons that lay just around the corner.

In the end, however, the first summer of Montreal big-league baseball was truly a season-long "love-in" for Montreal fans and players alike. As veteran Expos chronicler Dan Turner has phrased it, "it was the best of times" (Turner, 1983, 18); and as Canadian baseball historian William Humber has reported, big-time baseball was at long last back in Canada after nearly a century's absence (having departed with the deathknell of London's Lord Tecumsehs, an International Association team way back in 1878):

> There were some unforgettable heroes in those early days. To lessen the sting of being hit by the pitcher, Ron Hunt stood in the way of balls tossed by the pitching machine in practice . . . The old Delormier Downs spirit was reincarnated in the open air of Jarry Park, led by (what was then an innovation) an organist . . . celebrants included the Jarry Park dancer, the peanut vendors, beer in the ballpark, and the public address announcer's dramatic introductions . . . John Bah-ka-BELL-ah gave this one player more local fame than anything he ever did upon the field . . . the team's uniforms which appear drearily conservative today were the sartorial talk of the league . . . the Expo cap became a national symbol (Humber, 1983, 134).

In gratitude to their loyal fans at season's end, Expos players initiated a yearly ritual that would soon come to underscore the special style of team, organization, and city alike: on the season's final day each player would be introduced to the adoring fans, tip his hat, leave the cherished uniform cap on a table at mid-field, then trot down the left-field line to the clubhouse. A special lottery drawing was then held for the cherished mementos of a departed summer's play.

If the Montreal Expos had enjoyed a most typical first expansion season, their sophomore campaign must be rated in hindsight as anything but duly typical. Never in the history of expansion franchises has any newly minted ballclub jumped so dramatically in on-field performance between its first and second summers. Never before or since has the National or American League seen anything like the 21-game improvement in the won-lost column or the 32-game jump in league standings that the still-wet-behind-the-ears Montreal contingent put together in 1970. Staub was again the batting hero with 30 dingers, Ron Fairly led the regulars with a respectable .288 BA, and shortstop Bobby Wine keyed a much-improved defense by exchanging his league-high standard in errors for a league-best in double plays. There was team offensive balance as well, as five starters (Fairly, Wine, Laboy, Staub, Bateman) and one reserve (Bailey) knocked in more than 50 runs apiece. The pitching hero was Carl Morton (18–11, 3.60 ERA), ably assisted by Steve Renko (13–11, 4.32 ERA) and reliever Claude Raymond (fourth in the league with 23 saves). It was again a last-place finish, of course, but this was last place with a difference! Fifth place was a mere half-game away at season's end, and fourth place was but three games (as opposed to last year's 35-game margin) from reach this time around.

Colorful Diamond Characters in Colorful Baseball Flannels

> *Never mind. Nobody's perfect. A great pool of talent has been accumulated, and someone should be saluted for accumulating it.*
>
> Dan Turner, The Expos Inside Out

Things looked exceptionally bright as the Montreal National League ballclub entered a new decade in just its third season of play. The 1970 season had been more than merely competitive; Gene Mauch's hustling charges had improved by a remarkable 21 games in the won-lost column over their maiden season and—while still anchored in last place—had surprisingly found themselves at season's end only 16 games off the pace of the front-running Pirates and a half-game behind the fifth-place Phillies. The Expos already featured a large stash of bright young stars: Rusty Staub had just pounded 30 roundtrippers while valuable utility man Bob Bailey had polled 28; 26-year-old Carl Morton had surprisingly proved one of the league's most successful righthanders with an 18–10 mark (3.60 ERA); Mack Jones at age 31 and with 36 homers in his first two Montreal seasons seemed capable of several more fine campaigns; Quebec native son Claude Raymond had ranked fourth best in the circuit with 23 saves and had just enjoyed a career season in his 10th full big-league campaign. Enthusiastic fans filled Jarry Park with their bodies and their souls as 1.4 million attended home games, an increase of more than 200,000 over the inaugural summer in Montreal. Montreal players, executives, and fans had plenty of reason for rampant optimism on the eve of the 1971 campaign: a mere 10-game improvement in the won-loss column for season number three might well be sufficient to provide the earliest first-division finish in expansion baseball history.

And if the Expos were not yet quite fully competitive in the early seasons of the 1970s, they were certainly a most colorful outfit each and every time they took to the diamond. This "color" started, of course, with the bright red-white-and-blue outfits which Expos players donned upon the field of play. In the words of one early local favorite, catcher John Bateman, the Expos looked something like an ABA basketball team, resplendent in their non-traditional tricolor beanies and matching barber-pole stretch-silk uniforms (Turner, 1983, 12). But bold fashion statement went far beyond the uniforms themselves. Rusty Staub, for one, cut a flamboyant image with his rotund figure, compact swing, and flaming red mane duly befitting his French-Canadian sobriquet as "La Grand Orange" ("The Great Orange One"). Staub has been described by one baseball historian as "never resembling an athlete so much as a 205-lb. Sherlock Holmes who'd taken an intense interest in the game of baseball . . . whose broad, curious world view attracted him to the study of history and gourmet cookery" (Shatzkin, 1990, 1,039). "He leads the league in idiosyncrasies," another Staub observer once remarked about the man who would eventually retire after 22 big-league seasons with 2,716 base hits, but who would never again during his baseball sojourn enjoy anything like the idolization which made him a Canadian national hero during those first three expansion seasons spent in Montreal. And in addition to Staub there was a colorful supporting cast as well: Coco Laboy, whose alliterative name and flamboyant on-field style were as renowned as his butcherous play at third base; Mack Jones, whose long-ball heroics earned instant folk-hero status after he slammed a first-ever round-tripper upon Canadian soil on April 14, 1969, and whose two grandslams later the same season immediately assured lasting immortality, with the left-field bleachers being rechristened "Jonesville" in his honor by the local patrons; Bill Stoneman, who captivated a nation with his no-hit pitching almost before locals could recite the full National League lineup from memory, and who was equally well-known as the easiest pitcher to strike out in big-league history (having fanned 53 times in 77 at-bats during his rookie 1969 season).

Much of the characteristic charm surrounding the young and exciting Expos team in those earliest seasons came, however, largely from the powerful personality of veteran manager Gene Mauch. By the date of his eventual retirement two full decades later Mauch would establish a nearly unmatched reputation for longevity, piloting more games (3,941) over more seasons (26) than any man in major league history save the venerable Connie Mack, the charismatic John McGraw, and the much-maligned Bucky Harris. Only Mack and Harris lost more games than Gene Mauch; and no other major league skipper would manage as long and yet never enjoy the sweet reward of a single World Series appearance. Mauch's reputation throughout his career was not so much that of a loser, however, as it was that of a leader blessed with the ability to turn struggling young clubs into serious league contenders seemingly overnight. Mauch's second season as an untried 36-year-old-field boss with the Phillies in 1961 resulted in a pathetic 47–107 ledger; yet the following summer he had his charges playing at .500 (81–80) for a remarkable 34-game turnaround. His second of seven seasons in Montreal also brought an improvement of over 20 games. And the veteran Mauch would work his magic once again in California in 1982, molding a 51-game-winner of the previous season into a 93-game-winning division title team. Mauch was also to be remembered as a sharp tactician (the most frequent complaint was that he overmanaged) and a quiet leader who displayed firm confidence in every man on his ballclub and played his entire roster more frequently than almost any other veteran manager in the game. "I play guys when I want to," Mauch remarked, "so they'll always be ready when I have to . . . I don't consider myself to be a motivator of players . . . I think it's an insult to a ballplayer to have to be motivated" (Shatzkin, 1990, 686).

The Expos of the early 1970s also enjoyed the benefit of playing in one of baseball's most colorful ballyards—Jarry Park. What is most often remembered about the cozy confines of Jarry Park (which supposedly seated only 28,000 fans, though often accommodated several thousand standees as well) is its cramped quarters (perhaps the very essence of its lasting charm), its rare historical distinction as the site of the first big-league games ever played outside of the United States, its precedent-setting and odd-sounding bilingual public address system, and the oddly situated public swimming pool, a frequent recipient of home run balls poked beyond the right-field fence. Jarry Park was a delightful single-deck structure with seats extending to the foul poles (both standing at 340 feet from home plate) and a gently sloped open bleacher section sweeping across left field. While this open structure offered Montreal fans absolutely no protection from the often bitter early and late-season Quebec elements for eight full seasons, it did provide some of the best seats and most intimate ballpark views found in any National League city. For only in Jarry Park could fans watch early-season action from a free and intimate perch upon snowbanks which sat in icy splendor beyond the right-field fence. No team (except perhaps the neighboring Toronto Blue Jays, which a decade later moved from quaint Exhibition Stadium to the enclosed SkyDome), therefore, has ever experienced a more traumatic change of venue than the Montreal Expos and their fans when the 1977 campaign was finally launched in the huge saucer-shaped Olympic Stadium.

The optimism-drenched 1971 season, once it arrived, did not provide the continued improvement expected as a matter of due course by local Expos watchers both at home and around the remainder of the league. While the team was able to climb one notch in the standings (from sixth to fifth), it actually fell two games in the won-loss column and slid nine-and-a-half games further off the pennant pace. Power fell off as well, as Staub dipped from 30 to 19 homers and the team itself stood dead last in the Eastern Division in longball production. Pitching showed a distinct downturn as well: while Bill Stoneman rebounded from a poor sophomore campaign with a career-best 17–16 mark (3.14 ERA) and a league-leading 39 starts, Carl Morton unexpectedly slumped to a lackluster 10–18 (4.79 ERA), thus leaving Steve Renko (15–14, 3.75 ERA) as the only other dependable Montreal starter. Divisional worsts in team fielding (.976) and team ERA (4.12) told much of the story for the 1971 Expos, an altogether inconsistent team which scored more frequently than only five other National League competitors while at the same time giving up more opponent's tallies than any other Senior Circuit club.

With the shocking departure of Rusty Staub during the 1971 off-season, Montreal fans soon experienced their first bitter taste of the economic realities which constitute the business known as major league baseball. For three short seasons Staub had been an unrivaled crowd favorite and, for an athlete not on ice skates, his status as national sports hero throughout Canadian provinces stretching from Quebec westward to British Columbia was unparalleled. But the demands of building a competitive ballclub prompted Montreal management to deal Rusty Staub to the New York Mets by April 1972 in exchange for what appeared to be the nucleus of a future major league lineup: shortstop Tim Foli, first baseman Mike Jorgensen, and outfielder Ken Singleton. The deal proved sound in the long run if not popular in the short haul, as Foli would man the shortstop post capably for the next five seasons, Jorgensen would supply power and defense over the same stretch, and Singleton (currently an Expos TV broadcaster) would enjoy three fine seasons and slam 23 homers in 1973 before eventually being dealt to Baltimore for hurler Dave McNally and outfielder Rich Coggins. With Staub's departure from the Expos outfield at the outset of the 1972 campaign, the team turned to veterans Ron Fairly and Bob Bailey for new offensive output. And each would come through with reasonable flair in future seasons, Fairly pacing the team in roundtrippers (with 17) the first post-Staub summer and Bailey doing so (with 26) during the second.

Montreal baseball seemingly moved from the "age of expansion" to the "era of respectability" during the 1974 season, a second-straight fourth-place finish. For the second campaign in a row Mauch's men had come down the stretch just a whisker shy of .500, owning 79 victories and tucked safely in fourth place, 8½ games off the pace and a scant half-game out of the third spot. The 1973 season had seen the Expos finish only 3½ games off the lead in a tight four-team race between New York's Mets (the eventual winners), the Cardinals of St. Louis, Pittsburgh's Pirates, and the brash Montrealers; yet it was an unexpected repeat performance in 1974 that suggested to the baseball world at large that perhaps Mauch had not merely done it with mirrors in 1973. The expansion-era of Expos baseball seemed to formally mature into adulthood, however, with the departure of the skipper Gene Mauch at the end of the 1975 campaign. As in his first managerial tenure with the Phillies and in later stints at Minnesota and Anaheim, Mauch showed by 1975 that he was far more adroit at turning teams from also-rans into contenders than he was at molding contenders into league champions. After climbing within clear sight of the top rung for two successive campaigns, the 1975 outfit again floundered and fell into a last-place tie with the Cubs, a dozen games under the break-even point and 17½ markers from the top spot. As Gene Mauch packed his bags at the end of the disappointing 1975 campaign, heading for his third managerial stop in the Twin Cities of Minnesota, Montreal front-office brass were now faced with their first managerial decision since the pre-expansion draft days of autumn 1968. And the eventual choice quickly proved to be one of the worst front-office blunders in the 20 years of Canadian National League baseball history.

The choice of both club president John McHale and righthand man Jim Fanning for the task of guiding Expos fortunes upon Mauch's departure was a complete baseball unknown—Karl Otto Kuehl—a 39-year-old veteran of the minor league coaching scene with no major league playing experience and few credentials for the post. Kuehl was to survive but 128 games into his first and only disastrous big-league campaign, departing in mid-August with his disoriented team standing at 43–85, deeply entrenched in last place, and careening at breakneck speed toward a 55–107 record that would barely miss replicating the embarrassing inaugural expansion season of seven summers earlier. Replacement skipper Charlie Fox provided little immediate relief as interim boss at season's end, winning but 12 of the club's final 34 contests, a losing standard (.353) which was only percentage points above that accomplished by Kuehl.

In the end the transitional seasons of 1975 and 1976 were notable only for a few outstanding individual performances by a handful of seasoned Expos veterans and a spattering of promising newcomers.

Despite missing a month of the 1975 season with hepatitis, hurler Dale Murray paced all N.L. relievers with 15 wins, then racked up 13 saves and a league-leading 81 appearances the following summer. Boasting an impressive fastball, Murray also compiled a remarkable two-year streak (between August 1974 and August 1976) of 247.1 innings without allowing an opponent's home run, the longest such string of the entire post-World War II era. Meanwhile, southpaw starter and reliever Dan Warthen posted his only career winning season, a respectable 8–6 mark (with a fine 3.11 ERA), during an exceptional 1975 rookie campaign which saw him finish third among the league's moundsmen in strikeout effectiveness (6.86 strikeouts per nine innings pitched). Of course this was hardly the tandem of Steve Carlton and Jim Lonberg hurling for the pennant-winning Phillies in 1976, or the duo of Jon Matlack and Jerry Koosman mowing down N.L. hitters for the Mets that same season. In fact, it wasn't even a match for the dependable duo of Bill Stoneman (weaver of two no-hitters between 1969 and 1972) and Steve Renko (author of two one-hitters within a single month of 1971) with which the Expos themselves had begun the decade only a few seasons earlier.

Great Expectations Reach a Hollow Climax in Quebec

> *What I do object to violently is the notion which apparently prevails here that a baseball game is merely the central attraction in a giant carnival. Music blares, clowns cavort and the game announcer sounds like a circus ringmaster, introducing each batter as if he had come directly from a command performance before the crowned heads of six countries.*
>
> Art Hill, I Don't Care If I Never Come Back

A new era dawned for Canadian baseball with the opening of the 1977 baseball season. Expansion baseball had now come to the Queen City of Toronto as well, and after eight summers the Montreal Expos were no longer the singular baseball story in the neighborly nation north of the border. In fact, almost from the day the fledgling Blue Jays of the American League first took the field in their quaint Exhibition Stadium the country of Canada (at least the large English-speaking portion) would take to its heart a new favored team. Suddenly and noticeably the Expos were dropped to second-son status, like the White Sox in Chicago or the old Browns in St. Louis. And ironically, this turn of events would come at precisely the moment when the Montreal ballclub was opening an exciting new era of its own—one that would see it playing in a bold new stadium and becoming at last a truly competitive team in the National League baseball wars.

Olympic Stadium (home of the 1976 Summer Olympic Games) opened for National League play on April 15, 1977, when a crowd of

57,592 greeted the Expos and Philadelphia Phillies for a somewhat lackluster home opener which saw the Phillies predominate 7–2 and Ellis Valentine provide the brief moment of hometown excitement with a towering homer and both Expo RBIs. The huge new saucer-shaped arena which the Expos now called home would perhaps account for an imminent surge in Montreal attendance equally as much as any improved league play over the coming seasons; yet this was not quite the futuristic domed venue that Expos management had long coveted. Plans for a retractable canvas roof had been temporarily suspended in 1976 as a result of construction strikes and soaring cost over-runs on the $770 million facility, and it would not be until the summer of 1989, a dozen seasons later, that the 200,000 square-foot, 65-ton moveable canvas arena covering would finally become fully operational. But the Olympic Stadium was a management dream when compared with cramped and revenue-thin Jarry Park, and eventual expansion to a seating capacity of 60,011 would make this ballpark one of only four in either league (alongside Anaheim, Cleveland, and Philadelphia) with a seating capacity listed at 60,000-plus for major league baseball.

The 1977 season, the first to be played in the Expos' plush new palace home, brought a surge reminiscent of the heady 1970 season. Like their forerunner of seven seasons earlier, the 1977 Expos were able to register a rare improvement of 20 full games in the league standings over their previous season's outing, winning exactly 20 more contests (75) than in 1976 and finishing 20 games closer to the top as well (16 games behind the champion Phillies). The fifth-place Expos were rewarded for this noticeable reversal with 1.4 million paying customers in 1977, more than double the 1976 attendance which had dipped to an all-time franchise low of 646,704. And to show that this was not a one-season aberration, the ballclub then climbed to fourth place in 1978, one game better in the win column and again pulling 1.4 million enthusiastic patrons through the turnstiles. And all this fortuitous upsurge could not help but be attributed at least partially to the arrival of veteran manager Dick Williams, who had already won three league pennants in Oakland and a fourth in his rookie campaign in Boston. While the first seven Montreal seasons had worn the indisputable stamp of laid-back skipper Gene Mauch, this new phase in the evolution of Canada's first big-league ballclub—destined to last through five exciting years until the strike-torn season of 1981—would soon enough bear the unmistakable signature of emotional and hard-bitten manager Dick Williams.

The 1978 Montreal season also witnessed the best-ever single-season pitching performance by an Expos hurler, as Ross Grimsley became the club's first and only 20-game winner in over two full decades of franchise play. Possessing a variety of slow-pitch deliveries, Grimsley had starred for the powerful Cincinnati Reds teams of the 1971–75 period, pitching a two-hitter in Game Four of the 1972 N.L.C.S. and winning two World Series contests that same autumn. Coming to Montreal as a high-priced free agent at the outset of the 1978 campaign, after a brief sojourn in Baltimore (including an 18–13 1973 season), the free-spirited lefty would enjoy a single career season with the Expos, before dropping to 10–9 (5.36 ERA) in 1979 and then departing for Cleveland by early-season 1980. Yet for the 1978 season Ross Grimsley stole much of the thunder from veteran righthander Steve Rogers, actually the club's most dependable hurler during the second half of the seventies and early eighties. While Rogers would post double-figure victory totals every summer between 1977 and 1983—once reaching 19 wins in his career campaign of 1982— he would never quite reach the lofty level of the charmed 20-victory circle that was Grimsley's special prize in his first and only effective Montreal summer.

The surges of 1970 and 1977 were only forerunners to the 1979 National League pennant carnival. For the 1979 Expos ballclub of Manager Dick Williams would burst upon the National League like an unleashed blast of arctic air, nearly paralyzing everything in its path as it charged to 95 victories (16 better than any previous Montreal club) and outpaced every league rival but one—the power-laden and pitching-rich Pirates featuring Willie Stargell, Dave Parker, and company. The margin of defeat was but two games, and a marathon home-field loss to the Pirates on September 18—in a game which stretched for only 11 innings but was prolonged by two rain delays, logged in at 6 hours and 11 minutes, and finally ended with Stargell's dramatic two-run homer off Dale Murray—was the contest which tipped the season's final balance.

The last summer of the seventies and the first of the newly minted eighties were a true highwater mark in Montreal baseball history. What had begun in 1979 continued full-force in 1980 as catcher Gary Carter led a balanced attack with 29 homers, Andre Dawson and Ellis Valentine both hit well above .300, and Steve Rogers and Scott Sanderson paced the mound corps by winning 16 games apiece. While the victory total slipped slightly, from 95 to 90, the result was yet another tight pennant scrap which saw the Montrealers again in second slot, this time losing out by a single game to the surprising and equally pennant-hungry Phillies of Manager Dallas Green. Although it seemed an ominous pattern that was developing—a multi-talented team that just couldn't seem to clinch the big victories when autumn championships were on the line—it was better than kissing pennant contention good-bye just about the time the first warm June breezes blew across the wintry climes of southern Quebec.

A bright new gate attraction for Montreal in 1980 was speedster Ron LeFlore, a one-time convicted burglar who had been signed by the Detroit Tigers in 1974 (discovered by Manager Billy Martin while playing for the Jackson State Prison team) and had subsequently enjoyed six productive seasons in Tiger stripes, hitting .300 on three separate occasions and leading all American Leaguers in runs scored in 1978. But LeFlore's distinctive trademark was the stolen base, of which he would register 455 over the course of a nine-year career. Picked up by Montreal at a bargain price (little-used reliever Dan Schatzeder) after a salary dispute ended his welcome in Detroit, the speed merchant LeFlore would enjoy only a single season in the National League before being lost as a free agent to the American League White Sox. But it was a most memorable year indeed, bringing with it a league-leading 97 steals, a level of thievery bested by only four other major leaguers (Rickey Henderson, Maury Wills, Lou Brock, and Vince Coleman) across the decades. LeFlore's brilliant baserunning was usually matched by his comic ineptitude afield, as well, and when the newest Expos hero stole his 62nd base two-thirds of the way through the 1980 season he inadvertently provided one of the most comical moments in franchise history. As the huge Olympic Stadium message board commemorated the moment by noting that exactly 115 summers earlier the first steal in baseball history had been recorded, a self-satisfied LeFlore decided to take momentary respite to admire his prodigious accomplishment, and was promptly picked off second base!

If the 1979 and 1980 seasons had represented a sudden surge to prominence in Montreal, the 1981 campaign which followed would be one of constant surprise and unprecedented event as well. This was, after all—by almost any conceivable standard—one of the weirdest seasons in all baseball history. An assault on fan patience in the form of an unfortunate players' union strike had disrupted the season and wreaked havoc with normal championship play. And as if fans had not suffered enough at the hands of players' brutal actions, management was soon to strike their own blow at the most cherished of baseball traditions. A makeshift playoff system was hastily arranged when season's play resumed on August 1, and it was indeed a system which made little sense in terms of anything but that almighty "Golden Egg" of the sporting business—television revenue. In a laughable attempt to create even more revenue-producing post-season games, the owners decreed *post facto* that the season would be viewed as two distinct segments and that division winners of the half-season "pennant races" would first clash to determine L.C.S. combatants. The result was (almost predictably!) that the team with the best season record in the N.L. East, St. Louis, was not invited to playoff action; nor were the N.L. West pacesetters (Cincinnati) featuring the best overall season record in all of baseball. But if teams like Cincinnati and St. Louis suffered unduly in the face of inventive entrepreneurship, Montreal (two games behind the Cardinals, but second-half winners by a scant half-game over St. Louis) and Philadelphia (overall third-place finishers, yet first-half winners by the mere accident of standing 1.5 games ahead of St. Louis when strike action commenced) were surprising if undeserving beneficiaries.

The 1981 season was not all plusses for the Expos, however, despite a credible 60–48 ledger and charity playoff appearances against the Phillies and Dodgers. For this was also a season that witnessed perhaps the worst trade in club history.[6] In what had by now seemingly become a typical move, the Expos front office had cashed in proven talent for unproven if promising new blood, this time by sending second baseman Tony Bernazard (a solid performer in several forthcoming seasons with both the White Sox and Indians) to Chicago in a pre-season swap for journeyman pitcher Rick Wortham (a sore-armed lefty who would never pitch a single inning in Montreal nor even win another big-league game). This ill-advised deal probably cost the Expos at least a pennant or two, as the second base slot remained a permanent hole wrecking an otherwise solid Montreal lineup over the next several near-miss pennant-losing campaigns (see further enlightening discussion of the ill-fated Bernazard deal in Turner, 1983, 193).

Two notable events did occur within a five-day period at Olympic Stadium during mid-summer 1981. On May 6 (while suffering through a 13–5 crushing at the hands of the lowly San Diego Padres) Expos batters tied an obscure slugging record when Mike Gates, Tim Raines, and Tim Wallach slammed consecutive ninth-inning triples, a performance which left them one shy of the big-league standard for consecutive three-base hits. Four days later, on May 10, Charlie Lea provided one of the biggest shocks of a truly shocking season when he hurled the first no-hitter in Olympic Stadium history, a 4–0 whitewashing of the San Francisco Giants in the second game of a Mother's Day Sunday doubleheader. Lea's performance was most surprising in light of the fact that he had been sporting a 7.36 ERA at the time and hadn't pitched a complete game in any of his previous 21 major league starts. Yet these were only momentary sidelights of a long (if interrupted) summer of National League play. The Expos were competitive if not dominating throughout the 1981 season, and in the end they played just well enough down the stretch to earn a post-season appearance under the new and unpopular dual-playoff format by taking two of three in a season-final series with the Mets at Shea Stadium. A makeshift playoff series with the Phillies would see the Montrealers emerge victors by the narrow count of three-games-to-two, the rubber match going to Montreal on the strength of brilliant six-hit shutout pitching and clutch 2-RBI hitting by the ever-dependable veteran hurler Steve Rogers.

Post-season play in October 1981 was perhaps the most exciting brief epoch of our Montreal major league saga. Having duly dispatched the Phillies on October 11 behind Steve Rogers' shutout effort, it was a confident ballclub that debuted in N.L.C.S. play on the West Coast two days later. And a two-game split in Los Angeles (the Game Two win coming on the strength of a Ray Burris five-hit whitewash and three base hits by offensive star Tim Raines), coupled with another Steve Rogers complete-game masterpiece in the Montreal opener, left the Expos needing only a split in two final contests on home soil. But it was not to be, as Dodgers hurlers Burt Hooton, Bob Welch, and Steve Howe combined on a five-hitter of their own in Game Four to set the stage for the most dramatic finish yet on record for Senior Circuit L.C.S. play. Following a day's delay due to rain, and after Fernando Valenzuela and Ray Burris had locked in a brilliant 1–1 standoff for eight gripping innings, veteran outfielder Rick Monday launched a heart-wrenching ninth-inning two-out homer off Steve Rogers which cleared the distant center-field fence and squelched the decade-long World Series dreams of a fledgling big-league baseball nation. For three successive seasons the Montreal Expos had come within a narrow hair's breadth (this last time within a single pitch!) of bringing a coveted first National League Championship and a first World Series cameo to the sports-crazy nation of Canada. And never in the first 21 years of franchise history would they again come quite so close.

Boys of Autumn Provide Baseball's Perennial Disappointment

> *These were the Boys of Autumn, and their time had finally come. Late August had been cruel, so cold that maple trees had turned red and dropped their leaves a month ahead of time. But September was warm, and a warm World Series at Olympic Stadium wasn't out of the question.*
>
> *Dan Turner*, The Expos Inside Out

One measure of the Montreal Expos' brief yet still unfulfilled history lies in assessment of this team's remarkable penchant for late-season play. At least through the middle years of franchise history the Expos demonstrated remarkable adeptness at late-season play—

despite their frequent ineptitude for late inning rallies in individual games, or even their later fondness (1987–1989) for folding in pennant races by early August. Certainly between 1978 and 1982—during their first burst of glory as a league contender—Montreal dominated all other National League division winners from wire to wire during regular-season play. A mythical composite standings of National League teams which had won division titles and also played at above a .500 clip over this four-year stretch would appear as follows (Turner, 1983, 186):

Team (1979–1982)	W	L	Pct.	GB
Montreal Expos	**331**	**261**	**.559**	—
Philadelphia Phillies	323	270	.545	8½
Los Angeles Dodgers	322	275	.539	11½
Houston Astros	320	277	.536	13½
Pittsburgh Pirates	311	277	.529	18
St. Louis Cardinals	311	277	.529	18
Cincinnati Reds	306	287	.516	25½

Yet despite this apparent overall league superiority, the Montreal ballclub had very little to show in the way of pennant glory or post-season play. The Cardinals, Phillies, Dodgers, and Pirates during this same stretch all went on to garner World Championship flags. Even the lowly Atlanta Braves, who were actually under .500 over the entire stretch between 1978 and 1982, had managed to capture a divisional championship in the stretch run of 1982. The failure of the Expos to bring home a winner during this period, however, certainly didn't come as a result of collapse in the late pennant weeks of September. Between 1979 and 1981 the Expos actually went 64–37 (a remarkable .634 winning percentage) after September 1, registering the best late-season record in all of baseball by a wide margin (Turner, 1983, 176). In the late seventies and early eighties the Expos were indeed baseball's "Men of Autumn" in the Senior Circuit; unfortunately, autumn reached only to the end of September within the plastic confines of Olympic Stadium, and a long winter of Hot Stove League waiting was the standard fare in Quebec long before World Series play began each crisp fall season.

Another manner of assessing the history of the Montreal Expos is in terms of the four colorful men who have manned the third base slot for this franchise over the 20 years of its National League baseball sojourn. First came the memorably named Coco Laboy (1969–1970), perfect reflection of the colorful ineptness of expansion baseball. The 29-year-old Puerto Rican rookie led the ballclub with 83 RBIs during the inaugural franchise season, then slumped to a .199 sophomore batting average and was relegated to the bench after only two brief summers of expansion glory. Laboy was followed to the hot corner by heavy-hitting Bob Bailey (1971–1974) who, like his teammates, provided plenty of thrills and much entertainment yet only an also-ran's share of team wins during the four seasons he manned the post. A one-time Pittsburgh Pirates bonus baby (reportedly signed for a record $175,000 in 1961), Bailey exhibited with his lackluster fielding the precise comic ineptitude which is the joy and trademark of expansion baseball. Laconic Expos Manager Gene Mauch is reputed to have commented often about his sometimes exasperating third sacker that "Bailey means wood; Bailey doesn't mean leather" (Shatzkin, 1990, 38); and an anonymous opponent once supposedly charged that "Bailey is called Beetle around the league since he fields like a cartoon character" (Shatzkin, 1990, 38). Montreal fans were less one-sided in their view of the heavy-hitting Bailey, however, maintaining what can only be described as a love-hate relationship with the lead-footed streak hitter who grounded into 216 career double plays and yet at the time he was traded away in December 1975 (to Cincinnati for pitcher Clay Kirby) was ensconced as franchise career leader in nine of 10 major batting categories.

The remainder of the 1970s—a period of steady progress which brought a heady rise in the National League standings from sixth (1976) to fifth (1977) to fourth (1978) to second (1979–1980)—was characterized by the stable Larry Parrish (1975–1981), the third major keeper of the hot corner for the baseball capital of French-speaking Canada. A Topps All-Rookie team member in 1975 and Montreal Player of the Year in 1979, the broad-shouldered Parrish was a fitting representative for a bold new epoch of baseball respectability in Montreal. An adequate fielder (he led the league in double plays at his position in 1976 and in putouts in 1981) and fine hitter, Parrish had established himself as the club career leader in several offensive categories (games, at-bats, hits, doubles) by the time he was shipped to Texas for heavy-hitting first sacker Al Oliver in late spring training in 1982. The current decade of high hopes and bitter disappointments, on the other hand, has been as much as anything the era of Parrish's replacement, Tim Wallach. Inheriting the position in Spring Training 1982, Wallach established himself quickly among the league's finest hot corner performers, tying for the circuit's top spot in RBIs among third basemen his rookie season, setting club records for sophomore homers (28) and RBIs (97), and leading National League third basemen in putouts for three straight seasons (1983–1985). Like the Expos themselves, however, Wallach exploded on the scene in the early 1980s (when he homered in his first official big-league at-bat), then faded to mediocrity as the decade progressed. Before rebounding with a true "career" offensive season in 1987 (26 roundtrippers, .298 BA, and a league-leading 42 doubles), Wallach had struggled through four offensive seasons in which his average dipped as low as .233 (1986) and .246 (1984). His fielding was equally erratic, alternating between banner defensive summers in 1984 and 1985 (as league-leader in putouts, assists, and double plays) and lackluster ones in 1982 (.948 fielding percentage) and 1986 (when his error totals equalled those for double plays). Tim Wallach over the past eight seasons has seemed the very mirror image of the Montreal Expos franchise itself: alternating on-field brilliance with slumps of big-league proportion, and climbing precariously near the summit at his position each season, while never standing by year's end quite at the top of the heap.

And if the Expos era of the 1980s is in this one sense the era of Tim Wallach at third base, it is in still another respect the decade owned by Tim Raines upon the basepaths. Without a doubt Raines has been the most colorful and most consistent performer in Montreal franchise history. Bursting on the scene with an American Association batting title (.354 at Denver) and *The Sporting News* Minor League Player of the Year honors in 1980, "Rock" Raines debuted dramatically in the majors with four straight stolen base titles (1981–1984) and a close second-place finish (behind the Dodgers' Fernando Valenzuela) in 1981 Rookie-of-the-Year balloting. A switch-hitter who began as a second baseman in the minors but played almost exclusively in the outfield after his arrival in Montreal, Raines reached career highs in steals (90) and runs scored (133) in 1983, established a major league mark with a lofty 87.4 percent success rate over his first 300 big-league steal attempts, then crowned his early successes with a National League batting title (.334) in 1986 and third-place finish (.330) in the 1987 batting race as well. Since his batting title year of 1986, however, Tim Raines' meteoric career has been somewhat tarnished by scandals, controversies, and injuries. Rumors of drug abuse have dogged his recent seasons in Montreal. Opting for free agency in the spring of 1987, the Montreal speedster found that alleged owners' collusion concerning free-agent signings had left him without an offer, forcing a begrudging return to the Canadian team's roster. A move to the cleanup spot in the lineup after Andre Dawson's 1987 free-agent departure worked to boost Raines' power numbers (18 homers and 68 RBIs in 1987) yet deplete his stolen base totals (50 in but 59 attempts that same season). Injuries and a first-ever stint on the disabled list brought a disappointing 1988 campaign which saw a .270 BA and 33 stolen bases compiled over only 109 game appearances. Yet despite some lessening of his overall impact on the league in recent summers, Tim Raines remains the all-time major league career leader in stolen base percentage (585 successes in 675 attempts for an .867 ratio), a distinction he has held consecutively since May 18, 1984, when he took over from Willie Wilson of the Kansas City Royals with his 300th career stolen base attempt.

While Tim Raines was establishing himself as a household name in the province of Quebec and across the National League during the strike-ruined season of 1981, the Montreal National League ballclub was itself gamely rebounding from what was destined to remain both the high-water mark campaign as well as the emotional low-point of franchise history. If 1981 had ended with a discordantly sour note for both Expos players and fans, however, the mid-summer of 1982 would soon bring another milestone event in the team's unfolding saga. For on July 13, 1982, Olympic Stadium would proudly showcase Canada's premier major league All-Star Game, a gala ceremonial event which would pack 59,057 patrons into the saucer-shaped stadium to watch a first-ever big league mid-summer classic held outside the United States. That several Expos players were actually destined for heroic roles in baseball's most glorified exhibition game was but fitting dessert for the Expos faithful in attendance. Steve Rogers, now in his 10th Montreal season, was the starting and winning pitcher in a 4–1 triumph which marked the 11th straight victory for the Senior Circuit. Al Oliver, on his way to a league batting title and RBI crown in his first Expos season, contributed some important offense as well, stroking a double and a single and scoring a crucial run for the winners. And to add yet one final joyous moment to an already delightful hometown experience for enthralled Expos fans, Gary Carter would single home Oliver with the final run for the Nationals in the bottom of the sixth frame.

Despite exasperating near misses during three preceding seasons, the Expos remained highly competitive in 1982 and 1983, staying in the thick of the National League pennant race both summers. Led by the booming bats of new acquisition Al Oliver (the first league batting champion in franchise history) and veterans Gary Carter and Tim Wallach (who smacked 29 and 28 homers respectively and tied for the club lead in RBIs at 97), Manager Jim Fanning's club eventually wilted in the stretch for a third-place finish, six games behind the pacesetting Cardinals. The following summer brought a new manager in ex-big-league outfielder Bill Virdon, as Fanning reluctantly gave up managerial duties to return to front-office duty. The results were largely the same, however: third slot and a respectable eight lengths behind pennant-winning Philadelphia. In the end the final ledger of these two seasons could be nothing but deeply disappointing, however, as fan expectations had been high after the cameo playoff appearance of 1981 and nearly all the baseball pundits—from *TSN* to Thomas Boswell to Bill James—had picked Fanning's club as a runaway pennant choice at the outset of the 1982 campaign. And if pennant defeats were not sufficiently damning, the Expos lost $3 million at the gate in 1982, despite drawing 2.3 million fans and maintaining the most lucrative TV contract in all of baseball (Turner, 1983, 195). The high cost of booming player salaries and those ever-present inequities in the U.S.-Canadian dollar exchange rate were making profitable baseball an extremely difficult proposition for a team located in the province of Quebec, especially during the first full explosion of free agency which characterized the early years of the resurgent 1980s. Staying competitive in the marketplace (largely the responsibility of majority owners Charles Bronfman and Hugh Hallward—the recognized business moguls) was suddenly proving even more difficult than staying competitive on the National League fields of play (largely the responsibility of majority owner John McHale—the acknowledged baseball man).

If the last team fielded by Jim Fanning and the first led by Bill Virdon were still seemingly only a player or two away from championship-caliber performance, by the outset of the 1984 season it was becoming increasingly clear that the Expos were suddenly an aging team headed for a drastic fall. The second base problems had never been adequately resolved after the disastrous trade of Tony Bernazard in 1981 and the subsequent shocking dismissal of problem-child Rodney Scott before mid-season of 1982. Warren Cromartie had played the last of his seven up-and-down seasons in the outfield during 1983, and Al Oliver was surprisingly peddled away to San Francisco after two brief but productive seasons in Montreal tricolors. Chris Speier, who had brought a veteran's invaluable experience if not the league's flashiest glove to the shortstop slot for six full seasons, had been dealt away as well (to St. Louis) by mid-season 1984. Cincinnati legend Pete Rose (a sure gate attraction as he closed in on his 4,000th big-league base hit) had been signed as an expensive free-agent in January, yet Rose offered little enough hope of contributing as a regular starter. And the pitching staff which broke from Spring Training camp in 1984 was undeniably an aging and battle-weary crew: Steve Rogers had won in double figures for the final time in 1983; Bill Gullickson and Charlie Lea were now battling tired arms; and a staff which had paced the Senior Circuit in shutouts in 1983 would fall all the way to sixth place in this department by the following summer.

Thus, the 1984 Montreal season would not surprisingly bring the first losing Expos campaign in six summers, a dismal fifth-place finish which found the patchwork Canadian team a full 18 games off the league-leading pace set by Chicago's resurgent and surprising Cubbies. It was equally small surprise that Bill Virdon was dispatched as the Expos' field leader with only 30 games remaining in the disappointing season, though it was admittedly something of a mild shock that Virdon was temporarily replaced near season's end by none other than special assignments coach and ex-skipper Jim Fanning. One highlight of this largely dismal 1984 campaign was a rare abbreviated perfect-game no-hitter by Expos hurler Dave Palmer (in St. Louis on April 21), an unusual rain-shortened five-inning affair which would stand as only the fourth no-hitter in club history and only the 20th abbreviated version during present-century major league play. Ironically, this feat would soon be duplicated by another Montreal hurler, Pascual Perez, whose rain-shortened five-inning mastery of the Phillies at Veterans Stadium in September 1988 would not only be the next Montreal masterpiece, but also the next abbreviated no-hit affair as well.

The clearest signal of the numerous changes surrounding the Montreal ballclub came in December of 1984, however, when a block-buster transaction saw popular catcher Gary Carter swapped to the New York Mets for four promising players, including infielder Hubie Brooks, catcher Mike Fitzgerald, outfielder Herm Winningham, and promising minor league hurler Floyd Youmans. If the trade brought four potential starters for one and thus made sense at the time, Carter's departure was indeed a blow for the local faithful who had for 10 full seasons followed the burgeoning career of the first true franchise superstar. For exactly a decade "The Kid" had been a fixture in Mon-treal and the very backbone of the Expos franchise. While not always entirely popular with his teammates (who sometimes voiced the opin-ion that he was a camera hog and publicity hound), the ebullient Gary Carter was perhaps baseball's premier catcher in the late seventies and early eighties—at least after the retirement of Hall-of-Famer Johnny Bench of Cincinnati. Above all else, Carter was a rugged and durable player known primarily for his outstanding clutch hitting (10 career grand slams), his astute handling of pitchers, and his overall brilliant defensive play. A *TSN* Rookie-of-the-Year in 1975, Gary Carter had established his defensive pre-eminence among the league's backstops between 1977 and 1982, leading the circuit in most chances six times, in putouts five times, in assists four times, and in double plays three times. It certainly didn't help assuage feelings among Montreal fans when Carter's replacement, Ed Fitzgerald, hit 74 points below "The Kid" during the 1985 season, while knocking in 69 fewer runs, blasting 30 fewer homers, and registering 414 fewer putouts behind the plate than did Carter from his new post with divisional rival New York.

Another signal of change in Montreal at the outset of the 1985 season was the arrival of new manager Buck Rodgers, the seventh skipper in 17 short seasons of franchise history (one field boss for every 2.43 campaigns). Under the even-tempered and stone-faced Rodgers the Expos would enjoy three third-place finishes over the next four unspectacular seasons. If this was a welcomed rebound after the subterranean campaign of 1984, on the one hand, it was hardly the long-awaited arrival in baseball's promised land so long anticipated by increasingly impatient Montreal faithful.

There was nothing remotely spectacular about the first several ballclubs guided by Rogers, yet little embarrassing either: one brief dip below .500 and 29½ games off the pace in 1986, followed by a climb to 20 games over the break-even point and four games out at the end of the following season. With Raines winning a batting title in 1986 and Tim Wallach and Andres Galarraga emerging among the league's slugging stars in 1987 and 1988, the Expos had again seemed to find a way to remain competitive, yet never to challenge seriously for the league's top spot.

If the loss of Gary Carter had been a severe blow to the Expos' pennant chances in 1985, the departure of another Montreal star slugger would have equal impact the very next season. Since his rookie-of-the-year campaign in 1977 (19 HRs, 65 RBIs, .282 BA), Andre Dawson had teamed with Gary Carter as one of the most potent offensive tandems in the entire National League. During the 1977–1984 stretch Dawson and Carter had, in fact, accounted for 373 homers, scored 1,364 runs, knocked home 1,344 more tallies, and enjoyed a total of seven 25-plus home run seasons between them. Yet the slugging outfielder had grown increasingly unhappy with the conditions of playing on astroturf and in front of French-speaking fans in Olympic Stadium. Dawson was apparently so unhappy in Montreal, in fact, that despite a reportedly long-term $2 million offer and the collusively-limited free-agent market, "The Hawk" signed on with the Chicago Cubs during the 1986 off-season, accepting a blank contract and receiving a 1987 salary far below his obvious free-market value. Montreal's loss and Chicago's gain was almost immediately evident as daytime baseball and true turf outfields seemed to quickly rejuvenate Dawson's tired legs and sharpen his batting eye; Dawson would soon poll 49 homers and register 137 RBIs (both big-league bests) on his way to a career season and runaway MVP honors during the 1987 National League campaign.

The seasons of 1987 and 1988 were played out as respectable if not serious division contenders. Buck Rodgers' 1987 ballclub won 91 games and finished only four games off the mark. Had Andre Dawson still been in camp to bolster the league's third lowest home run production, or had a true pitching ace emerged from a staff of steady if unimpressive hurlers (Neal Heaton paced the group with only 13 victories), pennant fever might well have swept through the Montreal citizenry well past the final sweltering days of August. The 1988 club, by contrast, was 10 games off the 1987 pace in the won-loss column and 16 games further off the pennant pace, yet still ensconced comfortably in the respectable third slot of the competitive Eastern Division. A rare highlight of the late 1988 season, of course, was the strange September no-hit effort of unpredictable Montreal moundsman Pascual Perez.[7] By duplicating Dave Palmer's earlier oddity of a rain-shortened five-inning no-hitter (the club's fifth no-hit effort in 20 seasons), Perez also became the first hurler to accomplish a no-hit game of any variety in the 17 seasons of play in Philadelphia's cavernous Veterans Stadium.

Pascual Perez had, of course, generated considerable excitement in Montreal and throughout the league long before his destined date with pitching immortality on September 24, 1988. Joining the Expos as a free-agent castoff in 1987, after several unfortunate bouts with drug dependency and a year outside of organized baseball in 1986, the frenetic Dominican hurler quickly established himself as one of the most successful hurlers (7–0 in 1987 and 12–8 in 1988) and colorful characters of Montreal franchise history. A true baseball "hot dog" and "flake" of the classic mold, the rail-thin righthander had sported a crowd-pleasing reputation around the circuit from his earliest seasons with the Atlanta Braves. Perez soon drew crowds to applaud such antics as shooting batters with an imaginary finger-gun, pounding balls into the mound at inning's end and running full-speed to the dugout, and developing his own version (the "Pascual" pitch) of the once-famous looping "eephus" delivery of an earlier decade.

By the summer of 1989 a revamped Expos team—without the slugging and defense of Carter and Dawson but still featuring the spray hitting and unbridled speed of star outfielder Tim Raines, plus the long-ball punch of third sacker Tim Wallach and first baseman Andres Galarraga—had scrapped and clawed its way seemingly back into National League contention. This sudden Montreal success was seemingly the result of properly blending patiently nurtured home-grown talent with a needed transfusion of fresh blood from outside the organization. Having taken over in mid-season of 1988 as vice president for player personnel and general manager, youthful Dave Dombrowski (at 32 the youngest decision maker in big-league baseball) had filled key holes in the Montreal lineup by acquiring veteran shortstop Spike Owen from Boston and experienced righthanded hurler Kevin Gross from Philadelphia in vital pre-season transactions. And after continued criticism from fans and baseball pundits over the loss of franchise players Carter and Dawson in recent seasons, the Montreal management this time around was determined to give at least the appearance of trying to win and to win big during the promising 1989 campaign. The unfortunate result of this altered stance might today be deemed the worst mid-season trade in recent National League history.

On May 25, 1989, the Montreal Expos shocked the baseball world by sending a trio of highly promising young arms (Randy Johnson, Brian Holman, and Gene Harris) to the Seattle Mariners for talented but unhappy lefthanded flamethrower Mark Langston. Langston, one of the most dominant lefties of the decade and reigning American League strikeout king in 1984 (his rookie campaign), 1986, and 1987, had long coveted an escape from cellar-dwelling and low-paying Seattle, and the Junior Circuit ballclub was equally eager to deal their ace before free agency set him free at season's end. Nearly every contending team in both leagues desired Langston, and thus the Canadian-based Montrealers had hardly been considered a likely candidate for his service. It was indeed a risky move, as Langston would most likely depart frigid Montreal for a warmer climate and the highest bidder immediately upon conclusion of his expiring 1989 contract. And the pitchers lost in the transaction might well constitute the bulk of an entire future successful mound corps. Yet by the time the Expos swung the Langston deal, it seemed that this might indeed be the long-awaited (at least in Quebec) "Year of the Expo"—the pieces all seemed to be there once a dominant mound ace had been obtained. The offense of Raines, Wallach, Galarraga, and Hubie Brooks was effective if not overwhelming. Langston seemed the needed centerpiece of a solid staff, and indeed he broke from the gate in Montreal with several stellar starts (including a winning 12-strikeout effort versus San Diego in his debut on May 28). The Expos excelled at winning tight games during the early season going, and a pair of one-run victories in Los Angeles the final weekend of May lifted the ballclub into second place in a tight four-team race that would remain hotly contested until the second full week of September.

Mid-season was an exciting time in Montreal, and no moments were more exciting than those in the first few games when Langston was delivering his blazing fastball and tantalizing curve for his new Canadian employers. By the All-Star Break Mark Langston was 6–2 and the Expos sat in first place with a game and a half lead. First place was not relinquished, in fact, until a seven-game losing streak on the road in Pittsburgh, New York, and Chicago during the first week of August spelled the beginning of the end for what had earlier seemed a potential dream season for the rebounding Montrealers. By the second week of September another three-game sweep at the hands of the pennant-bound Cubs in Chicago dropped the Expos a full eight games off the pace and virtually out of contention.

By season's end, neither team involved in the Langston trade had seemed to "break the bank" with the year's most celebrated trade. Langston himself finished the season with three defeats in his final four starts and a closing 12–9 mark (2.39 ERA and 175 strikeouts in

177 innings). Randy Johnson (baseball's tallest-ever player at six-foot-ten) flopped in Seattle at 7–9 (4.40 ERA), and Harris and Holman were 9–14 between them. But the Seattle trio is young and Randy Johnson, especially, promises huge dividends somewhere down the road. Mark Langston may still be the best lefthander in baseball, but an off-season free-agent signing (making the flamethrower the highest-paid pitcher of all-time) soon assured that the California Angels and not the Expos would be reaping all the benefits of Langston's extraordinary pitching talents.

One moment of the late 1989 season does seem to demand brief reliving—the longest and most dramatic game in Expos history and certainly one of the strangest contests in recent National League annals. Played in Olympic Stadium on the night of August 23, this seemingly endless draw stretched for 22 scoreless innings and six and one-quarter hours before Rick Dempsey's solo homer against Dennis Martinez brought the Dodgers a 1–0 triumph. While bending the patience of weary fans to the limit this unusual contest managed to establish only one new major league record of note—22 consecutive innings without a base on balls, thus equaling a big-league standard set by the Pirates and Giants way back in July of 1913. Yet if this strangest of ball games was not filled up with new records it was indeed crammed with extraordinary occurrences. Montreal mascot Youppi, for one, set some sort of "unofficial mascot record" by being ejected from the field of play in the top of the 11th inning, only to return to the scene in the bottom of the 13th, now restricted to a safe spot atop the home team dugout. Later a throw from center-fielder Dave Martinez hit cutoff man Spike Owen in the "gluteus maximus," forcing the Montreal shortstop to remain standing for much of the remainder of the game. And in the 16th inning Expos outfielder Larry Walker apparently scored on a sacrifice fly, only to have the apparent game-winner nullified on an appeal play with two umpires already in the tunnel on their way to the locker room.

With Langston not quite living up to lofty expectations during late-season outings, the Expos sputtered at season's end and fell to an even .500 performance for the second straight season, failing once more to be a factor down the final stretch of the divisional race. What was worse, the ballclub had seemingly mortgaged its immediate future with the ill-advised Mark Langston deal. This was made all the more dramatically clear by early season of 1990 when Brian Holman barely missed a first-ever Seattle no-hitter, only a few scant weeks before Randy Johnson actually pitched one for his new American League employers. Meanwhile further free-agent departures by seasoned hurlers Pascual Perez (to the New York Yankees) and Bryn Smith (to the St. Louis Cardinals) meant that the continually revamped Expos had to rely once again on talented yet inexperienced young pitching from the farm system (Mark Gardner, Chris Nabholz, Mel Rojas, and Bill Sampen) which could once more only be sufficient to hold them in the 1990 pennant race until the telling dog days of late July and early August. By late season the game but outmanned Montreal team had fallen far off the National League pace.

As the always colorful Expos rounded out their first quarter-century of franchise history in the initial seasons of the 90's, it was both the best and worst of times (as it had almost always been!) for baseball's only French-speaking city. A heavy irony seemed to hang over everything that involved this quixotic baseball franchise. As the fortunes of the Expos' junior circuit Canadian counterpart in Toronto continued to soar wildly toward a world championship in 1992, enthusiasm was on the wane for what had once been the north country's only big-league franchise. Despite a host of talented youngsters on the roster, the loss of veteran showpieces like Tim Raines (traded to the White Sox in 1991) and Gary Carter (retired after returning to the Expos for a single curtain-call 1992 campaign) caused fans to stay away in droves. The collapse of part of the support structure in Olympic Stadium just before the close of 1991 necessitated a bizarre season-ending month-long roadtrip and fueled speculation about whether the Expos would even call Montreal home for the 1992 pennant chase. Both 1993 NL expansion ballclubs pilfered front office staff wholesale (including prized GM Dave Dombrowski) from the senior Canadian team. Yet despite such setbacks the Expos surprised in 1992 with a hustling young ballclub under new skipper Felipe Alou that copped second slot and posted 87 victories. With budding stars like Canadian slugger Larry Walker and flashy infielder Delino DeShields, the Expos now seemingly stand posed to follow their Toronto counterparts onto the very pinnacle of America's national pastime.

Notes

1. The team nickname commemorates the showcase Canadian National Exposition held in Montreal during 1973. This author is considerably indebted to Richard Griffin, the Montreal Expos' talented Media Relations Director, for the updated Expos statistics cited herein. Readers interested in further explorations of this ballclub should first consult Dan Turner's *The Expos Inside Out* (1983) for a comprehensive overview of the franchise (through 1982), and then tackle Brodie Snyder's entertaining paperbacks (see bibliography) for the day-by-day sagas of the 1979 and 1981 seasons, to date the highlight years of franchise history.

2. The Expos logo has spurred almost as much controversy and debate as the garish tri-colored uniform design, both of which have been fixtures as team trademarks since Opening Day of Year One. In way of official explanation, the *1990 Expos Media Guide* offers the following clarification: "The Expos

logo is composed of three letters, the largest of which is the overall stylized M for Montreal. Represented in the lower left of the logo is a lower case e for Expos and on the righthand side of the logo, in blue, is the letter b for baseball." Somehow it sounds a lot more convincing than it actually looks. For years the local wags of Montreal have insisted the logo instead contains a stylized "cb" standing for the initials of majority owner Charles Bronfman (an interpretation the club vehemently denies); others suggest that it is perhaps a graphic representation of a bat and ball, a constantly needed reminder to its wearers of the game they supposedly play.

3. Charles Lea of the Expos owned the only other no-hitter to occur on Canadian soil previous to the 1990 season, since the Expos themselves had never been no-hit by the opposition at home, and no American League hurler had tossed a no-hitter in Toronto against the Jays before Dave Stewart turned the trick at the SkyDome on June 30, 1990.

4. Following is a complete roster of original Expos, selected in the National League Expansion Draft on October 14, 1968; players are listed here in the actual order drafted:

Drafted Player	Position	Taken From	Seasons with Expos
Manny Mota	Outfield	Pittsburgh	1969
Mack Jones	Outfield	Cincinnati	1969–1971
John Bateman	Catcher	Houston	1969–1972
Gary Sutherland	Second Base	Philadelphia	1969–1971
Jack Billingham	Pitcher	Los Angeles	none
Donn Clendenon	First Base	Pittsburgh	1969
Jesus Alou	Outfield	San Francisco	none
Mike Wegener	Pitcher	Philadelphia	1969–1970
Dranon Guinn	Pitcher	Atlanta	none
Bill Stoneman	Pitcher	Chicago	1969–1973
Maury Wills	Shortstop	Pittsburgh	1969
Larry Jackson	Pitcher	Philadelphia	none
Bob Reynolds	Pitcher	San Francisco	1969
Dan McGinn	Pitcher	Cincinnati	1969–1971
Jose Herrera	Outfield	Houston	1969–1970
Jim Williams	Infield	Cincinnati	none
Angel Hermoso	Infield	Atlanta	1969–1970
Jim "Mudcat" Grant	Pitcher	Los Angeles	1969
Jerry Robertson	Pitcher	St. Louis	1969
Don Shaw	Pitcher	New York	1969
Ty Cline	Outfield	San Francisco	1969–1970
Gary Jestadt	Infield	Chicago	1969
Carl Morton	Pitcher	Atlanta	1969–1972
Larry Jaster	Pitcher	St. Louis	1969
Ernie McAnally	Pitcher	New York	1971–1974
Jim Fairey	Outfield	Los Angeles	1969–1972
Coco Laboy	Third Base	St. Louis	1969–1973
John Boccabella	Catcher	Chicago	1969–1972
Ron Brand	Catcher	Houston	1969–1971
John Glass	Pitcher	New York	none

5. Ibid.

6. While Dan Turner considers the Bernazard-for-Wortham deal of December 12, 1980, to be perhaps the worst of John McHale's many player transactions, John Reichler (in his *Baseball Trade Register*, 1984) offers the following list of all-time-worst Montreal trades (of course, this list was compiled long before the Mark Langston deal, as was Dan Turner's relative assessment of the Tony Bernazard deal):

1. Traded Ken Singleton and Mike Torrez to the Baltimore Orioles for Dave McNally, Rich Coggins, and Bill Kirkpatrick (December 4, 1974)

2. Traded Andre Thornton to the Cleveland Indians for Jackie Brown (December 10, 1976)

3. Traded Don Stanhouse, Gary Roenicke and Joe Kerrigan to the Baltimore Orioles for Rudy May, Randy Miller, and Bryn Smith (December 7, 1977)

4. Traded Mike Marshall (pitcher) to the Los Angeles Dodgers for Willie Davis (December 5, 1973)

5. Traded Don Carter and $300,000 to the Cleveland Indians for Manny Trillo (August 17, 1983)

7. A further irony surrounding Pascual Perez's rain-shortened no-hitter was the fact that it was duplicated by his brother in 1990. When Melido Perez of the Chicago White Sox no-hit the New York Yankees on Friday, July 13, 1990, in a game shortened to six innings by rainfall, the Perez sibling tandem became the first and only brother combination in baseball history to own such questionable yet official truncated hitless masterpieces.

References

Frommer, Harvey. 1976. "Affaire de Coeur: The Expos." In *A Baseball Century: The First 100 Years of the National League,* edited by Jeanne McClow, 169–75. New York: Rutledge Books.

Hill, Art. 1980. *I Don't Care If I Never Get Back—A Baseball Fan and His Game.* New York: Simon and Schuster.

Humber, William. 1983. *Cheering for the Home Team: The Story of Baseball in Canada.* Toronto, Ont.: The Boston Mill Press.

Reichler, Joseph L. 1984. *The Baseball Trade Register.* New York: Macmillan Publishing Company.

Shatzkin, Mike, ed. 1990. *The Ballplayers: Baseball's Ultimate Biographical Reference.* New York: William Morrow.

Snyder, Brodie (with illustrations by Terry Mosher). 1979. *The Year the Expos Almost Won the Pennant.* Toronto, Ont.: Virgo Press.

———. 1981. *The Year the Expos Finally Won Something!* Toronto, Ont.: Checkmark Books.

Turner, Dan. 1983. *The Expos Inside Out.* Toronto, Ont.: McClelland and Stewart Publishers.

Annotated Bibliography

Bjarkman, Peter C. "Montreal Expos." In *The 1989 Left Field Baseball Book,* edited by Elliot Regenstein and Tony Formo, 176–80. Ithaca, N.Y.: Left Field Publications, 1989.

———. "Montreal Expos." In *The 1990 Left Field Baseball Extravaganza,* edited by Elliot Regenstein and Tony Formo, 64–73. Ithaca, N.Y.: Left Field Publications, 1990.

Irreverent but informative evaluations of the disappointing 1988 and 1989 Montreal Expos seasons, contributed as part of a complete series of capsule team summaries featured in this popular underground baseball annual published by SABR members Elliot Regenstein and Tony Formo. The 1989 essay explores ups and downs of a young Expos team which wilted during the pennant home stretch of 1988, and features minor league prospects looming on the horizon with the Expos' stellar Indianapolis Triple A ballclub (the winner of American Association pennants for four consecutive summers, 1986–89). The 1990 article utilizes Bill James' *Game Score Theory* to assess a perplexing Montreal pitching staff which labored during the second straight disappointing pennant failure in 1989. Both essays wrestle with the two prominent questions surrounding Montreal ballclubs in the 1980s: Why do the Expos always fold so precisely on schedule in late August? and Why do franchise-type Expos players (Gary Carter, Andre Dawson, Hubie Brooks, Mark Langston, Bryn Smith, Pascual Perez) always seem to pack their bags and head south (literally) just when this franchise seems to be on the verge of finally putting together a winning roster?

Frommer, Harvey. "Affaire de Coeur: The Expos." In *A Baseball Century: The First 100 Years of the National League,* edited by Jeanne McClow, 169–75. New York: Rutledge Books, 1976.

Lively capsule portrait of the first eight summers of Montreal Expos baseball which together constitute the "Jarry Park Years" in Expos history. One chapter in a handsome coffee-table volume celebrating the 100th anniversary of National League play, this text is illustrated with a dozen attractive color and black-and-white photographs of game action and team personalities. Special amenities of bilingual baseball in Canada are featured throughout as Frommer captures the unique flavor of the earliest and most wacky (yet still somehow innocent) seasons of Montreal Expos expansion baseball.

Humber, William. *Cheering for the Home Team: The Story of Baseball in Canada.* Toronto, Ont.: The Boston Mill Press, 1983. 150 pp.

The most comprehensive essay available on baseball's Canadian origins and the Canadian history of North America's national pastime, including: the story of Canada's only legitimate major league championship team; barnstorming Japanese Canadian teams; black players in Canadian baseball, from the nineteenth century to Jackie Robinson's debut in Montreal; Canadian nationals in the big leagues; and finally the birth of the Blue Jays and Expos as the "big show" comes north of the border in 1969 (Expos) and 1977 (Blue Jays). Lavishly illustrated with rare black-and-white photographs, this handsome coffee-table volume was once praised by reviewer George Bowering as a must for Canadian baseball fans: "There should be a copy in the parlour of every baseball fan and everyone at all interested in Canadian memorabilia over the past 150 years."

Lee, Bill, with Dick Lally. *The Wrong Stuff.* New York: The Viking Press, 1984 (New York: Viking Penguin, 1985). 242 pp.

One of the most zany and colorful baseball flakes ever to take the mound in the major leagues, Bill Lee toiled for the Montreal Expos his final four seasons (1979–82) after a decade of service in Boston. In this no-holds-barred autobiography and freewheeling memoir, "Spaceman" Lee plays it every bit as fast, loose, and funny in print as he did on the big-league diamond and in the Boston and Montreal clubhouses. While much of the text focuses on Lee revealing his own personal universe, as well as on his longer Boston pitching career, there is much material as well on the four zany summers spent in Montreal, including an explanation of the infamous incident in which the free-spirited pitcher walked out on the Expos in protest against the release of a valuable teammate and friend— second baseman Rodney Scott. From first to last this is a most delightful and highly unorthodox baseball journey.

Robertson, John. *Rusty Staub of the Expos.* Scarborough, Ont.: Prentice-Hall of Canada, 1971. 186 pp.

Intending to capitalize on the immense fan appeal of Montreal's most popular player, this thinly veiled autobiography (in collaboration with Montreal daily sports columnist John Robertson) takes on the shape of an intimate dialogue between Rusty and the everyday fan of Montreal baseball. Staub's career is traced from early years in New Orleans, through his first eight big-league seasons with the Houston Astros, down to his trade to Montreal and the start of his stardom. Rusty passes on to the fans his insider's insights and opinions on such diverse matters as a baseball player's methods of off-season conditioning, detailed preparations for the upcoming season in spring training, tips on techniques for the aspiring young ballplayer, and anecdotes relating to other teams and rival players. Also provided are one player's frank personal views of behind-the-scenes wheeling and dealing by big-league owners, and the complicated maneuvering often involved in trading a player from one club to another. This book is a delightful read for fans wanting a glimpse of the seldom-seen business side of baseball.

Shaw, Bill. *Montreal Expos*. Major League Baseball Team History Series. Mankato, Minn.: Creative Education Publishing Company, 1982. 48 pp.

Heavily illustrated thin historical text written for a juvenile audience and coming in the wake of the Expos' single divisional title season of 1981. Part of a series covering all 26 big-league clubs, this small volume is perhaps one of the least objectionable in a collection of hastily written and poorly researched capsule histories produced by a team of authors not much more up-to-date (and probably even less so) on their baseball history than their juvenile readers themselves. At least Shaw manages to get most of the facts straight (not always the case with this series) as he weaves an interesting short narrative on the flavor of early expansion seasons with Canada's first big-league team. But there is virtually nothing here that an average informed adult fan won't already know.

Snyder, Brodie (with illustrations by Terry Mosher). *The Year the Expos Almost Won the Pennant*. Toronto, Ont.: Virgo Press, 1979. 233 pp.

Expomania exploded across all of Canada in 1979 as the Expos not only enjoyed their first-ever winning season but actually challenged briefly for a National League pennant. Two national newspaper award winners, Montreal sportswriter Brodie Snyder and political cartoonist Terry Mosher (a.k.a. Aislin) of the Montreal *Gazette*, team here to provide an intimate inside look at the ballclub and its incredible season. All the details are here: what happened and how and why; what the players and front-office executives of the ballclub did and felt and said throughout the summer, from the first spring training pitch to the final disappointing out of the season. Complete 1979 statistics, an all-time Expos 10-year player roster (complete through the 1979 season), and detailed statistical information on the Expos over their first decade—all are featured within a valuable appendix which concludes this "must-read volume" for all Montreal Expos diehards.

————. *The Year the Expos Finally Won Something!* Toronto, Ont.: Checkmark Books, 1981. 319 pp.

From the opening of spring training in West Palm Beach to the final thrilling moments of their memorable playoff game with the Los Angeles Dodgers, sportswriter Brodie Snyder captures the excitement of the Montreal Expos' unprecedented 1981 winning season. Day-by-day, through victory and defeat, and the uncertainty of the players' strike, Snyder chronicles events that led the Expos to their most amazing year ever. Mosher (a.k.a. Aislin) provides more than two dozen delightful illustrations, and the author includes 36 pages of complete statistics on the first dozen years of franchise history, on the full 1981 regular season, and on 1981 post-season play as well (including complete box scores).

Turner, Dan. *The Expos Inside Out.* Toronto, Ont.: McClelland and Stewart
   Publishers, 1983. 203 pp.
   A loving fan's tribute and informal team history by the popular host of
   an Ottawa public affairs television program. This is perhaps the most
   entertaining and informative book yet devoted to Canada's first major
   league ballclub. Beginning with the first historic game in 1969, Turner
   guides the reader through a comprehensive 15-year history of the team,
   its players, and its on-field and front-office management. His lively narrative leads up to the great drama of the 1982 season, when the Expos
   were favored by just about every baseball prognosticator to swagger into
   Canada's first World Series. With deft journalism, Turner explores what
   precisely went wrong with that highly touted 1982 Montreal club which
   fell ultimately to a disappointing third in the final league standings. This
   is a fine portrait of the Expos written with love, humor, and respect, and
   one offering an intimate inside look at such diamond stars as Carter,
   Dawson, Rogers, Raines, and Cromartie—the heart of Montreal's best
   and yet most disappointing team in club history.
———. *Heroes, Bums and Ordinary Men: Profiles in Canadian Baseball.* Toronto,
   Ontario: Doubleday Canada Limited, 1988. 280 pp.
   Assessment of Canada's contributions to big-league baseball, seen mainly
   through portraits of some of the handful of Canadians who have made
   it to the big time and enjoyed noteworthy (Fergie Jenkins, Reggie Cleveland) or momentary (Reno Bertoia, Claude Raymond) major league careers. Turner provides personal and human stories about young men's
   dreams of sharing the spotlight on major league playing fields, and of
   moments of true glory enjoyed by the few Canadians who have managed
   to get there.

Year-by-Year Standings and Season Summaries

Year	Pos.	Record	Pct.	GB	Manager	Player	BA	Player	HR	Player	W-L	ERA
1969	6th	52–110	.321	48.0	Mauch	Staub	.302	Staub	29	Stoneman	11–19	4.39
1970	6th	73–89	.451	16.0	Mauch	Fairly	.288	Staub	30	Morton	18–11	3.60
1971	5th	71–90	.441	25.5	Mauch	Staub	.311	Staub	19	Stoneman	17–16	3.14
1972	5th	70–86	.449	26.5	Mauch	Fairly	.278	Fairly	17	Torrez	16–12	3.33
1973	4th	79–83	.488	3.5	Mauch	Hunt	.309	Bailey	26	Renko	15–11	2.81
1974	4th	79–82	.491	8.5	Mauch	W. Davis	.295	Bailey	20	Torrez	15–8	3.58
1975	5th	75–87	.463	17.5	Mauch	Parrish	.274	Jorgensen	18	Murray	15–8	3.97
1976	6th	55–107	.340	46.0	Kuehl / Fox	Foli	.264	Parrish	11	Fryman	13–13	3.37
1977	5th	75–87	.463	26.0	Williams	Valentine	.293	Carter	31	Rogers	17–16	3.10
1978	4th	76–86	.469	14.0	Williams	Cromartie	.297	Valentine	25	Grimsley	20–11	3.05
								Dawson	25			
1979	2nd	95–65	.594	2.0	Williams	Parrish	.307	Parrish	30	Lee	16–10	3.04
1980	2nd	90–72	.556	1.0	Williams	Dawson	.308	Carter	29	Rogers	16–11	2.98
1981	3rd	30–25	.545	4.0	Williams	Cromartie	.304	Dawson	24	Rogers	12–8	3.41
	1st	30–23	.566	+0.5	Fanning	Raines	.304					
1981*	2nd	60–48	.556	2.0								
1982	3rd	86–76	.531	6.0	Fanning	Oliver	.331**	Carter	29	Rogers	19–8	2.40
1983	3rd	82–80	.506	8.0	Virdon	Oliver	.300	Dawson	32	Rogers	17–12	3.23
1984	5th	78–83	.484	18.0	Virdon / Fanning	Raines	.309	Carter	27	Lea	15–10	2.89
1985	3rd	84–77	.522	16.5	Rodgers	Raines	.320	Dawson	23	Smith	18–5	2.91
1986	4th	78–83	.484	29.5	Rodgers	Raines	.334**	Dawson	20	McGaffigan	10–5	2.65
1987	3rd	91–71	.562	4.0	Rodgers	Raines	.330	Wallach	26	Martinez	11–4	3.30
1988	3rd	81–81	.500	20.0	Rodgers	Galarraga	.302	Galarraga	29	Martinez	15–13	2.72
1989	4th	81–81	.500	12.0	Rodgers	Raines	.286	Galarraga	23	Martinez	16–7	3.18
1990	3rd	85–77	.525	10.0	Rodgers	Wallach	.296	Wallach	21	Sampen	12–7	2.99
1991	6th	71–90	.441	26.5	Rodgers/ Runnells	Calderon	.300	Calderon	19	D. Martinez	14–11	2.39
1992	2nd	87–75	.537	9.0	Runnells/Alou	Walker	.301	Walker	23	D. Martinez	16–11	2.47

*Split Season Totals (Players' Union Strike).
**Led National League

Career Batting Leaders (1969–1992)

Games Played	Andre Dawson	1,443	
At Bats	Andre Dawson	5,628	
Runs Scored	Tim Raines	934	
Hits	Tim Raines	1,598	
Batting Average (300 or	Al Oliver	.315	
more games)	Tim Raines	.301	
Home Runs	Andre Dawson	225	
Grand Slam Home Runs	Gary Carter	7	
Multiple Home Run Games	Tim Wallach	8	
Inside-the-Park Home	Tim Wallach	2	
Runs	Gary Carter	2	
	Ellis Valentine	2	
Runs Batted In	Tim Wallach	905	
Stolen Bases	Tim Raines	634	
Doubles	Andre Dawson	295	
Triples	Tim Raines	81	
Total Bases	Andre Dawson	2,679	
Walks	Tim Raines	775	
Consecutive Games Played	Rusty Staub	259	1970– 1971

Career Pitching Leaders (1969–1992)

Innings Pitched	Steve Rogers	2,839	
Earned Run Average (start- ing pitcher)	Steve Rogers	3.17	
Wins	Steve Rogers	158	
Losses	Steve Rogers	152	
Strikeouts	Steve Rogers	1,621	
10-Plus Strikeout Games	Bill Stoneman	8	
Walks	Steve Rogers	876	
Games	Steve Rogers	399	
Shutouts	Steve Rogers	37	
Saves	Jeff Reardon	152	
Games Started	Steve Rogers	393	
Complete Games	Steve Rogers	129	
No-Hit Games	Bill Stoneman	2	1969, 1972
One-Hit Games	Steve Rogers	4	

All-Time Expos Career and Season Records *(continued)*

Single-Season Batting Records

Batting Average (350 ABs)	Tim Raines	.334	1986
Home Runs	Andre Dawson	32	1983
Home Runs (left-handed)	Rusty Staub	30	1970
Home Runs (rookie)	Andre Dawson	19	1977
Home Runs (month)	Rusty Staub	12	August 1970
Home Runs (consecutive games)	Andre Dawson	4	1985–86
	Mitch Webster	4	1985
Pinch-Hit Home Runs	Hal Breeden	4	1973
Runs Batted In	Tim Wallach	123	1987
Runs	Tim Raines	133	1983
Hits	Al Oliver	204	1982
Singles	Tim Raines	140	1986
Doubles	Warren Cromartie	46	1979
Triples	Rodney Scott	13	1980
	Tim Raines	13	1985
	Mitch Webster	13	1986
Slugging Percentage	Andre Dawson	.553	1981
	Larry Parrish	.551	1979
Extra Base Hits	Andres Galarraga	79	1988
Stolen Bases	Ron LeFlore	97	1980
Pinch Hits	Jose Morales	25	1976
Sacrifice Hits	Larry Lintz	23	1974
Sacrifice Flies	Andre Dawson	18	1983
Strikeouts	Andres Galarraga	153	1988
Fewest Strikeouts (502 at-bats)	Dave Cash	29	1970
Walks	Ken Singleton	123	1973
Intentional Walks	Tim Raines	26	1987
Hit-by-Pitch	Ron Hunt	50	1971
Total Bases	Andre Dawson	341	1983
Hitting Streak	Warren Cromartie	19	1979
	Andre Dawson	19	1980
Consecutive Base Hits	Andre Dawson	8	1983
Most Hits by Pitcher	Steve Renko	24	1973
At-Bats	Warren Cromartie	659	1979
Games	Rusty Staub	162	1971
	Ken Singleton	162	1973
	Warren Cromartie	162	1980

All-Time Expos Career and Season Records *(continued)*

Single-Season Pitching Records

ERA (starting pitcher)	Mark Langston	2.39	1989
	Dennis Martinez	2.39	1991
ERA (relief pitcher)	Dale Murray	1.03	1974
Wins (starting pitcher)	Ross Grimsley	20	1978
Wins (relief pitcher)	Dale Murray	15	1975
Losses	Steve Rogers	22	1974
Strikeouts	Bill Stoneman	251	1971
Walks	Bill Stoneman	146	1971
Saves	Jeff Reardon	41	1985
Games	Mike Marshall	92	1973
Complete Games	Bill Stoneman	20	1971
Games Started	Steve Rogers	40	1977
Shutouts	Bill Stoneman	5	1969
	Steve Rogers	5	1979, 1983
Innings Pitched (starter)	Steve Rogers	302	1977
Innings Pitched (relief)	Mike Marshall	179	1973
Runs Allowed	Steve Rogers	139	1974
Earned Runs Allowed	Steve Rogers	126	1974
Hits Allowed	Carl Morton	281	1970
Home Runs Allowed	Carl Morton	27	1970
	Steve Renko	27	1970
	Bill Gullickson	27	1984
Wild Pitches	Steve Renko	19	1974
Hit Batsmen	Bill Stoneman	14	1970
Consecutive Games Won	David Palmer	8	1979
	Charlie Lea	8	1983
	Tim Burke	8	1985
Consecutive Games Lost	Steve Renko	10	1972
Consecutive Scoreless Innings	Woodie Fryman	32.2	1975

7

New York Giants-
San Francisco Giants
A Tale of Two Cities
FRED STEIN

The Giants came to New York in time for the 1883 season as the National League replaced moribund franchises in Troy, New York and Worcester, Massachusetts with clubs in New York and Philadelphia. The Giants (known as the "Gothams" from 1883 to 1885) were purchased by New York City factory owner John B. Day and James Mutrie, an energetic sports promoter. Day and Mutrie operated the independent New York Metropolitans baseball club which they had formed in 1881. In 1883 Day and Mutrie entered the "Mets" in the American Association and simultaneously began to build the National League Gothams.

Day and Mutrie stocked the Gothams with the cream of the Troy club's crop, players such as future Hall of Famers catcher Buck Ewing, first baseman Roger Connor, and pitcher Mickey Welch. Pitcher and jack-of-all-trades John Montgomery "Monte" Ward, another future Hall of Famer, was obtained from the Providence club. And several members of the Mets, including new Gothams manager John Clapp, were transferred in order to fill the Gothams' 13-man roster.

The Gothams played their first game on May 1, 1883, defeating Boston in a ragged 7–5 victory. The game was played at the first Polo Grounds, at 110th Street between Fifth and Sixth Avenues in Manhattan. The first Gothams lineup had catcher Buck Ewing leading off. The other players, in batting order sequence, were first baseman Roger Connor, center-fielder Monte Ward, left-fielder Pat Gillespie, right-fielder Mike Dorgan, pitcher Mickey Welch, second baseman Ed Caskins, shortstop Dasher Troy, and third baseman Frank Hankinson. Sparked by Captain (and actual field manager) Ewing, Connor, and Welch, the Gothams finished their first season in sixth place but within a respectable four games of .500. In 1884 the same trio led the club to a fifth-place finish.

The National League had set admission prices at 50 cents per person compared with the "lower class" American Association's 25 cents admission charge. Accordingly, in 1885, John Day concentrated on building up the more profitable Gothams, even at the expense of his 1884 pennant-winning Mets. He moved Mets manager Jim Mutrie over to manage the Gothams and transferred Mets star righthander Tim Keefe to the Gothams. With these substantial additions, plus stellar play by Welch, Connor, Ewing, and outfielders "Orator Jim" O'Rourke and Mike Dorgan, the Polo Grounders vaulted into second place, just two games behind baseball immortal Cap Anson's Chicago White Stockings. Mutrie's jubilant, postgame victory shouts as his good-sized charges won ("My big fellows! My Giants! We are the people!") led to the team's adoption of the name "Giants" in 1886.

The Giants, carried along by Keefe and Welch who registered 61 of the club's 84 wins, copped their first pennant in 1888 with relative ease over Cap Anson's club. Keefe won 19 consecutive games, which remains a tie for the major league record. In 1889 the Polo Grounders were the beneficiaries of 55 wins accumulated by Welch and Keefe, and they closed out the decade with another pennant.

The situation for the Giants changed drastically for the worst in the 1890s. City officials unexpectedly informed the Giants that their property was being taken over for city use, and Day hastily arranged to move the Giants to the Manhattan Field site further uptown at 155th Street and Eighth Avenue. The Giants played their earlier 1890 home games in Jersey City and Staten Island before moving into the second Polo Grounds on July 8, 1890.

The Giants sustained a more serious blow with the advent of the Players League in 1890. The new league was formed by the Brotherhood of Professional Baseball Players after a series of unresolved player-owner confrontations came to a head in 1889. The New York entrant in the Players League persuaded most of the Giants to join it. Of the players who carried the Giants to successive National League titles in 1888 and 1889, only Mickey Welch and outfielder "Silent Mike" Tiernan remained with the National League club. The Players League lasted only one year, but the Giants suffered large attendance losses and managed to survive only because President Arthur Soden of the National League's Boston team and a few others put up the money to keep the valuable New York franchise alive. But Day and Mutrie were ruined financially.

In March 1890 the Indianapolis club withdrew from the National League and its owner, John T. Brush, sold his best players, most notably fireballing righthander Amos Rusie, to the Giants. Regardless, the decimated Giants finished in sixth place in 1890. With the demise of the Players League after the 1890 season, the Giants purchased the larger Players League club's playing site adjoining the Polo Grounds, renamed it the "new Polo Grounds," and moved in for the next 67 years. The Polo Grounders regained enough of their old players—Ewing, Connor, Keefe, O'Rourke, outfielder George Gore, and infielder Danny Richardson—to climb back up to third place in 1891.

In 1892 the National League and the American Association patched up their differences and together formed a 12-club league with a split season. The Giants, with John Day in deep financial trouble, joined the coalition. Under stockholder pressure, Day released Mutrie as manager and replaced "Smiling Jeems" with Pat Powers. Powers' club finished an unspectacular eighth in 1892, his only managerial year.

Former Giants star Monte Ward, one of the key Players League figures, managed the Giants in 1893 and 1894. The second-place Giants played the pennant-winning Baltimore Orioles for the Temple Cup in 1894, and Ward's club beat the champions in four straight games. It was learned later that several Baltimore players had agreed to split their shares with Giants players, thereby explaining an uncharacteristically nonchalant performance by the storied Orioles.

C. C. Van Cott was the Giants president in 1893 and 1894, having replaced the financially crippled Day. Andrew Freedman, a New York insurance dealer and Tammany Hall political operator, bought controlling interest from Van Cott on January 24, 1895. Freedman conducted the club in a frenetic, uncoordinated manner during the eight years of his stewardship (1895–1902), continually antagonizing anyone with whom he came in contact. The Giants managed to finish in the first division only once despite no less than 17 managerial changes by the abrasive Freedman.

Star players of the Freedman years included shortstop-third baseman George Davis, infielder Kid Gleason, outfielders Mike Tiernan and George Van Haltren, and pitchers Amos Rusie, Cy Seymour, and Jouett Meekin. Davis succeeded Ward as Giants manager in 1895 when Davis was only 24. Managerial headaches had little effect upon Davis's playing performance as he hit well over .300 in each of his nine years with the club. He still holds the Giants' consecutive-game hitting record, with 33 in 1893.

Amos Rusie, elected to the Hall of Fame in 1977, won 230 games during his eight seasons with the Giants. The big Indiana righthander, possessor of a blinding fastball, led the National League in strikeouts in five of these seasons. A proud man, he sat out the 1896 season when Freedman deducted a $200 fine levied in 1895 from his 1896 contract. Rusie brought suit to recover his 1896 salary because the club "had prevented him from following his profession." He won his point and his money when all of the National League clubs chipped in to pay his 1896 salary, thereby avoiding a legal showdown on the reserve clause of player contracts. Rusie was a valuable Giant to the last; he was traded to Cincinnati in 1899 in a deal which brought the Giants the great righthander, Christy Mathewson.

Things improved for the Giants during the 1900–1910 period. The blundering Freedman left the Polo Grounds scene in 1902. Before he left he made one of his few certifiably wise decisions—he hired Baltimore Orioles manager John McGraw as Giants field boss, a move that made the Giants the most successful National League team for the next 25 years. McGraw assumed control of the Giants on July 19, 1902, bringing with him such talented Baltimore players as righthanded pitcher Joe "Iron Man" McGinnity, catcher Roger Bresnahan, and first baseman Dan McGann.

The 1902 Giants were a lost cause. Even the dynamic McGraw and his imported talent could not prevent a cellar finish. But in 1903 John T. Brush bought controlling interest in the Giants from the discredited Freedman, and the completely liberated McGraw drove his club to a second-place finish. The Giants' resurgence was led by McGinnity (31–20) and Mathewson, who won 30 games for the first of four times with the Giants. During the month of August the rubber-armed McGinnity pitched and won an incredible three complete-game doubleheaders.

The Giants came on strong in 1904, winning the pennant by 13 games over Chicago. Between them Mathewson, McGinnity, and Luther "Dummy" Taylor won a total of 95 games. There had been a World Series in 1903, the American League's first year of operation, but John Brush remained contemptuous of the new league and did not permit the Giants to play the Boston Red Sox, who had won the American League pennant.

The year 1905 was a virtual carbon copy of 1904 as the powerful Giants won the pennant over Pittsburgh by nine games. Mathewson, McGinnity, and righthander Leon "Red" Ames accounted for 74 Giants wins, and McGraw's offensive stars were centerfielder "Turkey Mike" Donlin, leftfielder Sam Mertes, and catcher Roger Bresnahan. The Giants defeated Connie Mack's Philadelphia Athletics in the World Series, 4 to 1, in a beautifully pitched "Shutout Series." Mathewson was brilliant, pitching three shutouts, and McGinnity shut out the A's for the Giants' other win. The Athletics' only win came when Chief Bender beat McGinnity, 3–0.

The Giants did not win another pennant during the 1900–1910 period, but they were competitive in every season. The innovative McGraw personally had a major impact on the game itself. For example, his use of the platoon system—specialized deployment of players—changed baseball strategy and was a prototype of later managers' sophisticated maximization of player skills. The highly emotional little Irishman motivated his players as no manager had yet done and, in so doing, roused fans, both for and against the Giants. As famed sportswriter Grantland Rice wrote: "His very walk across the field in a hostile town is a challenge to the multitudes."

McGraw's impact upon the emotional level of fans led the Giants into a continuous series of controversial and often wildly exuberant scenes. In August 1904, for example, Giants catcher Frank Bowerman slugged a fan who had been riding him hard throughout a game in Cincinnati. The aggrieved fan, holding his badly cut jaw, claimed that McGraw had "ordered the assault." A week later, overenthusiastic Giants fans celebrated an exciting doubleheader victory at the Polo Grounds by nearly trampling McGraw as he left the Giants dugout for the clubhouse. Several fans tried to carry McGraw off the field in triumph, but they dropped him and wildeyed rooters walked all over the prostrate McGraw, nearly crushing him and injuring his ankle severely.

Christy Mathewson's brilliance shone through the McGraw-generated turmoil. "Big Six" became the fans' idol early in the 1900s, not only because of his great pitching and famous "fadeaway" (screwball), but because of his personal style. Unlike the rough-and-ready McGraw, Matty came across as a cool, gentlemanly craftsman who pitched as though he were playing chess. He preferred outguessing hitters to terrorizing them with brute speed. He did not specialize in strikeouts but, with his superb control and guile, induced hitters to tap weakly to his fielders.

Other Giants of early 20th-century vintage also drew special attention from the fans and writers. Tough, aggressive outfielder Mike Donlin spent six highly successful years with the Giants, interspersed with years out of the game when he pursued a career in vaudeville. Roger Bresnahan was a future Hall of Famer and innovative catcher who in 1906 became the first receiver to wear shinguards and the first player to wear a head protector when batting. Second baseman "Laughing Larry" Doyle was a solid, upbeat player who coined the phrase, "It's great to be young and a Giant." Third baseman Art Devlin was the classic McGraw-type player whose steadiness and aggressiveness compensated for his average hitting performance. And alcoholic righthander Arthur "Bugs" Raymond intrigued the fans with his occasional brilliance on the mound and his heavy drinking, although his weakness led to his death at 30. (Raymond's favorite practice was to trade baseballs for drinks at bars near the ballpark.)

The 1911–1920 period began unhappily on April 14, 1911, when a fire of undetermined origin ravaged the Polo Grounds and demolished much of the structure. The Giants accepted an offer by the Yankees to use Hilltop Park, the American Leaguers' home park at 168th Street and Broadway in Manhattan. The Giants played there until they returned to the rebuilt and enlarged Polo Grounds on June 28, 1911. The decade was marked by three straight pennant wins during the 1911–1913 period, a precipitous drop into last place in 1915, and a rebuilding program that carried the Giants to another pennant in 1917 and second-place finishes through the 1920 season.

Lefthander Richard "Rube" Marquard matured from a four-game winner in 1910 to a 24-game victor in 1911, and that improvement brought McGraw's club the pennant. The Giants repeated in 1912 and 1913 as Mathewson, Marquard, and righthander Jeff Tesreau provided continued great pitching. The offensive load was carried by Fred Merkle (whose famous "boner" in failing to touch second base on a game-winning hit had nullified a crucial win and cost the Giants the 1908 pennant), Larry Doyle, rightfielder Red Murray, centerfielder Fred Snodgrass, and full-blooded Indian catcher John "Chief" Meyers.

The Giants failed completely in their World Series appearances of 1911–1913. They lost to the Athletics in 1911 and 1913 so convincingly that Giants rooters could accept these losses philosophically. But the loss to the Red Sox in 1912, on Snodgrass's "$30,000 muff" of an easy flyball, was difficult to take.

On November 26, 1912 Giants' President Brush died, and he was succeeded by his son-in-law Harry N. Hempstead. Hempstead, who knew nothing about baseball, relied for advice on Club Secretary John B. Foster rather than McGraw. The resulting front-office friction continued until McGraw characteristically reestablished complete control over club operations a few weeks later.

After a second-place finish in 1914 the Giants fell apart in 1915, finishing in last place for the only time in McGraw's 30-year managerial tenure. The season was notable only because widely heralded 1912 Olympic star Jim Thorpe joined the Giants (he proved allergic to curveballs and didn't stay) as did future Hall of Famer George "High-pockets" Kelly. McGraw cleaned house and brought the Giants up to fourth place in 1916 with help from outfielder Benny Kauff, the "Ty Cobb" of the collapsed Federal League. In midseason McGraw traded his friend Christy Mathewson to Cincinnati, where Matty took over as manager.

The 1916 Giants were models of inconsistency. The club lost eight straight games in April, then reeled off a string of 17 consecutive victories in May, all of them on the road. Finally, the Giants escaped to fourth place from deep in the second division with a record 26-game winning streak in September. The retooled Giants won the 1917 pennant by a 10-game margin. This was an unexpectedly easy flag considering that the Giants had only one 20-game winner (lefthander

Ferdie Schupp with a 21–7 record), only two .300 hitters (center-fielder Benny Kauff and left-fielder George Burns), and only one hitter with more than 68 RBIs (third baseman Heinie Zimmerman had 102). The Giants lost the World Series to the Chicago White Sox, four games to two.

McGraw's club wound up the decade with second-place finishes in 1918 and 1919, but not without some taint of the game-throwing scandals which surfaced in the 1919 Black Sox affair. The Giants had obtained fancy-fielding first baseman Hal Chase from Cincinnati early in 1919 after the Reds had suspended the shady Chase for "indifferent play" in August 1918. The Reds also had charged Chase with attempting to influence players to throw games, but he was acquitted by the National League's Board of Directors.

Three future Hall of Famers joined the club as the decade neared its end—outfielder Ross "Pep" Youngs, infielder Frank Frisch (fresh off the Fordham University campus), and first baseman George Kelly (back from the minors). In addition, polished lefthander Art Nehf came over from the Braves and righthander Jesse Haines arrived from the Cubs.

The Giants changed hands on January 14, 1919, when the club was purchased for more than one million dollars from the Brush estate by a syndicate headed by New York stockbroker Charles A. Stoneham, New York City Magistrate Francis X. McQuade, and John McGraw. Stoneham was elected president, McQuade treasurer, and McGraw vice president while continuing as field manager.

The Giants sparkled in the first half of the 1920s, then frustrated McGraw and their fans by barely falling short in the second half. The 1920s also found the Giants in a losing struggle with the up-and-coming Yankees for supremacy in New York. On May 14, 1920 the Giants informed the Yankees that the American Leaguers' lease to use the Polo Grounds would not be renewed after the 1920 season. No reason was given although it was obvious that the wide acclaim for the Yanks' recently acquired Babe Ruth had been a great irritant. Yankees Owner Jacob Ruppert responded angrily that the Giants "had gone back on their word," the understanding that had been in effect since the Yanks began using the Polo Grounds in 1912. The eviction order was rescinded a week later, but the bitter Ruppert began immediate efforts to obtain a site for the Yankees' own ballpark.

The Giants won the first of four consecutive pennants in 1921 as Kelly, shortstop Dave Bancroft, Frisch, Youngs, and veteran outfielder George Burns led the offense and Art Nehf anchored the pitching staff. The turning point in the season came in late August when the Giants, 7½ games behind league-leading Pittsburgh, took five straight games from the overconfident Pirates at the Polo Grounds. McGraw's club went on to defeat the Yankees 5 games to 3 in the first "Subway Series."

The Polo Grounders repeated in 1922 with the same personnel, winning the pennant with relative ease and again defeating the Yankees in the World Series. The Giants' second straight World Series win over the hated Yankees was noteworthy because McGraw's pitchers held Babe Ruth to only two hits, and the second game was called surprisingly "on account of darkness" with the score tied at three-all and the sun high in the sky. There was such an uproar at the decision of Umpire George Hildebrand to call the game that Commissioner Kenesaw M. Landis ordered the receipts of more than $120,000 sent to New York City charities and veterans groups.

The Giants welcomed the 1923 season in a Polo Grounds which had been expanded to its ultimate 55,000 seating capacity. The original 15,000 bleacher seats were reduced by two-thirds, as many of the old bleacher seats in left center and right center were converted to covered, double-decked grandstands. This was the last significant addition to the Polo Grounds except for lights for night games, which were installed in 1940. It left the elongated, bathtub-shaped park with short foul lines (257 feet to right and 280 feet to left) and bleachers some 455 feet from the plate.

The Polo Grounders won their third straight pennant in 1923, led offensively by leftfielder Emil "Irish" Meusel, Frisch, Kelly, and Youngs. But the Giants lost the World Series to the Yankees, now ensconced in brand new Yankee Stadium. The key figures in the Series were Ruth, who hit .368 with three homers, and the Giants' Casey Stengel, who clubbed .417 and won two games with home runs.

The Giants nosed out Brooklyn in 1924 for their fourth straight flag. This was substantially the same cast that had won pennants the past three years, with the addition of shortstop Travis Jackson (replacing Bancroft), center-fielder Hack Wilson, and part-timers first baseman Bill Terry and third baseman Fred Lindstrom. The Washington Senators beat the Giants in a seven-game Series. Giants reliever Jack Bentley lost to the great Walter Johnson in the bottom of the ninth of the deciding game when the Senators' Earl McNeely poked an easy bouncer that hit a pebble and hopped over Lindstrom's head.

Hampered by inadequate pitching, the Giants did not win another pennant in the 1920s. Equally as galling, they began to play an increasingly more obvious second fiddle to the mighty Yankees with each passing year, and McGraw's frustration grew correspondingly. Still, the Giants remained a star-studded club through the 1920s despite McGraw's inability to bring another pennant to New York. Ross Youngs was a great outfielder and hustler who hit .322 over a 10-year career. His playing days ended abruptly with the onset of a serious kidney ailment that took his life in 1927 when he was only 30.

Bill Terry was considered the finest-fielding first baseman of his day, and his .341 lifetime average is among the highest of modern-era players. Memphis Bill was a powerful, straightaway hitter who specialized in blasting line drives into the power alleys. Travis Jackson was the classic "ballplayer's ballplayer," widely respected and liked by both players and fans. He was a great shortstop with good range, a rifle arm, superb bunting and hit-and-run talents, and surprising power considering his slight build.

Mel Ott's brilliant career with the Giants began in 1925 when he joined the club just before the season ended, as a scared 16-year-old catcher referred to McGraw by a New Orleans friend. Ott played his first Giants game at 17 and became the regular right fielder in 1928. The most popular Giants player of his time, Master Melvin carried the club's offense for most of his 22 seasons with the Giants. Carl Hubbell, a stylish, screwballing lefthander from Oklahoma, carried the Giants' pitching load as effectively as his bosom buddy Ott spearheaded the offense. Noted for his ability to win crucial games, King Carl retired in 1943 to become the Giants' farm club supervisor, a position he held for more than 30 years.

Freddy Fitzsimmons, a stout and stout-hearted knuckleballer from Indiana, joined the Giants in 1925. Famed for his unusual "turntable" delivery (he turned his back to the hitter and appeared to look out to center field before delivering his pitch), the righthander won 170 games as a Giant before he was traded to Brooklyn in 1937 in Terry's worst deal ever. Fred Lindstrom was a talented third baseman-outfielder who came to the Giants as an 18-year-old in 1924. Lindstrom had an impressive 231 hits in both the 1928 and 1930 seasons, winding up with a .311 career batting average.

The decade ended with the front office in turmoil. On December 24, 1929 officers of the Giants filed a $200,000 damage suit against Francis X. McQuade, a major stockholder who had been deposed as club treasurer after serving in that post for nine years. The suit charged McQuade with seeking to "wreck and destroy" the club. McQuade filed a countersuit. After long and arduous litigation the New York Supreme Court ordered the Giants to pay McQuade back salary but refused to order his reinstatement as treasurer. The Giants successfully protested the payment order to a higher court, leaving McQuade out in the cold.

In the 1930s the Giants were dominated by three great players—Terry, Hubbell, and Ott. Terry hit .401 in 1930 (the last National Leaguer to hit .400), just missed winning the National League batting title in 1931 by the narrowest of margins, then replaced McGraw as manager in 1932. Memphis Bill, making excellent use of his skills as a superb defensive strategist, took the Giants to a surprise World Championship in 1933 and to pennants in 1936 and 1937. Hubbell was the Giants' pitching leader and Ott the club's offensive bellwether through the decade.

The 1930s began with two more first-division finishes by the Giants but without McGraw's coveted 11th National League pennant. McGraw's 1930 club managed to remain in the running through August, but wound up in third place. The story was the same in 1931 when the Giants finished well behind the pennant-winning Cardinals. McGraw's health, poor for some time, worsened in 1932, and the jumpy, easily irritated manager lost control of his players. The club floundered through April and May. Then, on June 3 an ill and aging McGraw stepped down and Terry was named to succeed him. McGraw died less than two years later, on February 25, 1934.

Under Terry the disorganized, last-place Giants regrouped and managed a sixth-place finish. Terry began maneuvering to improve the club as soon as the season ended. He swung a major deal with the Cardinals, obtaining second-string catcher Gus Mancuso. (Mancuso would be a key figure in three pennant wins.) Lindstrom, openly unhappy because he felt that he would be McGraw's successor, was traded to the Pirates. In other off-season moves, pitchers Waite Hoyt and Clarence Mitchell were released and catcher Frank "Shanty" Hogan was sold back to the Braves.

Terry inherited several excellent players from McGraw, beginning with first baseman Terry himself. Travis Jackson was still around, although hampered by knee ailments. Mel Ott, beginning his eighth year with the Giants at 24, was the club's only authentic power hitter and one of the best defensive right fielders in the game. Leftfielder JoJo Moore, a gaunt, hollow-cheeked Texan with a great throwing arm, had shown promise. Second baseman Hughie Critz was the other regular holdover from the McGraw years.

The Giants had a number of talented pitchers. Hubbell was the staff leader and Fitzsimmons was an established starter. Terry was high on Hal Schumacher, a determined, sinkerball-throwing righthander who had pitched for the club in 1931 and 1932. Other pitchers included LeRoy "Tarzan" Parmelee, whose nickname derived from his wildness; righthander Ray Starr, who had come from the Cardinals in the Mancuso deal; lefthander Al Smith; and Adolfo Luque, a wily, 43-year-old Cuban righthanded relief pitcher whose National League career dated back to 1919 when he pitched for Cincinnati.

The Giants, picked to finish in sixth place in the annual Associated Press poll of sportswriters, surprised the experts by holding third place on Memorial Day. Well suited to the dead ball that had come into

National League use in 1933, the Giants began to win a series of low-scoring games and moved into first place to stay in June. Hubbell, Fitzsimmons, Schumacher, and Parmelee rotated starting assignments and pitched effectively, and Luque, Starr, and the all-purpose Hubbell excelled in relief. Mancuso proved a steadying influence behind the plate. Rookie shortstop Blondy Ryan was an adequate, and occasionally inspiring, substitute for Jackson. Ott led the hitters as expected.

The Giants defeated Joe Cronin's Washington Senators in a five-game Series as Hubbell and Ott excelled. King Carl won the opening game at the Polo Grounds 4–2, supported by Master Melvin's three-run homer and four-for-four hitting performance. Hubbell took the fourth game 2–1, and Ott won the last game with a 10th-inning home run to give the Giants a 4–3 decision.

A triumphant Bill Terry attended the annual major league meetings in New York in January 1934 and talked with several of the writers about prospects for the coming season. On the edge of the group stood the *New York Times'* Roscoe McGowen, who normally covered the Dodgers. In the beginning he paid little attention to the conversation. But when Terry was questioned about the other clubs, McGowen became more attentive. He asked, "How about Brooklyn, Bill?" Terry turned to him and smiled. "Brooklyn, I haven't heard anything about them. Are they still in the league?" Everybody laughed and everybody printed the remark.

Terry, never known for his subtlety, had responded lightly, but it didn't come out that way in the writers' stories. Thousands of letters poured into the Giants' offices, all of them from irate Dodgers fans. The Dodgers had left their rooters cold since falling deep into the second division, but Terry's offhand comment had fired them up. Wait until the season started. Their team would show Terry whether Brooklyn was still in the league!

The Giants were favored to repeat and they played up to that form, leading the league handily by the time the All-Star Game was played in early July. Terry piloted the National League squad in the second game of the new mid-summer series at the Polo Grounds on July 10. The National League's 9–7 loss was not the enduring story of the game; Hubbell's remarkable pitching was. The great lefthander struck out five future Hall of Famers in a row—Babe Ruth, Lou Gehrig, Jimmy Foxx, Al Simmons, and Joe Cronin.

On Labor Day the Giants resided comfortably in first place, six games ahead of St. Louis and Chicago. But by mid-September Terry's club was faltering badly while the "Gas House Gang" Cardinals, sparked by Dizzy Dean, were streaking, and the clubs were tied with two games left to play. The relaxed Dodgers, well out of the running, came into the Polo Grounds to complete the season.

Terry probably had given very little thought to the Brooklyn fans during the season when the Giants were riding high and the Dodgers were floundering in the second division. But now, at the rain-swept Polo Grounds that final Saturday of the season, the Dodger fans were out in force. They taunted all of the Giants unmercifully, including Ott and Jackson who normally were cheered even at Ebbets Field. But they saved their choicest epithets for Terry—one of the most gentle being, "Is Brooklyn still in the league, Terry? You'll find out, you cocky bum. We'll show you." And show Terry the Dodgers did. They took the Giants in two games, while the Cardinals won twice to capture the pennant. Within the context of the historic Giants-Dodgers rivalry, it was a bad year for the second-place Giants and a triumphant year for Casey Stengel's sixth-place Dodgers.

The 1935 Giants team was essentially unchanged except for the important addition of scrappy little shortstop Dick Bartell, who was obtained from the Phillies. So were the results. A good start, with the Giants leading the league through much of the season; then the Terrymen falling before a tough western club, this time the Cubs, who steamrollered to the pennant with a 21-game winning streak. Terry made one important trade after his second straight disappointing loss, acquiring utility infielder Burgess Whitehead from the Cardinals. Several of the writers questioned whether the slight Whitehead had the stamina to play a full season, but the intelligent North Carolinian proved them wrong.

Club President Charles A. Stoneham died on January 6, 1936. He was the last survivor of the triumvirate that had purchased the Giants in 1919. A week later, 32-year-old Horace C. Stoneham replaced his father. Stoneham, a convivial man who virtually forced his managers to match him drink for drink, remained the Giants' president for the next 40 years. Popular Eddie Brannick, who had been associated with the Giants since he was a small boy running errands for John McGraw, became the club secretary.

After a good start the 1936 Giants slipped badly, and they fell into fifth place at the All-Star break. Losing the first game of a double-header on July 15, the Terrymen were 11 games off the pace. But they captured the second game when Terry, playing courageously on a badly crippled knee and against his doctor's advice, came off the bench and led the club with a single, double, and triple. This valiant effort revived the Giants, who rebounded sharply to win 39 of their next 47 games and to rocket into first place and remain there for the rest of the season. Bartell and Whitehead stabilized the defense, and Mancuso had his best year since 1933. But the blue-chip performers, as always, were Hubbell and Ott. Hubbell, called the "Meal Ticket" (to the proud Terry's disgust), racked up a league-leading 26 wins, finishing the season with 16 straight victories. Stocky little Ott had a league-leading 33 homers and 135 RBIs.

The Giants lost the World Series to the overpowering Yankees in six games. Hubbell won the first game, and Schumacher held on tenaciously to win the fifth game. But the Giants were overmatched by the Gehrig-DiMaggio-Dickey-Ruffing powerhouse that had won the American League flag by a cool 19½ games.

The Giants repeated as pennant winners in 1937 on the strength of 20-game winning seasons by Hubbell and rookie lefthander Cliff Melton, powerful hitting by Ott, and some late-season hitting heroics by outfielder Jimmy Ripple as well. The key to the season came when Terry benched weak-hitting third baseman Lou Chiozza, replacing him with the versatile Ott, and inserted Ripple in right field in Ott's position. Hubbell won his first eight decisions of the campaign, running his two-season consecutive-game winning streak to 24, before the Dodgers, his career-long nemesis team, broke the string on Memorial Day. The 1937 World Series was a virtual replay of the 1936 Series. The Giants again were badly overmatched as Hubbell recorded their only victory.

The Polo Grounders were also-rans for the rest of the decade. The 1938 club started brilliantly, holding first place by midseason. But Terry's club faltered after the All-Star break and the team finished deep in third place, the downswing largely attributable to serious elbow ailments suffered by Hubbell and Schumacher. After the season Terry engineered a major trade with the Chicago Cubs, exchanging Bartell, Mancuso, and center-fielder Hank Leiber for their opposite numbers—shortstop Billy Jurges, catcher Ken O'Dea, and outfielder Frank Demaree. First baseman Zeke Bonura, a potent hitter but with no discernible mobility afield, was obtained from Washington. Regardless of the trades the Giants sank into fifth place in 1939, by far their worst showing under Terry's leadership. To make matters worse, as the decade ended the hated Dodgers moved past the Giants into third place.

The Giants' melancholia persisted through the 1940s. The Polo Grounders finished sixth in 1940 and fifth in 1941, Terry's last two years as manager. Hal Schumacher led the pitching staff in wins both years, with a meager 13 in 1940 and 12 in 1941. First baseman Babe Young and catcher Harry Danning were the most effective hitters in 1940, and Ott, troubled with vision problems, had his first poor hitting season. Meanwhile, the Giants continued to lose in attendance and local prestige as the revived Dodgers came in second in 1940 and won the pennant in 1941.

Mel Ott was named to replace Terry on December 2, 1941, just five days before Pearl Harbor. Master Melvin was a surprise managerial choice, primarily because of his quiet, unassuming personality and his lack of managing experience. Terry, long desirous of moving into the front office, became the director of the Giants' rapidly shrinking farm system operation.

Ott's regime began on a high note. New York fans, writers, and players rejoiced in the likable slugger's appointment, and his quick trade for the Cardinals' slugging Johnny Mize made a big hit. It also paved the way for an unexpectedly strong third-place finish as Ott and Mize blasted the pitching-poor Giants to victory after victory. But the Giants' fortunes plummeted in 1943 as the club lost a disproportionately large number of regulars to the military. When the Giants gathered at their Lakewood, New Jersey, training camp (all clubs were required to train near their home cities because of transportation and fuel shortages caused by the war effort), regulars Danning, Mize, Young, and Willard Marshall were in the service, and several other Giants were expected to be called up at any time.

The undermanned Giant sank deep into the second division early in the season, the one bright spot coming on June 5 when Hubbell, approaching 40 and in his final playing season, threw a brilliant one-hitter against the Pirates for his 250th career win. As the 1943 season drew to a merciful close, Ott was signed to a three-year player-manager contract, and the freshly retired Hubbell signed a long-term pact as farm system director, the post formerly held by Bill Terry. With the U.S. military effort at its peak of activity, the Giants' farm system consisted only of the Jersey City team of the International League, the Class D Bristol, Tennessee, club in the Appalachian League, and a small scouting staff.

The 1944 club managed a fifth-place finish, reflecting the fact that other National League teams had lost even more talent to the military than the Polo Grounders since the outset of the 1943 campaign. The Giants repeated their 1944 performance in 1945—a fifth-place finish and never in pennant contention. The year's highlight game came on August 1 when Ott blasted the 500th home run. (At the time, the second highest National League home run total was owned by Rogers Hornsby with 302.)

The first post-World War II year started promisingly. The Giants purchased catcher Walker Cooper from the Cardinals for $175,000, a lot of money in 1946. In addition, the Giants acquired highly ballyhooed pitcher-outfielder Clint "Hondo" Hartung from Minneapolis. Then, with no warning before the season opened, several Giants players jumped to the Mexican League, a newly formed "outlaw" league operated by Mexican businessman Jorge Pasquel. Within six weeks the Giants lost outfielder Danny Gardella; first baseman Napoleon Reyes; pitchers Adrian Zabala, Sal Maglie, Harry Feldman, and Ace Adams;

second baseman George Hausmann; and reserve first baseman Roy Zimmerman. Adams had been the Giants' relief anchor since 1942, and his loss was a particularly heavy blow to Ott's pitching-starved team. None of the other National League clubs suffered a comparable loss to the Mexican League, and the Giants' pennant chances ended there.

The 1946 season began poorly. Ott injured his knee and played very little for the balance of the season. Cooper broke a finger. The overrated Hartung flopped as an outfielder and was tried as a pitcher. The pitching was woeful, and Adams was missed badly as game after game slipped away because of poor relief pitching. The club stumbled through June making little headway, then settled in last place to stay. The only achievement of note was the club's home attendance of 1,243,773, which far exceeded the club record set in 1945. After the season ended there were rumors that San Francisco baseball legend Frank "Lefty" O'Doul would replace Ott, but Mel was retained.

The 1947 club, which finished in fourth place, was a reinforced version of the 1946 team, yet without the injuries. Rookie righthander Larry Jansen shone through the cloud of pitching ineptitude with a remarkable 21–5 season, and second baseman Bill Rigney, along with young outfielders Bobby Thomson and Carroll "Whitey" Lockman, supplied the slow-moving Giants with needed pep and speed. But the big story was the Giants' home run-hitting power—they were affectionately referred to as "the windowbreakers" by the Polo Grounds faithful. By the All-Star break the Giants were in third place, but only because the powerful offense continually bailed out a weak pitching staff. National League club records for home runs fell as the Giants homered in 18 straight games and exceeded the Yankees' all-time major league record total of 182. Ott's blasters wound up with 221 homers, a 154-game season record at the time.

Giants fans, despite their deep fondness for Ott, continually debated his merits as a manager. Some said he couldn't handle pitchers. Others faulted his tendency to play for one run late in the game despite his pitchers' inability to hold leads. Many felt vaguely that he was "too nice" to be a winning manager. But, examined in retrospect, Ott's failure to win was essentially a matter of poor pitching.

The 1948 season began with Ott's future as Giants manager on the line. After a good start, the club faltered and Horace Stoneham decided to change managers. He announced his move on July 16, 1948, with the Giants in fourth place, and what a change! Dodgers manager Leo Durocher was named to replace Ott. A man Giants rooters detested for his abrasive style, as well as his Dodgers affiliation, was taking the place of their longtime hero, dismissed contemptuously by Durocher a few years before as a "nice guy."

Lippy Leo was uncharacteristically restrained as the Giants finished an undistinguished fifth in 1948. But he took direct action when the Giants showed no improvement in 1949. This, incidentally, was the first season in which black players—in this case Monte Irvin and Hank Thompson—played for the Giants. Durocher began to clean house long before the season ended. Cooper, having a poor season and never a Durocher admirer, was traded to Cincinnati. Mize, hitting .263 with a mere 18 home runs, was sold to the Yankees in time to star in the World Series against the Dodgers. During the winter the Giants made a whopper of a deal in which they sent outfielder Willard Marshall, third baseman Sid Gordon, and shortstop Buddy Kerr to the Braves for second baseman Eddie Stanky and shortstop Alvin Dark. Durocher was well on the way to having "his kind of team" as the decade ended.

The Giants moved up to third place in 1950, finishing only five games behind Philadelphia's famous pennant-winning Whiz Kids. Stanky and Dark played superbly and the pitching improved. After a so-so year in 1949, Jansen rebounded to win 19 games. And the Giants got a big break when Maglie returned from Mexico a tough, seasoned pitcher who had mastered the art of nicking the inside corner of the plate to the point that he was nicknamed "The Barber" because of the close shave he gave hitters.

The 1951 club started slowly and Durocher made some crucial lineup changes. Lockman and Irvin switched positions, Lockman moving to first base and Irvin to left field, and Thomson was replaced in center field by a young fellow who had been terrorizing pitchers for Minneapolis—Willie Mays. After going hitless in his first 12 at-bats, Mays stroked his first major league hit off Warren Spahn, a towering home run off the left-field grandstand roof at the Polo Grounds. Shortly after, the effervescent Mays began to spark the club with his spirited play and morale-boosting good nature. Still, as late as August 11, the Giants were a distant 13½ games behind Charlie Dressen's league-leading Dodgers. Durocher's club bounced back dramatically and cut the Dodgers' lead to five games with an inspired 16-game winning streak, then pulled dead even as the regular season ended.

In the three-game playoff for the pennant, Giants righthander Jim Hearn beat Ralph Branca 3–1 in the first game, but the Dodgers squared matters as Clem Labine defeated righthander Sheldon Jones 10–0. The deciding game, on October 3, proved to be the most memorable in baseball history. Losing 4–1 in the bottom of the ninth, the Giants' chances were dim as they faced powerful righthander Don Newcombe.

Alvin Dark opened with a bloop single to right. For some unexplained reason, Dressen had first baseman Gil Hodges playing a step behind the baserunner even though Dark was highly unlikely to steal because his run was meaningless. Mueller, a bat magician, grounded a single to right into the large gap provided by Hodges' positioning near first base. Irvin popped to Hodges, but Lockman came through with a sliced double past third base, scoring Dark and moving Mueller to third. Mueller injured his ankle sliding into the bag and Clint Hartung ran for him. Meanwhile, Dressen removed the tiring Newcombe and brought in Branca.

With one out, men on second and third, and the Giants losing 4–2, Bobby Thomson stepped in to hit as Willie Mays moved into the on-deck circle. The first pitch was a called strike as Branca threw a waist-high fastball. And here is the way longtime Giants announcer Russ Hodges described the action that followed:

> Bobby batting at .292. He's had a single and a double and he drove in the Giants' first run with a long fly to center . . . Hartung down the line at third not taking any chances . . . Branca throws . . . (pause) . . . THE GIANTS WIN THE PENNANT! THE GIANTS WIN THE PENNANT! THE GIANTS WIN THE PENNANT! . . . Bobby Thomson hits into the lower deck of the leftfield stands. THE GIANTS WIN THE PENNANT! THE GIANTS WIN THE PENNANT AND THEY'RE GOING CRAZY! THE GIANTS WIN THE PENNANT! THE GIANTS WIN THE PENNANT!

After hitting the ball, Thomson left the plate with his usual greyhound speed, then slowed down as the ball hooked into the lower stands about 20 feet above the outstretched glove of leftfielder Andy Pafko, some 315 feet from home plate. The Giants mobbed Thomson as he leaped high and planted both feet on the plate. The thunderstruck Dodgers began to move off the field like zombies, except for the indomitable Jackie Robinson,who stood near second base making sure that Thomson touched each base.

The Polo Grounds was a madhouse as Giants fans shrieked joyfully, pounded each other in unabashed ecstasy, and raced onto the field to intercept their heroes before they could escape to the clubhouse in deep center field. Long after the game, Giants enthusiasts could be seen in the stands and on the field shouting, dancing, and hugging complete strangers. The high point came when Thomson emerged from the clubhouse, stood at the top of the stairs, and waved to the crowd.

The jubilation at the Polo Grounds was matched all over the city as Russ Hodges' voice carried throughout the area. When the "Miracle at Coogan's Bluff" happened, it was 3:58 p.m. Within a few seconds the entire city (with the notable exception of the borough of Brooklyn) reacted. Motorists blew their horns in jubilation, and the din continued in city streets and on school campuses for the next couple of hours. The

Giants' loss to the Yankees in a six-game World Series was completely anticlimactic.

The Giants finished in second place in 1952 as the Dodgers regrouped and came on strong to win. Irvin missed most of the year with a broken ankle, and Mays was called up by the Army early in the season. Hearn, Maglie, and rookie reliever Hoyt Wilhelm carried the pitching load as Jansen faltered, but the Giants were completely outclassed. Durocher brought back memories of the McGraw days, drawing three separate suspensions for umpire-baiting in a three-week period.

With Mays in the service for the entire season, 1953 was a leaner year, and the Giants fell back to fifth place. The Giants were out of the race by mid-August, and Charlie Dressen counted them out with the accurate, if ungrammatical, pronouncement, "The Giants is dead." The season was marked by particularly bitter Giants-Dodgers games. On September 4, Clem Labine and Jansen threw at several opposing hitters, and Jansen narrowly escaped being spiked when Duke Snider and Jackie Robinson dropped bunts down the first-base line in futile attempts to retaliate for close pitches. Then, two days later, Dodgers right-fielder Carl Furillo climaxed several seasons of hard feelings with Durocher when, after being hit on the wrist with a pitched ball, Furillo raced to the Giants dugout to engage Lippy Leo in a memorable brawl.

The 1954 season provided a pleasant surprise as the Giants came back to win the pennant. The offense was paced by the booming bat of the returned Willie Mays. Lockman, Dark, and outfielder Jim "Dusty" Rhodes came through repeatedly in the pinch to pull out close games. Mays barely beat out Giants right-fielder Don Mueller to win the batting title. Lefthander Johnny Antonelli, a former bonus baby obtained from the Braves, led the pitching staff with a brilliant 21–7 record. Righthander Marv Grissom and Wilhelm were the other pitching standouts as the Giant beat out the Dodgers by five games. The Giants went on to sweep a strong Cleveland club in four straight in the World Series. The Series is remembered best for a marvelous over-the-shoulder catch by Mays on Vic Wertz's long smash to deep center field at the Polo Grounds, which cut short a budding Indians rally.

In 1955 the club slipped back to third place, 18½ games behind another powerful Dodgers club. The Giants had three new regulars: first baseman Gail Harris, second baseman Wayne Terwilliger, and catcher Ray Katt. None of them came through, the pitching was mediocre, and another great 51-homer season for Mays was wasted. Durocher's contract also ran out and was not renewed.

Billy Rigney, who had managed the Giants' farm club in Minneapolis in 1954–55, succeeded Durocher in 1956. But the Giants finished sixth as Brooklyn's "Boys of Summer" won again. The story was the same in 1957—a sixth-place finish, inept pitching except for righthander Ruben Gomez, and a generally mediocre club with weaknesses relieved only by the brilliant play of Mays and the occasional power hitting of outfielder Hank Sauer.

In 1955 it had become public knowledge that Dodgers President Walter O'Malley wanted to move his club out of tiny, outmoded Ebbets Field. At the same time Horace Stoneham was looking for another home for his team as well. With the Polo Grounds slated to be demolished and replaced by a housing development, it was rumored that Stoneham was considering renting Yankee Stadium—full cycle from the early 1920s when the Yanks were ousted from the Polo Grounds by John McGraw. After long, fruitless negotiations between the Dodgers and Brooklyn borough officials, O'Malley openly expressed his disenchantment with the situation and his interest in moving his team to Los Angeles. At the same time Stoneham announced that he had received an attractive offer to relocate the Giants to San Francisco. Finally, on August 19, 1957, Stoneham announced that the Giants would move to the Bay Area in time for the 1958 season. Asked how he felt about taking the Giants from New York's youngsters, Stoneham replied, "I feel badly about the kids, but I haven't seen many of their fathers at games lately." Stoneham's reference was to the attendance at the Polo Grounds, which had fallen from almost 1.2 million in 1954 to less than 630,000 in 1956.

The Giants played their last game at the Polo Grounds on September 29, 1957, losing to the Pirates, 9–1. Mrs. John McGraw, a devoted Giants rooter even in the many years since her husband's death, lamented tearfully, "I still can't believe it. This would have broken John's heart. New York will never be the same." The other fans simply stood there, then trudged sorrowfully out of the Polo Grounds. The Giants' historic 75-year stay in New York was over.

* * *

The extreme depression in New York was matched by high excitement, enthusiasm, and anticipation in California's Bay Area as West Coast fans awaited the arrival of the Giants for the 1958 season. But there also was a degree of apprehension as proud Californians showed some reluctance to adopt a team with emotional ties to New York. It was for that reason, more than any other, that the brilliant Mays was not embraced immediately as one of their own by West Coast fans.

Held back by mediocre pitching, the 1958 club finished in third place, 12 games behind the pennant-winning Milwaukee Braves. Beginning with an 8–0 Opening Day victory over the equally new Los Angeles Dodgers, the Giants exhibited a powerful offense. They sparked the enthusiasm of their fans with several dramatic comebacks. The club also enhanced its popularity by winning 16 of 22 games with the arch-rival Dodgers (the Giants' best record against the Dodgers since 1937), while drawing almost 1.3 million paying customers to tiny, 22,900-capacity Seals Stadium (Candlestick Park was still in the planning stage).

The 1959 club led the league as late as September, but fell before the rush of the more experienced Dodgers, despite strong performances by righthanders "Toothpick Sam" Jones and Jack Sanford, Antonelli, Mays, Orlando Cepeda, and rookie Willie McCovey. With eight games remaining, the Giants led the Dodgers by two games. But Rigney's young club couldn't hold the advantage, losing a three-game series to the Dodgers and falling to third place.

The 1960s would see the Giants move into Candlestick Park, win a pennant, and showcase the talents of Mays, Cepeda, McCovey, and pitchers Juan Marichal, Gaylord Perry, and Mike McCormick. The highly rated 1960 club began the season splendidly but collapsed in midseason to finish in fifth place, with Manager Bill Rigney fired early in the season. For the third straight year, the Giants brought up another future great when high-kicking righthander Juan Marichal arrived on the heels of Cepeda and McCoury and threw a one-hitter against the Phillies in his first start. Also on the plus side, the team moved into newly built Candlestick Park and set an attendance record (1,795,356) that would stand for 27 years.

Alvin Dark took over the managerial reins in 1961, and the Giants completed a major deal before the season, trading discontented Johnny Antonelli to Cleveland for outfielder Harvey Kuenn. The resurgent Giants finished in third place, carried by the booming bats of Mays and Cepeda, who led the league with 46 homers and 142 RBIs. Giants fans finally warmed to the redoubtable Mays, who underscored a great season with a four-home-run, eight RBI performance on April 30. The chilly, whipping winds which swept across Candlestick Park and affected player performance gained wide attention, especially during the 1961 All-Star Game when Giants relief ace Stu Miller was forced into a balk by a heavy wind gust which blew him off the mound. The wind problem was reduced somewhat several years later with the closing of the large open area behind the outfield.

The 1962 pennant race bore a remarkable resemblance to the 1951 campaign. The Dodgers, who lost the great Sandy Koufax late in the season because of a circulatory problem, led by 5½ games when they visited San Francisco for a three-game series in August. But the Giants took three straight, helped by the use of a time-worn baseball tactic. They slowed down Dodgers basestealing star Maury Wills by watering down the baseline between first and second bases. The gambit prompted Jim Murray of the *Los Angeles Times* to write, "An aircraft wouldn't have run aground. . . . They found two abalone under second base."

With three games remaining on the Giants' schedule the day before the regular season ended, the Giants split a doubleheader with Houston while the Dodgers lost to the Cardinals, moving the Giants to within one game of the first-place Dodgers. The final day fairly dripped with tension. While Billy O'Dell and Stu Miller held Houston to one run, a home run by catcher Ed Bailey tied the game until Mays clouted an eighth-inning homer for a 2–1 win. Meanwhile Giants announcers Russ Hodges and Lon Simmons relayed the Dodgers-Cardinals play-by-play to their listeners and Giants fans cheered as the Cardinals defeated the Dodgers 1–0 on a ninth-inning home run. Similar to 1951, the Giants had forced a playoff with their ancient rivals.

Vivid reminders of the 1951 playoff abounded as the two teams prepared to open their best of three series at Candlestick Park. Leo Durocher, now a Dodgers coach, wore the same T-shirt he had worn during the 1951 playoff finale. Dark, who captained the Giants in 1951, was asked if he had brought along anything from the 1951 classic. Dark replied with a tight grin, "Yeah, Willie Mays!"

The Giants won the opener 8–0, courtesy of lefthander Billy Pierce's 13th straight home-field victory and two homers by the irrepressible Mays. Back in Los Angeles, the Dodgers overcame a five-run deficit to take the second game 8–7. The deciding game was played at Dodgers Stadium on October 3, 11 years to the day after the Bobby Thomson miracle. The Dodgers led 4–2 as the Giants came up in the top of the ninth. With righthander Ed Roebuck pitching, Mays singled off his glove to run the score to 4–3 with the bases loaded. Righthander Stan Williams relieved the shaken Roebuck, but Cepeda lifted a sacrifice fly to tie the game. A wild pitch sent Mays to second base, and an intentional walk reloaded the bases. Jim Davenport then drew a walk, forcing home the go-ahead run. Pierce retired the Dodgers in order in the bottom of the ninth, and the jubilant Giants had repeated their 1951 triumph.

The World Series with the favored Yankees was much closer than might have been expected, and several rainouts added to the suspense. The Series lasted 13 days before the Giants went down on their last at-bat in the seventh game on October 16. The two clubs simply traded victories after the Yankees won the opener at Candlestick Park, then met in the seventh game back at Candlestick. With righthanders Ralph

Terry and Jack Sanford pitching, the Yanks led 1–0 and Terry took a two-hit, 1–0 shutout into the bottom of the ninth. Matty Alou beat out a bunt and took third on Mays' two-out double. Stretch McCovey, who had homered off Terry earlier in the Series, smoked a low liner that Yankee second baseman Bobby Richardson grabbed just to his left. Giants fans sat rooted in their seats for some time after, contemplating the unkind fates which had directed McCovey's rifle shot just a few feet too close to Richardson.

The 1963 Giants slipped to third place, and the 1964 club finished in fourth place in Dark's last managerial year. The season was marked by Mays' 42 homers, another magnificent year for Marichal, and a 31-homer rookie season by third baseman Jim Ray Hart. Rookie manager Herman Franks, formerly a reserve catcher for the Giants in New York, replaced Dark and guided the 1965 club to the first of five consecutive second-place finishes. Mays was the National League MVP, McCovey was brilliant, and Marichal delivered a 22–13 season. Marichal's fine performance was marred unfortunately by a bat-swinging altercation with Dodgers catcher John Roseboro which resulted in the Dominican hurler's fine and suspension.

The 1966 Giants stayed close to the Dodgers as Marichal and righthander Gaylord Perry had a combined 46 wins and Mays, McCovey, and Hart supplied the power. The 1967 pitching staff was bolstered when the Giants re-acquired lefthander Mike McCormick. McCormick won the Cy Young Award with a 20–10 season. But Perry fell to a hard-luck 15–17 record, and an injury hampered Marichal. The aging Mays slipped badly and solid hitting by McCovey and Hart failed to take up the slack as the Giants finished in second place, well behind the Dodgers.

The Giants averaged over 91 victories during five consecutive second-place finishes from 1965-69. Hal Lanier, a Giants infielder during the period, summed up the Giants' frustration with the analysis: "We just weren't fundamentally sound. The Giants always waited for the home run. We could hit the ball with anyone and we had some pretty good pitching, but we never seemed to do the little things we needed to do in the close games." Herman Franks blamed the Giants' frustration on a factor with which shortstop-second baseman Lanier was unlikely to agree. Said Franks, "The main reason we didn't win a couple of pennants was our double play combination. I can still remember several games we blew because we couldn't turn a double play."

After a mediocre start in 1970, Clyde King, who had replaced Herman Franks in 1969, was fired. Charlie Fox, a peppery catcher for the New York Giants, took over. The Giants' performance improved under Fox, as the club finished in third place. Fox had his best managerial year in 1971 when he directed the club to the Western Division title, beating out the Dodgers by a game.

In 1972 the Giants began a long-term slide toward mediocrity, finishing fifth with a 69–86 record, the first time the club had a losing season since moving to San Francisco. The season also was notable because Mays was traded to the New York Mets on May 11 for righthander Charlie Williams and $150,000 in a deal made primarily for economic reasons. However, the fundamental reasons for the Giants' decline were a serious injury to McCovey which sidelined him midway in the campaign and a disastrous pre-season trade of Gaylord Perry to Cleveland for lefthander "Sudden Sam" McDowell.

The Giants rebounded to take third place in 1973 with an 88–74 record on the strength of a brilliant season by outfielder Bobby Bonds. Lefthander Ron Bryant enjoyed his career season (24–12), and outfielder Gary Matthews won the Rookie of the Year Award. Marichal's great career with the Giants ended after the 1973 season as he was sold to the Red Sox following an 11–15 swan song. McCovey also left the Giants (temporarily, as it developed) in a post-season deal with the Padres.

The Giants slipped badly in 1974, and Fox was replaced in midseason by Wes Westrum, yet another former Giants catcher from the New York days. Stoneham, who was in a serious financial squeeze, had committed the Giants to a youth movement but the fifth-place club simply was not competitive. The 1975 team improved somewhat, finishing in third place, but was never in the hunt against the powerful Cincinnati Reds. The lackluster field performance resulted in a sharp drop in home attendance. The 1974–75 combined attendance at Candlestick barely exceeded one million, and Stoneham ran low on operating funds. As a result, he reluctantly sold the club to Labatt's Breweries of Toronto, pending League approval, ending 57 years of Stoneham family ownership. The Giants appeared headed for Canada, subject to League approval.

San Francisco Mayor George Moscone obtained a temporary restraining order against the transfer, and city officials hunted frantically for new owners who would keep the franchise in the Bay Area. San Francisco financier Bob Lurie, a past member of the Giants Board of Directors, was willing, but he was financially unable to go it alone. At the last minute Moscone found Arizona cattleman Bud Herseth, who agreed to participate with Lurie. Within minutes of the 5 p.m. deadline imposed by the League, Lurie and Herseth had pooled financial resources enabling the Giants to stay in San Francisco. Moscone issued the dramatic (and to New York Giants fans ironic) statement, "Bobby Thomson lives!"

After two mediocre years the Giants improved in 1978, leading the league for most of the season and finishing in third place. Joe Altobelli, hired to pilot the club in 1977, was voted Manager of the Year, and General Manager Spec Richardson was voted top executive of the year as the Giants more than doubled their home attendance to 1.74 million. The keys to the club's improvement were the winter acquisition of lefthander Vida Blue, who delivered an 18–10, 2.79 ERA performance, lefthander Bob Knepper, who was equally effective, and the emergence of young outfielder Jack Clark as a potent long-ball hitter.

The 1979 Giants were a disappointment as the team sank to fourth place and a sub-.500 season. Victimized by inept pitching, Altobelli was deposed in September and replaced by the third-base coach Dave Bristol. Clark and first baseman Mike Ivie carried the offensive load, and McCovey, reclaimed from San Diego, supplied the season's highlight when he hit his 512th career home run to surpass Mel Ott's National League record for lefthanded hitters.

The Giants had run-of-the-mill clubs through the early years of the 1980s, but the franchise's fortunes took a turn for the better during the second half of the decade. The 1980 club improved on the record of the previous year but nevertheless finished in fifth place, held back by mediocre pitching. Frank Robinson replaced Dave Bristol before the 1981 season, becoming the first black National League manager, a distinction he had achieved in the American League when he managed the Cleveland Indians in 1975. The Giants finished fourth in 1981 and moved up in 1982 as they finished only two games off the pace in third place, carried along by a strong second-half showing. General Manager Tom Haller, who had replaced Spec Richardson, shook up the starting rotation, replacing veterans Doyle Alexander and Vida Blue with rookies Bill Laskey and Atlee Hammaker. Greg Minton had a team-record 30 saves, and Jack Clark led the hitting attack.

The Giants fell back to fifth place in 1983. After a miserable second half dropped the Giants to a mere five games out of last place, the front office talked about sweeping changes. Despite the front office's concern, the 1984 squad was essentially unchanged except at first base where free-agent Darrell Evans, who had defected to Detroit, was replaced by Al Oliver. The Giants deceived everyone by playing extremely well in spring training, then slumped badly early in the season. They fell to 10 games out by May 1 and trailed by 16 games by midseason. With two years remaining on his contract, Frank Robinson was fired in early August, and the Giants collapsed completely, finishing in last place, 30 games under .500.

After the club's dismal 1984 performance, the general feeling at Candlestick Park was that the 1985 team would have to do better—after all, the law of averages was on the Giants' side. But the law of averages was temporarily repealed as the club suffered through its worst season in the history of the franchise (62–100) and became the first non-expansion club of the expansion era to lose 100 games in a season. Popular, easy-going Jim Davenport took over the team in 1985, but there was little he could do to offset the ineptness of the club, which finished a cool 38 games below .500.

There was a profound improvement in the overall team leadership on September 8, 1985, when General Manager Tom Haller and field leader Davenport were replaced by Al Rosen and Roger Craig. Rosen, a former star third baseman for Cleveland in the 1950s, had been a successful executive both in and out of baseball. Craig was a highly respected pitching coach who was noted for successfully teaching the delivery of the split-fingered fastball. For the first time in many years the Giants appeared to be developing both a potentially successful strategy for winning and the leadership to implement such a plan.

Giants President Bob Lurie, intent on not playing at Candlestick Park in 1986, publicly discussed plans for playing home games in Oakland or Denver. It was not until January 1986 that Giants fans could even be certain that the club would remain in San Francisco for the season. These off-field events were the setting for one of the most satisfying seasons in the team's history.

Craig started boldly by giving starting jobs to two rookies—first baseman Will "The Thrill" Clark and second baseman Robby Thompson. The club had a fine start and enjoyed its first winning April since 1973. Most pleasing, the team exhibited Craig's confident, gung-ho (referred to by Craig as "Hum-Baby") attitude. Despite many roster moves and lineup changes, the Giants topped their division at the all-Star break for the first time since 1978. The club suffered the loss of team leader Jeffrey Leonard for the final two months of the season but still managed a solid third-place finish to become only one of 10 teams since 1900 to attain a winning record (83–79) after losing 100 games the previous season.

Individually, Mike Krukow's 20–9 season stood out (the first Giants' 20-game winner since 1973), and newcomer Candy Maldonado's 17 pinch hits set a club record. When Leonard went down for the season, Maldonado replaced him and finished the season with a team-leading 18 home runs and 85 RBIs. Clark and Thompson played superbly, and Thompson was named National League Rookie of the Year. But individual statistics do not do the 1986 Giants justice. It was the club's character and Craig's confidence that triggered their improvement. There were more than 40 come-from-behind victories, no less than 26 of them during the team's final at-bat.

Hoping to build upon their fine 1986 season, the Giants looked forward to 1987. However, they struggled during the early going, playing only .500 ball through the All-Star break. Then the razor-sharp Rosen came through. He shook up the club, trading oft-injured Chris Brown (there were reports of Brown's unwillingness to play with pain) and pitchers Mark Davis, Mark Grant, and Keith Comstock to San Diego for third baseman Kevin Mitchell and pitchers Craig Lefferts and Dave Dravecky. The stocky, powerful Mitchell perked up the team's offense, but nevertheless the Giants trailed the first-place Reds by five games beginning a series in Cincinnati in early August.

Craig's club caught fire, sweeping the Reds four straight to move within a game of the lead. Will Clark sparkled as the Giants took over the lead for good in late August, the smooth-swinging New Orleans native batting .440 with eight homers and 18 RBIs in a 14-game period. As the club fought for the pennant, the aggressive Rosen gave them another lift, picking up righthanders Don Robinson and Rick "Big Daddy" Reuschel in two separate deals with the Pirates.

At the time of the acquisition of the portly, well-seasoned Reuschel, the Giants were only four games above .500. With the big fellow firing a pair of two-hit games and going 5–3, the Giants went 27–13 down the pennant stretch run. The pennant clincher came in San Diego on September 28 when the newly acquired Robinson hit a tie-breaking homer in the eighth, then also held off the Padres for the mound win.

The Giants' first division title since 1971 was marked by a sound, all-around team performance under Manager of the Year Craig's skilled leadership. Will Clark, Jeffrey Leonard, Chili Davis, Candy Maldonado, and Bob Brenly carried an offense which tied for the league lead in run production and also led with 205 home runs. Jose Uribe and Robby Thompson provided the defensive agility that produced a league-leading 183 double plays. Starters Mike LaCoss, Kelly Downs, Atlee Hammaker, and relievers Scott Garrelts and Don Robinson were the principal contributors as the staff led the league with a 3.68 ERA.

The Giants carried the League Championship Series with the Cardinals to a full seven games. In a losing cause, Jeffrey Leonard was the MVP, whacking a home run in each of the first four games and hitting .417. He also gained the enmity of the Cardinals and their rooters by trotting slowly around the bases after each homer with a scornful one flap (hand) up and one down routine. The irrepressible Clark also was outstanding with a .360 performance. The key play of the series came in the sixth game when right-fielder Candy Maldonado lost a flyball in the lights as Dravecky lost a 1–0 heartbreaker.

Fortified by the addition of outfielder Brett Butler, the Giants played well early in the 1988 season and were in second place at the All-Star break, within 2½ games of the league-leading Dodgers. As it turned out, the week before the break would prove to be the Giants' highest point of the year. Giants' pitchers recorded three consecutive shutouts for the first time since 1960, and the hitters hammered out a five-homer, 21–2 win over the Cardinals on July 9. The last home run, hit by infielder Ernest Riles, was number 10,000 for the 106-year-old franchise. But after the midseason break, the club fell quickly apart, losing five straight games and falling eight games off the pace. Hampered by injuries and weak hitting, the Giants fell back, ultimately finishing in fourth place, 11 1/2 games behind the division-leading Dodgers.

The 1988 season was distinguished by fine individual accomplishments, as Butler and Clark finished at or near the top of the league in a number of offensive categories. But in the final analysis it was a deeply disappointing and sometimes tragic season. Injuries forced starting pitchers Mike Krukow, Kelly Downs, Mike LaCoss, Terry Mulholland, and Dave Dravecky out of action. Jose Uribe suffered the most devastating loss of all when his wife died while giving birth. All in all, and despite the Giants' third best attendance ever (1,786,482), 1988 was one of the Giants' unhappiest years.

The 1989 squad started well and Rosen, realizing the club was capable of going all the way, strengthened the bullpen in June by obtaining ace reliever Steve "Bedrock" Bedrosian from the Phillies. But the big story was the powerhitting duo of Mitchell and Clark (later to be voted MVP and runner-up, respectively), one of the most potent hitting combinations of the 1980s. By the All-Star break, with the Giants leading their division by two games, Mitchell had 31 home runs and 81 RBIs. Clark, with a batting stroke reminiscent of Ted Williams, was hitting .332 with 60 RBIs. The consistent Giants moved along steadily to top their division by three games, spearheaded by Mitchell and Clark, solid years by Butler and Thompson, and sound pitching by Garrelts (league-leading 2.28 ERA), Reuschel, Don Robinson, Bedrosian, and Craig Lefferts. Mitchell led all major league hitters in home runs (47), RBIs (125), total bases (345), slugging percentage (.635), and extra-base hits (87). Clark barely missed winning the National League batting title, with a .333 average, tied for the lead in runs scored (104), and ranked second in hits (196).

Giants lefthander Dave Dravecky provided the season's most dramatic story. Sidelined after post-1988 season surgery for the removal of a cancerous tumor on his pitching arm, Dravecky astounded the baseball world with a 4–3 win against Cincinnati on August 10 in his first comeback start of the season. In his next outing, against Montreal, Dravecky led after a three-hit, six-inning shutout, when his weakened arm snapped as he threw a pitch. He fell to the ground as though shot. The Giants held on to win the game for Dravecky, although several players were near tears as the pitcher was carried off the field, his career over.

The Giants won the pennant showdown by defeating the Cubs, four games to one, in the National League Championship Series. Clark led the club with a magnificent .650 (13 for 20) and eight RBI performance which earned him the series MVP honor. Opening in Chicago, the Giants won the first game, sparked by Clark's monster four-for-four, two-homer, six-RBI game; lost the second game; then wore down the Cubs with three straight wins in Candlestick Park. Clark carried the Giants to a 3–2 win in the final game with a crucial triple and a two-run single to drive in the game-winning runs. Mitchell, third baseman Matt Williams, and Robby Thompson shared the remaining hitting honors, driving in 19 of the Giants' 29 runs, with each player matching Clark with two homers apiece.

Craig's club lost the World Series to the overpowering Oakland Athletics in four straight, in what will always be remembered as the "Earthquake Series." The A's defeated the Giants easily in the first two games at Oakland on the strength of powerful pitching performances by righthanders Dave Stewart and Mike Moore. The teams moved to Candlestick Park for the third game on October 17, most of the experts having already written off the Giants' chances.

Much of the crowd of 62,000 was still filing into Candlestick, milling about the runways or standing in concession lines, when a devastating earthquake hit at 5:04 p.m., 20 minutes prior to the game's scheduled start. The entire stadium shook violently and power immediately went out, abruptly eliminating all lights and terminating television and radio broadcasts. The players raced onto the field, waving their families down to join them as police kept fans off the field. Miraculously, there were no serious accidents or injuries as the stunned fans soberly left the ballpark. Baseball Commissioner Fay Vincent, just named to succeed the late A. Bartlett Giamatti, conferred with area and team officials, rescheduled Game Three for October 24, then moved it back to October 27 as the Bay Area struggled slowly to regain some semblance of normalcy.

The third and fourth games were anticlimactic as Stewart and Moore repeated their earlier performances. Stewart mowed down the Giants in Game Three as Oakland hit five home runs to tie a 61-year-old Series record. The longest Series ever (in elapsed time) ended the next night when Moore held the Giants to two runs over six innings as the multi-talented A's took a six-run lead, then held off a valiant, last-ditch Giants effort. The Giants, who never threatened to win any of the games, took their defeat philosophically, recognizing the overwhelming superiority of the Athletics. As the unflappable Craig put it, "Let's face it, everyone picked us to finish third or fourth before the season, and I'm proud that my guys did as well as they did against a great team. We'll be back." And with that, the Giants closed the book on the season and prepared to enter the 1990s, upbeat and optimistic. The only unhappy note—shortly after the Series, San Franciscans voted against a proposal to build a larger stadium, leading to concern that the Giants eventually would move from the Bay Area.

And it was this concern that would disorient a once proud Giants ballclub throughout much of the coming seasons. Seemingly all the news swirling around the Giants had to do with front office machinations and what now seemed a certain loss of the ballclub from the Bay Area. Frustrated in his attempts to find a local buyer and soured himself on club ownership by multiple taxpayer rejections of new stadium funding, Bob Lurie shocked baseball's family in August 1992 by announcing that he was indeed selling to St. Petersburg interests bent on moving the Giants to Florida in time for the 1993 campaign. Only an eleventh hour rejection of the Florida bid by a majority of NL owners in early November, along with a patchwork local ownership team pulled together by league officials unwilling to permit yet another franchise shift, was able to salvage the Giants once again for increasingly apathetic San Francisco fans. Whether the rescue was indeed permanent or merely a temporary postponement was very much an open question as the battered San Francisco Giants limped warily into the 1993 spring season.

Annotated Bibliography

Alexander, Charles C. *John McGraw*. New York: Viking Penguin, 1988. 358 pp.
> This thoroughly researched and well-written book provides the ultimate coverage of the life and times of John McGraw. It is especially valuable for its discussion of McGraw's formative years before he entered professional baseball and during his famous playing days in Baltimore.

Durocher, Leo. *Nice Guys Finish Last*. New York: Simon and Schuster, 1975. 448 pp.
> Written in his characteristically pungent style, a significant portion of Durocher's book tells of his days as Giants manager from 1948 to 1955. He writes of his problems in dealing with heavy-drinking Giants owner Horace Stoneham and of the Giants' "miracle" pennant win in 1951.

Durso, Joseph. *The Days of Mr. McGraw*. Englewood Cliffs, N.J. Prentice-Hall, 1969, 243 pp.
> This book, while essentially a reiteration of material contained in Frank Graham's classic *McGraw of the Giants*, nevertheless contains sufficient

original material to justify reading by students of the game and of the Giants.

Fleming, Gordon H. *The Dizziest Season.* New York: Morrow, 1984. 320 pp.
This work describes the Dizzy Dean-led "Gashouse Gang" St. Louis Cardinals' surge to the 1934 World Championship. The book comprises newspaper accounts from 1933 and 1934 about the Cardinals (accompanied by the author's explanatory notes), and in the telling, the Giants' heartbreaking season is vividly described.

Graham, Frank. *McGraw of the Giants.* New York: Putnam, 1944. 265 pp.
This masterful book describes McGraw's years with the Giants from the viewpoint of a writer who traveled with the team for much of that time. Graham's anecdotes are enhanced by his deft use of dialogue which gives the reader the impression of being a participant in the goings-on.

Hynd, Noel. *The Giants of the Polo Grounds.* New York: Doubleday, 1988. 396 pp.
A thorough recount of the Giants' 75 years in New York. Hynd retells many of the old anecdotes in a modern, hip-style which may be described either as "entertaining" or as "irritating" depending on the reader's taste.

Kiernan, Thomas. *The Miracle at Coogan's Bluff.* New York: Crowell, 1975. 284 pp.
Kiernan relives the magical 1951 season, both by describing it in graphic detail and by having the participating players describe it in their own words. His use of the old players' descriptions represents effective employment of the retrospective approach mastered so effectively by Roger Kahn in his *Boys of Summer.*

King, Joe. *The San Francisco Giants.* Englewood Cliffs, N.J.: Prentice-Hall, 1958. 215 pp.
Written just prior to the first Giants season in San Francisco in 1958, this book provides a general history of the franchise and assessment of its prospects before beginning operations in San Francisco.

Mathewson, Christy. *Pitching in a Pinch.* New York: Putnam, 1912. 306 pp.
Mathewson's rediscovered book (actually ghostwritten by sports writer John Wheeler) provides superb descriptions of John McGraw's celebrated use of baseball strategy, psychology, and discipline and provides an accurate reflection of the great pitcher's cool, scholarly approach to the game.

McGraw, John J. *My Thirty Years in Baseball.* New York: Boni and Liveright, 1923. 265 pp.
Fresh off two straight World Series victories over the hated Yankees, McGraw writes triumphantly of his own outwitting, and his club's outplaying, of the Giants' crosstown rivals.

McGraw, Mrs. John J. *The Real McGraw.* New York: D. McDay, 1953. 336 pp.
Written almost 20 years after her husband's death, Mrs. McGraw describes the private McGraw and her view of events in which he played an important part.

Peters, Nick. *Giants Almanac.* Berkeley, Calif.: North Atlantic Books, 1988. 188 pp.
This book updates (through the 1987 season) and expands upon the San Francisco seasons covered in *Giants Diary.* It excludes coverage of the New York years.

Stein, Fred. *Under Coogan's Bluff.* Glenshaw, Penn.: Chapter and Cask, 1981. 145 pp.
This book describes the Terry and Ott managerial years (1932 to 1948) from the perspective of a devoted Giants fan.

Stein, Fred, and Nick Peters. *Giants Diary.* Berkeley, Calif.: North Atlantic Books, 1987. 374 pp.

This is a comprehensive review of the 1883 to 1986 period, providing detailed discussion of (a) day-to-day highlights of each season; (b) a general history of the Giants franchise; (c) biographical sketches of great Giants players; (d) a description of Giants players' participation in World Series and All-Star games; (e) complete team and player statistics; (f) player nicknames; and (g) a complete roster of Giants players during the 103-year period.

Year-by-Year Standings and Season Summaries

Year	Pos.	Record	Pct.	GB	Manager	Player	BA	Player	HR	Player	W-L	ERA
1883	6th	46–50	.479	16.0	Clapp	Connor	.357	Ewing	10	Welch	27–21	2.73
1884	5th	62–50	.554	22.0	Price Ward	Connor	.317	Connor McKinnon	4 4	Welch	39–21	2.50
1885	2nd	85–27	.759	2.0	Mutrie	Connor	.371	Ewing	6	Welch	44–11	1.66
1886	3rd	75–44	.630	12.5	Mutrie	Connor	.355	Connor	7	Keefe	41–21	2.53
1887	4th	68–55	.553	10.5	Mutrie	Ward	.338	Connor	17	Keefe	35–19	3.10
1888	1st	84–47	.641	—	Mutrie	Ewing	.306	Connor	14	Keefe	35–12	1.74
1889	1st	83–43	.659	—	Mutrie	Tiernan	.335	Connor	13	Keefe	28–13	3.31
1890	6th	63–68	.481	10.5	Mutrie	Glasscock	.336	Tiernan	13	Rusie	29–30	2.56
1891	3rd	71–61	.538	13.0	Mutrie	Tiernan	.306	Tiernan	17	Rusie	33–20	2.55
1892	8th	71–80	.470	31.5	Powers	Ewing	.310	Lyons	8	Rusie	33–28	2.88
1893	5th	68–64	.515	19.5	Ward	Davis	.362	Tiernan	15	Rusie	29–18	3.23
1894	2nd	88–44	.667	3.0	Ward	Doyle	.369	Davis	9	Rusie	36–13	2.78
1895	9th	66–65	.504	21.5	Davis Doyle Watkins	Tiernan	.347	Van Haltren	8	Rusie	22–21	3.73
1896	7th	64–67	.489	27.0	Irwin	Tiernan	.369	Tiernan	7	Meekin	26–14	3.82
1897	3rd	83–48	.634	9.5	Joyce	Davis	.358	Davis	9	Rusie	29–8	2.54
1898	7th	77–73	.513	25.5	Joyce Anson	Van Haltren	.312	Joyce	10	Seymour	25–17	3.18
1899	5th	60–90	.400	42.0	Day Hoey	Davis	.346	O'Brien	6	Carrick	16–26	4.65
1900	8th	60–78	.435	23.0	Ewing Davis	Selbach	.337	Hickman	9	Carrick	19–21	3.53
1901	7th	52–85	.380	37.0	Davis	Van Haltren	.342	Davis	7	Mathewson	20–17	2.41
1902	8th	48–88	.353	53.5	Fogel Smith McGraw	McGann	.300	Brodie	3	Mathewson	14–17	2.11

Year	Pos.	Record	Pct.	GB	Manager	Player	BA	Player	HR	Player	W-L	ERA
1903	2nd	84–55	.604	6.5	McGraw	Bresnahan	.350	Mertes	7	McGinnity	31–20	2.43
1904	1st	106–47	.693	—	McGraw	McGann	.286	McGann	6	McGinnity	35–8	1.61
1905	1st	105–48	.686	—	McGraw	Donlin	.356	Dahlen	7	Mathewson	31–8	1.27
								Donlin	7			
1906	2nd	96–56	.632	20.0	McGraw	Seymour	.320	Strang	4	McGinnity	27–12	2.25
								Seymour	4			
1907	4th	82–71	.536	25.5	McGraw	McGann	.298	Browne	5	Mathewson	24–13	1.99
1908	2nd	98–56	.636	1.0	McGraw	Donlin	.334	Donlin	6	Mathewson	37–11	1.43
1909	3rd	92–61	.601	18.5	McGraw	Doyle	.302	Murray	7	Mathewson	25–6	1.14
1910	2nd	91–63	.591	13.0	McGraw	Snodgrass	.321	Doyle	8	Mathewson	27–9	1.90
1911	1st	99–54	.647	—	McGraw	Meyers	.332	Doyle	13	Mathewson	26–13	1.99
1912	1st	103–48	.682	—	McGraw	Meyers	.358	Merkle	11	Marquard	26–11	2.57
1913	1st	101–51	.664	—	McGraw	Meyers	.312	Doyle	5	Mathewson	25–11	2.06
								Shafer	5			
1914	2nd	84–70	.545	10.5	McGraw	Burns	.303	Merkle	7	Tesreau	26–10	2.37
1915	8th	69–83	.454	21.0	McGraw	Doyle	.320	Merkle	4	Tesreau	19–16	3.29
								Doyle	4			
1916	4th	86–66	.566	7.0	McGraw	Robertson	.307	Robertson	12	Perritt	18–11	2.62
1917	1st	98–56	.636	—	McGraw	Kauff	.308	Robertson	12	Schupp	21–7	1.95
1918	2nd	71–53	.573	10.5	McGraw	Kauff	.315	Burns	4	Perritt	18–13	2.74
1919	2nd	87–53	.621	9.0	McGraw	Youngs	.311	Kauff	10	Barnes	25–9	2.40
1920	2nd	86–68	.558	7.0	McGraw	Youngs	.351	Kelly	11	Toney	21–11	2.65
1921	1st	94–59	.614	—	McGraw	Frisch	.341	Kelly	23	Nehf	20–10	3.63
1922	1st	93–61	.604	—	McGraw	Stengel	.368	Kelly	17	Nehf	19–13	3.29
1923	1st	95–58	.621	—	McGraw	Frisch	.348	Meusel	19	Scott	16–7	3.89
1924	1st	93–60	.608	—	McGraw	Youngs	.356	Kelly	21	Bentley	16–5	3.78
1925	2nd	86–66	.566	8.5	McGraw	Meusel	.328	Meusel	21	Barnes	15–11	3.53
1926	5th	74–77	.490	13.5	McGraw	Jackson	.327	Kelly	13	Fitzsimmons	14–10	2.88
1927	3rd	92–62	.597	2.0	McGraw	Hornsby	.361	Hornsby	26	Grimes	19–8	3.54

Year	Pos.	Record	Pct.	GB	Manager	Player	BA	Player	HR	Player	W-L	ERA
1928	2nd	93–61	.604	2.0	McGraw	Lindstrom	.358	Ott	18	Benton	25–9	2.73
1929	3rd	84–67	.556	13.5	McGraw	Terry	.372	Ott	42	Hubbell	18–11	3.69
1930	3rd	87–67	.565	5.0	McGraw	Terry	.401	Ott	25	Hubbell	17–12	3.76
1931	2nd	87–65	.572	13.0	McGraw	Terry	.349	Ott	29	Fitzsimmons	18–11	3.05
1932	6th	72–82	.468	18.0	McGraw / Terry	Terry	.350	Ott	38	Hubbell	18–11	2.50
1933	1st	91–61	.599	—	Terry	Terry	.322	Ott	23	Hubbell	23–12	1.66
1934	2nd	93–60	.608	2.0	Terry	Terry	.354	Ott	35	Schumacher	23–10	3.18
1935	3rd	91–62	.595	8.5	Terry	Terry	.341	Ott	31	Hubbell	23–12	3.27
1936	1st	92–62	.597	—	Terry	Ott	.328	Ott	33	Hubbell	26–6	2.31
1937	1st	93–57	.625	—	Terry	Ripple	.317	Ott	31	Hubbell	22–8	3.20
1938	3rd	83–67	.553	5.0	Terry	Ott	.311	Ott	36	Gumbert	15–13	4.01
1939	5th	77–74	.510	18.5	Terry	Bonura	.321	Ott	27	Gumbert	18–11	4.32
1940	6th	72–80	.474	27.5	Terry	Demaree	.302	Ott	19	Schumacher	13–13	3.25
1941	5th	74–79	.484	25.5	Terry	Bartell	.303	Ott	27	Schumacher	12–10	3.36
1942	3rd	85–67	.559	20.0	Ott	Mize	.305	Ott	30	Lohrman	13–4	2.56
1943	8th	55–98	.359	49.5	Ott	Witek	.314	Ott	18	Adams	11–7	2.82
1944	5th	67–87	.435	38.0	Ott	Medwick	.337	Ott	26	Voiselle	21–16	3.02
1945	5th	78–74	.513	19.0	Ott	Ott	.308	Ott	21	Mungo	14–7	3.20
1946	8th	61–93	.396	36.0	Ott	Mize	.337	Mize	22	Koslo	14–19	3.63
1947	4th	81–73	.526	13.0	Ott	Cooper	.305	Mize	51	Jansen	21–5	3.16
1948	5th	78–76	.506	13.5	Ott / Durocher	Gordon	.299	Mize	40	Jansen	18–12	3.61
1949	5th	73–81	.474	24.0	Durocher	Thomson	.309	Thomson	27	Jones	15–12	3.34
1950	3rd	86–68	.558	5.0	Durocher	Stanky	.300	Thomson	25	Jansen	19–13	3.01
1951	1st	98–59	.624	—	Durocher	Irvin	.312	Thomson	32	Maglie	23–6	2.93
1952	2nd	92–62	.597	4.5	Durocher	Dark	.301	Thomson	24	Maglie	18–8	2.92
1953	5th	70–84	.455	35.0	Durocher	Mueller	.333	Thomson	26	Gomez	13–11	3.40
1954	1st	97–57	.630	—	Durocher	Mays	.345	Mays	41	Antonelli	21–7	2.30

Year	Pos.	Record	Pct.	GB	Manager	Player	BA	Player	HR	Player	W-L	ERA
1955	3rd	80–74	.519	18.5	Durocher	Mays	.319	Mays	51	Antonelli	14–16	3.33
1956	6th	67–87	.435	26.0	Rigney	Brandt	.299	Mays	36	Antonelli	20–13	2.86
1957	6th	69–85	.448	26.0	Rigney	Mays	.333	Mays	35	Gomez	15–13	3.78
1958	3rd	80–74	.519	12.0	Rigney	Mays	.347	Mays	29	Antonelli	16–13	3.28
1959	3rd	83–71	.539	4.0	Rigney	Cepeda	.317	Mays	34	Jones	21–15	2.83
1960	5th	79–75	.513	16.0	Rigney / Sheehan	Mays	.319	Mays	29	Jones	18–14	3.19
1961	3rd	85–69	.552	8.0	Dark	Cepeda	.311	Cepeda	46	Miller	14–5	2.66
1962	1st	103–62	.624	—	Dark	F. Alou	.316	Mays	49	Sanford	24–7	3.43
1963	3rd	88–74	.543	11.0	Dark	Cepeda	.316	McCovey	44	Marichal	25–8	2.41
1964	4th	90–72	.556	3.0	Dark	Cepeda	.304	Mays	47	Marichal	21–8	2.48
1965	2nd	95–67	.586	2.0	Franks	Mays	.317	Mays	52	Marichal	22–13	2.13
1966	2nd	93–68	.578	1.5	Franks	McCovey	.295	Mays	37	Marichal	25–6	2.23
1967	2nd	91–71	.562	10.5	Franks	J. Alou	.292	McCovey	31	McCormick	22–10	2.85
1968	2nd	88–74	.543	9.0	Franks	McCovey	.293	McCovey	36	Marichal	26–9	2.43
1969	2nd	90–72	.556	3.0	King	McCovey	.320	McCovey	45	Marichal	21–11	2.10
1970	3rd	86–76	.531	16.0	King / Fox	Bonds	.302	McCovey	39	Perry	23–13	3.21
1971	1st	90–72	.556	—	Fox	Bonds	.288	Bonds	33	Marichal	18–11	2.94
1972	5th	69–86	.445	26.5	Fox	Speier	.269	Bonds	26	Bryant	14–7	2.90
1973	3rd	88–74	.543	11.0	Fox	Maddox	.319	Bonds	39	Bryant	24–12	3.54
1974	5th	72–90	.444	30.0	Fox / Westrum	Rader	.291	Bonds	21	Caldwell	14–5	2.95
1975	3rd	80–81	.497	27.5	Westrum	Joshua	.318	Matthews	12	Montefusco	15–9	2.24
1976	4th	74–88	.457	28.0	Rigney	Herndon	.288	Murcer	23	Montefusco	16–14	2.84
1977	4th	75–87	.463	23.0	Altobelli	Madlock	.302	McCovey	28	Halicki	16–12	3.31
1978	3rd	89–73	.549	6.0	Altobelli	Madlock	.309	J. Clark	25	Blue	18–10	2.79
1979	4th	71–91	.438	19.5	Altobelli / Bristol	Ivie	.286	Ivie	27	Blue	14–14	5.01

Year	Pos.	Record	Pct.	GB	Manager	Player	BA	Player	HR	Player	W-L	ERA
1980	5th	75–86	.466	17.0	Bristol	Whitfield	.296	J. Clark	22	Blue	14–10	2.97
1981*	4th	56–55	.505	11.0	Robinson	May	.310	Clark	17	Alexander	11–7	2.90
1982	3rd	87–75	.537	2.0	Robinson	Morgan	.289	J. Clark	27	Laskey	13–12	3.14
1983	5th	79–83	.488	12.0	Robinson	Leonard	.279	Evans	30	Laskey	13–10	4.19
1984	6th	66–96	.407	26.0	Robinson Ozark	Gladden	.351	J. Davis Leonard	21 21	Krukow	11–12	4.56
1985	6th	62–100	.383	33.0	Davenport Craig	Brown	.271	Brenly	19	Garrelts	9–6	2.30
1986	3rd	83–79	.512	13.0	Craig	Brown	.317	Maldonado	18	Krukow	20–9	3.05
1987	1st	90–72	.556	—	Craig	Aldrete	.325	W. Clark	35	LaCoss	13–10	3.68
1988	4th	83–79	.512	11.5	Craig	Butler	.287	W. Clark	29	Reuschel	19–11	3.12
1989	1st	92–70	.568	—	Craig	W. Clark	.333	Mitchell	47	Garrelts	14–5	2.28
1990	3rd	85–77	.525	6.0	Craig	Butler	.309	Mitchell	35	Burkett	14–7	3.79
1991	4th	75–87	.463	19.0	Craig	McGee	.312	Williams	34	T. Wilson	13–11	3.56
1992	5th	72–90	.444	26.0	Craig	Clark	.300	Williams	20	Swift	10–4	2.08

*Split Season Totals (Players' Union Strike).

All-Time Giants Career and Season Records

Career Batting Leaders, 1883–1992

	Career Total		New York (1883–1957)		San Francisco (1958–1992)	
Games Played	W. Mays	2,992	M. Ott	2,730	W. Mays	2,095
At Bats	W. Mays	10,881	M. Ott	9,456	W. Mays	7,578
Runs Scored	W. Mays	2,062	M. Ott	1,859	W. Mays	1,480
Hits	W. Mays	3,283	M. Ott	2,876	W. Mays	2,284
Batting Average	B. Terry	.341	B. Terry	.341	O. Cepeda	.308
Home Runs	W. Mays	660	M. Ott	511	W. McCovey	468
Runs Batted In	W. Mays	1,903	M. Ott	1,860	W. McCovey	1,503
Stolen Bases	M. Tiernan	428	M. Tiernan	428	B. Bonds	263
Strikeouts	W. Mays	1,526	M. Ott	896	W. McCovey	1,355

Career Pitching Leaders, 1883–1992

	Career Total		New York (1883–1957)		San Francisco (1958–1992)	
Innings Pitched	G. Perry	5,352	C. Mathewson	4,769	J. Marichal	3,443
Earned Run Average	C. Mathewson	2.13	C. Mathewson	2.13	G. Lavelle	2.82
Wins	C. Mathewson	372	C. Mathewson	371	J. Marichal	238
Losses	T. Keefe	225	C. Mathewson	187	J. Marichal	140
Winning Percentage	C. Mathewson	.665	C. Mathewson	.665	J. Marichal	.630
Strikeouts	G. Perry	3,534	C. Mathewson	2,499	J. Marichal	2,281
Walks	A. Rusie	1,704	A. Rusie	1,701	J. Marichal	690
Games	H. Wilhelm	1,070	C. Mathewson	633	G. Lavelle	647
Shutouts	C. Mathewson	78	C. Mathewson	78	J. Marichal	52
Saves	G. Lavelle	127	A. Adams	49	G. Lavelle	127
Games Started	G. Perry	690	C. Mathewson	550	J. Marichal	446
Complete Games	C. Mathewson	434	C. Mathewson	433	J. Marichal	244

All-Time Giants Career and Season Records (*continued*)

Single-Season Batting Records, 1883–1992

	New York Seasons (1883–1957)			San Francisco Seasons (1958–1992)		
Batting Average (502 ABs)	B. Terry	.401	1930	W. Mays	.347	1958
Home Runs (right-handed)	W. Mays	51	1955	W. Mays	52	1965
Home Runs (left-handed)	J. Mize	51	1947	W. McCovey	45	1969
Runs Batted In	M. Ott	151	1929	O. Cepeda	142	1961
Hits	B. Terry	254	1930	W. Mays	208	1958
Singles	B. Terry	177	1930	W. Mays	135	1958
Doubles	B. Terry	43	1932	W. Mays	43	1959
Triples	G. Davis	27	1893	W. Mays	12	1960
Slugging Percentage	W. Mays	.667	1954	W. McCovey	.656	1969
Extra Base Hits	W. Mays	87	1954	W. Mays	90	1962
Stolen Bases	M. Ward	111	1887	B. Bonds	48	1970
Pinch Hits	S. Leslie	22	1932	C. Maldonado	17	1986
Strikeouts	G. Kelly	92	1920	B. Bonds	189	1970
Total Bases	B. Terry	392	1930	W. Mays	382	1962
Hitting Streak (consecutive games)	G. Davis	33	1893	J. Clark	26	1978
Grand Slam Home Runs	S. Gordon	3	1948	W. McCovey	3	1967
On-Base Percentage	M. Ott	.458	1930	W. McCovey	.458	1969

All-Time Giants Career and Season Records *(continued)*

Single-Season Pitching Records, 1883–1992

	New York Seasons (1883–1957)			San Francisco Seasons (1958–1992)		
ERA	C. Mathewson	1.14	1908	J. Marichal	2.10	1969
Wins	M. Welch	44	1885	J. Marichal	26	1968
Losses	A. Rusie	34	1890	R. Sadecki	18	1968
Winning Pct.	J. McGinnity	.814	1904	J. Marichal	.806	1966
(20 or more decisions)		(35–8)			(25–6)	
Strikeouts	T. Keefe	361	1883	S. Jones	209	1959
Walks	A. Rusie	289	1890	V. Blue	111	1979
Saves	M. Grisson	19	1954	G. Minton	30	1982
Games	H. Wilhelm	71	1952	G. Lavelle	77	1984
				M. Davis	77	1985
Complete Games	J. McGinnity	46	1903	J. Marichal	30	1968
Shutouts	C. Mathewson	11	1908	J. Marichal	8	1969
Innings Pitched	W. Welch	557	1884	G. Perry	329	1970
Consecutive Games Won	T. Keefe	19	1888	J. Sanford	16	1962
Consecutive Games Lost	R. Marquard	19	1912	N/A		
	R. Marquard	12	1914			

8

New York Mets
From Throneberry to Strawberry:
Baseball's Most Successful Expansion Franchise

PETE CAVA

Meet the Mets, meet the Mets
Step right up and greet the Mets
Bring your kiddies, bring your wife
Guaranteed to have the time of your life
Because the Mets are really sockin' the ball
Knockin' those homeruns over the wall
East Side, West Side, ev'rybody's comin' down
to meet the M-E-T-S, Mets of New York town.

Words and music by Ruth Roberts and Bill Katz
Copyright © 1963 & 1969 Michael Brent Publications,
Inc.

The New York Mets have been baseball's most successful expansion franchise. Period. In their brief history, the Mets have produced four Cy Young Award winners, two home run champions, five earned run average leaders, four Rookie of the Year Awards, four division titles, three pennants, and two World Series triumphs. The team's farm system is an unmatched model, and the Mets have been among the leaders in attendance going back to their first season in Shea Stadium.

Theirs is a record that some original franchise teams would envy. To many fans the Mets are the epitome of glamor and baseball sophistication: a team that has been able to produce in the harsh glare of the Big Apple's light fantastic. The Mets of the 1980s were what John McGraw's Giants, the Boys of Summer from Brooklyn, and the Yankees of Ruth, Gehrig, DiMaggio, and Mantle were to earlier generations of New Yorkers.

But it wasn't always like this.

The Mets' story begins shortly after the Dodgers and the Giants crossed the Hudson for good. In their wake swirled confusion and alarm. Mayor Robert Wagner appointed a panel to investigate the possibilities of a new National League team for New York. Wagner's committee consisted of former Postmaster General James Farley, Bernard Gimbel of department store fame, realtor Clinton Blume, and an energetic young attorney, Brooklyn-born William Shea.

Although not the committee chairman, Shea was the group's cleanup hitter. Shea courted the Phillies, Reds, and Pirates, but each team decided their futures weren't in New York.

The 1958 season began with no National League team in New York City for the first time in this century. Shea's strategy began to shift. If he couldn't bring an established team to New York, maybe he could create one. But expansion was a nasty word to baseball's hierarchy. National League President Warren Giles was on record as saying, "Who needs New York?"

If Shea was going to joust with windmills, he wanted the best Sancho Panza available. He went after 77-year-old Branch Rickey, the man who had pioneered the farm system and opened baseball to blacks. Rickey, itching in semi-retirement, went to work with Shea immediately. In July 1959 Shea and Rickey announced the formation of the fledgling Continental League. The proposed eight-team league would include a New York franchise. The prospect of a rival league must have sent shivers up the spines of the baseball establishment, since four decades earlier, the upstart Federal League had raided players and sent salaries skyrocketing. Organized baseball had wound up in court, with the Feds charging violations of the antitrust laws.

Antitrust laws were again a hot topic in 1959. For most of the decade baseball's exemption had been under government scrutiny. The threat of a new league, together with full-scale government investigation, was too much for the Lords of Baseball. Rickey and Shea milked the scene for all it was worth, blasting the big-league owners for a "total lack of loyalty to the communities which support their enterprises." A bill that would have abolished baseball's immunity from the antitrust laws was defeated by a slim margin in 1960. Both leagues began to discuss "expansion from within."

At a meeting in August major league officials offered to accept four Continental League franchises as part of their expansion plans. Shea and Rickey quickly accepted. On October 17 National League club owners unanimously passed a resolution that would bring New York and Houston into the circuit. Thus was born the New York Metropolitan Baseball Club, Inc.

The man behind most of the early moves in Met history was a business associate of Joan Payson, the team's principal owner. He was a Wall Street broker named M. Donald Grant, a former member of the New York Giants board of directors. Grant asked Rickey to stay with the club as general manager, but Rickey's terms—complete control of the club and a $5 million budget—killed the deal. Rickey faded out of the scene.

Meanwhile, events in the Bronx would have a profound effect on the new club's administrative makeup. On the day after the N.L. voted to expand, the Yankees fired their 70-year-old manager, Casey Stengel. The Yanks cited Casey's age and the need for a youth movement. A few weeks later the Yanks retired George Weiss, their general manager. The affable Stengel and the phlegmatic Weiss had been odd-couple partners in what had been baseball's dominant team in the postwar era. Now both were adrift. Donald Grant wanted Weiss as his G.M. Weiss's settlement with the Yanks precluded him from serving in that capacity. Grant resolved the situation deftly, naming Weiss president of the club.

In March 1961 the New York State Assembly voted for a bond that would build a new stadium for the team in Flushing Meadows. But there was no chance for the new park to be ready by 1962. When the Yanks nixed the idea of sharing their stadium with the Mets, it became official: the Mets' first home would be the Polo Grounds, the oddly shaped arena that had once been home to Christy Mathewson, Bill Terry, Carl Hubbell, and Willie Mays.

On May 8, 1961 Joan Payson announced the official nickname for the new club, based on a write-in contest by fans. The name "Mets" won out over a field that included Continentals, Skyliners, Jets,[1] Meadowlarks, Burros, Skyscrapers, NYB's, and Avengers. The name Mets was a natural, considering the team's corporate title. It harkened back to nineteenth-century baseball in New York, when the Metropolitans of the old American Association were the city's hardball kingpins. New York baseball writers, especially Dan Daniel of the old *World Telegram*, had been using the name for some time.

Well in the background of the Mets was owner Joan Payson. A true New York blueblood, she was the epitome of the gracious, well-bred sports magnates of a distant era. Many of today's owners should have taken lessons from this charming woman, who was as much at home in New York social circles as she was behind the home dugout, rooting for her team like any other rabid fan.

George Weiss was busy putting the team together. For six months the word was out that he wanted Casey Stengel to manage the Mets. Stengel, with 50 years of experience in the game—including service with all three New York teams—was a gnarled, bowlegged legend. To the baseball writers, Stengel was a kind of Mark Twain in baseball shoes, spending large chunks of his off-duty time in hotel bars, where he'd regale them with stories of seasons past. Stengel wasn't easily wooed. Finally, calls from Mrs. Payson and Donald Grant did the trick.

On September 29, 1961 the Mets made it official. Casey was coming back. Now all Stengel needed was a few players. And on October 10, he got them.

For the expansion draft, the eight National League clubs had created a pool made up of 15 players from each team. Seven of these had to have been on a big-league roster as of August 31. The draft was to be conducted in three tiers. First, the two new franchises were allowed to pick 16 players (two from each team) for $75,000 each. Next, if the expansion teams opted, they could select one more player from each team at $50,000 a head. After these picks, the Mets and Houston would each be permitted to make "premium picks." Each club would make one player available in this phase of the draft. The Mets and Colt .45's would each be allowed four selections in this round.

Houston won a coin toss for the right to pick first. When the Mets' turn came, they selected a 31-year-old journeyman catcher named Hobie Landrith from the Giants. At the time Landrith had a career batting average of .231. Stengel defended the selection with irrefutable logic: "You gotta have a catcher," he explained, "or you'll have a lot of passed balls."

In subsequent history, number one draft selections have changed the history of sports franchises. Basketball's New York Knicks turned from also-rans to world champs after making Willis Reed a top pick. Joe Namath lent authenticity to an entire league when football's New York Jets made him their number one choice. Landrith never did join Namath and Reed in New York's pantheon of sports legends. Ironically, he would soon be traded for the man who became the symbol of the early Mets.

The entire list of the new Mets included:

- $125,000 "premium picks": pitchers Jay Hook (Reds) and Bob Miller (Cardinals); infielder Don Zimmer (Cubs); outfielder Lee Walls (Phillies).
- $75,000 picks: pitchers Craig Anderson (Cardinals), Roger Craig (Dodgers), Ray Daviault (Giants), Al Jackson (Pirates); catchers Chris Cannizzaro (Cardinals), Choo Choo Coleman (Phillies), Hobie Landrith (Giants); infielders Ed Bouchee (Cubs), Elio Chacon (Reds), Sammy Drake (Cubs), Gil Hodges (Dodgers), Felix Mantilla (Braves); outfielders Gus Bell (Reds), Joe Christopher (Pirates), John DeMerit (Braves), Bobby Gene Smith (Phillies).
- $50,000 picks: pitcher Sherman Jones (Reds); outfielder Jim Hickman (Cardinals).

The 22 selections cost Mrs. Payson $1.8 million. The new cast had a distinct New York flavor: Zimmer, Craig, and Hodges had all played for the Dodgers in Brooklyn. The Mets would further build on this theme during the off-season. They acquired Johnny Antonelli, twice a 20-game winner with the Giants of the Polo Grounds, and Billy Loes, a Long Island native who once claimed he lost a ground ball in the sun while pitching for the Dodgers in a World Series game.[2] Before the year was out the Mets acquired from the Reds yet another ex-Dodger, second baseman Charlie Neal. Two of George Weiss's better acquisitions were outfielders Richie Ashburn and Frank Thomas. Ashburn came from the Cubs and Thomas from the Braves for an aggregate sum of $225,000.

In October ground was broken at 126th Street and Roosevelt Avenue in Queens for a new 55,000-seat stadium. The Mets took care of other housekeeping chores: television rights were assigned for $6 million and, since the franchise and players had cost around three million, the team was now solvent. The Mets hired three announcers; Lindsay Nelson, best known as NBC's top football commentator; Bob Murphy, a nine-year broadcasting veteran with the Red Sox and Orioles; and former N.L. home run king Ralph Kiner. The trio would remain intact for the next 17 years.

Lindsay Nelson's decision to switch from network announcing to the Mets was a surprise. "I had observed," Nelson said, "that, generally speaking, network sports announcers did not tend to live to a ripe old age. On the other hand, I had noticed that baseball announcers seemed to go right on forever. Bob Elson had been calling balls and strikes since the beginning of time. Harry Caray must have started with Abner Doubleday, and was still going strong."

* * *

The Mets, Branch Rickey opined, had drafted players who "are about to climb down the other side of the hill." That was the master plan. While the Houston Colt .45's would play in virgin territory, the Mets would be performing in the shadows of legends. The team's heavy New York accent (Weiss, Stengel, Hodges, Zimmer, Craig, etc.) was no accident. Robert Creamer, Stengel's biographer, explains: "(Weiss) chose them with a certain practical cynicism. He based the team's future on his staff of scouts, which he felt would discover and sign exemplary prospects who would blossom into a respectable team in five or six years. For the time being, though, he had to attract customers to the ballpark."

Stengel was a vital part of the master plan, and the old man played the role to perfection. He even came to New York to help publicize the Mets at the 1961 Thanksgiving Day Parade in Manhattan. "I may be able to sell tickets with my face," said Casey.

Street and Smith's Yearbook picked the Mets for eighth place, ahead of Philadelphia and Houston. The Mets were analyzed as a "respectable club with the possible exception of pitching." Spring training was a busy time for Stengel and his coaching staff of Solly Hemus, Rogers Hornsby, Red Kress, Cookie Lavagetto, and Red Ruffing. They tried desperately to put together a team from the salvageable parts in camp. The Mets finished the spring with 12 wins and 15 defeats. The big news was a win over the Yankees in the first-ever meeting between the two teams on March 22. The Yanks downplayed the importance of the game but Stengel, realizing the propaganda benefits, played it for all it was worth. The Mets won dramatically in the bottom of the ninth and the outcome made the front page of the New York *Daily News*.

A 28-year-old former track star from Drury College in Springfield, Missouri, hustled his way onto the Mets roster that spring. His name was Rod Kanehl, and he had come to camp as the property of the Mets' Syracuse (International League) farm club. Kanehl had been purchased from Nashville (Southern League), a Reds' affiliate. Kanehl had broken in with McAlester (Sooner State League) in 1954.[3]

Stengel recalled Kanehl leaping over a fence to catch a fly ball years earlier in a Yankee camp. "Hot Rod," who played every position except pitcher and catcher, soon became hot copy for the New York reporters. They called him a "splinter from the Yankees bench." Kanehl was destined to become an early crowd favorite at the Polo Grounds, but a knee injury in mid-August slowed him down. In typical Kanehl style he tried to conceal the injury to stay in the lineup, but his batting average dropped from .284 to .248.

When the team broke camp, the following players headed north:

- Pitchers: Craig Anderson, Roger Craig, Ray Daviault, Jay Hook, Al Jackson, Ken MacKenzie, Bob Moorhead, Sherman Jones, Clem Labine, Herb Moford, Bob Miller.
- Catchers: Choo Choo Coleman, Chris Cannizzaro, Joe Ginsberg, Hobie Landrith.
- Infielders: Ed Bouchee, Elio Chacon, Gil Hodges, Felix Mantilla, Jim Marshall, Charlie Neal, Don Zimmer.
- Outfielders: Richie Ashburn, Gus Bell, John DeMerit, Joe Christopher, Jim Hickman, Rod Kanehl, Bobby Gene Smith, Frank Thomas.

It was a team that managed to commit the oldest baseball sins in the newest kinds of ways. Ashburn batted a respectable .306. Thomas, who had spent three years in a Carmelite seminary earlier in life, parked 34 home runs. Al Jackson, a lithe southpaw out of the Pirates' system, threw four shutout victories. The team managed 40 wins in 160 tries. Only two teams in history—the 1916 Philadelphia Athletics and the 1935 Boston Braves—had compiled lesser winning percentages. The 120 losses were enough for a league record that still stands.

The Mets used 45 players that first year. For many, service with the original Mets was like the mark of Cain. Eighteen of them never appeared again in a major league contest.[4] Not one of the players is currently in the Hall of Fame, even though Hodges belongs and Ashburn is worthy.

The Mets' first game, scheduled for April 10 in St. Louis, was rained out. That was the last break the team got for the rest of the season. The following day Stengel threw this lineup at the Cardinals: Ashburn cf, Mantilla ss, Neal 2b, Thomas lf, Bell rf, Hodges 1b, Zimmer 3b, Landrith c, Craig p. The Mets lost, 11–4. The first run scored against the Mets came in the first inning when Roger Craig balked in a run from third base. It was an omen of things to come. Gil Hodges hit the first home run ever struck by a Met, in the fourth inning.

After a ticker-tape parade up lower Broadway, the Mets played their first game in the Polo Grounds on April 13. They lost again, this time by a 4–3 margin to the Pirates before a crowd of 12,447 who braved the wet, cold weather to see the inaugural game.[5] The Mets lost their next game, and the next game after that. And they kept right on losing through their first nine games, tying a major league record. From the vantage point of the announcer's booth, Lindsay Nelson observed: "(They) looked like the Light Brigade at Balaclava. They bravely took the field each day and were systematically destroyed."

Finally on April 23 the Mets broke the ice in a 9–1 win over the Pirates at Forbes Field. Jay Hook, an engineering student from Northwestern University, allowed five hits for the victory. "I may pitch Hook every day," Stengel noted.

There was a brief period in May when the Mets overtook the Cubs and Houston in the standings and moved into eighth place, a kind of Prague Spring in upper Manhattan. Reality set in with the brutality of a Stalin tank, however. The Mets started a 21-game losing streak on May 21. It lasted through June 6. In July they lost 11 straight. And in August they managed a 13-game losing skein. On June 30 Sandy Koufax of the Dodgers threw a no-hitter at the Mets. Cardinal Stan Musial contributed to the horror with three homers in a 15–1 slaughter at the Polo Grounds in July.

Sensing disaster, George Weiss began to make changes early in the season. In late April he picked up a pair of catchers after Stengel made some unnerving discoveries about his receivers: Hobie Landrith could catch, but had no arm; Chris Cannizzaro could throw, but couldn't catch; and Choo Choo Coleman could catch low pitches, but little else.[6] Asked why Coleman stayed in the lineup when the only pitches he could catch were those in the dirt, Stengel answered: "Them are the only ones the other teams ain't hitting."

One early trade with the Reds brought a lefthanded Bob Miller to New York; giving the Mets a league lead in the Bob Miller department. Traveling secretary Lou Niss roomed the two Bob Millers together on road trips. His logic was that anyone trying to reach Bob Miller would be sure to find him.[7]

The most significant addition of the year was a balding first baseman named Marv Throneberry, the best hitter ever produced by the West Tennessee Throneberrys.[8] Maybe it was Marvin Eugene Throneberry's acronymic initials. Whatever it was, the fans loved him and he came to symbolize the Mets in their year of living futilely. Throneberry had been a hot prospect in the Yankee chain, hitting 118 home runs in three seasons with the Yanks' Denver (American Association) affiliate. After a few lackluster seasons in the Bronx, he was dealt to Kansas City and from there to Baltimore. On May 9 Throneberry joined the Mets. The Mets, ironically, gave up Hobie Landrith—their first pick in the expansion draft—to the Orioles on June 6 as the player to be named later in the deal.

When Gil Hodges' cranky knee gave out, Throneberry took over at first. He quickly became the quintessential New York Met. A mocking reporter hung the "Marvelous Marv" tag on the big Tennessean, but the Polo Grounds fans took him to heart. "Trouble was," former *Long Island Press* reporter Jack Lang recalls, "the fans loved him more for his mistakes than they did for the little talent he showed." Throneberry managed to wear the goat's horns even in triumph. Trailing the Cubs one afternoon by a 3–0 score, he hit an apparent triple with two men on base. The Cubs appealed that Throneberry had missed first. Throneberry was promptly called out. Enraged, Stengel scuttled out to argue. The second base umpire intercepted him. "Forget it Case," said the ump. "He missed second, too." "Well, I know damn well he didn't miss third," Stengel shot back. "He's standing on it."

The unusual became commonplace. Richie Ashburn, a skilled center fielder with the Phillies for most of his 15-year career, found he was having communication problems with shortstop Elio Chacon, a Venezuelan whose command of English was limited. On pop flies to center, Ashburn and Chacon had some near collisions. To resolve the problem, the enterprising Ashburn learned the Spanish phrase for "I got it." Soon he was able to put his new linguistic skills to use in a game against Cincinnati. On a short flare over second, Ashburn came in as Chacon raced out. "Yo lo tengo!" shouted Ashburn. Chacon backed off and Ashburn, settling under the ball, was promptly bowled over by left-fielder Frank Thomas.

Stengel managed to maintain his sense of humor through most of the year. After one show of particular ineptitude, however, he railed: "Can't *anybody* play this here game?" The remark, converted into "Can't anybody here play this game?" became a verbal emblem of the Mets' first year. Popular New York columnist Jimmy Breslin used it as the title of a 1963 book that immortalized the sometimes humorous, always entertaining first year of New York expansion baseball.

One of Casey's toughest days on the job came after the Mets swept a twinbill in Milwaukee. En route to Houston, the Mets' flight was delayed and rerouted. They finally arrived close to 12 hours after their original flight was supposed to leave Milwaukee. Stengel had been his convivial self throughout the marathon journey, entertaining reporters and anyone else who would listen. Finally heading to his hotel room after being without sleep for 24 hours, Stengel told road secretary Lou Niss: "If anyone wants me, tell them I'm being embalmed."

Despite the mounting losses, the fans loved it all. And they turned out in droves. Mets' attendance was 922,530, the second-best attendance in baseball history for a last-place team.[9] The fans rocked the Polo Grounds with the rhythmic chant of "Lets-Go-Mets!" soon banners began appearing. At first management tried to quash this phenomenon. But George Weiss, sensing a movement, soon relented. The messages, usually scrawled on bedsheets, became a regular feature below Coogan's Bluff. One memorable banner proclaimed: "To err is human, to forgive is a Mets fan." "Cranberry, Strawberry, we love Throneberry," appeared on one sheet. Another offered what may have been the only logical advice: "Pray," was all it said.

The season ended on a fitting note when Joe Pignatano hit into a triple play in what was his final major league at bat. But the fans—by now dubbed the New Breed—looked like they'd be back for more in 1963. One fan, who'd seen every inning of every Mets home game in 1962, explained it in Jimmy Breslin's book: "I had sixteen box seats. And I had thrills you couldn't count. It was the greatest summer of my life."

* * *

Pedants explain the popularity of New York's National League team—the "Amazin' Mets," Stengel had called them during the maiden voyage—in many ways. They were counterculture. The times were a-changin', and antiheroes were in. Social revolution, which would reach the brim later in the decade, was beginning to brew. Somehow John F. Kennedy and the Beatles wind up as a part of this rationale.

Most of this would have been news to the fans who jammed into the Polo Grounds in those early years. Actually, it was pretty simple. National League baseball was back, and that's what they wanted. And the Mets were born at a time when a large chunk of the population was either into or approaching adolescence. Oh, not that the glandular changes in Gotham's youths contributed to the celebration of the Mets. But the teenage years, when those first, tentative steps are taken toward independence, self-confidence, and self-expression, are the time when personal identities are forged. For this sizable segment of the New Breed, the team was a mirror. And above all, the Mets were a hell of a lot of fun, and there was always hope for a better tomorrow. Lindsey Nelson summed it up nicely: "The Met fans survived and multiplied. They yelled and cheered and hoped and prayed—and often they laughed to keep from crying. Bad jokes were made by people who misunderstood and mistakenly thought the Met fans cherished a loser."

Management tried to shore up the 1963 team with a series of off-season deals. The acquisition that caused the biggest stir came on April 1. On that date the Dodger Alumni Club acquired a new member: The Duke of Flatbush, Edwin Snider. Snider, whose years of stardom in Brooklyn would eventually lead to a niche in Cooperstown, wasn't thrilled. "Being sold was humiliating enough," he recalled in his autobiography, "but being sold to the New York Mets in those days seemed like the ultimate humiliation. They were the worst team in baseball."

On Opening Day at the Polo Grounds the Mets faithful let Snider know how they felt. Hanging from the stands was a banner that read: "Welcome home Duke. We still love you." The experience of losing 111 games, however, was too much for the Duke. After the season he was dealt to the Giants, where he finished out the string.

There were improvements. The Mets lost nine fewer games. The eight straight losses at the start of the season were one less than the year before. One of Stengel's new recruits was a scrapper picked up from Milwaukee named Ron Hunt, who would finish second only to Pete Rose in Rookie-of-the-Year balloting. Carlton Willey, another ex-Brave picked up before the year's start, won three of his first four decisions for the Mets. He pitched four shutouts and, despite a 9–14 slate, finished with a commendable 3.14 earned run average. But mostly the Mets served up leftovers from the previous year. Tracy Stallard, obtained from Boston, lost 17 of 23 decisions. Newcomer Al Moran hit a weak .193 at short (despite flashes of brilliance afield). The entire team could muster only a .219 batting average.

The Mets' first win of the year was powered by the kids. In a 4–3 triumph over Milwaukee, Ed Kranepool, the $85,000 bonus baby from James Monroe High School in the Bronx, hit his first major league homer. Ron Hunt doubled in two runs in the bottom of the ninth. The old order began to give way slowly. By early May, Marv Throneberry was gone, shipped to the Mets' Buffalo farm team.[10] Gil Hodges left later that month. His knees ravaged by injury, Hodges was through as a player. The Mets gave Hodges a break and dealt him to the Washington Senators, where he took over as manager.

In a separate waiver deal the Senators sent veteran outfielder Jimmy Piersall to New York. Stengel remembered Piersall from his days as a star Red Sox flyhawk. "That guy who wears my number," the Old Man called him (both wore uniform number 37 when they were in the American League). Piersall—who had suffered a mental breakdown earlier in his career—was a colorful if sometimes eccentric player. His Met career lasted just 60 days, but he contributed to team folklore when he hit his one hundredth career home run on June 23 at the Polo Grounds. Piersall celebrated the landmark by running the bases backwards. "There's only room for one clown on this team," muttered Stengel, and a month later, Piersall was released.

The highlight of the year for the Mets didn't come in a regular season game. Instead it came in an exhibition contest with the Yanks on June 20. Before a packed house at Yankee Stadium the Mets beat the Bronx Bombers, 6–2. Forget that the Yanks, en route to a fourth straight pennant, had fielded their scrubs. The Mets won, and the newspapers played it up. Score another triumph for Stengel in the battle for hearts and minds.

The attendance continued to climb. They went over the million mark by early September and finished with 1,080,108 when they closed down the Polo Grounds on September 18. Still, the Polo Grounds had never seen such futility. When Carlton Willey's grand slam led the way in a 14–5 win over Houston, it marked the end of a 15-game losing streak. When Tracy Stallard presented Stengel with a win on his birthday at the end of July, it snapped a major-league-record 22 straight road losses. Roger Craig lost 18 straight. The final loss in the streak came on an errant pickoff throw that allowed the winning run to score from first.[11]

Amid the horror were seeds of hope. A kid from Mobile named Cleon Jones made his debut in the Mets outfield in September. The scouts had signed youngsters like Bud Harrelson and Dick Selma during the year. But these recruits were a long way off. Stengel bluntly assessed his players during a game against the Reds: "You look there into the Cincinnati dugout and what do you see? All mahogany. Then you look at our bench and all you see is driftwood."

* * *

On April 17, 1964 the Mets opened William A. Shea Stadium—named for the man who had midwifed the ballclub—and before the year was out some 1,732,597 fans had passed through the turnstiles.

Only the Dodgers drew more. And the Mets had attracted over 400,000 more customers than the Yankees, who had won their fifth straight pennant. The Mets meanwhile finished last for the third straight year.

When Al Jackson whitewashed Pittsburgh five games into the season, the Mets were off to their quickest start. Meanwhile, prospects like Ron Swoboda, Tug McGraw, and Jerry Koosman would sign with the Mets before the year was out. The Mets had landed a capable pitcher in the off-season when they picked up Jack Fisher from San Francisco in a supplemental expansion draft.[12] But the pitching staff suffered an early setback when a line drive caromed off Carlton Willey's jaw. Unable to eat solid food, Willey's strength atrophied and he lost weight. He tried to come back, but developed a sore arm and was never the same.

At the end of May the Mets hooked up in a doubleheader with San Francisco in what turned out to be one of the most memorable days in baseball history. The Giants easily won the first game. The nightcap got under way at 4:02 p.m. By 11:25 that night the contest was over.

The umpires went through 22 dozen baseballs. The concessionaires ran out of hot dogs. The two teams had used 41 players. And the Mets lost, 8–6, when the Giants scored twice in the top of the 23rd. Another three innings would have tied the major league record for the longest game in history. Three weeks later the Mets were again awash in history.[13] On June 21 Jim Bunning of the Phillies threw a perfect game at them. At the time, only eight perfect games had been pitched in all of major league history. Shea Stadium had seen one in only its third month in the big leagues.

By August Casey Stengel was an old man in a dry month. At 74 his detractors said he was too old to manage.[14] Stories began to circulate that he catnapped in the dugout during games. Rumor had it that Stengel would soon be replaced by Alvin Dark, the San Francisco manager. It wasn't Casey's fault, but the act was getting old. The team wasn't going anywhere without better players. In late September the Mets took a step in the right direction when Bing Devine, who'd helped to fashion the Cardinals into pennant winners, joined the front office. And in the off-season the Mets obtained from the Giants the man who would eventually take over for Stengel. Yet it was not Alvin Dark.

* * *

From the beginning the master plan had been to build from within. While shopworn "name" players entertained in New York, Casey Stengel was imploring the Youth of America to enlist in the Mets' system. Met scouts kept the promise. By 1965 talents like Cleon Jones, Bud Harrelson, and Jerry Koosman were on display at outposts in Buffalo, Williamsport, Auburn, Greenville, and Marion. From Texas, veteran scout Red Murff filed this report on an eighteen-year-old high school pitcher: "Has the best arm I've ever seen in my life. Could be a real power pitcher some day."

Murff had been watching Nolan Ryan, whom the Mets would select in baseball's first-ever draft that summer. Ken Boswell, Steve Renko, and Jim McAndrew were among the Mets' other top picks.[15] That spring one of the first products of the Youth Movement came north with the big club. He was Ron Swoboda—"Suh-boda," Stengel called him. A L'il Abner in flannels, Swoboda had been signed off the University of Maryland campus a year earlier. For him, the only limit seemed to be the sky.

At seventy-four, Stengel could still separate the wheat from the chaff. His assessment of a burly catcher named Greg Goossen is a masterpiece: "He's twenty years old," Stengel observed, "and in ten years he has a chance to be thirty."[16]

With the youngsters still learning the trade in the minors, the front office brought in more old, familiar faces. From the Braves came Warren Spahn. Two seasons earlier Spahn, at age forty-two, had won 23 games. After a 6–13 season the Braves sold him to New York. Yogi Berra, unceremoniously dumped by the Yankees after winning a pennant in 1964, joined the Mets as a coach. And Eddie Stanky, once a favorite with Giant fans at the Polo Grounds, signed on as director of player development. Almost overlooked was the addition of Wes Westrum to the coaching staff. Westrum, a catcher for the Giants before their move west, came to the Mets with Cookie Lavagetto, an Oakland resident, leaving the Mets for San Francisco. Berra and Stanky, both experienced managers, looked like probable successors to Stengel. It was Westrum who would be the Old Man's personal choice.

For a while there were signs of hope. In spring training Gary Kroll and Gordie Richardson combined to no-hit the Pirates. When the season began, it took only three game for the Mets to post their first win of the year. Spahn looked like he'd found the Fountain of Youth in Queens, wrapping a pair of complete-game wins around his 44th birthday.

Soon the Mets went flat, settling into last place for good in mid-May. The strain began to show on Stengel. He was forced to field lineups consisting of "plumbers"—his term for players who wouldn't have made the final cut with his fabled Yankee teams.

Casey's last stand was presaged on May 10 at West Point. The Mets were on hand to play an exhibition game with the cadets. Stengel slipped and broke a wrist. His detractors used the incident as one more excuse to call for Casey's ouster. "He's too old to manage," carped

Jackie Robinson, never a Stengel fan. "He sleeps on the bench. He should quit." When Stengel's finish came, it came quickly. And, as often happens, no one even realized it at the time. Just five days short of his 75th birthday, Casey fell again, this time after an Old-Timers Day celebration at Shea Stadium. Shortly after a party at Toots Shor's, Stengel slipped and broke a hip. Westrum was named interim pilot. Everyone figured he'd keep the seat warm until Old Case could come back. Old bones, of course, are slow to heal. And Edna Stengel, Casey's wife, was urging him to retire. So was Met management. Faced with a long recuperation, Casey Stengel called it quits on August 30. Within seven months he would be inducted into the Hall of Fame.

Stengel wasn't the only casualty. Young Ron Hunt suffered a shoulder separation in May and missed two-thirds of the season.[17] Al Jackson and Jack Fisher were also victimized: Jackson suffered through 20 defeats while Fisher endured 24 losses despite a 3.93 earned run average. The Mets won 50 game and lost 112. Warren Spahn managed only two more wins and was released in July. The Mets closed the season on a sour note, managing just two runs in their last 49 innings. But the New Breed kept the faith: More than 57,000 fans turned out in June for a doubleheader with the Dodgers. The Mets lost both games.

It was the little victories that sustained the faithful, like the night Reds' pitcher Jim Maloney threw 10 no-hit innings at the Mets. But while Maloney was striking out 18 New York batters, a pair of Met pitchers were blanking his teammates. A home run by Met outfielder Johnny Lewis in the top of the 11th was the game's only score.

The unusual win was the only one the Mets could manage during a 16-game stretch. Another joyful moment came in July when the Mets finally beat Sandy Koufax for the first time. Outdueling the Dodger stalwart was one of Stengel's kids, a gutsy southpaw named Tug McGraw.

* * *

Westrum officially took over as manager shortly after Stengel's retirement. During the winter of 1966 the Mets picked up veterans Ken Boyer and Ed Bressound and, although few noticed, they acquired a young catcher from Houston named Jerry Grote.

It would be a breakthrough year. After an Opening Day loss the Mets won two games in a row. Finally the team had more wins than losses. The heady business continued. In July the Mets won more games than they lost—another team first!—with an 18–14 slate. That month the Amazins won seven straight, sweeping a pair of doubleheaders in two days.

The quiet Westrum blended the youngsters with the veteran players. Cleon Jones took over an outfield post and hit .275. Ed Kranepool, a veteran at age 21, led the team with 16 homers. Boyer, his best years behind him at 35, knocked in 66 runs. But it was pitching that made the difference. For the first time in team history no Met pitcher lost 20 games. Jack Fisher, Dennis Ribant and Bob Shaw each won 11. Shaw—picked up from the Braves in June—won his first four decisions for the Mets. His 11–10 slate was the first-ever winning record by a Met regular starter.

The Mets topped the Phillies in the first game of an August doubleheader for a team-record 54th win. They finished with 66 victories, avoiding both the basement and 100 losses for the first time. The Cubs dropped into last place, 7½ games behind the Mets. With the Yankees dropping into last place in the A.L., the Mets were suddenly the toast of the town. Almost two million fans flocked to Shea Stadium.Westrum's contract was promptly renewed for the 1967 season.

All of the improvements would pale in comparison to the events of a five-week span before the start of the season. On February 24, 1966 the Braves signed a University of Southern California righthander named Tom Seaver. The Braves, however, had violated baseball rules by inking a player whose collegiate season was in progress. On March 2 the commissioner's office voided the deal. Seaver's collegiate eligibility had ended when he'd signed the contract and, with nowhere to go, he became a free agent.

The Indians, Phillies, and Mets matched the Braves' $50,000 offer. On April 2 Commissioner William Eckert wrote the name of the three teams on slips of paper. He placed them into a hat and closed his eyes. The slip he plucked out read "Mets." Seaver signed the next day. Commissioner Eckert, whose term is scarcely remembered, had altered forever the course of Met history.

In June, 1966, however, the Mets proved that luck is not always the residue of design. With Reggie Jackson available, they made catcher Steve Chilcott the top pick in the draft. Chilcott never played a game in the big leagues.

* * *

In a season of hope deferred, the Mets slipped back into the cellar in 1967. They won 61 games and lost 101. The previous summer George Weiss had retired and Bing Devine moved in. Devine kept in motion throughout the year, trying to find a winning combination. A record 54 players toiled for the Mets during the 1967 season.

Devine had retooled the Cardinals into pennant winners. He had similar plans for the Mets. He surrounded himself with capable front-office men like Whitey Herzog, a former outfielder whose roots were in the Yankee organization. Devine moved Herzog up from the Met coaching ranks and the club's farm system began operating on all cylinders.[18]

Tommy Davis came from the Dodgers in a winter trade for Jim Hickman and Ron Hunt. The Mets picked up pitchers Don Cardwell from Pittsburgh and Ron Taylor from Houston. During the regular season Key Boyer went to the White Sox for future considerations, veteran third sacker Ed Charles came over from Kansas City, and reliever Cal Koonce arrived from the Cubs.

Outfielder Don Bosch was emblematic of the Mets' year. Picked up in the same deal that brought Don Cardwell, Bosch was touted as the next Willie Mays in centerfield. When Westrum first saw the 5'10" Bosch in spring camp, he wasn't impressed. "My god," moaned the old backstop, "they sent me a midget." For Bosch, the gift of promise was fatal: intimidated by the harsh glare of New York's light fantastic, he hit a buck-forty and was soon back in the minor leagues.

Still, there were good tidings: Ron Swoboda hit .281. Bud Harrelson, a lithe Californian, took over at shortstop and showed signs of brilliance. And the Young Lochinvar out of the west, Tom Seaver, joined the club after one season at Jacksonville, winning 16 games with a 2.76 earned run average.[19]

* * *

"The New York Mets were the worst team in the league," observed former major league outfielder Curt Flood in his book, *The Way It Is*: "When some of the youngsters showed signs of becoming first-rate professionals, Gil Hodges was named manager and they became serious." How the Indiana-born Hodges, one of the best-loved sports figures in New York history, became manager of the Mets is one of those ironic chapters in the team's history.

The old Brooklyn star was married to Joan Lombardi, a local girl. Gil and Joan had maintained their home in Flatbush even after the Dodgers moved west. Hodges, since leaving the Mets to manage Washington, had led the Senators from the cellar to sixth place. Hodges had been a Marine platoon leader in the Pacific during the Second World War. One of the strongest men in baseball, he was known as a peacemaker on the oft-tumultuous Dodger teams of the fifties. Ralph Kiner recalls Hodges as "a man who ruled with quiet strength. At times he could be patient; at other times he could be forceful."

Johnny Murphy, Bing Devine's chief lieutenant, began clandestine negotiations with his counterpart for the Senators, George Selkirk. Devine was fully aware that Murphy and Selkirk had been teammates on the Yankees from 1934 through 1942.

The story broke during the 1967 World Series: The Senators would release Hodges from his contract. He would manage the Mets in 1968.[20] Immediately the players sensed a change. "When some of us got together (during the winter), we all felt like we couldn't wait to start the season," Ron Swoboda told *Sports Illustrated* the following spring.

Johnny Murphy took over as general manager when Bing Devine left to return to the Cardinals. Murphy, the man who engineered Hodges' return, was a native New Yorker who had gone to Fordham University. He'd been an outstanding relief pitcher with the Yanks and had been with the Mets since the beginning.

During the winter catcher J. C. Martin and outfielder-first baseman Art Shamsky came to the Mets. Martin, much-admired by Hodges when he played for the White Sox, came as the player-to-be-named-later in the Ken Boyer deal. Shamsky arrived from the Reds. In the biggest off-season trade, the Mets picked up center-fielder Tommy Agee, the A.L. Rookie of the Year for 1966, plus infielder Al Weis from the White Sox in return for Jack Fisher, Tommy Davis, and a pair of throw-ins. The trade reunited Agee and Cleon Jones—they had been high school teammates in Mobile, Alabama—and the Mets hoped that Agee would succeed where Don Bosch and others had failed.

But the big trade wouldn't pay dividends for at least a year because an errant fastball struck Agee behind the ear during the first exhibition game and he never got untracked. The team suffered through a 9–18 spring season, the worst to date. Hodges and his coaching staff were unperturbed. Calmly, they assessed their players.[21]

As usual the Mets lost their season opener. But the next day rookie Jerry Koosman gave up only four hits in a 4–0 win over the Dodgers. Older members of the New Breed reserved judgment: they were used to false alarms.[22] Then Koosman gave the Mets their first-ever win in a home opener, shutting out the Giants. He went on to win his first four decisions, proving he was no flash in the pan. With Swoboda hitting seven home runs during April, the Mets began to serve notice. Ever inclined to the uncommon, the Mets hooked up in a 24-inning duel with Houston at the Astrodome in April. The six-hour, six-minute contest ended when a potential double-play ball went through the legs of shortstop Al Weis and the Astros won, 1–0.

Koosman impressed throughout the season. In September he blanked Pittsburgh for the Mets' 67th win of the season, a team record. The Mets finished with 73 wins, their best performance to date. Pitching was the team's trademark. Koosman finished with 19 wins, seven shutouts, and a 2.08 earned run average, all team records.[23] Tom Seaver became the first Met to strike out 200 batters. Nolan Ryan whiffed 133 in 134 innings. Ryan's pitching hand tended to blister, however, and trainer Gus Mauch came up with an unusual solution. "(Mauch) went to a delicatessen in the Bronx," explained Met announcer Lindsey Nelson, "and got a small jar of pickle brine and he instructed Ryan to soak his fingers rather continuously in the pickle brine in order to toughen the skin." Mauch would cut the blisters to let the blood drain before each soaking. The result was a mixture that Ryan's fellow Mets dubbed a "bloody Nolan."

The pitching staff's 2.72 earned run average was second only to the pennant-winning Cardinals. Attendance shot back up, with 1,781,657 customers visiting Shea Stadium. The year ended on a frightening note, however. During a night game in Atlanta on September 24 Hodges suffered chest pains. The next day it was announced that the Big Man had suffered a mild heart attack.

* * *

"Man will walk on the moon before the Mets win a pennant," the pundits proclaimed earlier in the decade. Of course, they were right. But not by much. The Mets' performance in the 1969 baseball season is usually mentioned in the same breath as the parting of the Red Sea. Starring in the title role of "Oh, God!," George Burns utters this memorable line: "My last miracle was the sixty-nine Mets."

Actually, the Mets' march to the World Series was no more a miracle than the Apollo lunar expedition. Chances for both had once been remote. But diligent preparation, execution, and leadership made each a reality. Had Gil Hodges been in charge of the space program, man might have made it to the moon a few years ahead of schedule. Hodges was back in 1969, 25 pounds lighter and in excellent health.

Baseball had expanded again, with San Diego and Montreal joining the National League. *Street and Smith's* praised the young Met pitchers, but projected New York for last in the six-team N.L. East Division, behind the fledgling Expos. And when Montreal topped the Mets 11–10 on Opening Day, it looked like another long year in Queens.

The team started out slowly. Gary Gentry, a newcomer out of Arizona State, joined Seaver, Koosman, Don Cardwell, and Jim McAndrew in the starting rotation.[24] Koosman, bothered by shoulder ailments, began to come around in May. But McAndrew's pitching hand blistered and Nolan Ryan pulled a thigh muscle.

By May 21 the team had won 18 of 36 games, the first time a Met squad had been at .500 that far into the season. A week later the team began an 11-game win streak. But just when everyone was healthy, National Guard duty began to deplete the starting lineup. Hodges' keystone combination of Ken Boswell and Bud Harrelson was called away for extended periods. So was Tug McGraw, back with the team as a reliever.

Still, this was the most competitive Met squad ever seen. Joe Durso analyzed the club's new-found self-respect in *Amazing: The Miracle of the Mets*:

> Outside of (Ed) Kranepool and (Cleon) Jones, none of them had been around during the comedy days . . . It had taken a half dozen years to find talent, but (George) Weiss, (Bing) Devine and (Johnny) Murphy had beat the bushes to find it. Then they turned the talent over to bright, young hard-working supervisors like (director of player development) Whitey Herzog . . . Joe McDonald, the director of minor league operations, a methodical and energetic type, Nelson Burbrink, the director of scouting, who had pursued some of the 1969 Mets in schoolyards; Wes Stock, a former pitcher who was now the minor league pitching coach; and a scouting staff led by three longtime baseball men—Bill Kelly, Sheriff Robinson and Bob Scheffing. . . .

And at the heart of it was Hodges, quickly establishing himself as one of the game's top managers. On the morning of June 15 the Mets had won 30 games and lost 26. They were second to the Cubs. By day's end they had lost to the Dodgers, 2–1. And they had pulled off one of the shrewdest trades in their brief history. From Montreal the Mets picked up 33-year-old first baseman Donn Clendenon.[25] Hodges began to alternate the big righthanded hitter with Kranepool. The trade paid immediate dividends. "In his first sixteen games," recalls Jack Lang, "Clendenon drove in either the lead run or the winning run and the Mets continued to win."

In early July the Mets, with seven straight wins under their belt, were poised for their first crucial series as the Cubs came to town. Hodges's outlook was typically austere: "I don't believe you can have a big series in July," he opined. There was no love lost between the Mets and Cubs. An earlier series at Wrigley Field spawned a beanball duel that turned into a near riot.

The Mets trailed 3–1 in the ninth inning of the first game when a misplayed fly ball turned into a triple, leading to three runs and a come-from-behind New York triumph. The Cubs fumed. "It's ridiculous," muttered Cub third baseman Ron Santo. "There's no way the Mets can beat us." The Mets won again the next day. Tom Seaver came within three outs of a perfect game. Only a leadoff single by Jimmy Qualls in the ninth marred Seaver's 4–0 performance. Qualls, ironically, had only 30 other hits in his brief major league career. He had started in place of Don Young, the rookie who had botched the fly ball a day earlier. The Cubs recovered and won the next day. A reporter asked Leo Durocher, the Cubs' mercurial manager, if these were the real Cubs. "No," shot back Leo the Lip, "those were the real Mets." A week later in Chicago the two teams met again. the Cubs won the first game, but the Mets, powered by an Al Weis homer, won 5–4 the following day. Weis's drive landed on Waveland Avenue. The Mets took the rubber game with Weis homering again. The Cub lead was cut to three games.

Weis's eight-year major league home run total was now up to six. Unlike the towering drive in the second game, this homer landed in the bleachers. "Weis has lost a little power," Hodges drily confided to *Newsweek's* Paul Zimmerman.

At home in Glendale, California, Casey Stengel followed the Mets with interest in their new role as pennant contenders. "This club plays better baseball now," he told Joseph Durso of the *New York Times*. "Several of them look fairly alert."

In the next few weeks the Mets played more like their old selves. They lost 14 of 25 games, including three straight to the Astros. In one game Houston scored 10 runs in one inning, and Hodges observed what he took as a lack of hustle from Cleon Jones. Striding from the dugout, the Big Man walked purposefully to left, casting a cold eye upon Jones. A moment later Hodges, followed by Jones, trudged back to the dugout. The Met public relations department said later Jones came out because of a leg injury. In reality, Hodges had served notice to every man in Met flannels: nothing less than 100 percent effort would be tolerated.[26]

On July 17, midway through the bleak spell, two American astronauts walked on the moon. The Mets, 9½ games back of the Cubs and in third place, had the day off.

The Mets recovered from the Houston debacle, winning 12 of their next 13. Suddenly they were right back in the race. When Seaver beat Philadelphia 5–1 on September 1 for his 20th win—a Met first—the Mets were suddenly trailing the Cubs by only four games. A few days later the Cubs came to New York, now up by only 2½.

Chicago's Bill Hands opened the bottom of the first by dusting Tommy Agee. Jerry Koosman started the next frame by drilling Cub Ron Santo in the elbow. The Cubs, particularly the truculent Leo Durocher, got the message: don't try it again. Agee took revenge when he homered his next time up. Koosman struck out 13 in a 3–2 Met victory. Chicago's lead dropped to half a game the next day when the Mets won again. Suddenly the Cubs looked like toolmakers and stackers of wheat. For the New Yorkers, the hiss now became a roar. A day later a doubleheader sweep of the Expos put the Mets in first place to stay.

The Mets won 22 of their last 27 games. In St. Louis, Cardinal lefthander Steve Carlton struck out 19 Mets, a record performance.

Incredibly, the New Yorkers won anyway, by a 4–3 margin with Ron Swoboda driving in all the Met runs with a pair of homers. Even the losses were remarkable: The Pirates' Bob Moose threw a no-hitter at them on September 20. Four days later Gary Gentry's shutout win over the Cards gave the Mets the Eastern Division title. Finishing the year with 100 wins and 62 defeats, Hodges had brought them where no Met team had gone before.

Pitching had been the team's strength. Seaver had won 25 games, including his last 10 in a row. Koosman was 17–9 for the year. The rookie Gentry chipped in with 13 wins. Met pitchers registered 28 shutouts and Tug McGraw had saved 35 games. Cleon Jones and Tommy Agee, the boys from Mobile, had supplied most of the punch. Jones hit .340 and Agee clubbed 26 home runs. Hodges had platooned brilliantly, getting maximum performances from Swoboda and Art Shamsky in right and from Clendenon and Kranepool at first base.

Before the first-ever N.L. Championship Series against the Western Division champion Atlanta Braves, Hodges honestly appraised his team for Jack Lang: "I really didn't think we'd come as far as we did as fast as we have," said Hodges. "But now that we're here I see no reason to stop." And they didn't, sweeping the Braves in three games. They did it, oddly enough, with hitting, winning by scores of 9–5, 11–6, and 7–4. Although the Met pitchers were raked for five earned runs a game, the hitters batted .327 with six homers. "They beat the hell out of us," said Atlanta Manager Lum Harris.

The World Series matched the Mets against the Baltimore Orioles, a solid team of veterans. Three years earlier many of these same Orioles had knocked over the Dodgers in a stunning four-game sweep. The Orioles featured stalwarts like Frank Robinson, Brooks Robinson, Boog Powell, Jim Palmer, Mike Cuellar, and Dave McNally. To them the Mets were upstarts. "Who the hell is Rod Gaspar," they taunted, mocking a Met rookie outfielder who had hit .228 in a part-time role.

The Orioles were heavy favorites and, when the Series opened in Baltimore, they showed why: Don Buford hit Seaver's first pitch for a homer and Cuellar pitched a complete game victory.

The second game was a pitchers' duel between Koosman and McNally. Clendenon's fourth-inning homer gave Koosman a slim cushion, which he held through six innings. A leadoff single for the Orioles in the seventh—their first hit of the game—led to a run and a 1–1 tie. But the Mets scored the deciding run in the top of the ninth with two out when Ed Charles, Jerry Grote, and Al Weis stroked consecutive singles. Ron Taylor came out to the bullpen to snuff out a Baltimore rally and save the win for Koosman. With the Series tied, the action shifted to Shea Stadium.

Over 56,000 fans turned out for the first World Series game played in New York in five years. If the Orioles were baseball's aristocracy, Met fans had been the oppressed and downtrodden since their beginning. And Bastille Day was just around the corner.

The Mets scored first in Game Three on a leadoff homer by Tommy Agee. Gary Gentry doubled in two more in the second. By the time Ed Kranepool homered in the eighth the Mets had a 5–0 lead that stood up. Tommy Agee's two fielding gems had staved off at least two Oriole rallies. Agee snared a line drive in the fourth, saving a pair of runs, and in the ninth made a diving, one-handed catch at the warning track with the bases full.

More fielding artistry saved the day in Game Four. Hodges sent Seaver to the mound while the Orioles countered with Cuellar. Clendenon's second-inning homer gave the Mets a 1–0 lead which Seaver protected into the ninth, thanks largely to a fine catch by Cleon Jones in left. The Orioles threatened in the ninth when back-to-back singles put runners at the corners with one out. What happened next was as close to miraculous as the Mets got all year. Brooks Robinson lined a drive to right. Ron Swoboda took off to his right at full speed. As the ball arced toward the turf, Swoboda dove head first. Inches from the ground, the ball stuck in his glove. The catch was one of the greatest in Series history. It was, Swoboda recalled years later, "as big a surprise to me as anyone in the stands. I had to dive for the ball, and when I left the ground I had no idea it would hit my glove." The runner at third tagged on the catch, but Swoboda had prevented the Orioles from taking the lead. With the score still 1–1 in the bottom of the 10th the Mets rallied. With runners on first and second, Hodges sent J. C. Martin up to hit for Seaver. Martin bunted. Pitcher Pete Richert charged toward the plate and fired to first. The ball ricocheted off Martin's left wrist. Scoring the winning run from second was Rod Gaspar, inserted moments earlier as a pinch runner. Incredibly, the Mets were one win away from taking a World Series.[27]

In the fifth game the Orioles went up 3–0 courtesy of home runs by McNally, their starting pitcher, and Frank Robinson, both in the third inning. The Mets struck back in an unusual way in the sixth. A low inside pitch sent Cleon Jones sprawling. Jones got up and, dusting himself off, started for first. Ump Lou DiMuro called him back. Jones protested, claiming the pitch had struck him in the foot. DiMuro held fast until Hodges came out with the ball. Hodges showed the ump where it was smudged by polish from Jones's shoe. DiMuro recanted and waved Jones to first.[28] Clendenon followed with his third home run of the Series and the Oriole lead dropped to 3–2. An inning later Al Weis homered to tie the score. It was the little infielder's first roundtripper at Shea Stadium.

The Mets took the lead in the eighth. Jones doubled off reliever Eddie Watt. Swoboda's single along the left-field line put the Mets ahead. Swoboda scored when Jerry Grote's bouncer to the left side was bobbled. Koosman took the mound in the ninth with a 5–3 lead. After a walk, Koosman retired the next two batters. Davey Johnson came up as the Orioles' last hope. Johnson lifted a fly ball to Jones in left, who caught the ball and sank to one knee. An entire city—and a large chunk of America—wildly celebrated.[29]

Miraculous? Not for the men who played the game. The Mets had done it with some of the best pitching, the tightest defense, and the timeliest hitting ever seen in Series play. Hodges had taken 25 talented men and turned them into World Champions. Tom Seaver summed up the season succinctly: "Miracle," said Tom Terrific, "my eye."

* * *

Fortune's favorites in 1969, the Mets reaped the rewards: Donn Clendenon was the Series MVP. Seaver won the Cy Young Award and Hodges won every managerial award available. Soon after, tragedy struck: Johnny Murphy, honored as executive of the year by *The Sporting News*, suffered a fatal heart attack at the end of the year. He was 61 years old.

Only a few weeks earlier Murphy had made several deals at baseball's winter meetings, trades that would hopefully keep the Mets on top in the coming year. One deal brought lefthander Ray Sadecki from the Giants. Another brought thirdbaseman Joe Foy, a Brooklyn native, from Kansas City.[30]

The Mets finally won an Opening Day game and, picking up right where he'd left off, Seaver won his first six starts. In late April he tied a major league record by striking out 19 San Diego Padres. For a month in midseason New York won 20 of 27 games and briefly took over first place. The hitting improved. Clendenon, used sparingly at the start, hit .288 with 22 home runs while Tommy Agee belted 24 with a .286 average. In September the Mets moved in front again, tying Pittsburgh for a couple of days before finally dropping out of the race for good.

It was pitching, of all things, that betrayed the Mets as they fell to third behind Pittsburgh and Chicago. Seaver won 18 games with a 2.81 earned run average, but there was little else to applaud. A sore elbow hampered Koosman. Shoulder ailments held Gentry to nine wins in 18 decisions. Nolan Ryan—who had shown signs of greatness in April, striking out 15 Phillies in one game—won just seven games. The Mets were still tops in New York, however. Attendance was up to almost 2.7 million. But change was inevitable, if this team was again to challenge for a pennant.

* * *

Bob Scheffing, a veteran baseball man, had replaced Johnny Murphy in the club's top administrative slot. And Donald Grant, Mrs. Payson's top advisor for baseball matters, was by now a presence in the front office. The Mets gave up on Joy Foy, a washout in his one year with the team. Another Brooklynite, handsome Bob Aspromonte, came in from Houston as the latest hot corner candidate.[31]

On the eve of the 1971 season the Mets cut off Ron Swoboda's buttons and threw away his stripes, dealing him to Montreal. The Mets felt they'd waited as long as they could for the former Series hero to develop into a first-rate hitter. Swoboda's replacement in right was switch-hitting Ken Singelton, a local kid from Hofstra University.

Starting out fast, the Mets were atop their division by June. But in July they lost 20 of 29 games and the bottom dropped out. The Mets finished in a tie for third. Seaver was again magnificent, winning 20 games with a 1.76 ERA. His 289 strikeouts were a league record for righthanded pitchers. Tug McGraw and Danny Frisella were bullpen stalwarts. But Jerry Koosman was a cause for concern: arm miseries limited him to six wins against 11 losses.

More change was also in the offing. In December the Mets dealt for veteran California Angel shortstop Jim Fregosi. The plan was for Fregosi to take over at third base, where Aspromonte had failed to produce. The Mets gave up four players to California, including Nolan Ryan. Ryan had asked to be traded, and the Mets figured Ryan, like Ron Swoboda, might never live up to his enormous potential. Gil Hodges approved the trade, proving that, at times, even the gods are crazy.

* * *

"The mystique of the Mets," wrote baseball historian Donald Honig, "had been predicated on two wildly opposing extremes—Stengel's lovable losers and Hodges' astonishing winners." Hodges had led the Mets out of the desert and by spring of 1972 there was hope of a renaissance. Two youngsters up from the minors—lefty Jon Matlack and slugger John Milner—were cause for joy. Jim Fregosi broke a thumb in the first spring game but the Mets, undaunted, won 15 of 23 in the exhibition season. Hodges called it the best club he'd managed.

Spring training ended abruptly when the players association voted to go out on strike on the last day of March. The walkout left Hodges and three of his coaches—Eddie Yost, Rube Walker, and Joe Pignatano—in West Palm Beach with time on their hands. Hodges' fourth staff member, Yogi Berra, had gone to Miami to spend time with family and friends. On Easter Sunday Hodges and his lieutenants opted for a round of golf. After 18 holes they headed back. In their hotel parking lot they made dinner plans Hodges would never keep: suddenly the Big Man fell backwards to the ground, the victim of a massive heart attack. Two days short of his 48th birthday, the man who was most responsible for the team's metamorphosis was dead.

Callously, the Mets made two announcements on the day of Gil Hodges' funeral in New York. They announced that they had obtained outfielder Rusty Staub from Montreal for Ken Singleton, Tim Foli, and Mike Jorgensen.[32] They also announced that Yogi Berra was the new manager. The strike of 1972 lasted 13 days and cut into the first week of the regular season. When play resumed the Mets picked up where they'd left off in Florida. Under Berra the team looked like pennant contenders.

Then on May 11 came the news that—almost 21 years to the day he'd first arrived in New York—Willie Mays, old and stricken, was coming home.[33] Joan Payson had been a Mays fan when both were connected with the New York Giants. She'd once tried to bring Mays to the Mets with an offer of a million dollars, which the Giants owner- ship had rejected. But the San Francisco fans had never warmed to Mays, whom they identified with New York. They politely acknowl- edged Mays' greatness, saving their adulation for players like Orlando Cepeda and Willie McCovey, who had come of age not in the Polo Grounds, but in Candlestick Park.

As June rolled around the Mets were in contention, a veteran club with solid pitching. Then the injuries began. On June 3 an inside pitch struck Staub's right wrist. Rusty continued to play until he could no longer grip a bat. The pitch had fractured a bone. In July the entire outfield was maimed as both Cleon Jones and Tommy Agee joined Staub on the sidelines. Fregosi and shortstop Bud Harrelson were disabled. Manager Berra, wrote Jack Lang, "resembled a Continental Army general seeking volunteers." During one stretch the Mets had only 10 healthy players available for duty.

For the third straight year the Mets wound up in third place. Seaver's 21 wins were tops, with rookie Jon Matlack contributing 15 victories. McGraw added 27 saves and a 1.70 ERA from the bullpen. Milner, the other first-year man, led the club with 17 homers but the offense was otherwise woeful.

Still, the New Breed kept coming in droves and the attendance figures topped two million for the fourth straight year. The Mets, no longer lovable losers, were far from worldbeaters. Four years after the World Series triumph, they had settled into mediocrity.

* * *

If there is a miracle year in Met history, 1973 is it. In 1972 the Mets had been riddled by injuries; by mid-season of 1973 they looked like they'd been visited by a Biblical plague. Nevertheless, Yogi Berra would become the second manager in history to win pennants in both leagues.[34]

By the end of April the Mets looked like contenders. Then the incredible string began:

- At the end of the month sophomore slugger John Milner went on the disabled list with a pulled hamstring.
- On May 8 a line drive caromed off the head of pitcher Jon Matlack. He suffered a mild concussion.
- A pitched ball struck Rusty Staub's left hand three days later. Staub eventually wound up on the DL and the injury hampered him throughout the season.
- In the same game Jerry Grote suffered a broken right forearm.
- A few days later Willie Mays came out of the lineup for 14 days with a sore shoulder.
- Catcher Jerry May, picked up from the Royals to replace Grote, sprained his left wrist. When he got back in the lineup, May then pulled a hamstring.
- The month of June began with Cleon Jones going on the disabled list with a sore right wrist.
- Rookie outfielder George Theodore was struck in the eye by a pitched ball. Fortunately, the injury wasn't serious. A month later, however, Theodore wound up disabled when a collision left him with a fractured hip.
- The day after Theodore was struck in the face, Bud Harrelson went out of the lineup with a fractured left hand.
- Shortly after returning to active duty Harrelson was disabled a second time, this time at the end of July with a broken sternum.

All told eight Mets (including Harrelson twice) spent time on the disabled list, missing a total of 183 games. Adding to Berra's woes was a total collapse by the Met bullpen. His ace, Tug McGraw, was 0–5 by mid-August with a paltry 13 saves. "If you ain't got a bullpen," noted Berra, "you ain't got nothin'."

As the injuries mounted the Mets sank further in the standings. Last by the end of June, they were still in the basement by the All-Star break. With no team in the Eastern Division able to take control, however, the Mets were only 7½ games back. It was Tug McGraw who fueled the miracle. With the team floundering in July, board chairman Donald Grant visited the clubhouse. According to Met historian Dennis D'Agostino, Grant's homily centered around confidence, faith, and the team believing in itself. The clubhouse was silent as the sermon ended. As Grant started to leave, McGraw leaped up, yelling, "He's right! He's right! Just believe! You gotta believe!" In the next few weeks, McGraw's words would become the team's battle cry.[35]

In August Harrelson returned and Berra was able to field his regular lineup for the first time since May. On August 22 McGraw won his first game. Nine days later the team fought their way out of last place for good. Jerry Koosman caught fire, throwing 31⅔ scoreless innings. Ex-Brave George Stone won eight games down the stretch. And McGraw was . . . well, unbelievable, with three wins and seven saves in 11 outings.

By mid-September, with the New Yorkers 2½ back of the division-leading Pirates, the two teams squared off for five straight contests. The Mets split the first two games in Pittsburgh, then won three straight from the Bucs at Shea. The middle game produced a play that could only be described as miraculous. With the score tied in the top of the 13th and Richie Zisk on first, Pirate reserve Dave Augustine drilled a deep drive to left. Cleon Jones watched helplessly as the ball sailed over his head. Instead of reaching the seats, the ball landed at the edge of the wall and bounced straight up, still in play, and fell directly into the glove of an incredulous Jones. Jones quickly fired the ball to cutoff man Wayne Garrett, who relayed it perfectly to catcher Ron Hodges. Hodges tagged out Zisk at home plate. In the bottom of the frame Hodges drove in Jones from second base for the winning run.

When Tom Seaver beat the Pirates the next day, the Mets were in first place. They also reached the .500 mark for the first time since May. Berra had said all along that the Mets were the only team in the division that hadn't had a hot streak. Now they were smoldering. Between September 1 and October 1 the Mets won 20 and lost eight. McGraw posted 12 saves, won another five, and had an 0.88 earned run average through his last 19 games.

A win over the Cubs on October 1 gave the Mets their second Eastern Division crown. Earlier in the year Yogi Berra had put it best: "It ain't over 'til it's over." For the N.L. Championship Series the Mets faced the awesome Cincinnati Reds. "If you examined the comparative talents of the two teams," recalls broadcaster Lindsey Nelson, "it looked like a joke. This was the Big Red Machine—this was Bench and Rose and all those folks."

Showing no prejudice, the Miracle Mets beat the heavily favored Reds in five games. Midway through the series, Pete Rose slid into Bud Harrelson on a force at second. The 190-pound Rose came up swinging at the 155-pound Harrelson, producing a bench-clearing brawl.[36]

The World Series matched the Mets against Oakland. These were Charlie Finley's Swingin' A's, in the middle of three straight trips to the Fall Classic. The Mets bravely clawed their way to a three-games-to-two lead. But when the Series shifted back to Oakland for the last two games, the miracle ran out of gas. The A's won both games to put away the title.[37]

* * *

Reminiscing on the Mets' second pennant, Whitey Herzog said the club "gave up too much for that one year of glory. It was a long time before they even got close to winning again."[38]

The Mets fell to fifth in 1974 with a 71–91 record. Injuries were again a factor. The worst ailment was a sciatic condition that limited Tom Seaver to 11 wins against as many defeats. Tug McGraw, yesterday's hero, was no help. The entire relief corps saved only 14 games. "A lot of guys," said a beleaguered Yogi Berra, "save that many all by themselves."

* * *

Change was in the air in 1975. Joe McDonald became general manager, replacing Bob Scheffing, who had retired. McDonald, a Staten Island native and a Fordham graduate, had been around since the beginning, initially as the Mets' radio/television statistician.

McDonald sought a stronger bullpen and more offense. Tug McGraw rode the tradewinds to Philadelphia while Dave Kingman, a moody San Francisco slugger, came to New York. Brooklyn native Joe Torre, a Most Valuable Player in 1971 with St. Louis, arrived as the new third baseman.

The offense rebounded. Kingman broke Frank Thomas's 12-year-old club record for homers with 36 and Rusty Staub became the first Met to knock in more than 100 runs in a single season, with 105. These were the glad tidings. The bad news was that, by the end of the year, the Mets were tied for third place with an 82–80 record and both Yogi Berra and Cleon Jones were gone.

Injured at the start of the season, Jones stayed in Florida when the club traveled north. Early one morning St. Petersburg police arrested Jones after discovering the outfielder in a parked van on a main street wearing nothing more than a frown.

Jones and Berra clashed during a game in July when the manager told his malingering player to go to left field as a late-inning defensive replacement. Jones refused. Berra wanted to suspend him. Joe McDonald and Donald Grant tried to dissuade Berra, who held fast. On July 26 Berra announced that Jones had been released. "I did what I had to do," said Yogi.

On August 6 Berra was also gone. Taking over as manager was former shortstop Roy McMillan, a Met coach since 1973. Under McMillan the Mets made a brief run for the pennant, pulling to within four games of first by September 1. But McMillan's final slate of 26 wins and 27 losses convinced the front office he wasn't the answer. At the end of the year the Mets announced that Joe Frazier, named

Minor League Manager of the Year for guiding Tidewater to the International League pennant, would take over the reins for 1976.

Toward the end of the season Casey Stengel died and Joan Payson passed away five days later. "Now so many who had done so much for the Mets were gone," said broadcaster Ralph Kiner. "George Weiss, Johnny Murphy, Gil Hodges, Casey Stengel and Joan Payson, the president of the club since its inception. An era had ended."

* * *

"Joe Frazier has all the qualifications you would want in a manager," said G.M. Joe McDonald. "He wins." Frazier played for four clubs in four seasons in a brief league career that stretched from 1947 to 1956. His big-league managerial career would be even briefer. Frazier guided the Mets to 10 more wins than losses in the Bicentennial Year, good for third place.

Again, injuries stalled the Mets. Dave Kingman broke his own club record for homers with 37, but suffered ligament damage in his left thumb and missed a quarter of the season. Mike Vail, Rusty Staub's replacement, missed most of the season due to an off-season injury. A year earlier, Vail's .302 performance down the stretch made Staub expendable; the big redhead had been dealt to Detroit.

Tied for first in mid-May, the team settled into mediocrity soon after. Joe McDonald and Tom Seaver got into a contract squabble that almost resulted in the star pitcher's dismissal. A story leaked that Seaver was headed to the Dodgers, roiling the Met faithful. McDonald recanted, signing Seaver instead to a complex contract that made the righthander the best-salaried player in team history.

Seaver tailed off to 14–11, but Jerry Koosman won 20 games for the first time in his career, going 21–10 for the year. Joe Torre moved from third to first, dragging his best years behind him. The articulate Torre's name began to circulate as a managerial candidate.

* * *

By 1977 the Mets were no longer kingpins in New York. The Yankees were in the middle of three straight World Series appearances, and the Mets' dwindling attendance figures reflected their wretchedness afield. With the big club floundering, the farm system wasn't producing either. Free agentry was the law of the land and, while the Yanks had signed Reggie Jackson and others to fat contracts, the Mets abstained. Donald Grant had set a limit on how much the Mets would spend on free agents.

More dissent ravaged the team. Seeing the amounts lavished on free agents by other teams, Tom Seaver and Dave Kingman asked for salary increases. Grant, now in virtual control of the team, refused.

Kingman announced he would play out his option and the rift between Seaver and Grant widened. With the Mets fumbling their way to 15 wins in their first 45 games, Grant replaced Joe Frazier with the available Joe Torre.

The feud between Seaver and Grant turned acrimonious as members of the press took sides. When Seaver and management finally seemed to resolve matters, *New York Daily News* sports editor Dick Young blasted Seaver for requesting contract renegotiation. Young implicated Nancy Seaver, Tom's wife, as the reason for the pitcher's discontent. When Seaver learned of Young's column, he was furious and demanded to be traded immediately. On the night of June 15 the Mets' first authentic hero tasted the bitter bread of banishment. Seaver went to the Reds for four players. On a night soon dubbed the "Midnight Massacre," the Mets also sent Kingman packing. The team's all-time home run leader was off to San Diego.[39]

The players the Mets received would never equal Seaver or even Kingman in the hearts of Met fans. Red Smith of the *New York Times* wrote:

> Tom Seaver has been one of the finest pitchers in the game. . . . He is his own man, thoughtful, perceptive and unafraid to speak his mind. Because of this, M. Donald Grant and his sycophants put Seaver away as a troublemaker. They mistake dignity for arrogance.

For the first time since 1967 the team dropped into last place. Jerry Koosman lost 20 games, the first Met hurler in a dozen years to suffer that fate. Four years removed from a World Series appearance, the New York Mets were again doormats.

* * *

The Mets started the 1978 season with three straight wins. Unfortunately they won only 63 more times and finished last yet again. Joe Torre suffered for the sins of the front office. The team he inherited was a pale reminder of the Hodges/Berra years. A couple of newcomers performed capably: John Stearns, picked up from the Phillies as Jerry Grote's replacement, set a league record for catchers with 25 stolen bases. Craig Swan led the league in earned run average and outfielder Lee Mazzilli—a native New Yorker and a favorite of the young female fans—hit .273 and stole 20 bases.

The season would be Donald Grant's last as chairman of the board. In November Lorinda de Roulet, Mrs. Payson's daughter, took over the position. "It just seemed like the time to do it," she quipped.

* * *

Lorinda de Roulet had promised that the Mets would enter the free agent market. As spring training rolled around in 1979, the only new talent arriving in New York was via the trade route. A deal with

Minnesota for Jerry Koosman left Ed Kranepool as lone survivor of the 1969 season.[40]

The first rumors that the Mets were for sale began circulating in March. Denied vigorously by the Payson family, the rumors persisted throughout the season. The Mets finished last again, barely avoiding 100 losses with a 63–99 record. In 38 home dates after the All-Star break, the team won only six times. Met fans, once renowned for their stoicism, stopped coming. The team drew fewer than 800,000 customers.

Financially the team was in shambles. Mrs. de Roulet had borrowed heavily from her father, Charles Payson, who was never a baseball fan despite his late wife's passion for the game. By the end of the year the Payson family had reached the limit. They were finished as owners of the Mets.

* * *

Twenty-four days into the new decade Fred Wilpon and Nelson Doubleday bought the Mets for more than $21 million. The franchise had cost just $2 million 18 years earlier.[41]

The new owners brought in Frank Cashen to right the club. Cashen had been Baltimore's general manager during the Orioles' halcyon days of 1966 through 1975. Joe McDonald was siderailed into a vice presidential post. Cashen immediately opened the Met checkbook, signing pitcher Craig Swan to a five-year contract worth over $3 million. Clearly, the Mets were willing to spend money in order to contend.[42]

Neither was the farm system ignored. That summer the Mets had the top pick in the amateur draft and they selected a six-foot, six-inch outfielder from Crenshaw High School in Los Angeles named Darryl Strawberry. Here's how one Major League Scouting Bureau report described the youngster: "Very tall, slender build. Large neck, wide shoulders, Good frame that will develop added strength. Long arms, big hands. Still growing. No injuries, no glasses."

Relying on speed and a good young bullpen, Torre moved the club to fifth place. While admen dreamed up feathery slogans like "The Magic is Back," the Mets surged briefly in mid-season before dropping off to 67–95. Attendance went back over the million mark and Torre received a two-year contract.[43]

Gradually, Frank Cashen had brought old Oriole hands into the Met front office. By 1981 he had on board Lou Gorman, Al Harazin, and Joe McIlvaine, all trusted aides during his Baltimore years. Two old crowd favorites also returned to the Mets in 1981 as Cashen signed free agent Rusty Staub and traded with the Cubs for Dave Kingman.

With the year split by a midseason players' strike, the Mets had two chances for post-season play. The commissioner's office declared that the first-place teams from both halves would meet to determine the divisional winner. In the pre-strike part of the season the Mets went 17–34—good for fifth place—and were 24–28 the rest of the way, moving up a notch. On the last day of the season Cashen informed Torre that he would not be back as manager.

* * *

Torre's successor for 1982 was another hometown boy: George Bamberger, a Staten Islander who had pitched briefly for the New York Giants in the fifties. Bambi was Cashen's man, having served as Baltimore's pitching coach for many years before managing the Milwaukee Brewers.

Cashen brought in George Foster, once a devastating part of the Big Red Machine, to fortify the offense. The hope was that Foster and Kingman would provide the Met lineup with a powerful one-two punch. Foster, at 34, never lived up to the advance billing and Kingman, while hitting 37 homers, batted only .204. The defense was pathetic and the pitching was subpar. Craig Swan, coming back from rotator problems, led the staff with 11 wins. Neil Allen, quickly becoming one of the league's best closers, suffered a variety of ailments and was virtually lost to the team after June. Sophomore center-fielder Mookie Wilson chipped in with a solid year—58 stolen bases and a .279 batting average—but the Mets finished last again.[44]

* * *

The 1983 season began on a joyous note: Tom Seaver was back with the Mets. Cashen brought the 38-year-old Seaver back from Cincinnati, and when he was announced as the starting pitcher on Opening Day, the Met faithful gave Seaver a five-minute ovation. The team showed little early improvement, however, and Cashen, in need of a quick fix, brought up Darryl Strawberry from Tidewater. Strawberry had only 16 games at the AAA level under his belt. George Bamberger, whose first managerial stint had been ended by a heart attack, decided the risk wasn't worth it. He stepped down in early June, with coach Frank Howard taking the job on an interim basis.

At the trading deadline Cashen obtained Keith Hernandez from St. Louis for Neil Allen and pitcher Rick Ownbey. The arrival of Hernandez, a former league MVP and batting champion, gave the Mets a valuable team leader.[45]

Strawberry, young in limbs but mature in talent, hit .257 with 26 homers and won N.L. Rookie of the Year honors. He joined Seaver (1967) and Jon Matlack (1972) as Met players so honored. Strawberry,

Hernandez, Mookie Wilson, third baseman Hubie Brooks, and reliever Jesse Orosco offered hope for the future. *Baseball America* proclaimed the Mets the best organization in baseball, citing the revitalized farm system. Ron Morris said of the Mets:

> The Mets' success in the minor leagues is as much a credit to Steve Schryver, their director of minor league operations, as it is to (Lou) Gorman, (Joe) McIlvaine and (Frank) Cashen. Gorman brought Schryver to the Mets from the Seattle Mariners in 1982, where the two had worked together.
>
> Gorman says Schryver has helped develop "the Mets Way" in the minor leagues, a way he says will begin to produce results next season and in 1985.

* * *

During the 1983 World Series Frank Cashen announced that another old Oriole, Davey Johnson, would manage the Mets in 1984. Some felt that a New York team needed a "name" manager, but Johnson would prove to be a wise choice. He'd managed many of the Mets' top prospects at Jackson (Texas) and Tidewater and, in 1983, he had guided the Tides to the AAA World Series title. In Baltimore Johnson had been one of Earl Weaver's most apt pupils. "He always asked intelligent questions," Weaver said of his old second baseman.

In January an embarrassing gaffe almost undid all the good work of the Met front office. Tom Seaver, left unprotected on the Met roster, was claimed by the Chicago White Sox as compensation for a free-agent signing. The Mets, Jack Lang observed, "were devastated" by the loss of Seaver. "The criticism that followed Cashen in the next few days," said Lang, " was as harsh as that Grant had received when he first traded Seaver in 1977." But after the Mets' surprising second-place finish, the fans were willing to forgive Cashen. The Mets won 90 games; only Gil Hodges' 1969 team had won more.

At the start of the season Cashen and Johnson clashed over rookie pitcher Dwight Gooden, just 19 years old and two years removed from Tampa's Hillsborough High School. Cashen thought the young pitcher needed more seasoning while Johnson wanted to keep Gooden in New York. Gooden's 19 wins and 300 strikeouts in 191 innings at Lynchburg (Carolina) were all the credentials Johnson needed.[46] Gooden began the year as part of Johnson's rotation along with veterans Craig Swan, Mike Torrez, and Dick Tidrow. By mid-season Johnson dispatched the vets, going instead with youngsters Ron Darling, Walt Terrell, and Sid Fernandez.[47]

Amazingly, Johnson and his youthful pitching staff made a strong run for the pennant. In first place as late as the end of July, the Mets wound up second to another surprise team, the Chicago Cubs. Gooden won 17 games. His 276 strikeouts broke Herb Score's record for rookies. Things were looking up in Queens.

* * *

In the off-season Frank Cashen picked up infielder Howard Johnson from Detroit and catcher Gary Carter from Montreal. The deal with the Expos gave the Mets a solid backstop to go with their talented young pitchers. To some, the Mets were obvious favorites in the N.L. East as the 1985 season opened.[48]

But disaster struck in May with the Mets already atop the division with an 18–8 record. Attempting a shoestring catch, Darryl Strawberry tore the ligaments in his right thumb and went out for seven weeks. "It was our darkest hour," said Davey Johnson. During a brief stretch the Mets played like they were back in the Polo Grounds. On June 11 they lost to the Phillies, 26–7. It was their worst defeat in history.

Then on July 4 in Atlanta they went 19 rounds with the Braves in a game that concluded at four in the morning. Rain delayed the contest,which was to be a prelude to a Fourth of July fireworks exhibition. The game dragged on until the top of the 18th, when the Mets took a 12–11 lead. The Braves, out of players by the bottom of the frame, were forced to send up pitcher Rick Camp with two outs and the bases empty. Camp's career batting average was .062. He promptly homered to tie the game again. Finally, in the 19th inning, the Mets nailed down a 16–13 victory. Braves management then proceeded with the fireworks display for those patriotic souls still on hand in the pre-dawn hours of July 5.

Without Strawberry the Mets played .500 ball. Gooden was incredible: the 20-year-old would finish with 24 wins and only four losses. Fireballing Gooden had eight shutouts and an earned run average of 1.53. The Cubs seemed likely to repeat, if the Mets couldn't win. But at season's end it was Whitey Herzog's Cardinals in first place. Davey Johnson told his charges before the season ended: "we're going to win it all next year."

* * *

After two straight years of second place, the Mets went into their silver anniversary season as heavy favorites. "The Mets have the best young pitching in baseball," declared *Street and Smith's*, "the best young slugger in Strawberry, the best catcher in Carter, the best N.L. first baseman in Hernandez . . . and the noisiest fans."

Petersen's Pro Baseball was even more emphatic: "With the return of a fine young pitching staff and veteran sluggers it won't be a miracle this time when they go all the way." Early in the year Davey Johnson set the tone: "We don't just want to win," he said, "we want to dominate." When the season ended the Mets were clearly baseball's dominant team. They won 108 games and finished 21½ games on top of the N.L. East.

Along the way the Mets' high-spirited style left opposing teams in high dudgeon. High-fiving, jiving, and gamboling their way to victory, the Mets engaged in four on-field brawls. Tracy Ringolsby, writing for *Baseball America*, dubbed them the "despised team of baseball."[49]

Manager Johnson made all the pieces fit. Newcomer Bob Ojeda, obtained from Boston, teamed with Dwight Gooden, Ron Darling, Sid Fernandez, and Rick Aguilera in the starting rotation. Roger McDowell and Jesse Orosco were formidable in relief. With center-fielder Mookie Wilson injured in the spring, Johnson inserted Lenny Dykstra in the starting lineup. When Wilson came back, Dykstra stayed in center and Wilson moved to left, platooning with hard-hitting rookie Kevin Mitchell. Teamed with ex-Twin Tim Teufel at second, Wally Backman hit a career-high .320. Keith Hernandez, Gary Carter, and Darryl Strawberry contributed mightily, but in the end third baseman Ray Knight, who battled his way into everyday status, stole the show.[50]

In the N.L. Championship Series the Mets went up against an old nemesis, the Houston Astros. Since infancy the Astros had pestered their crib-mates. Even in the great 1969 campaign the Texans had won 10 of 12 games with the Mets. The Mets' chief tormentor was Astro pitcher Mike Scott, a former Met whose 18–12 record made him the ace of the Houston staff. Scott's 306 strikeouts and 2.22 earned run average were due chiefly to a split-fingered curve taught to him by Roger Craig, the old Met mainstay. "If everyone threw like that," Keith Hernandez said of Scott, "I don't think this game would make it. It would be too damned boring."[51]

At Houston Scott beat Gooden in the first game, but the Mets evened the series the next day, beating old friend Nolan Ryan. Back at Shea Lenny Dykstra's two-run homer in the bottom of the ninth put the Mets ahead, two games to one. "The last time I hit a home run in the bottom of the ninth to win a game was in Strat-O-Matic," said Dykstra.

Scott came back the next day to even the score at two games apiece. The fifth game matched Gooden and Ryan. Neither was still around, however, when Gary Carter's single in the bottom of the 12th gave the Mets a 2–1 win. A Houston win in the sixth game would mean a seventh game in the Astrodome with Scott primed and ready to pitch again. The game went 16 innings, lasting four hours and 42 minutes. The Mets survived a two-run Astro rally in the final half inning to win, 7–6. "That has to be the greatest game that ever lived," a drained Gary Carter exclaimed as the Mets celebrated their first pennant in 13 years.

The Red Sox, meanwhile, won the American League title. Boston and New York have always been baseball rivals. Hardly a man was now alive who could recall the 1912 World Series between the Sox and John McGraw's New York Giants (Boston's Smokey Joe Wood won three games to turn back the Jints), but many could still recall the 1949 American League pennant race (the Yankees beat the Sox for the title on the last day of the season) and Bucky Dent's 1978 home run at Fenway off Mike Torrez is a nightmare from which some Boston fans are still trying to awaken.

The Mets got off to an egregious start, losing the first two games of the Series in Shea Stadium. The Mets came back to even the Series with two straight wins, but Boston slammed Dwight Gooden around in Game Five to go up three games to two.

In Game Six the Red Sox had the Series all but bagged. With two out and the bases empty at Shea, they led 5-3. Hits by Gary Carter, Kevin Mitchell, and Ray Knight, followed by a wild pitch, tied the score. The next batter, Mookie Wilson, tapped a grounder to first baseman Bill Buckner. The ball skipped under Buckner's glove, giving the Mets a 6–5 win and sending the Series to a seventh game.

The Red Sox took a 3–0 lead into the sixth inning when the Mets knotted the score. In the seventh Ray Knight's homer put the Mets on top for good. The more than 55,000 fans at Shea celebrated as Jesse Orosco set the Bosox down in order in the ninth. The final score was the Mets 8, Red Sox 5. Knight, who'd come close to drawing his outright release at the start of the year, hit .391 against the Sox and was voted Series MVP.

* * *

The Mets' 1986 triumph would be their only World Series title of the decade. Dissent and injury kept the Mets from a repeat performance in 1987 and the next year they ran up against someone else's miracle. In 1989 the Cubs paid back a 20-year-old grudge.

For a change, the Mets had hitting in 1987. Darryl Strawberry finally had the kind of year everyone had long predicted for him, with 39 home runs and a .284 average. Taking over at third after Ray Knight left as a free agent, Howard Johnson belted 36 homers. Left-fielder Kevin McReynolds, coming over in a winter trade with San Diego, hit .276 with 29 four-baggers.

Injuries riddled the vaunted Met pitching staff. At various times Roger McDowell, Bob Ojeda, Rick Aguilera, Sid Fernandez, David Cone (obtained in March from Kansas City), and Ron Darling were *hors de combat*. The biggest setback came in April when Dwight Gooden entered a drug rehabilitation clinic. Two months later Gooden returned, but the Mets had struggled without him.

Whitey Herzog again had the Cardinals in contention, helped by the Mets' internal strife. Mookie Wilson and Lenny Dykstra, tired of platooning in center, both asked to be traded. Feelings were strained when Wally Backman and Lee Mazzilli—who'd returned the previous year for a second tour of duty with the Mets—accused Strawberry of not giving 100 percent. By now team harmony was in worse shape than the pitching staff.

The Mets got as close as 1½ games in September, but the Cardinals held on. Davey Johnson tied a league record with 90 wins in his first four seasons as the Mets finished 92–70. At campaign's end, Frank Cashen announced that after the 1988 season, Johnson would become a special assistant to the club owner, giving up field boss responsibilities.

* * *

In their first game of 1988 the Mets set a record for homers in a season opener with six circuit blasts against the Expos. Yet it would be pitching that would bring the New Yorkers their second division title in three years. The biggest surprise of the year was David Cone, who became a starter when Rick Aguilera was injured. Cone won 20 games, losing just three. His 2.22 earned run average and 213 strikeouts were both second in the league. Darryl Strawberry hit 39 homers, tying his own club record and taking over the lead in career roundtrippers by a Met with 186.

When the year was over the Mets were 100–60. Davey Johnson had tied Al Lopez's major league record of 90 wins in each of his first five managerial seasons.[52] The Mets led the league in homers (152), runs scored (703), earned run average (2.91), and strikeouts (1,100) and turned back brief challenges by the Pirates and Expos. Yet there were signs of mortality. A pulled hamstring sidelined Keith Hernandez for most of June and July. Gary Carter's seven home runs in April and May put him just one away from the 300th of his career. It was August, however, before Carter finally reached the milestone.

Still, there was two-time Minor League Player of the Year Gregg Jefferies, who came up from Tidewater to play third, hitting .321 down the stretch. In the League Championship Series the New Yorkers went up against the Dodgers, a team they'd beaten 10 times in 11 meetings during the regular season. It would be the Dodgers' year, however, as they swept the Mets in seven games in the N.L.C.S., followed by a World Series defeat of the powerful Oakland Athletics.

The Mets took a two-games-to-one lead over Los Angeles, and were within three outs of winning the fourth game when Dodger catcher Mike Scioscia's homer off Dwight Gooden knotted the score. Kirk Gibson's homer in the top of the 12th gave the Dodgers a 5–4 lead. Orel Hershiser then made a rare relief appearance to cement the win for L.A.

Less than 12 hours later the Dodgers won again, sparked by another Gibson homer. Cone beat ex-Met Tim Leary to set the stage for the seventh game, but to no avail. Hershiser, turning post-season play into his own personal showcase, ended the Mets' year with a 6–0 shutout. "Seven months, gone like that," reflected Met captain Keith Hernandez.[53]

* * *

The Mets were picked to win again in 1989, bolstered by "more arms than a banana republic army," as veteran writer Maury Allen phrased it. *USA Today* declared that the Mets "have the talent to dominate. They ought to romp." "Comebacks by Keith Hernandez, Gary Carter and Bob Ojeda," observed *The Sporting News* "would seem to make repeating automatic."[54]

Davey Johnson was back for another year at the helm, the plan to move him into the front office shelved, at least temporarily. A downward trend started even before the Ides of March. Darryl Strawberry complained about his status as the sixth-highest salaried player on the team and, on March 1, declared that he would leave camp if matters weren't resolved. During a team photo session the next day, Strawberry and Keith Hernandez tangled over Strawberry's statement. "Rightfielder Darryl Strawberry finally hit his cutoff man," quipped *Sports Illustrated's* Steve Wulf. Strawberry departed soon after the incident, but returned a few days later and made peace publicly with Hernandez. Strawberry insisted, however, that he would leave New York as soon as he became a free agent after the 1990 season.

To accommodate Gregg Jefferies, everyone's pre-season pick for Rookie of the Year, the Mets tried to deal Howard Johnson to Seattle. The package also was to include Sid Fernandez for lefthander Mark Langston, a Mariner pitcher on the verge of free agency. Jefferies couldn't get untracked in Florida, hitting safely once in his first 21 at-bats. Manager Johnson fortuitously opposed the deal. With Jefferies shifting to second HoJo took command at third, leading the Mets with 36 homers and a .287 batting average. Fernandez's 14–5 record was the best on the staff.

Injuries took their toll: Hernandez went down with a broken kneecap; Carter underwent knee surgery; a broken toe and a sore shoulder kept Strawberry out of the lineup for 20 games. The worst blow of all came when Dwight Gooden, the Met stopper, was lost for two months. Gooden was the victim of a torn shoulder muscle. Just as they had two years earlier, the Mets struggled without Gooden in the rotation.[55]

At the All-Star break the Mets were in third place behind Montreal and Chicago. The injuries and inconsistent pitching held them to a 45–39 record. Met management, trying to ignite the team, went to market. They got Juan Samuel from the Phillies in return for Lenny Dykstra and Roger McDowell. They picked up Long Island native Frank Viola from the Twins in exchange for Rick Aguilera and four prospects.[56] In yet another deal, Mookie Wilson went to Toronto for pitcher Jeff Musselman.

Nothing went right. Samuel was a bust in center, eventually demanding to be traded. Viola, thanks mainly to a lack of hitting support, won four of nine decisions with the Mets. Johnson seemed to change his lineup daily in search of the right combination.

The Mets' penchant for the bizarre surfaced on June 25, when they tied an arcane record. In a 5–1 win over the Phils, they went through an entire nine-inning game without a single assist. Only once before in major league history had there been a big-league game with no assist.[57]

Going into September the Mets trailed Chicago by only 2½ games, but couldn't put together a sustained run at the Cubs. As the season moved into the final weeks, Manager Johnson urged Darryl Strawberry to assume a leadership role. "Strawberry does for leadership," *Chicago Tribune* columnist Bernie Lincicome noted acidly, "what Roseanne Barr does for the bikini."

In mid-September Johnson benched Strawberry and left-fielder Kevin McReynolds for leaving the dugout with a game against the Cubs still in progress. When the Mets staged a ninth-inning rally, Strawberry had to be summoned from the clubhouse. He struck out with the bases loaded. Strawberry reiterated his intent to leave. "I want to play on the West Coast," he said during the season's final week. "A change of scenery would be good for me." Gary Carter, relegated to the unaccustomed role of third-string catcher, also expressed his displeasure to the media. By mid-September he and Davey Johnson were no longer speaking to one another about the catcher's role with the club.

Maybe it was a cynic's miracle. Maybe it was the Bleacher Bums' revenge, paid back with 20 years' interest. When the season ended the Mets, at 87–75, were six games behind the division-winning Chicago Cubs. "The New York Mets," observed *United Press International's* Joe Illuzzi, "proved this season it takes more than talent." The Mets, Illuzzi claimed, "lacked continuity and togetherness."

There were rumblings that Johnson would not be brought back for a seventh season in 1990. *Sports Illustrated* reported that Frank

Cashen respected Johnson's record, but Vice-President Joe McIlvaine was disturbed by Johnson's "disregard for fielding ability, his obsession with home runs and his failure to discipline his players." McIlvaine said that the team "reflects the personality of the manager," adding enigmatically that "people can read into that whatever they want to." Johnson's views on the disappointing season were philosophical. "When you're going good it doesn't get any better than being in New York," he said. "But when you're going bad, it doesn't get any worse."

And things would indeed get considerably worse for both Johnson and the Mets before too many more exciting ballgames played out their course in lively Shea Stadium. Despite a second-place finish, Johnson would not last out the 1990 campaign. And replacement skipper Bud Harrelson would receive even less patience from management, remaining at the helm for only a single disappointing 5th-place pennant chase the following summer. Doc Gooden had overnight become a mediocre moundsman, Darryl Strawberry had departed via free agency for the Los Angeles Dodgers, and the once-proud Mets had now become thoroughly unspectacular also-rans.

Jeff Torborg, the third club bench boss in as many seasons, brought little to the 1992 campaign to win the hearts of increasingly alienated Mets supporters. Heavy-hitting outfielder Bobby Bonilla earned much press with a $26-million free agent contract at the outset of the summer, yet his 19 homers and .249 BA over an injury-riddled 128 games earned more boos than cheers from the frustrated Shea faithful. Three years into the 1990s there was indeed very little joy in Mudville!

Notes

1. The city's American Football League franchise was then still known as the Titans.

2. Both Antonelli and Loes would retire before spring training.

3. Kanehl's teammates at McAlester included twins Roy and Ray Mantle, Mickey's siblings.

4. Those who ended their careers with the Mets in 1962 were Elio Chacon, Richie Ashburn, Gene Woodling, Ed Bouchee, Rick Herrscher, Joe Pignatano, Sammy Drake, Harry Chiti, John DeMerit, Joe Ginsberg, Bob (Lefty) Miller, Ray Daviault, Herb Moford, Larry Foss, Wilmer Mizell, Sherman Jones, Dave Hillman, and Clem Labine.

5. Among the crowd was a 17 year old from the Castle Hill section of the Bronx who had cut classes at James Monroe High School to attend the game. On September 22 the Mets pressed him into service. He stuck around for the next 17 years. The kid from Castle Hill was Ed Kranepool, the first player ever developed by the Mets. Kid Kranepool, who had broken most of Hank Greenberg's records at James Monroe, came to the game with the blessing of the Mets, if not his high school. Kranepool was the club's guest for their first game.

6. One of the catchers obtained in April was veteran Harry Chiti, who came from the Indians for a player to be named later. Chiti was subsequently

dealt to Cleveland's Jacksonville (Southern League) affiliate. He became the first player in major league history to be traded for himself.

7. The Mets obtained Bob (Righty) Miller for their Opening Day third baseman, Don Zimmer, who had recently broken an 0-for-34 slump with his first hit of the year. "They traded him while he was hot," noted one wag.

8. Marv's older brother Faye hit .235 with three American League teams in eight seasons. Marv bested him with a .237 average in his seven-year career.

9. Only the Detroit Tigers, cellar dwellers in 1952, had done better with 1,026,846.

10. Throneberry hit .176 at Buffalo in 88 games and soon faded into memory. But his last day with the Mets was one of his most memorable. According to Ralph Kiner, Throneberry was sent down on May 9, 1963. "After everyone had said goodbye and the clubhouse had emptied," Kiner recalled, "he pulled off his New York uniform for the last time, showered, dressed, packed his gear, and began his journey. He didn't get far. The clubhouse door was locked from the outside. It was only after a half hour of commotion that his cries were heard and he was allowed to leave. No Met ever went out in more fitting style."

11. Craig's agony finally ended on August 9 when Jim Hickman's grand slam gave him a 7–3 win over the Cubs. For the big righthander, 1963 was a galling year. He lost five games by 1–0 scores, finishing with a 5–22 record despite a 3.78 earned run average. Craig became the first National League hurler to suffer consecutive 20-game losing seasons since 1934.

12. Guilt over the original expansion draft may have been the reason for this supplemental round. The Mets took Fisher and first baseman Bill Haas, a Dodger farmhand. The acquisition of Fisher made the Mets an answer to the trivia question: What club included in its starting rotation the men who served up to Roger Maris his 60th and 61st home runs? Fisher (with Baltimore) and Stallard (with Boston) were the victims, in that order. Fisher had shown a flare for history-making in 1960, when he gave up a home run to Ted Williams in the Kid's final major league at bat.

13. It wasn't a total loss, though. After 32 innings of baseball the Mets had lost only two games. And an exhibition contest with their Williamsport (Eastern League) farm club scheduled for the next day was mercifully rained out.

14. One of Stengel's greatest detractors was an obscure radio personality named Howard Cosell. Monday Night Football was yet to be invented.

15. In the draft, held June 9, 1965, the Kansas City Athletics picked first, taking Arizona State outfielder Rick Monday. The Mets drafted next, selecting a British-born pitcher from Billings, Montana, named Les Rohr. This was not one of the Mets' better picks. The six-foot, five-inch southpaw won 2 games and lost 3 in parts of three seasons at Shea Stadium, and soon sank out of the major leagues. Rohr is chiefly remembered as the pitcher of record in the 24-inning, 1–0 loss to Houston in 1968.

16. Stengel was still a good judge of baseball talent. Goossen had a great 1965 campaign at Auburn (New York-Pennsylvania League), batting .305 with 24 homers. His six-year major league career stats, however, show a .241 average with 13 roundtrippers in 193 games. When Goossen celebrated his 30th birthday, he'd been gone from the big league for five years.

17. Hunt was dealt to the Dodgers for the 1967 season. He enjoyed a 12-year career, batting .273 for the Mets, Dodgers, Giants, and Expos. He specialized in getting hit by pitched balls. In 1971 he was hit 50 times, a major league record that still stands.

18. Herzog, as director of player development, successfully shaped the team's farm system. "I was probably the best player development man who

ever drew breath," Herzog immodestly recalls. "Two years after I took the job, the Mets won the World Series, and we did it with young players whom I had rushed through the system . . . I moved them along as fast as I could, and cleaned house of all the old, stagnant guys in the system. We went with kids at all levels and pushed them hard." Herzog spent seven years with the Mets, moving on in 1972 after being passed up for the managerial post.

19. Seaver became the first member of a last-place team to win National League Rookie of the Year honors. He also became the first Met player to win a major award.

20. In return for Hodges, the Mets sent pitcher Bill Denehy to Washington, also with a reported $100,000. A southpaw, Denehy won one and lost seven for the Mets in 1967. Denehy's career record shows a 1–10 slate. The Mets had showered larger sums on oafish draft picks, so the trade for Hodges rates as one of the premier bargains in team history.

21. Every member of the Met staff had New York ties. Holdover Yogi Berra, of course, had starred with the Yankees as a player and manager. Joe Pignatano, Rube Walker, and Eddie Yost came from Washington with Hodges. Piggy and Rube were ex-Dodgers and Yost, who had played for the Senators, Tigers, and Angels, was a Brooklyn native with a master's degree from New York University.

22. Two other Mets had thrown shutouts in their first seasons. They were Grover Powell in 1963 and Dick Rusteck in 1967. Neither won another game. Met fans were, by now, habitual skeptics.

23. Scout Red Murff had signed Koosman when the big Minnesotan was averaging 18 strikeouts per game for an army team at Fort Bliss, Texas. Koosman's batterymate was the son of a Shea Stadium usher, who wrote his father about the talented lefty. Murff originally tendered Koosman a $1,600 bonus. Koosman held out for higher stakes. Murff reduced his offer. Koosman finally signed for $1,200. "I figured I'd better sign," said Koosman, "before I owed them money."

24. McAndrew, from Lost Nation, Iowa, had posted an excellent 2.28 ERA the year before, despite a 4–7 record.

25. To the Expos, for Clendenon, went pitchers Steve Renko, Bill Cardon, and Dave Colon, plus third baseman Kevin Collins. Only Renko, with 134 career wins, amounted to anything in the majors. As for Clendenon, his arrival in Queens came via a circuitous route: After eight years in Pittsburgh, he'd been selected by Montreal in the expansion draft. When he told the Expos he had no intention of playing in Montreal, he was dealt to Houston for Rusty Staub and Jesus Alou. Clendenon promptly announced his retirement. The Astros wanted the trade nullified. New commissioner Bowie Kuhn intervened, arranging for two players to be substituted for Clendenon. This sated the Astros. The Expos then offered Clendenon a heftier contract, and his "retirement" ended.

26. "Nobody knew what was going on," Tug McGraw told Dave Kaplan of the *New York Daily News* years after Hodges' walk. " . . . when Gil kept walking to left . . . I don't think people took the incident seriously. But the players realized that this man expects more of us than we ever dreamed of."

27. Controversy ensued after Martin's bunt. The Orioles claimed Martin was inside fair territory when hit by Richert's throw. Home plate umpire Shag Crawford ruled that there was no intentional interference on Martin's part. Earlier in the game Crawford had ousted the Orioles' feisty skipper, Earl Weaver, for protesting a call. It was the first time a manager had been thrown out of a Series game in 34 years.

28. The play was eerily similar to one in a 1957 World Series contest between the Yanks and Braves. A Braves batter was awarded first base when

shoe polish on the ball proved he'd been hit by the pitch. The Braves batter, ironically, was also named Jones.

29. The same Davey Johnson would return to New York after his playing days ended, this time as the Met manager.

30. The trade for Foy, for whom the Mets had great hopes, was one of the worst in team history. Foy was a complete flop while Amos Otis, who went to the Royals as part of the deal, developed into a standout batter. Otis hit .277 in a 17-year career as a star outfielder.

31. Bob Aspromonte was destined to be the last of the Brooklyn Dodgers. He'd had one at-bat for the Brooks in 1956 after graduation from Lafayette High School, Sandy Koufax's alma mater. When Aspro called it quits after one year with the Mets, he was the last former Brooklyn Dodger still active in the major leagues.

32. The Staub deal had been all but completed at the time of Hodges' death. For Whitey Herzog, the player development director, the trade was a step in the wrong direction. "You have to be crazy to give up three starters for one player," Herzog explained in his autobiography. "We had guys in our system who could have helped the Mets dominate baseball in the 1970s— players like Foli and Jorgensen and Amos Otis—and we gave them up." Herzog claims it was Donald Grant's mistrust of using players from the minors that undid the Mets in the years to come.

33. Mays came to the Mets six days after his 41st birthday. In return the Mets sent the Giants pitcher Charlie Williams and a reported $50,000.

34. Another old Yankee manager, Joe McCarthy, had won pennants in two leagues. Marse Joe won with the Cubs in 1929 before leading the Yanks to eight World Series appearances in the thirties and forties.

35. Jack Lang says that Grant thought—justifiably, according to some Met players—that the free-spirited McGraw was mocking Grant's speech. Perhaps with tongue in cheek, McGraw explained to Grant that he was trying to back up the chairman's words. Whatever the puckish southpaw's intent, "You Gotta Believe!" became as famous a slogan as "Remember the Alamo."

36. Met fans may have forgiven Rose for besting Ron Hunt for National League Rookie of the Year Honors, but his assault on Harrelson was another matter. When Rose trotted out to left in the bottom of the inning, the fans showered him with debris. The barrage stopped only after the intercession of several Met players. For years afterward, Rose was jeered lustily every time he played in New York.

37. Mays retired after the World Series. Not long after hitting his 660th— and final—carrier home run, Mays said the 1973 season would be his last. On "Willie Mays Night" àt Shea Stadium on September 25, a tearful Mays said it was time for him to "say goodbye to America." The Say Hey Kid had one last moment of glory in the Series. In the Mets' 10–7 win in Game Two, Mays's single in the top of the 12th put the Mets in the lead.

38. By the time the Mets were again contenders, Herzog was rooting against them as manager of the Cardinals. Herzog left the Mets before the 1973 season to manage the Washington Senators.

39. Dick Young, one of the most widely read New York sportwriters, was as popular as Benedict Arnold after his role in the Seaver trade. Never one to flinch when he felt he was in the right, Young's stance on Seaver came back to haunt him five years later when he ended a 45-year association with the *Daily News* to join the New York *Post*. Since Young had two years remaining on his *Daily News* contract, his detractors had a field day.

40. In return for Koosman, dealt to the Twins in December 1978, the Mets received a pair of minor league pitchers. One of them was Jesse Orosco,

who would play an important role in the team's future. Kranepool, destined to be the last of the original Mets, occupied a special place in Joan Payson's heart. Perhaps it was the fact that both her son and Kranepool's father had been killed in action during the Second World War at the Battle of the Bulge. Mrs. Payson had a standing order that Kranepool was to remain a Met throughout his career. Kranepool retired after 1979 season, one of the most popular players in team history.

41. Fred Wilpon, a real estate mogul, had been a batting practice pitcher for the Brooklyn Dodgers as a youngster. He had pitched for Brooklyn's Lafayette High School on a team whose first baseman was Sandy Koufax. Nelson Doubleday's forebears had dabbled in book publishing and, according to popular myth, the invention of popular sports. The original agreement gave the Doubleday Publishing Company 95 percent control of the Mets with Wilpon holding the remaining five percent. At the end of the 1986 season, Doubleday and Wilpon bought the club from the publishing firm as equal partners.

42. Soon after, Swan suffered rotator cuff problems and never really lived up to his potential.

43. The relationship between Cashen and Torre was strained early in the year when the manager insisted on keeping pitcher Tim Leary, a promising second-year pro out of UCLA, on the Met roster. Cashen wanted to farm out the youngster for more seasoning. Leary injured his arm in his first start and never developed with the Mets.

44. The 1982 season wasn't a total loss. Lee Mazzilli, the man Mookie Wilson had replaced in center, was dealt to Texas for a pair of promising pitchers, Walt Terrell and Ron Darling. And the Mets' top pick in the summer draft was another gifted young hurler, Dwight Gooden.

45. The paths that brought Hernandez to New York and Allen to St. Louis are tinged with intrigue. By 1983 Allen, his confidence gone, claimed he had a drinking problem. Said announcer Ralph Kiner, "Hell, my good friend Phil Harris spilled more than Allen drank." Allen's problems made him expendable. Meanwhile in St. Louis, Hernandez was in Manager Whitey Herzog's doghouse. Hernandez had been using drugs; his problems with cocaine became public knowledge during hearings in Pittsburgh two years later. Herzog had pledged to assist any player who would come to him for help with substance abuse. Soon afterward Herzog, privately calling Hernandez a "lying son-of-a-bitch" to one St. Louis reporter, dealt the first baseman to the Mets. Hernandez maintains that his personal problems had nothing to do with the trade. "The White Rat got rid of me," he said, "because he didn't like me."

46. Still fresh in Cashen's memory was the Tim Leary affair of 1981, when then-manager Joe Torre insisted on keeping the young pitcher in the major leagues against the general manager's better judgement.

47. Fernandez had been one of the Dodgers' brightest pitching prospects. The Mets picked him up in December 1983, after a 13–4 record with 209 strikeouts in 153 innings with San Antonio (Texas League).

48. In return for Carter the Mets sent the Expos Hubie Brooks (moved from third to short late in 1984), pitcher Floyd Youmans, catcher Mike Fitzgerald, and outfielder Herm Winningham. The Mets gave up Walt Terrell for Johnson. Both were excellent trades for the Mets, although the *New York Post* didn't agree. One *Post* story likened the Terrell-Johnson trade to the Nolan Ryan-for-Jim Fregosi fiasco of 1971.

49. The best-remembered battle that year involving Met players didn't even count in the official statistics. It took place outside Cooter's, a Houston

nightclub, during July. Four players tangled with two off-duty policemen. The altercation ended with infielder Tim Teufel and pitchers Ron Darling, Rick Aguilera, and Bob Ojeda spending the night in police custody.

50. Knight came to the Mets in a 1984 deal with Houston. After part-time duty in 1985, Knight got off to a great start in 1986 and took control at third base.

51. Scott's major league record was 14–27 when the Mets dealt him to Houston in December of 1983. Craig taught the split-fingered curve to Scott at the request of Al Rosen, Houston's general manager at the time. Scott's success with the pitch had the rest of the league convinced that he was doctoring baseballs.

52. Lopez did it with Cleveland from 1951–55.

53. Two controversies contributed to the Mets' first failure to win a League Championship Series. Before the second game David Cone, writing a column for the *New York Daily News*, disparaged Orel Hershiser as "lucky" and likened L.A. reliever Jay Howell to a high school pitcher. Dodger manager Tommy Lasorda used Cone's statements to stir up his players. During the third game Howell was booted by the umpires after the Mets protested the pine tar on his glove. Howell drew a two-game suspension, another event that galvanized the Dodgers.

54. Late in the 1988 season, Ojeda accidentally severed the middle finger of his pitching hand while using electric hedge clippers. Ojeda would come back with a 13–11 record in 1989.

55. Not even Davey Johnson was exempt. The Met skipper had to follow a rigorous diet and exercise program due to a recurrent back problem.

56. Along with Aguilera, the Mets sent the Twins pitchers David West, Kevin Tapani, and Tim Drummond in return for Viola. Hurler Jack Savage went from the Mets to Minnesota at the end of the season as the player to be named later. The arrival of Viola gave the Mets the two starting pitchers in what many consider the greatest game in collegiate baseball history. Pitching for St. John's in a 1981 NCAA Northeast Regional, Viola matched blanks with Yale's Ron Darling for 11 innings. Darling threw no-hit ball at the Redmen until the 12th, when St. John's scored the game's only run. Not long after joining the Mets, Viola drew a starting assignment against Orel Hershiser. For the first time in major league history, two Cy Young Award winners from the previous year were matched in regular season play. The historic moment came on August 28 when Viola, collecting his first major league hit in the process, blanked the Dodgers 1–0. The win was a costly one for Manhattan delicatessen owner Abe Lebewohl. Lebewohl had promised a free salami to anyone who came to his shop with a ticket stub from a game won by Viola. Viola's parents had been regular customers at Lebewohl's Second Avenue Deli before moving to Florida. Viola's win over Hershiser came in Los Angeles. Eight hours later New Yorker Stuart Baron walked into Lebewohl's deli with a ticket stub from the game. Baron had ordered the ticket by phone the night before and had it sent from Los Angeles via air express. Lebewohl's one-pound salami carried a $7 price tag. Baron's ducat cost $4, but the ticket vendor's commission and delivery sent his outlay up to $14. The episode proved, as *The Sporting News* archly noted, "there's no such thing as a free lunch."

57. That was on July 4, 1945, by the Cleveland Indians in a game against the New York Yankees. "Consider there have been more than 125,000 major league games," wrote Marc Topkin of the *St. Petersburg Times*. "In that time there have been more than 200 no-hitters, 13 perfect games and nine unassisted triple plays. But only two no-assist games."

References

Breslin, Jimmy. 1963. *Can't Anybody Here Play This Game?* New York: The Viking Press.

Cohen, Richard M., David S. Neft, and Jordan A. Deutsch. 1979. *The World Series.* New York: The Dial Press.

Cohen, Stanley. 1988. *A Magic Summer: The '69 Mets.* San Diego: Harcourt Brace Jovanovich, Publishers.

Creamer, Robert W. 1984. *Stengel: His Life and Times.* New York: Simon & Schuster.

D'Agostino, Dennis. 1981. *This Date in New York Mets History.* New York: Stein and Day.

Durso, Joseph. 1970. *Amazing: The Miracle of the Mets.* Boston: Houghton Mifflin Company.

Hernandez, Keith, and Mike Bryan. 1986. *If At First. . . . A Season With the Mets.* New York: McGraw-Hill Book Company.

Herzog, Whitey, and Kevin Horrigan. 1987. *White Rat: A Life in Baseball.* New York: Harper & Row.

Honig, Donald. 1986. *The New York Mets: The First Quarter Century.* New York: Crown Publishers, Inc.

Izenberg, Jerry. 1987. *The Greatest Game Ever Played.* New York: Henry Holt and Company.

Johnson, Davey, and Peter Golenbock. 1986. *Bats.* New York: G.P. Putnam's Sons.

Kiner, Ralph, with Joe Gergen. 1987. *Kiner's Korner: At Bat and on the Air—My 40 Years in Baseball.* New York: Arbor House.

Lang, Jack, and Peter Simon. 1986. *The New York Mets: Twenty-five Years of Baseball Magic.* New York: Henry Holt and Company.

Mays, Willie, with Lou Sahadi. 1988. *Say Hey: The Autobiography of Willie Mays.* New York: Simon and Schuster.

Nelson, Lindsey. 1985. *Hello Everybody, I'm Lindsey Nelson.* New York: Beech Tree Books, William Morrow and Company, Inc.

Polner, Murray. 1982. *Branch Rickey: A Biography.* New York: Atheneum Publishers.

Reichler, Joseph. 1988. *The Baseball Encyclopedia.* New York: Macmillan Publishing Company.

———. 1984. *The Baseball Trade Register.* New York. Macmillan Publishing Company.

Snider, Duke, with Bill Gilbert. 1988. *The Duke of Flatbush.* New York. Kensington Publishing Corp.

Zimmerman, Paul D., and Dick Schaap. 1969. *The Year the Mets Lost Last Place.* New York: The World Publishing Company.

Annotated Bibliography

Breslin, Jimmy. *Can't Anybody Here Play This Game?* New York: The Viking Press, 1963. 124 pp.

    Breslin's hilarious recapitulation of the Mets' first season. His dedication speaks volumes: "To the 922,530 brave souls who paid their way into the Polo Grounds in 1962. Never has so much misery loved so much company."

Cohen, Stanley. *A Magic Summer: The '69 Mets.* San Diego: Harcourt Brace Jovanovich, 1988. 319 pp.

Cohen's premise is that the '69 Mets—despite the fact that they were not a remarkable team taken individually—have an identity all their own, like the '27 Yankees, the '34 Cardinals, and the '55 Dodgers. Interviewing many of the team members 17 years after their championship season, Cohen presents an interesting account of Hodges, Seaver, Koosman, Agee, Jones, et al.

Creamer, Robert W. *Stengel: His Life and Times*. New York: Simon and Schuster, 1984. 349 pp.

Creamer's other biography, *Babe: The Legend Comes to Life*, is an American classic. His portrayal of the Old Perfesser is in the same class. The portions dealing with Stengel's career as Met Manager are a must. Creamer retells the agony and the humor with equanimity.

D'Agostino, Dennis. *This Date in New York Mets History*. New York: Stein and Day, 1981. 222 pp.

Indispensable trove of Metsiana, written by one of the all-time Met trivia kings. The book provides a day-by-day history of the Met franchise, an all-time Met roster, information on the origin of the Mets, and much more. A smorgasbord of abstruse information on the Mets' first 20 years.

Durso, Joseph. *Amazing: The Miracle of the Mets*. Boston: Houghton Mifflin Company, 1970. 242 pp.

Durso covered the Mets from their infancy through the championship year. The *New York Times* reporter's rendition traces the path many of the team's key players took to the season of glory in '69. Want to know who it was who polished Cleon Jones's famous shoes prior to that Series game with the Orioles? In Durso's book, you could look it up. . . .

Hernandez, Keith, and Mike Bryan: *If at First . . . A Season With the Mets*. New York: McGraw-Hill Book Company, 1986. 329 pp.

The Met first baseman's account of the 1985 season, game-by-game, with information on his youth, his years with the Cardinals, and his life outside baseball interspersed throughout. Interestingly contrasted with his manager's book, which chronicles the same year.

Honig, Donald. *The New York Mets: The First Quarter Century*. New York: Crown Publishers, Inc., 1986. 148 pp.

The Official 25th Anniversary Book of the Mets, written by one of baseball's foremost historians. Although lacking the pithy insights of a beat reporter (a la Jack Lang), Honig's rich prose makes this one of the best of the Met histories. Loaded with illustrations (both black and white and color), Honig's book takes the reader up through the 1985 season.

Izenberg, Jerry. *The Greatest Game Ever Played*. New York: Henry Holt and Company, 1987. 175 pp.

Can one League Championship Series launch a thousand words? Game Six of the Mets-Astros matchup in 1986 sired an entire book by this *Newark Star-Ledger* reporter. At first glance, this is for Met fans only; a closer look shows a detailed account of one of baseball's greatest games, with interesting insights into the lives of the men who played in it.

Johnson, Davey, and Peter Golenbock. *Bats*. New York: G.P. Putnam's Sons, 1986. 316 pp.

Johnson's version of the 1985 season makes for interesting reading when compared with Hernandez's book. It gives a parallel version of why moves are made, when viewed from the manager's side of the dugout. If Johnson keeps on winning the way he has in his first six seasons, this will probably not be a definitive work. But it does provide insights into the burgeoning career of a top big-league manager.

Kiner, Ralph, with Joe Gergen. *Kiner's Korner: At Bat and on the Air—My 40 Years in Baseball*. New York: Arbor House, 1987. 238 pp.

> One of baseball's premier home run threats, Kiner joined the Met broadcasting team at the outset and has never left. Written with *New York Newsday* columnist Gergen, the book takes its name from Kiner's postgame show. Humorous, entertaining, and insightful, Kiner's seen it all in his years with the Mets . . . and lived to tell about it.

Lang, Jack, and Peter Simon. *The New York Mets: Twenty-Five Years of Baseball Magic*. New York: Henry Holt and Company, 1986. 223 pp.

> Jack Lang is the only daily beat writer who has covered the Mets continuously since their first year. He and Peter Simon have produced the sine qua non for the serious Met fan. Lang's knowledge of the team, its history, the bright moments, and the dark corners make this one of the best team history books ever written. Plenty of stats and ample photos are this feast's dessert.

Nelson, Lindsey. *Hello Everybody, I'm Lindsey Nelson*. New York: Beech Tree Books, William Morrow and Company, Inc., 1985. 430 pp.

> An affable, articulate Tennessean, Lindsey Nelson joined the Met broadcasting team in 1962 and stayed around for 17 years. His autobiography provides wonderful portraits of a variety of subjects: His budding television career as a University of Tennessee student, his service in World War Two, life behind the mike as a network football announcer and, of course, a view from the broadcast booth of the Mets in action in bad times and good. Nelson reveals a warm side seldom seen in sports. There are sections about his family life—particularly his relationship with a daughter who has Down's Syndrome—that will make you forgive him those terrible sports jackets.

Zimmerman, Paul D., and Dick Schapp. *The Year the Mets Lost Last Place*. New York: The World Publishing Company, 1969. 223 pp.

> The basic premise of this book is that the games of July 8–16 were "crooshal" in the Mets' ascent to the pennant in 1969. This includes some great insights into the Mets-Cubs series during that period. There's a bizarre sidebar about a man who murdered his wife because she wanted to watch *Dark Shadows* while he wanted to watch the ballgame. And you always thought the Bleacher Bums were violent . . . .

Year-by-Year Standings and Season Summaries

Year	Pos.	Record	Pct.	GB	Manager	Player	BA	Player	HR	Player	W-L	ERA
1962	10th	40–120	.250	50.5	Stengel	Mantilla	.275	Thomas	34	Craig	10–24	4.52
1963	10th	51–111	.315	48.5	Stengel	Hunt	.272	Hickman	17	Jackson	13–17	3.96
1964	10th	53–109	.327	40	Stengel	Hunt	.303	C. Smith	20	Jackson	11–16	4.27
1965	10th	50–112	.309	47	Stengel Westrum	Kranepool	.253	Swoboda	19	Jackson	8–20	4.35
1966	9th	66–95	.410	28.5	Westrum	Hunt	.288	Kranepool	16	Ribant	11–9	3.21
1967	10th	61–101	.377	40.5	Westrum Parker	Davis	.302	Davis	16	Seaver	16–13	2.76
1968	9th	73–89	.451	24	Hodges	Jones	.297	Charles	15	Koosman	19–12	2.08
1969	1st	100–62	.617	+8	Hodges	Jones	.340	Agee	26	Seaver	25–7	2.21
1970	3rd	83–79	.512	6	Hodges	Agee	.286	Agee	24	Seaver	18–12	2.81
1971	3rd	83–79	.512	14	Hodges	Jones	.319	Agee	14	Seaver	20–10	1.76
								Kranepool	14			
1972	3rd	83–73	.532	13.5	Berra	Staub	.293	Milner	17	Seaver	21–12	2.92
1973	1st	82–79	.509	+1.5	Berra	Millan	.290	Milner	23	Seaver	19–10	2.08
1974	5th	71–91	.438	17	Berra	Jones	.282	Milner	20	Koosman	15–11	3.36
1975	3rd	82–80	.506	10.5	Berra McMillan	Unser	.294	Kingman	36	Seaver	22–9	2.38
1976	3rd	86–76	.531	15	Frazier	Millan	.282	Kingman	37	Koosman	21–10	2.70
1977	6th	64–98	.395	37	Frazier Torre	Randle	.304	Henderson	12	Espinosa	10–13	3.42
								Milner	12			
								Stearns	12			
1978	6th	66–96	.407	24	Torre	Mazzilli	.273	Montanez	17	Espinosa	11–15	4.72
1979	6th	63–99	.389	35	Torre	Mazzilli	.303	Youngblood	16	Swan	14–13	3.30
1980	5th	67–95	.414	24	Torre	Henderson	.290	Mazzilli	16	Bomback	10–8	4.09

Year	Pos.	Record	Pct.	GB	Manager	Player	BA	Player	HR	Player	W-L	ERA
1981	5th	17–34	.333	15	Torre	Brooks	.307	Kingman	22	Allen	7–6	2.96
	4th	24–28	.462	5.5								
1981*	5th	41–62	.398	18.5								
1982	6th	65–97	.401	27	Bamberger	Wilson	.279	Kingman	37	Swan	11–7	3.35
1983	6th	68–94	.420	22	Bamberger/ Howard	Wilson	.276	Foster	28	Orosco	13–7	1.47
1984	2nd	90–72	.556	6.5	Johnson	Hernandez	.311	Strawberry	26	Gooden	17–9	2.60
1985	2nd	98–64	.605	3.0	Johnson	Hernandez	.309	Carter	32	Gooden	24–4	1.53
1986	1st	108–54	.667	+21.5	Johnson	Hernandez	.310	Strawberry	27	Ojeda	18–5	2.57
1987	2nd	92–70	.568	3	Johnson	Hernandez	.290	Strawberry	39	Gooden	15–7	3.21
1988	1st	100–60	.625	+15	Johnson	McReynolds	.288	Strawberry	39	Cone	20–3	2.22
1989	2nd	87–75	.537	6	Johnson	Johnson	.287	Johnson	36	Fernandez	14–5	2.83
1990	2nd	91–71	.562	4	Johnson/ Harrelson	Magadan	.328	Strawberry	37	Viola	20–12	2.67
1991	5th	77–84	.478	20.5	Harrelson	Boston	.275	Johnson	38	Cone	14–14	3.29
1992	5th	72–90	.444	24	Torborg	Magadan	.283	Bonilla	19	Fernandez	14–11	2.73

*Split Season Totals (Players' Union Strike).

All-Time Met Career and Season Records

Career Batting Leaders (1962–1992)

Games Played	Ed Kranepool	1,853
At Bats	Ed Kranepool	5,436
Runs Scored	Darryl Strawberry	662
Hits	Ed Kranepool	1,418
Batting Average	Keith Hernandez	.297
Home Runs	Darryl Strawberry	252
Runs Batted In	Darryl Strawberry	733
Stolen Bases	Mookie Wilson	281

Career Pitching Leaders (1962–1992)

Innings Pitched	Tom Seaver	3,045.1
Earned Run Average	Tom Seaver	2.57
Wins	Tom Seaver	198
Losses	Jerry Koosman	137
Strikeouts	Tom Seaver	2,541
Walks	Tom Seaver	847
Games	Tom Seaver	401
Shutouts	Tom Seaver	44
Saves	Jesse Orosco	107
Games Started	Tom Seaver	395
Complete Games	Tom Seaver	171

Single-Season Batting Records (1962–1992)

Batting Average (502 ABs)	Cleon Jones	.340	1969
Home Runs	Darryl Strawberry	39	1987
			1988
Home Runs (righthanded)	Dave Kingman	37	1976
			1982
Runs Batted In	Howard Johnson	117	1991
Hits	Felix Millan	191	1975
Singles	Felix Millan	155	1973
Doubles	Howard Johnson	41	1989
Triples	Mookie Wilson	10	1984
Slugging Percentage	Darryl Strawberry	.583	1987
Extra Base Hits	Howard Johnson	80	1989
Game-Winning RBIs	Keith Hernandez	24	1985
Sacrifices	Felix Millan	24	1974
Stolen Bases	Mookie Wilson	58	1982
Pinch Hits	Rusty Staub	24	1983
Strikeouts	Tommy Agee	156	1970
	Dave Kingman	156	1982
Total Bases	Howard Johnson	319	1989
Hitting Streak	Hubie Brooks	24	1984
Grand Slam Home Runs	John Milner	3	1976
Hit by Pitch	Ron Hunt	13	1963

All-Time Met Career and Season Records *(continued)*

Single-Season Pitching Records (1962–1992)

ERA (150 innings)	Dwight Gooden	1.53	1985
ERA (100 innings)	Jesse Orosco	1.47	1983
Wins	Tom Seaver	25	1969
Losses	Roger Craig	24	1962
	Jack Fisher	24	1965
Winning Pct. (10 decisions)	Terry Leach	.917	1987
Strikeouts	Tom Seaver	289	1971
Walks	Nolan Ryan	116	1971
Saves	John Franco	33	1990
Games	Roger McDowell	75	1986
Complete Games	Tom Seaver	21	1971
Games Started	Jack Fisher	36	1965
	Tom Seaver	36	1970
			1973
			1975
Shutouts	Dwight Gooden	8	1985
Innings Pitched	Tom Seaver	291	1970
Home Runs Allowed	Roger Craig	35	1962
Consecutive Games Won (season)	Dwight Gooden	14	1985
Consecutive Games Lost (season)	Roger Craig	18	1963
Wild Pitches	Jack Hamilton	18	1966

9

Philadelphia Phillies
Swooning In The Shadow of the Miracle Whiz Kids

PETER C. BJARKMAN

The Phillies have had their ups and downs through the years, but with few exceptions the club never has been dull.—Frederick G. Lieb and Stan Baumgartner

As the dried leaves peel off baseball's annual calendar in rapid and regular succession, fans in every big league city can count on eventually having their regular turn at pennant thrills, World Series glories, superstar sluggers and unhittable twirlers. That is, in at least most cities. Somehow the gods of baseball never have smiled very long on the American League club in St. Louis, nor the National League franchise in Philadelphia. For decades the Cubs have seemed preordained losers and the Red Sox and Tigers manage always to ruin a brief moment of glory with long stretches of draining ineptitude. Nowhere, however, is this prolonged saga of losing more firmly entrenched than in the historical City of Brotherly Love. What other team has ever lost 23 games in a row, or finished in the second division for 29 summers of one thirty-year stretch, or lost a guaranteed pennant after having a six-game cushion with but a dozen contests to play? Even the lowly Browns, slapstick Cubs, or failure-bound Red Sox and Tigers can't boast such valleys of miserable performance as these.

Not that the Philadelphia senior circuit ballclub has not known its moments of glory and prodigious performance. This was the franchise, after all, that for years boasted a pitcher seldom equalled and never bettered in all of baseball's lengthy annals. Matchless Grover Cleveland Alexander toiled without support for the better part of a decade for the usually hapless Phils. And before Alexander the Phillies could also parade batting wizard Nap Lajoie for several seasons before he became the first triple crown winner in a new upstart circuit operating across town. The Phils—let it be remembered—gave baseball its first "greatest outfield of all time" when Sliding

Billy Hamilton, Sam Thompson and Ed Delahanty took up residence in Baker Bowl during the final decade of the game's maiden century. And even while mired deep in the cellar during the lively decade of the thunder-filled thirties the team from Philadelphia provided the most spectacular offensive fireworks and entertaining on-field glovework ever witnessed from a basement-bound ballclub.

When the current century creased in the middle and opened the last great decade of the "old game" of pre-television play, a wet-behind-the-ears bunch of upstarts would ride the arm of a matchless hurling machine named Robin Roberts to a rare pennant and thus etch themselves into baseball lore as one of the diamond's most cherished single-season wonders. As if one thrilling eleventh-hour victory of legendary proportions were not quite sufficient, three decades later the 1980-edition of the Philadelphia National League ballclub would somehow survive one of the most exciting pennant playoffs in history to wrap up the long-suffering team's first and only world championship flag. And on that singular Phillies World Series champion performed perhaps the most talented home-run slugging third sacker, as well as one of the most gifted southpaw hurlers, ever to thrill hometown throngs during the long saga of baseball's colorful history.

And there have been other moments and heroes that Philadelphia ballfans across the generations could point to with a goodly measure of local pride. Here for decades stood one of the most stately and legendary among old style brick and concrete baseball cathedrals. A centerfielder once patrolled the spacious gardens of that park who many contend was kept from immortality only by the fact that he performed in an era of other matchless centerfielders playing in the baseball media capital of Gotham to the north. Richie Ashburn stood proud as one of the most steady and valued performers in the fifties golden era of pre-expansion baseball. Great pitchers too have worn the Phillies pinstripes down through the years—Jim Bunning, Rick Wise, Kirby Higbie, Bucky Walters, Claude Passeau, Chris Short, John Denny, Jack Sanford, Art Mahaffey, Steve Bedrosian. The trouble was always that these overworked hurlers were usually not around in those seasons when the Phils' roster was loaded with any free-swinging fence-killing sluggers; and the batsmen themselves only seemed to crop up when pitching was at a distinct premium in Philly. Yet such marvelous sluggers they often were—Chuck Klein, Lefty O'Doul, Cy Williams, Dolf Camilli, Harry Walker, Del Ennis, Greg Luzinski. And, of course, 500-homer-club member Mike Schmidt.

From Nap Lajoie to Mike Schmidt it has taken a thick skin indeed to be a committed Phillies fan. In the end, the Phillies have always somehow managed to entertain their faithful, even though they have rarely rewarded decades of true suffering with an incomparable thrill of autumn victory. As baseball historian Donald Honig has whimsically noted, senior circuit pennants seemed always to come around in Philadelphia with the frequency of Halley's famed comet. Yet in a game founded in the life-mirroring rhythms of nature's seasons and mellowed with the bitter wine of defeat, nowhere have true fans gotten any more reward for their long resignation to teams of mediocrity and their patient acceptance of diamond doormats. You rarely went to Baker Bowl or Shibe Park or Veterans Stadium to cheer on a pennant rush in the early autumn. But as a hardcore Phillies fan you hardly ever failed to find some form of thrilling baseball in those stately and storied venues either.

Biggest Surprise of Baseball's Second Century

"There was a real convulsion in the National League standings at the finish of the 1949 season. People had to look twice to make sure they weren't seeing things. The Phillies were in third place."—Frederick G. Lieb and Stan Baumgartner

It's a safe claim that no team has ever had an entire century of league history boil down so easily within the shared public imagination to a single glorious summer of triumph or a single celebrated team of momentary duration. Yet when one thinks of the Phillies one is almost always left with a single memorable lineup planted in the mind's eye. This is an everyday roster which boasts nearly the stature of the Murderer's Row Yankees, the Gashouse Gang Cardinals, or the Boys of Summer Dodgers. It is a lineup etched indeliably into the memories of ballfans of the forties and fifties even if they grew up far from Shibe Park in Philadelphia and rooted for teams like the Red Sox or Dodgers or Tigers or Cardinals. It is a batting order for all ages, lodged in the realm of pure fantasy where flights of baseball legend meet the mundane stuff of everyday baseball history.

The Whiz Kids Batting Order

CF	Richie Ashburn
SS	Granny Hamner
LF	Dick Sisler
RF	Del Ennis
3B	Willie "Puddin' Head" Jones
C	Andy Seminick
2B	Mike Goliat

1B	Eddie Waitkus
P	Robin Roberts
Relief	Jim Konstanty

While ordinary fans and even seasoned baseball writers like the well-travelled Fred Lieb may have been shocked by the rise of the Phillies to contention and victory in the dawn of the television age, baseball insiders were not taken quite so off guard by such unanticipated events. Robin Roberts, for one, later reflected that the 1950 Philadelphia team was no real surprise around the National League circuit. Roberts spoke enthusiastically on the heels of that fateful 1950 campaign: "We finished sixth in 1948, then third in '49. So while a lot of people may have been surprised when we won the pennant in 1950, that didn't include us. We were a relaxed, cocky bunch of guys; we knew we could play ball" (quoted by Honig, 1992, 136).

It is almost a cliche, familiar to each and every dedicated fan with an eye toward the game's history, that baseball's most exciting teams are almost never the most talent-laden outfits. One need only recall the sport's most unforgettable Cinderella teams to verify this seeming fixed law of baseball legend and myth. The 1951 Giants come readily to mind, as well as the 1934 Cardinals and perhaps the 1960 Pirates. Or one could consider the 1967 Red Sox and even the 1991 worst-to-first Atlanta Braves. These were all clubs of superior talent and a sprinkling of superstars—Dizzy Dean in St. Louis in 1934, Yaz with the Bosox and Clemente with the Buccos. Yet young Roberto Clemente was still wet-behind-the-ears in 1960, as was Mays with Bobby Thomson's Giants. For these were all miracle teams that featured ballclub personality and not individual player personalities, and they were also clubs that always seemed to do it with mirrors. They were charmed teams that came out of nowhere and then usually faded once again almost as quickly. These were all clubs, as well, that unexpectedly exchanged rags for riches, then felt uncomfortable with such success and thus rapidly donned their familiar rags once more, in order to continue their regular dance of mediocrity.

Such Cinderella teams also often feature inspirational stories of struggle against human suffering and adversity off the field as well as on. The Whiz Kid Phillies had their share of Cinderella status here too. First sacker Eddie Waitkus would literally return from the near-dead in 1950, overcoming a life-threatening injury from the previous summer. In a plot almost too contrived for fiction, Waitkus had been gunned down in a Chicago hotel room by an over-zealous female admirer. He was thus a featured player in one of baseball's most legendary bizarre events, proving a stranger-than-fiction plot line for Bernard Malamud's popular baseball novel *The Natural* and the eventual classic baseball film of the same title. And southpaw Curt Simmons would only two seasons later match Waitkus's comeback courage while himself battling back from a domestic injury that had severed part of a foot and thus left his marvelous pitching motion in serious jeopardy.

The infield and outfield boasted by the Phils were admittedly almost as good as any in the league, save perhaps the one in Brooklyn. But Willie Jones and Granny Hamner were no Jackie Robinson and Pee Wee Reese. And while Del Ennis and Dick Sisler could slug the baseball and Ashburn shagged fly balls with the best, a lineup of Ennis, Jones, Sisler and Waitkus hardly sent pitchers quaking like the ones billing Snider, Hodges and Campanella, or Bobby Thomson, Monte Irvin and Whitey Lockman. For one thing the Phillies' hitting was solid but hardly spectacular. While second sacker Mike Goliat was the only regular batting under .250 that summer, only Ennis and Ashburn topped .300. Ennis did pace the league in RBI (126) while three others (Sisler, Hamner, Jones) contributed more than 80 apiece.

It was in the realm of pitching—that 90% portion of victory so touted by every manager and sportswriter—that the Phillies had built their pennant fortunes. Roberts had showed steady promise and proved dominant by the time the 1950 campaign had rolled around. Curt Simmons was not yet ready to enjoy his best years, but the 1950 season demonstrated the slight lefty's true promise. The true key to the Phillies pennant successes at the century's midpoint was a robust starting rotation (Roberts 3.02, Simmons 3.40, and Bob Miller 3.57) which allowed the club—so long reputed as the league's pacesetter for futility in this crucial statistical category—to pace the National League with the circuit's lowest staff ERA figure (3.50).

But the truly magical element for the Whiz Kid Wonders of Eddie Sawyer was the miracle season of veteran Jim Konstanty. Here we find baseball's consummate one-season wonder. Breaking in with the Cincinnati Reds in the talent-thin wartime season of 1944, the bespectacled righthanded six-footer would amass only a modest 66 victories across eleven big league campaigns, though he did manage to win far more than he lost (.579 winning percentage). A heretofore journeyman reliever and sometime starter, Konstanty would suddenly double his previous total of 16 big league wins with the output of his pinnacle 1950 campaign. Statistics that were otherwise commonplace across ten other summers (9-5, 3.25 ERA in 1949) became suddenly incomparable for the single season in which they were most needed and most capable of translating into pennant race insurance. The senior statesman of the Whiz Kid corps at age 33, Konstanty appeared in a league-high 74 contests (23 better than his nearest challenger, Murray Dickson of Pittsburgh); his 22 saves more than doubled his nearest rival (Pittsburgh's Bill Werle with 8) in an era of starting pitching when the "save" was hardly so commonplace. That Konstanty was the backbone of Phillies pitching is underscored by the fact that the league MVP anchored a staff which maintained the league's best ERA while ranking only fifth in complete games produced by its starters.

The pennant race of 1950 was itself a grueling affair. In the guise of the Cinderella outfit that they certainly were, the Phils could apparently only win a pennant the hard way. The club buoyed by high hopes coming off the successful 1949 campaign, edged to the top by mid-season (July 25) and then hung on desperately throughout the dog-day summer months. It was indeed a balanced league that year, as the Giants didn't yet have Mays and the Dodgers were a pitcher or two away from the dominance they would soon show their rivals. Yet the Phils almost crumbled anyway, nearly transforming into the "Fiz Kids" under the stretch-run heat of September. The Dodgers soon made a furious charge in the season's final days and were able to eclipse a nine-game Phillies margin over the final two hectic weeks. The Phillies especially sagged on the road down the tortuous home stretch, winning only two of eight before a final head-to-head weekend, while the pursuing Brooklyn club took eight straight with their final pennant rush.

The final game of that exhausting season was one of the most memorable in National League history. Its potential status as the National League's most dramatic contest ever played is diminished perhaps only by the fact that it would be ironically succeeded and surpassed by an infamous Brooklyn collapse at the hands of Ralph Branca and Bobby Thomson only twelve months later. Manager Eddie Sawyer would now send his ace Robin Roberts to the mound for this most crucial game in 75 seasons of ballclub history. It was a dangerous choice, indeed, as Roberts would be making his fourth start in eight days and had already failed in four recent efforts to attain an elusive season's 20th victory. Don Newcombe—himself in the process of earning a reputation for failure by faltering in the final-day pennant-deciding game of three consecutive seasons—was sharp on the hill that day for the Brooklyn Bums, as was Roberts for the Phils. "Puddin' Head" Jones singled in the first run of the contest in the visitor's sixth to unlock a masterful pitching duel; but a fluke homerun by Pee Wee Reese that stuck into the right field screen in that same inning continued the tension-filled deadlock before a fanatical and partisan Ebbets Field crowd.

The entire season thus came down to two final and almost unbearably dramatic innings. It seemed safe for the home club when Roberts faltered in the ninth, allowing a free pass to Cal Abrams and a single to Reese which moved the pennant-clinching run into scoring position at second. Here one of baseball's strange and frequent twists of fate unfolded, however, and the best of managerial strategy exploded in a spate of ill-fortune for the Brooklyn team. With slugging Duke Snider at bat the Phillies sensed that manager Charlie Dressen would attempt an unorthodox bunt, sacrificing one of his best hitters to move the game-winner to third. While the Phils' infield thus charged the anticipated bunt, centerfielder Richie Ashburn rushed in toward second to back up any anticipated throw in that direction. The Phillies were outguessed, however, as Snider lashed a vicious single to center; yet the charging Ashburn was now in perfect position to field the liner on a single bounce and unleash a crucial throw plateward. Held close to the bag by shortstop Hamner, the helpless Abrams was a sitting duck when he charged toward the plate on the heels of Snider's clutch base hit. Having dodged a season-ending bullet, Roberts intentionally passed Robinson and calmly retired sluggers Furillo and Hodges on a pair of tame fly balls.

Thus the stage was set for the most dramatic homer of Phillies history, and perhaps of league history as well if one excepts only the pennant-winning blow by Thomson and the World Series clincher a decade latter off the bat of Bill Mazeroski. A tiring Roberts was allowed to lead off the tenth and responded with an unlikely single against Newcombe. Now the season would unexplicably unravel for Newcombe as well as the Brooklyn team and fans, all with the swiftness of an unexpected lightning bolt. Waitkus blooped a single and Ashburn trying to bunt failed and thus forced Roberts at third. Then Sisler strode to the plate, already owning three singles off Newcombe on the day and now staring destiny straight in the eye. Sisler like the legendary Casey took a strike, fouled off a second pitch, and then let a third offering go by only inches from the outside corner. But the forth pitch would be one for the record books. Sisler unleashed a mighty swing from the left side of the plate and lofted a Newcombe fastball skyward for a crushing opposite field homer. Silence struck among the legions of Dodgers faithful while euphoria broke out only a hundred miles to the south among the sparser throngs of Phillies fanatics. The Philadelphia National League club was shockingly in the World Series for the first time in more than a generation of diamond play.

The World Series, of course, would prove about as anti-climactic as it could possibly be for Philly fans. If the Dodgers provided a decade-long road block in the senior circuit, there was now the insurmountable hurdle of the New York Yankees over in the American League. The Phillies quickly redonned their paupers rags for World Series play and were swept away in four straight contests by a Yankee pitching staff of Vic Raschi, Allie Reynolds, Ed Lopat and Whitey Ford. Roberts (1.64 ERA) and Konstanty (2.40 ERA) held up their end of the bargin, with an assist from Ken Heintzelman (1.17 ERA) in game three, and only the final contest (5–2) provided more than a one-run margin of defeat for the chagrinned Phillies. Yet given a second chance at a world title after thirty-five years, the Philadelphia club could still boast of only a single game of World Series victory.

In the end the greatest legacy of the Whiz Kids is precisely the fact that no other franchise is as singularly associated with one short season and one single group of ballplayers. There were indeed better players (with the possible exception of Robin Roberts) waiting down the road during the next two decades. Pitchers like Jim Bunning and Rick Wise would eventually be brought on board. Dick Allen would only a decade later provide the kind of dramatic slugging that Philadelphia teams of the early fifties lacked. Yet it remains that no other Phillies ballclub ever drenched themselves in quite the same charisma as that enjoyed by Sawyer's youngsters for one brief summer. It was indeed a magical time. And when these same players proved unequal to the task in subsequent campaigns, their failures only seemed to enhance the legend of that one glorious summer of franchise history.

To understand just how bleak Philly baseball history has been across the years that have preceded and followed the marvelous Whiz Kid season, one need only look at the composite standings drawn from six 20th-century decades that preceded baseball's modern-day expansion era.[1]

Composite NL Standings	Pre-Expansion Era	1901-1960	60 Seasons
1. New York-San Francisco Giants	5033-4064 .555 Pct.	46 Winning Seasons	15 Pennants
2. Chicago Cubs	4804-4327 .526 Pct.	34 Winning Seasons	10 Pennants
3. Pittsburgh Pirates	4751-4361 .521 Pct.	41 Winning Seasons	7 Pennants
4. St. Louis Cardinals	4682-4431 .514 Pct.	36 Winning Seasons	9 Pennants
5. Brooklyn-Los Angeles Dodgers	4651-4451 .511 Pct.	32 Winning Seasons	10 Pennants
6. Cincinnati Reds	4397-4726 .482 Pct.	21 Winning Seasons	3 Pennants
7. Boston-Milwaukee Braves	4151-4938 .457 Pct.	21 Winning Seasons	4 Pennants
8. Philadelphia Phillies	3893-5130 .432 Pct.	15 Winning Seasons	2 Pennants

This is what Philadelphia fans who rooted for the National League club had to face summer-in and summer-out. Owning a league-record low total of 15 winning seasons (out of sixty!) and but two pennants, the Phils also amassed a league high 13 seasons with

100 or more losses and 26 summers (43% of the total) with 90 or more defeats. This is losing baseball elevated to its highest art form. And such comparisons with rival senior circuit clubs do not even consider the Phillies' ongoing competition through 1954 with an inter-city rival American League team. Connie Mack's crosstown Athletics often plumbed equal depths, yet the A's also boasted an array of championship seasons. Connie Mack's team was widely accepted as the city's often wayward and thoroughly inconsistent yet nonetheless lovable step child. The cellar-dwelling Phillies, on the other hand, were more often than not a mere civic embarrassment. But for one brief moment of Whiz Kid glory it all didn't seem to matter. And, by contrast, the Whiz Kids themselves are today only magnified in their achievement by the vacuum of losing in which their triumphs forever remain encased.

Alexander the Great, and a Half Century in the Senior Circuit Cellar

"The Phillies haven't coddled their fans. While other teams developed, or at least tried to develop, winners, the Phillies of the twenties and thirties stayed in business by helping the competition. Assisted by the other seven clubs, the Phillies were a halfway house to the majors for youngsters, to unconditional release for fading veterans. If there is merit in being ahead of the times, credit the old Phillies for fielding teams that anticipated wartime baseball."—Harvey Frommer

By the time the baseball ledger opened its dusty leaves upon the twentieth century, the Phils of Philadelphia had already established themselves as a familiar institution along the banks of the Schuylkill River. Legendary baseball historian Fred Lieb remembers back to his youth in the City of Brotherly Love to recall what once may have been on the minds of numerous young Phillies fans between the turn of the century and the great 1919 World Series betting scandal which effectively ended baseball's more innocent age. Lieb reminisces that "the first generalization I remember arriving at was that teams whose city name started with the letter "B"—Baltimore, Boston, and Brooklyn—were always at the top. As a loyal Philadelphian, this irked me. The scorecards all too often showed that our hometown favorites, the Phillies, would collect a lot of hits and score enough runs to win most games, but were always being topped by one of those annoying 'B' teams" (1977, 13).

When it comes to heroic diamond feats, the first half-century of modern Phillie history reduces itself rather simplistically to but four brief tales, all promising much but in the end always signifying preciously little. First there was the single and surprising pennant run of 1915, a flag won with comparative ease behind the slugging of Gavvy Cravath (who won his third straight longball title that year), the incomparable hurling of Alexander the Great, and the able backup moundsmanship of Erskine Mayer (21–15) and Al Demaree (14–11). Then there was the continued mound mastery of the club's single lonely Hall-of-Fame hurler of the first half-century, baseball's arch tragic figure, "Old Pete" Alexander. A third would be the brief and altogether spectacular (and largely misplaced) slugging displays of baseball's first true "live-ball" era, while the fourth chapter would have to recount the artful batsmanship of teammates Chuck Klein and Lefty O'Doul that flared up suddenly and then vanished just as rapidly in the first half of the free-swinging thirties. The remaining forty or more odd seasons all seemed but a vast and unredeemed wasteland.

Phillie baseball appropriately started off on a familiar enough foot. The first National League game ever played was fittingly lost by a team representing Philadelphia (Boston's Quakers bested Philadelphia's Athletics on April 22, 1876 by a 6–5 count). Perhaps glimpsing their unpromising future, this first team to represent the city almost immediately suffered total collapse and promptly seceded from official scheduled play. Philadelphia returned to the league under the managership of Alfred J. Reach in 1883 and immediately established an altogether too-familiar pattern. The team now at least sported a friendly name, since it was subsequently known as the Phillies. And Reach's men foreshadowed the future in yet another dubious manner, setting an all-time futility standard even for this city of regular losers by posting an incredibly inept 17–81 mark. Diminutive John Coleman would suffer extreme individual indignities upon the mound, himself posting 48 of the team losses while hurling 772 laborious innings. This first Phillies team thus established an indelibly negative tone for much future Philadelphia baseball.

The Philadelphia club did conclude the 19th century on something of a high note of false optimism. The 1899 team sported two of the game's great hitters of the pioneer dead-ball era in Delahanty and Lajoie. Yet both soon jumped to the newly minted American circuit founded by Ban Johnson. Thus still another Phillies pattern was established, a practice of spawning and losing talent that began with Delahanty and Lajoie, reached heights of absurdity with the double sale of Chuck Klein, and remained a haunting presence at the nearer end of the century with the premature peddling of Ryne Sandberg and Dave Stewart. Many of the city's best young National League stars could be counted upon to enjoy their finest big-league summers as ex-Phillies leading pennant charges in the league's other venues. William Baker (1913–1930) enjoyed a reputation around the circuit as an owner bent on surviving financial hardship through regular fire sales of whatever homegrown talent was now seasoned enough to bring a profit to the owner and a pennant to any other city. Dave Bancroft, Pete Alexander, and Emil "Irish" Meusel would all fit this pattern of cheaply auctioned homegrown ballplayers. Manager Pat Moran (1915–1918) once unwisely dared to protest Baker's sale of regulars and was summarily fired for his insubordinate concerns. Moran would then sign on in rival Cincinnati and immediately led the Reds to their first-ever flag during the 1919 ill-fated Black Sox season.

The lone pennant of the first half century came during the brief glory rush of 1915 and was a culmination of several seasons of solid performance. Actually the Phils might have won it all a full season earlier, had it not been for the messy talent war which broke out in baseball's own backyard (Federal League cash lured away four dependable starters in shortstop Mickey Doolan, second sacker Otto Knabe, and pitchers Tom Seaton and Ad Brennan). But if the Phils were stripped of talent by Federal League raiders, they were left with enough raw firepower to make a shambles of the 1915 National League, despite the lowest winning percentage (90–52, .592) of any pre-1926 pennant winner. Arguments can be made that never did a team win a pennant so exclusively on the work of one man as did the Phils in 1915. Alexander, now four seasons beyond the greatest rookie campaign ever enjoyed by a major league pitcher, again pocketed more than a full third of the team's victories (31 of 90). He also led the circuit in almost all major pitching categories: .756 winning percentage, 1.22 ERA, 36 complete games, 376.1 innings pitched, 12 shutouts, 241 strikeouts.

Yet even the awesome mound presence of Alexander was insufficient to prevent the Phillies from methodically losing their first post-season playoff appearance. Boston's Red Sox were more than ready to challenge the National League's greatest mound ace, and an astute Beantown skipper had his club primed for facing Philly's most serious defensive threat. Bill Carrigan had instructed his ballclub that the strategy would have to be to win early and thus not face the great Alexander on three separate occasions (cf. Frommer 141). But a more tangible strategy impacting on the Series outcome had to do with shifting ballpark venues, and in fact it was the issue of ballpark architecture which sabotaged the Phillies more than anything else. Boston opted to boost Series attendance (and thus hometown profits) by borrowing the spanking new and larger ballpark of their National League cousins. Braves Field and its expansive layout would soon rob Phillie slugger Gavvy Cravath of several potential homers in games three and four, turning bleacher blasts into harmless rainmaking putouts. Next a revamped Baker Bowl would ironically reward Boston's Harry Hooper with a pair of perhaps unmerited yet nonetheless decisive circuit blasts in game five. Stating that his motive was "allowing more of our fans to see such an important contest" Bill Baker padded his own gate receipts by erecting temporary bleachers in the center field expanses of Baker Bowl. When Hooper's line drives reached the makeshift grandstand and the Series came to an abrupt end, however, for the first time the press and fans were vocal about what was widely perceived as owner Baker's cheapskate tactics.

A final footnote to the 1915 Series remained. By succumbing to Alexander in the opener, Boston's Ernie Shore would long wear the dubious distinction of being the only hurler ever to lose a World Series match to the Phillies. The Philadelphia club, it turned out, would not win another Series game between that 1915 lidlifter and 1980's Fall Classic opener 65 seasons later.

After one momentary fling the Phillies were now largely done and buried. This was clearly not the case for the combative Alexander. Again in 1916 and 1917 he proved every bit as effective around the circuit. In both seasons the diminutive righthander would once again win over thirty. He would also pace the league in victories and ERA (1.55, 1.68), as well as in starts (45, 44), complete games (38, 35), innings pitched (388.2, 387.2), shutouts (with an all-time record 16 in 1916) and strikeouts (167, 201). And down the road lay more than a decade of further big league mastery, including several brilliant seasons with the Chicago Cubs and a couple with the emerging powerhouse Cardinals in St. Louis.

Yet while Alexander hurled so brilliantly, few Phils ever hit the ball with any sustained authority. Not in the seasons surrounding the nation's first great world war. And a true irony of Phillies history was also that each time the batsmen finally arrived the hurlers seemingly had taken the previous train out of town. Thus when slugging picked up in the twenties and thirties pitching became as rare in Philadelphia as an enthusiastic and overflowing crowd in sparsely populated Baker Bowl.

If it is true that Boston owner Harry Frazee ranks first in the annals of ballclub ruination for his peddling of Babe Ruth in order to bankroll his Broadway theater exploits, surely William Baker deserves a runner-up prize for unloading Pete Alexander for the purpose of increasing his own coffers at the expense of ballclub competitiveness. And if the Red Sox slid from championship contention for decades after the "Curse of the Bambino" reigned down upon the franchise, the Phillies simply self-destructed altogether after the infamous sale of Alexander.

Baker decided his own showcase piece was expendable once it appeared that the great hurler was subject to military draft on the eve of World War I and thus might be lost forever to the cannons of war. Fearing the potential ruination of a cash investment, the crafty (and surprising modern in this regard) Baker peddled his star to the Cubs for $55,000 and a truckload of worthless talent in the guise of a broken-down catcher with one of baseball's all-time colorful nicknames (Pickles Dillhoefer) and a journeyman hurler with one of the game's most undeserved monikers ("Iron-Mike" Prendergast, who won but 41 big-league contests in six full seasons). If the Red Sox after Ruth were contenders but never again world champions, the Phillies after Alex faced a fan's lifetime of not even reaching pretender's status. For the next three decades the press nationwide would dub them the "Phutile Phillies" and the label was clearly merited by a ballclub that took up thirty seasons of unrelieved residence in the second division, broken exactly in the middle by a 1932 peek into the stratosphere of fourth place. Twelve times over these three decades the club dressed more than 100 players in a single campaign, exactly the same number of times they lost more than 100 games in a campaign, and 13 seasons saw the team anchored in either a seventh or eighth-place grave.

Between the departure of Alexander and the sudden birth of the Whiz Kids, then, it might be claimed that the Philadelphia Phillies had only two legitimate reasons for existing. One was to provide big league apprenticeships for an endless supply of talented youngsters destined to lead pennant charges in other league cities. The other was to inflate league standards for both team batting average (while they maintained a position in the upper echelon of hitting clubs during the early 1930s and boasted club averages over .280 three different summers) and staff ERA (where the last-place staff mark remained well above 4.00 throughout the same stretch and reached the absurd record level of 6.71 in 1930's aberration of a slugging campaign). The Phillies seemed to have yet another function, of course, and that was to guarantee each and every summer that no other ballclub would have to face the agonies of last place.

In all this saga of woeful hurling laced with robust slugging stands one single season which today seems to defy the fan's freest imaginings. That season came in 1930, a year when the league's moguls were rumored to have lightened the ball in the hopes of inflating attendance, and the hitters responded by launching an avalanche of base hits upon their hapless rival moundsmen. When hard economic times gripped the nation and the soup lines grew long, there was certainly no depression in the land when it came to the batting averages and other offensive numbers of baseball's batsmen.

Several notes mark the wildly bizarre 1930 season, a summer that rightly merits a full chapter of its own (and one that indeed did receive treatment in a lively 1990 book by veteran baseball historian William B. Mead). This series of facts and events provide some insight into the impact of the free-swinging game that captivated fans around the league that summer and brought new legions of fans everywhere but to the empty grandstands of excitement-filled Baker Bowl.

1. Chuck Klein set all-time club hitting records in a half-dozen categories (doubles with 59, RBI with 170, runs with 158, total bases with 445, slugging at .687), yet he led the hit-crazy circuit in only two (doubles and runs scored).

2. Klein also enjoyed two club-record 26-game batting streaks, pounding the ball at a .485 clip during the first spree which stretched a full month from mid-May to mid-June.

3. The same slugging Chuck Klein proved his double worthiness by registering a major league record 44 outfield assists.

4. This last achievement clearly followed from the Philly pitching staff's astronomical ERA record—a staff composite of 6.71, based on 1,199 runs allowed. The Phils had an easy time with making doubleplays and registering a flock of outfield assists, of course, since the opposition often had the sacks jammed with enemy runners.

5. The club as a whole hit .315 (second only to the Giants, who fared far better in the standings) but finished dead last. The average score of a Phillies' game in 1930 was 8-6, which indicated that the worthless hurlers could undo almost any amount of labor the robust batters provided. And this team slugging mark was no aberration. Over the next several seasons the Phils continued to rank as one of the circuit's top hitting (and worst pitching) outfits.

6. And if pitching were not shabby enough, the staff was embarrassed further by a management ploy to return a broken and ineffective Alexander to the mound. Alex—suffering from the dual curse of alcoholism and epilepsy—returned to boost attendance and hopefully garner a league-record 374th mound triumph (he stood tied with Christy Mathewson behind only Cy Young). But it was the bottle that won in the end, and thus the Hall-of-Famer sadly never reached this one final career goal.

Most of the glorious slugging of this era was done by two robust portside swingers—Chuck Klein and Lefty O'Doul. And both soon suffered the fate of all Phillies stars: they were traded away as rapidly as their booming bats would bring a handsome market price for the profit-minded owner. If Bill Baker saw profit-by-player-auction as his main business strategy, soon there would be another figure in the boss's seat who held a similar passion for continuing these regular fire sales in order to survive in the rugged world of ballclub ownership. At the close of the 1930 offensive explosion Baker had continued his uncontrolled dealings by shipping off O'Doul (who hastened matters by clamoring for a higher salary) to Brooklyn for a truckload of lesser players, then peddling a pitcher and shortstop to Pittsburgh for unknown (but promising) infielder Dick Bartell. These deals were fortunately the last for the penurious owner who died suddenly in December 1930. The strangest of all the front office maneuvers ochestrated by Baker, however, was the one by which he willed the largest part of his interest in the club to his longtime secretary, Mrs. May Mallon Nugent. This paved the way for Baker's business manager, Gerry Nugent, Sr., to gain full operating control of the team and thus continue the tradition of talent peddling with a vengeance. Baker's inefficient style would now be replaced with a much more efficient approach to ballclub mismanagement.

The League actually encouraged Nugent's rampant profiteering. The Cardinals, behind Branch Rickey, as well as other league clubs played along with a system that seemed to spread talent around and thus gave the appearance of thwarting the danger of an overproductive St. Louis farm system. Nugent didn't himself invest in a costly farm system for breeding talent. He simply ran a profitable one at the big league level, thus providing winners for fans in almost every city but hometown Philadelphia. Now more players of promising stature regularly came and went—Jimmie Wilson, Dolf Camilli, Bucky Walters, Claude Passeau and Kirby Higbie were among them. The most outrageous set of transactions involved slugging hero Klein who was sold off twice and then twice again reacquired. No fool when it came to trading up for bankroll profits, the crafty Nugent landed $65,000 from the Cubs for the still-potent Klein in 1933, then collected another $50,000 for bringing him back a little worse for wear in 1936. Klein would nonetheless enjoy one unmatched day's work upon his return in 1936, poking four homers in spacious Forbes Field on July 10 and thus becoming the first National Leaguer since Delahanty to accomplish such a single-game feat. But on the whole the former slugger was but a shadow of himself (he hit only eight homers over five seasons after being reacquired a second time from Pittsburgh in 1940) during his two return visits to Baker Bowl and Shibe Park.

Two additional slugging rarities occurred at the height of baseball's freest swinging era in the hitter-friendly confines of claustrophobic Baker Bowl. In 1932 Burt Shotton's offensive-minded club was able to boast all three top RBI men in the senior circuit. This was an event that had never previously occurred over a third of a century of modern-era baseball, nor would it occur again across the final two-thirds of the present century. And in the following summer of 1933 Philly sluggers residing on both sides of town—Klein of the Phils and Jimmy Foxx of the Mackmen—would garner the prized triple crown. It again would be the only time such a feat was registered—two triple crown champions lodged in the same big league city. For the A's of Connie Mack, of course, Foxx and his fence-bashing would mean another American League title. For Klein and the Phillies, however, it all translated into yet another summer in the solid concrete of seventh place.

Three historical oddities also attached themselves to the 1935 season and to a Phillies ballclub that was always long on color if short on winning baseball. On May 24 it would be the Phils who would provide the visiting opposition while a pioneering Cincinnati franchise launched big league nighttime baseball. Philadelphia was of course the loser under the first arc-lights, dropping a 2–0 decision to the Reds and their ace hurler Paul Derringer. Six days later a remarkable "first" would be balanced by a nostalgic "last" as Baker Bowl provided the scene for Babe Ruth's final big league game, with the equally hapless Boston Braves in town for the occasion. And on a positive if equally arcane note, the 1935 Philadelphia pitching staff was destined to climb one notch above last place in the ranking of team ERA totals, the single season between 1918 and 1942 that a Phillies mound corps was not dead last in this most crucial of all pitching categories.

Much of the rampant hitting in Philadelphia, of course, may have resulted as much from the unique local ballpark as it did from the free-swinging style popularized by Ruth and his imitators. Here was indeed one of the most character-filled ballparks in big league annals. Baker Bowl boasted a number of unique elements—a crazy outfield angle where center field clubhouse met right field wall, three grazing sheep who tended to lawnmowing duties between games, and a noticeable hump in the midst of center field where an underground railroad tunnel ran smack beneath the ballpark.

But the charming venue was also by the thirties an unquestionably dangerous fire trap after seasons of neglect and ill-repair. Fred Lieb remembers fans shielding themselves with scorecards from falling rusty bolts which often rained down from the grandstand roof. Yet the most humorous anecdote surrounding the old park probably is the one that involves an imposing sign painted on the right field wall. This Lifebuoy soap advertisement occupying almost all of the outfield fence displayed an oversized message endorsing the popular locally made product—"The Phillies use Lifebuoy"—and to this some wags supposedly added the crude but visible message ". . . and they still stink!" This seemed to be the final appropriate word on both the ballpark and the era of its greatest glories.

Baker Bowl would eventually see its demise as the Phillies' cosy hit-laced home. Years of neglect by penny-pinching management and the ravages of time eventually turned the once proud park into a mere scrapheap. Thus it was no surprise when the city's National League club finally moved in alongside their junior circuit rivals in the stately concrete baseball palace known as Shibe Park. The Phillies joined the Mackmen over on Lehigh Avenue on July 4, 1938, and remained there for 33 long seasons. The most immediate result of this relocation was a slight surge in always welcomed ballpark attendance. But an equally decisive impact was the sudden dip in hometown batting prowess. Once housed in the spacious and pitching-friendly confines of Shibe Park, the formerly musclebound Phillies suddenly but not surprisingly tumbled to the second lowest team batting average in the senior circuit.

The club inaugurated their new home with a holiday double-header against Boston that drew far more than the usual Baker Bowl sprinkling of disinterested spectators. The park was a comfortable fit, at least until the mid-1950s and the post Whiz Kid era when the Athletics left the city on their own odyssey west and the neighborhood and stadium itself began to deteriorate almost as fast as the National League club still living there. Prior to the 1953 campaign the park would be formally rechristened as Connie Mack Stadium—only providing further ghostly reminders of an unhappy past once Mack and his American Leaguers departed and left the hapless Phils as sole tenants. By the late fifties the Phillies had begun to make small decorative changes in a futile effort to modernize a ballpark that had already seen better days, and soon it was apparent that the Phutile Phils were again as saddled with a decaying arena of play as they had been for so many bleak summers in decrepit Baker Bowl.

Once past the pennant exploits of 1915, the hurling of Alexander, the slugging of O'Doul and Klein, and the romance of Baker Bowl and Shibe Park, the remaining chapters of the Phils story are indeed little more than high comedy. The free-swinging decade of the thirties, especially, saw an abundant supply of such diamond high jinks. Ex-catcher Jimmie Wilson eventually succeeded ex-catcher Burt Shotton and hung on to the bench for nearly five seasons (1934–1938). This was quite a survival record on a ballclub that never rose above seventh place and never won as many as sixty-five games in any single campaign.

Yet the darkest comedy and diamond slapstick was saved for the war years of the forties, in Philadelphia just as much as around the remainder of the baseball world. Only an inexplicable climb to a lofty spot on the seventh-place perch in 1937 and again in 1943 prevented the Phils from stringing together an incredible run of ten straight last-place finishes. Fat Freddy Fitzsimmons was the manager from 1943 to 1945 and the talented pitcher who rang up a respectable .598 career winning percentage could muster no better than a .367 winning ledger as a hapless skipper. The lineup was stocked from top to bottom with has-beens like hurler Schoolboy Rowe and never-to-bes like lifetime 13-game-winner Ike Pearson. Harry Walker did provide some momentary excitement for the locals by earning a 1947 batting title, after he had been traded from the Dodgers upon making it widely known in Brooklyn that it was against his southern ethics to play alongside Jackie Robinson. There were a few additional bright spots like Vince DiMaggio (19 HRs in 1945), Ron Northey (22 HRs in 1944) and Ken Raffensberger (13–20 in 1944). But the lesser of the DiMaggios never lived up to his classic blood lines. And the hardthrowing Raffensberger, in the best Phillies tradition, would save his blossoming and thus his victories for a later reincarnation out in Cincinnati.

This team was so bad that it resorted to headline-grabbing ploys like signing an aging and ineffective local hero, Jimmie Foxx, who returned to Shibe Park in a National League uniform and filled in for awhile as batting practice sideshow and even part-time pitcher. And to shake the embarrassment of its true identity, the ballclub even resorted to a change in team name—for a few short wartime summers the Phillies were by fiat redubbed the Blue Jays. But old traditions die hard and soon both the familiar moniker "Phillies" and the endless losing it represented were restored to their rightful place in Shibe Park.

One especially stark example of the manner in which the generous Phillies benefitted other ballclubs around the league in this period while constantly shortchanging the all-too-patient (and all-too-sparse) hometown rooters came with the saga of a light-hitting third sacker named Bucky Walters, an unheralded arrival with 1934's lackluster club. Ex-backstop and current skipper Jimmie Wilson was sagacious enough to note the lively arm of his unpromising prospect. Thus Walters was promptly converted to mound duty and was soon mowing down National League batters with great regularity. A weak-sticking infielder was thus miraculously converted into a respectable hurler in Philly and then (once the inevitable "for sale" sign was draped upon his shoulders) a legitimate mound ace in Cincinnati. And while Philadelphia fans and management never fully benefitted from this conversion, the forward-thinking Jimmie Wilson fittingly did. Dropped as manager in 1938 the nine-lived Wilson next turned up as a backup catcher for the championship Reds of 1939 and 1940, just in time to ride Walters' arm to a couple of well-deserved World Series paychecks.

And while on-field play was often only short of laughable, front office intrigues with this ballclub proved just as bizarre. In the midst of the war years, for example, rival owners grew ultimately weary of the punchless and dull clubs that Nugent was sending on the road to visit league ballparks. No one could draw a crowd when the hapless Phillies were in town. Thus the league's top brass quietly buried the Nugent ownership and effected a secretive transition to local lumber tycoon William Cox. Ford Frick, NL president, himself officially engineered the backroom deal. But if the Baker and Nugent ownerships could be best described as slow bleeding of the ballclub, Cox and his impetuous ways brought an immediate and almost fatal hemorrhaging. Cox hired veteran Bucky Harris as skipper then interfered and feuded with his manager from the first day. When Harris was shown a quick exit for demanding a free-hand in managing, Bucky wasted little time in letting Commissioner Landis know all about his boss's gambling activities. No friend of those who would wager on league games, righteous Judge Landis in one of his final important acts rang a quick deathknell for the Cox ownership.

In less than a year the league was ochestrating another transfer of the Philadelphia franchise, this time to a respected vice-president of the huge DuPont Corporation. Robert Carpenter Sr. made it clear in public statements that he was buying the team for his son to operate. And though an amateur at ballclub management, Robert Carpenter Jr. was no blind meddler when it came to the business of sports entrepreneurship. He was intelligent enough about his mission, for example, to hire a front office genius in Herb Pennock, to whom he turned over much of the responsibility as chief architect of a rebuilding era. Yet even before Carpenter could work his influence on rebuilding the Phillies some further intrigue surrounded the comings and goings in the Philadelphia front office. Rumors circulated that a young Bill Veeck had made a reasonable offer with serious intent to purchase the ballclub. But the dangerous Veeck was rumored to be scheming to purchase a full roster of Negro League standouts and bring them unannounced into the all-white big league circuit. Of course the Veeck offer never got off the ground since Landis and a bevy of arch-conservative owners were still very much in control of the segregated baseball world.

By the late 1940s and throughout the immediate post-war boom years, however, it was obvious that a change was finally rolling into view for long-suffering fans of the hapless Phils. Once the Carpenters were in control of National League fortunes in Shibe Park an entirely new strategy for operation became apparent to the most casual baseball observer. In five years the new owners spent more than half a million dollars acquiring promising young talent to stockpile in a previously thin farm system. Curt Simmons was signed for a $65,000 bonus in 1947 and Roberts was lured for another $25,000 a single summer later. The signing of Roberts was itself an intriguing story as the youngster was lured to a Phils' tryout in Chicago and then resisted two handsome offers out of loyalty to an earlier pledge (he had promised several other ballclubs that he would audition for them as well) before eventually inking a substantial Phillies offer.

The Nugent philosophy had been completely reversed and a welcomed new mode of operation was now to cultivate high-priced home grown talent for the purpose of building a winner and not for the pocket-lining mission of enriching the pool of trade bait. Seminick (1944), Hamner (1944), Ennis (1946), Jones (1947), Simmons (1947), Roberts (1948) and Ashburn (1948) all soon emerged from short apprenticeships in the revamped Philadelphia farm system. By 1946 the team had climbed to the top of the second division as the nation and the league climbed out from under the ravages of the war years. Three seasons later the ballclub was resting dizzily in third. In only half a decade the Carpenters had miraculously taken a basement team with almost no scouting system and preciously little reserve minor league talent and transformed it into a legitimate pennant contender.

Mediocre But Seldom Dull in the Glorious Fifties and Turbulent Sixties

"For the Phillies, the year of black crepe occurred in 1964."— Donald Honig

The image of the fifties Phillies—once the glorious Whiz Kids season faded to dim memory—is a rather simple and boring one. There was Robin Roberts toiling bravely for almost unimaginable numbers of innings. There was a bevy of slow-footed sluggers—free-swinging backstop Stan Lopata, reliable pinch-hitter Smoky Burgess, fence-crunching Wally Post, disappointing Bill "Swish" Nicholson. There was the stellar centerfield play of Richie Ashburn who would set new standards for defensive play (Honig 132) and win two batting titles to boot before the decade was out.[2] And there was always a secure spot towards the rear of the National League pack.

Between 1951 and 1957 the Phillies seemed to own fourth and fifth spot in the annual league standings. Only 1953—a third-place deadheat with the Cardinals—provided any diversion from this painfully predictable pattern. Steve O'Neill, Sawyer's replacement, engineered a run into the first division that particular summer which managed to move his charges up a notch in the standings, despite four less victories than a year earlier and a gapping 22 game deficit to the runaway champion Dodgers. Roberts matched Milwaukee's Warren Spahn with 23 victories, including 28 complete games pitched over two seasons before being knocked from the hill on July 9 by heavy-hitting Brooklyn. Simmons provided considerable support at 16-13, more amazing still in light of a lawn mowing accident in the late spring that severed part of the southpaw's toe and almost ended both his season and promising mound career. Del Ennis continued to dent outfield fences and scatter bleacher occupants in 1953 with 29 homers as well, while Ashburn slapped singles and doubles at a .330 pace and inched closer to the NL batting titles he would eventually garner in 1955 and 1958. At the same time the fleet Philadelphia centerfielder paced the senior circuit with 205 base hits, five more than Stan Musial in St. Louis. Such progress unfortunately paid little dividend for jovial Steve O'Neill, however, who like Eddie Sawyer before him was fired unceremoniously (July 15, 1954) as soon as his ballclub slipped back deep into the thick of the pack.

Robin Roberts, meanwhile, was relentlessly establishing his own legend as a true mound phenomenon of the otherwise pitching-poor decade of the fifties. Owning masterful control which allowed him to complete most games on but 70–75 pitches, Roberts was thus able to hurl regularly on as little as two days' rest and work over 300 innings for six straight seasons without ever walking over 77 enemy batters. Between 1952 and 1956 Robin paced the circuit in complete games, finishing 140 of 191 starts over that truly remarkable span. The first year of Roberts' peak stretch witnessed a dazzling 28–7 mark (30 complete games and but 45 walks in 330 innings), the most NL wins since Dizzy Dean garnered the same number in 1935. Robin Roberts rarely ever beat himself, and a more potent supporting cast over the course of a lengthy 19-year career would likely have increased many fold the 286 career wins (234 with Philadelphia) of this six-time 20-game winner.

There were clear enough reasons to explain a sudden Phillies collapse after 1950. And most of those reasons were named Dodgers, Giants and Milwaukee Braves. What the steady decline of the mid-fifties proved in Philadelphia was that the mere signing of promising young talent was not of itself quite enough to sustain a lengthy run in the league's upper echelons. The Dodgers may have dropped a fluke game to the Phils with a pennant on the line in 1950 (just as they would blow another the following season to Bobby Thomson's heroics), but the organization that Rickey and O'Malley had now built in Brooklyn was too rich in talent to be regularly denied. For every Ashburn and Roberts in Philadelphia the Giants too had a Mays and an Antonelli. And the Braves (with Aaron) and Pirates (behind Clemente) were now also coming on like true gangbusters as the decade rapidly progressed.

The luster was also wearing rapidly off a clean-cut Phillies image engendered by the popular Whiz Kid contingent. As baseball now entered the age of integration full force and black stars like Robinson, Mays, Aaron and Clemente led pennant charges in Brooklyn, New York, Milwaukee and Pittsburgh, the old traditions of racial bigotry seemed to linger on like bad weather in Philadelphia, long after they were admirably cleared from other league cities. If a ballclub indeed reflects its community in both spirit and identity, the Phils were proving by their pronounced inaction on the integration front that the "City of Brotherly Love" was indeed an unfortunate misnomer when it came to spreading baseball brotherhood. Of course it had been the Phils and manager Ben Chapman that had so rudely treated Robinson to taunts and intolerance when he boldly arrived on the scene. And it would now be the Phillies who would hold out inexplicably as the very last segregated team in the senior circuit.

When Jackie Robinson announced his own retirement in January 1957 he released a terse public statement questionning why if thirteen big league clubs could play with black athletes three others still couldn't. Within two months of Robinson's challenge the Philadelphia ballclub reluctantly reached outside its own racially pure farm system to purchase the contracts of shortstop John Kennedy from the Negro League Kansas City Monarchs and Cuban infielder Chico Fernandez from the Brooklyn Dodgers. It was Kennedy who would formally bust the color barrier with the Phils, on April 22, then ironically lose his five-game career to a severe shoulder injury after only two big-league at-bats. Fernandez would thus by default become the first regular Phillies black player, manning the shortstop slot for much of the next two summers. Only the Detroit Tigers and Boston Red Sox of the American League were slower in bringing black players into the big time.[3] And all three clubs seemed to suffer proportionally in the league standings for their backward-looking and seemingly racist sins of omission.

The five seasons at the end of the fifties and outset of the turbulent sixties (1958–1962) saw the Philadelphia Phillies again hit rock bottom. The 1961 club in particular brought back nightmarish visions of the hapless sluggers of the hopeless 1930s. This team not only lost 107 games over the course of a single season (outstripped in losing only by the 1928, 1942 and 1945 editions), but dropped a major league record 23 in a row during one horrendous stretch that lasted from July 29 through August 20. The outfield of Tony Gonzalez (who would eventually hit over .300 three times during the decade), Johnny Callison and Don Demeter (acquired from the Dodgers that spring) showed promise enough. A Cuban youngster with the un-Hispanic-sounding name of Tony Taylor also flashed defensively at second, while Art Mahaffey (11–19) and Chris Short (6–12) demonstrated irregular prowess upon the mound. But promise and potential won very few games in 1961. Business seemed to be unfolding quite as usual in the basement surroundings of Shibe Park (which by now had been renamed Connie Mack Stadium prior to the 1953 campaign) and wherever else the Phillies took there defeat-riddled sideshow on the road. A single season before the hapless 1961 club went on its record losing rampage, for example, the equally lackluster 1960 outfit (59–95, 8th place) demonstrated its own special brand of punchlessness. Twice in the same summer were the Phillies no-hit victims of the Milwaukee Braves talented pitching staff. First Lew Burdette allowed only a hit batsman to reach the basepaths during an August 18th 1–0 blanking.[4] Then Warren Spahn repeated the trick (allowing but two walks) in a September 16th rematch, again in Milwaukee's County Stadium.

As if to prove that even mediocrity is capable of unfolding levels of increasing severity, next came the decade of the sixties—appropriately known in Philadelphia as the "Age of Gene Mauch" and marked by a stream of unspectacular summers interrupted with a single spectacular collapse. And what a remarkable collapse it truly was! For the 1964 Phillies will always live in league annals as the complete antithesis of the glorious Whiz Kids—a ballclub known to future generations for its dream-smashing nosedive rather than its heartstopping eleventh-hour heroics.

Gene Mauch had come on board on the immediate heels of Eddie Sawyer's second departure, a single game into the 1960 pennant race. Sawyer himself had walked away on Opening Day, remarking that he had now reached age forty-nine and wished to live long enough to see fifty. Over the first four agonizing summers of what would eventually stretch into a 26-year big league managerial career, the crafty Mauch slowly constructed the jigsaw puzzle of a winning ballclub. His 1964 Phillies thus entered their most fateful campaign already loaded with potential young superstars. At third there was Richie Allen, a brash rookie slugger known from "Day One" as much for his outrageous individualism, ongoing spats with management, and total disregard for team discipline as for his always lethal batting stroke. In the outfield roamed Johnny Callison who would be both an All-Star Game hero and a runner-up in the NL MVP balloting that very season. And on the hill there was Jim Bunning, newly arrived from the Detroit Tigers and destined to be the first hurler since Cy Young himself to hurl 100 victories and post 1,000-plus strikeouts in both leagues. The 1964 season itself unfolded quietly enough, with the drastically improved Phils holding down the top spot by mid-July and building a 7½ game cushion by mid-August.

The 1964 final month collapse didn't officially begin until September 21st. At that juncture the club still maintained a seemingly insurmountable 6½ game lead over three neck-and-neck challengers with but a dozen contests to play. In the next two weeks, however, the Phils flushed away ten straight games while the Cardinals (winners of eight in a row), Reds (winners of nine straight), and Giants (victors in seven of nine contests) all set out on relentless rampages. By the final weekend the Giants had fallen slightly off the pace, while the Phils themselves could only hope for a last-minute tie if (and only if) the now-leading Cardinals were defeated and the Phils prevailed against the Reds. The combination of a Phils win and Cardinal defeat would indeed have meant a three-way tie and a first-ever coinflip playoff round-robin. But it didn't happen, since the Philadelphia Sunday shellacking of Cincinnati was too-little-too-late in the face of a pennant-clinching Cardinals win against the Mets.

NL Standings for September 21st			Final NL Standings on October 4th		
Contenders	W-L	GB	Contenders	W-L	GB
Philadelphia	90-60	—	St. Louis	93-69	—
St. Louis	83-66	6.5	**Philadelphia**	92-70	1
Cincinnati	83-66	6.5	Cincinnati	92-70	1
San Francisco	83-67	7.0	San Francisco	90-72	3

There was little joy in Pennsylvania's Mudville after the horrendous collapse in the final days of the ill-fated 1964 campaign. And yet the season had given the partisans much to cheer. For one thing there was a franchise record 92 victories, as well as a new club standard (1,425,891) at the turnstiles. The team's first exciting black star, Richie Allen, had posted numbers (.318 BA, 29 HRs, 91 RBI, 201 hits) spectacular enough to walk away with NL rookie-of-the-year honors. And there had also been the marvelous mound feats of Jim Bunning who posted 19 victories and the circuit's fifth best ERA (2.68). In the midst of the campaign Bunning had even earned immortality for himself and thrills for everyone else with the first perfect game performance of modern National League history.[5] Jim Bunning's flawless masterpiece came against the Mets at Shea Stadium in the lidlifter of a June 21 twin bill. Eighteen-year-old Rick Wise was nearly as effective with a three-hit shutout in the nightcap (his first big league victory), thus giving the Bunning-Wise combo a record for the lowest doubleheader hit total across the entire history of National League play.

Bunning pitched well after 1964 (winning 19 games three times and 17 once in his four Philadelphia seasons) and was often aided on the hill by two other contributing moundsmen. Maturing lefty Chris Short became a big winner and one of the best portsiders in club annals by topping 17 victories four times between 1964 and 1968. And veteran righty Larry Jackson arrived from Chicago in time to tack two final 13-victory campaigns onto this 14-year sojourn through the National League. Others from the ill-fated 1964 club would also hang on for the full course of this lingering decade of disappointments. Richie Allen, for one, would only slowly wear out his welcome as an always productive if unpopular slugger, peaking with 40 roundtrippers in 1966. One unique moment for Allen came with a game-winning homer in baseball's first-ever indoor game (April 12, 1965, in Houston's Astrodome); a second arrived four seasons later in the form of a full month's suspension at the hands of skipper Bob Skinner for missing a twi-night doubleheader during mid-season 1969. But Allen's independent ways finally wore altogether thin by decade's end and he would be eventually peddled to the Cardinals for proven receiver Tim McCarver and equally flaky outfielder Curt Flood (who himself chose to battle baseball's reserve clause in court rather than report to his new NL team). Gene Mauch would last almost four more seasons himself and upon his firing in June 1968 Mauch had rung up the longest managerial tenure (eight-plus seasons) in Philadelphia Phillies history.

Making one of the most egregious front office misjudgements in recent decades, Phillies management reached an ill-advised decision after the 1964 debacle that the ballclub was indeed preciously close to a pennant and could be pushed over the edge with only the slightest amount of tinkering. Carpenter thus tried to win with trades over the next several campaigns and failed miserably in his effort. Acquiring first sacker Bill White and shortstop Dick Groat from St. Louis and hurlers Larry Jackson and Bob Buhl from Chicago—seasoned veterans all—the team nonetheless tumbled to fourth by 1966, despite 87 victories. The final two Phillies editions before divisional play slid to fifth (Mauch's final full year at 82–80) and then seventh (76–86), the latter team outpacing only expansion stumblebums New York and Houston in the final ten-team league pennant chase. Equally telling was the fact that the same 1968 ballclub stood tenth in the league in batting and sixth in run production as well.

Thus a clear badge of continuing ineptitude had to do with the Phillies' on-going reputation as the senior circuit's most frequently punchless ballclub. The latest proof came when the Phils yet again fell victim to no-hit pitching, this time at the hands of a mere expansion team playing in only its second week of big league competition. The infant Montreal Expos could soon boast of the earliest franchise no-hitter ever recorded when unheralded Bill Stoneman, making just his fifth big league start, twirled perfection at the host club on April 17 in venerable Connie Mack Stadium. Only slightly more than 6,000 somnolent Philadelphians were on hand for the 7–0 blanking, which amazingly occurred in only the ninth game ever played by the fledgling Expos. Yet one long-time Phillie who may have gloated upon the occasion was ex-skipper Gene Mauch, now handling the bench duties for the expansion Montrealers.

By the end of the decade it was still painfully apparent in the proud city housing the Liberty Bell and Independence Hall that the Phils were again going absolutely nowhere, and getting there in a hurry. A drastic overhaul seemed necessary if the baseball at Shibe Park was to avoid becoming as outmoded and seedy as the surrounding neighborhood and ramshackle ballpark in which it was still being played.

New Home and Hopes for the Seditious Seventies and Exploding Eighties

"When the Phillies finally came up with one fine team in the late 1970s and early 1980s, the present imposed itself on the past. Sports commentators wrote nostalgia pieces that denigrated Connie Mack's Athletics in comparison with the powerful National League team. A franchise that at least had a few great moments now suffered in memory in comparison to the actually hapless Phillies."— Bruce Kuklick

If ever a baseball club underwent a radical facelifting and a sudden change in corporate image, then it was the Philadelphia Phillies between the close of the unsettled sixties and the launching of the tradition-bashing seventies. A considerable part of this drastic ballclub facelift had to do with the shift of hometown venue in which Bob Carpenter's teams strutted their usually inadequate stuff. Indeed October 1, 1970, was a sad day for the city's veteran baseball watchers as the local National League club closed down their longtime residence on Lehigh and 21st with a 2–1 10-inning finale against the Montreal Expos. Decades of fan frustration aimed at the local losing ballclub mingled with over-exuberant souvenir hunting as the modest throng in attendance erupted upon the field at game's end and made a shambles of the old ballpark in but a few frenzied moments.

Not to be outdone in modernization by their chief league rivals in St. Louis, Pittsburgh and Cincinnati, the long-time occupants of outmoded and decaying Connie Mack Stadium opened the doors on a pristine new multi-purpose oval just in time for the hope-filled 1971 campaign. Veterans Stadium had been constructed despite three-and-a-half years of frustrating delays at a then-lofty cost of $49.5 million and shared its site in South Philadelphia with existing 100,000-seat John F. Kennedy Stadium (football) and eventually with The Spectrum (the city's plush NBA arena) as well. Seating 64,454 for baseball, The Vet now provided Philly with the third largest baseball venue in either circuit (only Cleveland's Municipal Stadium and California's Anaheim Stadium could hold more). Opening night (April 10, 1971) of the new structure successfully drew the largest Pennsylvania baseball crowd to date (55,532) and the partisans thrilled to a Jim Bunning victory over Montreal, spiced by the dropping of a ceremonial first pitch from a hovering helicopter and by a game-clinching Don Money roundtripper. While a club record 1,511,233 fans continued to hum the turnstiles that first summer, however, their only reward was yet another humdrum last-place finish, 67-95 and 30 games off the front-running pace of the state-rival Pirates. The Vet had now moved the Phillies into the modern era, and the price of that move was soon to be a modest upgrade in performance matched by a equal dip in former local color.

There were other things about the Phillies ballclub that looked different yet had little or nothing to do with the venue in which they performed. One was uniforms, as the familiar and colorful white and red pinstripped flannels with "Phillies" emblazoned across the front—a fixture since the Whiz Kid era—were jetisoned in 1970 for a more stylized futuristic look. New nylons sported a stylized "P" logo as replacement for the traditional club name, smaller and more modern numerals, piping all the way up the sides to the armpits, and a deeper burgundy shade of red for the trim coloring and pinstripping. Road uniforms would be further modernized with blue background replacing the traditional grey after 1973 and thus producing something of an embarrassing pajama look. A wave of nostalgia during the early 1990s, however, would result in eventual 1992 reinstitution of the once-favored bright red piping and "Phillies" lettering which had been harbinger of the fifties and sixties.

Another drastic overhaul came in the form of personnel, with a large part of the roster shift beginning at the manager's end of the bench. The "Age of Mauch" was clearly over by 1970 as long-time farm system employee Frank Lucchesi was appointed to hopefully end the string of five consecutive second division finishes. Lucchesi had never played in the big leagues, yet nineteen summers as a minor league bench boss (14 with the Phillies organization) had hopefully readied him for the Herculean task at hand. And the new manager had been supplied with a flood of fresh talent to nurse toward a more competitive daily lineup. Seasoned slugger Deron Johnson inherited the first base job from Richie Allen and responded with 27 homers in 1970 and 34 more in 1971. Larry Hisle and Oscar Gamble made failed debuts in Philadelphia's outfield before taking their slow-developing talents over to the junior circuit. Denny Doyle provided steady if unspectacular service at second base while the left side of the infield was handed to a pair of young defensive wizards named Don Money and Larry Bowa. Money would quickly establish a league record of 163 consecutive chances without error, a standard he would later replicate in the junior circuit as well during his sojourn in Milwaukee. Bowa, for his part, would perform 12 of his 16 seasons in a Phillies' uniform and retire after 2,222 games at shortstop owning the major-league mark for highest lifetime fielding average (.980) at that position. Joe Hoerner (1.97 ERA as reliever in 1971) and Wayne Twitchell (13–9, 2.50 ERA in 1973) provided fresh mound work, while Willie Montanez enjoyed a spectacular 1971 rookie season (30 HRs, 99 RBI) before coming back to earth in subsequent years.

The biggest dividend-paying personnel shifts, however, came in the form of two broadshouldered sluggers—both local farmhands—plus a remarkable lefthanded pitcher soon plucked from the trader's market. Mike Schmidt arrived on the scene late in 1972 for 13 brief games and the first of his unchallenged club-record 548 homers. That same season a "Baby Bull" named Greg Luzinski (himself eventual author of 307 career dingers) enjoyed his first productive summer with 18 roundtrippers and 68 RBI. Together Schmidt and Luzinski would soon provide the made-over Phils with the league's heaviest double-artillery of the second half of the decade.

And if future Phillies' fortunes hung on two home-ground strongboys in the batter's box, they hinged as well on the arrival of the greatest portside hurler in a century of ballclub history. Five-year veteran Steve Carlton was plucked from St. Louis after puzzling bookend campaigns in which he had been both a 19-game loser and a 20-game winner. Soon "Lefty" was altogether dazzling opponents at The Vet with the greatest single-season mound show since the pre-World War I exploits of "Old Pete" Alexander. Unwilling to meet Carlton's $75,000 salary demand after his turn-around 1971 season, the Cardinals had unloaded the flaky southpaw straight up for Rick Wise, in what was perhaps the most fortuitous Phillies' trade ever engineered by front-office caretakers.

Once in Philly Carlton would waste no time in establishing both the unique personality and unsurpassed talent which made him one of baseball's top drawing cards. Off the field Lefty instituted a policy of total silence with the print and electronic media, a stance which would bathe him in controversy for two decades. More important to diamond diehards was one of the greatest individual single-season performances in senior circuit history. Laboring for a last-place ballclub that managed but 59 total victories and ranked ninth in the circuit in batting and eleventh in run production, Carlton wrapped up a club-first Cy Young Award with individual statistics that almost defy the imagination: 27 wins (versus but 10 defeats), 346 innings pitched, 310 strikeouts, 1.97 ERA, 30 complete games, 8 shutouts, 15 straight wins, 22 victories in his final 25 outings. Only flawless defense on the left side of the Phils infield (Money at third and Bowa at short) seems to provide even partial explanation for Carlton's history-shaping season.

A revamped image for the Philadelphia nine did not, however, mean an immediate climb in the league's standings. Manager Lucchesi suffered through one season in fifth slot and two in sixth. But he did patiently develop Larry Bowa, sticking with the light-sticking shortstop against a flood of fan protests when Bowa's obvious defensive wizardry didn't seem to make up for his rookie shortcomings with the stick. Such judgments of talent aside, Lucchesi would be gone by late 1972 in the backwash of two tailend finishes. Danny Ozark, the next bench boss on board, began his own seven-year tenure with a third-straight basement finish. The onfield record did nonetheless improve by a dozen games under Ozark and the team batting average jumped thirteen points as well under the influence of Luzinski's slugging and the spray hitting of Del Unser and Bill Robinson. And the youthful playing talent was matched on the management front with the naming of Ruly Carpenter (only 32 years of age) to succeed his father at the owner's desk. The Phillies thus now also owned the youngest club president in baseball, and one whose lineage and training boded well for sound future front office strategy.

Perhaps the most exciting individual performer during these early rebuilding years in the pristine new venue of Veterans Stadium was veteran righthanded flamethrower Rick Wise, a promising prospect of the late sixties who finally established himself as staff ace in the first new season of more spacious ballpark surroundings. The even-tempered Wise was the year's big winner at 17–14 in 1971, and on June 21st of that season he enjoyed a performance at Cincinnati that certainly rivals any in league history when it comes to ultimate fantasy outings in a hurler's professional career. In his dream game Wise authored a rare Phillies no-hitter, also becoming the first and only moundsman ever to sock two homers (he had six for the total season) during his own hitless masterpiece. Clearly the biggest bonus of Wise's sudden surge in performance, however, was that his astronomical rise in stock would provide the trade bait necessary to lure future Hall-of-Famer Carlton from St. Louis. Before he was done Wise would win nearly 200 ball games with five different clubs. Yet it would be his ordained fate to be remembered simply as the player who was traded for the incomparable Steve Carlton.

It was Mike Schmidt's second full season that finally saw the revitalized Phillies make their first lethal assault on the rest of the division. Though he had batted only an anemic .196 for his rookie campaign, by his 1974 sophomore season Schmidt had already dislodged the slick-fielding Money (traded to Milwaukee) at the hot corner and thus had launched a career that would one day end with accolades as the greatest all-around third sacker in baseball history. With Schmidt pounding out 36 homers and necomer Dave Cash now teaming at the keystone with Bowa, Ozark's crew finally made its long-anticipated run. The Phils would even lead the circuit for 51 days that summer, only fading to third after a devastating 12–17 September. Schmidt became the first Phillie to win a homerun derby since Chuck Klein in 1933.[6] Perhaps only the loss of Luzinski to season-ending injury had blocked a divisional title in this first season of renewed slugging. The 1975 campaign, buoyed by Luzinski's return with 120 RBI, was also one of steady improvement. Again Philadelphia challenged, this time with a spot in first as late as August 18 and an eventual second-place resting spot behind Pittsburgh. But it was 1976 that saw the Phils truly explode upon the league with their first ever 100-victory campaign and a comfortable nine-game lead over the still-pesky Pirates at the wire. Schmidt (38 homers) and Carlton (20–7) again were the expected on-field and clubhouse leaders. For only the third time in their history the Philadelphia Phillies could boast of being champions, even if this time the prize was a devalued divisional flag and not a true National League pennant. In the end the only negative coloring on a heady Bicentennial summer enjoyed by the nation's most historic city had to be a sudden and decisive three-game whipping by the western division Cincinnati Reds in the October showdown for a National League flag.

The newly crowned division champions had little enough trouble repeating. In fact they produced a near carbon copy by posting an identical 101-61 season's ledger and a five-game cushion over familiar rival Pittsburgh. Good things were soon enough to come in threes for this ballclub that had so long suffered as a hopeless yearly also-ran. The 1978 edition of Ozark's sluggers was again a divisional champion, this time by a less-than-comfortable 1½-game margin over those self-same Pirates. Yet it was becoming painfully apparent that despite their summer-long frontrunning play the Phils were still not quite ready to solve the mysteries of post-season competition. In both 1977 and 1978 it was the Los Angeles Dodgers who rudely derailed the Phillies' World Series plans, both times by an identical and comfortable three-games-to-one playoff margin. Mike Schmidt had special difficulties with the added tensions of NLCS performance, tumbling to an embarrassing .063 batting mark in 1977 (one harmless single in 16 plate appearances) and improving that mark to only .200 the following October.

Danny Ozark's final season at the helm in Philadelphia was one of bitter disappointment. After dominating other eastern clubs three summers running the Phillies' usually strong pitching succumbed to numerous injuries which effectively eliminated two top starters, Dick Ruthven and Larry Christenson. Ineffective play and a tumble all the way to fourth cost Ozark his job by late August. This despite a huge publicity coup with the free-agent signing of one of baseball's most popular players, long-time Cincinnati Reds star Pete Rose. And also despite a surge with Rose in the lineup (slamming 208 hits in his pursuit of Ty Cobb's all-time record) and an all-time club attendance mark of 2.7 million hometown admissions. Suddenly it appeared as though the Phillies' crowning glory moment—so long awaited—had somehow come and gone without achievement of that one truly coveted prize of World Series play.

Yet as the new decade opened the Phillies were once again back on track. Farm director Dallas Green (a journeyman pitcher with the club in the early sixties) had succeeded Ozark for what was originally supposed to be only an interim assignment. Green seemed to fit comfortably into his new role, however, and was still hanging around as the 1980 campaign opened on a somewhat sluggish note, with the Phils playing under .500 ball for the first month, then climbing steadily into a first-place berth by Memorial Day. The summer of 1980 seemed somehow special from the beginning as the Philadelphia club clawed and scratched under Green and refused this time around to play themselves out of a pennant race. A torrid battle with Montreal and Pittsburgh expanded through August and into late September and the entire campaign fittingly came down to a final weekend head-to-head matchup with Montreal that found the two clubs in a dead-heat for the title. Green's charges would finally clinch their fourth divisional flag in dramatic fashion when unanimous league MVP Mike Schmidt belted an eleventh-inning two-run game-winning homer on the season's penultimate day.

Schmidt's heroics (his 48 homers had set a new big-league mark for third sackers) and the Phillies' successful late-season charge were only preludes to more explosive fireworks yet to come. Post-season play of 1980 was not only the most exciting Philadelphia had ever known; it may well have been the most heart-stopping in a full century of senior circuit play. Cy Young winner Carlton staked the Phils to a 1–0 NLCS lead over Houston in the post-season lidlifter. It was a lead which failed to hold up as the Astros rallied in the next two contests, both heated extra-inning affairs. A third-straight see-saw extra-inning tussle then saw the Phillies again knot the Series when Luzinski and Manny Trillo both doubled in runs during a tenth-frame Phils' uprising. As though there had not already been enough energy-sapping tension, crucial game five also extended into overtime when the Phillies struck for five in the eighth, only to see the Astros rebound for two of their own in the same frame to force extended play. Mercifully the exhausting series was put to rest when Elliot Maddox doubled home Del Unser with the tally that at long last handed the Phillies their first National League flag in thirty exasperating seasons.

Perennially downtrodden Philadelphia fans now sensed—perhaps for the first time ever—that they finally had a true team of destiny on their hands. For one thing the 1980 World Series would match the local heroes with a Kansas City Royals outfit that had also recently failed miserably in three straight cracks (1976–1978) at league championship play. Nonetheless, the Royals offered explosive offense (George Brett batted .390 that summer) and stingy pitching (Dennis Leonard boasted 20 victories and Larry Gura 18) of their own, plus an apparent ability to rebound just as effectively as the Houston Astros or the never-say-die Phillies themselves.

The National Leaguers jumped out to a two-game margin in high-scoring affairs that were rescued by bullpen aces Tug McGraw and Ron Reed. The Royals then returned the fire in their own home park to even the Series, benefitting from the long-ball power of first baseman Willie Mays Aikens. Aikens grabbed headlines when he established a milestone of his own by providing the first-ever feat of two multiple-homer games within the same Series. As fortunes continued to shift wildly, Tug McGraw then became the man-of-the-hour, winning game five in relief and saving the final sixth contest by twice pitching out of bases-loaded jams. Despite McGraw's final mound heroics (and 1.17 ERA), Mike Schmidt was finally a post-season MVP on the strength of two vital homers and seven RBI, while receiver Bob Boone played a crucial offensive role as well with a Series-best .412 BA. The hoops and hollers which soon exploded up and down the Delaware River had little to do with statistics or individual heroics, however, while they had everything to do with the fact that for the first time ever the Phillies were undisputed champions of the entire baseball world.

The Phillies rolled into the early 1980s with a good deal of apparent momentum still on their side. A labor-wrecked and thus much-diluted season of 1981 brought continued respectability (a third-place divisional finish) but its share of disappointment as well (including a 3–2 loss to Montreal during the jerry-rigged extra play-off round between first and second half-season Eastern Division pacesetters). The strange year of 1981 was not only one of upheaval throughout the strike-plagued game, but in the Phillies long-stable front office as well. After four decades of dedicated progressive ownership, the Carpenter family had finally decided to sell out their interests in the ballclub. Ruly Carpenter was reportedly alarmed by the seemingly uncontrolled escalation in players' salaries and club operating expenses and was thus more than happy to hand over club ownership for $30 million to a syndicate headed by Bill Giles, son of former Cincinnati GM and National League president, Warren Giles.

In baseball as in life, fortune swings with the regularity of the shifting New England weather. The summer of 1982 brought re-newed hope with a club that resurged to runner-up slot in the division behind the continued production of Schmidt (35 HRs) and Carlton (23–11, 3.10 ERA). And by 1983 the Phillies were back on top, riding the Cy Young arm of John Denny to a six-game divisional cushion over Pittsburgh and a relatively easy three-games-to-one NLCS triumph against the west coast Los Angeles Dodgers. This was again a team with a new identity, one dubbed affectionately by local press wags as "The Wheez Kids"—clear reference to an obvious contrast between the legendary league champs of 1950 and the advanced age of most key performers on this team's veteran roster. Joining Rose in his fifth Philadelphia season were his two stellar teammates of the Big Red Machine era in Cincinnati. Veterans Joe Morgan and Tony Perez were now on board for brief free-agent stopovers that would last but this single championship campaign.

The World Series of 1983 was only the fourth in club history and thus could hardly be termed a genuine letdown. Yet there certainly had to be a good deal of disillusionment among diehard Phillies fanatics concerning events which soon transpired in late October 1983. Much of that disappointment had to do with another post-season failure by Mike Schmidt. Smitty slumped to a horrendous one-for-twenty Series performance and thus outstripped previous post-season failures with an unthinkable .050 BA and failure to produce a single RBI or even an extra-base whack. Philly's down-the-street neighbors from Baltimore hardly broke a sweat as the Orioles rode the .385 hitting of Series MVP Rick Dempsey and a 1.60 staff ERA to a relentless four-games-to-one pasting of the once-again punchless Phils.

By the mid-1980s the old standbys as well as the temporary stopovers were beginning to leave in droves. Rose was quick to go, taking his free agent act on to Montreal before the start of the 1984 season. Morgan and Perez departed at the same time, having stayed long enough only for a single pennant dash as members of the Phils. The battery of John Denny and Bo Diaz would also exit by the middle of the decade, both peddled to Cincinnati in separate deals before the conclusion of 1985. Schmidt (who would not retire until early 1989) and Carlton (whose strained rotator cuff and fading fastball led to final release in June 1986) stayed on, but the glory years were now well past for both. Schmidt would win his final HR and RBI titles in 1986 while Carlton had already seen his final 20-victory season the summer before the thrilling Wheez Kid pennant run.

Only the Philly Phanatic, one of baseball's most colorful modern-day performing mascots, continued to strut his stuff proudly in Veterans Stadium after 1984. One spectacular season was turned in, nonetheless, by Steve Bedrosian, a hard throwing reliever who had found his way to Veterans Stadium from Atlanta's Braves, arriving with Milt Thompson in a December 1985 four-player transaction. The righty reliever set the National League on fire throughout 1987, recording 12 straight saves at season's end (a record at the time) and also accumulating a league-best 40 saves. For his yeoman efforts "Bedrock" pulled down both the Fireman-of-the-Year and NL Cy Young awards in a rare pitching double.[7] And Bedrosian, like Rick Wise before him, soon proved as valuable in the marketplace as on the pitcher's hill. After his lofty saves count dipped by a dozen the following summer "Bedrock" was eventually dealt to San Francisco in a blockbuster 1989 transaction that brought hard-hitting third sacker Charlie Hayes and future no-hit hurler Terry Mulholland into town.

The Phillies of the early 1990s were aptly known around the circuit as baseball's "dirtiest" team. This epithet of course had nothing to do with unsportsmanlike play. Instead it arose from the same storehouse of colorful diamond imagery as the term "Gas House Gang" that had once adorned another dynamic National League club over in St. Louis decades earlier. The designation was popularized by the more poetic among local sportswriters as response to the usual soiled appearance of the Philly uniforms and the bone-crunching style of all-out skull-crashing play that was a frequent cause of stained flannels and wrinkled caps. This was a ballclub that was long on relentless hustle if not on victories.

The single player most representative of this gritty style and appearance was a hard-nosed centerfielder who even raised memories of Richie Ashburn crashing outfield fences three decades earlier. Lenny Dykstra came to the Phils as a New York Mets (mid-season 1989) castoff seemingly earmarked for spot platoon duty. But soon Lenny Dykstra was a huge boxoffice hit in the domain of Brotherly Love. Most of Dykstra's lasting love affair with the often-fickle Philly fans came during the 1990 season when the pugnacious outfielder opened the campaign with a torrid batting display that carried him to a sizzling .418 mark by June 4th. It couldn't last for a spunky hitter who was batting at only a .268 lifetime clip over the five previous seasons, yet the inevitable fall-off still left the Phillies' sparkplug with a .325 average, fourth best in the circuit, and an NL-best 192 base hits.

Dykstra was also a throwback to tobacco-chawing ballplayers of an earlier era, always as controversial and colorful away from the ballpark as he was valuable upon the diamond. A high-speed automobile accident would cost him much of the 1991 season and rumors of huge gambling losses (involving card playing and fortunately not baseball betting) threatened his career status in the Commissioner's Office as well. Two other Phillies of the early nineties also mirrored the devil-may-care playing-style inspired by Dykstra. One was San Diego Padres castoff John Kruk who assumed the first-base slot and slugged away at a .291 clip in 1990 and then pounded the ball for a .323 standard (third best in the league) in 1992. A second was workman-like catcher Darren Daulton, a hard-nosed backstop with a lethal stick who led the senior circuit in 1992 with 109 RBI (the most by a Philly backstop since Stan Lopata's 95 in 1956) and constructed countless lethal roadblocks in the neighborhood of homeplate.

There were also a few exceptional highlight moments at the dawn of the new decade. One was a no-hit masterpiece spun before the hometown fans, the first such event in the Phillies' lengthy history. Lefthander Terry Mulholland provided the most exhilarating pitching performance of many a season with his 6–0 Veterans Stadium whitewashing on August 15, 1990, of his former teammates, the San Francisco Giants. Soon the Phillies were part of another no-hitter, as well, only the sixth ever thrown in ninety-plus seasons by a moundsman on their own side of the pitching matchup. This time it was promising Tommy Greene who turned the trick in Montreal's Olympic Stadium (May 23, 1991) for a 2–0 blanking of the usually offensive-minded Expos. Yet while the Phillies received some surprise pitching performances, hitting often failed to live up to expectations. Outfielder Von Hayes exasperated the faithful by never sustaining the lumber-swinging potential flashed in a 1986 .305 season. And the arrival of long-time league homerun star Dale Murphy from Atlanta would provide little but disappointment as the fading slugger fought a seemingly losing battle against late-career injury in a futile effort to reach the 400-plateau in career roundtrippers.

An accent on rebuilding remained the hallmark of a new Phillies management philosophy well into the fresh decade of the 1990s. While veteran journeymen like Lenny Dykstra and John Kruk continued to pace the offensive attack, new sluggers like first-base prospect Rickie Jordan (who overcame a string of 1992 injuries to hit .304 in 276 plate appearances) and Dave Hollins (switch-hitting third sacker who belted 27 1992 roundtrippers) adequately replaced the fading veteran Dale Murphy in the heart of the Philly order. Despite a sixth-place finish in 1992, the youth movement under new skipper Jim Fregosi now promised another imminent climb in the senior circuit standings.

Thus it has been a true rollercoaster ride for fans of the Philadelphia Phillies, and most of that ride has been a dizzying breakneck ascent toward the cold cement of the National League cellar. But such is baseball that—even here in the netherworld of Baker Bowl, Shibe Park or the saucer-like Veterans Stadium—true diehards might still dredge up memories of an all-star lineup culled from decades lost, a roster capable of conjuring the diamond's hero-drenched past. Even the downtrodden Phillies fan might construct a potent fantasy lineup of all-time batsmen and hurlers to do any big-league city proud.

The All-Time Philadelphia Phillies Mythical Team
OF   Chuck Klein (1928–1933, 1936–1939, 1940–1944)*
OF   Richie Ashburn (1948–1959)**
OF   Del Ennis (1946–1956)
1B   Richie "Dick" Allen (1963–1969, 1975–1976)#
2B   Granny Hamner (1944–1959)##
3B   Mike Schmidt (1972–1989)**

SS   Larry Bowa (1970–1981)
C   Bob Boone (1972–1981)
RHP   Grover Cleveland Alexander (1911–1917, 1930)*
RHP   Robin Roberts (1948–1961)*
LHP   Steve Carlton (1972–1986)**
*Hall-of-Famer
**Future Hall-of-Famer
#Also played third base
##Also played shortstop

What fan could resist a team featuring the second winningest pitcher of all-time (Alexander), the seventh best career home run slugger (Schmidt), the only southpaw hurler ever to surpass 4,000 career strikeouts (Carlton), the winningest righthander of baseball's most glorious "Golden Decade" (Roberts), the best defensive centerfielder of the nostalgia-rich decade that featured Mantle, Snider and Mays (Ashburn), and the all-time leader in big league games caught (Boone)? How, indeed, could any franchise featuring such immortals have possibly finished in the cellar more times than any other century-old ballclub?

Perhaps a new baseball century on the horizon will hold better fortunes for its losingest franchise. Perhaps there will be other glory days and even a pennant or two for baseball's real-world "Mudville" and its long-suffering diehards. But whenever baseball's first full century is recalled the image of the club in Philadelphia will have to be one of annual losers and all-too-often big-league bumpkins. Even such a city and such a ballclub has had its larger-than-life stars and its eventual championship dream. Even here there was a Pete Alexander, a Richie Ashburn, a Robin Roberts and a Mike Schmidt. Trouble was that Philly fans usually had to live a lifetime of seasonal suffering between each rare visit of such immortals. And only in the single summer that marked the century's Continental Divide did a whole ballclub of such proven winners inexplicably arrive for a brief summer's fling at glory. Even the most fanatical Whiz Kid booster would thus find little enough excuse to agree with comedian W.C. Fields—that on the whole he or she would rather be in Philadelphia!

Notes

1. The post-expansion era has hardly been kinder to the hapless Phillies, though unsurpassed bumbling has often been happily replaced by mere mediocrity. While the first six decades of the present century saw the senior circuit dominated by the Giants, Cubs and Pirates, it has been the Reds, Dodgers, and Cardinals who have surged to the fore over the past three

decades, along with those always steady Pirates who share the state of Pennsylvania with the usually undermanned Phils. The Phillies did, of course, have nearly as many winning seasons in the 30-year post-expansion era as they did in twice that many seasons before baseball took up wholesale franchise shifting. Also the club did move into the middle of the pack, at least now topping all the other regular yearly losers. On the other hand, they passed only two pre-expansion teams, and this was due largely to a spate of winning across a mere five seasons that closed out the 1970s and opened up the decade of the eighties.

Composite NL Standings	Post-Expansion Era 1961–1992			32 Seasons
1. Cincinnati Reds	2782-2326 .545 Pct.	25 Winning Seasons	6 Pennants
2. Los Angeles Dodgers	2773-2342 .542 Pct.	23 Winning Seasons	8 Pennants
3. Pittsburgh Pirates	2691-2393 .529 Pct.	20 Winning Seasons	2 Pennants
4. St. Louis Cardinals	2660-2445 .521 Pct.	21 Winning Seasons	6 Pennants
5. San Francisco Giants	2622-2496 .512 Pct.	20 Winning Seasons	2 Pennants
6. **Philadelphia Phillies**	2520-2590 .493 Pct.	14 Winning Seasons	2 Pennants
7. Montreal Expos (1969)	1854-1966 .485 Pct.	11 Winning Seasons	0 Pennants
8. Milwaukee-Atlanta Braves	2457-2644 .482 Pct.	14 Winning Seasons	2 Pennants
9. Houston Colt 45s-Astros (1962)	2388-2571 .482 Pct.	10 Winning Seasons	0 Pennants
10. Chicago Cubs	2427-2674 .476 Pct.	9 Winning Seasons	0 Pennants
11. New York Mets (1962)	2305-2637 .466 Pct.	14 Winning Seasons	3 Pennants
12. San Diego Padres (1969)	1722-2102 .450 Pct.	7 Winning Seasons	1 Pennant

2. Honig (131–132) and others have built the argument that Richie Ashburn is perhaps the most unjust case of all, when it comes to those truly deserving players left out of the Cooperstown shrine. Certainly the defensive numbers alone seem to argue for Ashburn as a Hall-of-Famer: he holds a share (with Max Carey) of the record for most years (9) leading in putouts for an outfielder, owns the record for most years (4) with 500-plus putouts and most years (9) with 400-plus putouts. Six of the top ten season's totals for outfielder putouts were turned in by Richie Ashburn. It is probably the presence of Mantle, Snider and Mays in the same decade, and the fortune of those latter three to have played in the constant media glare of baseball's media Mecca, that best explains Ashburn's ongoing slight. Ashburn himself has, since his playing days, enjoyed a successful second baseball career as long-time Phillies' radio play-by-play broadcaster.

3. Kuklick suggests that the Philadelphia team's largely all-white lineup, set against the black urban neighborhood which housed Connie Mack Stadium (nee Shibe Park), was an important part of the ballclub's malaise throughout the decades of the fifties and sixties. Kuklick at one point observes that: "The Phillies believed they had no future in North Philadelphia, where the problems of the city centered and where their team played poorly. As its commitment to alternatives far from 'the black belt' grew, the franchise allowed Connie Mack Stadium to fall into disrepair, contributing to disinvestment in the area. The dirty and unkempt park mirrored the down-at-the-heels team" (158–159).

4. Seventeen different pitchers in all have authored no-hit games versus the all-too-often punchless Philadelphia Phillies over the course of the 20th Century, including the very first such masterpiece in which Frank "Noodles" Hahn victimized the hapless Phils at Cincinnati on July 12, 1900. This total makes the Phillies the most frequently no-hit ballclub of major league his-

tory. A complete listing of hitless whitewashes against the Philadelphia National League ballclub is as follows:

Pitcher	Date	Team	Game Score	Location
*Noodles Hahn	July 12, 1900	Cincinnati	Reds 4, Phillies 0	Cincinnati
George Wiltse	July 4, 1908	New York	Giants 1, Phillies 0	New York
Jeff Tesreau	September 6, 1912	New York	Giants 3, Phillies 0	**Philadelphia**
George Davis	September 9, 1914	Boston	Braves 7, Phillies 0	Boston
Jess Barnes	May 7, 1922	New York	Giants 6, Phillies 0	New York
Dazzy Vance	September 13, 1925	Brooklyn	Dodgers 10, Phillies 1	Brooklyn
Jim Wilson	June 12, 1954	Milwaukee	Braves 2, Phillies 0	Milwaukee
Sal Maglie	September 25, 1956	Brooklyn	Dodgers 5, Phillies 0	Brooklyn
Lew Burdette	August 18, 1960	Milwaukee	Braves 1, Phillies 0	Milwaukee
Warren Spahn	September 16, 1960	Milwaukee	Braves 4, Phillies 0	Milwaukee
Don Nottebart	May 17, 1963	Houston	Colt '45s 4, Phillies 1	Houston
Sandy Koufax	June 4, 1964	Los Angeles	Dodgers 3, Phillies 0	**Philadelphia**
George Culver	July 29, 1968	Cincinnati	Reds 6, Phillies 1	**Philadelphia**
Bill Stoneman	April 17, 1969	Montreal	Expos 7, Phillies 0	**Philadelphia**
Bill Singer	July 20, 1970	Los Angeles	Dodgers 5, Phillies 1	Los Angeles
Burt Hooton	April 16, 1972	Chicago	Cubs 4, Phillies 0	Chicago
Bob Forsch	April 16, 1978	St. Louis	Cardinals 5, Phillies 0	St. Louis

*First big-league no-hitter of the 20th Century

5. Only six Philadelphia Phillies moundsmen have spun ultimate masterpieces against the opposition during 92 full seasons of 20th-Century play. Terry Mulholland was surprisingly the first and only to do so before the home crowd—over the full nine decades of the present century—when he achieved perfection against the San Francisco Giants on August 15th of 1990. A complete listing of Phillies no-hitters is provided here:

Pitcher	Date	Opponent	Game Score	Location
Chick Fraser	September 18, 1903	Chicago	Phillies 10, Cubs 0	Chicago
Johnny Lush	May 1, 1906	Brooklyn	Phillies 6, Dodgers 0	Brooklyn
*Jim Bunning	June 21, 1964	New York	Phillies 6, Mets 0	New York
Rick Wise	June 23, 1971	Cincinnati	Phillies 4, Reds 0	Cincinnati
Terry Mulholland	August 15, 1990	San Francisco	Phillies 6, Giants 0	**Philadelphia**
Tommy Greene	May 23, 1991	Montreal	Phillies 2, Expos 0	Montreal

*First perfect game in modern National League history

6. Despite the endless string of unenviable records and second division finishes that have clouded each and every decade, the City of Brotherly Love has not been totally shut out when it comes to individual offensive and defensive ballplaying heroes. The Phillies have indeed managed to land their share of single season league leaders in all major batting and pitching categories. Five Phils have paced the circuit in batting average: Sherry Magee (1910), Lefty O'Doul (1929), Chuck Klein (1933), Harry Walker (1947) and Richie Ashburn (1955, 1958). Four others have been home run champions for a combined total of 21 different seasons: Cliff "Gavvy" Cravath (1913–1915, 1917–1919), Cy Williams (1920, 1923, 1927), Klein (1929, 1931–1933) and future Hall-of-Famer Mike Schmidt (1974–1976, 1980–1981, 1984, 1986). The only Phillies' triple crown winner, of course, was Chuck Klein during his phenomenal 1933 season (.368 BA, 28 HRs, 120 RBI). Only two have paced the league in the hallmark of good pitching, ERA: "Old Pete" Alexander (1915–1917) and Steve Carlton (1972). But

seven have paced the circuit in strikeouts: Alexander (1912, 1914–1917), Tom Seaton (1913), Kirby Higbie (1940), Robin Roberts (1953–1954), Jack Sanford (1957), Jim Bunning (1967) and, of course, Carlton (1972, 1974, 1980, 1982–1983). And six different Phillies moundsmen have bested all rivals in season's victory totals: Alexander (1911, 1914–1917), Seaton (1913), "Jumbo" Jim Elliott (1931), Roberts (1952–1954), Carlton (1972, 1977, 1980, 1982) and John Denny (1983).

   7. Three men in Philadelphia uniforms have copped the league's cherished MVP honors (Chuck Klein in 1932, Jim Konstanty in 1950, Mike Schmidt in 1980–1981 and 1986), while three as well have earned Cy Young Awards for their superb moundsmanship (Steve Carlton in 1972, 1977, 1980 and 1982; John Denny in 1983; Steve Bedrosian in 1987). Twice have the Phillies also boasted a league rookie-of-the-year winner (Jack Sanford in 1957 and Richie Allen in 1964). Yet no managers wearing the Phils' colors have ever been tabbed as the senior circuit's skipper-of-the-year, given that this award had not yet been conceived at the time Eddie Sawyer worked his Whiz Kid miracles way back in 1950.

References

Frommer, Harvey. "Pride in Philadelphia: The Phillies" in: *A Baseball Century: The First 100 Years of the National League,* edited by Jean McClow, 140–151. New York: Rutledge Books, 1976.

Honig, Donald. *The Philadelphia Phillies: An Illustrated History.* New York: Simon and Schuster, 1992.

Lieb, Frederick G. and Stan Baumgartner. *The Philadelphia Phillies.* New York: G. P. Putnam's Sons, 1953.

Lieb, Frederick G. *Baseball As I Have Known It.* New York: Coward, McCann & Geoghegan Company, 1977.

Lieb, Frederick G. *The Baseball Story.* New York: G. P. Putnam's Sons, 1950.

Mead, William B. *Two Spectacular Seasons: 1930 (The Year the Hitters Ran Wild) and 1968 (The Year the Pitchers Took Revenge).* New York: Macmillan and Company, 1990.

Tygiel, Jules. *Baseball's Great Experiment: Jackie Robinson and His Legacy.* New York: Oxford University Press, 1983.

Annotated Bibliography

Like National League pennants in Baker Bowl and Shibe Park, comprehensive histories of the Phillies have been a distinct rarity. The original Putnam volume by Fred Lieb and Stan Baumgartner stands out as one of the finest (and also rarest for today's baseball book collector) from that landmark series and remains the standard treatment on the Philadelphia ballclub over the first half of the 20th century. Honig's most recent illustrated history fills a gap with its up-to-date account, despite the author's often sketchy approach to season-by-season reportage. No scholarly and comprehensive tome exists, however. Two of Lieb's other books, while not about the Phillies exclusively, do provide some interesting tidbits. And, ironically, the best "stadium book" ever written is devoted to the very ballpark where the Phillies spent a goodly part of their modern history. Kuklick's study of Shibe Park and its environs can be taken as a cautionary tale of the decay of a professional baseball franchise as well as the decay of a big league ballplaying venue. Below is a comprehensive listing of all legitimate Philadelphia Phillies histories, along with selected biographies and other sources which treat team history and important team personalities.

Archibald, Joe. *The Richie Ashburn Story*. New York: Julian Messner Publishing Company, 1960. 186 pp.
    The only available biography of the Phillies' two-time batting champion opens with an account of boyhood years in Nebraska and his struggles to become a major league ballplayer. This juvenile-market account traces Ashburn's minor league career plus eleven seasons with the Phillies, concluding with a trade to the Chicago Cubs prior to the 1960 season.

Bartell, Dick (with Norman L. Macht). *Rowdy Richard: A Firsthand Account of the National League Baseball Wars of the 1930s and the Men Who Fought Them*. Berkeley, California: North Atlantic Books, 1987. 186 pp.
    The National League's first All-Star Game shortstop here reminisces about an 18-year action-filled big league career during baseball's powerpacked decades of the thirties and forties. Chapter 4—"Playing on the Brink of Bankruptcy"—focuses on Bartell's four frustration-filled seasons (1931–1934) with the lowly Philadelphia Phillies.

Bunning, Jim (as told to Ralph Bernstein). *The Story of Jim Bunning*. Philadelphia: J. B. Lippincott Company, 1965. 180 pp.
    The life of the Phillies' ace pitcher of the mid-sixties is scrutinized from his youth in rural Kentucky through the infamous pennant-collapse season of 1964, his first in the National League. Included are Bunning's early career with the Detroit Tigers, his 1964 trade to the Phillies, and also his remarkable perfect game of June 1964 against the New York Mets in Shea Stadium (seemingly the occasion which prompted this autobiographical book). One highlight is the radio play-by-play excerpts of Bunning's perfect game (with By Saam, Jim Gordon and Richie Ashburn at the microphone) which open, close and intersperse the thin volume.

Bodley, Hal. *The Team That Wouldn't Die*. Wilmington, Delaware: Serendipity Press, 1981. 418 pp.
    The future *USA Today* baseball columnist here recaps the finest single season in Phillies' history, the 1980 campaign which saw a usually downtrodden ballclub win its first and only World Series title. Box scores from season's play and profiles of all players from the proudest of all Phillies teams (Schmidt, Carlton, McGraw, Rose, Perez, Boone, Luzinski, and others) provide the bulk of this fast-paced text.

Doyle, Ed. *The Forgotten Ones*. Philadelphia: Doyle Publications, 1974. 35 pp.
    Doyle provides the only book or monograph discussing the distinguished big-league career of Chuck Klein, one of the foremost NL sluggers of the lively Baker Bowl era. This unfortunately thin paperback volume makes the strongest possible case for inclusion of both Klein (eventually elected in 1980) and Joe Sewell (elected in 1977) in

baseball's Hall of Fame at Cooperstown. Klein's entire big-league career is detailed here with considerable precision.

Frommer, Harvey. "Pride in Philadelphia: The Phillies" in: *A Baseball Century: The First 100 Years of the National League,* edited by Jean McClow, 140–151. New York: Rutledge Books, 1976.

This lively, compact and heavily illustrated team portrait traces the rollercoaster ride of Phillies history from the 19th Century through the mid-1970s. Highlighted are the 1915 and 1950 World Series appearances; the spendthrift ownerships of Baker, Nugent and Cox; the slapstick play of the thirties and forties; the star-crossed fortunes of manager Gene Mauch; and the rebuilding of the ballclub in the early seasons of Mike Schmidt, Steve Carlton and Greg Luzinski. This chapter is part of a full set of NL team portraits within a handsome coffee table volume celebrating the senior circuit's 1976 centennial season.

Hochman, Stan. *Mike Schmidt, Baseball's King of Swing.* New York: Random House, 1983. 132 pp.

An intimate portrait of the slugging future Hall-of-Fame third baseman, beginning with his days as a youngster in Dayton, Ohio, and continuing throughout his collegiate (Ohio University), minor league, and major league ballplaying careers. Published deep into Schmidt's career, this portrait covers eleven of his eighteen big league seasons.

Honig, Donald. *The Philadelphia Phillies: An Illustrated History.* New York: Simon and Schuster, 1992. 256 pp.

The latest in Honig's growing series of potboiler coffee table team histories (following similar volumes on the Cubs, Cardinals and Reds), this is easily the best of the lot and the one most likely to appeal to fans of the particular ballclub treated. Not that this book escapes entirely from criticisms levied at the others—viz., the author's chatty narrative style, uninspired black and white photos consisting mainly of posed publicity head shots, absence of statistical appendices or the usual information-filled year-by-year timelines. Instead, the book holds its appeal as a more-than-adequate capsule history of one of our oldest and most ignored big league ballclubs. This value springs, of course, from the almost total absence of good Phillies team histories after Lieb and Baumgartner's 1953 Putnam volume. Honig, simply put, doesn't have much to compete with here, and his full volume club history thus fills a very large void in the existing baseball literature.

Kuklick, Bruce. *To Every Thing A Season: Shibe Park and Urban Philadelphia, 1909-1976.* Princeton, New Jersey: Princeton University Press, 1991. 237 pp.

Kuklick's blending of urban history with the story of one of the nation's most colorful lost big league ballparks results in the finest historical treatment ever provided on baseball's playing venues—either collectively or individually. Kuklick explores race relations, urban decay and renewal, class and ethnicity, and the modern-day commercialization of sport, persuading the reader of how each of these topics relates vitally to an understanding of Philadelphia's valued ballpark and its role as an important cultural and social institution. Shibe Park, after all, long bound generations of the city's residents to a rich cultural and emotional context known as big league baseball. And with the rise and fall of America's first steel and concrete ballpark (built in 1909 and demolished in 1976) the reader witnesses the function and passing of a particular kind of American urban community, one that has now largely vanished by century's end.

Lieb, Frederick G. and Stan Baumgartner. *The Philadelphia Phillies*. New York: G. P. Putnam's Sons, 1953. 246 pp.

Early history of the Phillies from 1883 through the 1952 season is detailed with this pioneering study, perhaps the most difficult Putnam title to locate in today's rare and used baseball book market. Better than half the book concentrates on the ballclub's first thirty-five seasons, but four final chapters relate details of the building and triumphs of Eddie Sawyer's storied 1950 Whiz Kids team. Baumgartner was himself a Phillies and Athletics pitcher (eight seasons in the teens and twenties) before becoming a popular Philadelphia sportswriter. Lieb is author of a half-dozen Putnam team histories and biographies and arguably the best baseball historian of the first half of the 20th century.

Lewis, Allen. *The Philadelphia Phillies: A Pictorial History*. Virginia Beach, Virginia: JCP Corporation, 1981. 176 pp.

This magnificently illustrated volume traces the history of the Philadelphia Phillies with the aid of rare pictures, as well as intelligent text drawn from the club's very first 19th-century years through the 1980 world championship season. The resulting handsome book is coffee table size, and its distinguished author is a member of the writer's wing of the Baseball Hall of Fame in Cooperstown.

Lewis, Allen and Larry Shenk. *This Date in Philadelphia Phillies History*. New York: Stein and Day Company, 1979. 295 pp.

A day-by-day listing of important events in Phillies history is the main thrust of this book, but it also contains numerous lists, box scores of significant games, statistics and club records, plus many other facts and figures about the National League ballclub. The coverage extends down through the 1978 season, and the format is identical to other "This Date in . . ." books which make up this series, itself covering nearly a dozen different professional baseball and football franchises.

Paxton, Harry. *The Whiz Kids*. New York: David McKay Publishers, 1950. 167 pp.

The Phillies' first pennant in thirty-five years is the subject of Paxton's short and largely uninspired spin-off volume. The story begins with the construction of the Whiz Kids by Bob Carpenter and Herb Pennock and progresses throughout the unfolding of the dramatic 1950 pennant chase. Profiles are offered on all regular players (Ashburn, Roberts, Konstanty, Jones, Hamner, Sisler, Simmons, etc.) and coaches, as well as on Whiz Kid manager Eddie Sawyer.

Richter, Ed. *View from the Dugout*. Philadelphia: Chilton Book Company, 1964. 149 pp.

In an insightful look at youthful manager Gene Mauch and his Philadelphia Phillies during the 1963 season, particular attention is paid here to Mauch's offbeat philosophies and his radical managerial techniques, as well as to his highly personal views on the game of baseball. This volume takes on special poignancy in view of the Phillies' 1964 stretch-drive collapse which immediately followed it's publication.

Segar, Charles (Editor). "Phillies" in: *75th Anniversary Official History of the National League*. New York: Jay Publishing Company, 1951, pp. 46–53.

Thumbnail histories of each of the eight NL ballclubs contain approximately a dozen pages of text interspersed with artful black and white action and portrait photos. The occasion for this volume was the 1951 75th anniversary of league play, and the Phillies chapter thus came flush on the heels of the surprising Whiz Kid pennant triumph. Due to the timing of the volume this is perhaps the one and only Phillies portrait that can legitimately end on a definite high note.

Sowell, Mike. *July 2, 1903—The Mysterious Death of Hall-of-Famer Big Ed Delahanty.* New York: Macmillan Publishing Company, 1992. 326 pp.

The date alone provides all necessary clues to the subject matter of this fascinating detective story which traces circumstances surrounding the mysterious and premature death of Hall-of-Fame slugger Ed Delahanty. Sowell weaves much of his tale around events concerning the ill-fated outfielder's final season with the Washington ballclub, yet much of the background of Delahanty's marvelous dozen campaigns in Philadelphia during the final decade-plus of the 19th century is recounted as well. This is by far the most comprehensive biography devoted to one of the greatest forgotten stars of ancient Phillies history.

Ward, Martha. *Star Southpaw.* New York: G. P. Putnam's Sons, 1975. 126 pp.

A juvenile-market sketch of future Hall-of-Fame hurler Steve Carlton, this brief biography opens with Carlton's childhood years and progresses through his early pitching career with both the St. Louis Cardinals and Philadelphia Phillies. Only two of Carlton's six 20-win seasons are included for treatment, however, along with one of his four Cy Young award summers.

Yeutter, Frank. *Jim Konstanty.* New York: A. S. Barnes and Company, 1951. 181 pp.

A spinoff of the Whiz Kid storybook pennant triumph, this well-written juvenile profiles the "one-season wonder" relief ace of the Philly ballclub. Focus is mostly upon Konstanty's single spectacular season of 1950, a year in which the Phillies' bullpen stopper became the first reliever ever to capture a league's MVP award. Some attention is also devoted to Konstanty's early career with Cincinnati and Boston, as well as his arrival in the Brotherly Love city only two brief summers before his phenomenal pennant-clinching season.

Year-by-Year Standings and Season Summaries

Year	Pos.	Record	Pct.	GB	Manager	Player	BA	Player	HR	Player	W-L	ERA
1883	8th	17–81	.193	46	R.Ferguson Purcell	E. Gross	.397	4 Tied with	1	Coleman	12–48	4.87
1884	6th	39–73	.348	45	Wright	Manning	.271	Manning	5	C. Ferguson	21–25	3.54
1885	3rd	56–54	.509	30	Wright	Mulvey	.269	Mulvey	6	C. Ferguson	26–20	2.22
1886	4th	71–43	.623	14	Wright	Fogarty	.293	Farrar	5	C. Ferguson	30–9	1.98
1887	2nd	75–48	.610	3.5	Wright	Andrews	.325	Wood	14	Casey	28–13	2.86
1888	3rd	69–61	.531	14.5	Wright	Clements	.245	Wood	6	Buffinton	28–17	1.91
1889	4th	63–64	.496	20.5	Wright	Thompson	.296	Thompson	20	Buffinton	27–17	3.24
1890	3rd	78–53	.591	9.5	Wright	Hamilton	.325	Clements	7	Gleason	38–17	2.63
1891	4th	68–69	.496	18.5	Wright	Hamilton	.340	Thompson	8	Gleason	24–22	3.51
1892	4th	87–66	.569	16.5	Wright	Hamilton	.330	Connor	12	Weyhing	32–21	2.66
1893	4th	72–57	.558	14	Wright	Hamilton	.380	Delahanty	19	Weyhing	23–16	4.74
1894	4th	71–56	.555	18	Irwin	Thompson	.404	Thompson	13	Taylor	23–13	4.08
1895	3rd	78–53	.595	9.5	Irwin	Delahanty	.399	Thompson	18	Taylor	26–14	4.49
1896	8th	62–68	.477	28.5	Nash	Delahanty	.397	Delahanty	13	Taylor	20–21	4.79
1897	10th	55–77	.417	38	Stallings	Delahanty	.377	Lajoie	10	Taylor	16–20	4.23
1898	6th	78–71	.523	24	Stallings Shettsline	Delahanty	.334	Flick	7	Piatt	24–14	3.18
1899	3rd	94–58	.618	9	Shettsline	Delahanty	.408	Delahanty	9	Donahue	21–8	3.39
1900	3rd	75–63	.543	8	Shettsline	Flick	.378	Flick	11	Fraser	16–10	3.14
1901	2nd	83–57	.593	7.5	Shettsline	Delahanty	.354	Delahanty	8	Donahue	22–13	2.60
						Flick		Flick	8			
1902	7th	56–81	.409	46	Shettsline	Barry	.287	Barry	2	White	16–20	2.53
1903	7th	49–86	.363	39.5	Zimmer	Thomas	.327	Keister	3	Duggleby	15–18	3.75
1904	8th	52–100	.342	53.5	Duffy	Titus	.294	Dooin	6	Fraser	14–24	3.25
1905	4th	83–69	.546	21.5	Duffy	Thomas	.317	Magee	5	Pittinger	23–14	3.10
1906	4th	71–82	.464	45.5	Duffy	Magee	.282	Magee	6	Sparks	19–16	2.16
1907	3rd	83–64	.565	21.5	Murray	Magee	.328	Magee	4	Sparks	21–8	2.00
1908	4th	83–71	.539	16	Murray	Bransfield	.304	Bransfield	3	McQuillan	23–17	1.53

Year	Pos.	Record	Pct.	GB	Manager	Player	BA	Player	HR	Player	W-L	ERA
1909	5th	74–79	.484	36.5	Murray	Bransfield	.291	Titus	3	Moore	18–12	2.10
1910	4th	78–75	.510	25.5	Dooin	Magee	.331	Magee	6	Moore	21–15	2.58
1911	4th	79–73	.520	19.5	Dooin	Luderus	.301	Luderus	16	Alexander	28–13	2.57
1912	5th	73–79	.480	30.5	Dooin	Paskert	.315	Cravath	11	Alexander	19–17	2.81
1913	2nd	88–63	.583	12.5	Dooin	Cravath	.341	Cravath	19	Seaton	27–12	2.60
1914	6th	74–80	.481	20.5	Dooin	Becker	.325	Cravath	19	Alexander	27–15	2.38
1915	1st	90–62	.592	+7	Moran	Luderus	.315	Cravath	24	Alexander	31–10	1.22
1916	2nd	91–62	.595	2.5	Moran	Cravath	.283	Cravath	11	Alexander	33–12	1.55
1917	2nd	87–65	.572	10	Moran	Cravath / Whitted	.280 / .280	Cravath	12	Alexander	30–13	1.86
1918	6th	55–68	.447	26	Moran	Luderus	.288	Cravath	9	Hogg	13–13	2.53
1919	8th	47–90	.343	47.5	Combs	Meusel	.305	Cravath	12	Meadows	8–10	2.47
1920	8th	62–91	.405	30.5	Cravath	Williams	.325	Williams	15	Meadows	16–14	2.84
1921	8th	51–103	.331	43.5	Donovan / Wilhelm	Williams	.320	Williams	18	Meadows	11–16	4.31
1922	7th	57–96	.373	35.5	Wilhelm	Walker	.337	Williams	26	Meadows	12–18	4.03
1923	8th	50–104	.325	45.5	Fletcher	Henline	.324	Williams	41	Ring	18–16	3.76
1924	7th	55–96	.364	37	Fletcher	Williams	.328	Williams	24	Hubbell	10–9	4.83
1925	6th	68–85	.444	27	Fletcher	Harper	.349	Harper	18	Ring	14–16	4.37
1926	8th	58–93	.384	29.5	Fletcher	Williams	.345	Williams	18	Carlson	17–12	3.23
1927	8th	51–103	.331	43	McInnis	Leach / Wrightstone	.306	Williams	30	Ulrich	8–11	3.17
1928	8th	43–109	.283	51	Shotton	Leach	.304	Hurst	19	Benge	8–18	4.55
1929	5th	71–82	.464	27.5	Shotton	O'Doul	.398	Klein	43	Willoughby	15–14	4.99
1930	8th	52–102	.338	40	Shotton	Klein	.386	Klein	40	Collins	16–11	4.78
1931	6th	66–88	.429	35	Shotton	Klein	.337	Klein	31	J. Elliott	19–14	4.27
1932	4th	78–76	.506	12	Shotton	Klein	.348	Klein	38	Collins	14–12	5.27
1933	7th	60–92	.395	31	Shotton	Klein	.368	Klein	28	Holley	13–15	3.53
1934	7th	56–93	.376	37	Wilson	Moore	.343	Camilli	12	Davis	19–17	2.95
1935	7th	64–89	.418	35.5	Wilson	Moore	.323	Camilli	25	Davis	16–14	3.66

Year	Pos.	Record	Pct.	GB	Manager	Player	BA	Player	HR	Player	W-L	ERA
1936	8th	54–100	.351	38	Wilson	Moore	.328	Camilli	28	Passeau	11–15	3.48
1937	7th	61–92	.399	34.5	Wilson	Whitney	.341	Camilli	27	Walters	14–15	4.75
1938	8th	45–105	.300	43	Wilson Lobert	Weintraub	.311	Klein	8	Passeau	11–18	4.52
1939	8th	45–106	.298	50.5	Prothro	Arnovich	.324	Marty Mueller	9 9	Higbe	10–14	4.85
1940	8th	50–103	.327	50	Prothro	May	.293	Rizzo	20	Higbe	14–19	3.72
1941	8th	43–111	.279	57	Prothro	Etten	.311	Litwhiler	18	Podgajny	9–12	4.62
1942	8th	42–109	.278	62.5	Lobert	Litwhiler	.271	Litwhiler	9	Hughes	12–18	3.06
1943	7th	64–90	.416	41	Harris Fitzsimmons	Dahlgren	.287	Northey	16	Rowe	14–8	2.94
1944	8th	61–92	.399	43.5	Fitzsimmons	Northey	.288	Northey	22	Schanz	13–16	3.32
1945	8th	46–108	.299	52	Fitzsimmons Chapman	Wasdell	.300	DiMaggio	19	Karl	9–8	2.99
1946	5th	69–85	.448	28	Chapman	Ennis	.313	Ennis	17	Rowe	11–4	2.12
1947	T7th	62–92	.403	32	Chapman	Walker	.363	Seminick	13	Leonard	17–12	2.68
1948	6th	66–88	.429	25.5	Chapman Cooke Sawyer	Ashburn	.333	Ennis	30	Leonard	12–17	2.51
1949	3rd	81–73	.526	16	Sawyer	Ennis	.302	Ennis	25	Meyer	17–8	3.08
1950	1st	91–63	.591	+2	Sawyer	Ennis	.311	Ennis	31	Roberts	20–11	3.02
1951	5th	73–81	.474	23.5	Sawyer	Ashburn	.344	Jones	22	Roberts	21–15	3.03
1952	4th	87–67	.565	9.5	Sawyer O'Neill	Burgess	.296	Ennis	20	Roberts	28–7	2.59
1953	T3rd	83–71	.539	22	O'Neill	Ashburn	.330	Ennis	29	Roberts	23–16	2.75
1954	4th	75–79	.487	22	O'Neill Moore	Burgess	.368	Ennis	25	Roberts	23–15	2.97
1955	4th	77–77	.500	21.5	Smith	Ashburn	.338	Ennis	29	Roberts	23–14	3.28
1956	5th	71–83	.461	22	Smith	Ashburn	.303	Lopata	32	Roberts	19–18	4.45
1957	5th	77–77	.500	18	Smith	Ashburn	.297	Repulski	20	Sanford	19–8	3.08

Year	Pos.	Record	Pct.	GB	Manager	Player	BA	Player	HR	Player	W-L	ERA
1958	8th	69–85	.448	23	Smith / Sawyer	Ashburn	.350	Anderson	23	Roberts	17–14	3.24
1959	8th	64–90	.416	23	Sawyer	Bouchee	.285	Freese	23	Conley	12–7	3.00
1960	8th	59–95	.383	36	Sawyer / Cohen / Mauch	Taylor	.287	Herrera	17	Roberts	12–16	4.02
1961	8th	47–107	.305	46	Mauch	Gonzalez	.277	Demeter	20	Mahaffey	11–19	4.10
1962	7th	81–80	.503	20	Mauch	Demeter	.307	Demeter	29	Mahaffey	19–14	3.94
1963	4th	87–75	.537	12	Mauch	Gonzalez	.306	Callison	26	Culp	14–11	2.97
1964	T2nd	92–70	.568	1	Mauch	Allen	.318	Callison	31	Bunning	19–8	2.63
1965	6th	85–76	.528	11.5	Mauch	Rojas	.303	Callison	32	Bunning	19–9	2.60
1966	4th	87–75	.537	8	Mauch	Allen	.317	Allen	40	Short	20–10	3.54
1967	5th	82–80	.506	19.5	Mauch	Gonzalez	.339	Allen	23	Bunning	17–15	2.29
1968	T7th	76–86	.469	21	Mauch / Myatt / Skinner	Gonzalez	.264	Allen	33	Short	19–13	2.94
1969	5th	63–99	.389	37	Skinner / Myatt	Allen	.288	Allen	32	Wise	15–13	3.23
1970	5th	73–88	.453	15.5	Lucchesi	Taylor	.301	Johnson	27	Wise	13–14	4.17
1971	6th	67–95	.414	30	Lucchesi	McCarver	.278	Johnson	34	Wise	17–14	2.88
1972	6th	59–97	.378	37.5	Lucchesi / Owens	Luzinski	.281	Luzinski	18	Carlton	27–10	1.97
1973	6th	71–91	.438	11.5	Ozark	Unser	.289	Luzinski	29	Twichell	13–9	2.50
1974	3rd	80–82	.494	8	Ozark	Montanez	.304	Schmidt	36	Lonborg	17–13	3.21
1975	2nd	86–76	.531	6.5	Ozark	Johnstone	.329	Schmidt	38	Carlton	15–14	3.56
1976	1st	101–61	.623	+9	Ozark	Maddox	.330	Schmidt	38	Carlton	20–7	3.13
1977	1st	101–61	.623	+5	Ozark	McBride	.316	Luzinski	39	Carlton	23–10	2.64
1978	1st	90–72	.556	+1.5	Ozark	Bowa	.294	Luzinski	35	Carlton	16–13	2.84
1979	4th	84–78	.519	14	Ozark / Green	Rose	.331	Schmidt	45	Carlton	18–11	3.62
1980	1st	91–71	.562	+1	Green	McBride	.309	Schmidt	48	Carlton	24–9	2.34

Year	Pos.	Record	Pct.	GB	Manager	Player	BA	Player	HR	Player	W-L	ERA
1981	1st	34–21	.618	+1.5	Green	Rose	.325	Schmidt	31	Carlton	13–4	2.42
	3rd	25–27	.481	4.5								
1981*	3rd	59–48	.551	2.5								
1982	2nd	89–73	.549	3	Corrales	Diaz	.288	Schmidt	35	Carlton	23–11	3.10
1983	1st	90–72	.556	+6	Corrales/Owens	Lefebvre	.310	Schmidt	40	Denny	19–6	2.37
1984	4th	81–81	.500	15.5	Owens	Hayes	.292	Schmidt	36	Carlton	13–7	3.58
1985	5th	75–87	.463	26	Felske	Schmidt	.277	Schmidt	33	K. Gross	15–13	3.41
1986	2nd	86–75	.534	21.5	Felske	Hayes	.305	Schmidt	37	Rawley	11–7	3.54
1987	4th	80–82	.494	15	Felske/Elia	Thompson	.302	Schmidt	35	Rawley	17–11	4.39
1988	6th	65–96	.404	35.5	Elia/Vykovich	Thompson	.288	James	19	K. Gross	12–14	3.69
1989	6th	67–95	.414	26	Leyva	Kruk	.300	V. Hayes	26	Parrett	12–6	2.98
1990	4th(T)	77–85	.475	18	Leyva	Dykstra	.325	V. Hayes	17	Combs	10–10	4.07
1991	3rd	78–84	.481	20	Leyva/Fregosi	Kruk	.294	Kruk	21	Mulholland	16–13	3.61
1992	6th	70–92	.432	26	Fregosi	Kruk	.323	Daulton	27	Schilling	14–11	2.35
								Hollins	27			

*Split Season Totals (Players' Union Strike).

All-Time Phillies Career and Season Records

Career Batting Leaders

Games Played	Mike Schmidt	2,404
At Bats	Mike Schmidt	8,352
Runs Scored	Mike Schmidt	1,506
Hits	Mike Schmidt	2,234
Batting Average	Billy Hamilton	.362
Home Runs	Mike Schmidt	548
Runs Batted In	Mike Schmidt	1,595
Singles	Richie Ashburn	1,811
Doubles	Ed Delahanty	432
Triples	Ed Delahanty	151
Slugging Percentage	Chuck Klein	.546
Extra Base Hits	Mike Schmidt	1,015
Total Bases	Mike Schmidt	4,404
Stolen Bases	Billy Hamilton	508
Pinch Hits	Greg Gross	117
Strikeouts	Mike Schmidt	1,883
Walks	Mike Schmidt	1,507
Grand Slam Home Runs	Mike Schmidt	7

Career Pitching Leaders

Innings Pitched	Robin Roberts	3,740
Wins	Steve Carlton	241
Losses	Robin Roberts	191
Winning Percentage	Grover Alexander	.676
Strikeouts	Steve Carlton	3,031
Walks	Steve Carlton	1,252
Games	Robin Roberts	529
Shutouts	Grover Alexander	61
Saves	Steve Bedrosian	103
Games Started	Steve Carlton	499
Complete Games	Robin Roberts	372

Single-Season Batting Records

Batting Average	Ed Delahanty	.408	1899
Home Runs	Mike Schmidt	48	1980
Home Runs (lefthanded)	Chuck Klein	43	1929
At Bats	Juan Samuel	701	1984
Runs Batted In	Chuck Klein	170	1930
Runs Scored	Billy Hamilton	196	1894
Hits	Lefty O'Doul	254	1929
Singles	Lefty O'Doul	181	1929
	Richie Ashburn	181	1951
Doubles	Chuck Klein	59	1930
Triples	Sam Thompson	27	1894
Slugging Percentage	Chuck Klein	.687	1930
Extra Base Hits	Chuck Klein	107	1930
Sacrifices	Kid Gleason	43	1905
Stolen Bases	Billy Hamilton	115	1891
Pinch Hits	Doc Miller	20	1913
Strikeouts	Mike Schmidt	180	1975

All-Time Phillies Career and Season Records *(continued)*

Total Bases	Chuck Klein	445	1930
Walks	Mike Schmidt	128	1983
Hitting Streak	Billy Hamilton	36	1894
Grand Slam Home Runs	Vince DiMaggio	4	1945
On-Base Percentage	Billy Hamilton	.523	1884
Hit by Pitch	Phil Bradley	16	1988
Single-Season Pitching Records			
Earned Run Average	Grover Alexander	1.22	1915
Wins	Kid Gleason	38	1890
Losses	John Coleman	48	1883
Winning Percentage	Robin Roberts	.800	1952
Strikeouts	Steve Carlton	310	1972
Walks	Tom Vickery	184	1890
Saves	Steve Bedrosian	40	1987
Games	Kent Tekulve	90	1987
Complete Games	John Coleman	59	1883
Games Started	John Coleman	61	1883
Shutouts	Grover Alexander	16	1916
Innings Pitched	John Coleman	538	1883
Home Runs Allowed	Robin Roberts	46	1956
Consecutive Games Lost	John Coleman	12	1883
	Russ Miller	12	1928
	Hugh Mulcahy	12	1940
	Ken Reynolds	12	1972
Consecutive Games Won	Steve Carlton	15	1972
Wild Pitches	Jack Hamilton	22	1962
Hit Batters	Fred Mitchell	19	1903
	Jim Bunning	19	1966
Balks	Steve Carlton	11	1979

10
Pittsburgh Pirates
The Art of the Comeback
PAUL D. ADOMITES

As Spring Training 1985 was about to begin, Pirate General Manager Harding "Pete" Peterson said, "This is the most important year in Pirate history."

People who liked baseball in Pittsburgh in 1985 must have wondered what spell had been cast on them, what deal they had made with what devil, to have to suffer through such a dreadful year—arguably one of the worst *any* fans have *ever* had to deal with.

It wasn't just that their team was terrible (they would finish last for the second straight year and easily lose 104 games); Pirate fans had lived through lean years of bad baseball before. It wasn't just the *way* they were terrible; this was no crowd of lovable losers (with the exception of the always-hustling Tony Peña and the heroic Rick Reuschel). These guys were awful, yet acted as though they deserved Hall-of-Fame voting for staying awake in the outfield. The team featured George Hendrick, for whom "moody" and "sullen" are too charitable, Jason Thompson, in a three-year slump, the onset of which coincided with the signing of a multi-million dollar contract, and newest acquisition Steve Kemp who, having told no one about his recent shoulder surgery, was all but useless.

Holding the rank of team captain was Bill Madlock, whose secret to winning three batting titles seemed to be "keep playing time to a minimum"—only twice did he squeak within 20 hits of 200 in a season. It was almost a guarantee that Madlock would spend much of every September riding the bench with one injury or another. This is the same Madlock who, instead of showing the leadership his "title" indicated, was quick to resign his captaincy when things got hairy, and a week later would announce, "I'm sick of watching us play." This is also the same Madlock who ballooned to 230 pounds (on a less-than-six-foot-frame) and offered this excuse: "They didn't encourage us to take care of ourselves, so I just let myself go." Some leader!

"Managing" this bunch was the eternally optimistic Chuck Tanner, who announced to the world that "You just can't tell when a guy is using cocaine," thereby defining his own ignorance. On July 31 of

1985, with his team 44 games below .500, Mr. Tanner was heard to say, "The Pirates haven't quit." (A month later they completed a 19-game losing streak.) This was the same Chuck Tanner who, as the team crumbled around him, announced to the new owners he felt he deserved the job of general manager. When the team was sold, he minced no words with new owners: "I want more control or I'm gone." The decision to let him go didn't take hours. He went to Atlanta to manage there. Upon accepting the post, he showed his keen insight into baseball and people once more, stating "Atlanta is not a fifth-place team, and I intend to change that quickly." Under Chuck's staunch leadership, they finished sixth.

Professional incompetence wasn't the only source of Pirate woe that year. Personal tragedy was there as well. The infant son of star pitcher and star grumbler John Candelaria fell into the family swimming pool in Florida on Christmas Eve. The child never regained consciousness, and died November 15. A seventeen-year-old stadium cleanup employee walking across the bridge to downtown Pittsburgh after work the night of May 20 was attacked and fatally stabbed—for thirty cents.

Even worse, Pirate owners, the Galbreath family, had put the team up for sale November of 1984. But no one was buying. More than a dozen groups were interested, but most were from out of town (Washington, D.C., Indianapolis, Donald Trump). Despite Dan Galbreath's strident claim ("I can sell the Pirates to anyone I want"), he was far from free to unload the team. Three years earlier, to cut himself a better deal and free more money for player salaries, he had renegotiated the lease on Three Rivers Stadium (and sold 48 percent of the team to pay off old bills), and after more than a year of negotiations, obtained a new lease through 2010—a lease that was absolutely ironclad. It included what one lawyer called a "Hell or high water" clause.

So anyone who wanted the Pirates would have to keep them in Pittsburgh. And that was definitely a losing proposition. While the Pirates had value, they had little value if they stayed home. There was much talk that Pittsburgh was really a football town, that Pittsburghers just wouldn't watch baseball ("Too slow" . . . ."Too many blacks" . . ."A lousy organist" were some of the inane reasons people gave when asked). Yet no one from the city had the energy or money to offer the Galbreaths their asking price.

This was a city that won the World Championship in 1979, but finished 10th in the league in attendance. They repeated at 10th in 1981 and 1983, and were dead last in bodies in the seats in 1982 and 1984. So it's not surprising only seven people signed up for the Pirate fantasy camp. A local sportswriter promoted a "Ballot by Ballpark" day for June 30. His message: This team isn't worth watching. But it's important that we let the world know we can still support baseball in this town. Or we may have none at all. The result? An ambivalent 31,384 people showed up.

By the middle of May the list of potential buyers had shrunk to three. The Galbreaths' desperation was evident. The team had lost over $6 million in 1984. Losses for 1985 were expected to exceed that.

Desperation was showing elsewhere too. To boost sagging ratings, the Pirate broadcast group resurrected a legend. Bob Prince, the Voice of the Pirates for nearly 30 years and one of the most colorful (and beloved) figures in the city's sports history, was hired from a sickbed to return to the broadcast booth. Prince had been fired 10 years earlier in a territorial squabble with executives of Westinghouse Electric Corporation (parent company of KDKA, Pirate flagship broadcasting station).

And despite a ravaged voice and frail constitution, what a comeback "the Gunner" made: the first inning he broadcast was for a game against the Dodgers. The usually surehanded men from Los Angeles went haywire and handed the Bucs nine runs. In the next inning Jason Thompson headed to the plate, and "the Gunner" said, "Jason, old boy, put one out of here now and we'll have a little of everything." Thompson promptly skied a homer into the right-field seats, which prompted Prince to say to his booth partner, "If this keeps up, you can carry me out of here on my shield." But that would be the last inning Prince ever did for the Pirates. Five weeks later he was dead.

There were other attempts to harken back to a brighter past. Willie Stargell was hired as first-base coach, but, more portly than ever, all he did was block the view of the fans down the right-field line when he took his first base coaching station. The Pirates signed Roberto Clemente Junior on February 22. He looked like his father, but that was all. After hitting .186 in the minors, he was released in September. To add irony to injury, it was the silver anniversary of the greatest year in Pirate history: the 1960 team's implausible World Series upset of the legendary Yankees.

Sale or no sale, it was clear that even the lame duck owners had had enough of General Manager Pete Peterson. He was fired, replaced by the man he had replaced (another historical allusion)—Joe L. Brown. Brown was to serve on an interim basis till the team could be sold and a new GM found. Brown knew he could help his bosses by getting rid of some of the deadest of the dead wood. So before the season was out, complaining Candelaria, grim Hendrick, buck-passing Madlock, and chunky Al Holland were all history.

While all this was going on, there was also "The Drug Investigation." In a city where baseball was flat on its back, with a rotten team for sale to no one, seven local men were under grand jury investigation for cocaine sales. While none of these characters was big-time in any sense of the word, some of their best customers had been baseball players. Three or four of them had been Pirates.

For weeks during Spring Training there had been a daily parade to the Pittsburgh federal courthouse of ballplayers: Keith Hernandez, Dave Parker, Enos Cabell, Jeffrey Leonard, Lee Mazzilli, Dale Berra, Rod Scurry, Tim Raines, Al Holland, Lonnie Smith. Sportswriter Bruce Keidan quipped, "There is no truth to the rumor that Dale Berra was placed in a witness protection program, disguised as a major league shortstop and started at Three Rivers Stadium to keep him away from crowds."

Having been traded for Kemp, Dale Berra wasn't around by the time the 1985 season happened. Yet he was quick to criticize the "rotten morale" he saw as a Pirate (his drug use had nothing to do with it, of course), and he didn't change his style. In May he was arrested in Kansas City for indecent exposure; in August he was the second of two Yankees thrown out at home on the same play: the White Sox' Carlton Fisk tagged one, then waited a second or two for Dale to enter his range before putting the tag on him as well. Dale Berra didn't play much after that.

Pittsburgh, recently selected "Most Livable City in America" by a national publisher, was becoming a national baseball joke. In fact, a billboard on a major Pittsburgh highway was altered to highlight the fact. The copy read "The #1 City Has the #1 Drug Store," but the real name of the drugstore was painted out, replaced by "The Pirate Clubhouse." A local paper ran a "Sports Drug Roundup" feature. Familiar jokes about "The Pits" and "City of Chumps" were being resurrected. At the same time the baseball Players Union decided it was time for a brief strike.

Even the Pirates' advertising agency wasn't immune. In reference to that year's theme line, one wag noted, "The Bucs *are* 'Bringing it Back' . . . they're resurrecting memories of 1952."

1952—Not Just Losers, Laughingstock

Although the torment was more intense in 1985, 1952 was also a year of legendary suffering. All the Pirates did that year was lose more games in one season than any other team since 1916. And unlike their counterparts of the 1980s, the 1952 Buccos weren't fat cats, drug takers, umpire baiters, or a bad bunch of boys. They were churchgoers. They were amiable. They just couldn't seem to get the hang of this baseball thing.

The 1952 season was not an isolated incident.The Pirates began a string of mediocrity in 1934, and for the next 12 years, they were able to squeeze out only two second-place finishes and one third-place finish. The rest: two fifths, one sixth, and six fourths. Not bad, but far from good. Then they went downhill fast.

In 1946 the Pirates began the dramatic tailspin that hung on for decades. They finished last or next to last 10 of the ensuing 12 years. They *earned* their place in infamy. In fact, if you rule out the glorious three-year swing of 1958–1960, the mini-era crowned by the seemingly divinely inspired upset of the dreaded Yankees in the World Series, the Pirates managed to finish in the first division of the National League only twice between 1946 and 1965.

Opening Day 1946 featured the unveiling of a young slugger from New Mexico named Ralph Kiner. Kiner quickly captured the interest of the fans of Pittsburgh. He hit the ball far. Even in Forbes Field, where a righthanded hitter like Ralph had to bang the ball 365 feet just to get it to the left-field corner, the 23-year-old smacked 23 homers and led the National League.

Fans took to Kiner. That prompted a crop of new owners, led by Columbus, Ohio, real estate financier John Galbreath (and aided by crooner Bing Crosby), to buy the team in August from Bill Benswanger, son-in-law of its first twentieth-century owner, Barney Dreyfuss. The Bucs finished seventh. The following year the new owners bribed former Detroit slugging star Hank Greenberg to join the team. They paid the Tigers $50,000 for his contract (which was remarkable, since he had already announced his intended retirement, and gave him $80,000 to play one season (a hard salary to turn down).

Then they changed the park to help him out. A bullpen was installed in left field, which shortened the home run distances—down the line by 30 feet and to the power alley in left center by 51 feet.

The concept, as they say, flew. Greenberg slugged 25 homers (nine into the new bullpen), Kiner hit 51 (13 into the new space), second most ever by a National Leaguer. Johnny Mize of the Giants tied him for the league lead. Attendance leaped from 749,000 to 1,283,000. The Pirates had a hit show; people loved coming to see Kiner's home runs. It didn't seem to matter that the team all around him was miserable.

Kiner's team topped a million in attendance in 1947, 1948, 1949, and 1950, with a team that finished last, fourth, sixth, and again last. Greenberg lasted just one year, but his presence set a style. General Manager Roy Hamey stocked the club with retreads like Kirby Higbe, Roger Wolff, Dixie Walker, Harry Gumbert, and Hank Borowy.

The Pirates thought they had the solution in 1950, when they back-room maneuvered the biggest signing bonus ever paid to anyone: $100,000 to a lefty pitcher from Lomita, California—Paul Pettit. Most major league teams wanted Pettit, but rules forbade signing anyone who hadn't graduated from high school. So the Pirates danced around the rule: they had a talent scout sign him to a movie and television contract for $85,000 six months before graduation. Then when the diplomas were handed out the Bucs brought his contract from the scout and tossed in $15,000 to sweeten the deal. N.L. owners were outraged, but without reason. Pettit never even hinted at his promise, and he was out of the bigs after just 31 innings.

The owners looked for a Moses to lead them from the wilderness. They thought they found him in Branch Rickey—a legendary baseball personage, the architect of greatness with the Dodgers and Cardinals, the man whose very mode of speech echoed forthrightness and a hundred more all-American virtues, a preacher, and a teacher. Rickey was the "Mahatma," an acknowledged baseball genius with half a century of experience in the game.

Rickey took charge in November of 1950, and made a mark on the team the first day of Spring Training in 1951. He held a team meeting and lectured the young Bucs on attitude and behavior. His speech was entitled "Why Last Place?" and in it he announced a strict 11:30 curfew and the banning of alcohol consumption *anywhere*. Not in the clubhouse, not on the trains, not even a glass of wine with dinner.

Then he started innovating. He moved Ralph Kiner to first and decided first baseman Dale Long (though a lefty) should become a catcher. He introduced "the cradle," a device made of wooden slats which he had seen in cricket practices, for learning how to react to ground balls. He told manager Meyer to wear civilian clothes in the dugout (a la Burt Shotton), and gave a perfectly Rickey reason: it would "lengthen his career." He set up a replica of Dodgertown at the Pirates Deland, Florida, minor league facility. He lectured the team on morality: "A happily married player is a good player. Single men are matrimonial cowards." Because he believed catcher Ed Fitzgerald was lacking aggressiveness, the Bible-quoting Rickey surprisingly offered him $100 each time he punched an opponent. It was no wonder that within three weeks Pittsburgh cartoonists and columnists were openly making fun of Rickey. One writer accused him of doubletalk; another wondered why he hadn't tried a lefthanded shortstop, as final proof the game had been taken over by "Barnum and Bailey."

Rickey's first team was six games better than the last, and out of last place, but the fans weren't intrigued. Attendance fell below one million. However, Rickey was just getting started. The 1952 team was both his crowning glory and his eventual downfall.

The 1952 season was called "The Year of the Youth Movement." It started a lifelong career for Joe Garagiola, telling stories about how bad the team was. Rickey announced a "Five Year Plan" and signed 435 prospects. The approach made sense. Yet somehow it didn't look right. On Opening Day, for example, the Pirates started a six-foot-six third baseman, Dick Hall (who later became a decent pitcher) and a five-foot-two shortstop, Clem Koshorek. They made road trips with only 18 players. And it was the first time in 20 years that the paternal figure of Honus Wagner was no longer with the team as a coach.

The Youth Movement split their first four games, then didn't win again for a long time. After 13 games they had been outscored 90–38. In game 14 George Metkovich broke out of an 8 for 42, no homer slump with three homers against the Braves to land victory number three. When the team dropped game 15 to Jim Hearn of the Giants 13–5, the local headline announced "Back in Stride!"

The punchless Bucs scored but one run (total) in their 18th, 19th, and 20th games of the season. When they won their fourth game (the season's 21st) on five Phillie errors and began a road trip, the papers noted: "Road tour is welcomed by Bucs. 3–13 at home." A late May fistfight between Pirate coach Bill Posedel and Reds catcher Andy Seminick was called "the most excitement at Forbes Field this season." When it was sour, it was sour. In a "Ronnie Kline Night" honoring the young pitcher, the Bucs blasted out to a 6–0 lead off Warren Spahn. But Ronnie couldn't hold on, and was knocked out in the fifth, unable to snare the win.

By June 21 the Dodgers had whipped the Bucs 10 straight times. By June 23 Bob Friend was the first major league pitcher to have 10 losses under his belt. On the Fourth of July, the Pirates swept the Reds in a double header. The two wins were the team's 20th and 21st of the year.

As resoundingly awful as this team was, Rickey's plan was actually taking hold. By 1951 both Bob Friend and Vernon Law were pitching mainstays. Rickey selected tiny Roy Face from the Brooklyn draft list in 1953. He did the same the following year, "pirating" Roberto Clemente from the Dodger organization.

But the signing that had the greatest impact on the team was that of local boy Dick Groat, whom Rickey signed in June of 1952, the day after his graduation from Duke University.

A mature 22, a basketball All-American, Groat didn't need minor league seasoning. He made his major league debut as a pinch hitter two days after he signed. In his second game his first major league hit drove in the team's first two runs in an 8–1 victory. He spent 1953 and 1954 in the service, but from 1955 through 1962 he *was* the Pirates. A quiet, prematurely balding young man who typified the work ethic mentality of his home town, he made himself into a solid hitter—swatting over .300 three times as a Pirate. As a team player he was unsurpassed, an absolute artist on the hit-and-run, a deft shortstop.

However, by the time the dust settled, the Pirates had lost 112 times. The only team they beat eight times (out of 22) was the Cubs. The Dodgers toppled them 19 times.

Rickey sensed the need for a major deal. Not just a prospect-for-prospect swap, but a mega-deal, a headline-making deal. He did it on June 3, 1953. Less than an hour before the Pirates were to play the Cubs, Ralph Kiner, the only man to have led or tied for the lead in homers his first seven big-league seasons, was swapped to the opposing clubhouse. Along with Metkovich, Garagiola, and pitcher Howie Pollet, Kiner brought the Pirates Preston Ward, Toby Atwell, Gene Hermanski, Bob Addis, and Bob Schultz.

Pittsburgh was stunned. Yet for all the noise it caused at the time, the deal had precious little impact on the history of either team. Neither club improved because of it. Kiner was out of baseball two years later.

Yet a few years later, after Rickey was gone, another trade of a well-liked young slugger *did* turn the tide for the Pirates. In fact, it gave them a World Championship.

1960—The Magic

The Pirate team Rickey had built around Skinner, Virdon, Clemente, Groat, Mazeroski, Friend, Law, and Face was a talented group. A second-place finish in 1958 had the town's hopes up and the team's attendance back over the million mark for the first time since 1950. But a few pieces were still missing. On January 15, 1959, Manager Danny Murtaugh made this request at a Pittsburgh sports banquet: "Give me a winning lefthanded starter and some offensive power behind the plate." Sixteen days later he had his wish.

GM Joe L. Brown swapped longtime power hitter Frank Thomas. Another Pittsburgh native, the quiet slugger of Polish extraction had been trade bait for years. When the deal finally happened, Thomas was joined by pitchers Ron Blackburn and (great name) Whammy Douglas, and outfielders Johnny Powers and Jim Pendleton, in going to the Reds for Smokey Burgess (offensive-minded catcher), Harvey Haddix (lefthanded starter and winner), and Don Hoak (third-base fireball). Thomas went on to become a trivia question—Who was the only player to appear in the last game the Giants played in the Polo Grounds and the first game the Mets played there? Meanwhile, Haddix, Hoak, and Burgess helped the Bucs become World Champs.

An overweight Mazeroski and Friend slowed the team down to fourth in 1959. Brown wouldn't stand pat. In December he traded Dick Hall to the Kansas City Athletics for catcher Hal Smith. In May he sent minor league second baseman Julian Javier (whose career path looked dim behind Mazeroski) to the Cardinals for veteran lefty Wilmer "Vinegar Bend" Mizell. All the pieces were now in place. The Pirates came scampering home.

It was the greatest season in Pittsburgh baseball history. The 1960 Pirates were a team for which everything clicked. They got spectacular defense from the infield of Hoak, Groat, and Bill Mazeroski. Outfielders Clemente and Virdon both had great range and Roberto's arm may have been the best in baseball history.

The pitching staff was durable if unspectacular. Law won 20 games and the Cy Young Award. Friend was among the league leaders with a 3.00 ERA and a sturdy 276 innings pitched. Mizell added 13 wins in a Pirate uniform. Haddix captured 11 more. Although Face wasn't able to match his 17 consecutive victories of 1959, he still tucked 10 wins and 24 saves under his arm. Their team ERA was one-tenth of a run behind the league leader. The staff allowed no losing streak more than four games all year (each time it happened, Vern Law ended it).

The offense was seamless. Virdon and Groat formed an impressive hit-and-run combo, and Groat led the league with a .325 average. Dick Stuart and Rocky Nelson at first combined for 30 homers and 118 RBIs. Clemente drove in more than 90 runs and scored nearly as many. The catching tandem of Smith and Burgess had almost identical .295 averages. The team led the league in runs scored (only 12 fewer than the Yankees, by the way).

The personalities could have been sent in by central casting: Murtaugh the gruff Irish manager, a renowned tobacco spitter; Hoak, the blazing leader at third; Groat, the silent leader at short; Maz, the youthful defensive wizard at second. Dick Stuart had a swagger worthy of the title "Pirate," and Rocky Nelson was an antique curio with a cockeyed stance dusted off for one last show. Clemente was passion personified; excellence was all that mattered to him. Burgess was the roly-poly pure hitter ("Get him out of bed on Christmas morning and he'll go two-for-four").

Vern Law was ice; Bob Friend was smooth; Harvey Haddix was "The Kitten"; Roy Face was called into the game by Murtaugh holding his arm out waist-high—"the little guy." The nonstars came through as well. Pitchers Fred Green, Joe Gibbon, and Tom Cheney contributed. Outfielder "Attsa My Boy" Gino Cimoli provided some clutch hits and clubhouse tomfoolery.

But no sub did more than Dick Schofield. When a Lew Burdette pitch fractured Groat's wrist on September 6, unknown utility man Schofield (whose son has now surpassed him in major league glory) stepped in. It was one of the toughest clutch fill-in jobs in major league history. After all, the man he replaced would win both the batting title and the Most Valuable Player Award. "Ducky" hit .368 in 19 games, with four doubles, a triple, and seven RBIs.

Schofield's performance was indicative of a remarkable style of play evident on the whole team: steadfast refusal to fail. They showed it quickly. April 17 was Easter Sunday and the Pirates took the first game of a doubleheader from the Reds 5–0. Going into the last of the ninth in the second game, the Reds were holding onto a 5–0 lead themselves. But Hal Smith belted a three-run homer (he would do that again in October), and Bob Skinner cracked a two-run smash to drive in the tying and winning runs.

Power wasn't their only weapon. Another typical game happened in July: Losing to the Dodgers 2–1 in the 10th, the Bucs came back when Joe Christopher scored from second on Clemente's infield hit. Then, when Stuart popped a single into short right, Clemente scored the winning run *from first*. Amazingly, they won 23 games that season in their final at-bat. Bob Prince christened Forbes Field "The House of Thrills."

Danny Murtaugh's post-season analysis: "We won the pennant in Spring Training. What happened is everybody hit camp so full of pep and ginger you'd have thought it was opening day. I figured out how to save that spirit and base hits for the games that counted later on. I just cut the veterans' time in the batting cage in half. We had the world's greatest bunch of pouters. But when the season started it was like opening a cage and letting the lions out."

But in fan memory the 154 games the Pirates played that season against the National League can't compare with the seven they played against the American League in October—against the New York Yankees.

Even today just the name of that awesome array of superhuman sluggers instantly evokes a chill in the hearts of us oldtime fans. There was, quite bluntly, never anything like them in sports history. Their 1960 World Series appearance was their 26th since 1921. A Pirate fan who could remember the last time the Yanks had missed the Series *back-to-back years* was 16 years old. The Yankees *always* won, and almost always won the World Series, too. A novel by Douglas Wallop entitled *The Year the Yankees Lost the Pennant* was obviously to be categorized under "Fantasy."

And the scrapping Bucs delivered a World Series performance that ignited the nation and left them dancing in the streets in Pittsburgh.

The story has become familiar. The Yankees beat the Pirates soundly at first. Twice Whitey Ford turned their bats to mush, shutting them out while his team scored 10 and 12 runs, respectively. In another game the Yanks stampeded to a 16–3 trouncing. None less than Red Smith called it "A grisly parody of sport."

But in between the Yankee assault, the Pirates were putting together moments of their own. They scored three runs in the first inning of Game One and took a 6–4 win. Vern Law had a big hit in Game Four to drive in a key run and the Buccos prevailed, 3–2. Another three-run inning (the second) in Game Five was all they needed to win, 5–2.

Don Hoak reflected, "That sixth game loss [to Ford, 12–0] was the turning point for the team, emotionally. We had a short meeting and everybody agreed we already had a great year. We could get beat 15 to nothing tomorrow, but still would have had a great season. We were more relaxed for the seventh game than any time in the Series."

It came down to Game Seven. It would be, if not the greatest game in baseball history, at least the greatest Seventh Game. If not the strangest game ever in post-season play, certainly the weirdest game ever to determine a championship.

One thing was missing from the Series up to this point. The Yankees hadn't seen the legendary Pirate comeback capability. The Bucs had overcome single-run deficits twice in the Series—once in the first inning, once in the fifth. No big deal.

In the first inning of Game Seven, Skinner walked and Rocky Nelson cracked a 2–1 pitch over the right-field screen, giving the Bucs a 2–0 lead. The Forbes Field faithful were delirious. In the second inning Yogi Berra cracked a line drive over third base that Don Hoak dived for and knocked down; he then skidded on the ground, and stood up in plenty of time to nab Berra. According to sportswriter Bill Surface, Hoak's dive was even tougher than it looked—and it was called "impossible" in the newspapers. No one knew—and the intense competitor Hoak wasn't telling—that he was suffering from an agonizing inflammation of the prostate gland and a fever of 103 degrees.

A two-out single by Virdon netted two more Pirate runs in the second. Skowron's fifth-inning solo homer nudged the Yanks closer. They exploded in the sixth. A walk, two singles, and a towering Berra home to right on the first pitch put the men from New York out in front 5–4.

Roy Face's third inning of relief was the eighth, and he began it with a new catcher. A pinch runner in the seventh had taken Smokey Burgess out of the game. Hal Smith was now in. Maris and Mantle went down easily. But Berra walked, Skowron chopped a single to third, Blanchard singled, and Boyer doubled. The Yanks took a three-run lead into the bottom of the eighth.

But these were the comeback Pirates, the never-say-die "Battling Buccos." Cimoli batted for Face to lead off and lined a single to right. Virdon chopped at a pitch and bounced a double-play grounder toward Yank shortstop Kubek. Tony Kubek seemed confused. He stopped, started, backed up, then came forward. A wicked hop off the famous rock-hard Forbes Field infield caught him in the throat. Two on, none out, Kubek out of the game. Groat singled to drive in a run, and Bobby Shantz, who had thrown five scoreless innings of clutch relief, was removed for Jim Coates. Coates, never Shantz's equal as a fielder (no one was), was a likely target for a Skinner bunt. "Doggie" put it down successfully, and runners moved up to second and third. Virdon refused to challenge Maris's arm on Nelson's short fly to right. Two were out.

Roberto Clemente cracked a one-hopper behind first, and Skowron, guarding the lines, had him played perfectly. Unfortunately Coates didn't. Clemente outhustled the gangly Coates to the bag. Safe! The Pirates had come back—again—to within one run. Hal Smith, 30-year-old journeyman catcher, was up. Smith had two singles and no RBIs in seven previous Series plate appearances.

Coates pushed the count to 1–2. Former Yankee farmhand Smith barely checked his swing on the next pitch. Ball two. Hal timed the next Coates offering perfectly and sent it soaring over the left-center-field fence. The Pirates had come back from three runs down to take a two-run lead with one of the most clutch home runs in World Series history. The Pirates were three outs away from the Championship. But the Yanks weren't through.

Bob Friend was called in to close out the ninth. But the Yankees had shot large holes in Friend's hurling throughout the Series and this inning was no exception. Quick singles by Richardson and ex-Buc Dale Long knocked Friend from the game. Harvey Haddix, starter and winner of Game Five, replaced him.

Maris popped to Hal Smith, who was still probably bubbling inside. But Mantle rippled a single to right and the Yanks were within a run. And then Mantle surprised everyone.

He pulled a dazzling piece of clutch base running. On Berra's grounder, seeing that Nelson had touched first, removing the force at second, Mantle ducked around Rocky and dived back into first. The game was tied at 9. Mantle's remarkable heads-up hustle had turned a Series-ending double play into a game-tying run. The Yanks had pulled out some comeback magic of their own.

Bill Mazeroski led off the last of the ninth against Ralph Terry. The second pitch was not as high as the first, and Maz belted it to left center, just over the fence. With one swing, Bill Mazeroski had 1) completed one of the most remarkable comebacks in World Series history; 2) given Pittsburgh its first baseball champion in 35 years; 3) washed from memory the glorious poke of Hal Smith and Mantle's sensational backwards run; and 4) (sadly) assured that he (Mazeroski) would never receive his deserved spot in the Hall of Fame.

Because of that winning homer, most baseball fans dump Maz in the category of Al Weis or George Whiteman (World Series heroes who were mediocre ballplayers with limited careers). The truth is that Maz was nothing less than the greatest fielding second baseman in history, and holder of more fielding records than any other man alive.

The 1961 Pirates Yearbook opens with a two-page spread full of photographs of Pittsburghers literally dancing in the streets, celebrating this awesome baseball event. But that Pirate team was nowhere near a dynasty. Even though it had Hall of Famer Clemente, and deserving Hall of Famer Mazeroski, the rest of the club was made up of typical Pittsburgh players—hard-working, unspectacular. It took a lot of magic for it all to come together in such a grand year for a city so starved for winners.

What Happened Next

The failures that would bring the Pirates back into mediocrity were textbook examples of a team too in love with its moment of glory to see its shortcomings. Of course the Buccos added their own uniquely Pirate twists.

One was overweight. Every year teams that win championships have many of their players invited to banquets around the country, where cholesterol-heavy gravy dinners and late nights of alcohol and story-telling are the rule. Although this was more the case in earlier days, it still holds true today. Then, too, if *his* team had won it all, the delightful bonus of a World Series check meant a player wouldn't have to work; he could take it easy for the off-season. More banquets, no work worries—it was easy to add a few pounds of lard.

Although Danny Murtaugh allegedly whistled with delight when he was able to fit into his 1961 uniform without difficulty, the same wasn't true for his players. Another big loss for the team was Vernon Law, who had injured his ankle, the story goes, when Gino Cimoli tried to force some pennant champagne on the Mormon minister. Favoring his foot, Law next hurt his arm.

A plummet to sixth in 1961 was followed by a comeback of sorts to fourth in 1962. But by then another peculiar Pirate front-office trait revealed itself: The desire to trade for pitching, and the almost total inability to get any. Within two days in November that year Joe L. Brown swapped big-time slugger Dick Stuart for questionable Red Sox hurler Don Schwall, then sent longtime team mainstay Dick Groat to the Cardinals for the totally average Don Cardwell. Don Hoak was traded the following week as well.

The Groat trade was the one the Pirate fans couldn't understand. No one was more closely identified with the team. Groat had come on board during that disastrous 1952 season and was league MVP during the championship year. Everyone knew that Groat had hoped to become a Pirate coach and manager. After he expressed betrayal and bitterness, his consummate professionalism reappeared. He became a key man on the Cards World Champions of 1964. Even though he still lives in the Pittsburgh area, to this day Groat refuses any formal contact with the Pirates.

The Pirates responded to this influx of new pitching talent by finishing eighth in a 10-team league. Attendance was down 300,000. The coaching staff was cut to save money. Yet Brown and Murtaugh, World Series memories still fresh, could chirp: "We still have a good nucleus. There's no need for a big change."

Although no one said it at the time, in a very real sense the 1958–60 seasons and Branch Rickey had saved the Pirates for Pittsburgh. With their rotten record (since 1934) and their awful attendance, the Galbreath group could have been forgiven for selling out to one of the several cadres of New York investors who wanted to bring National League baseball back to the Big Apple. And when Rickey proposed his Continental League in the early 1960s, with a New York franchise as its center, the National League voted for expansion and people quit talking about a Pirate sale.

But just as Dick Groat, the basketball-playing shortstop, was the center of the Pirates championship team of 1960, another shortstop, who also played basketball, was the key member of the first Pirate dynasty.

1900—Dreyfuss Arrives

In the first eighteen years of professional baseball in Pittsburgh, the team was able to finish in the first division only twice— a second-place finish in the American Association in 1886 earned them a spot in the National League, where they were once again a doormat, though they managed to reach as high as second in 1893. Originally the Alleghenies, because they played in the city of Allegheny (now the North Side of Pittsburgh), they became the Pirates officially in 1892 when they assumed the nickname that had been hung on them pejoratively for signing Louis Bierbauer when he returned from the Players' League. Philadelphia thought they had owned Bierbauer.

Then Barney Dreyfuss arrived. Dreyfuss, a 125-pound German immigrant, had worked his way up from whiskey barrel cleaner for the Bernheim distillery in Louisville, Kentucky, to credit manager. The Louisville American Association team was connected to "whiskey money," and Dreyfuss brought some stock. Before long he used his shrewd business sense to become club treasurer, then owner. Dreyfuss was known for being his own scout, making notes when he heard of a good performance, then buying bargain-priced players to build a team.

But by the end of the last decade of the nineteenth century, the powers of the National League had decided to drop four of their 12 teams. Dreyfuss's Louisville nine was one of them. He pulled some strings to find out which current team was in trouble, and made a deal with the Pittsburgh club's owners. Dreyfuss would get half interest in the club if he would bring some of his better Louisville players with him.

Since the League had not yet officially dumped Louisville, the transfer of players was done as a trade, the biggest ever; $25,000 and five Pittsburghers for 14 Louisville players.

Among the players Dreyfuss brought from his Kentucky crew were second baseman Claude Ritchey, third sacker Tommy Leach, and pitchers "Deacon" Phillippe and Rube Waddell. Good players all.

But the key men were left-fielder and manager Fred Clarke, and a hulking, bowlegged first baseman/third baseman/outfielder, John Peter "Honus" Wagner.

Wagner was the best of a family of rugged athletes—five boys from a coal town a few miles south of Pittsburgh. The alternative to life in a coal mine was life on a ball field or in a gym, and the Wagner boys were always in one or another. Like Dick Groat, Honus enjoyed playing basketball. For 20 years he and his brothers toured the country in the off-season as professional cagers, a fact which nettled Dreyfuss, naturally.

It is unlikely that a scout today would notice Wagner; his body strayed too far from the standard athletic model. His arms seemed long enough for his knuckles to drag on the ground. His legs were too bowlegged, his shoulders too broad. Although his hands and feet were large, his fingers were thick. Yet this unlikely physical specimen became the greatest player of his time at the position demanding the most raw physical skill—shortstop. In fact, Honus Wagner is the only position player of his era who still holds his place on baseball's All-Time Team.

Although Dreyfuss's Louisville crew had never reached the first division, the combined organization was loaded. In addition to the hot shots from the South, the Bucs had quality pitchers in Jack Chesbro, Jesse Tannehill, and Sam Leever. Outfielder Ginger Beaumont, an original Pirate, could hit up a storm. As a rookie he had six singles and scored six runs in one game. Wagner began the 1900 season as the right fielder, and ended it as the third baseman. At the end of May the Buccos were in fourth, but by the end of June they had moved up to third. Streaks in August and September put them into second, where they finished the campaign.

In the next 14 years their worst finishes would be two descents to fourth. The Pirates were the first great team of the twentieth century. The 1901–'02–'03 teams were league champions every year. The 1902 crop was especially strong. Legendary sportswriter Grantland Rice later listed them as one of five best in history (along with Baltimore 1895, Cubs 1907, Philadelphia 1911, and Boston 1897) (granted many teams lost several players to the new American League [fair-dealing Dreyfuss kept most of his]). The 1902 Pittsburgh team still dominated their league more than any team has before or since. They won 103 times, and took the pennant by 27½ games. Fred Lieb said that "the ripsnortin' Pirates were [quickly] so far in front that the rest of the league couldn't even follow their foam."

Wagner led the circuit in runs, doubles, RBIs, slugging average, and stolen bases. He was second in total bases. Ginger Beaumont led all hitters with a .357 average, 24 points more than Sam Crawford. Ginger also led the league in hits. "Wee" Tommy Leach was the power guy, netting more triples and homers (6!) than anyone else in the league. Three pitchers had more than 20 wins, with Chesbro's 28 leading the pack.

But toward the end of the season Dreyfuss got word that catcher Jack O'Connor was acting as agent for the American League, and had solicited Chesbro, Davis, and Tannehill. Dreyfuss fired them all. In 1903 Chesbro, Tannehill, and O'Connor became members of the brand new New York Highlanders, who would grow into the well-known New York Yankees. In 1904 Chesbro would set the twentieth-century record for wins in a season.

Despite the loss of the 48 wins Tannehill and Chesbro had delivered, the 1903 team was still strong enough to capture the N.L. flag again. Then Barney Dreyfuss resurrected an old idea. The war between the N.L. and the upstart A.L. had cooled. Player contract disputes had been settled. So Dreyfuss challenged the owner of the Boston Pilgrims, winners of the American League title, to a series that would determine "World's Champions."

Back in the 1880s the National League champs frequently played the American Association winners in a post-game exhibition series, sometimes glorified into "World's Championship," sometimes not. But the format changed from year to year (one year they played more than 20 games from coast to coast) and no one had a handle on what a championship should truly be. When the AA closed its doors in 1892, so did the idea of a World Series.

The "First Modern World Series" was a grand success. Income topped $55,000, attendance was more than 100,000. But the Pirates' decimated pitching (Chesbro and Tannehill were gone, Leever had an injured shoulder, and Ed Doheny had a mental breakdown before the Series and would spend the rest of his life in an insane asylum) couldn't hold a 3–1 lead. The Boston team, led by excellent pitching from Cy Young and Bill Dineen, took the Series in eight games. Dreyfuss proved his generosity; he divvied *his* share of the monies among his team. Because Killilea didn't follow suit, the Pirates are the first, last, and only team that lost a World Series but made more than the winners.

The next five years the National League was ruled by John McGraw's Giants and Frank Chance's Cubs, with the Bucs in there scrapping. In 1909 Barney Dreyfuss built Forbes Field. Exposition Park, in old Allegheny, on the river, was frequently flooded. Outfielders were known to play in six inches of water; the whole field was damp all the time. People laughed at Dreyfuss when he chose a site for his new Park in the Schenley Farms, about three miles east of downtown. "It's out in the sticks," one said. Someone else pointed out, "There's nothing there but a livery stable, a hothouse and a few cows." But when Dreyfuss was done, he had given baseball its first concrete-and-steel ballpark (with an amazing seating capacity of 25,000, 5,000 more than any other), and had given the city a gem of architectural pleasure that Pittsburgh fans still wax eloquent about at a moment's urging.

The Pirates responded to their new ballpark by outdistancing the National League again, winning 110 games, which gave them a 6½-game lead over the Cubs, who won "only" 104. Clarke, Wagner, and Tommy Leach were the only starting holdovers from the 1903 pennant winners, and Leach had moved from third base to the outfield. Wagner had settled in at shortstop, winning his sixth batting title in the past seven years. His new keystone partner was "Dots" Miller, an able student of Honus's infield erudition. George Gibson was solid behind the plate, and the new pitching staff included Howie Camnitz and Vic Willis, both 20-game winners, and Lefty Leifield, who took 19 decisions. Even venerable Deacon Phillippe and Sam Leever each pitched in with eight.

But when the World Series began against the Detroit Tigers (playing in their third consecutive post-season classic), Manager Fred Clarke started the baby-faced (though 27 years old) Babe Adams. Behind his decision is an interesting anecdote that points out a fascinating difference between the game then and now. The animosity between the leagues had cooled as far as courts and legal challenges were concerned, but the fire still burned on the field. Before Game One, National League President John Heydler remarked to Clarke that he had seen the Senators' Dolly Gray stymie the potent Tigers in a regular-season game. Heydler felt that rookie Buc Babe Adams' delivery resembled Gray's. Given the scouting report from the president of the league, Clarke concurred. Babe Adams soon became the first man to win three games in a seven-game Series.

The 1909 Championship also featured the first Series skirmish between the two batting champions, Wagner and Ty Cobb, and the Pirates won that one, too. Cobb could produce only a .231 average and two stolen bases. Wagner hit .333 and pilfered six. Clarke belted two homers, Tommy Leach had four doubles among his nine hits. Both teams battled hard, winning alternate games; this was the first Series to go the distance, to come down to a one-game championship. Scrappy play, spikings, and unusual umpiring made this one of the most dramatic in the early history of the championship clashes. The Pirates celebrated their seven-game victory with a parade through downtown Pittsburgh, and were joined by 5,000 fans. When the Mayor tried to address the crowd, he was ignored—till he began banging on the podium with a baseball bat.

The following year the Pirates brought up a 20-year-old switch hitting outfielder born Maxmilian Carnarius, called familiarly Max Carey. Carey became the greatest base stealer in Pittsburgh history, with 49 more than Wagner and 270 more than the third-place finisher.

But the Pirate magic had dimmed. The following years they finished third, third, second, and fourth, yet were never closer than 10 games from the leaders. In 1912 "Chief" Owen Wilson, a powerful Indian, smacked 36 triples. No one in baseball history has been within 10 of Wilson's remarkable record. Wilson also belted 11 homers, to tie for third in the league. Yet the fans didn't seem interested. The 1912 season was called by the local press "probably the worst financially in Pittsburgh's baseball history." The gate fell off 138,000 to 346,231.

Then Dreyfuss was suckered in by another "big deal." After the 1913 season Wilson, popular second baseman Dots Miller, and three other Bucs were swapped to the St. Louis Cardinals for first baseman Ed Konetchy, third baseman Mike Mowrey, and pitcher Bob Harmon. The 1914 team started the season by capturing 15 of their first 17 games, then stumbled, and fell all the way to seventh place.

Konetchy and Mowrey left in a hurry, joining the exodus to the Federal League in 1915. A 41-year-old Wagner had a remarkable 1915 season, playing in all 156 of the team's games, hitting 32 doubles, 17 triples, and six homers. But the Bucs finished fifth, and Fred Clarke retired to his Kansas ranch, taking up mule raising and oil drilling. "After handling ballplayers for many years, handling mules should be easy," he observed. Clarke's retirement put the final period on the Bucs' first glory era.

Under Manager Jimmy Callahan they fell to sixth. Sixty games into the 1917 season, Honus Wagner was given a chance to pilot the club, but backed off after only five games—he didn't take to it. Former

Penn State football coach Hugo Bezdek was the manager for the last-place finish in 1917, and fourth places in 1918 and 1919. Erstwhile Buc catcher George Gibson could do no better than fourth his first season.

Despite the solid pitching of Wilbur Cooper (he would lead the staff in starts and wins every year from 1917 through 1922), the Bucs missed the presence of their superhero, Wagner, who had left the game after the 1917 season. Dreyfuss found the solution in one of the most aptly nicknamed players in major league history—"Rabbit" Maranville.

Maranville joined fellow fun-lovers with good nicknames, Charlie "Jolly Cholly" Grimm, "Possum" Whitted, and "Cotton" Tierney, to form a quartet that rapped National League pitching and could be counted on to hoist a few, strum their banjos, and harmonize a lively tune.

But their first year together struck a sour note for the Buccos. Up by 7½ games on August 24, they dropped five straight to McGraw's Giants in the Polo Grounds. The effect on the standings could have been overcome; the effect on morale couldn't. They finished four games back, and the quartet was blasted by Dreyfuss. John McGraw, always quick to gloat in victory, was heard to say, "You can't sing your way through this league."

But the Pirates had done more than just come close to a pennant. They were building their next solid team. In late 1920 they signed "Jughandle" Johnny Dewey Morrison, a lefty with a superior breaking ball, and the man who would define third base for years, Harold "Pie" Traynor.

When the 1921 doldrums slopped over into 1922, Manager Gibson was canned with the season one-third over and the Bucs flirting with the .500 mark. Replacing him was coach Bill McKechnie who had been a Federal League manager at the tender age of 28. McKechnie had earned a reputation of being as shrewd a repository of baseball knowledge as he was a devout elder of his church (his nickname, "Deacon," was not ironic).

Maranville and his crowd, including the wild Indian Chief Moses Yellowhorse, bedeviled the religious McKechnie at every turn. But the team was jelling—they pounded the juiced-up "Ruth" ball for a team .308 average and completed the season tied for third, eight games behind the men from the Polo Grounds. They won two more games in 1923 and three more than that in 1924, finishing third both years. In September of 1923 Hazen "Kiki" Cuyler made his debut with a splash.

And Dreyfuss had had enough of his "banjo players." In the off-season Grimm and Maranville (along with steady pitcher Cooper) were gone, sent to the Cubs for infielder George Grantham, pitcher Vic

Aldridge, and rookie first sacker Al Niehaus. Buc fans hated the deal; the banjo boys were great fun, Cooper was as steady as any pitcher the Bucs had in this century, and the credentials of the newcomers were suspect.

But the fans could not have been more wrong, because the Pirates soon finished first and the Cubs dead last—for the first time in the Chicagoans' 72-year history. The Pirates rolled over the league, slipping below first for a total of three days between June 29 and July 23 and never again thereafter. Resurrected from retirement to help with coaching duties, mule-handler Fred Clarke supplied the inspiration.

No one on the team had a bad year. Aldridge tallied 15 wins; Morrison, Ray Kremer, and Emil Yde each won 17; and Lee Meadows led the staff with 19 victories. The lowest hitting average among the regulars was .298; the team scored 84 more runs than the next-best team, and also led the league in hits, doubles, triples, RBIs, walks, stolen bases, batting, and slugging averages. Carey led the league in steals; Cuyler in runs scored and triples; and only two players out-reached his .357 average.

Then they met a legend in the World Series: Walter Johnson. At age 36 Johnson had made his first World Series appearance the year before, and landed his first win in the bizarre seventh game in which not one, but two balls bounced over Giant third baseman Freddy Lindstrom's head to tie, then win the game (and the Series) for the Nats and Johnson.

"The Big Train" was still splendid in his 19th season in the bigs, notching 20 wins against seven defeats. Both the Pirates and Senators had won their leagues by identical 8½ game margins. Fans around the country seemed to feel the Washingtonians had the edge; gamblers, however, favored the Bucs.

Johnson was true to form in Game One, hurling a masterful five-hitter to top the Bucs 4–1. For Game Two all the players wore black armbands in memory of Giant superstar Christy Mathewson, who had died the previous night. The Pirates won 3–2, aided by Washington shortstop and just-named league Most Valuable Player Roger Peckinpaugh's second and third errors of the Series. The Bucs led Game Three 3–2 till the last of the seventh, when a surprise bunt by Goose Goslin loaded the bases and the Nats scored twice to snatch a 4–3 win. Johnson collected his second victory in Game Four, a six-hit whitewash.

Down three games to one, the Pirates faced history. No team had ever come back from a deficit that large to win a seven-game Series. But with their backs pressed firmly against the wall, the Pirates took the fifth game against spitballer Stan Coveleski, with Vic Aldridge throwing a savvy eight-hitter. Then the Pirates battled to a tense 3–2 win in Game Six, with Ray Kremer holding the Nats to just six hits.

The game scheduled for October 14 was rained out by a powerful deluge.

The field was still in poor shape when the sun dawned through cold and drizzly skies the morning of October 15. But Commissioner Landis wanted the game played. And play they did.

Washington blew Aldridge out of the box in the very first inning, sending him to the clubhouse showers by scoring four times before Aldridge had retired two men. The great Walter Johnson held a 4–0 lead. By the third inning the drizzle had become a steady downpour.

A three-run rally in the last of the third brought the Bucs to within one run, but the Senators reopened the distance between them with two more in their half of the fourth. By the fifth, Fred Lieb said, "A dark mist hung over the field, and the outfielders looked like ghoulish figures in the general gloom."

But Johnson couldn't hang on. The Bucs tallied a solo run in the fifth. They added two more to tie in the seventh, aided greatly by Peckinpaugh's *seventh* Series error. After driving in the tying score, Traynor's attempt to break the tie by stretching his triple into a homer failed.

Peckinpaugh broke the tie with a solo homer in the eighth. In the last of the eighth, Johnson called for the groundskeepers for the eighth time to bring sand to keep the mound's footing as clean as possible. What Walter didn't know was that the men who brought out the wheelbarrows full of sand had been keeping it soaked under a garden hose. Johnson would get no advantage from the Pirates this day.

With two outs, Earl Smith doubled. Carson Bigbee matched Smith's hit and the game was tied. Second baseman Eddie Moore was walked, but Peckinpaugh couldn't make the play at second for the force, and was charged with Series error number *eight*. (There was only one non-Peckinpaugh Series error by the Senators.) The bases were loaded for Kiki Cuyler, who shot a line drive down the right-field foul line. He and all three of his teammates crossed the plate, but the umpires ruled a ground-rule double. Two runs were plenty for the Bucs. No Senator reached against Red Oldham in the ninth, and the Bucs had attained the championship by coming back from a three-game-to-one deficit and beating Walter Johnson in the rain.

The Series had much noisy aftermath. It was wisely decided that announcement of MVP winners would not take place till the Series was over. American League President Ban Johnson criticized Senator Manager Bucky Harris in a post-Series wire for letting Johnson remain in the game: "You sacrificed a World's Championship for our league through your display of mawkish sentiment." And Grantland Rice described Walter Johnson's defeat in a glorious extended metaphor: "They caught old Barney, the western grizzly, with his foot in a steel trap yesterday and clubbed him to death. They found (him) hooked and helpless with nothing left but a snarl and a growl as they hammered him into a shapeless mass of fur and gore."

The Pirates' second World Championship club may well have been the greatest Pirate team of all. Their season-long statistical leadership was one element in measuring their quality. Their steadfast refusal to be cowed by Johnson and the Nats, and their unprecedented comeback, are further indications of their greatness.

The Bucs slipped in 1926, scoring 150 fewer runs and stumbling to third. A big blow-up between Manager McKechnie and right-hand man Fred Clarke shattered morale. Babe Adams, Carson Bigbee, and Max Carey threatened to strike unless Clarke was removed from the team (hence the name, "ABC Incident"). The three were disposed of in one day.

But the season was not without promise. Kremer had a spectacular season, and the Pirates brought up a new outfielder to join Cuyler and Carey. Rookie Paul Waner led the league in batting average (.336), on-base percentage, and triples. He was second in slugging average, walks, and runs scored. Baseball hadn't seen the likes of a fresh new hitter like this in years.

But Dreyfuss knew that McKechnie had lost the team's confidence, and the owner replaced "The Deacon" with former Tiger shortstop (who had played against the Bucs in the 1909 Series) Donie Bush. Bush got the team rolling again, and they took the National League crown by a game and a half over the Cardinals. This year the manager/player rift was between Kiki Cuyler and Bush, and the hot new star was Paul Waner's younger brother, Lloyd. The little Waner hit .355, and slapped 198 singles (still the season record) among his 223 hits (still the rookie record).

Pie Traynor added another excellent defensive year and rapped the ball at a .342 clip. Dreyfuss re-obtained Carmen Hill (whose name always seemed to be prefaced by "the bespectacled") from Indianapolis and Hill won 22 games to go with Kremer's 19–8 and Meadows' 19–10 records. As another wearer of glasses, Meadows gave the Pirates the all-time season record for wins by pitchers with specs.

The Pirates' biggest problem was that they had to face what many call the Greatest Team of All-Time in that 1927 Series: the potent New York Yankees. These were the Yankees of Ruth and Gehrig's 107 home runs, 339 RBIs, and slugging averages of .772 and .765.

The Yanks swept the Pirates, but not with "Murderers Row" power. Ruth homered twice, but no one else did. The Yankees took the first game 5–4. Three of their runs were unearned.

In Game Two the men from New York took advantage of two walks, a wild pitch, and a hit batsman to score the three runs in the eighth that gave them a 6–2 victory. They had their only big inning of the Series in the seventh frame of Game Three, when they scored six runs with the help of Ruth's three-run smash. But they won Game Four in the bottom of the ninth with two outs on John Miljus's second wild pitch of the inning. It was hardly the stuff of legend.

But it was the Pirates' last gasp at a championship for 33 years. The team slumped to fourth in 1928, then spent the next six years three times each in fifth and second.

The Mediocre Years

In 1931 Barney Dreyfuss's son Sam, who had been in line to replace his dad as the boss, died of pneumonia at age 36. Dreyfuss called upon his son-in-law, Bill Benswanger, to help him run the team. By the following February the elder Dreyfuss, too, was dead, and Benswanger was completely in charge.

The arrival of Arky Vaughan in 1932 gave the team their second great-hitting shortstop of franchise history. That same year George Gibson was called back for his second tour as a Pirate manager. George did well, bringing the team in just a handful of games behind the Cubs, now managed by none other than banjo-playing Charlie Grimm himself.

In 1933 a familiar figure showed up at Benswanger's door—a stocky, broad-shouldered, bowlegged man with big hands and a large nose. Honus Wagner had never been comfortable out of baseball, and he had been there for 15 years. He asked for a job—"one wearing a uniform." Benswanger hired him as a coach.

Gibson was fired 50 games into the 1934 season, replaced by another old favorite, Pie Traynor. But the attempt to recapture the old magic of Traynor and Wagner didn't work from the bench and coaching box. The Pirates began their longest spell of mediocrity. The famous second-place finish in 1938 because of Gabby Hartnett's late September homer was a fluke; the team had been slumping before the big belt, and was defeated promptly 10–1 the next day, when they had a chance to make up for the Hartnett poke.

That same year an aged Babe Ruth was making his last turn around baseball as a Boston Brave. A Pittsburgh sportswriter told Traynor, "Don't worry about the Babe today; I had him out till 5 a.m." The useless Ruth hit three home runs that day. One was the first ever smacked all the way over the right-field grandstand in Forbes Field.

The Bucs would eke into second in 1943, and again in 1948. But, all things considered, the Pirates were a fair-to-poor team from 1934 through 1965. Attendance, which had fractured the 800,000 mark in the pennant years of 1925 and 1927 stumbled as low as 260,000 and bounced as high as 604,000 before the World War-II-ending season of 1945. Kiner's arrival lifted ticket sales past a million for four consecutive years, but that soon dropped off as well. From 1958–61 they again pushed past the million mark. But they finished sixth under Danny Murtaugh in 1964, attendance was just over 750,000, and Murtaugh was replaced by Harry Walker.

Walker was a non-stop, sometimes abrasive talker. But he did know hitting. Under his tutelage the Pirates acquired Matty Alou from the Giants in 1966. Alou, one-third of the famous all-brother outfield, had seen his average slip into the .230s. Walker taught him to hit down on the ball. Matty won a batting title, with a .342 mark in 1966, then followed it up with years of .338, .332, and .331.

But Harry's success with hitting was more than balanced by his lack of success with pitching. Even Vernon Law, the taciturn Mormon, publicly criticized Walker's mishandling of the starting pitching as the reason for the Bucs' collapse in 1966.

So what did the Pirates do? They traded for Dennis Ribant and Juan Pizarro. Walker was gone by the middle of 1967, replaced by none other than Danny Murtaugh. The team wound up sixth in a 10-team race. And of course the Pirates traded for some more pitching. This time they swapped Woody Fryman (who would win 129 more major league games in 16 more seasons) to obtain Jim Bunning (who would win 32 more in four years, only 14 with the Bucs). Incidentally, the Pirates threw in three minor leaguers in the deal, one of whom turned out to be future Milwaukee regular Don Money.

For the 1968 season the team was given a battery of psychology tests to determine their motivation, while new manager Larry Shepard motivated them to another sixth-place finish. A young pitcher named Steve Blass won 18 games. In 1969 the Pirates brought up a crop of rookies who couldn't stop hitting the ball: Al Oliver was an outfielder and first baseman, Bob Robertson played first, too; and it didn't seem to matter that Richie Hebner didn't think defense was proper behavior for grown men (Jim Rooker: "I didn't care that Hebner doesn't *dive* after balls that go by him; I just wish he'd *flinch*"). But they could hit. The Pirates' great team of the 1970s was taking shape.

The Lumber Company

The young crop of Pirates finished third in 1969. Joining Hebner and Oliver were young pitchers Dock Ellis and Bob Moose. The Pirate investment in Latin American scouting and the charisma of Clemente were paying off. The Bucs catcher in 1969 was a perpetually grinning Panamanian line-drive hitter named Manny Sanguillen. But Manager Shepard wasn't doing a good job of pleasing General Manager Joe L. Brown. Shepard badgered Brown to trade Roberto Clemente. Brown refused. Shepard was relieved of his duties when the season still had five games to go.

A few days after the season ended the Pirates announced their "new" manager; Danny Murtaugh was returning for his third stint in the job. Less than an hour after Murtaugh's hiring, Don Hoak, third baseman from the 1960 Champions, who had been grooming himself for the Pirate managerial job, was dead of a heart attack while chasing car thieves near his home.

After seven years in the big leagues, the large and gregarious Bucs outfielder Willie Stargell was beginning to make his presence felt as a team leader. His sunny disposition led one writer to call him "The Ernie Banks of the Bucs." During Spring Training, he brashly predicted the Pirates would win the pennant. Most experts were picking them for fourth.

Stargell was right; the experts wrong. The Bucs moved into their new home, Three Rivers Stadium, and won their division in 1970. They repeated in 1971, then won the League Championship series and the World Series. The National League East title was theirs again in 1972, 1974, and 1975. The Bucs finished second to a strong Phillies team for 1976–78, but returned with vengeance in 1979, again winning the division, L.C.S., and World Series. In the decade of the 1970s the Pirates finished as low as third only once—and then only 2½ games back. Twice they defeated more highly regarded Baltimore Orioles teams in thrilling seven-game World Series. The Bucs easily ranked with the Oakland A's and Cincinnati Reds as the three greatest teams of that era.

What is interesting about these Pirates teams is that they didn't keep the same basic lineup for a long period of time, and keep winning with it, as the Reds and Oakland did. Only one player was on both the 1970 and 1979 teams: the personable Stargell, and he changed positions, taking Robertson's first base job in 1975.

Some changes were the function of age. Bill Mazeroski ended his career as a regular in 1970. Dave Cash took the spot Maz had held since 1956. Others were deliberate shifts to maximize strengths. And at least one was the result of a tragedy.

Longtime Pirate Bill Virdon earned the managerial post for 1972, replacing Murtaugh. The Bucs lost the lead in the final inning of the final game of the League Championship Series when Bob Moose threw a wild pitch to give the Reds the pennant.

But between the 1972 and 1973 seasons, the Pirates were dealt a more crushing defeat when "The Great One," Roberto Clemente, died tragically in a New Year's Eve plane crash while attempting to deliver supplies to Nicaraguan earthquake victims. Clemente's dedication to his fellow man in Latin America was no put-on. The team was devastated. Virdon was unable to cope. In a strange move, he tried to make catcher Sanguillen into a right fielder, thereby awarding Roberto's job to his closest friend. Whether or not the symbolic pressure was too much for the emotional Sanguillen is difficult to say, but it is certain that he was no outfielder, and some claim that this "experiment" ruined his arm as a catcher for the rest of his career, as well. But that was only part of Virdon's stumbling.

Stargell was moved to first, Bob Robertson to left, then the two were switched back again two days before the season started. Ultimately, young slugger Richie Zisk earned the right-field job. Injury-prone (but a spectacular fielder when healthy), Gene Alley lost his job to Dal Maxvill. Starter Steve Blass suddenly lost all the skills that had made him a valuable star. He was unable to throw strikes in a game, although he seemed to have lost nothing when he threw in the bullpen.

With 26 games left in the season, Danny Murtaugh returned once more. It's not surprising the Pirates didn't win in 1973.

Pitching was changing, too. By 1973 mainstays Ellis and Moose were joined by Bruce Kison, Luke Walker, and Dave Giusti. By 1974 the Pirates had traded for starters Jim Rooker, Jerry Reuss, and Ken Brett as well.

Cash was gone in a trade and rookie Rennie Stennett took over at second. The Panamanian was keystoned at short with a young Dominican, Frank Taveras, whose glove would make no one forget Alley, but who sparked a Pirate return to base-stealing as an offensive weapon. The tag line "The Lumber Company" became "Lumber and Lightning."

The 1974 Bucs team overcame an early-season slump to claim first place, then fell back. But they recovered, and came back from a 4–0 deficit on the final night of the season to win the division title. They had won their division for the fourth time in five years, yet attendance dropped more than 200,000. It was the first strong indication that Pittsburghers weren't in love with their baseball as they had once been.

New blood on the 1975 team included Dave Parker in right field and 21-year-old John Candelaria, both of whom would contribute glory, then be major players in the team's fall during the early 1980s. After the 1975 season the team fired local institution/announcer Bob Prince. A local restaurant chain turned off the taps for Iron City Beer (a team sponsor) in protest.

From 1975 to 1976 the Pirates starting lineup didn't change—the first time that had happened in the decade. But the Bucs added some bench strength with the acquisition of capable right hand power hitter Bill Robinson. But the familiar bugaboo arose again: the Pirates made another ill-conceived swap for pitching—trading Willie Randolph to get Doc Medich from the Yanks.

After the 1976 season Danny Murtaugh retired for the fourth time, and that December he died. Joe L. Brown followed his longtime pal into retirement. Harding "Pete" Peterson, former minor league catcher in the Pirate organization and scout, took over Brown's job. It didn't take Peterson long to irritate both the fans and the press. Sports columnist Bob Smizik remarked, "In just 21 days Peterson built up a larger credibility gap than Brown did in 21 years."

A few days later Peterson traded his catcher, Manny Sanguillen, for a manager, Chuck Tanner. And Peterson kept dealing, picking up Goose Gossage and Terry Forster, both of whom would last only one season before joining the free-agent market. In March of 1977 he sent six players to Oakland for Phil Garner, Tommy Helms, and pitcher Chris Batton. Those departing Pittsburgh were the backbone of the Pirate farm system: outfielders Tony Armas, Dave Augustine, and Mitchell Page, plus pitchers Doc Medich, Rick Langford, and Doug Bair. Garner became a catalyst for the Pirate champions of 1979, and a fan favorite. But it seemed clear that Peterson had been skunked. Armas would belt more than 240 home runs for several teams before he was through; the three pitchers would win nearly 200 games before their careers ended. (In fact, Doug Bair was still active in 1989—as a Pirate.) The year of the trade Rennie Stennett hit .336, but was out of the lineup after breaking his leg in August. In the off-season the Bucs traded Al Oliver as well for veteran hurler Bert Blyleven.

On August 12 of 1978 the Pirates were 11½ games out of first, with a record of 51–61. Then they got red hot, winning 37 of their next 49. Four games back, the Bucs began the season's final series on a Friday night with a doubleheader against the first-place Phillies. Pittsburgh won both games in their final at-bat to cut the Phillies' lead in half. Star of the comeback was the remarkable Dave Parker, who had fractured his jaw in a home plate collision as he tried to score the winning run in the ninth inning on July 4. But he returned, wearing a makeshift football helmet at bat and on the basepaths, and hit over .400 for the month of September. Despite all the pennant race excitement, Pirate attendance again fell below one million.

It all finally came together in 1979. Thirty-nine-year-old Willie Stargell found enough zip in his windmill bat to slug 32 homers and drive in 82 runs. Early-season acquisition Tim Foli solidified the infield defense, and was a good hit-and-run man behind speedster Omar Moreno, who swiped 77 bases. Mid-season acquisition Bill Madlock hit .328 as a Buc. Parker ripped 25 homers with a .310 average. Bill Robinson popped 24 homers himself.

The pitching staff had eight men who won eight games or more, but not one who won 15. The key was the spectacular rotating bullpen of skinny sidearming righthander Kent Tekulve, stocky lefty Grant Jackson, and mercurial fireballer Enrique Romo. Teke appeared 94 times, Romo 84, and Jackson 72. It wasn't uncommon for Tanner to use all three in the same inning.

The team was loud, and loved it. Parker and Stargell were a pair of rollickers. Willie handed out "Stargell stars" for exceptional performance, to be sewn on the recipient's cap. The disaffecteds, Foli, Madlock, and Garner, relished the chance to play for a winner. The team had a wonderful time, called themselves the "Family," after one of their favorite disco songs, and came back from a 3–1 deficit in the World Series to upend the favored Baltimore Orioles. Stargell was National League, L.C.S., and World Series Most Valuable Player.

But cracks were showing. The hard-working—and winning— football Steelers had captured the hearts and minds of the fans. They seemed so different from the bothersome Bucs. Parker's million-dollar contract and braggadocio didn't sit well with fans suffering through a steel industry depression. His weight problems became obvious as well. Talk of a player strike was viewed as absurd even by union loyalists in Pittsburgh. Bert Blyleven had a much-publicized falling out with Chuck Tanner, and Peterson obligingly swapped the pitcher for a fistful of nobodies. In 1980 the team drew 1.6 million fans and lost $2.1 million at the same time.

Before the 1981 season Pirate owners, the Galbreaths, sued to break their lease with the city for the stadium. When Three Rivers Stadium had been built, the Bucs were the "fat cats" and the Steelers the poor relatives in town. When baseball free agency arrived, the Pirates began using the money they made from ballpark concessions to pay players, and the stadium fell into disrepair. It took over a year to settle the dispute, and the settlement included an ironclad lock-in date till the year 2010.

A spurt to second by Tanner's 1983 Bucs could have been a fluke, or it could have been the result of a good team going cocaine-bad. At any rate, by the time the 1985 season rolled around the team was at the absolute bottom of a downward spiral.

The group that ultimately bought the team from the Galbreaths was a unique conglomerate. Thirteen corporations, with the city's help, turned things around. Under the guidance of new General Manager Syd Thrift and field manager Jim Leyland, the Bucs made a strong move in the last half of 1987 to tie for fourth. Then they started 1988 with a bang, challenging the Mets early. In the end they finished 15 games out, but they were in second place.

When it came to the century's final decade, the ill-starred Buccos were somehow able to capture a unique distinction within the baseball world held before them by perhaps only the "Boys of Summer" Brooklyn Dodgers of the nostalgia-laden fifties. This was an inexplicable ability to dominate the senior circuit for a string of summers and yet still own the universal image of a consistent baseball loser. Three straight seasons the Pittsburghers parlayed the explosive bats of Barry Bonds (NL MVP in 1991 and 1992) and Bobby Bonilla (lost via free agency to the Mets in 1992), as well as the consistent hurling of Doug Drabek (1990 Cy Young winner), into runaway Eastern Division titles. And three straight seasons Leyland's team saw their World Series dreams suddenly go up in smoke during lackluster NLCS performances. In 1990 (4–3 loss to Cincinnati) and 1991 (4–3 loss to Atlanta) the Pirates were seemingly sabotaged by the prolonged post-season hitting slumps of Bonds and Bonilla. Then after fighting back from a 3–1 deficit and forcing a deciding seventh game with the Atlanta Braves once again in 1992, shabby defense was responsible for an embarrassing blown 2–0 ninth-inning lead and a third consecutive year on the sidelines. As Bonds prepared to follow Bonilla into free agency during the winter of 1992, disillusioned Pirates fans were sullenly resigning themselves to an unhappy conclusion that their time had both come and gone without a single deserved turn on the championship dance floor.

Annotated Bibliography

Burtt, Richard L. *The Pittsburgh Pirates: A Pictorial History.* Virginia Beach, Va.: Jordan and Company, 1977.
   A broad pictorial overview. Interestingly, the photos of the oldtimers are better than the more modern versions. Reminiscences by longtime Pittsburgh baseball writer Les Biederman provide splashes of color.
Eckhouse, Morris, and Carl Mastrocola, *This Date in Pittsburgh Pirates History.* New York: Stein and Day, 1980.
   Pirate stats, trades, and rosters, plus a long history of the 1979 World Series Champions. Most helpful: season-by-season leaders in 10 offensive categories.
Groat, Dick, and Bill Surface, *The World Champion Pittsburgh Pirates.* New York: Coward-McCann, Inc., 1961.
   Also written to capitalize on a championship, the "Pirate history" takes up half the space of the 1960 season and Series writeups. But the quotes from 1960 are priceless.
Lieb, Frederick. *The Pittsburgh Pirates.* New York: G.P. Putnam's Sons, 1948.
   The definitive history, both in breadth and depth, of the team's first 61 National League seasons.
———. *The Story of the World Series.* New York: G.P. Putnam's Sons, 1965 (revised edition).
   What happened, game-by-game, told by a man who was there to see it all unfold. As pleasurable as solid baseball history gets.

Year-by-Year Standings and Season Summaries

Year	Pos.	Record	Pct.	GB	Manager	Player	BA	Player	HR	Player	W-L	ERA
1900	2nd	79–60	.568	4.5	Clarke	Wagner	.381	Williams	5	Tannehill	20–6	2.88
1901	1st	90–49	.647	+7.5	Clarke	Wagner	.353	Beaumont	8	Phillippe	22–12	2.22
1902	1st	103–36	.741	+27.5	Clarke	Beaumont	.357	Leach	6	Chesbro	28–6	2.17
1903	1st	91–49	.650	+6.5	Clarke	Wagner	.355	Leach Beaumont	7	Leever	25–7	2.06
1904	4th	87–66	.569	19	Clarke	Wagner	.349	Wagner	4	Leever	18–11	2.05
1905	2nd	96–57	.627	9	Clarke	Wagner	.363	Wagner	6	Phillippe	22–13	2.19
1906	3rd	93–60	.608	23.5	Clarke	Wagner	.339	Nealon	3	Willis	22–13	1.73
1907	2nd	91–63	.591	17	Clarke	Wagner	.350	Wagner	6	Willis	22–11	2.33
1908	T2nd	98–56	.636	1	Clarke	Wagner	.354	Wagner	10	Maddox	23–8	2.28
1909	1st	110–42	.724	+6.5	Clarke	Wagner	.339	Leach	6	Camnitz	25–6	1.62
1910	3rd	86–67	.562	17.5	Clarke	Wagner	.320	Flynn	6	Adams	18–9	2.24
1911	3rd	85–69	.552	14.5	Clarke	Wagner	.334	Wilson	12	Adams	22–12	2.34
1912	2nd	93–58	.616	10	Clarke	Wagner	.324	Wilson	11	Hendrix	24–9	2.58
1913	4th	78–71	.523	21.5	Clarke	Viox	.317	Wilson	10	Adams	21–10	2.18
1914	7th	69–85	.448	25.5	Clarke	Viox	.265	Konetchy	4	Cooper	16–15	2.12
1915	5th	73–81	.474	18	Clarke	Hinchman	.307	Wagner	6	Vaughn	20–12	2.87
1916	6th	65–89	.422	29	Callahan	Hinchman	.315	Carey	7	Mamaux	21–15	2.53
1917	8th	51–103	.331	47	Callahan Wagner Bezdek	Carey	.296	Fischer	3	Cooper	17–11	2.36
1918	4th	65–60	.520	17	Bezdek	Cutshaw	.285	Cutshaw	5	Cooper	19–14	2.11
1919	4th	71–68	.511	24.5	Bezdek	Stengel	.293	Stengel	4	Cooper	19–13	2.67
1920	4th	79–75	.513	14	Gibson	Carey	.289	Bigbee	4	Cooper	24–15	2.39
1921	2nd	90–63	.588	4	Gibson	Cutshaw	.340	Grimm Whitted Carey	7 7 7	Cooper	22–14	3.25
1922	T3rd	85–69	.552	8	Gibson McKechnie	Bigbee	.350	Russell	12	Cooper	23–14	3.18

Year	Pos.	Record	Pct.	GB	Manager	Player	BA	Player	HR	Player	W-L	ERA
1923	3rd	87-67	.565	8	McKechnie	Grimm	.345	Traynor	12	Morrison	25-13	3.49
1924	3rd	90-63	.588	3	McKechnie	Carey	.297	Cuyler	9	Cooper	20-14	3.28
1925	1st	95-58	.621	+8.5	McKechnie	Cuyler	.357	Wright	18	Meadows	19-10	3.67
								Cuyler	18			
1926	3rd	84-69	.549	4.5	McKechnie	P. Waner	.336	Grantham	8	Kremer	20-6	2.61
								Wright	8			
								P. Waner	8			
								Cuyler	8			
1927	1st	94-60	.610	+1.5	Bush	P. Waner	.380	Wright	9	Hill	22-11	3.24
								P. Waner	9			
1928	4th	85-67	.559	9	Bush	P. Waner	.370	Grantham	10	Grimes	25-14	2.99
1929	2nd	88-65	.575	10.5	Bush	Traynor	.356	Grantham	15	Kremer	18-10	4.26
					Ens							
1930	5th	80-74	.519	12	Ens	P. Waner	.368	Grantham	18	Kremer	20-12	5.02
1931	5th	75-79	.487	26	Ens	P. Waner	.322	P. Waner	10	French	18-16	3.02
1932	2nd	86-68	.558	4	Gibson	P. Waner	.341	P. Waner	8	Meine	19-13	2.98
								Grace	8			
1933	2nd	87-67	.565	5	Gibson	Vaughan	.314	Suhr	10	French	18-13	2.72
1934	5th	74-76	.493	19.5	Gibson	P. Waner	.362	Suhr	14	Hoyt	15-6	2.92
					Traynor							
1935	4th	86-67	.562	13.5	Traynor	Vaughan	.385	Vaughan	19	Blanton	18-13	2.59
1936	4th	84-70	.545	8	Traynor	P. Waner	.373	Suhr	11	Lucas	15-4	3.17
1937	3rd	86-68	.558	10	Traynor	Vaughan	.354	Young	9	Bauers	13-6	2.87
1938	2nd	86-64	.573	2	Traynor	L. Waner	.313	Rizzo	23	Brown	15-9	3.79
1939	6th	68-85	.444	28.5	Traynor	P. Waner	.328	Fletcher	12	Klinger	14-7	4.36
1940	4th	78-76	.506	22.5	Frisch	Vaughan	.300	DiMaggio	19	Sewell	16-5	2.79
1941	4th	81-73	.526	19	Frisch	Vaughan	.316	DiMaggio	21	Butcher	17-12	3.05
1942	5th	66-81	.449	36.5	Frisch	Elliott	.296	DiMaggio	15	Sewell	17-15	3.41
1943	4th	80-74	.519	25	Frisch	Elliott	.315	DiMaggio	15	Sewell	21-9	2.55
1944	2nd	90-63	.588	14.5	Frisch	Russell	.312	Dahlgren	12	Sewell	21-12	3.18

Year	Pos.	Record	Pct.	GB	Manager	Player	BA	Player	HR	Player	W-L	ERA
1945	4th	82–72	.532	16	Frisch	Elliott	.290	Barrett	15	Strincevich	16–10	3.32
								Salkeld	15			
1946	7th	63–91	.409	34	Frisch Davis	Cox	.290	Kiner	23	Ostermueller	13–10	2.84
1947	T7th	62–92	.403	32	Herman Burwell	Kiner	.313	Kiner	51	Ostermueller	12–10	3.84
1948	4th	83–71	.539	8.5	Meyer	Walker	.316	Kiner	40	Chesnes	14–6	3.57
1949	6th	71–83	.461	26	Meyer	Kiner	.310	Kiner	54	Chambers	13–7	3.97
1950	8th	57–96	.373	33.5	Meyer	Murtaugh	.294	Kiner	47	Chambers	12–15	4.30
1951	7th	64–90	.416	32.5	Meyer	Kiner	.309	Kiner	42	Dickson	20–16	4.02
1952	8th	42–112	.273	54.5	Meyer	Garagiola	.273	Kiner	37	Dickson	14–21	3.56
1953	8th	50–104	.325	55	Meyer	O'Connell	.294	Thomas	30	Dickson	10–19	4.52
1954	8th	53–101	.344	44	Haney	Gordon	.306	Thomas	23	Littlefield	10–11	3.60
1955	8th	60–94	.390	38.5	Haney	Long	.291	Thomas	25	Friend	14–9	2.84
1956	7th	66–88	.429	27	Bragan	Virdon	.334	Long	27	Friend	17–17	3.47
1957	T7th	62–92	.403	33	Bragan Murtaugh	Groat	.315	Thomas	23	Friend	14–18	3.38
1958	2nd	84–70	.545	8	Murtaugh	Skinner	.321	Thomas	35	Friend	22–14	3.68
1959	4th	78–76	.506	9	Murtaugh	Stuart	.297	Stuart	27	Face	18–1	2.71
1960	1st	95–59	.617	+7	Murtaugh	Groat	.325	Stuart	23	Law	20–9	3.08
1961	6th	75–79	.487	18	Murtaugh	Clemente	.351	Stuart	35	Friend	14–19	3.85
1962	4th	93–68	.578	8	Murtaugh	Clemente	.312	Skinner	20	Friend	18–14	3.06
1963	8th	74–68	.457	25	Murtaugh	Clemente	.320	Clemente	17	Friend	17–16	2.34
1964	T6th	80–82	.494	13	Murtaugh	Clemente	.339	Stargell	21	Veale	18–12	2.73
1965	3rd	90–72	.556	7	Walker	Alou	.329	Stargell	27	Law	17–9	2.16
1966	3rd	92–70	.568	3	Walker	Clemente	.342	Stargell	33	Veale	16–12	3.02
1967	6th	81–81	.500	20.5	Walker Murtaugh	Clemente	.357	Clemente	23	Veale	16–8	3.64
1968	6th	80–82	.494	17	Shepard	Alou	.332	Stargell	24	Blass	18–6	2.13
1969	3rd**	88–74	.543	12	Shepard Grammas	Clemente	.345	Stargell	29	Moose	14–3	2.91

Year	Pos.	Record	Pct.	GB	Manager	Player	BA	Player	HR	Player	W-L	ERA
1970	1st	89–73	.549	+5	Murtaugh	Clemente	.352	Stargell	31	Walker	15–6	3.04
1971	1st	97–65	.599	+7	Murtaugh	Clemente	.341	Stargell	48	Ellis	19–9	3.05
1972	1st	96–59	.619	+11	Virdon	Oliver	.312	Stargell	33	Blass	19–8	2.48
1973	3rd	80–82	.494	2.5	Virdon	Stargell	.299	Stargell	44	Briles	14–13	2.84
1974	1st	89–74	.543	+1.5	Murtaugh	Oliver	.321	Stargell	25	Reuss	16–11	3.50
1975	1st	92–69	.571	+6.5	Murtaugh	Sanguillen	.328	Parker	25	Reuss	18–11	2.54
1976	2nd	92–70	.568	9	Murtaugh	Oliver	.323	Zisk	21	Candelaria	16–7	3.15
1977	2nd	96–66	.593	5	Tanner	Parker	.338	Robinson	26	Candelaria	20–5	2.34
1978	2nd	88–73	.547	1.5	Tanner	Parker	.334	Parker	30	Robinson	14–6	3.47
1979	1st	98–64	.605	+2	Tanner	Madlock	.328	Stargell	32	Candelaria	14–9	3.22
1980	3rd	83–79	.512	8	Tanner	Parker	.295	Easler	21	Bibby	19–9	3.33
1981	4th	25–23	.521	5.5	Tanner	Madlock	.341	Thompson	15	Rhoden	9–4	3.90
1981*	6th	21–33	.389	9.5								
	4th	46–56	.451									
1982	4th	84–78	.519	8	Tanner	Madlock	.319	Thompson	31	Tekulve	12–8	2.87
1983	2nd	84–78	.519	6	Tanner	Madlock	.323	Thompson	18	Candelaria	15–8	3.23
1984	6th	75–87	.463	21.5	Tanner	Lacy	.321	Thompson	17	Rhoden	14–9	2.72
1985	6th	57–104	.354	43.5	Tanner	Ray	.274	Thompson	12	Reuschel	14–8	2.27
1986	6th	64–98	.395	44	Leyland	Ray	.301	Morrison	23	Rhoden	15–12	2.84
1987	T4th	80–82	.494	15	Leyland	Bonilla	.300	Van Slyke	21	Dunne	13–6	3.03
1988	2nd	85–75	.531	15	Leyland	Van Slyke	.288	Van Slyke	25	Drabek	15–7	3.08
1989	5th	74–88	.457	19	Leyland	Bonilla	.281	Bonilla	24	Drabek	14–12	2.80
1990	1st	95–67	.586	+4	Leyland	Bonds	.301	Bonds	33	Drabek	22–6	2.76
1991	1st	98–64	.605	+14	Leyland	Bonilla	.302	Bonds	25	Smiley	20–8	3.08
1992	1st	96–66	.593	+9	Leyland	VanSlyke	.324	Bonds	34	Drabek	15–11	2.77

*Split Season Totals (Players' Union Strike).
**National League East, beginning of divisional play

477

All-Time Pirates Career and Season Records

Career Batting Leaders

Games Played	Roberto Clemente	2,433
At Bats	Roberto Clemente	9,454
Runs Scored	Honus Wagner	1,520
Hits	Roberto Clemente	3,000
Singles	Roberto Clemente	2,154
Doubles	Honus Wagner	556
	Paul Waner	556
Triples	Honus Wagner	231
Batting Average	Paul Waner	.340
Home Runs	Willie Stargell	475
Runs Batted In	Willie Stargell	1,540
Stolen Bases	Max Carey	688
Strikeouts	Willie Stargell	1,936
Extra Base Hits	Willie Stargell	953
Total Bases	Roberto Clemente	4,492

Career Pitching Leaders

Innings Pitched	Bob Friend	3,481
Wins	Wilbur Cooper	202
Winning Percentage	Sam Leever	.665
Strikeouts	Bob Friend	1,682
Strikeouts (lefthander)	Bob Veale	1,652
Walks	Bob Friend	869
Games	Elroy Face	802
Shutouts	Babe Adams	47
Shutouts (lefthander)	Wilbur Cooper	34
Saves	Kent Tekulve	158
Games Started	Bob Friend	477
Complete Games	Wilbur Cooper	263

Single-Season Batting Records

Batting Average (500 AB)	Arky Vaughan	.385	1935
Home Runs	Ralph Kiner	54	1949
Home Runs (lefthanded)	Willie Stargell	48	1971
Runs Batted In	Paul Waner	131	1927
Hits	Paul Waner	237	1927
Singles	Lloyd Waner	198	1927
Doubles	Paul Waner	62	1932
Triples	Owen Wilson	36	1912
Slugging Percentage	Ralph Kiner	.658	1949
Extra Base Hits	Willie Stargell	90	1973
Stolen Bases	Omar Moreno	96	1980
Strikeouts	Donn Clendenon	163	1968
Total Bases	Kiki Cuyler	366	1925
Hitting Streak	Danny O'Connell	26	1953
Runs Scored	Kiki Cuyler	144	1925

All-Time Pirates Career and Season Records *(continued)*

Single-Season Pitching Records

ERA (150 innings)	Wilbur Cooper	1.87	1916
Wins	Jack Chesbro	28	1902
Losses	Murry Dickson	21	1952
Winning Percentage	Elroy Face	18–1, .947	1959
Strikeouts	Bob Veale	276	1965
Walks	Marty O'Toole	159	1912
Saves	Jim Gott	34	1988
Games	Kent Tekulve	94	1979
Complete Games	Vic Willis	32	1906
Games Started	Bob Friend	42	1956
Shutouts	Jack Chesbro	8	1902
	Lefty Leifield	8	1906
	Al Mamaux	8	1915
	Babe Adams	8	1920
Innings Pitched	Burleigh Grimes	331	1928

11

San Diego Padres
The Saga of Big Mack
and Trader Jack
DAVID L. PORTER

The San Diego Padres story as a major league franchise since 1969 has been filled with the trappings of a soap opera. Sportswriter Steve Wulf has described Padre life as "baseball's comic soap opera" with "a plot synopsis that rivals anything in *Soap Opera Digest*."[1] The story features numerous losing records, second-division finishes, frequent managerial and player transactions, constant youth movements spiced with occasional ventures into the free-agent market, and abundant peaks and valleys. "Like a roller coaster," James Rothaus noted, "the Padre fans found themselves soaring to exciting peaks, followed by frightening dips and plunges."[2]

The Padres have experienced five stages in their relatively brief, 21-year history. The infant years (1969 to 1973) saw the club endure woeful hitting, pitching, and defense, last-place finishes, financial poverty, and a near move to Washington, D. C. The maturing years (1974 to 1978) witnessed the Padres being rescued by a generous Santa Claus, gaining financial stability, building respectability on the field, and compiling a first winning season. The transition years (1979 to 1981) saw the club struggle on the field, make frequent managerial and front-office changes, trade numerous veterans, and rely on younger players. The fulfillment years (1982 to 1985) witnessed the Padres achieve respectability on the field, improve dramatically at most positions, earn a first National League pennant, make their only World Series appearance, and retain first place through the 1985 All-Star Game. The rebuilding years (1986 to 1989) have seen the Padres develop another formidable contender with a few remaining veterans, an impressive farm system, and important acquisitions from other clubs.

The bustling metropolis on the southern border of sunny California had a long baseball heritage, as the San Diego Padres had played in the AAA Pacific Coast League from 1936 to 1968. In 1936 owner Bill Lane had shifted the Hollywood Stars franchise to San Diego. The Padres, named after the brave missionary fathers who first settled the region 400 years ago, captured the Shaughnessy playoffs in 1937 to be declared Pacific Coast League champions, but did not win another league title until 1954. Padre games were played at Lane Field, built with WPA funds at the foot of Broadway, until 1957. C. Arnholdt Smith, head of the U. S. National Bank and owner of an airline, taxi company, hotel, and tuna fleet, purchased the Padres in 1956 and moved them from Lane Field to beautiful Westgate Park in Fashion Valley in 1958. The Padres took Pacific Coast League pennants in 1962, 1964, and 1967, the last year Westgate Park was used. Soon the 50,000-seat, $27 million San Diego Stadium was constructed in Mission Valley in hopes of securing a major league baseball team. The stadium, financed by a voter-approved city bond issue, housed the 1967 San Diego Chargers professional football team and the 1968 Padres in their final Pacific Coast League campaign.[3]

Smith and Emil J. "Buzzie" Bavasi played key roles in securing a major league baseball franchise for San Diego. Smith consented to provide the $10.2 million franchise fee, borrowing over 90 percent of the money. Smith, who owned two-thirds of the club, also persuaded the City of San Diego to establish the Greater San Diego Sports Association. The Association formulated a game plan to sell the City of San Diego on the idea of securing a major league franchise. Bavasi, who had spent 25 years in the successful Brooklyn Dodger and Los Angeles Dodger organization and was very familiar with internal baseball operations, led the campaign for a major league team. Bavasi agreed to become club president and to own one-third of the club. His connections with Dodger owner Walter O'Malley helped San Diego's quest immensely.[4]

National League owners unanimously awarded franchises to the Padres and Montreal Expos on May 27, 1968 in Chicago. Bavasi had finally convinced National League owners that San Diego deserved a major league franchise. San Diego could support a major league baseball team with its growing population exceeding one million people. San Diego Stadium already contained ample seating capacity for major league baseball games. The city offered ideal weather for baseball play and the best climate among the competitors, including Montreal, Buffalo, New York, Milwaukee, Wisconsin, and Dallas, Texas. San Diego not only was a sports-minded city with a rich minor league baseball heritage, but had produced over 100 major league baseball players. Smith seemingly provided the club with solid financial ownership, while Bavasi had vast experience in baseball operations.[5]

The Infant Years (1969-73)

From the outset, Smith and Bavasi struggled to keep the Padres afloat financially and to secure the team public recognition as a major league club. The Padres needed to make major payments each year to meet the franchise fee obligations and initially lacked the cash flow to build a successful team. According to Bavasi, "There was never a lot of money from the start."[6] An enormous geographical disadvantage hindered the Padres in marketing operations. The City is bordered by the Pacific Ocean on the west, Mexico on the south, the desert on the east, and sprawling Los Angeles to the north, limiting likely Padre fan support to six miles to the west, 30 miles to the south, 20 miles to the east, and 30 miles to the north. The Los Angeles Dodgers had commanded enormous popularity in the San Diego area since 1958, compounding marketing problems. "San Diego," former Padre executive Elten Schiller remarked, "was Dodger territory. San Diegans listened to Dodger games, as announcer Vin Scully enthralled audiences. People did not switch allegiances until a new generation of dads came along."[7] The expansion agreement prevented the Padres from sharing in television revenues until 1972. "Now that's a major source of income to a club," former club publicist Irv Grossman remarked, "and it wasn't there."[8] Padre radio announcers could not entice a large audience away from Dodger games until a club identity was created with the public. The Padres also needed to lure San Diegans from other recreational activities, including golf, tennis, fishing, surfing, Sunday racing at Caliente, Sunday bullfights in Tijuana, backyard grilling, and beachgoing. "How," inquired Bavasi, "can you compete against the good life?"[9]

Bavasi recruited mainly former Dodger personnel to assist him and drafted young players for the initial Padre team. Dodger coach Preston Gomez, who stressed team organization and execution of fundamentals, was named the first Padre field manager. Former Dodgers Roger Craig, Wally Moon, and Sparky Anderson, along with local baseball personality Whitey Wietelmann, were selected as coaches. Duke Snider, legendary Dodger slugger, was hired to scout and broadcast games. Expansion rules allowed the Padres to select 30 players from other National League club rosters. The Padres drafted a few major league veterans, including outfielders Ollie "Downtown" Brown, Tony Gonzalez, and Clarence Gaston, first baseman Nate Colbert, and pitchers Al McBean, Billy McCool, and Dick Selma. Bavasi filled his roster with younger talent, hoping to build a contender in three or four years. "If we have to finish last," Bavasi philosophized, "we'd rather do it with youngsters who are learning and improving."[10] Coach Wietelmann admitted the Padres "got players the other teams did not want."[11]

The Padres, nevertheless, debuted auspiciously on April 8, 1969, by defeating the Houston Astros, 2–1, before 23,370 fans at San Diego Stadium, on their way to a three-game series sweep. The Padres starting lineup included Rafael Robles-ss; Bobby Peña-2b; Tony Gonzalez-cf; Ollie Brown-rf; Bill Davis-1b; Larry Stahl-lf; Ed Spezio-3b;

Chris Cannizaro-c; and Dick Selma-p. Selma hurled a five-hitter, striking out 12 batters, and did not allow a run after the first inning. Robles, the first Padre batter, reached base safely when second baseman Joe Morgan bobbled his grounder. Spezio homered in the fifth inning off Don Wilson to earn his place in Padre annals. An inning later, Brown doubled to score Peña with the winning run. Pitcher Johnny Podres remarked, "We didn't look like any expansion team tonight."[12]

The Padres honeymoon, however, ended abruptly. In 1969 the Padres finished last in the Western Division with a 52–110 record, 41 games behind the first-place team. The 613,327 home season attendance fell far short of the 800,000 Bavasi had expected. Nate Colbert supplied the main offensive power with 24 home runs and 66 RBIs, while Ollie Brown paced Padre batters with a .264 mark, hit 20 home runs, and drove in 61 runs for a club ranking last in most offensive categories. Starting pitcher Clay Kirby performed much better than his 7–20 record indicated. Starters Al Santorini and Joe Niekro shared the club lead in victories with eight, but the bullpen provided little relief.[13]

The 1970–73 seasons further disheartened Padre fans. The Padres struggled continuously in last place with records of 63–99 in 1970, 61–100 in 1971, 58–95 in 1972, and 60–102 in 1973. During that span, the sparse home attendance ranged between 550,000 and 645,000. The National League unfortunately scheduled many Padre home games in September because of favorable climate conditions when the club was mired hopelessly in the second division. On the brighter side, Padre sluggers Nate Colbert, Clarence Gaston, and Ollie Brown powered the club to third best in the National League in home runs (172) in 1970. In 1971 starting pitchers Dave Roberts and Clay Kirby helped Padre hurlers compile the National League's third best ERA (3.22).[14]

The abysmal team record sparked the club's first managerial change. Bavasi fired Preston Gomez, who had compiled a 180–316 managerial mark through late April 1972, and replaced him with Don Zimmer. Zimmer, a fiery competitor, stressing pitching and defense, had played with the Dodgers and managed in the Padre farm system. Zimmer kept the Padres out of last place until June 25, but his bold moves, such as demoting infielder Derrell Thomas for disciplinary reasons and keeping University of Oregon star infielder Dave Roberts on the roster, failed to stop the woeful Padre performances at the plate, on the mound, and on defense. Zimmer's injury-plagued 1973 squad included seven rookies and four sophomores and often fell below the 25-player limit. The Padres truly remained what Elten Schiller termed "a rag-tag outfit."[15]

Nate Colbert and Clarence Gaston supplied the main Padre offensive power during the infant years. Colbert slugged 163 home runs, knocked in 481 runs, scored 442 runs, and hit 130 doubles from 1969 to 1974, still ranking first in home runs, second in RBIs, fourth in runs scored, and fifth in doubles on the all-time Padre list. He set the Padre record for most season home runs (38) in 1970 and tied it two years later when he incredibly drove in nearly one-fourth of the team's 488 runs. On August 1, 1972, at Atlanta's Fulton County Stadium, Colbert attracted national attention by belting five home runs, driving in 13 runs, and recording 22 total bases in a doubleheader against the Braves. Colbert's RBI total remains a major league record, while his five home runs tied Stan Musial's major league mark. Infielder Dave Campbell recalled, "it was amazing how far Colbert could hit the ball on a consistent basis."[16] Gaston in 1970 became the first Padre regular to surpass the .300 plateau when he batted .318 and hit a career-high 29 home runs. Gaston's batting average catapulted an astounding 88 points that year. The powerful, speedy outfielder slugged 77 home runs and 29 triples for the Padres from 1969 to 1974. Among Padres Gaston still ranks fourth in home runs and fifth in triples.[17]

The mainstays of the pitching staff during the infant years were righthanders Clay Kirby and Steve Arlin. From 1969 to 1973 Kirby completed 34 of 170 starts, won 52 of 133 decisions, hurled seven shutouts, and struck out 802 batters in 1,128 innings. He still ranks second in strikeouts, third in starts, innings pitched, and complete games, fourth in shutouts, and fifth in victories among all-time Padres hurlers. On July 21, 1970, Clay Kirby hurled a masterpiece against the New York Mets at San Diego Stadium and was within three outs of tossing a no-hitter. The Padres, however, were losing, 1–0, on a first-inning walk, two stolen bases, and a groundout. Kirby started up to the plate with two men out and no runners on base in the eighth inning, but Manager Gomez called him back. The hometown crowd of 10,373 booed loudly when Clarence Gaston pinch hit for Kirby and struck out. Some irate fans jumped down from the box seats and looked for Gomez in the dugout. Police hustled the intruders away, as spectators booed the security. The Mets then tagged reliever Jack Baldschun for two runs in the ninth inning. Gomez had deprived Kirby of a golden opportunity to lift the last-place Padres psychologically and spark local interest in the team.[18] "Gomez," Steve Arlin recalled, "felt that's what he needed to do to win the game. He often pinch hit for pitchers in trying to generate runs."[19] In 1971 Kirby became the club's first 15-game winner. Besides ranking fourth in the National League with a team-record 231 strikeouts, he compiled an impressive 2.83 ERA and nearly pitched two consecutive no-hitters. A no-hitter was spun by Kirby for 7⅓ innings on September 13 at San Diego Stadium against the Houston Astros before John Edwards singled. Five days later he retired the first 21 San Francisco Giant batters at Candlestick

Park. Willie McCovey led off the eighth inning with a home run for the Giants' only hit.[20]

Steve Arlin, meanwhile, won 32 of 84 decisions for the Padres, nearly all coming between 1971 and 1973. Arlin, who still ranks third among Padre pitchers in shutouts (11) and fourth in complete games (31), paced National League pitchers from June 18 to July 18, 1972. His masterpieces included a one-hitter, a second one-hitter in the first 10 innings of another game, and three two-hitters. On July 18 Arlin hurled the best-pitched game in Padre history. He worked on a no-hitter against the Philadelphia Phillies with two men out in the ninth inning and had two strikes on Larry Bowa. After Padre manager Don Zimmer moved third baseman Dave Roberts in by 10 feet, Bowa bounced a single over Roberts' head. Bowa's grounder could have been fielded if Roberts had remained in his normal fielding position. Zimmer apologized to Arlin, who ironically led the major leagues in losses (21) that year.[21] Two other Padre pitchers set permanent club records. Roberts baffled opposition batters with a sparkling 2.10 ERA in 1971, while Fred Norman shut out six opponents in 1972.

The Padres' acute financial problems surfaced publicly during the 1973 season. On May 18 San Diego *Union* sports editor Jack Murphy published a startling story that owner C. Arnholdt Smith was struggling monetarily and wanted to sell the Padres. Smith, unbeknownst even to Buzzie Bavasi, secretly had juggled million of dollars to keep his massive financial empire afloat. The Padres lacked the money to acquire players on waivers, develop a strong farm system, or hire enough scouts to make the club competitive. "Nobody knew Smith's financial empire was tumbling," Elten Schiller remembered. "Smith was taking from Peter to pay Paul."[22] In June San Diego traded second baseman Dave Campbell to the St. Louis Cardinals and pitcher Fred Norman to the Cincinnati Reds to meet payroll. On May 29 Smith consented to sell the Padres to a Washington, D. C., group, led by wealthy grocer Joseph Danzansky, for $12 million. Danzansky gave Smith a $100,000 check as a down payment and was granted 45 days to complete financial arrangements, secure a lease from RFK Stadium, and gain support from National League owners. The Padres could not make major player changes without first consulting the Danzansky group.

The proposed sale, however, encountered numerous roadblocks. City Attorney John Witt notified National League President Chub Feeney that the Padres still had 15 years remaining on their 20-year stadium lease arrangement and warned that the city would file a $12 million breach of contract suit against the National League if the Padres left San Diego. The city later threatened to file a companion suit for $24 million and treble damages, raising the potential damages against the National League to $84 million. San Diego citizens, especially Little Leaguers, wrote protest letters and signed petitions to keep the Club in San Diego. In August the Internal Revenue Service claimed that Smith owed $22.8 million in back taxes and interest for 1969 and placed temporary liens on his properties in nine California counties.[23]

The Padres, therefore, continued under Smith's ownership for several more months. National League owners in early October tabled a vote on the proposed Danzansky sale to give Smith 30 days to complete financial arrangements with an unidentified wealthy California investor, who wanted to purchase the Padres outright and keep the club in San Diego. Mrs. Marjorie Lindheimer Everett, the mysterious investor, owned major stock in the Hollywood Race Track. Danzansky, who angrily replied, "The Washington group has been used,"[24] also protested when the Padres acquired high-salaried veterans Matty Alou from St. Louis, Willie McCovey from San Francisco, Glenn Beckert from the Chicago Cubs, and Bobby Tolan from Cincinnati without his consent. In early December the National League owners rejected Everett's bid by an 8–3 margin. Mrs. Everett had been involved in a bribery case resulting in the conviction of former Illinois Governor Otto Kerner. The National League owners then approved the sale of the Padres to the Danzansky group provided they would agree within 15 days to protect the league against legal action by the city. Vans were ready to move the club to Washington, D. C., while Topps Chewing Gum produced 1974 cards of 13 Padre players with the Washington inscription. The December 21 deadline, however, passed without any guarantee from Danzansky. Smith thus returned the $100,000 deposit check to the Danzansky group and sold the Padres a week later to Mrs. Everett for around $10 million. The National League owners in early January rejected the sale yet again, this time by a 9–3 margin.[25]

Chicagoan Ray Kroc, 72-year-old chairman and largest stockholder of the McDonald's Restaurant chain, then rescued the San Diego ballclub. The Chicago *Tribune* had published an article that the Padres were for sale. Kroc already had built the McDonald's hamburger operation into the nation's largest fast-food chain and had amassed a personal fortune estimated at $500 million. Kroc, who had always wanted to own the Chicago Cubs baseball club, paid Smith $12 million in cash for the Padres on January 25 and vowed to keep them in San Diego. "I just wanted a hobby," Kroc confided. "I'm in baseball so I can have fun. Money doesn't have anything to do with it."[26] San Diego players, management, and fans alike welcomed Kroc's move. "Kroc's buying of the club," Steve Arlin observed," was a great relief to the players."[27]

The Maturing Years (1974-78)

Ray Kroc's personal involvement soon began to turn the franchise around. Kroc, who vowed to build a contender gradually and let baseball authorities handle the front office and field manager operations, contrasted sharply with Smith. The new owner took much keener interest in the Padres. Steve Arlin recalled, "Smith did not care about the team. The players never saw him. Kroc, by contrast, was a great baseball fan."[28] Kroc also possessed the financial resources to make the Padres more competitive and to market the club more effectively. "His financial support," Los Angeles first baseman Steve Garvey reminisced, "gave the team money to change things."[29] Kroc bought the Padres an airplane to facilitate travel and installed a lounge for the players and their families. Pitcher Gary Lucas stressed, "Kroc came in at a time when the Padres had an identity problem and made the organization more credible."[30]

Two other major changes occurred before the 1974 season began. The Padres abandoned the old yellow uniforms and adopted a snappier white at home and gray on the road. John McNamara, a quiet, evenly dispositioned, sound baseball strategist, replaced Don Zimmer in February as manager. Zimmer had compiled a 114–190 mark in his two-year managerial tenure. McNamara had piloted the Oakland Athletics and coached for the San Francisco Giants.

Over 39,000 fans flocked to San Diego Stadium in early April to watch the Padres open their 1974 home season against the Houston Astros. The crowd cheered wildly when Kroc was introduced before the night game, showing affection and gratitude for the instant folk hero who had saved major league baseball for San Diego. By the eighth inning, however, the Padres had made several blunders and trailed, 9–2. Kroc grabbed the microphone and apologized to the startled, cheering crowd, "Ladies and gentleman, I suffer with you." After Kroc told the crowd that the loyal San Diego fans had "outstripped" the Los Angeles Dodgers by 8,000 fans in opening game attendance, a male streaker darted across the field. The ballpark turned into bedlam, as Kroc confessed, "I've never seen such stupid ballplaying in my life."[31]

Kroc's remarks infuriated the players, who contemplated boycotting the next game. Willie McCovey remarked, "This is a shocking thing. We may have played sloppy. But we're professionals and we know when the hell we play that way. We don't have to be reminded." Astros infielder Doug Rader exclaimed, "What does he think we are, short-order cooks or something?"[32] When the Astros returned to San Diego two months later, Kroc good-naturedly staged a chef's night and admitted free anyone wearing a chef's hat. Before that game, Rader approached home plate wearing a chef's hat and an apron and carrying a frying pan. Rader flipped the starting lineup card with a spatula and asked the umpires, "what's your pleasure—rare, medium, or well-done?"[33]

Financial stability slowly came to the struggling San Diego franchise. In 1974 the Padres drew over 1,075,000 spectators, smashing the previous attendance mark by around 431,000 people. "After five years of indifference," sportswriter Don Freeman noted, "the town has simply gone bananas over the Padres, from blue-collar Chula Vista to blue-chip La Jolla." The National Broadcasting Company ratings of Padre broadcasts by Jerry Coleman and Bob Chandler doubled in 1974.[34] Kroc's vow to create a contending club, the joy among San Diego fans that the club did not move, and special club promotions boosted both home attendance and radio ratings. The acquisition of veterans Alou, McCovey, and Beckert gave San Diego fans players they could recognize. Players promoted the Padres at McDonald's Restaurants and started endorsing various commercial products. Kroc initiated special promotions to draw San Diegans to home games. Elten Schiller enlisted San Diego businesses to finance the giving away of commercial products to fans on special promotion nights. "Kroc," according to club president Dick Freeman, "loved anything new and unique."[35] The owner hired the San Diego Chicken as the first team mascot and arranged for McNamara's Band to play at home games. Ted Giannoulas, a 5'4", 125-pound former journalism student from San Diego State University, amused millions of spectators and mimicked hundreds of players when colorfully attired in a henhouse costume as the San Diego Chicken.[36]

The Padres steadily improved under John McNamara from 1974 through 1976. In 1974 the 60–102 Padres finished last again. Fans saw little to cheer about that year aside from infielder Rich Morales becoming the first Padre to steal home and the club's 15-run outburst against the Philadelphia Phillies on July 17. The Padres traded veterans Nate Colbert, Clarence Gaston, and Derrell Thomas following the 1974 season and acquired several young pitchers, including Butch Metzger. In 1975 the Padres escaped the cellar for the first time with a 71–91 record and boosted club attendance by over 200,000 people. The Padres led the Western Division much of April and played well until numerous injuries decimated them after the All-Star break. San Diego again performed well the first half of 1976 and occupied second place in late June. A disastrous second-half slump, however, plunged the club to fifth place with a 73–89 mark.

Ray Kroc had instilled more enthusiasm and confidence in his squad. Before the 1975 season, Kroc hung a sign in the clubhouse that inspired his players, "Press on—nothing in the world can take the place of persistence. Persistence and determination alone are omnipotent." In early 1975, McNamara asserted, "Last year we didn't have the talent to stop a losing streak. This year we do." Infielder Mike Ivie added, "It feels good to come into a locker room knowing everybody is in a winning frame of mind."[37]

Padre pitching fortunes surged in 1975 and 1976. In 1975 San Diego hurlers led the major leagues in ERA into late June, as Randy Jones became the first Padre-developed superstar. Jones, who had lost 22 games in 1974, almost single-handedly gave pride and respectability to the once-pathetic Padres. Under rookie pitching coach Tom Morgan, Jones in 1975 became the first club 20-game winner with a 20–12 mark. Besides pacing National League pitchers with a 2.24 ERA, he tied Fred Norman's club shutout record (6) and finished second to Tom Seaver in the Cy Young Award balloting. Jones exhibited great control with his sinker ball, producing many ground balls and very short games. The sinker ball specialist tossed two one-hitters, two two-hitters, one three-hitter, and three four-hitters, and threw a scoreless ninth inning in relief to record a save for the National League in the 1975 All-Star Game. In 1976 he set season club records for wins (22), complete games (25), and innings pitched (315). Jones captured an incredible 16 of 19 decisions before the All-Star break and from May 17 to June 22 tied superstar Christy Mathewson's long-standing mark of 68 consecutive innings without surrendering a walk. Jones' 22–14 overall mark and 2.74 ERA helped him earn *The Sporting News* All-League Team honors for the second consecutive year. Seven of his losses were by one run, including three times when the Padres were shut out. Upon becoming the first Padre Cy Young Award winner, Jones commented, "It's a boyhood dream."[38] His feats came despite involvement in an automobile accident two months before the season ended and a subsequent arm operation for nerve fatigue. Pittsburgh Pirates coach Bob Skinner commented, "Randy's pitches are too good to take—and not good enough to hit," while Steve Arlin stressed, "Jones always kept his infielders in the game."[39] Jones still holds Padre career records for most starts (253), innings pitched (1,766), complete games (71), and shutouts (18), and ranks second in victories (92), third in strikeouts (677), and fourth in ERA (3.30). Former announcer Dave Campbell recalled, "People reveled in his success. He drew 10,000 to 15,000 additional people to games and received standing ovations even when warming up."[40] Butch Metzger, meanwhile, gave San Diego its best reliever up to that time with an 11–4 mark, 2.93 ERA, and 16 saves in 1976, becoming the first Padre to earn the National League Rookie Pitcher of the Year Award.

Dave Winfield and Willie McCovey supplied the main Padre offensive power in the mid-1970s. Winfield had joined the Padres in mid-1973 from the University of Minnesota, where he had been Most Valuable Player of the 1973 College World Series. Besides slugging 48 home runs from 1974 to 1976, he led the Padres in home runs (13) in 1976 and in RBIs (75) in 1974 and (76) in 1975. In 1975 Winfield was tied for the National League lead in home runs and was ranked near the top in RBIs before hurting his wrist in July. His batting average the next year soared to .283, a marked improvement of 16 points. "Winfield," Whitey Wietelmann claimed, "could do everything. He could run, field, throw, hit, hit with power."[41] The injury-prone McCovey, although past his prime, paced the Padres in home runs in 1974 (22) and 1975 (23), placed second in club RBIs both years, and equalled Hank Aaron's National League record by stroking his 15th career grand slam homer.

Following the 1976 season, the Padres entered the free-agent market for the first time. San Diego dramatically strengthened its bullpen by signing Rollie Fingers to a six-year contract worth $1.6 million and bolstered its power potential by inking outfielder Gene Tenace to a five-year $1.8 million contract. Fingers and Tenace both had starred on the championship Oakland Athletics club of the mid-1970s. The Cleveland Indians helped the Padres by trading center-fielder George Hendrick. These veterans boosted club attendance and paid immediate dividends. Fingers was named *The Sporting News* National League Fireman of the Year with an 8–9 mark and league-leading 35 saves in 1977, while Hendrick led the Padres with a .311 batting average and finished second on the club with 23 homers and 81 RBIs. At the same time, free agents Willie McCovey and Tito Fuentes left the team.[42]

These acquisitions, however, could not rescue the 69–93 Padres from a disappointing fifth-place finish in 1977. The Chicago Cubs' 23–6 shellacking of the Padres at Wrigley Field in mid-May set the tone for the disastrous season. Ray Kroc in late May fired Manager John McNamara, who had compiled a 224–310 mark since 1974. First base coach Alvin Dark, who previously had managed four major league clubs and produced three first-place finishers, subsequently guided the Padres to a 48–65 mark. Pitching mainstays Randy Jones and Butch Metzger did not repeat their dazzling 1976 performances. Jones underwent arm surgery and slumped to a 6–12 record, while Metzger was traded to St. Louis in mid-May. Dave Winfield paced the Padres in home runs (25) and RBIs (92), while three rookies—pitchers Bob Owchinko and Bob Shirley, and outfielder Gene Richards—showed considerable promise. Owchinko, *The Sporting News* National League Rookie Pitcher of the Year, won 9 of 21 decisions and hurled half the club's complete games (3). Shirley led the staff with 12 victories. Richards, among the best leadoff hitters in Padre history, set a major league record for most stolen bases (56) by a rookie.[43]

Several key personnel changes preceded the 1978 season. Buzzie Bavasi, club president for nine years, resigned in September 1977 because of a disagreement with Joan Kroc, the owner's wife. Bob

Fontaine, who had worked in the Dodger organization, was promoted from player personnel director to general manager and was encouraged to make trades and sign young players. The club budget for their minor league teams and scouting rose, enabling the Padres to sign several fine talented players.

In March 1978 the Padres fired Manager Alvin Dark only 17 days before the National League season opened. Dark, the victim of the earliest managerial change in major league history, was dismissed because of a player revolt, his failure to communicate with the front office, and his unwillingness to designate authority to his pitching, hitting, and other coaches. "We were getting a lot of feedback," Ray Kroc revealed, "from the players."[44] Several players had been unhappy with the complex strategy and rigid discipline that the born-again Christian manager had imposed. Gene Tenace claimed, "He put in so many trick plays and had so many signs that everyone was uptight."[45] Roger Craig, one-time Dodger pitcher and Padre pitching coach for six years, replaced Dark as manager.

The 84–78 Padres reached a major milestone in 1978, setting a club record for victories and surpassing the .500 standard for the first time. San Diego's home attendance increased by nearly 300,000 to 1,670,000 and remained steady after the All-Star break, as the club finished fourth in the Western Division only 11 games behind Los Angeles. The Padres, avoiding their usual second-half swoon, paced the National League clubs from June 20 to August 21 with a 37–22 record and remained in pennant contention through late August. Fontaine's personnel moves, along with Craig's field managing skills, improved Padre fortunes. Fontaine lured 39-year-old righthander Gaylord Perry from Texas in January 1978. That year Perry led the National League pitchers in wins (21), lost only six decisions, and boasted a 2.72 ERA, becoming the first hurler to garner the Cy Young Award in both leagues and becoming the oldest winner of the coveted pitching honor. *The Sporting News* named Perry to its All-League Team. Roger Craig contended, "I never saw a man who could get himself up so consistently."[46] "Perry," Steve Arlin reminisced, "really knew the game and made people think."[47] In late May 1978, Fontaine sent George Hendrick to St. Louis for pitcher Erik Rasmussen, who won 12 of 22 decisions that year. Seven rookies, including swift, acrobatic shortstop Ozzie Smith, joined the Padres in 1978. San Diego Hall of Champions director Frank Kern boasted, "Smith made hard plays look easy."[48] Manager Craig, a positive motivator, uplifted team spirits, proved an outstanding teacher, and gave his pitchers confidence. "Craig," infielder Tim Flannery recalled, "believed in his players and won their respect as a manager of men."[49]

Dave Campbell summed up the 1978 season by stating "a lot of guys put together good years."[50] For the first time, two Padre regulars batted over .300 in the same season. Dave Winfield batted .308, leading the Padres in homers (24), RBIs (97), doubles (30), and hits (181). Gene Richards batted .308 and swiped 37 bases in the leadoff role. The Padres ranked third in the National League in stolen bases (152), being paced by Ozzie Smith's 40. The Padres also furnished the league's second best pitching staff ERA (3.28), 1.15 fewer runs per game than the previous year. Perry, Jones, Erik Rasmussen, and Bob Owchinko formed an effective starting corps, while the bullpen saved 55 games. Fingers, recording a league-best 37 saves, repeated as the Senior Circuit's Fireman of the Year. Although struggling the first part of the season, the highly competitive Fingers pitched scoreless baseball for over one month and challenged opponents with his curves, sliders, and fastballs. Fingers saved 10 victories and completed 12 games for Perry. "Never in my 17 seasons," Perry declared, "have I had the good fortune of having a pitcher like Fingers in my bullpen."[51]

On July 11, 1978, San Diego hosted its first All-Star Game. A sellout crowd watched the National League stage a four-run eighth inning rally to triumph, 7–3. Dave Winfield, the first Padre All-Star Game starter and the National League's top vote getter, singled to left center field in the eighth inning and eventually scored. Fingers exhibited his usual dazzling control, hurling two shutout innings in relief. Fingers revolutionized relief pitching as one of baseball's first great bullpen artists. "Relief pitching," Steve Arlin remembered, "was not a very important thing until Fingers."[52]

The Transition Years (1979-81)

The 1979 through 1981 seasons saw the Padres plunge in the standings and change managers frequently. In 1979 the Padres suffered through a 68–93 fifth-place finish, as most veterans struggled. Dave Winfield, however, enjoyed his best season as a Padre and saved the club from last place with his 34 homers, .308 batting average, and league-leading and club record 118 RBIs. His post-season honors included being the first Padre to win a Gold Glove award and also making *The Sporting News* All-League Team. In October 1979 Jerry Coleman replaced Roger Craig, who had compiled a 152–171 record in his two seasons as manager. Coleman, a former New York Yankee infielder, had announced Padre games since 1972. The 72–89 Padres plummeted to last place in 1980, but ironically led the major leagues in stolen bases (239) and became the first major league team to have three players break the 50 stolen base barrier. Gene Richards, Ozzie Smith, and Jerry Mumphrey accomplished that feat with 61, 57, and 52 thefts, respectively. "The Padre strength," pitcher Gary Lucas stressed, "was speed."[53] Richards finished second in the National League in hits (193) and shared the league lead with 12 triples. Smith and Winfield both won Gold Gloves for their defensive prowess, while Fingers became the first pitcher to snare three Fireman of the Year awards. Six-foot, 7- inch, 280 pound Frank Howard, a former Los Angeles Dodger and Washington Senator slugger, in October 1980 replaced Manager Jerry Coleman, who returned to the broadcast booth. In the strike-shortened 1981 season, the Padres lost 20 of their first 30 games and struggled to their worst record (41–69) since 1974. Ozzie Smith won his second consecutive Gold Glove, but defensive and bullpen problems plagued the club. Howard was fired as manager that October.[54]

The front office also changed significantly from 1979 to 1981. In 1979 Commissioner Bowie Kuhn fined Ray Kroc a record $100,000 for tampering when the latter vowed he would pursue both Joe Morgan of the Cincinnati Reds and Graig Nettles of the New York Yankees when they became free agents. Kroc contemplated selling the club, but instead made several internal moves. First he turned the Padre presidency and team operations over to his son-in-law Ballard Smith, Jr. in August 1979 and authorized him to invest heavily in the free-agent market and to make trades. Smith, a former district attorney from Pennsylvania who had not been involved in baseball operations before, tried to make the Padre organization a family unit. "Smith," Dave Campbell noted, "created a family atmosphere and team harmony."[55] In September 1980 Jack McKeon, former Kansas City Royals and Oakland Athletics manager, became vice president of baseball operations and assumed Fontaine's responsibilities. Cigar-smoking McKeon, nicknamed Trader Jack, concentrated on developing a youth movement and laid the foundations for a strong club through trades and free-agent acquisitions. Following the 1980 season, McKeon unloaded 14 veterans. "The old players," McKeon contended, "were pretty much finished."[56] McKeon planned "to secure players at each position who could help his club win at least 50 percent of the games."[57] According to Steve Garvey, "McKeon was a good strategist with a vision for both the immediate season and the future and an excellent judge of the players' talents."[58]

San Diego lost Dave Winfield, who had been the Padres' most consistent offensive weapon in the late 1970s, to free agency after the 1980 campaign. Winfield still holds the club career records for RBIs (626) and ranks second in hits (1,134), runs scored (599), doubles (179), and home runs (154), third in triples (39), and fifth in batting average (.286) and stolen bases (133). San Diego management negotiated a renewal of Winfield's contract, but he and his agent Al Frohman demanded considerably more money. After the San Diego management balked, George Steinbrenner's New York Yankees signed the All-Star right fielder for $1 million. Winfield left without the Padres receiving any compensation. The star outfielder clearly wanted to play for New York, where he would gain more publicity. "Winfield," Tim

Flannery recalled, "did not want to go through another youth movement."[59]

Other veterans left San Diego in major transactions. The Padres traded Gaylord Perry to the Texas Rangers in February 1980. Perry had walked out near the end of the 1979 season, the last year of his contract, because of personal problems after compiling a 12–11 record. In December 1980 Rollie Fingers, Gene Tenace, and two other veterans were sent to the St. Louis Cardinals. Fingers, among the best relief pitchers in Padre history, had set club career (108) and season (37) records for saves, had paced the National League twice in saves, and had won 34 games from 1977 to 1980. The Padres traded Randy Jones to the New York Mets in December 1980 and Jerry Mumphrey to the New York Yankees in April 1981. These moves slashed the club payroll, but did not produce immediate dividends because the veterans could not be replaced very easily.[60]

Several acquisitions were made during the same period. Before the 1980 season, the Padres invested heavily in the free-agent market. They spent $1.95 million for Cleveland Indian righthander Rick Wise to replace Perry and $1.75 million for San Francisco Giant lefthander John Curtis, but neither fulfilled expectations. Wise won only 10 of 26 decisions during the next two seasons, while Curtis split 40 decisions from 1980 to 1982. The Padres in August 1980 obtained infielder Luis Salazar, who batted over .300 his first two seasons. The best San Diego addition during this period was catcher Terry Kennedy, part of an 11-player trade with the St. Louis Cardinals. The son of a former major leaguer, Kennedy batted over .300 his initial season and provided the Padres with power and a strong throwing arm. Kennedy joined the club shortly before San Diego Stadium was renamed Jack Murphy Stadium in 1981, within a year following the death of the San Diego *Union* sports editor who had lobbied intensely for a modern stadium and major league baseball and football franchises.[61]

The Fulfillment Years (1982-85)

San Diego enjoyed its greatest field success as a franchise under manager Dick Williams. In November 1981 the Padres signed former Brooklyn Dodger Williams, the 11th winningest all-time skipper with over 1,000 major league victories, to a three-year contract. Williams had guided the Boston Red Sox to the 1967 American League pennant and the Oakland Athletics to the 1972 and 1973 World Series titles and had led the Montreal Expos into contention. Utilizing a tough, no-nonsense approach, he stressed consistency and sound, fundamental baseball featuring solid pitching, speed, and defense. Pitcher Ed Whitson classified Williams as "a very strict manager, who expected 110 percent from his players."[62] Outfielder Tony Gwynn depicted Williams as "a winner who taught his players how to play the game, how to win, and how to be mentally tough."[63] "Players paid the price for mental mistakes and would sit on the bench," infielder Luis Salazar recalled.[64] Williams, an intense, demanding manager and aloof person, possessed a great knowledge of baseball, relied heavily on percentages, form charts, and statistics in making decisions, and hoped to instill a winning attitude and the importance of teamwork in his players. Infielder Steve Garvey called Williams "as good a baseball mind as I've ever played for."[65] "Williams," according to pitcher Eric Show, "always played the percentages."[66] Catcher Terry Kennedy stressed that Williams insisted "team play was in and excuses were out" and the players pick the team "by their own performances."[67]

Jack McKeon, meanwhile, made three trades with the St. Louis Cardinals before the 1982 season. The Padres secured outfielder Sixto Lezcano, traded light-hitting, Gold Glove shortstop Ozzie Smith for shortstop Garry Templeton in February 1982, and acquired pitcher Luis DeLeon. San Diego dealt Smith, the fourth leading Padre base stealer in history, because they anticipated losing him to free agency after the 1983 season. Smith's agent wanted $35 million for his client over a 25-year period. "Smith and the Padres," Elten Schiller remembered, "were miles apart financially."[68] The Padres did not want to lose Smith without compensation as had happened in the Dave Winfield case. Pitcher Gary Lucas remarked, "the Padres wanted compensation this time if they were going to lose someone."[69] Jack McKeon explained, "the Padres traded an All-Star shortstop for an All-Star shortstop."[70] Templeton, whom announcer Jerry Coleman termed "a remarkable athlete,"[71] possessed a fine career batting average, excellent range at shortstop, and a great throwing arm. Templeton still ranks third in club hits (999) and doubles (169), fourth in triples (32), and fifth in runs scored (380) and RBIs (377).[72]

McKeon also made two key acquisitions before the 1983 season. In November 1982 San Diego acquired starting pitcher Ed Whitson from the Cleveland Indians. The Padres became a legitimate contender on December 21, signing free-agent first baseman Steve Garvey to a five-year, $6.5 million contract. Garvey provided the righthanded power, defensive stability, and veteran leadership that the team had needed to become a quality baseball club. "Garvey," Jack McKeon remarked, "put the club close to where it wanted to be."[73] According to Ed Whitson, "Garvey gave leadership like Reggie Jackson. He was the center of attention and took the pressure off younger players."[74] Ticket sales increased dramatically following Garvey's signing. "Garvey," Dave Campbell stated, "gave the franchise legitimacy as a true superstar and integrated the team in the community."[75] Dick Freeman observed, "Garvey made a huge impact as a huge personality and enhanced the image of the Padres."[76]

Padre fortunes improved dramatically, as the squad compiled identical 81–81 records in both 1982 and 1983. In 1982 the Padres escaped the cellar for the first time in three years by finishing fourth with the fourth best record in franchise history. Williams' team set a club record by winning 11 consecutive games in April and stood only two games behind first-place Atlanta at the All-Star break. San Diego held second place until early August when several injuries and drug problems intervened. Rookie infielder Alan Wiggins underwent drug treatment after being arrested for cocaine possession and was suspended by Commissioner Bowie Kuhn. Second baseman Juan Bonilla subsequently received drug rehabilitation treatment.[77]

McKeon's trades and youth movement both paid dividends in the squad's improved pitching and offensive performances in 1982. Under new coach Norm Sherry, the Padres developed one of the National League's best pitching staffs. Lefthander Tim Lollar, acquired earlier from the New York Yankees, led San Diego starters with a 16–9 record and fine 3.13 ERA. Rookie starters Eric Show (10–6), Dave Dravecky (5–3), and Floyd Chiffer (4–3) surrendered less than three runs per game, while first-year reliever Luis DeLeon won 9 of 14 decisions, compiled 15 saves, and boasted a sterling 2.03 ERA. Kennedy led the Padres in batting (.295), home runs (21), and RBIs (97) and set a club record with 42 doubles. Sixto Lezcano supplied the righthanded power the club craved with 16 home runs, 84 RBIs, and a .289 batting average. Outfielder Tom Gwynn showed considerable promise, batting .289 in his first 54 major league contests.[78]

An injury-plagued 1983 season resulted in another fourth-place finish. Tony Gwynn broke his wrist in winter ball and missed the first part of the campaign. Steve Garvey dislocated his left thumb in a collision at home plate in late July and did not play the rest of the season. He was batting .294 with 14 homers and 59 RBIs when his consecutive game streak ended at 1,207, best in National League history and third highest in major league history. Opposing hurlers then pitched around Terry Kennedy, who was leading the club in nearly every offensive category and made *The Sporting News* Silver Slugger Team. Injuries also sidelined Garry Templeton, Ed Whitson, Tim Lollar, and 14-game winner Dave Dravecky, requiring the Padres to develop younger players. Tony Gwynn led the Padres in batting (.309) and strung together the major league's longest hitting streak at 25 games. Eric Show recorded 15 victories to pace the young pitching staff. Base-stealing became a major component of Williams' offense, as the Padres pilfered 179 bases. Wiggins overcame his initial drug problems to set a then club record with 66 stolen bases, while Bobby Brown hit in 21 consecutive games and stole 27 bases. Lefthander Mark Thurmond joined the Padres at midseason and finished with a 7–3 mark and 2.65 ERA. Dick Williams proclaimed, "We've got it going for us, now."[79]

The Padres dedicated their 1984 season to Ray Kroc, who had died on January 14 at age 81. As Jack McKeon eulogized, "The Padres had lost a great guy who was always interested in baseball and a genuine human being revering people who produced."[80] Joan Kroc, "a bubbling matriarch with a heart of golden arches,"[81] replaced her husband as owner. The St. Paul, Minnesota native had been a professional musician and music teacher for many years and music director of KSTP-TV before marrying Ray Kroc in 1969. An active philanthropist, she has given generously to such humanitarian concerns as substance abuse, world hunger, international peace, animal rights, hospice, and AIDS research. Her son-in-law, Ballard Smith, was also named as club president.[82]

Three major moves before the 1984 season solidified San Diego as pennant contenders. In a three-way deal in December 1983, the Padres secured relief pitcher Craig Lefferts and outfielder Carmelo Martinez from the Chicago Cubs. Free-agent Rich Gossage, then the most intimidating reliever in baseball with the New York Yankees, signed a multi-year contract worth over $6 million with San Diego on January 6. Gossage gave the club the bullpen stopper it had lacked since Rollie Fingers departed. The Padres solved their perennial third base problem by acquiring San Diego native, Graig Nettles, from the New York Yankees on March 30 for pitcher Dennis Rasmussen. Although 40 years old, Nettles remained an explosive hitter and fine infielder and provided valuable clubhouse leadership. Jack McKeon asserted, "Gossage made the club a contender and Nettles provided the last piece in the puzzle with steady third base play."[83] Tony Gwynn stressed, "these veterans knew how to win, taught the younger guys what it took to be successful, and supplied leadership through example."[84] On the other hand, the Padres lost veteran Gene Richards to free agency. Richards, who was unhappy with Dick Williams, ranked first in stolen bases (242), second in batting average (.291), third in runs scored (484), and fourth in hits (994) in Padre history.[85]

The Padres captured the Western Division title with an impressive 92–70 mark in 1984. San Diego surpassed the .500 mark for only the second time in franchise history and performed its best ever, finishing 12 games ahead of the Houston Astros and Atlanta Braves. The Padres won nine of 11 games in their first homestand and never relinquished first place after June 9. A 38–21 mark in June and July solidified their lead, as the other injury-ridden Western Division teams never really challenged. Jack McKeon recalled, "The Padres started great and had the division title won before the All-Star break."[86] Eric Show added, "The Padres won that year by default."[87] The Padres, who smashed a club attendance record by nearly 400,000 fans and drew 1,983,904 spectators, clinched the Western Division title on September 20. Pitcher Tim Lollar smashed a three-run homer, as the Padres defeated San Francisco to clinch at least a tie. Three hours later, Los Angeles downed Houston to clinch the Western Division title for the Padres.[88]

Two brawls on August 12 involving the Padres and Atlanta Braves solidified team unity. Atlanta pitcher Pascual Perez hit San Diego leadoff batter Alan Wiggins with his first pitch. Padre pitchers subsequently threw at Perez in each of his four plate appearances. Ed Whitson and Dick Williams were both ejected in the third inning. The first fight erupted when Craig Lefferts hit Perez with a pitch in the eighth inning. In the top of the ninth inning, Atlanta reliever Donnie Moore also hit Graig Nettles with a pitch, sparking a fierce fight. Altogether, 14 Braves and Padres were ejected from that single game. The umpires cleared both benches and both bullpens, and police lined both dugouts for the remainder of the game. Williams was fined $10,000 and suspended 10 days. Seven Padre players and two Padre coaches were also fined. "The brawl in Atlanta," Dave Campbell claimed, "woke the Padres up out of their doldrums."[89]

The youth and veterans blended together to produce the superb 1984 season. "The Padres," Steve Garvey reminisced, "were a well-balanced team with veterans and rookies."[90] The 24-year-old outfield tandem of Tony Gwynn, Kevin McReynolds, and Carmelo Martinez enjoyed fine campaigns. Gwynn waltzed to the major league batting title (.351), topped the National League in hits (213) and on-base percentage (.410), and paced the Padres in triples (10) and total bases (269). Gwynn, who stole 33 bases and struck out only 23 times in 606 at-bats, joined pitcher Mark Thurmond on *The Sporting News* All-League Team and shortstop Garry Templeton on *The Sporting News* Silver Slugger Team. McReynolds shared the club lead in home runs (20), batted .278, and knocked in 75 runs, while Martinez produced 66 RBIs. Alan Wiggins, converted to second base, ignited the offense as a leadoff hitter, setting team records in stolen bases (70) and runs scored (106), and topping the Padres in walks (75). "Wiggins," Ed Whitson recalled, "made all the difference in the world."[91] Garvey's 86 RBIs, Nettles' 65 RBIs and 20 home runs, and Terry Kennedy's contributions helped immeasurably. "The talent and experience of the veterans," Tim Flannery contended, "were crucial factors."[92]

The youthful starting pitchers performed better than anticipated in 1984. Eric Show led the Padre hurlers with a 15–9 record and 3.40 ERA, while Mark Thurmond and Ed Whitson compiled identical 14–8 records and 2.97 and 3.24 ERAs, respectively. Goose Gossage posted 10 victories, 25 saves, and a 2.90 ERA as the bullpen mainstay, while Craig Lefferts and Dave Dravecky combined for 12 wins and 18 saves. As Garry Templeton recalled, "speed, power, pitching, and defense produced the first-place finish."[93] The Padres improved their team batting average from .250 to .259 and their home runs from 93 to 109, as six players knocked in at least 57 runs. Padre pitchers lowered their team ERA from 3.62 to 3.48 and dramatically raised their shut-outs from five to a league-leading 17. In reflecting on the 1984 season, Dave Campbell noted, "lots of players performed up to their ability and even a few above their ability."[94] Eric Show explained, "Everyone had a good year. The team consistently executed the fundamentals."[95] Tony Gwynn added, "The team had a lot of heart and spunk. Nobody expected anything at the start."[96]

The National League Championship Series gave the San Diego franchise some of its most exciting and memorable moments. The Chicago Cubs dominated the Padres in the first two games at Wrigley Field. San Diego pitching disintegrated in the opening game, as the Cubs thrashed the Padres, 13–0. Chicago batters set National League playoff records with 16 hits, five home runs, and 13 hits off Eric Show and Greg Harris. Cubs starter Rick Sutcliffe surrendered only Steve Garvey's bunt single and Garry Templeton's bloop single while striking out eight in seven innings. The next day, the Cubs defeated the Padres, 4–2. The only Padre runs came on McReynolds' sacrifice fly in the fourth inning and Steve Garvey's single in the sixth inning, as the Cubs stood on the verge of ending their 39-year World Series famine.[97]

The Padres were amazed to find 3,000 to 5,000 fans greet them at Jack Murphy Stadium upon their return from Chicago. Their plane was three hours late leaving O'Hare Airport in Chicago and did not land at San Diego International Airport until around 10:30 p.m. "The players," Dave Campbell claimed, "already had given up and were talking about what they were going to do in the off-season."[98] "The players," Garry Templeton confessed, "weren't expecting anybody when thousands of screaming and hollering fans showed up. The fans were a tenth man, motivating the team and got their hearts pumping."[99] Bobby Brown stormed around the parking lot screaming through a bull horn, "Three in a row."[100] "Afterwards," Garry Templeton remarked, "the Padre players sensed that they could defeat the Cubs."[101] "The fans," Luis Salazar asserted, "turned things around."[102]

The Padres staged a dramatic comeback in what Tim Flannery fondly termed "four magical days."[103] The Padres snared the next three games from the Cubs to qualify for the World Series, becoming the first team to overcome a 2–0 deficit to take the Championship Series. Over 58,000 fans jammed Jack Murphy Stadium each night.

During player introductions at the third game, the usually non-emotional Garry Templeton waved his hat to the crowd. The fans then started applauding and cheering wildly. "Templeton's action," Jack McKeon maintained, "fired up the team further. You could probably hear the crowd all the way to Tijuana."[104] Steve Garvey claimed, "The cheering crowd won the game for us that night."[105] The Cubs led 1–0 in the bottom of the fifth inning, when Terry Kennedy and McReynolds both singled and scored on Garry Templeton's double. "Templeton's hit," Tony Gwynn observed, "gave the Padres the lead for the first time and confidence that they could come from behind."[106] The Padres ensured the victory with four runs the next inning. Tony Gwynn singled off Dennis Eckersley and came home on Graig Nettles' base hit. Terry Kennedy singled off reliever George Frazier before McReynolds slugged a three-run homer. The Cubs were baffled by Whitson's palm ball and fastball.[107]

Dramatic Game Four, won by the Padres, 7–5, featured Garvey's four hits and five RBIs. San Diego scored two runs off Cubs starter Scott Sanderson in the third inning. Garry Templeton singled and stole second base. Wiggins singled before Tony Gwynn's sacrifice fly tallied Templeton. Steve Garvey's double scored Wiggins. After the Cubs retaliated with three runs in the fourth inning, the Padres tied the game the next inning. Tim Flannery singled and moved to third base on a bunt and groundout. Garvey's single brought home Flannery. The Padres seized the lead in the seventh inning when Bobby Brown walked and stole second base. Reliever Tim Stoddard intentionally walked Gwynn. Garvey scored on Brown's single and Gwynn tallied on a passed ball. The Cubs knotted the score 5–5 in the eighth inning off Gossage. In the ninth inning, Cubs reliever Lee Smith surrendered a single to Gwynn. Garvey then drove a fastball into the right-center-field bleachers to win the game. "Time stood still," Garvey observed. "It was as if all sound stopped." Garvey knew "the Padres now had the home field advantage and, if they could stay close, they could win."[108] The five RBIs gave Garvey 20 career playoff RBIs, breaking Reggie Jackson's record.

Garvey's home run set the stage for the dramatic fifth game. The Cubs led 3–0 after five innings, as Rick Sutcliffe allowed just two weak singles. Padre relievers Andy Hawkins, Craig Lefferts, and Gossage shut out Chicago after the second inning. The Padres knotted the score in the sixth inning. Wiggins reached first base on a bunt, Gwynn singled, and Garvey walked. Wiggins and Gwynn scored on sacrifice flies by Graig Nettles and Terry Kennedy. The Padres plated four runs in the seventh inning, as Sutcliffe tired. Carmelo Martinez walked, was sacrificed to second base, and came home on Tim Flannery's ground ball through first baseman Leon Durham's legs. Wiggins sliced a single.

Gwynn's hard grounder took a bad hop by second baseman Ryne Sandberg for a double, tallying Flannery and Wiggins. Gwynn scored on Garvey's single, giving the Padres a 6–3 victory. Manager Jack McKeon remarked, "once the fifth game was tied, there was no way we would lose the game."[109] It is too bad that Ray Kroc had not lived to see the greatest moment in Padre history.

Padre batters and relief pitchers had performed brilliantly in the Championship Series comeback. "The Padres," McKeon boasted, "played the greatest baseball in franchise history."[110] Garvey enjoyed a brilliant series with a .400 batting average, seven RBIs, and eight hits to earn MVP honors. Gwynn's superb .368 batting average included three doubles and four singles. Templeton, Wiggins, and McReynolds all batted at least .300 and combined for 14 hits. Lefferts hurled four shutout innings in relief and earned two victories, while Dravecky allowed only two hits in six innings of relief. As Gwynn stated, "Everyone did his share. Confidence was the big key."[111]

The Padres' magic ended in the World Series, which the Detroit Tigers captured four games to one. A record 57,908 disappointed fans witnessed the Tigers edge the Padres, 3–2, in Game One. Detroit scored once in the top of the first inning off Mark Thurmond. In the bottom of the first inning, Garvey and Nettles singled off Jack Morris. Kennedy's double plated both Garvey and Nettles. In the fifth inning, Larry Herndon belted a two-run homer to give the Tigers the victory. The Padres rebounded in Game Two by a 5–3 margin. Detroit scored three runs off Ed Whitson in the first inning, but reliever Andy Hawkins hurled over five innings of one-hit ball. San Diego tallied once in the first inning on Nettles' sacrifice fly off Dan Petry and scored another on Bobby Brown's groundout. In the fifth inning Kurt Bevacqua, who had homered only once during the regular season, belted a three-run roundtripper into the left-field bleachers after Nettles walked and Kennedy singled. Reliever Lefferts struck out five batters in three innings to maintain the Padres' sole victory.[112]

Detroit swept the final three games at Tiger Stadium. San Diego pitchers walked a record 11 Tigers in the 5–2 Game Three loss. Maity Castillo's two-run homer highlighted a four-run outburst off San Diego starter Tim Lollar in the second inning. San Diego scored once in the third inning and plated another in the seventh inning on Gwynn's single, Garvey's double, and Nettles' sacrifice fly. Game Four saw the Tigers triumph, 4–2. Allen Trammell slugged a pair of two-run homers in the first and third innings off Eric Show. Jack Morris pitched a five-hit masterpiece, surrendering Terry Kennedy's second-inning homer and one run in the ninth inning. Relievers Dravecky, Lefferts, and Gossage hurled over five shutout innings. Detroit captured the finale, 8–4, to take its first World Series since 1968. The

Tigers dominated the last game after taking the first three contests by two runs or less. Mark Thurmond allowed three runs, including Kirk Gibson's two-run homer, in the first inning. San Diego scored once on Garvey's third-inning single and twice in the fourth inning on Bobby Brown's sacrifice fly and Wiggins' single. Gibson's fifth-inning single gave Detroit the permanent lead. Homers followed by Lance Parrish in the seventh inning off Gossage and by Bevacqua in the eighth inning off Willie Hernandez. Gibson's three-run roundtripper into the right-field upper deck off Gossage clinched the Tiger victory. Sparky Anderson became the first manager to take World Series titles in both leagues.[113]

San Diego batters hit a respectable .265 in the World Series, but ineffective starting pitching doomed the Padres. Kurt Bevacqua surprisingly paced Williams' club with a sparkling .412 batting average, slugging two home runs, two doubles, three singles, and four RBIs. "Bevacqua," Dave Campbell reminisced, "thrived on pressure and enjoyed five days of fame."[114] Wiggins and Templeton combined for 14 hits and compiled batting averages over .300, but Kennedy, Garvey, Carmelo Martinez, and Bobby Brown struggled offensively. The Padres lacked a dominant starting pitcher like Jack Morris. Mark Thurmond, Eric Show, Tim Lollar, and Ed Whitson all performed poorly, giving up more than one earned run per inning. Detroit batters shelled them for 17 runs, including 16 earned, in only 10⅓ innings. Allen Trammell, Kirk Gibson, and Larry Herndon hammered San Diego pitchers for 20 hits, five home runs, and 16 RBIs. "The San Diego starting pitchers," Dave Campbell noted, "could not survive the first three innings and always left the Padres behind."[115] Hawkins, Lefferts, Greg Harris, and Dravecky all relieved superbly, limiting the Tigers to one run and nine hits in 24 innings over the first four games. Luis Salazar boasted, "We got amazing help from our bullpen."[116]

Other factors influenced the World Series outcome. Detroit had won 35 of its first 40 games on the way to an excellent regular season and possessed a dominant starting pitcher in Morris. "Detroit," Ed Whitson commented, "had been consistent all year. They were bound and determined to win the World Series."[117] Garry Templeton added, "Detroit had an outstanding year. They had everything."[118] The Championship Series had drained the Padres physically and emotionally and left them without the same degree of intensity in the World Series. Steve Garvey admitted, "the Padres had an emotional let-down against Detroit."[119] Kevin McReynolds missed the entire World Series with a wrist injury, leaving a major power vacuum. Ed Whitson remarked, "McReynolds' injury killed us. It took power away from us."[120] The Championship Series and World Series, nevertheless, had given the Padres valuable playoff experience. "Our young players," manager

Dick Williams commented, "matured in the playoffs; there are no unseasoned players on this team anymore."[121]

The 1984 Padre season, in many respects, had resembled their 1978 campaign. Managers Roger Craig and Dick Williams got the maximum performances from their respective teams. Both times the Padres had played much better than anticipated and had not experienced a midseason swoon. The 1978 Padres had secured the first winning season in franchise history, while the 1984 club had earned the team's best season record ever. Veterans and younger players had blended very well. Batters and pitchers alike lived up to their potential as a team. Both teams executed fundamentals, plating runners in scoring position and stealing bases. Both squads boasted fine leadoff batters, who often stole bases and scored, as well as reliable bullpen stoppers.

Manager Dick Williams made winning the World Series the Padres' team goal for the 1985 season. McKeon strengthened the San Diego pitching staff during the off-season. On December 6 the Padres acquired starter LaMarr Hoyt, the 1983 American League Cy Young Award winner, from the Chicago White Sox for four players. Hoyt was regarded as one of the major league's best hurlers and was expected to lead the young pitching staff. "It was a good trade," McKeon insisted. "It was not Hoyt's fault that the team slumped in 1985."[122] San Diego also signed Tim Stoddard, former New York Yankee and Chicago Cub pitcher. Padre fans sensed that the club might be on the verge of a dynasty. The front office seemed to have unlimited financial resources to secure experienced players. "With everything we had going for us, we could have become one of the great franchises in baseball," Goose Gossage stated.[123]

The 1985 season indeed resembled the 1984 campaign through midseason. On opening night, a record regular-season crowd of 54,490 fans cheered the raising of the National League pennant in center field and saw a new $6.5 million Diamond Vision Scoreboard unveiled in right field. The Padres, sporting new pinstripe uniforms, led the Western Division by five games on July 4. Padre batters and pitchers performed well. LaMarr Hoyt captured 12 of his first 16 decisions before the All-Star break, while Andy Hawkins won his first 10 starts and established a club record by taking his first 11 decisions. The fine first-half season performance helped the Padres break the two-million attendance barrier for the first time. San Diego fielded its largest contingent ever at the All-Star Game in Minneapolis. The National League roster, managed by Williams, included five San Diego starters (Garvey, Templeton, Nettles, Gwynn, and Hoyt), two Padre reserves (Gossage and Kennedy), and some team coaches. Hoyt, the starting and winning pitcher, captured All-Star Game MVP honors, while Gossage earned a save.[124]

Padre fortunes, however, plunged dramatically after the All-Star break. In July the Padres lost 17 of 27 contests to fall five games behind Los Angeles. "The club blew it," Jerry Coleman explained.[125] The Padres eventually slumped to a disappointing 83–79 finish, in third place 12 games behind the Dodgers. The loss of leadoff hitter Alan Wiggins partly precipitated the decline. Joan Kroc refused to let Wiggins, who had suffered a drug relapse in April, play for the Padres anymore and traded him to the Baltimore Orioles. "Losing Alan changed the entire character of our offense," lamented Dick Williams.[126] "Wiggins was a team catalyst," Garry Templeton said. "The Padres could not find anybody to lead off and steal bases like him."[127] The Padres' stolen base production declined by 60 percent to a league-low 60, their runs by nine percent to 650, and their record in one-run games by 78 percent to 31–30. Padre batters did not deliver as many clutch base hits with two men out and runners in scoring position. Wiggins' loss may have hurt the batting performances of other Padres. Gwynn's batting average dropped to .317 in 1985 partly because he saw far fewer fastballs to hit without Wiggins batting ahead of him. Garvey, Kennedy, and McReynolds all slumped at the plate during the summer months. Injuries may have contributed to the team slump, forcing the Padres to use younger players. LaMarr Hoyt encountered arm trouble and won only four games after the All-Star break. Injuries sidelined Gossage much of August, hurting the bullpen. The impending strike also distracted player concentration. Jack McKeon contended, "the strike caused the July slump," while Gwynn maintained, "the strike divided the team."[128]

Padre players and the media increasingly grew disenchanted with Manager Williams. Williams experienced personality conflicts with several players including McReynolds, whose batting average and home run production plunged. Elten Schiller stated, "Williams was a stern taskmaster and very demanding, stepping on players' toes. A majority of the players were in the doghouse because of on-the-field things."[129] According to Whitey Wietelmann, "Williams played to win and didn't care if he hurt player feelings."[130] The media questioned Williams' decision to switch from a five-man to four-man rotation after the All-Star break. The Padres then lost 12 of their next 18 games before the two-day strike.

San Diego pitchers compiled an impressive 3.40 staff ERA, fourth best in the National League, in 1985. Despite the late-season arm trouble, LaMarr Hoyt boasted an excellent 16–8 mark and 3.47 ERA and hurled three shutouts. Andy Hawkins paced the staff with 18 victories in 26 decisions and wielded a fine 3.15 ERA. Starters Dave Dravecky and Eric Show combined for 25 additional wins, but the latter surrendered Pete Rose's historic record-breaking 4,192nd hit on September 11 at Cincinnati. Bullpen ace Gossage saved 26 games, took 5 of 8 decisions, and led the staff with a 1.82 ERA.[131]

The 1985 season had paralleled the 1979 campaign. Neither San Diego club performed up to expectations. The 1979 Padres plunged below the .500 mark, while the 1985 club floundered after the All-Star break. Padre veterans started aging and declining in productivity. Ace starters Gaylord Perry and LaMarr Hoyt missed crucial portions of their respective campaigns. Bullpen injuries diminished their effectiveness. Fundamentals were not executed well, as the Padres left numerous runners in scoring position and stole far fewer bases. The performances of the Padre leadoff batters declined markedly both seasons. Neither manager survived into the next season.

Turmoil marked the 1985-86 off-season. One year remained on Manager Williams' three-year contract at the end of the 1985 season. Williams wanted McKeon either to grant him a contract extension or let him resign with pay for the 1986 season. Williams initially agreed to buy out the contract when McKeon dismissed his close friend, Ozzie Virgil, as coach. Joan Kroc, however, wanted to retain Williams, negated the contract buyout, and rehired Virgil. Further discord surfaced when Williams dismissed coach Harry Dunlop. The night before spring training began in February 1986 at Yuma, Arizona, a settlement was reached. At an early morning press conference, the Padres announced that Williams would not be returning and that coach Virgil had resigned. The club faced a difficult assignment in replacing such a consistent winner as Williams. "Williams' leaving," Jerry Coleman confessed, "was hard to overcome."[132] He had become the first Padre manager to leave with a winning record, boasting a 337–311 mark over four years. A few days later, Hoyt entered a rehabilitation center for treatment of alcohol dependency. The period of fulfillment had ended abruptly.

The Rebuilding Years (1986–92)

With Williams' exodus, San Diego entered a rebuilding phase. Steve Boros, a low-key, computer-oriented former Oakland Athletics manager and director of the Padres' minor league instruction, replaced Williams. No time remained for Boros to prepare strategy or make plans regarding player personnel. Boros knew baseball well, lacked Williams' strictness, and gave the younger players more on-field time "Boros," according to Eric Show, "was a very kind manager and treated players like decent human beings."[133] Under Boros, the Padres struggled to a fourth-place finish and their worst mark (74–88) since 1980. Veteran starters Nettles, Garvey, Kennedy, and Templeton, as well as reserve Martinez, experienced sub-par seasons at the plate. Show and Dravecky, the club's premier starting pitchers, suffered season-ending injuries in August, as Padre pitchers saw their staff ERA soar to 3.99 and led the National League in home runs and walks surrendered.[134]

Younger Padres, developed in the farm system, salvaged the 1986 season. Gwynn batted .329, paced the National League in hits (211), tied for the league lead in runs scored (107), recorded a career-best 14 home runs, stole 37 bases, and snared the first of three consecutive Gold Gloves defensively. Gwynn's numerous honors included making the National League All-Star team, *The Sporting News* All-League team, and *The Sporting News* Silver Slugger team. McReynolds emerged as the Padres' top slugger with a .286 batting average, 26 homers, 96 RBIs, and a .504 slugging percentage. Rookie outfielder John Kruk batted .309, while rookie righthander Jimmy Jones debuted with a splendid one-hitter against Houston on September 21. Craig Lefferts and Lance McCullers furnished excellent relief. Lefferts led the National League in appearances (83), won 9 of 17 decisions, boasted a 3.09 ERA, and saved four games. McCullers finished 10–10 with a 2.78 ERA and five saves.[135]

The 1986 season virtually had repeated the earlier 1980 campaign. Both transition clubs suffered nearly identical losing records, with club attendance plummeting dramatically. Certain veteran players exhibited declining skills, while young players demonstrated considerable promise. Only one starter on either team batted over .300. A major power hitting outfielder left the club following each season because of stalled contract negotiations. In both instances, the Padre manager shouldered the blame for the team's sub-par performance and was replaced.

Several management decisions also stirred controversy. During the summer of 1986, President Ballard Smith announced that the Padres would no longer serve beer in the clubhouse after home games. The Padres had been notified that their insurance rates would rise if the club did not impose such a ban. Outspoken Goose Gossage protested, "They have Budweiser signs in the park so they can make money, but they don't want the players unwinding with a couple of beers after a game. How inconsistent and hypocritical is that?" Gossage called Ballard Smith "gutless" and accused Joan Kroc of "poisoning the world with her hamburgers."[136] Smith suspended Gossage indefinitely without pay on August 29. Gossage subsequently paid a $25,000 fine to charity and apologized publicly, stating that he and his family had enjoyed numerous fine meals at McDonald's.[137] Smith also stated that San Diego would offer only one-year contracts to those players refusing to include a drug-testing policy in their contracts. The Players Association protested the Padres' decision as unconstitutional. The policy change may have affected the case of free-agent Tim Raines of Montreal, who wanted to join the Padres and had experienced previous drug problems. After conducting negotiations with Raines, Smith suddenly announced without explanation that the Padres would not attempt to sign Raines. Raines probably would have joined the Padres had there not been collusion among the owners. No free agents were signed that winter by other clubs except Andre Dawson with the Chicago Cubs.

The Padres made several roster changes during the off-season, beginning with the dismissal of Manager Steve Boros in late October. "Boros," Jack McKeon claimed, "got caught up in a transition period. The players did not perform what they were capable of that year."[138] Larry Bowa, a diminutive, fiery shortstop, was elevated to the helm after only one year of minor league experience. In 1986 he had piloted the Las Vegas Stars farm club to the Pacific Coast League title. Bowa was more vocal, intense, and emotional than Boros, an overachiever who expected others to demonstrate his work ethic. The dedicated manager possessed a wealth of baseball knowledge and had mastered baseball strategy. A few days later, the Padres secured starting pitcher Storm Davis from the Baltimore Orioles. Veteran catcher Terry Kennedy, who ranks third in RBIs (424), fourth in doubles (158), and fifth in hits (817) and home runs (76), and pitcher Mark Williamson were sent to Baltimore.[139]

In December 1986, McKeon made a highly publicized trade with the New York Mets. He exchanged Kevin McReynolds and two other players for five young prospects, including infielder Kevin Mitchell. McReynolds had just completed the fourth year of a six-year contract. His agent had rejected the Padres' $4.5 million contract offer for five years and had made demands that the club could not meet. San Diego realized that McReynolds probably would file for free agency and wanted compensation. The Padres anticipated that Mitchell, a San Diego product, and the four other players would fill gaps at third base, second base, and in the outfield. The trade ultimately disappointed the Padres, who could not fill the power vacuum left by the departure of McReynolds. A month later, Hoyt's continued drug problems led to his release.[140]

Joan Kroc, meanwhile, nearly sold the Padres. She was involved heavily in various political and charitable causes in the San Diego community, while the San Diego media blamed Mrs. Kroc and Smith for not taking the steps it deemed necessary to improve the Padres. The marriage between Mrs. Kroc's daughter, Linda, and club president, Ballard Smith, was disintegrating. Steve Garvey headed a group that wanted to purchase the Padres, but Seattle Mariners owner George Argyros made the first offer. Argyros, a Newport Beach, California developer, wanted to sell the Mariners and buy the Padres by May 31 for a reported $60 million. The deal collapsed partly because Argyros could not find anyone willing to pay $45 million for the Mariners. The media also disclosed that Argyros operated the Seattle franchise too frugally. "The Seattle operation," Elten Schiller remarked, "was being run on a shoe string."[141] Other National League club owners also opposed selling the Padres to Argyros. Before the sale came to a vote, Kroc on May 29 dissolved the Argyros deal and took the club off the market. The San Diego community had given Mrs. Kroc a vast outpouring of public support and convinced her to keep the club. Frank Kern termed the Argyros transaction "the best deal that never happened."[142]

Ballard Smith, who gradually had removed himself from the intimate club operations since 1984, resigned as president in late May to pursue other business interests. Mrs. Kroc's daughter, Linda, was divorcing Smith and dating player-agent Jerry Kapstein. Smith also had alienated the San Diego press after calling them "bleeping flies." On June 10 former National League president Chub Feeney assumed the Padre presidency. Feeney's tenure proved unpopular. The San Diego media criticized Feeney because he spent too much time away from his club office and did not spend money on free agents or make many trades. "Feeney's ideas," Dave Campbell stated, "were antiquated. The game had passed him by."[143] Feeney also upset some Padre players when he mistook John Kruk for Lance McCullers at a luncheon. "Way to go, Lance," Feeney told Kruk. "You're finally starting to earn the money we're paying you."[144]

In 1987 San Diego plunged to last place in the Western Division with a 65–97 record. Poor pitching, hitting, and fielding doomed the Padres through early June to a 12–42 record. "The Padres," Dave Campbell stressed, "were on a pace to be worse than the 1962 New York Mets."[145] Steve Garvey, who suffered a career-ending shoulder injury in May, observed, "there was a lot of pressure on the team early in the season."[146] Manager Larry Bowa acted too intense, took losses too personally, and vented his frustration on Padre players in team meetings. Bowa shouted at players in clubhouse meetings, engaging in a verbal match in mid-May with normally soft-spoken rookie Stan Jefferson. According to Jack McKeon, "Bowa expected too much of his inexperienced players. You can't always get 100 percent from players."[147]

One of the most remarkable turnabouts in San Diego franchise history occurred. When the Padres fell 30 games below .500 in June, Bowa and McKeon made several major changes. San Diego dramatically improved both offensively and defensively, playing the best base-ball in the Western Division from June through August with a composite 42–38 mark. John Kruk, inserted at first base, batted .313 with 20 home runs and 91 RBIs. Veterans Tim Flannery and Randy Ready steadied the infield defensively at second base and third base. Carmelo Martinez moved to left field, improving his batting average to .273, slugging 15 home runs, and knocking in 70 runs. Pitcher Jimmy Jones, recalled from Las Vegas, won seven of his last 10 decisions.[148]

Tony Gwynn helped spark the Padres' sudden surge, leading the major leagues with a .370 batting average for his second National League batting crown. No National Leaguer had batted .370 since Stan Musial of the St. Louis Cardinals in 1948. Besides capturing a second straight Gold Glove award, Gwynn paced the National League with 218 hits for his third 200-hit season and ranked second in triples (13), stolen bases (56), and on-base percentage (.447). Gwynn, who had filed for bankruptcy in May 1987, confided, "I especially loved to come to the park and play baseball that year. Baseball took my mind off the bankruptcy problem."[149] Besides ranking first in Padre history in batting average (.332), runs scored (617), hits (1,354), and doubles (192), he remains second in triples (51) and stolen bases (221) and third in RBIs (446).[150] The dedicated, hard-working, personable Gwynn studied videotape continually to improve his hitting and worked on his fielding and throwing to become a more complete player. He demonstrates an excellent attitude and tremendous work ethic, frequently being the first player out on the field for practice before games. Jack McKeon remarked, "He can hit well for any manager. If we had nine Tony Gwynns, we would always do very well."[151] Garry Templeton described Gwynn as "a great player, great individual, and true professional, who loves to play baseball, and sets a great example for the younger players."[152] Jerry Coleman summed up, "Gwynn is the single most dedicated Padre. He is the greatest player they have ever had with such incredible dedication and work habits."[153]

Catcher Benito Santiago also made a dramatic impact on the club's improved fortunes in 1987. The then 22-year-old Puerto Rican earned National League Rookie-of-the-Year honors after batting .300, with 18 home runs and 79 RBIs. Santiago's 34-game hitting streak was the longest in the National League in 10 years and the most ever by a rookie. His exceptional throwing arm enabled him to pick runners off base, throw runners out attempting to steal, and prevent many runners on second base from scoring on singles. "It's a rarity," Garry Templeton observed, "when a catcher can throw, field, and hit like Benny."[154] Jerry Coleman, who has followed baseball since World War II, remarked, "Santiago has the best throwing arm I've ever seen. He stops runners from stealing."[155] "Santiago," Dave Campbell claimed, "has changed the baserunning strategy. Hardly anyone runs on him. Teams bunt rather than trying to steal."[156] *The Sporting News* Silver Slugger and All-League Teams included both Santiago and Gwynn.

A major transaction in mid-season accented the extent of the Padres' youth movement. On July 4 the Padres traded veterans Dravecky and Lefferts and third baseman Kevin Mitchell to the San Francisco Giants for third baseman Chris Brown and pitchers Mark Davis, Mark Grant, and Keith Comstock. The injury-prone Brown did not fulfill team expectations at third base, but the lefthanded Davis blossomed as a full-time reliever. Davis allowed only nine runs in his final 25 relief appearances and finished with a 5–3 mark and 3.18 ERA. Grant started initially before converting to a long relief role. McKeon knew the power potential of Mitchell, but the latter's erratic off-the-field behavior displeased the club.[157]

The 1987 season had resembled the 1981 campaign. Both clubs had relied heavily on younger players and finished in last place around the same number of games behind first place in the Western Division. The 1987 squad, however, performed much better in the second half than the 1981 unit. Club attendance dropped dramatically both times, although the strike prevented 26 home games in 1981. At least two starters on both teams hit over .300, with fine heavy-hitting catchers emerging both seasons. Both clubs suffered from ineffective starting pitching, but wielded formidable stoppers in the bullpen. No starter won over 10 games either campaign. In 1987 Ed Whitson surrendered a club record 36 home runs. Eric Show the same year beaned Chicago Cubs slugger Andre Dawson, causing wounds requiring 24 stitches and leading to a major bench-clearing brawl. The rookie managers did not endure long with either club.

The 1988 Padre campaign started like the 1987 season. San Diego opened 1988 with five consecutive losses and struggled to a 16–30 mark through May 27 under Larry Bowa. Bowa became more agitated with the increasingly disenchanted players and pressured them too much. The pitchers frequently lost leads, while the batters could not seem to score runners from second base. Tony Gwynn, bothered by a hand injury, was mired in the worst batting slump of his major league career, while Garry Templeton played with pain. John Kruk admitted, "Even God couldn't manage this team."[158] On May 28 Chub Feeney fired Bowa, who had compiled an 81–127 mark as manager.

Feeney selected Jack McKeon, who had two years remaining on his contract as general manager, as field manager. McKeon relished returning to the field 10 years after being fired as Oakland Athletics manager. In contrast to Bowa, McKeon encouraged the Padre players to relax and enjoy baseball. "My motto," McKeon confided, "is that the players should have fun. Fun is winning."[159] The Padres, McKeon stressed, should concentrate less on individual statistics and execute baseball fundamentals better. The fatherly McKeon talked to his players calmly, encouraged them, and soothed tempers. "McKeon," Jerry Coleman noted, "is a wise man who understands his team well and gets the most out of his players."[160] "The players," Whitey Wietelmann added, "are not afraid to make mistakes."[161] Garry Templeton explained, "McKeon changed the attitudes of players and made baseball more fun to play."[162]

McKeon's approach transformed the 1988 Padres into a winner. San Diego won its first six games under McKeon and compiled an excellent 67–48 mark under him, the second best National League record during that span. McKeon guided once floundering San Diego to a respectable 83–78 third-place finish, fourth best in franchise history. "What a comeback," Tony Gwynn exclaimed. "Finishing in third place, it was like us winning the pennant. We learned how to win."[163] McKeon confessed, "I only wish we had 30 more days in the season. I didn't think we'd turn it around this quickly."[164]

McKeon handled the team personnel shrewdly. Tony Gwynn was switched from right field to center field, while Carmelo Martinez moved from first base to left field. Although batting only .246 on July 2, Gwynn responded by hitting a torrid .367 in his final 73 games to finish at .313 for the season. Gwynn, named to *The Sporting News* Silver Slugger Team, not only won his third National League batting championship, but led the Padres with 70 RBIs. Carmelo Martinez belted 11 home runs and knocked in 34 runs in his final 38 games, leading the Padres in roundtrippers (18) and ranking second in RBIs (65). Jack McKeon switched Keith Moreland from left field to first base and inserted John Kruk in right field for the first time in his career. Rookie Roberto Alomar finished second in club batting and made numerous brilliant defensive plays at second base. Catcher Benito Santiago made *The Sporting News* All-League Team and won a Gold Glove, picking off eight runners and throwing out 45 percent of those attempting to steal.[165]

The Padre pitching staff flourished under McKeon and coach Pat Dobson. McKeon exuded more confidence in his starting pitchers, keeping them in games longer and conserving his bullpen. Dobson taught Padre pitchers how to hold runners on base better and how to deliver the ball more quickly to home plate. Eric Show enjoyed his best season with a 16–11 record, 3.26 ERA, and 13 complete games, winning nine of his final 10 decisions. Show ranks first among Padre pitchers in victories (94) and strikeouts (896), second in starts (218), innings pitched (1,497), and complete games (35), tied for second in shutouts (11), and fifth in ERA (3.43). Andy Hawkins and Ed Whitson, who developed an effective change-up, combined for 27 victories. In

June McKeon secured one-time Padre lefthander Dennis Rasmussen from the Cincinnati Reds for pitcher Candy Sierra. Rasmussen, who won 14 of 18 decisions for the Padres, asserted, "I always knew I could pitch like this. It was a matter of the Padres and Jack giving me the confidence to do it."[166] Mark Davis, who was named to the National League All-Star Team, became the dominant bullpen stopper the club sorely needed. Besides saving 28 games, Davis did not allow a home run after June 3 and established a club record by pitching 27 consecutive scoreless innings.

The 1988 Padres had exhibited similarities to the 1982 squad. Both clubs dramatically improved in the Western Division standings, vacating the cellar and finishing much closer to first place. Impressive winning streaks helped those clubs compile among the best records in franchise history. Experienced managers supervised the improved fortunes of both teams. Home attendance surged both times, especially in 1982. Padre pitching coaches worked very productively with the starting pitchers. Superior relief pitching and vastly improved hitting marked both clubs. Star free agents were signed after both seasons, filling significant gaps and leaving considerable optimism for the future.

Off the field, Chub Feeney engaged in a power struggle with Jack McKeon. Feeney did not want McKeon to continue serving as both vice president for baseball operations and field manager. McKeon, however, insisted that he could hold both positions simultaneously like Whitey Herzog had done with the St. Louis Cardinals. McKeon relinquished his vice president title in early September and signed a three-year, $1.3 million contract to remain as manager, being assured that he would handle most player personnel decisions. The same day, Feeney and agent Jerry Kapstein engaged in a shouting match over pitcher Andy Hawkins, whose contract was expiring. After Feeney mentioned the Hawkins disagreement on a pre-game show, Kapstein assailed Feeney in an impromptu press conference. The San Diego media and fans increasingly became disenchanted with Feeney. On Fan Appreciation Night in late September, two spectators paraded around Jack Murphy Stadium with a banner urging Mrs. Kroc to "Scrub Chub." Feeney, seated in a private box high above the field, acknowledged them with a one-finger obscene gesture. Feeney denied making the signal, but the video tape verified it. Feeney had signed a two-year contract the previous March, but resigned as president the next day and was replaced by Dick Freeman. Freeman mainly had worked on the financial side of club operations and had served as executive vice president.[167]

During the 1988-89 off-season, several transactions bolstered the Padres' prospects. On October 24 San Diego lured first baseman Jack Clark and pitcher Pat Clements from the New York Yankees for three players. The Padres hoped that Clark, who had hit 256 home runs and knocked in 904 runs in 14 major league seasons, would provide the power the Padres had lacked since the departure of Kevin McReynolds. In December, however, the New York Yankees enticed free agent pitcher Andy Hawkins to leave San Diego. Hawkins had ranked third in career victories (60), fourth in innings pitched (1,022), tied for fourth in shutouts (7), and fifth in starts (139) and strikeouts (489) among Padre pitchers. Bruce Hurst of the Boston Red Sox, the object of an intense bidding war, inked a three-year, $5.25 million contract with San Diego in December to give the Padres a quality lefthanded pitcher.[168]

The Padres enjoyed their second-best season in franchise history in 1989, finishing in second place with an 89–73 record only three games behind the San Francisco Giants. Several pre-season baseball publications had predicted the Padres would finish at or near the top of the Western Division. San Diego's excellent spring training performance augmented those predictions and, according to Dave Campbell, "had the town in a frenzy."[169] The Padre fortunes, though, sagged until early August, as its batters demonstrated inconsistent hitting, frequently produced less than three runs per game, often left numerous runners in scoring position, and stole relatively few bases. San Diego showed signs of ending its slump on July 17, setting a club record with a 17–4, 19-hit shellacking of the Pittsburgh Pirates. The Padres played superlative baseball from early August to mid-September, gaining considerable ground on the Giants. By the end of the 1989 season, San Diego ranked third in team batting (.251) and fifth in team ERA (3.38). Over two million fans, the second largest in franchise history, witnessed the dramatic club resurgence.[170]

The 1989 campaign witnessed several fine individual performances by Padre players. Tony Gwynn became the first National Leaguer since Stan Musial to win three consecutive batting titles. Gwynn, who batted .336 and led the league with 203 hits, made three hits in the final season game to edge Will Clark of San Francisco for the batting crown. Jack Clark displayed enormous power in late season. to pace the Padres in home runs (26) and RBIs (94). Roberto Alomar raised his batting average by season's end to .295, ranking third in the league in hits (184) and second in stolen bases (42). Outfielder Chris James, obtained from the Philadelphia Phillies for John Kruk in June, supplied valuable power with two grand slam home runs and 65 RBIs. Benito Santiago augmented his usual outstanding defensive skills with a late-season power surge, finishing second on the club with 16 home runs.[171]

Padre pitchers, meanwhile, performed well throughout the 1989 season. Mark Davis, who paced the staff with a club-record 44 saves and recorded a win or save in 48 of San Diego's 89 victories, became only the fourth reliever to win the National League Cy Young Award and also earned the Rolaids Relief Award. Besides compiling a brilliant 1.85 ERA, Davis converted nearly all save opportunities, averaged nearly one strikeout per inning, and did not allow a run in his final 24 innings. According to Dick Freeman, "Davis made a dramatic impact. I don't know where we would have been without him."[172] Ed Whitson led the starters with a 16–11 mark and 2.66 ERA, while Bruce Hurst compiled an almost identical 15–11 record and 2.69 ERA. Eric Show won eight games before suffering a season-ending back injury in July. Rookie Andy Benes, a member of the 1988 U. S. Olympic team and the Padres' number one draft pick the same year, filled the gap by winning six of nine decisions in late season.[173]

The 1989 season had resembled the 1983 campaign in several respects. Both clubs won at least half of their games, as free agents and trade acquisitions strengthened those teams. Injuries to veteran players, especially pitchers, enabled the Padres to give valuable experience to younger performers. Dick Williams and Jack McKeon guided the clubs to respectable records and remain the only mentors in franchise history to boast winning records. Two features, however, differentiated the 1983 and 1989 squads. The 1989 club, which possessed a much stronger bullpen, made a very dramatic comeback after the All-Star break and played perhaps the best baseball in the major leagues. The Padres also drew much better attendance in 1989 than in 1983.

The Padres had rebuilt once again to become a very formidable contender in the Western Division. San Diego still needs a leadoff hitter as the 1990 campaign dawns, someone the quality of Gene Richards or Alan Wiggins, who can get on base consistently, steal bases frequently, and score runs regularly. Utility infielder-outfielder Bip Roberts showed signs in 1989 of possibly fulfilling that role. The Padres also continued to lack a power-hitting outfielder in the mold of Kevin McReynolds, a player who can score runners consistently with two men out. Thus they engineered baseball's biggest off-season deal in acquiring slugging DH-outfielder-first sacker Joe Carter (A.L. home run runner-up) from Cleveland. Third base also remains a perennial problem for the Padres. The ballclub of 1989 did possess a wealth of skilled catchers in Benito Santiago, Mark Parent, and Sandy Alomar, Jr., and the latter was thus dealt off to the American League in the swap for Joe Carter. Another crucial loss at the conclusion of 1989 was Cy Young ace Mark Davis, signed to a huge free-agent contract by the Kansas City Royals of the rival league.

If there were bright spots for the constantly rebuilding Padres in the early seasons of the new decade, they came in the form of two sluggers acquired via the trade route. First sacker Fred McGriff justified a risky deal with Toronto for Joe Carter by slugging homers (a league-best 35 in 1992) as never before seen in franchise history. And third baseman Gary Sheffield turned around a lost career in Milwaukee to challenge for a triple crown in 1992. And yet the Padres were still the same old middle-of-the-pack club through it all, with little hope on the horizon for a true pennant challenge.

Notes

I am indebted to Dick Freeman, San Diego Padres president, and Bill Beck, Padres director of media relations, for graciously permitting me to interview various Padres personnel. Freeman, Elten Schiller, former Padres senior vice president of baseball operations; Dave Campbell, former Padres player and announcer; Jack McKeon, Padres manager; and Whitey Wietelmann, Padres clubhouse official, all provided me with invaluable information on club history. Interviews with Padres announcer Jerry Coleman; present Padres players Tony Gwynn, Eric Show, Garry Templeton, and Ed Whitson; as well as with former players Steve Arlin, Tim Flannery, Steve Garvey, Gary Lucas, and Luis Salazar, also enhanced my understanding of club history. I wish to thank Frank Kern, director of the San Diego Hall of Champions, for detailing both the Padres minor league and major league histories.

1. Steve Wulf, "Padres," *Sports Illustrated* 70 (April 5, 1989): 44.

2. James R. Rothaus, *San Diego Padres* (Minneapolis, Minn., 1987), 7.

3. Lowell Reidenbaugh, *Take Me Out to the Ball Park* (St. Louis, Mo., 1983), 242–47; Andy Strasberg and Mark Guglielmo, *Nineteen Summers: Padres 1969–1988* VHS; Frank Kern Interview, July 25, 1989; San Diego Hall of Champions, Balboa Park, San Diego, CA.

4. Elten Schiller Interview, July 24, 1989; Kern Interview, July 25, 1989; Dave Campbell Interview, July 24, 1989.

5. San Diego *Union*, May 29, 1968; Strasberg and Guglielmo, *Nineteen Summers*; Kern Interview, July 25, 1989; *The Sporting News Official 1969 Baseball Guide*, 174–81. For San Diego sports-mindedness, see Ray Kennedy, "San Diego Wins the Palm as Sports Town, U.S.A.," *Sports Illustrated* 49 (December 15, 1978–January 1, 1979): 48–50, 55–56, 58.

6. Jim Geschke, "Padres 20th Anniversary: The Building of Tradition 1969–1988, *Padres Magazine* 2 (September 1988): 28. For brief club history, see Joe Gergen, "San Diego Padres Survived a Most Humble Beginning," *Baseball Digest* 44 (February 1985): 55–58.

7. Schiller Interview, July 24, 1989.

8. Geschke, "Padres," 28.

9. Don Freeman, "San Diego Love Story: Two Big Macs With Lots of Trimmings," *Sport* 58 (September 1974): 80.

10. San Diego *Union*, October 15, 1968; Geschke, "Padres," 28; Strasberg and Guglielmo, *Nineteen Summers*. For player profiles from 1969 to 1989, see *San Diego Padres Yearbooks*, 1969–1985 and *San Diego Padres Media Guides*, 1969–1989.

11. Whitey Wietelmann Interview, July 21, 1989.

12. San Diego *Union*, April 9, 1969; Reidenbaugh, *Ball Park*, 247–48; Strasberg and Guglielmo, *Nineteen Summers*.

13. *The Sporting News Official 1970 Baseball Guide*, 165–67.

14. *San Diego Padres 1989 Media Guide*, 102; *The Sporting News Official 1971 Baseball Guide*, 157; *The Sporting News Official 1972 Baseball Guide*, 65.

15. San Diego *Union*, April 28, 1972; *The Sporting News Official 1973 Baseball Guide*, 136–37; Schiller Interview, July 24, 1989.

16. *San Diego Padres 1989 Media Guide*, 107; San Diego *Union*, August 2, 1972; Campbell Interview, July 24, 1989; Strasberg and Guglielmo, *Nineteen Summers*.

17. *San Diego Padres 1989 Media Guide*, 107.

18. *San Diego Padres 1989 Media Guide*, 104; San Diego *Union*, July 22, 1970; Reidenbaugh, *Ball Park*, 248; Bruce Nash and Allan Zullo, *The Baseball Hall of Shame 2* (New York, 1986), 114; Strasberg and Guglielmo, *Nineteen Summers*.

19. Steve Arlin Interview, July 26, 1989.

20. *The Sporting News Official 1972 Baseball Guide*, 65–66; San Diego *Union*, September 14, 19, 1971.

21. *San Diego Padres 1989 Media Guide*, 104; Arlin Interview, July 26, 1989; San Diego *Union*, July 19, 1972.

22. San Diego *Union*, May 18, 1973; Schiller Interview, July 24, 1989. Bavasi had stated that baseball in San Diego "might be the wrong game in the wrong town." Geschke, "Padres," 31.

23. San Diego *Union*, June 8, 13, 1973; *The Sporting News Official 1974 Baseball Guide*, 272–73; Freeman, "Love Story," 81.

24. *The Sporting News Official 1974 Baseball Guide*, 273–74.

25. *The Sporting News Official 1974 Baseball Guide*, 275–76. Irv Grossman recalled, "We were gone. Everything was in boxes. It was depressing. The whole 1973 season, the Padres were lame ducks." Geschke, "Padres," 31.

26. Freeman, "Love Story," 81; Strasberg and Guglielmo, *Nineteen Summers*; Geschke, "Padres," 31. For Kroc's background, see Ray Kroc and Robert Anderson, *Grinding It Out: The Making of McDonald's* (Chicago, 1985).

27. Arlin Interview, July 26, 1989.

28. Arlin Interview, July 26, 1989.

29. Steve Garvey Interview, July 27, 1989.

30. Gary Lucas Interview, July 25, 1989.

31. *The Sporting News Official 1974 Baseball Guide*, 285; Freeman, "Love Story," 81–82; San Diego *Union*, February 3, 1974, April 10, 1974; Strasberg and Guglielmo, *Nineteen Summers*.

32. Freeman, "Love Story," 82–83; Don Freeman, "San Diego Is Crowing About The Red Rooster," *Sport* 63 (September 1976): 61; Geschke, "Padres," 31.

33. Freeman, "Red Rooster," 61; Geschke, "Padres," 31.

34. Freeman, "Love Story," 79–80.

35. Schiller Interview, July 24, 1989; Dick Freeman Interview, July 25, 1989; Reidenbaugh, *Ball Park*, 248.

36. *San Diego Padres 1989 Media Guide*, 102; *The Sporting News Official 1975 Baseball Guide*, 150–53; San Diego *Union*, July 18, 1974, November 9, 19, 1974, December 7, 1974; *The Sporting News Official 1976 Baseball Guide*, 33–37; *The Sporting News Official 1977 Baseball Guide*, 36–40.

37. Ron Fimrite, "Playing Ketchup Out West," *Sports Illustrated* 42 (May 12, 1975): 26–27; Bob Hinz, *San Diego Padres* (Minneapolis, Minn., 1982), 22.

38. *The Sporting News Official 1976 Baseball Guide*, 35; *The Sporting News Official 1977 Baseball Guide*, 37; *New York Times*, November 3, 1976.

39. Pete Axthelm and Vern E. Smith, "The Amazing Randy," *Newsweek* 87 (June 21, 1976): 57; Arlin Interview, July 26, 1989.

40. *San Diego Padres 1989 Media Guide*, 104; Strasberg and Guglielmo, *Nineteen Summers*; Campbell Interview, July 24, 1989.

41. *San Diego Padres 1989 Media Guide*, 107; Dave Winfield with Tom

Parker, *Winfield: A Player's Life* (New York, 1988), 66–68, 76–91; Wietelmann Interview, July 21, 1989.

42. San Diego *Union*, December 9, 15, 1976; *The Sporting News Official 1978 Baseball Guide*, 165.

43. San Diego *Union*, May 18, 30-31, 1977; *The Sporting News Official 1978 Baseball Guide*, 162–66; *San Diego Padres 1989 Media Guide*, 8, 107.

44. Schiller Interview, July 24, 1989; San Diego *Union*, September 21, 1977, March 22, 1978; *The Sporting News Official 1979 Baseball Guide*, 317; Winfield and Parker, *Winfield*, 109.

45. *The Sporting News Official 1979 Baseball Guide*, 317–18.

46. *The Sporting News Official 1979 Baseball Guide*, 154–58; San Diego *Union*, January 26, 1978; Strasberg and Guglielmo, *Nineteen Summers*.

47. Arlin Interview, July 26, 1989.

48. San Diego *Union*, May 27, 1978; *The Sporting News Official 1979 Baseball Guide*, 154–55; Kern Interview, July 25, 1989.

49. Tim Flannery Interview, July 21, 1989.

50. Campbell Interview, July 24, 1989.

51. *The Sporting News Official 1979 Baseball Guide*, 154–55; Hinz, *Padres*, 33.

52. San Diego *Union*, July 12, 1978; Strasberg and Guglielmo, *Nineteen Summers*; Arlin Interview, July 26, 1989.

53. *The Sporting News Official 1980 Baseball Guide*, 143–47; Winfield and Parker, *Winfield*, 114; San Diego *Union*, October 2, 1979; Strasberg and Guglielmo, *Nineteen Summers*; *The Sporting News Official 1981 Baseball Guide*, 126–29; *San Diego Padres 1989 Media Guide*, 8; Gary Lucas Interview, July 25, 1989.

54. *The Sporting News Official 1981 Baseball Guide*; *The Sporting News Official 1982 Baseball Guide*, 47–48; San Diego *Union*, October 6–7, 1980, October 14, 1981.

55. Strasberg and Guglielmo, *Nineteen Summers*; San Diego *Union*, August 25, 1979; Campbell Interview, July 24, 1989.

56. San Diego *Union*, July 9, 1980, September 24, 1980; Jack McKeon Interview, July 21, 1989. For McKeon's role with club, see Jack McKeon and Tom Friend, *Jack of All Trades* (Chicago, 1988).

57. McKeon Interview, July 21, 1989; Strasberg and Guglielmo, *Nineteen Summers*. "We tried at the time," McKeon recalled, "to get players, quality players, at every position." Geschke, "Padres," 55.

58. Garvey Interview, July 27, 1989.

59. *San Diego Padres 1989 Media Guide*, 107; Winfield and Parker, *Winfield*, 123–36; Flannery Interview, July 21, 1989.

60. Geschke, "Padres," 55; San Diego *Union*, September 5, 1979, February 16, 1980, December 9, 16, 1980, April 2, 1981; *San Diego Padres 1989 Media Guide*, 104.

61. San Diego *Union*, November 20, 27, 1979, August 6, 1980, December 9, 1980; Reidenbaugh, *Ball Park*, 248.

62. San Diego *Union*, November 19, 1981; Ed Whitson Interview, July 22, 1989.

63. Tony Gwynn Interview, July 21, 1989.

64. Luis Salazar Interview, July 28, 1989.

65. Garvey Interview, July 27, 1989.

66. Eric Show Interview, July 23, 1989.

67. Rothaus, *Padres*, 33.

68. San Diego *Union*, December 11, 1981, February 12, 20, 1982; *San Diego Padres 1989 Media Guide*, 107; Schiller Interview, July 24, 1989.

69. Lucas Interview, July 25, 1989.

70. McKeon Interview, July 21, 1989.

71. Jerry Coleman Interview, July 23, 1989.

72. Kern Interview, July 25, 1989; *San Diego Padres 1989 Media Guide*, 107.

73. San Diego *Union*, November 19, 1982, December 22, 1982; McKeon Interview, July 21, 1989.

74. Whitson Interview, July 22, 1989.

75. Campbell Interview, July 24, 1989.

76. Freeman Interview, July 25, 1989.

77. *The Sporting News Official 1983 Baseball Guide*, 62–64; San Diego *Union*, July 22, 1982, August 8, 1982. See also John Curtis, "How We Did It," *San Diego Magazine* 34 (September 1982): 132–35.

78. *The Sporting News Official 1983 Baseball Guide*, 62–64; Bill Weurding, "The Making of a Pennant Contender," *San Diego Padres 1983 Official Yearbook*, 3–6.

79. *The Sporting News Official 1984 Baseball Guide*, 149–51; Rothaus, *Padres*, 34.

80. Strasberg and Guglielmo, *Nineteen Summers*; San Diego *Union*, January 15, 1984; Geschke, "Padres," 55; McKeon Interview, July 21, 1989. See also Mike Swenson, Charles Hrvatin et al., *A Dedicated Season: 1984 San Diego Padres Post Season Media Guide*.

81. Wulf, "Padres," 44.

82. *San Diego Padres 1989 Media Guide*, 2; San Diego *Union*, January 15, 1984; Strasberg and Guglielmo, *Nineteen Summers*.

83. San Diego *Union*, December 8, 1983, January 7, 1984, March 31, 1984; Strasberg and Guglielmo, *Nineteen Summers*; McKeon Interview, July 21, 1989. See also Steve Wulf, "The Best Team in Baseball," *Sports Illustrated* 60 (April 16, 1984): 18–23.

84. Gwynn Interview, July 21, 1989.

85. San Diego *Union*, April 1, 1984; *San Diego Padres 1989 Media Guide*, 107.

86. *The Sporting News Official 1985 Baseball Guide*, 115–17; McKeon Interview, July 21, 1989.

87. Show Interview, July 23, 1989.

88. *San Diego Padres 1989 Media Guide*, 102; Jim Geschke, "National League West Champions," in *World Series 1984 Program*, ed. Joseph L. Reichler, 39–43; San Diego *Union*, September 21, 1984.

89. San Diego *Union*, August 13, 1984; Ron Fimrite, "Take Me Out to the Brawl Game," *Sports Illustrated* 61 (August 24, 1984): 22–27; Campbell Interview, July 24, 1989.

90. Garvey Interview, July 27, 1989.

91. *The Sporting News Official 1985 Baseball Guide*, 115–17; Whitson Interview, July 22, 1989.

92. *The Sporting News Official 1985 Baseball Guide*, 115–17; Flannery Interview, July 21, 1989.

93. *The Sporting News Official 1985 Baseball Guide*, 115–17; Garry Templeton Interview, July 28, 1989.

94. *The Sporting News Official 1985 Baseball Guide*, 115–17; Campbell Interview, July 24, 1989.

95. Show Interview, July 23, 1989.

96. Gwynn Interview, July 21, 1989.

97. San Diego *Union*, October 3–4, 1984; Chicago *Tribune*, October 3–4, 1984; Strasberg and Guglielmo, *Nineteen Summers*.

98. Strasberg and Guglielmo, *Nineteen Summers*; Campbell Interview, July 24, 1989.

99. Templeton Interview, July 28, 1989.

100. Strasberg and Guglielmo, *Nineteen Summers*; Campbell Interview, July 24, 1989.

101. Templeton Interview, July 28, 1989.

102. Salazar Interview, July 28, 1989.

103. Flannery Interview, July 21, 1989.

104. Strasberg and Guglielmo, *Nineteen Summers*; San Diego *Union*, October 5, 1989; McKeon Interview, July 21, 1989. For summary of Championship Series games, see Steve Wulf, "You've Got to Hand It to the Padres," *Sports Illustrated* 61 (October 15, 1984): 28–34.

105. Garvey Interview, July 27, 1989.

106. Gwynn Interview, July 21, 1989.

107. San Diego *Union*, October 5, 1984; Chicago *Tribune*, October 5, 1984; Strasberg and Guglielmo, *Nineteen Summers*.

108. San Diego *Union*, October 7, 1984; Chicago *Tribune*, October 7, 1984; Strasberg and Guglielmo, *Nineteen Summers*; Garvey Interview, July 27, 1989.

109. San Diego *Union*, October 8, 1984; Chicago *Tribune*, October 8, 1984; Strasberg and Guglielmo, *Nineteen Summers*; McKeon Interview, July 21, 1989.

110. *The Sporting News Official 1985 Baseball Guide*, 195–200; McKeon Interview, July 21, 1989.

111. Gwynn Interview, July 21, 1989.

112. San Diego *Union*, October 10–11, 1984; Detroit *Free Press*, October 10–11, 1984. For summary of World Series games, see Steve Wulf, "Detroit Jumped All Over Them," *Sports Illustrated* 61 (October 22, 1984): 26–44.

113. San Diego *Union*, October 13–15, 1984; Detroit *Free Press*, October 13–15, 1984; Wulf, "Detroit Jumped," 26–44.

114. *The Sporting News Official 1985 Baseball Guide*, 215; Campbell Interview, July 24, 1989.

115. *The Sporting News Official 1985 Baseball Guide*, 215; Campbell Interview, July 24, 1989.

116. *The Sporting News Official 1985 Baseball Guide*, 215; Salazar Interview, July 28, 1989.

117. Whitson Interview, July 22, 1989.

118. Templeton Interview, July 28, 1989.

119. Garvey Interview, July 27, 1989.

120. Whitson Interview, July 22, 1989.

121. *The Sporting News Official 1985 Baseball Guide*, 115.

122. San Diego *Union*, December 7, 1984; McKeon Interview, July 21, 1989.

123. San Diego *Union*, January 18, 1985; Wulf, "Padres," 46.

124. *The Sporting News Official 1986 Baseball Guide*, 151–53; San Diego *Union*, July 17, 1985.

125. Coleman Interview, July 23, 1989.

126. *San Diego Padres 1989 Media Guide*, 102; *The Sporting News Official 1986 Baseball Guide*, 151.

127. Templeton Interview, July 28, 1989.

128. *The Sporting News Official 1986 Baseball Guide*, 151–53; McKeon Interview, July 21, 1989; Gwynn Interview, July 21, 1989.

129. Schiller Interview, July 24, 1989.

130. Wietelmann Interview, July 21, 1989.

131. *The Sporting News Official 1986 Baseball Guide*, 153.

132. Schiller Interview, July 24, 1989; Campbell Interview, July 24, 1989; San Diego *Union*, February 25–26, 1986; *The Sporting News Official 1987 Baseball Guide*, 21, 67.

133. San Diego *Union*, February 26, 1986; *San Diego Padres 1989 Media Guide*, 8; Schiller Interview, July 24, 1989; Show Interview, July 23, 1989.

134. *The Sporting News Official 1987 Baseball Guide*, 67.

135. *The Sporting News Official 1987 Baseball Guide*, 67–69; San Diego *Union*, September 22, 1986.

136. Wulf, "Padres," 48.

137. San Diego *Union*, August 30, 1986; Wulf, "Padres," 48.

138. *The Sporting News Official 1987 Baseball Guide*, 69; Gwynn Interview, July 21, 1989; San Diego *Union*, October 29, 1986; McKeon Interview, July 21, 1989.

139. Wulf, "Padres," 48; *San Diego Padres 1989 Media Guide*, 6; Campbell Interview, July 24, 1989; Garvey Interview, July 27, 1989; San Diego *Union*, October 31, 1986; *San Diego Padres 1989 Media Guide*, 107.

140. San Diego *Union*, December 12, 1986; Campbell Interview, July 24, 1989; McKeon Interview, July 21, 1989.

141. Schiller Interview, July 24, 1989; *The Sporting News Official 1988 Baseball Guide*, 14; Campbell Interview, July 24, 1989.

142. San Diego *Union*, May 30, 1987; Campbell Interview, July 24, 1989; Kern Interview, July 25, 1989.

143. San Diego *Union*, June 11, 1987; Wulf, "Padres," 48, 50; *The Sporting News Official 1987 Baseball Guide*, 69; Campbell Interview, July 24, 1989.

144. Wulf, "Padres," 48.

145. *San Diego Padres 1989 Media Guide*, 102; *The Sporting News Official 1988 Baseball Guide*, 159; Campbell Interview, July 24, 1989.

146. Garvey Interview, July 27, 1989.

147. McKeon Interview, July 21, 1989; San Diego *Union*, May 13, 1987.

148. *The Sporting News Official 1988 Baseball Guide*, 159–61.

149. *The Sporting News Official 1988 Baseball Guide*, 161; Strasberg and Guglielmo, *Nineteen Summers*; Gwynn Interview, July 21, 1989.

150. *San Diego Padres 1989 Media Guide*, 107.

151. Campbell Interview, July 24, 1989; Schiller Interview, July 24, 1989; McKeon Interview, July 21, 1989.

152. Templeton Interview, July 28, 1989.

153. Coleman Interview, July 23, 1989.

154. *San Diego Padres 1989 Media Guide*, 66–67; San Diego *Union*, August 26–October 4, 1987; Strasberg and Guglielmo, *Nineteen Summers*; Campbell Interview, July 24, 1989; Templeton Interview, July 28, 1989.

155. Coleman Interview, July 23, 1989.

156. Campbell Interview, July 24, 1989.

157. San Diego *Union*, July 5, 1987; *San Diego Padres 1989 Media Guide*, 30–31, 35; McKeon Interview, July 21, 1989; Kern Interview, July 25, 1989.

158. *The Sporting News Official 1989 Baseball Guide*, 35.

159. San Diego *Union*, May 29, 1988; Wulf, "Padres," 48; McKeon Interview, July 21, 1989.

160. McKeon Interview, July 21, 1989; Coleman Interview, July 23, 1989.

161. Wietelmann Interview, July 21, 1989.

162. Templeton Interview, July 28, 1989.

163. *The Sporting News Official 1989 Baseball Guide*, 35; *San Diego Padres 1989 Media Guide*, 8, 102.

164. *The Sporting News Official 1989 Baseball Guide*, 35, 37.

165. *The Sporting News Official 1989 Baseball Guide*, 35, 37.

166. *The Sporting News Official 1989 Baseball Guide*, 35, 37; *San Diego Padres 1989 Media Guide*, 104.

167. Wulf, "Padres," 48, 50; San Diego *Union*, September 15, 25–26, 1988; *The Sporting News Official 1989 Baseball Guide*, 22, 37; *San Diego Padres 1989 Media Guide*, 3.

168. San Diego *Union*, October 25, 1988, December 9, 1988; *Who's Who in Baseball 1989*, 27; *San Diego Padres 1989 Media Guide*, 104.

169. *USA Today*, October 2, 1989; Campbell Interview, July 24, 1989.

170. McKeon Interview, July 21, 1989; San Diego *Union*, July 18, 1989; *USA Today*, October 4, 1989.

171. *USA Today*, October 2, 4, 1989.

172. *USA Today*, October 2, 4, 1989, November 14–15, 1989; Freeman Interview, July 25, 1989.

173. *USA Today*, October 4, 1989.

References

Arlin, Steve. Interview, San Diego, Calif., July 26, 1989.

Axthelm, Pete, and Vern E. Smith. 1976. "The Amazing Randy." *Newsweek* 87 (June 21): 57.

Campbell, Dave. Interview, San Diego, Calif., July 24, 1989.

Coleman, Jerry. Interview, San Diego, Calif., July 23, 1989.

Curtis, John. 1982. "How We Did It." *San Diego Magazine* 34 (September): 132–35.

Fimrite, Ron. 1975. "Playing Ketchup Out West." *Sports Illustrated* 42 (May 12): 26–27.

———. 1984. "Take Me Out to the Brawl Game." *Sports Illustrated* 61 (August 24): 22–27.

Flannery, Tim. Interview, San Diego, Calif., July 21, 1989.

Freeman, Dick. Interview, San Diego, Calif., July 25, 1989.

Freeman, Don. 1976. "San Diego Is Crowing About the Red Rooster." *Sport* 63 (September): 57–63.

———. 1974. "San Diego Love Story: Two Big Macs with Lots of Trimmings." *Sport* 58 (September): 79–88.

Garvey, Steve. Interview, San Diego, Calif., July 27, 1989.

Gergen, Joe. 1985. "San Diego Padres Survived a Most Humble Beginning." *Baseball Digest* 44 (February): 55–58.

Geschke, Jim. "National League West Champions." In *World Series 1984 Program*, edited by Joseph L. Reichler, 39–43.

———. 1988. "Padres 20th Anniversary: The Building of Tradition 1969–1988." *Padres Magazine* 2 (September): 26–28, 31, 55, 61.

Gwynn, Tony. Interview, San Diego, Calif., July 21, 1989.

Hinz, Bob. 1982. *San Diego Padres*. Minneapolis, Minn.: Creative Education.

Kennedy, Ray. 1978–79. "San Diego Wins the Palm as Sports Town, U.S.A." *Sports Illustrated* 49 (December 25–January 1): 48–50, 55–56, 58.

Kern, Frank. Interview, San Diego, Calif., July 25, 1989.

Korn, Peter. 1984. "The Clean and Mean Machine." *Inside Sports* 6 (July): 24–31.

Kroc, Ray, and Robert Anderson. 1985. *Grinding It Out: The Making of McDonald's*. Chicago: Contemporary Books.

Lucas, Gary. Interview, San Diego, Calif., July 25, 1989.

McKeon, Jack. Interview, San Diego, Calif., July 21, 1989.

McKeon, Jack, and Tom Friend. 1988. *Jack of All Trades*. Chicago: Contemporary Books.

Nash, Bruce, and Allan Zullo. 1986. *The Baseball Hall of Shame 2*. New York: Pocket Books.
Reidenbaugh, Lowell. 1983. *Take Me Out to the Ball Park*. St. Louis, Mo.: The Sporting News.
Rothaus, James R. 1987. *San Diego Padres*. Minneapolis, Minn.: Creative Education.
Salazar, Luis. Interview, San Diego, Calif., July 28, 1989.
San Diego Padres Media Guide, 1969–1989.
San Diego Padres Yearbooks, 1969–1985.
Schiller, Elten. Interview, San Diego, Calif., July 24, 1989.
Show, Eric. Interview, San Diego, Calif., July 23, 1989.
The Sporting News Official 1969-1989 Baseball Guides.
Strasberg, Andy, and Mark Guglielmo. *Nineteen Summers: Padres 1969–1988* VHS.
Swanson, Mike, Charles Hrvatin et al. *A Dedicated Season: 1984 San Diego Padres Post Season Media Guide*.
Templeton, Garry. Interview, San Diego, Calif., July 28, 1989.
Weurding, Bill. "The Making of a Pennant Contender." In *San Diego Padres 1983 Official Yearbook*, edited by Laurence J. Hyman, 3–6.
Whitson, Ed. Interview, San Diego, Calif., July 22, 1989.
Who's Who in Baseball 1989.
Wietelmann, Whitey. Interview, San Diego, Calif., July 21, 1989.
Winfield, Dave, with Tom Parker. 1988. *Winfield: A Player's Life*. New York: W. W. Norton and Company.
Wulf, Steve. 1984. "The Best Team in Baseball." *Sports Illustrated* 60 (April 16): 18–23.
———. 1984. "Detroit Jumped All Over Them." *Sports Illustrated* 61 (October 22): 26–44.
———. 1989. "Padres." *Sports Illustrated* 70 (April 5): 42–50.
———. 1984. "You've Got to Hand It to the Padres." *Sports Illustrated* 61 (October 15): 28–34.

Annotated Bibliography

Freeman, Don. "San Diego Love Story: Two Big Macs with Lots of Trimmings." *Sport* 58 (September 1974): 79–88.

Freeman adroitly describes how the Padres nearly moved to Washington, D.C., after the 1973 season and how Ray Kroc rescued the club at the last moment, keeping it in San Diego. Kroc built up club attendance dramatically with various promotions and caused controversy when he denounced the Padre players over the stadium public address system on opening night in San Diego Stadium. Freeman's article profiles Kroc's career and several Padre players on the 1974 ballclub.

Geschke, Jim. "Padres 20th Anniversary: The Building of Tradition, 1969–1988." *Padres Magazine* 2 (September 1988): 26–28, 31, 55, 61.

Geschke, the editor of publications for the Padres, furnished an excellent, concise team history to commemorate the club's 20th anniversary. Geschke's article, which appeared in the Padres' game program for the final month of the 1988 season, recounts how San Diego was awarded a major league franchise in 1968, how the club struggled financially and on the field in the infant years, how Ray Kroc saved the ailing franchise in 1974, and how Jack McKeon built it into a winner in the early 1980s. Apt quotations by Padre officials Buzzie Bavasi, Irv Grossman, Ballard Smith, and McKeon are included.

Kroc, Ray, and Robert Anderson. *Grinding It Out: The Making of McDonald's.* Chicago: Contemporary Books, 1985, 274 pp.

Kroc's autobiography tells how he built up the McDonald's hamburger operation into the nation's largest fast-food chain and contains his observations, as well, as owner of the Padres from 1974 to 1984. Kroc bought the Padre franchise because he loved baseball as a hobby and he never viewed the purchase as a monetary proposition. The honest, frank owner initially infuriated Padre players by denouncing them in public on opening night, but quickly stabilized the franchise through popular fan promotions. The struggling franchise was built into a legitimate National League pennant contender when Kroc turned the daily field operations over to Jack McKeon and other experienced baseball executives.

McKeon, Jack, with Tom Friend. *Jack of All Trades.* Chicago: Contemporary Books, 1988. 267 pp.

McKeon's candid, sprightly autobiography portrays his role as general manager of the Padres from 1980 to 1988. In the early 1980s McKeon developed a youth movement, engineered trades, and acquired free agents to transform a last-place ballclub into a National League pennant winner. Appropriately nicknamed "Trader Jack," McKeon recalls how he improved the club step-by-step at every position. The ballclub was rebuilt by McKeon in the latter 1980s with a new combination of youth and experienced players. McKeon takes a fatherly approach toward his players and instills a winning attitude in them by encouraging them to relax and enjoy baseball.

Rothaus, James R. *San Diego Padres.* Minneapolis, Minn.: Creative Education, 1987. 46 pp.

This well-illustrated volume, which updates a 1982 work by Bob Hinz, is an anecdotal history of the Padres designed for a secondary school audience. Kroc's rescue of the Padres, the legacy of Willie McCovey, the "Never Say Die" spirit of the Padres from 1975 to 1980, the new hope manager Dick Williams brought to the club in 1982, the 1984 championship season, and the subsequent sweeping changes which the ballclub experienced are all featured. The text is filled with comments by numerous Padre managers and players as well.

Winfield, Dave, with Tom Parker. *Winfield: A Player's Life.* New York: W. W. Norton and Company, 1988. 290 pp.

Winfield, aided by novelist Tom Parker, candidly relates how he moved directly from being a multi-sport athlete at the University of Minnesota to the Padres, and recalls his experiences and achievements with the Padres from 1974 to 1980. The outspoken, proud Winfield comments about teammates and criticizes the San Diego management, detailing the contract problems which caused him to depart for the New York Yankees after the 1980 campaign. Winfield's work on behalf of the Foundation for Disadvantaged Youth is also stressed.

Wulf, Steve. "All My Padres." *Sports Illustrated* 70 (April 5, 1989): 42–50.

According to Wulf, the Padres, since 1974, have lived a full-fledged soap opera entitled "All My Padres"—complete with a cast of characters that would make daytime television drama proud. Wulf cleverly employs television soap opera themes similar to those found on such popular daytime fare as "Another World," "Dynasty," "The Young and the Restless," "One Life to Live," and "Search for Tomorrow," to depict the unfolding Padre franchise story. Numerous club struggles, both on and off the field, along with player and front-office transactions, are thoroughly discussed.

Wulf, Steve. "You've Got to Hand it to the Padres." *Sports Illustrated* 61 (October 15, 1984): 28–34.

Wulf provides a stirring account of the 1984 National League Championship Series, in which the Padres charged from behind to defeat the Chicago Cubs and take their first-ever National League pennant. Wulf captures here the drama both on and off the field in reviewing how the Padres made shocking playoff history. Padre fans will cherish reliving the parking lot scene, Garry Templeton's hat waving incident, Steve Garvey's dramatic home run, and other magic moments in the storybook Padre comeback. Several Padres also give their first-hand impressions of the Championship Series.

Year-by-Year Standings and Season Summaries

Year	Pos.	Record	Pct.	GB	Manager	Player	BA	Player	HR	Player	W-L	ERA
1969	6th	52–110	.321	41	Gomez	O. Brown	.264	Colbert	24	J. Niekro	8–17	3.70
1970	6th	63–99	.389	39	Gomez	Gaston	.318	Colbert	38	Dobson	14–15	3.76
1971	6th	61–100	.379	28.5	Gomez	O. Brown	.273	Colbert	27	Kirby	15–13	2.83
1972	6th	58–95	.379	36.5	Gomez	Gaston	.269	Colbert	38	Kirby	12–14	3.13
					Zimmer							
1973	6th	60–102	.370	39	Zimmer	D. Roberts	.286	Colbert	22	Arlin	11–14	5.10
1974	6th	60–102	.370	42	McNamara	Grubb	.286	McCovey	22	Freisleben	9–14	3.65
1975	4th	71–91	.438	37	McNamara	Fuentes	.280	McCovey	23	R. Jones	20–12	2.24
1976	5th	73–89	.451	29	McNamara	Ivie	.291	Winfield	13	R. Jones	22–14	2.74
1977	5th	69–93	.426	29	McNamara	Henrick	.311	Winfield	25	Shirley	12–18	3.70
					Skinner							
					Dark							
1978	4th	84–78	.519	11	Craig	Winfield	.308	Winfield	24	G. Perry	21–6	2.72
1979	5th	68–93	.422	22	Craig	Winfield	.308	Winfield	34	G. Perry	12–11	3.05
1980	6th	73–89	.451	19.5	Coleman	Richards	.301	Winfield	20	Fingers	11–9	2.80
1981	6th	25–33	.411	12.5	Howard	L. Salazar	.303	Lefebvre	8	Eichelberger	8–8	3.51
	6th	18–36	.333	15.5								
1981*	6th	41–69	.373	26								
1982	4th	81–81	.500	8	D. Williams	Kennedy	.295	Kennedy	21	Lollar	16–9	3.13
1983	4th	81–81	.500	10	D. Williams	Kennedy	.284	Kennedy	17	Show	15–12	4.17
1984	1st	92–70	.568	+12	D. Williams	Gwynn	.351	Nettles	20	Show	15–9	3.40
								McReynolds	20			
1985	T3rd	83–79	.512	12	D. Williams	Gwynn	.317	Martinez	21	Hawkins	18–8	3.15
1986	4th	74–88	.457	22	Boros	Gwynn	.329	McReynolds	26	Hawkins	10–8	4.30
1987	6th	65–97	.401	25	Bowa	Gwynn	.370	Kruk	20	Whitson	10–13	4.73
1988	3rd	83–78	.516	11	Bowa/McKeon	Gwynn	.313	Martinez	18	Show	16–11	3.26
1989	2nd	89–73	.549	3	McKeon	Gwynn	.336	J. Clark	26	Whitson	16–11	2.66
1990	4th(T)	75–87	.463	16	McKeon	Gwynn	.309	J. Clark	25	Whitson	14–9	2.60
						Roberts	.309					
1991	3rd	84–78	.519	10	Riddoch	Gwynn	.317	McGriff	31	Benes	15–11	3.03
1992	3rd	82–80	.506	16	Riddoch	Sheffield	.330	McGriff	35	Hurst	14–9	3.85

*Split Season Totals (Players' Union Strike).

All-Time Padres Career and Season Records

Career Batting Leaders (1969–1992)

Games Played	Tony Gwynn	1,463
At Bats	Tony Gwynn	5,701
Runs Scored	Tony Gwynn	842
Hits	Tony Gwynn	1,864
Batting Average	Tony Gwynn	.327
Home Runs	Nate Colbert	163
Runs Batted In	Dave Winfield	626
Stolen Bases	Gene Richards	242
Strikeouts	Nate Colbert	773

Career Pitching Leaders (1969–1992)

Innings Pitched	Randy Jones	1,766.0
Earned Run Average	Gaylord Perry	2.88
Wins	Eric Show	100
Losses	Randy Jones	105
Winning Percentage	Gaylord Perry	.660
Strikeouts	Eric Show	951
Walks	Eric Show	593
Games	Eric Show	309
Shutouts	Randy Jones	18
Saves	Rollie Fingers	108
Games Started	Randy Jones	253
Complete Games	Randy Jones	71

Single-Season Batting Records (1969–1992)

Batting Average (502 ABs)	Tony Gwynn	.370	1987
Home Runs	Nate Colbert	38	1970
Home Runs (lefthanded)	Fred McGriff	35	1992
Runs Batted In	Dave Winfield	118	1979
Hits	Tony Gwynn	218	1987
Singles	Tony Gwynn	177	1984
Doubles	Terry Kennedy	42	1982
Triples	Tony Gwynn	13	1987
Slugging Percentage	Dave Winfield	.558	1979
Extra Base Hits	Dave Winfield	71	1979
Game-Winning RBIs	Terry Kennedy	15	1982
	Steve Garvey	15	1984
Sacrifices	Ozzie Smith	28	1978
Stolen Bases	Alan Wiggins	70	1984
Pinch Hits	Merv Rettenmund	21	1977
Strikeouts	Nate Colbert	150	1970
Total Bases	Dave Winfield	333	1979
Hitting Streak	Benito Santiago	34	1987

All-Time Padres Career and Season Records *(continued)*

Grand Slam Home Runs	Nate Colbert	2	1972
	Dave Winfield	2	1976
	Dave Kingman	2	1977
	Kurt Bevacqua	2	1985
	Chris James	2	1989
On-Base Percentage	Tony Gwynn	.450	1987
Hit by Pitch	Gene Tenace	13	1977
Single-Season Pitching Records (1969–1992)			
ERA (100 innings)	Dave Roberts	2.10	1971
Wins	Randy Jones	22	1976
Losses	Randy Jones	22	1974
Winning Pct. (10 decisions)	Gaylord Perry	.778	1978
Strikeouts	Clay Kirby	231	1971
Walks	Steve Arlin	122	1972
Saves	Mark Davis	44	1989
Games	Craig Lefferts	83	1986
Complete Games	Randy Jones	25	1976
Games Started	Randy Jones	40	1976
Shutouts	Fred Norman	6	1972
	Randy Jones	6	1975
Innings Pitched	Randy Jones	315	1976
Consecutive Games Won (season)	Andy Hawkins	11	1985
Consecutive Games Lost (season)	Gary Ross	11	1969
Consecutive Games Lost	Gary Ross	11	1969
Wild Pitches	Steve Arlin	15	1972

12

St. Louis Cardinals
Baseball's Perennial Gas House Gang

STAN W. CARLSON

*The National League of Professional Baseball Clubs was
formed when Ulysses S. Grant was President of the United
States, General George A. Custer was about to be massacred
by Sioux Indians in the Battle of the Little Bighorn, there
were no telephones, automobiles, or airplanes, and the entire
land contained fewer than fifty million persons.*
Lee Allen, The National League Story

Spring is always a special season but spring in cities like St. Louis is
extra special because it marks the beginning of yet another season
of baseball.

Baseball in St. Louis is an old institution, dating back well beyond
the organizing of the National League. In a long and impressive
baseball history, the Redbirds came to prominence as the "Gas House
Gang" of the 1930s. In reality, it appears that the Cardinals have been
that type of team all through their history—colorful, competitive, and
above all else, exciting.

The first colorful figure in Cardinal baseball was named Chris
Von Der Ahe. He was a saloon keeper who was the guiding force
propelling the team—then called the Browns—to four straight titles
and a World Championship. Actually, the team wasn't even in the
National League when that early achievement was accomplished. Despite being called the Browns (the name of the future other St. Louis
team in the American League), these teams were the forerunners of
great Cardinal teams to follow.

When baseball was played on a field near Chris Von Der Ahe's
saloon, grocery store and beer garden, business was brisk—before the
game, during the game at tables adjacent to the playing field, and after
the game. Sundays were a real bonanza.

In the autumn of 1880 the Sportsman's Park Club and Association
was formed and capitalized with $5,000 worth of stock. At the early
meetings, $3,200 worth of stock in the organization was sold. President
of the new group was Chris Von Der Ahe. Another saloon keeper,
John W. Peckington, was vice president with A. H. Spink, secretary,

and W. W. Judy, the treasurer. Spink was from the Spink family that gained wide renown as publishers of the *Sporting News*.

The baseball stands at Grand Avenue Park were soon enough razed to make room for a new covered grandstand. Von Der Ahe opposed the new stands; he felt that beer sales would dwindle due to reduced thirst with a covered grandstand. A compromise was reached with the creation of sizable bleacher areas left exposed to bright sunlight.

Using the old name—the Browns—a team was organized and the new plant dubbed Sportsman's Park was duly opened with a game between the St. Louis nine and the Cincinnati Reds on May 22, 1881, a Sunday afternoon. Baseball and beer immediately became profitable partners. The balance of the original stock ($1,800) was announced as sold after a particularly profitable Sunday ball game. Chris Von Der Ahe himself was the buyer.

During the 1881 season the Dubuque (Iowa) Rabbits, a professional team, came to play in St. Louis. It was the first time some of the players had ever played baseball in a park with a fence around it. The club's first baseman was a lanky lad named Charles A. Comiskey. This same Comiskey later served as president of the Chicago White Sox and was a dominant figure in the nascent American League. Von Der Ahe took a liking to young Comiskey and hired him for the next season at $90 a month.

Baseball prospered in St. Louis and the town earned the reputation as a great baseball center. Teams from far away came to play, including the Philadelphia Athletics and the Brooklyn Atlantics. These games attracted large crowds and led to the organization of the American Association. Von Der Ahe's club was the St. Louis entry. The first manager of this team in the new league was Ed Cuthbert.

In 1883 Ted Sullivan was brought in to manage the St. Louis team. A player on the Dubuque Rabbits, he was hired by Von Der Ahe on Comiskey's recommendation. Ted had a wide player acquaintance and he is credited with assembling the personnel that went on to win four consecutive championships. Sullivan soon resented the constant interference from Von Der Ahe, however, and after a particularly violent confrontation he was finally fed up enough to quit. Chris Von Der Ahe, it seems, was constantly fining players for what he called stupid baseball.

To succeed Sullivan, Jimmy Williams was hired. He did a capable job and the then-named Browns finished in second place, just one game behind the leader. By the middle of the 1884 season, however, Williams also had a clash of personalities with Von Der Ahe and was promptly fired.

Comiskey was a born psychologist and had meanwhile established a firm relationship with the temperamental Chris Von Der Ahe. He avoided confrontations with the saloon keeper; he felt that his boss loved baseball and the money it produced, but actually knew nothing about the game. Comiskey felt it unwise to get angry over ignorance.

Chris Von Der Ahe, firing managers with frequency, found it difficult to get a qualified person to run his team. In desperation, he turned to Comiskey, insisting that he take over as manager.

Best Team in the World

Glory days for the St. Louis team followed. In the 1884 season the club finished fourth. Comiskey filled in the weak spots with better players and for the next four seasons—1885 to 1889—the team that was to become the Cardinals was the best baseball team in the world. Those teams were known as 10-man clubs. There were infrequent substitutions and 10 players carried the burden. Incidentally, that is the size of pitching staffs for modern ballclubs.

Comiskey originated the strategy of first basemen playing off the bag, fielding many plays that had formerly gone past and out into right field. The belief had been that the baseman couldn't get back to the bag if he played off it. Along with this, he taught the pitchers how to field balls hit on the first base side and even to cover first base when grounders pulled the baseman off the bag.

Comiskey introduced other bold innovations. He shifted his infield to conform with the hitting practices of the various batters. He also developed the idea of base coaches on first and third. Early coaching consisted mainly in badgering the opposing pitchers and catchers with personal insults. This led to confusion among the opposition and prompted the league to prescribe specific coaching boxes to keep coaching within bounds.

The 1885 St. Louis team had two pitchers: Bob Carruthers and Dave Foutz. In those days, even after an extra-inning game, the pitchers were ready and eager to play again the next day. As on modern college teams, pitchers would frequently play in the outfield when not pitching. Players often played hurt. Baseball in those early days was truly a pastime played mainly for fun and glory. Salaries were ridiculously low and players usually did not dispute salaries or contracts.

The 1885 series between St. Louis, champions of the Association, and the Chicago White Stockings, champions of the National League, failed to produce a winner. Each team won three games with the extra game ending in a tie. One of the games had been forfeited to Chicago and the St. Louis fans felt their team had been robbed. Outside of St. Louis, the general feeling was that the Chicago team, managed by

Adrian C. Anson, was the stronger. The Chicago team was also cocky and Anson informed St. Louis that if a 1886 World Series was played it would be on the basis of "winner take all."

The 1886 series began with the first game in Chicago. Clarkson of the White Stockings outpitched Foutz and Chicago won 6–0. Despite the defeat, the partial Chicago fans admired the dazzling infield play of St. Louis. Carruthers won the second game for St. Louis with a brilliant one-hit shutout, 12–0, to square the series.

Carruthers tried to pitch two days in a row and Chicago won again, 11–4. St. Louis evened the series with an 8–5 victory and then won the fifth game 10–3. In the sixth game, with 12,000 St. Louis fans in attendance, Chicago took an early 3–0 lead. The score was tied on a triple in the eighth inning, and the game went into extra innings.

In the 10th inning Curt Welch crowded the plate and Chicago pitcher Clarkson nicked him. The umpire waved Welch to first base but the crowd grew wild and Chicago manager Anson, spending more than 15 minutes arguing, convinced the umpire to reverse his decision. The ruling was that Welch had tried to get hit. He returned to bat and singled. Foutz followed with a grounder through the box. The Chicago shortstop, Williamson, eager to make a force play, fumbled the ball and both runners were safe.

Robinson sacrificed, moving the runners to second and third base with only one out. Clarkson seemed reluctant to throw the next pitch but the delay only made him more edgy. Finally he made the pitch—a throw so high that Kelly, the catcher, didn't even attempt to leap for it. Curt Welch raced home and in a "hot dog" gesture slid gracefully over the plate. It was called the $15,000 slide.

It is interesting to note that the total attendance for the 1886 series was 40,000 with gate receipts of $13,920.10. Half of this total was divided among the 12 members of the St. Louis team, amounting to $580 each. Von Der Ahe received the other half of the receipts, $6,960. By contrast, when the Cardinals won their first modern pennant in 1926, each player received $5,584.51 and the Cardinal club received a check for $163,595.97.

St. Louis was back in the National League in 1892. The team was still called the Browns but later they were to be called the Perfectos. The glory days of Chris Von Der Ahe were fading; his days in the National League were not happy ones, either artistically on the field or financially. The fans were also unhappy—Von Der Ahe was finally financially strapped and his property was sold by court order.

To stop the constant wrangling, the National League expelled the old St. Louis club and awarded the franchise to Frank DeHaas Robison, president of the American Baseball and Exhibition Company. Frank Robison was already the owner of the Cleveland club and he transferred the best of his players to St. Louis and sent the members of the old St. Louis squad in turn to Cleveland.

At this time, 1899, the succession of modern ownership for the St. Louis ballclub in the National League was established. The team nickname was changed from Perfectos to Cardinals. The new label was pinned on the team by a St. Louis baseball writer. Frank DeHaas Robison owned and operated the Cardinals until his death in 1905. At that time his brother, Stanley, took charge. Stanley Robison died in the spring of 1911 and the baseball property was inherited by his niece, Mrs. Helene Hathaway Robison Britton. She was the daughter of Frank and with her takeover the team had the distinction of having the only female major-league owner.

This period in the history of the Cardinals was far from impressive. There was a procession of managers with a fourth-place finish the highest, and that only achieved once. In 1900 Managers Oliver Tebeau and Louis Heilbroner piloted a club that won 65 games while losing 75 to tie for a fifth-place finish.

For the next three seasons Patsy Donovan managed the Cardinals. His 1901 team finished fourth with 76 victories. The following year his team won only 56 games while losing 78 for sixth place in the standings. Still on the downgrade, in his final season Donovan saw his team finish dead last with a skimpy 43 wins. The team drew but 263,538 patrons that season.

"Kid" Nichols was the 1904 manager. He piloted the team to 75 wins and a fifth-place finish. He was replaced during the next season, first by Jimmy Burke and then by Matthew Robison. The team finished sixth.

For the next three seasons (1906–09) John J. McCloskey was the pilot. His first two teams each won 52 games—finishing seventh and eighth. In his third and final season, 1908, he again finished in the league cellar with only 49 wins.

Roger Bresnahan followed in the ever-changing parade of managers. He managed Cardinals teams for four seasons, 1909–12. His first two teams finished seventh with 54 and 63 victories. The 1909 team drew 299,982 fans and his 1910 team had a comparatively impressive attendance of 363,624. The 1911 team won 75 games while losing 74 for a fifth-place finish and his 1912 team won 63 games to come home sixth.

The 1911 team is worthy of special mention. Roger Bresnahan, who is considered one of the greatest catchers of all time, had the fans excited despite the overall poor Cardinal season. This team drew a year-long attendance of 447,768. On this aggregation, Big Ed Konetchy was the first baseman, Miller Huggins, later a successful Yankee manager, was at second base, with Arnold Hauser at shortstop and

Mike Mowrey at third. In the outfield there was Rube Ellis, Steve Evans, and Rebel Oakes. This was the era of playing managers and Bresnahan did most of the catching. Harry Sallee was the ace of the pitching staff. Other hurlers were the two Lowdermilks, Grover and Louie, and Bob Harmon. In midseason the Cardinals were only three games out of first place in a tight race that had five clubs contending. It was the Giants, however, who finally won the coveted pennant.

The Cardinal team was in a train wreck just after midseason in 1911. Nobody was seriously injured but the devastating experience may well have contributed to the fifth-place finish that year. Bresnahan, known as the "Duke of Tralee," was often rough talking, and in his final season he was caught in frequent heated arguments with the club's female owner. Bresnahan had a five-year contract but Mrs. Britton insisted on firing him. The titular head of the St. Louis Cardinals at this time was E. A. Steininger, a distinguished businessman who kept far removed from the ongoing Bresnahan-Britton dispute. Later, from 1913 to 1916, Mrs. Britton installed her husband, Schuyler P. Britton, popularly known as "Skip," as club president.

Mrs. Britton really ran the operation. She was a strikingly attractive woman who attended all the major league meetings. She kept the organization in disarray much of the time, however. It was she who hired and fired the managers. And later she dismissed Skip Schuyler as well with a decree of divorce.

In 1913 Miller Huggins was hired as manager. In his first season the club finished last with 51 wins and 99 losses. The next season the Cardinals won 81 games to finish third—and with a greatly increased attendance of 346,025. In 1915 the team won 72 games and finished sixth. In his fourth season, Huggins piloted his club to 60 wins against 93 losses to tie for seventh place. In his final season as manager of the Cardinals (1917), Huggins led the club to a third-place finish with 82 victories. After that season the New York Yankees lured him away and in Gotham he became one of the outstanding managers of all time.

In 1917 Mrs. Britton decided to sell the team and she informed her attorney James C. Jones and Manager Miller Huggins of her plans. She suggested that they might want to buy the club. Huggins was interested but before he could secure the necessary backing, Jones had organized a syndicate to purchase the baseball club and the ballpark. The purchase price was $375,000 but Jones waived his $25,000 legal fee to reduce the price to $350,000.

Branch Rickey was brought to the Cardinals by new owner James Jones in 1916. Jones had consulted the newspapermen who covered the team—asking them for suggestions for a baseball man to serve as president of his new St. Louis organization. The response was practically unanimous—Jones was told that the man for the job was Branch Rickey.

Rickey was an idea man with a lot of savvy. He was with the other St. Louis club, the Browns, owned by Phil Ball. Ball had received Rickey as part of the package when he purchased the club as part of the settlement of the Federal League war. Phil Ball had not wanted Rickey as part of the deal but when the Cardinals wanted him he decided he wouldn't give him up. Rickey took the matter to court and won, becoming president of the reorganized Cardinals.

In his new post Rickey decided he couldn't compete with some of the other well-heeled clubs. His response was the creation of the farm system. It was his idea to take young baseball players of promise, sign them to low-budget salaries, develop them in the minor league chain, and then bring the better ones to the parent club for stardom. Other baseball men didn't agree with Rickey's philosophy but after the system became successful all baseball clubs eventually developed such farm systems.

The creation of the farm system by St. Louis was just one of many baseball innovations originating with the Cardinals. The man who drew up the league's constitution was a native of St. Louis, Judge Orrick C. Bishop. He was a practicing court judge and he also drafted the first baseball player's contract. That early contract was complete, including a reserve clause, a controversial inclusion, but an integral part of the structure of organized baseball down through the years. Another native of this Mississippi River waterfront town invented the hot dog, now an integral part of attendance at any ball game. The Sunday doubleheader—two games in one day for a single admission—also got its start in St. Louis.

The 1876 St. Louis team had been a charter member of the National League but after one season they withdrew. St. Louis was out of the league from 1877 to 1884. Later, from 1887 to 1891, the St. Louis club again dropped out. But from the time of the organization of the first professional team, St. Louis has always had a professional ballclub in some league or other.

In 1918, with the world at war, baseball, especially in St. Louis, was at a low ebb. The Cardinals were managed by Jack Hendricks. Attendance was down and the club finished in last place with 51 victories and 78 losses.

Branch Rickey returned from service in World War I and in 1919 he assumed the double role as club president and field manager. Rickey was a better administrator than manager but he piloted the team for six and a half seasons. The 1919 team, with 54 wins and 83 losses, finished seventh.

At this time Sam Breadon also became a part of the St. Louis Cardinal organization. Teaming with Rickey, he gave the club perhaps the greatest two-man combination that ever ran a baseball team. Breadon, an enthusiastic fan, was a young automobile dealer who had been persuaded by a friend, Warren "Fuzzy" Anderson, to invest in the Cardinals. Breadon purchased $200 worth of stock. Later, after attending a promotional banquet, he met Rogers Hornsby and other team stars, and he bought another $1,800 worth of stock. In a few more years he became a major stockholder and president of the Cardinals.

The combination of Breadon and Rickey was a strange one. Breadon liked parties, with highballs and pleasant company. Rickey was a teetotaler and religious to the point that he didn't attend baseball games on Sunday. The two had a deep respect for each other. Sam Breadon sifted Branch Rickey's many ideas, culling out the impractical ones and exploiting the better ones. Together, they built baseball's earliest farm system to develop fledgling players.

The Cardinals moved from Robison Field, where they had taken up residence in the 1890s, back to Sportsman's Park in 1920. The season was just average—75 victories and 79 defeats for a fifth-place finish. Attendance remained average as well—325,845 passing through the turnstiles.

Rogers Hornsby, Cardinal Superstar

In 1921 Rickey managed his Cardinals to a third-place finish. The team came home tied for third the following year. The 1922 team was highlighted by the performance of Rogers Hornsby. The Rajah won the league's triple crown with 42 home runs, 152 runs batted in, and a .401 batting average.

Hornsby, one of the great hitters in baseball history, had been signed by scout Bob Connery for a small sum in 1915. It was also Hornsby, one story has it, who indirectly gave Rickey the idea of developing a farm system.

The Cardinals were at the Polo Grounds in New York, playing the New York Giants. On a ground ball, hit to shortstop Johnny Lavan, the infielder fielded the ball and without looking fired it toward first base. The throw hit Hornsby, the second baseman, in the head and he fell to the ground unconscious. The night before, Charles A. Stoneham, the Giants owner, had offered Rickey $350,000 for Hornsby and was turned down. Stoneham chided Rickey and said it was a mistake to turn down the offer. Now, with Hornsby knocked out, Rickey painfully envisioned the loss of $350,000. Hornsby made a full recovery but Rickey decided then and there that he would find other Hornsbys on sandlots and in colleges and develop them into major league stars. Thus came about the seeds of development for a farm club system.

In 1923, with 79 wins and 74 losses, the Cardinals finished in fifth place and the next year they climbed to sixth with 65 victories. A bright spot in the 1924 season was again Rogers Hornsby's hitting. He won the National League batting crown with a .424 average, the highest batting mark in the league since 1900. A few seasons earlier, bases on balls counted as hits. If this rule had still been in effect, Hornsby would have had a whopping batting average of well over .500.

Branch Rickey, now recognized as possibly the finest front-office operator in the history of baseball, was, as we have already indicated, much less effective as a field manager. Breadon had long wanted to relieve Rickey of running the team on the field. Rickey was an articulate man who conversed on a level far beyond the intelligence of the players. He originated the practice of blackboard lectures and addressed the players much in the manner of a college professor addressing his classes. Many of the players had no idea of what he was trying to put across.

In the spring of 1925 Sam Breadon planned on switching managers and he told Rickey of his plan. Rickey, who wanted to continue as field director of the team, protested vigorously. He declared that the team was in a building stage and he needed one more season to completely mold the team.

Breadon had already made up his mind but he didn't want to embarrass Rickey who had finally consented to step down. At Spring Training Rickey was to announce that Burt Shotton, one of the team's coaches, would take over as manager. Rickey then reconsidered and refused to abide by the agreement. Breadon waited and waited and then finally went to the Cardinal camp. Rickey said he had changed his mind and pleaded his case to continue as manager. Breadon finally agreed.

Rickey's extension as manager was brief. In late May, with the club not doing well, Sam Breadon joined the team at Pittsburgh and observed Memorial Day by firing Branch Rickey as field manager and then appointing him as general manager of the team. Then, instead of appointing Burt Shotton, a Rickey supporter, he appointed second baseman Rogers Hornsby as the new pilot.

Hornsby, who had tremendous respect for Rickey, didn't want the job. Furthermore, as a playing manager, he was afraid it would detract from his play and his hitting. Yet he reluctantly took the position and the Cardinals in turn rallied. With 77 wins and 76 losses, and an attendance of 405,297, the club finished in fourth place. Hornsby himself had another great offensive year, winning the triple crown with 39 home runs, 143 runs batted in, and a batting average of .403.

Cardinals Win Their First World Series

The year 1926 was a major milestone in the history of baseball in St. Louis. In his first full year as manager, Rogers Hornsby had piloted the Cardinals to a pennant in the National League with 89 victories and 65 losses. Attendance had been high, too, with 681,575 patrons turning out to watch a revamped and exciting Cardinals ballclub.

In a seven-game World Series, the Cardinals defeated the New York Yankees, four games to three, to become World Champions for the first time in club history. It was, however, to be only the first of nine eventual world titles in 15 pennant-winning seasons and World Series appearances down the road. The 1926 Series turned out to be an exceptionally dramatic one, full of spectacular plays and featuring plenty of hard-hitting diamond excitement that would eventually become a St. Louis Fall Classic tradition.

The Yankees presented a star-studded lineup, one featuring the immortal Babe Ruth along with Earl Coombs and Bob Meusel in the outfield; and with Lou Gehrig, Tony Lazzari, Mark Koenig, and Joe Dugan comprising the infield. A talented New York pitching staff included Herb Pennock, Bob Shawkey, Urban Shocker, Walter Ruether, and Waite Hoyt. The catchers were Hank Severeid and Pat Collins.

The Cardinals had their manager, Rogers Hornsby, at second base with Jim Bottomley at first, Tommy Thevenow at shortstop, and Lester Bell at third base. Among the pitchers were Grover Cleveland Alexander, Bill Sherdel, Jess Haines, and Art Reinhart.

New York won the opening game, 2–1, as Pennock bested Sherdel. Alexander won over Shocker, 6–2, in the second game and St. Louis took the Series lead by winning the third game with Jess Haines, a knuckleballer, shutting out Dutch Ruether and the Yankees, 4–0. In the fourth game the Yanks evened the series with a display of power as Waite Hoyt bested Art Reinhart, 10–5. The Yankees went ahead in the fifth game when Pennock again shaded Sherdel, 3–2. This was the last game at Sportsman's Park for the Series.

The Cardinals showed they still had life in the sixth game, played at Yankee Stadium. The Series was squared with a 10–2 St. Louis win. Alexander recorded the crucial victory.

On a misty, dark day at Yankee Stadium, the seventh game of the 1926 World Series was played out. Going into the seventh inning, Cardinal pitcher Jess Haines had a 3–2 lead when he developed a blister on his finger from throwing the knuckleball. The bases were loaded and Tony Lazzari, always a dangerous hitter, was at bat. At that point, Hornsby summoned Alexander from the bullpen. Alexander, as was his wont, had celebrated fully his victory of the night before and Hornsby wondered if his ace was in any shape to pitch. Alexander assured his manager that he was ready, after being reminded that the bases were all occupied with Yanks and that the batter was indeed the dangerous Lazzari.

Lazzari lofted a tremendous foul fly on one of his swings but then harmlessly struck out. Alexander finished the game, holding the Yankees hitless for two and a third innings.

All through the early stages of the 1926 pennant-winning season, Sam Breadon had praised Rogers Hornsby and predicted many years of managerial success for the slugging second baseman. However, friction soon enough developed between Hornsby and Branch Rickey. Money was a thorny problem much of the time with the Cardinals. Rickey scheduled exhibition games in small towns on open dates to build extra revenue. In the midst of a torrid pennant race, Hornsby, on the other hand, became extremely angry over these additional bookings—feeling that his battle-weary players deserved the sparse time off.

Breadon wanted to please his manager above all else, so the club boss tried to cancel these extemporaneous barnstorming exhibition games. Telegrams were even sent telling of Hornsby's opposition to such contests and asking for the desired cancellations. Some towns refused to cancel these attractions, however. After the Cardinals had lost one tough league game, Breadon entered the clubhouse to inform his irritable manager that the team would have to meet a commitment as the promoters had refused to cancel. Hornsby read the riot act to his boss, Breadon.

Breadon was enraged at Hornsby's insubordination. He felt that he had been insulted and belittled by an employee in front of other employees—the ballplayers. He soon decided that despite the League Championship and World Series victory, the manager must go. Fans and baseball people were stunned during the Christmas season of 1926 when the announcement came that Hornsby had been traded to the New York Giants for two players—Frankie Frisch and Jimmy Ring, a pitcher. Cardinal fans were up in arms; they threatened to boycott the team. Verbally and in letters to sports editors of local newspapers, team followers declared they would no longer pass through the turn-stiles at Sportsman's Park. Sam Breadon was suddenly a very unpopular man.

Bob O'Farrell, a catcher, was selected to succeed Hornsby as manager in 1927 and quickly proved popular with both fans and players. Frankie Frisch had a great season and the team battled for a repeat pennant. The Cardinals finished second, with 92 victories, and might have won another pennant if not for injures to shortstop Tommy Thevenow and other key players. The attendance boycott did not materialize, however, as the team drew 763,615 fans.

Breadon and Rickey, having experienced the thrills of victory, now would not be satisfied with anything less than another winner. Bill McKechnie, who had come to St. Louis from Pittsburgh as a coach for Manager O'Farrell, received the nod to pilot the 1928 Cardinals. The team copped the pennant with 95 wins and 59 losses. Attendance continued to soar—to 778,147 paid admissions.

In the World Series that followed, the Cardinals met an invincible Yankee team with the New York nine making quick work of the Series with a four-game sweep. The Yankees were paced by Babe Ruth and Lou Gehrig: the Bambino had three home runs in one game and batted .625 for the series; Gehrig had a .545 batting average and had six hits, four of them home runs. He batted in nine runs as well.

With the four-game loss to the New York Yankees in the 1928 World Series, Breadon felt that Bill McKechnie lacked the inspirational qualities necessary for winning. He fired McKechnie and brought in Billy Southworth, a winning manager at Rochester in the International League. By July of 1929, with the Cardinals floundering, Breadon admitted he had blundered in his shuffling of managers, however. Southworth was sent back to Rochester and Bill McKechnie was recalled to finish the season. The team finished fourth and attendance dipped to nearly half that of the preceding season.

McKechnie, one of baseball's finer gentlemen, had no bitterness against his treatment by Breadon, yet while the Cardinal boss was preparing to extend a new contract, McKechnie was lured away by a long-term job offer with the Boston Braves.

Charles "Gabby" Street, a coach on the Cardinal staff in 1929, was hired to manage the 1930 team. Also known as the "Old Sargeant," Street, who had been bogged down by his activities off the playing field, was hired partly because Breadon felt Street could keep Grover Alexander on the straight and narrow path for effective pitching.

Gabby Street inherited a great ballclub and he was popular with his players. The team responded by becoming the first Cardinal team to win back-to-back pennants—in 1930 and 1931. The 1931 team won 101 games and, as with all winning teams, the attendance soared.

The World Series opponents for the St. Louis team both years were Connie Mack's Philadelphia Athletics. In the 1930 Series the Athletics won, four games to two. Both teams hit poorly with the Athletics batting only .197 and the Cardinals only .200. Bill Hallahan won for St. Louis in the third game, 4–0, and Jess Haines hurled a 3–1 Cardinal win in the fourth game.

The 1930 Series defeat was avenged in 1931 in an action-packed Series that went the full seven games. The Cardinal attack was led by John "Pepper" Martin, also known as the "Wild Horse of the Osage." He batted .500, collected 12 hits and stole five bases. Bill Hallahan and Burleigh Grimes each posted two victories.

The 1931 St. Louis team stands as one of the best Cardinal teams of all time. Jim Bottomley was the first baseman; Frank Frisch, a hitting and fielding star, was at second; Charlie Gelbert, a young infielder getting better, was at shortstop; and third base was handled by Sparky Adams in the main with Jake Flowers and Andy High as replacements. High was also an expert pinch hitter.

In the outfield Pepper Martin was in center field, flanked by Chick Hafey in left field and either George Watkins or Wally Roettger in right field. Gus Mancuso and Jimmy Wilson handled the catching with the pitching staff including Paul Derringer, Bill Hallahan, Burleigh Grimes, and Sylvester Johnson. Jim Lindsey was the relief ace of the staff.

There was a considerable change in the St. Louis National League team when the 1932 season rolled around. The great loyalty that had developed seemed to be gone altogether, and there was friction everywhere among the players. The team finished in a tie for sixth place with 72 victories and 82 losses. Gabby Street had suddenly lost his managerial magic. The situation continued to worsen into the following season, until July of 1933, when Breadon decided a move was necessary. He was fond enough of Street, yet he felt the team needed new management and thus Frank Frisch was brought in. The team showed little immediate improvement under Frisch, finishing in fifth place with 82 wins.

Frisch and the Dean Brothers

Frankie Frisch, known as the "Fordham Flash" for his collegiate days, piloted the 1934 Cardinals to the League Championship and a World Series victory. This colorful 1934 club quickly became known as the "Gas House Gang"—named by the team's lippy shortstop, Leo "The Lip" Durocher. This team was one of the very best box-office aggregations to ever play baseball.

The 1934 Cardinals won the pennant on the last day of the season, with 95 victories. During the regular season, the Dean brothers, Jerome "Dizzy" and Paul "Daffy," had combined to win 49 games. In the World Series against Detroit, they each won two games.

Jerome "Dizzy" Dean had joined the Cardinals in 1930. In the final game of that season he pitched a three-hit game against the Pittsburgh Pirates. However, he spent the entire 1931 season at Houston because of his undisciplined behavior. His brother Paul joined the club in 1934, brought up from Columbus.

In the final game of the 1934 Series, played at Detroit, Joe Medwick slid hard into third base, drawing boos and the ire of the Tiger fans. Fruit, vegetables, bottles, and other debris were thrown at Medwick by the fans in the left-field bleachers when he took his place in the field. Crowd behavior became so disruptive that baseball Commissioner Kenesaw Mountain Landis finally decreed that Medwick should leave the game to protect the Cardinal outfielder and to prevent those in attendance from becoming involved in a full-scale riot.

On that colorful 1934 team, James "Ripper" Collins was at first base. He was a switch-hitter who stroked the long ball. At second base, playing-manager Frank Frisch was a major star; Leo "Lippy" Durocher was the shortstop and Pepper Martin held down third base. In the outfield, Ernie Orsatti and Chick Fullis covered center field with Jack Rothrock in right field and Joseph "Ducky" Medwick in left. Medwick was a notorious bad-ball hitter. Bill Delancy did the catching. In addition to the Dean brothers, Jerome and Paul, the Cardinal pitching staff included three southpaws (Bill Hallahan, Bill Walker, and Jim Mooney) along with righthanders Jess Haines and Tex Carleton.

There are colorful stories galore about the two Deans—especially "Dizzy." It is interesting that Jerome got his nickname in an exhibition game, due to his pitching skill and not his antics. He was dubbed "Dizzy" because he made the opposing batters dizzy with his pitching stuff. Eastern sports writers pinned the label "Daffy" on Paul Dean as an alliterative to "Dizzy." Paul was the opposite of the loud, gregarious Jerome—quiet and attentive.

While at Houston during the 1931 season, Dizzy Dean met Patricia Nash. Within 48 hours they were married and in addition to being his wife she became his governor, stabilizer, and especially his financial guardian. It has often been said that the two Deans were underpaid. They were, however, paid salaries comparable to those of other stars, receiving the regular raises that were common to baseball of the day. Dizzy had no regard for or comprehension of money and he bought anything that appealed to him. The Cardinal front office picked up the tabs for much of this, including hotel bills, automobiles, and much else.

Dizzy Dean pitched as well as he had to. He challenged the hitters, pitching to the batter's greatest strength. He had a strong right arm, a great curve ball and a change of pace that maddened the league's hitters. His fastball was blazing—sometimes he threw a whole game that was almost entirely fastballs. He also had great baseball instincts. In the season that he won 30 games (1934) and lost only seven, he can be visualized as winning 40 games if he had seriously set his mind to doing so.

Pitching in the 1937 All-Star Game, Dizzy received an injury that led to the end of his career. He suffered a broken toe and with the fracture still bandaged, he returned to pitching. Throwing with the broken digit, he developed an unnatural motion in favoring the injury and did something irreparable to his pitching-arm muscles. He never regained the effectiveness of his fastball. In the spring of 1938 he was traded to the Chicago Cubs for two pitchers, Clyde Shoun and Curt Davis, and $185,000 in cash.

An interesting episode in the Dean saga occurred in 1934. Playing at their home field on Sunday, August 12, Dizzy and Paul pitched a doubleheader and both lost their games. The team left for Detroit that night to play an exhibition game, but when Manager Frisch checked the player personnel he found the Deans were missing. Dizzy was at the country home of a friend, eating fried chicken.

Frisch fined Dizzy $100 and Paul $40. They refused to pay or appear on the field so Frisch suspended them. In the clubhouse Dizzy Dean tore up two uniforms—one to give vent to his anger and the other to oblige the press photographers. The Cardinals, minus their two star pitchers, won seven of the next eight games, but chances for a pennant were slim without them.

Dizzy appealed to Commissioner Landis, expecting a favorable ruling, but the judge ruled against them. They then took their medicine, and returned to the team. When the New York Giants faltered down the stretch drive, the Cardinals came on strong and won the pennant with 95 victories.

Frank Frisch lasted for three more full seasons and part of a fourth—the longest tenure of any Cardinal manager up until this time. His 1935 team finished second with 96 wins and an attendance of 517,805. The 1936 team tied for second and the ballclub the next year finished fourth. That year (1937) Joe "Ducky" Medwick won the league's triple crown with 31 home runs, 154 runs batted in, and a .374 batting average.

Late in the 1938 season Frisch was replaced by Mike Gonzales. The team finished in sixth place and experienced rather poor attendance. Branch Rickey thus made a replacement recommendation for the 1939 season. Ray Blades, who had long been closely associated with Rickey, was selected to pilot the Cardinals. Blades managed the team to a second-place finish and greatly increased attendance, well over 400,000. Blades also replaced pitchers with reckless abandon, a system that worked in 1939 but floundered the next season.

The Cardinals finished third in 1940 and Blades was replaced during the season by Mike Gonzales who in turn was replaced by Billy Southworth. The 1940 season brought night baseball to St. Louis, first with the American League Browns and then with the Cardinals.

Johnny Mize also set a season's home run record for St. Louis that year when he hit 43 round-trippers.

The Stan Musial Era

Billy Southworth's second tenure as manager of the Cardinals resulted in a five-year hitch that was perhaps the most successful in the history of the St. Louis franchise. Billy managed his first full season (1941) to a second-place finish, winning 97 games, usually enough for a pennant, against 56 losses. A bright spot of the 1941 season was the arrival of Stan Musial. Musial had started out in the Cardinal farm system as a lefthanded pitcher but arm trouble led to his development into a slugging outfielder. Before he had finished his baseball career, Musial had contributed much to Cardinal success and had put numerous new hitting standards into the record books.

In 1942 Southworth's Cardinals won a whopping 106 games against only 48 losses to win the League Championship. The first-place finish boosted attendance for the year to 571,626. Despite the fact that the 1942 Cardinals were a wartime club, they presented a star-studded lineup during a period when many baseball teams were critically short on talent. Stan Musial joined Enos Slaughter and Terry Moore in the outfield to give the Redbirds one of baseball's all-time best trio of flychasers.

In the infield Johnny Hopp held down first base, backed up by Ray Sanders. Jimmy Brown was the second baseman with George Kurowski over at third. Newcomer Marty Marion, who quickly became "Mr. Shortstop," anchored the center of the infield.

The 1942 Cardinals had a brother combination as its leading battery. Walker Cooper was the catcher with his brother, Mort, the mainstay of the pitching staff. Other pitchers were Ernie White, a lefthanded clutch performer; a rookie, Johnny Beazley; Howie Pollet and Max Lanier, both southpaws; and a capable relief hurler, Harry Gumbert.

The Yankees were a heavy odds-on favorite to overwhelm the Cardinals in the 1942 World Series. The New Yorkers took the first game, with Red Ruffing holding the Cards hitless until two were retired in the eighth inning. (Terry Moore eventually singled to ruin Ruffing's near no-hitter.) The Cardinals then rallied for four runs in the ninth frame, knocking the shaken Ruffing from the box after he had been within one putout of a two-hit shutout; yet the rally was not quite enough to salvage Game One.

The Cardinals did roar back to take four straight games and thus score one of the greatest upsets in World Series history. Rookie Johnny Beazley bested Ernie Bonham, 4–3, to win the tightly contested second game, while Ernie White pitched a sparkling shutout for a 2–0 win in manager who could instill some of the old Gas House Gang spirit into the team. Eddie's 1952 team finished third and his team the next season finished tied for third as well.

Fred Saigh might have remained as owner and president of the St. Louis Cardinals for a long time but he was charged with federal income tax evasion and given a heavy fine and a prison term of 15 months. On February 20, 1953, the club was sold to Anheuser Busch, Inc., one of America's leading breweries. August A. Busch, Jr. became club president. Sportsman's Park was renovated by the new owners and renamed Busch Stadium.

Despite the fact that Stanky managed the team to only a sixth-place finish in 1954, attendance remained high at over a million. In a doubleheader against the New York Giants at Busch Stadium on May 2, Stan Musial hit five home runs. In 1955 the Cardinals were mired in seventh place and Eddie Stanky was fired during the season. For the balance of the campaign the replacement was Harry Walker. The seventh-place finish was the lowest for the club since 1932, and reflecting the team's performance, attendance was also down.

For the next decade there was a parade of managers in an ongoing campaign to make the Cardinals a pennant contender again. Frank Lane came into the front office in 1956 as general manager. The field manager was Fred Hutchinson. Freddie's first team finished fourth, 17 games behind Brooklyn, after looking like a pennant contender the first couple of months of the season. Frank (known as "Trader") Lane incurred the anger of the press and fans with three major trades in the space of a month. He peddled pitcher Harvey Haddix; Bill Virdon, the 1955 Rookie of the Year; Jackie Brandt, an outstanding rookie; and Red Schoendienst, a stalwart infielder.

Hutchinson had a second-place team in 1957. A bright spot of the season was the appearance of new players who gave promise of helping the Cardinals to resume winning ways. Newcomers included Ken Boyer at third base and Don Blasingame at second. Larry Jackson was a pitcher of considerable promise.

During the 1957 season veteran Stan Musial established a National League record for endurance as he extended his total of consecutive games played to 895 before an injury benched him. The accident occurred on August 22 when Musial tore a muscle and chipped a bone in his shoulder blade as he swung at and missed a high, outside pitch. Musial did win the batting title that season with a .351 average.

Frank Lane was gone after two years and Fred Hutchinson was also fired during the 1958 season, replaced by Stan Hack with the Cardinals finishing tied for fifth place. On May 13, pinch hitting in the sixth inning, Stan Musial collected a two-base hit against the Chicago Cubs at Wrigley Field. This dramatic hit was the 3,000th hit of Musial's outstanding career.

Solly Hemus was installed as manager in 1959 and his team that year finished seventh. The next season his team finished third. During the 1961 season Hemus was replaced by Johnny Keane as the team ended the season in fifth place. In 1962, with Keane as manager, the Cardinals finished sixth. Stan Musial, approaching his 42nd birthday, made a solid bid for his eighth batting title as he hit .330. Yet Musial eventually fell short as Tommy Davis of the Los Angeles Dodgers won the crown with a .346 mark.

In 1963, with Johnny Keane still the manager, the Cardinals finished in second place with 93 victories. Stan Musial, who had won seven National League batting titles in his 22-year career with St. Louis (he had a lifetime batting average of .331), announced his retirement. His famous number six became the first Cardinal number to be retired.

Johnny Keane reached the top as he piloted the 1964 team to a pennant in his final year as manager. In the World Series the Cardinals defeated the Yankees, four games to three. Many players contributed to the 1964 Series success. Pitcher Bob Gibson won two games, Ken Boyer hit a grand slam home run to win the fourth game, and Tim McCarver smashed a 10th-inning home run to win the fifth game. McCarver topped the Cardinal hitters in the Series with a .478 average. Roger Craig and Ron Taylor were valuable in pitching relief roles.

Red Schoendienst at the Helm

For 12 seasons, beginning in 1965, St. Louis Cardinal baseball teams were managed by Albert "Red" Schoendienst. The two preceding years Schoendienst had been a coach and before that had been a Cardinal player for two hitches for a total of 14 years. As a manager, his teams compiled a total of 1,028 victories. He piloted the team to pennants in 1967 and 1968 and the Cardinals finished second in 1971, 1973, and 1974.

In Schoendienst's first season as manager, the Redbirds won 80 games and finished in seventh place. The next season, 1966, the team finished sixth with 83 victories.

On May 8, 1966, the Cardinals closed the old Busch Stadium with a 10–5 loss to the San Francisco Giants. On May 12 the team opened the new Busch Memorial Stadium by defeating the Atlanta Braves, 4–3 in 12 innings. The winning run was scored when Lou Brock singled with the bases loaded to drive in Curt Flood. The winning pitcher was Don Dennis while the losing hurler for the Braves was Phil Niekro. The first Cardinal to record a hit in the new stadium was Mike Shannon, who knocked a first-inning single. Atlanta's Felipe Alou hit two home runs in this game. Later in the season the Cardinals hosted the All-Star Game at the new park.

Game Three. In the fourth game Mort Cooper was knocked out but Pollet and Lanier in relief gave the Cards a 9–6 victory.

Johnny Beazley won his second Series game in the fifth meeting by a 4–2 score. Whitey Kurowski, who had hit a decisive triple in the second game, poled a two-run homer in the ninth inning of the fifth game to clinch the Series for the surprising Cardinals.

After the 1942 season Branch Rickey moved to Brooklyn and close observers of the game were of the opinion that the St. Louis Cardinals organization would find Rickey irreplaceable and would rapidly deteriorate. The Cardinal stars were getting older and there seemed to be no adequate replacements. Sam Breadon, always concerned about the financial side of the operation, may have felt that this was true. Breadon's health was also a factor; the time seemed ripe to sell the club. There were some immediate inquiries, yet the team wasn't sold until after the 1947 season.

In the next two seasons, 1943 and 1944, Billy Southworth piloted the Cardinals to two more National League pennants and another World Series victory. Both years the team won 105 games while losing 49.

The Yankees, in the 1943 Series, evened the record between the two clubs at two apiece. The New Yorkers defeated the Redbirds, four games to one. The key play in the Series occurred in the third game. In the eighth inning, with the Cardinals leading 2–1, Johnny Lindell of the Yankees crashed into third baseman Whitey Kurowski on a sacrifice bunt, jarring the ball loose. Billy Johnson then tripled to drive in three runs and the Yankees went on to score five runs in the inning and coasted to victory. The Yankees took the next two games for the championship.

The 1944 World Series was the only one that was an all St. Louis affair with the Cardinals against the American League Browns. The Redbirds won the Series, four games to two, in a dramatic six-game set highlighted by outstanding pitching. A total of 92 batters struck out, 49 of them mowed down by Cardinal hurlers and 43 by Browns moundsmen. Leading hitter of the Series for the Cardinals was Emil Verban with a .412 average.

Southworth's 1945 team won 95 games for a second-place finish. In a move that bordered on tampering, the new owners of the Boston Braves approached Southworth with a lucrative offer. The Boston owners contacted Sam Breadon and asked for a release for the coveted skipper. Reluctantly, Breadon gave consent—he didn't want an unhappy manager. Searching for a new field boss, Breadon selected a man who had been a veteran in the Cardinal organization but at the time was in the oil and insurance business. The choice was Eddie Dyer.

With 98 victories, Dyer piloted the Cardinals to a pennant in his first season. For the first time home crowds in St. Louis topped a million in paid attendance. In a seven-game World Series, the Cardinals won the October Classic against Boston, four games to three.

Ace pitcher Harry (the Cat) Brecheen won three of the four Cardinal Series victories. It was a thrilling Series. In the last half of the eighth inning of the deciding game, Enos Slaughter singled and then scored all the way from first base on Harry Walker's hit to left center field. This reckless base running sprint surprised the relay man, Johnny Pesky, and when he hesitated, Slaughter scored the winning run. Walker advanced to second base and was credited with a double. The Cardinals were clear underdogs in this series as powerful Boston was led by slugger Ted Williams. After falling behind, three games to two, the Cardinals rebounded to take the deciding sixth and seventh games.

For the next three seasons Dyer's Cardinals finished in second place each season with 89 wins in 1947, 85 victories in 1948, and an impressive 96 victories in 1949—usually enough to win a pennant. Attendance all three years was well over a million fans.

The Cardinals were almost sold during the 1947 season but a leakage of tips led Breadon to call off the negotiations. Fred Saigh, a corporate and tax lawyer, led a group of Texas oil men in the inquiries that were eventually called off.

Breadon told the ballplayers in midseason that he was not selling the team. Later, he changed his mind and negotiations were resumed with Fred Saigh and his partner, Robert E. Hannegan. In the fall Breadon announced with deep emotion that the team had been sold. Hannegan was Postmaster General in the cabinet of President Harry Truman; he resigned that post to become president of the St. Louis Cardinals.

The club was purchased for about $4 million with the assets including more than $2 million, part of which was earmarked for a new baseball park. Hannegan served as president of the ballclub until after the 1948 season when, in failing health, he sold out his share of the club to Saigh who thus became president and virtually sole owner of the team.

In 1948 Stan Musial won his third National League Most Valuable Player Award. He had previously won that honor in 1943 and 1946. In 1948 Musial led the league in almost every batting department. His batting average was .376 and he led as well in runs (135), hits (230), and total bases (429). He hit 46 doubles and 18 triples, batting in 131 runs. His leading slugging percentage was .702.

The Cardinals played the first night game season opener in St. Louis in 1950. The team finished in fifth place that year in what proved to be the last season for Dyer.

Marty Marion piloted the Cardinals for a single season; his 1951 club finished third. Eddie Stanky took over in 1952 as Saigh sought a

After winning the 1967 league pennant with 101 victories and enjoying a paid attendance above two million, the Cardinals met the Boston Red Sox and defeated them in a seven-game World Series, four games to three. Ace Bob Gibson pitched three complete-game victories and Lou Brock gave a superstar performance, topping all Series hitters with a .414 batting average. He also set a Series record by stealing seven bases. Gibson limited the Red Sox to 14 hits in the three games he hurled. Roger Maris batted .385 and drove in seven runs, a Cardinal Series record.

The Cardinals repeated as league champions in 1968 with 97 victories. In the World Series that followed, St. Louis had a three-games-to-one lead but their opponents, the Detroit Tigers, rebounded and won the final three games for their first Series title in 23 years.

During the 1968 season Denny McLain of the Detroit Tigers won 31 games, but in the Series Mickey Lolich was the star, winning three games including the 4–1 victory over the Cardinals in the decisive seventh game. Bob Gibson in turn won two games for the Redbirds. Gibson set records by striking out 17 Tigers in the first game and a total of 35 for the Series, breaking his own standard of 31 set against the Yankees in the 1964 Series.

Bob Gibson won 22 games and lost nine during the 1968 season. He tossed 13 shutouts, had a winning streak of 15 games, and allowed only 38 earned runs in 304 innings for a fabulous earned run average of 1.12. This was a major league record for a pitcher working more than 300 innings. Gibson won the National League Cy Young Award and was named the league's Most Valuable Player.

The 1968 pennant represented the last title season for Red Schoendienst. His 1969 team finished tied for fourth place and his 1970 aggregation was again in fourth place. After finishing second in 1971, the Cardinals were again fourth-place finishers in 1972. The next two seasons, 1973 and 1974, the Cardinals finished second and in 1975 the team finished in a tie for third place. In his final season as manager, 1976, Schoendienst piloted his club to a fifth-place finish.

The Era of Gibson and Brock

The seventies was the Cardinal era of Lou Brock and Bob Gibson. It was also the period of numerous sparkling Redbird performances. In September of 1969, for starters, Steve Carlton struck out 19 New York Met batters in nine innings to set a major league record, although Carlton lost the game, 4–3. In 1970 Gibson won his second Cy Young Award, capturing 23 games while losing but seven. In 1971 Joe Torre took the league batting title with an average of .363 and was fittingly named the circuit's Most Valuable Player.

That same year Gibson pitched his first no-hit game, defeating Pittsburgh 11–0 on August 14, 1971. Brock became the first major league player to steal 50 or more bases in seven consecutive seasons. Schoendienst, as well, got into the act, setting a longevity record by completing his seventh season as a Cardinal manager in 1971.

In 1972 Bob Gibson extended his big-league record to nine seasons of registering 200 or more strikeouts. Brock extended his base-stealing as well to eight seasons of 50 or more steals. During the 1972 season Gibson recorded his 2,786th strikeout, the most career whiffs by a National League righthanded hurler at the time. In 1973 Gibson moved into second place on the all-time strikeout list, Joe Torre registered his 2,000th hit and his 1,000th run-batted-in, and Brock stole his 600th base. In the process Lou also moved into ninth place on the all-time list and set a further record by stealing 50 or more bases for nine consecutive seasons.

Lou Brock stole 118 bases in 1974 to break the one-season mark and move from ninth to second place on the career stolen bases list. Bob Gibson struck out his 3,000th batter to become the second pitcher in baseball history to reach that figure. The Cardinals had the third highest attendance in their history in 1974 with 1,838,413 paid customers. That season the Cardinals and the New York Mets played the longest night game in major league history, 25 innings. St. Louis was the winner when Bake McBride scored from first base on two errors. McBride won Rookie of the Year honors. In 1975 Bob Gibson retired after a glorious 17-year career with the Cardinals. He was honored for his 251 career victories on Bob Gibson Day with a standing-room-only crowd on hand. Lou Brock got his 2,500th hit and stole his 800th base that same season. The Cardinals had a "jacket day" which drew 50,548 fans, the largest regular season crowd in St. Louis baseball history. Al Hrabosky recorded 13 victories and 22 saves to be named "Fireman of the Year." With an average of .332 Ted Simmons finished second in the league batting race.

Lou Brock closed to within 27 of matching Ty Cobb's stolen base record in the 1976 season. The next year, on August 29, Brock broke Cobb's career record for stolen bases by pilfering his 893rd base in a game against San Diego.

The 1977 team, managed by Vernon Rapp, finished third in the N.L. standings. Shortstop Garry Templeton became the youngest major leaguer to record 200 hits in a season; he also led the majors with 18 triples. Ted Simmons set the record for home runs by a Cardinal catcher with 22 round-trippers. But perhaps the greatest long-range effect on Cardinals baseball occurred when Astroturf was installed that year upon the grounds of Busch Memorial Stadium.

The 1978 St. Louis team, with a fifth-place finish, had three managers during the course of the season. Vernon Rapp, the manager of the 1977 team, was first replaced in early spring by Jack Krol, who was in turn succeeded by Ken Boyer before the season ended. Boyer continued as manager in 1979 with the Cardinals finishing third. In 1980 Jack Krol was returned as field manager, but he was quickly replaced by Whitey Herzog and then old-hand Red Schoendienst before the finish of the campaign, one which saw the team finishing in fourth slot. Bob Forsch, a 20-game winner in 1977, pitched a no-hit ball game against the punchless Philadelphia Phillies on April 16, 1978.

On August 8, 1979, Lou Brock collected his 3,000th career hit and in September he stole his 938th and final career base to culminate his brilliant career as baseball's all-time stolen base leader. Also in 1979, Keith Hernandez won the N.L. batting title with an average of .344 and was quickly named co-winner (along with Hall-of-Famer Willie Stargell of Pittsburgh) of the MVP award. Garry Templeton led the senior circuit in hits, 211, and banged out 19 triples. Templeton became the first switch hitter to achieve 100 hits both righthanded and lefthanded, having an even 100 hits from the right side of the plate and 111 from the left. Catcher Ted Simmons knocked out 26 home runs to cap a fine St. Louis offensive season.

In 1980 third baseman Ken Reitz set a National League fielding record for third basemen with only eight errors. In June Manger Boyer was replaced by Whitey Herzog. In August General Manager John Claiborne was fired and replaced by Herzog as well. Schoendienst served as interim field manager for the balance of the season, as Whitey became acclimated to his new front-office responsibilities. In late October, however, Herzog was back on the field as he assumed the dual role of both general manager and field boss.

Modern Cardinals under Herzog

The 1981 campaign was a split season due to the highly unpopular Players'–Union strike. This was a season when the owners' revised playoff format for the strike-shortened schedule wreaked havoc upon normal baseball logic. The Cardinals finished second in each half of the season, yet had the best overall season-long record in the Eastern Division, giving them a first-place finish with 59 wins and 43 losses. It was to little avail, however. Finishing second in each of the two sections of the schedule caused St. Louis to miss the bizarre playoffs.

The Cardinals did have a championship team again in 1982, however. In order to concentrate more fully on his field managing duties, Whitey Herzog stepped down as general manager on Opening Day, with Joe McDonald taking over all front-office duties. The move paid off handsomely—the Cardinals were out of first place only 48 days during the entire summer's season.

In the league playoffs the Redbirds swept by the Atlanta Braves, three games to none. In their 13th post-season classic, the Cardinals played the upstart Milwaukee Brewers and won again, four games to three. The Cards were down at one point, three games to one, yet battled back to capture the final two games and the coveted World Series trophy as well.

In a rain-delayed contest that took five hours to complete, the Cardinals took the crucial Series' sixth game with rookie John Stuper on the mound. Joaquin Andujar won two games and Bruce Sutter was credited with one victory and two saves. During the season Sutter had a part in almost half of the team's victories. Rookie Willie McGee hit two home runs and made two spectacular fielding plays. Darrell Porter was named Series Most Valuable Player.

In the seasons from 1982 through 1989, the St. Louis team drew more than two million fans each year. The championship team of 1987 drew a whopping 3,072,121 paid admissions.

Whitey Herzog's 1983 team finished fourth, 11 games out of first place. The team was inconsistent but climbed to within a half game of the division lead before embarking on a 13-game road trip. Failure of the starting pitchers to produce soon caused the ballclub to take a nose-dive out of contention. The team set a new club record with 207 stolen bases. Bob Forsch pitched his second no-hit game and shortstop Ozzie Smith won his fourth straight gold glove.

In 1984 the Cardinals were up a notch, finishing third. The team stole 220 bases and Bruce Sutter tied the major league record for saves with 45. Joaquin Andujar won 20 games.

The 1985 St. Louis team got off to a slow start, losing their first four games and then reaching a .500 percentage with seven wins and seven losses. Herzog's team then lost four more games and it wasn't until they reached 20 wins and 20 losses that they achieved a .500 level again. Early in September, with five losses in six games, the Cardinals trailed the Mets by a game with but 25 games remaining. The Redbirds then won 14 of the next 15 and took the 1985 division title with 101 victories. Willie McGee was the league batting champion with a .353 average and was also the National League Most Valuable Player. Joaquin Andujar and John Tudor each won 21 games. Danny Cox had 18 wins and Willie McGee and Ozzie Smith each won gold gloves for fielding prowess. Whitey Herzog was fittingly selected as senior circuit Manager of the Year.

In the league playoffs the Cardinals lost the first two games to the Los Angeles Dodgers and then won the next four. The final game was highlighted by a three-run ninth-inning blast by N.L.C.S. hero Jack Clark.

In the 1985 World Series against cross-state rival Kansas City, the Cardinals won the first two games on the road and then lost four of the next five contests when the team mysteriously failed to hit. Kansas City won Game Three before John Tudor shut out the Royals for a 3–0 St. Louis victory in Game Four. The Royals fought back to win Game Five by a 6–1 mark. In Game Six the Cardinals had a 1–0 lead heading for the ninth frame. The first Kansas City batter reached base on a disputed umpire's call, and the Royals went on to score twice for a controversial victory, 2–1. The seventh game was no contest. The Kansas City team took home the championship by breezing in an 11–0 romp, marked by a memorable and unfortunate emotional outburst by ejected Cardinal hurler Joaquin Andujar.

The 1986 Cardinals went into reverse. After the first two months of play the team was mired in last place, yet they bounced back to finish third. Ozzie Smith won his seventh straight gold glove. Rookie Todd Worrell led the league in saves with 36 and was named Rookie of the Year. Cardinal attendance was above two million for the fifth consecutive year and the team drew the 75th million fan in the history of the franchise stretching back to 1900. The team also drew the 50 millionth fan to see the Cardinals play under the ownership of Anheuser-Busch.

Despite injuries to key players the 1987 Cardinal team hovered around first place most of the first half of the season. On July 3 the Cardinals enjoyed a 9½-game lead but by September 19 this had dropped to 1½ games. A doubleheader sweep of the Expos on September 29 led to the pennant-clinching victory over Montreal on October 1. The year 1987 was fantastic at the turnstiles, as well, with attendance totaling 3,072,121 paying fans. This made St. Louis the third club in major league history to surpass the single-season three million mark in attendance.

The 1987 World Series opened against the Minnesota Twins at the Metrodome in Minneapolis. The Twins took the first two games, aided in part by the unfamiliarity with the dome surroundings by the Cardinal players. Returning to St. Louis, the Cardinals took three games in a row to even up and then go ahead in the Series.

Returning to Minneapolis for Game Six, the Cardinals took a 5–2 lead in the fifth inning but home runs by Don Baylor and Kent Hrbek helped the Twins to a come-from-behind 11–5 victory.

In the deciding seventh game Twins pitcher Frank Viola allowed two runs in the second inning. In the sixth inning, with the score tied at 2–2, Greg Gagne singled to give the Twins a 4–2 triumph and the championship. This was the first World Series ever in which the home team won each of the seven games.

In 1988 the Cardinals finished fifth as the champions of the year before struggled with a lack of offensive power and key injuries. New players with youth have been added to bolster the departure of some of the veterans. The Cardinals plan to be a team to contend with in the seasons to come.

Whitey Herzog, in turn, was known and respected by the players and baseball administrators and was probably the best manager in baseball during the 1980s. He kept the Cardinals in contention most years and his sudden resignation early in the 1990 campaign was a severe blow to club prospects for the 1990s.

On September 29, 1989, August A. "Gussie" Busch, Jr., at the age of 90, died at his home in suburban St. Louis after a brief illness. He was the owner, president, and chief executive officer of the St. Louis Cardinals. Gussie Busch had become president of the St. Louis baseball club on February 20, 1953, when Anheuser-Busch purchased the team from Fred M. Saigh for $3,750,000. Busch took great pride in driving a six-horse hitch of Clydesdale horses around Busch Stadium for the sixth World Series the Cardinals participated in during his tenure. St. Louis won three of these. In 1987 the Cardinals drew more than 3 million paid admissions. On the night of Busch's death, the club again went over three million in paid attendance. Gussie Busch was one of baseball's most influential owners—he contributed much to the grand old game of baseball.

Annotated Bibliography

Borst, Bill. *Baseball Through a Knothole: A St. Louis History*. St. Louis, Mo.: Krank Press, 1980. 120 pp.
    A fan's loving perspective on the drama, the heroes, and the memories of Maroons, Browns, and Cardinals baseball history down through the years. Self-published and with a small scattering of photographs, this volume is strongest for its brief portraits of St. Louis (mostly Cardinals) Hall-of-Famers, and for its capsule summaries of team histories, epoch by epoch, including hard-to-find material on the origins and evolution of the nineteenth-century St. Louis National League ballclub.
Broeg, Bob. *Baseball's Redbirds, a Century of Cardinals Baseball in St. Louis*. St. Louis, Mo.: River City Publishers, 1981. 219 pp.
    A standard team history by a veteran (since 1945) St. Louis *Post-Dispatch* baseball writer. Broeg's highly readable franchise chronicle is delightfully colored by his years with the team and his close personal associations with many of its players, providing an intimate and often witty portrait of great St. Louis Cardinal baseball moments and unmatched Cardinals personalities.
Brosnan, Jim. *The Long Season*. New York: Harper and Row Publishers, 1960. 278 pp.

A classic portrait of baseball from inside the major league locker room, as recounted by the game's first and best "literary" ballplayer. A witty, perceptive, and outspoken chronicle of a pitcher's life from the February opening of Spring Training through the final out of October. A relief specialist and veteran of nine big-league seasons, Brosnan recounts life with the 1959 Cardinals.

Fleming, Gordon H. *The Dizziest Season: The Gashouse Gang Chases the Pennant.* New York: William Morrow and Company, 1984. 311 pp.

A day-by-day re-creation of the 1934 National League pennant race, when the Gashouse Gang battled to the last two games of the season against the rival World Champion New York Giants. Fleming collects and annotates contemporary press reports of this dramatic baseball summer, and the results are unmatched portraits of one of baseball's most colorful teams and pennant races ever.

Hood, Robert E. *The Gashouse Gang.* New York: William Morrow and Company, 1976. 242 pp.

A less distinguished portrait of the Dizzy Dean-era Cardinal team which captured the nation's imagination and became as noted for its colorful characters and off-field pranks as for its quite considerable baseball accomplishments. This is the team which featured, as well, a supporting cast of Pepper Martin, Joe "Ducky" Medwick, Lippy Leo Durocher, Ripper Collins, Dazzy Vance, Paul "Daffy" Dean, Jesse Haines, and player-manager Frankie "the Fordham Flash" Frisch. Hood focuses on the dramatic 1934 pennant race and on the players which made this team so memorable.

Leptich, John, and David Barauowski. *This Date in St. Louis Cardinals History.* New York: Stein and Day Publishers, 1982. 235 pp.

Done in the standard format of the Stein and Day team chronology series, this work presents Cardinals baseball history in terms of memorable events (accomplishments, records, important milestones, birth and death dates, etc.) for each calendar date. Also featured are a photo section, World Series boxscores, all-time individual leaders in important batting and pitching categories, plus all-time team rosters and nickname sections.

Lieb, Frederick G. *St. Louis Cardinals: The Story of a Great Baseball Club.* New York: G. P. Putnam, 1944. 213 pp.

Complete only through the World War II years, this is the standard team history from the classic series of franchise portraits issued by Putnam during the forties and fifties. Lieb was the premier baseball historian of his age, and this loving book brings to life the great Cardinals teams of the first half of the century, with special focus on the Gashouse Gang teams of Dean, Frisch, Pepper Martin, and Joe Medwick, and the young Cardinals team of Musial, Slaughter, Marty Marion, and Johnny Mize, which dominated the late thirties and early forties.

Meany, Thomas. "Little Big Man: The 1942 Cardinals." In *Baseball's Greatest Teams*, 31-44. New York: A. S. Barnes, 1949.

Combative Billy Southworth, one of the most successful skippers in franchise history (three pennants and two seconds in five short seasons as a full-time manager), leads the wartime Cardinals to perhaps their best season ever, and to a surprising romp over the Yankees in the 1942 World Series. This was the first Yankee Series defeat in nine appearances dating back to 1926; it was also the launching of a Cardinal ballclub starring Musial, Slaughter, Kurowski, Max Lanier, and Mort and Walker Cooper, that would dominate the National League throughout most of the remaining years of the war-torn decade.

Neuman, Jeffrey. *The Cardinals: The Complete Record of Cardinals Baseball*. New York: Collier-Macmillan, 1983. 504 pp.

An early entry in the Macmillan series of statistical team histories, replete with photos, graphs, charts, and extensive SABRmetric summaries of a century of Cardinals' National League baseball. One of the most extensive and user-friendly sources for numerical career records for all former Cardinals players, as well as team and individual club records for many useful pitching and batting categories. Boxscores and linescores for post-season play are a standard highlight of this series.

Stockton, J. Roy. *Gashouse Gang and a Couple of Other Guys*. New York: A. S. Barnes, 1945. 283 pp.

An intimate and often romanticized look at the Cardinals of the Gashouse Gang era, with a primary emphasis on the incomparable pitching tandem of Dizzy and Daffy Dean. The "Other Guys" here turn out to be Cleveland ace hurler Bob Feller, and "them Phillies" of the National League baseball wars, baseball's truest doormats of the World War II era.

Stockton, J. Roy. "The St. Louis Cardinals." In *The National League*, edited by Ed Fitzgerald, 168-211. New York: Grosset and Dunlap, 1966.

A standard chatty team chronicle in one of the best-known earlier anthologies of baseball franchise histories. Beginning with some of baseball's most glorious traditions—the birth of the ballpark hotdog and the Sunday doubleheader—the Cardinals' contributions to major league luster and lore are traced up to the early Bob Gibson years of 1964–65, and to the verge of the great pennant triumphs at the end of that glorious decade of the volatile sixties.

Tiemann, Robert L. *Cardinal Classics: Outstanding Games from Each of the St. Louis Baseball Club's 100 Seasons, 1882-1981*. St. Louis, Mo.: Baseball Histories, Inc., 1982. 268 pp.

An overview of some of the Cardinals' most memorable moments down through the seasons, from the nineteenth-century glory days of Chris Von Der Ahe and Charles A. Comiskey, through the unforgettable slugging of Rogers Hornsby and buffoonery of the Gashouse Gang, down to the age of Stan Musial in the fifties and the domination of Bob Gibson in the sixties. Through the retelling of some of the team's most memorable individual games, the St. Louis Cardinal legacy comes to life.

Honig, Donald. *The St. Louis Cardinals: An Illustrated History*. New York: Prentice-Hall Press, 1991. 244 pp.

The initial offering in a series of formula ballclub histories by this same author (others include the Chicago Cubs, Cincinnati Reds and Philadelphia Phillies, with more certain to follow). While an adequate beginning book for anyone altogether illiterate in Cardinals baseball lore, this volume will certainly disappoint the serious St. Louis ballclub afficionado. The weakness of this particular volume lies in Honig's whirlwind tour through facts and stories already handled deftly—with more inspiration and in far more detail—by baseball scholars like Fred Lieb, Bob Broeg and Robert Tiemann. And for a picture book, this tome suffers equally from the hundreds of grainy black and white photos, the great majority of which are merely uninteresting posed headshots.

Year-by-Year Standings and Season Summaries

Year	Pos.	Record	Pct.	GB	Manager	Player	BA	Player	HR	Player	W-L	ERA
1900	6th	65–75	.464	19.0	Tebeau / Heilbroner	Burkett	.363	Donlin	10	Young	20–18	3.00
1901	4th	76–64	.543	14.5	Donovan	Burkett	.382*	Burkett	10	Harper	23–13	3.62
1902	6th	56–78	.418	44.5	Donovan	Donovan	.315	Smoot	3	O'Neill	18–14	2.93
								Barclay	3			
1903	8th	43–94	.314	46.5	Donovan	Donovan	.327	Smoot	4	Brown	9–13	2.60
1904	5th	75–79	.487	31.5	Nichols	Beckley	.325	Brain	7	Nichols	21–13	2.02
1905	6th	58–96	.377	47.5	Nichols / Burke / Robinson	Smoot	.311	Smoot	4	Taylor	15–21	3.44
								Grady	4			
1906	7th	52–98	.347	63.0	McCloskey	Bennett	.262	Grady	3	Taylor	8–9	2.15
1907	8th	52–101	.340	55.5	McCloskey	Murray	.262	Murray	7	Karger	15–19	2.03
1908	8th	49–105	.318	50.0	McCloskey	Murray	.282	Murray	7	Raymond	15–25	2.03
1909	7th	54–98	.355	56.0	Bresnahan	Konetchy	.286	Konetchy	4	Beebe	15–21	2.82
1910	7th	63–90	.412	40.5	Bresnahan	Konetchy	.302	Ellis	4	Lush	14–13	3.20
1911	5th	75–74	.503	22.0	Bresnahan	Evans	.294	Konetchy	6	Sallee	15–9	2.76
1912	6th	63–90	.412	41.0	Bresnahan	Konetchy	.314	Konetchy	8	Sallee	16–17	2.60
1913	8th	51–99	.340	49.0	Huggins	Oakes	.291	Wilson	7	Sallee	18–15	2.70
1914	3rd	81–72	.529	13.0	Huggins	Miller	.290	Bescher	9	Doak	20–6	1.72
1915	6th	72–81	.471	18.5	Huggins	Synder	.298	several	4	Doak	16–18	2.64
1916	8th	60–93	.392	33.5	Huggins	Hornsby	.313	Hornsby	6	Doak	12–8	2.63
1917	3rd	82–70	.539	15.0	Huggins	Hornsby	.327	Cruise	8	Ames	15–10	2.71
1918	8th	51–78	.395	33.0	Hendricks	Hornsby	.281	Hornsby	6	Packard	12–12	3.50
1919	7th	54–83	.394	40.5	Rickey	Hornsby	.318	McHenry	8	Goodwin	11–9	2.51
1920	6th	75–79	.487	18.0	Rickey	Hornsby	.370*	Hornsby	10	Doak	20–12	2.53
1921	3rd	87–66	.569	7.0	Rickey	Hornsby	.397*	Hornsby	21*	Doak	15–6	2.59
1922	4th	85–69	.552	8.0	Rickey	Hornsby	.401*	Hornsby	42	Pfeffer	19–12	3.58
1923	5th	79–74	.516	16.0	Rickey	Hornsby	.384*	Hornsby	17	Haines	20–13	3.11

Year	Pos.	Record	Pct.	GB	Manager	Player	BA	Player	HR	Player	W-L	ERA
1924	6th	65–89	.422	28.5	Rickey	Hornsby	.424*	Hornsby	25*	Sothoron	10–16	3.57
1925	4th	77–76	.503	18.0	Rickey Hornsby	Hornsby	.403*	Hornsby	39	Sherdel	15–6	3.11
1926	1st	89–65	.578	+2.0	Hornsby	Bell	.325	Bottomley	19	Rhem	20–7	3.21
1927	2nd	92–61	.601	1.5	O'Farrell	Frisch	.337	Bottomley	19	Alexander	21–10	2.52
1928	1st	95–59	.617	+2.0	McKechnie	Hafey	.337	Bottomley	31	Sherdel	21–10	2.86
1929	4th	78–74	.513	20.0	McKechnie Street Southworth	Hafey	.338	Bottomley Hafey	29 29	Johnson	13–7	3.60
1930	1st	92–62	.597	+2.0	Street	Frisch	.346*	Hafey	26	Grimes	13–6	3.01
1931	1st	103–53	.656	+13.0	Street	Hafey	.349	Hafey	16	Hallahan	19–9	3.29
1932	7th	72–82	.468	18.0	Street	Orsatti	.336	Collins	21	D. Dean	18–15	3.30
1933	5th	82–71	.536	9.5	Street Frisch	Martin	.316	Medwick	18*	D. Dean	20–18	3.04
1934	1st	95–58	.621	+2.0	Frisch	Collins	.333	Collins	35	D. Dean	30–7	2.66
1935	2nd	96–58	.623	4.0	Frisch	Medwick	.353	Collins Medwick	23 23	D. Dean	28–12	3.11
1936	2nd	87–67	.565	5.0	Frisch	Medwick	.351*	Mize	19	D. Dean	24–13	3.17
1937	4th	81–73	.526	15.0	Frisch	Medwick	.374	Medwick	31	Warneke	18–11	4.53
1938	6th	71–80	.470	17.5	Frisch Gonzalez	Mize	.337	Mize	27	Weiland	16–11	3.59
1939	2nd	92–61	.601	4.5	Blades	Mize	.349*	Mize	28*	Davis	22–16	3.63
1940	3rd	84–69	.549	16.0	Blades Gonzalez Southworth	Mize	.314	Mize	43*	Warneke	16–10	3.14
1941	2nd	97–56	.634	2.5	Southworth	Mize	.317	Mize	16	McGee	16–10	3.80
1942	1st	106–48	.688	+2.0	Southworth	Slaughter	.318*	Slaughter	13	White	17–7	2.40
1943	1st	105–49	.682	+18.0	Southworth	Musial	.357	Musial Kurowski	13 13	M. Cooper M. Cooper	22–7 21–8	1.78 2.30
1944	1st	105–49	.682	+14.5	Southworth	Musial	.347	Kurowski	20	M. Cooper	22–7	2.46

Year	Pos.		Record	Pct.	GB	Manager	Player	BA	Player	HR	Player	W-L	ERA
1945	2nd		95–59	.617	3.0	Southworth	Kurowski	.323	Kurowski	21	Barrett	21–9	2.74
1946	1st	**	98–58	.628	+2.0	Dyer	Musial	.365	Slaughter	18	Pollett	21–10	2.10
1947	2nd		89–65	.578	5.0	Dyer	Musial	.312	Kurowski	27	Munger	16–5	3.37
1948	2nd		85–69	.552	6.5	Dyer	Musial	.376	Musial	39	Brecheen	20–7	2.24
1949	2nd		96–58	.623	1.0	Dyer	Musial	.338	Musial	36	Pollet	20–9	2.77
1950	5th		78–75	.510	12.5	Dyer	Musial	.346	Pollet	28	Pollet	14–13	3.29
1951	3rd		81–73	.526	15.5	Marion	Musial	.355	Staley	32	Staley	19–13	3.81
1952	3rd		88–66	.571	8.5	Stanky	Musial	.336	Staley	21	Staley	17–14	3.27
1953	3rd		83–71	.539	22.0	Stanky	Schoendienst	.342	Musial	30	Haddix	20–9	3.06
1954	6th		72–82	.468	25.0	Stanky	Musial	.330	Musial	35	Haddix	18–13	3.57
1955	7th		68–86	.442	30.5	Stanky Walker	Musial	.319	Musial	33	Arroyo	11–8	4.19
1956	4th		76–78	.494	17.0	Hutchinson	Musial	.310	Musial	27	Dickson	13–8	3.07
1957	2nd		87–67	.565	8.0	Hutchinson	Musial	.351	Musial	29	Jackson	15–9	3.47
											McDaniel	15–9	3.49
1958	5th		72–82	.468	20.0	Hutchinson Hack	Musial	.337	Boyer	23	S. Jones	14–13	2.88
1959	7th		71–83	.461	16.0	Hemus	Cunningham	.345	Boyer	28	McDaniel	14–12	3.82
1960	3rd		86–68	.558	9.0	Hemus	Boyer	.304	Boyer	32	Broglio	21–9	2.74
1961	5th		80–74	.519	13.0	Hemus Keane	Boyer	.329	Boyer	24	Sadecki	14–10	3.72
1962	6th		84–78	.519	17.5	Keane	Musial	.330	Boyer	24	Jackson	16–11	3.75
1963	2nd		93–69	.574	6.0	Keane	White	.304	White	27	Broglio	18–8	2.99
1964	1st		93–69	.574	+1.0	Keane	Flood	.311	Boyer	24	Sadecki	20–11	3.68
1965	7th		80–81	.497	16.5	Schoendienst	Flood	.310	White	24	Gibson	20–12	3.07
1966	6th		83–79	.512	12.0	Schoendienst	Cepeda	.303	Gibson	17	Gibson	21–12	2.44
1967	1st		101–60	.627	+10.5	Schoendienst	Flood	.335	Cepeda	25	Hughes	16–6	2.67
1968	1st		97–65	.599	+9.0	Schoendienst	Cepeda	.301	Cepeda	16	Gibson	22–9	1.12
1969	4th	***	87–75	.537	13.0	Schoendienst	Brock	.298	Torre	18	Gibson	20–13	2.18
1970	4th		76–86	.469	13.0	Schoendienst	Torre	.325	Allen	34	Gibson	23–7	3.12
1971	2nd		90–72	.556	7.0	Schoendienst	Torre	.363	Torre	24	Carlton	20–9	3.56

Year	Pos.	Record	Pct.	GB	Manager	Player	BA	Player	HR	Player	W-L	ERA
1972	4th	75–81	.481	21.5	Schoendienst	M. Alou	.314	Simmons	16	Gibson	19–11	2.46
1973	2nd	81–81	.500	1.5	Schoendienst	Simmons	.310	Simmons	13	Wise	16–12	3.37
1974	2nd	86–75	.534	1.5	Schoendienst	Smith	.309	Torre	13	McGlothen	16–12	2.70
						McBride	.309	R. Smith	23			
1975	3rd	82–80	.506	10.5	Schoendienst	Simmons	.332	R. Smith	19	Hrabosky	13–3	1.67
1976	5th	72–90	.444	29.0	Schoendienst	Brock	.301	Cruz	13	Denny	11–9	2.52
1977	3rd	83–79	.512	18.0	Rapp	Templeton	.322	Simmons	21	B. Forsch	20–7	3.48
1978	5th	69–93	.426	21.0	Rapp	Hendrick	.288	Simmons	22	Denny	14–11	2.96
					Kroll							
1979	3rd	86–76	.531	12.0	Boyer	Hernandez	.344	Simmons	26	S. Martinez	15–8	3.26
1980	4th	74–88	.457	17.0	Boyer	Hernandez	.321	Hendrick	25	Vuckovich	12–9	3.41
					Kroll							
					Herzog							
					Schoendienst							
1981	2nd	30–20	.600	1.5	Herzog	Hernandez	.306	Hendrick	18	B. Forsch	10–5	3.19
	2nd	29–23	.558	0.5								
1981‡	1st	59–43	.578	+2.0								
1982	1st	92–70	.568	+3.0	Herzog	L. Smith	.307	Hendrick	19	Andujar	15–10	2.47
1983	4th	79–83	.488	11.0	Herzog	Herr	.323	Hendrick	18	Stuper	12–11	3.68
1984	3rd	84–78	.519	12.5	Herzog	McGee	.291	Green	15	Andujar	20–14	3.34
1985	1st	101–61	.623	+3.0	Herzog	McGee	.353	Clark	22	Tudor	21–8	1.93
1986	3rd	79–82	.491	28.5	Herzog	O. Smith	.280	Van Slyke	13	Tudor	13–7	2.96
1987	1st	95–67	.586	+3.0	Herzog	O. Smith	.303	Clark	35	Tudor	10–2	3.84
1988	5th	76–86	.469	25.0	Herzog	McGee	.292	Brunansky	22	DeLeon	13–10	3.67
1989	3rd	86–76	.531	7.0	Herzog	Guerrero	.311	Brunansky	20	Magrane	18–9	2.91
1990	6th	70–92	.432	25.0	Herzog	McGee	.335*	Zeile	15	Tudor	12–4	2.40
					Schoendienst/							
					Torre							
1991	2nd	84–78	.519	14.0	Torre	Jose	.305	Zeile	11	B. Smith	12–9	3.85
1992	3rd	83–79	.512	13.0	Torre	Gilkey	.302	Lankford	20	Tewksbury	16–5	2.16

*Led National League.
**Defeated Brooklyn in two-game playoff, 2–0.
***National League East (first season of divisional play).
‡Split Season Totals (Players' Union Strike).

All-Time Cardinals Career and Season Records

Career Batting Leaders (1900–1992)

Games Played	Stan Musial	3,026
At Bats	Stan Musial	10,972
Runs Scored	Stan Musial	1,949
Hits	Stan Musial	3,630
Batting Average (300 or more games)	Rogers Hornsby	.359
Total Bases	Stan Musial	6,134
Walks	Stan Musial	1,599
Doubles	Stan Musial	725
Triples	Stan Musial	177
Home Runs	Stan Musial	475
Runs Batted In	Stan Musial	1,951
Hitting Streak (consecutive games)	Rogers Hornsby	33 (1922)
Stolen Bases	Lou Brock	888
Pinch Hits	Steve Braun	60

Career Pitching Leaders (1900–1992)

Innings Pitched	Bob Gibson	3,885.0
Earned Run Average (400-plus innings)	John Tudor	2.52
Wins	Bob Gibson	251
Losses	Bob Gibson	174
Winning Pct. (50 decisions)	John Tudor	.705 (62–26)
Strikeouts	Bob Gibson	3,117
Walks	Bob Gibson	1,336
Games	Jesse Haines	554
Shutouts	Bob Gibson	56
Saves	Bruce Sutter	127
Games Started	Bob Gibson	482
Complete Games	Bob Gibson	255

Single-Season Batting Records (1900–1992)

Batting Average (350 ABs)	Rogers Hornsby	.424	1924
Home Runs	Johnny Mize	43	1940
Runs Batted In	Joe Medwick	154	1937
Runs	Rogers Hornsby	141	1922
Hits	Rogers Hornsby	250	1922
Singles	Jesse Burkett	180	1901
Doubles	Joe Medwick	64	1936
Triples	Tom Long	25	1915
Slugging Percentage	Rogers Hornsby	.756	1925
Extra Base Hits	Stan Musial	103	1948
Sacrifice Hits	Harry Walker	36	1943
Stolen Bases	Lou Brock	118	1974
Pinch Hits	Vic Davalillo	24	1970
Strikeouts	Jack Clark	139	1987
Fewest Strikeouts (153 Games)	Frankie Frisch	10	1927
Total Bases	Rogers Hornsby	450	1922

All-Time Cardinals Career and Season Records *(continued)*

Grand Slam Home Runs	Jim Bottomley	3	1935
	Keith Hernandez	3	1977
Hit by Pitch	Lou Evans	31	1910
Games	Bill White	162	1963
	Curt Flood	162	1964
	Ken Boyer	162	1964
At Bats	Lou Brock	689	1967
Walks	Jack Clark	136	1987

Single-Season Pitching Records (1900–1992)

ERA (150 innings)	Bob Gibson	1.12	1968
ERA (lefthanded)	Howie Pollet	1.75	1943
Wins	Dizzy Dean	30	1934
Losses	Grant McGlynn	25	1907
	Art Raymond	25	1908
Winning Pct. (10 decisions)	Howie Krist	1.000 (10–0)	1941
Strikeouts	Bob Gibson	274	1970
Walks	Bob Harmon	181	1911
Saves	Lee Smith	47	1991
Games	Todd Worrell	75	1987
Complete Games	Jack Taylor	39	1904
Games Started	Bob Harmon	41	1911
Games Finished	Bruce Sutter	63	1984
Shutouts	Bob Gibson	13	1968
Innings Pitched	Grant McGlynn	352.1	1907
Home Runs Allowed	Murry Dickson	39	1948
Hits Allowed	Jack Powell	351	1901
Runs Allowed	Jack Powell	194	1900
Consecutive Games Won	Bob Gibson	15	1968
Consecutive Games Lost	Bill McGee	9	1938
	Tom Poholsky	9	1951
	Bob Forsch	9	1978
Wild Pitches	Fred Beebe	15	1907
			1909
	Dave LaPoint	15	1984
Hit Batsmen	Gerry Staley	17	1953

13

Colorado Rockies
Rocky Mountain High, For Awhile
PETER C. BJARKMAN

Colorado Rockies Pre-History

Expansion sagas have always been the cruelest joke our national pastime has to foist upon its dedicated legions of unwavering fans. The 1961 Washington Senators, leading the thin ranks of rooters in the nation's capital to pine nostalgically for those earlier legitimate Senators ragtag outfits who were always "first in war, first in peace, and last in the American League" but at least looked something like big league pretenders. Gene Woodling, Coot Veal and Pete Burnside were hardly a fair overnight exchange for Harmon Killebrew, Jim Lemon and Camilo Pascual! The 1962 New York Mets who established standards for futility and ineptitude that left a whole nation of ballfans wondering "Can't anybody here play this game?" And the 1969 Seattle Pilots, lasting only a single lackluster season in a sport whose rock solid foundations are longevity and unwavering franchise stability.

Media pundits and self-appointed baseball experts unanimously agreed well in advance of November 17, however, that the 1992 baseball expansion draft would be quite different from those four laughable roster-filling expansion lotteries (1961, 1962, 1969 and 1977) of baseball's past history. And as a result, the add-on ballclubs stocked by this current round-robin would likely have a quite different look from the lame also-ran outfits of seasons long lost—forgettable and uncompetitive teams that had to fill out opening-day batting orders with a pathetic list of "has-beens" and "never-weres" named Steve Bilko, Albie Pearson, Dale Long, Jay Hook, Jim Hickman, Ken Aspromonte, Marv Throneberry, Joe Foy, Mack Jones, Mike Hegan, Angel Hermoso, Don Mincher, Coco Laboy, Ollie Brown, Ruppert Jones, Bob Bailor, and Dave Lemanczyk.

The prime reasons for such a different flavor to this 1992 expansion giveaway were altogether obvious, perhaps even to inexperienced baseball watchers. This time around players would be chosen from both leagues and not just from a single circuit as in 1969 (Pilots, Royals, Expos and Padres) and 1977 (Mariners and

Blue Jays). More dramatically, high-salaried big-ticket-item ballplayers were not likely to be protected on the 15-man lists of "untouchables" allowed each existing club this time around. The World Champion Toronto Blue Jays would throw established stars like Jack Morris, Kelly Gruber and Jimmy Key onto the offering table; New York's Mets would risk losing slugger Eddie Murray, while Chicago's White Sox would gamble with productive RBI-man George Bell and former saves-king Bobby Thigpen. Issues governing player personnel had, after all, changed drastically from bygone years of diamond play. Before it was a simple matter of protecting your best hitters and throwers; on-field playing talent alone was the sole yardstick in making such crucial roster decisions. Now a beleaguered general manager had to take into consideration thorny issues of long-term contracts, huge and sometimes unwanted salaries, fine-print contract conditions on trades, and other such dollars-and-cents matters. The result was that high-profile players like Lee Smith (Cardinals), Candy Maldonado and Manny Lee (Blue Jays), Kirk McCaskill (White Sox), Otis Nixon (Braves), Shawon Dunston (Cubs) and others of similar proven talent would be available for plucking by anyone with a teeming bank account and a clear penchant for financial suicide.

Another factor—true baseball people considered it the most important if least publicized factor—was not to be overlooked either. The frenetic (even scientific) scouting activities of these new teams over the past season were altogether unprecedented in baseball history. For better than fifteen months the Rockies (under scouting director Pat Daugherty and player development director Dick Balderson) and their rivals, the embryonic Florida Marlins (led by counterparts Gary Hughes and John Boles), had scanned the majors and minors from big-time to bush leagues and from spring planting to autumn harvest in a sweeping search for the very best in available young slugging, hurling, fielding and baserunning talent.

In the afterglow of November's historical Draft Day '92, few could dispute that it had been the Rockies of Colorado who had best exploited these novel features of this 1992 drafting format. While the Florida Marlins followed a timeworn and familiar path of past expansion drafts and opted for a long and risky look into the dim future, the team from Denver seemed driven by a philosophy of building as much as possible for the season immediately at hand. Thus with the very first round of the November 17th draft the Rockies came close, indeed, to filling out what might be anything but an embarrassing Opening Day line-up for April 5, 1993. First the outfield was stocked with the likes of Jerald Clark (Padres), Alex Cole (Pirates), and Texas Rangers designated hitter Kevin Reimer (though this latter pick would be quickly traded to Milwaukee for more talented flychaser Dante Bichette). Then the infield was glued together with New York Yankees hot corner star Charlie Hayes at third, promising Cincinnati Reds utility man Freddie Benavides and Los Angeles Dodgers hopeful Eric Young forming a classy keystone combination, veteran Andres Galarraga (acquired a day earlier through free agency) at first, and Chicago Cubs journeyman Joe Girardi behind the plate. Torrid mound prospect David Nied, the overall first selection, would obviously be an Opening Day starting pitcher, Milwaukee's Darren Holmes (4–4, 2.55 ERA in 1992) the middle reliever, and Scott Aldred (Tigers) or Willie Blair (Astros) the makeshift veteran closer.

Projected Draft-Day Colorado Rockies Starting Lineup

CF Alex Cole
SS Freddie Benavides
LF Jerald Clark
3B Charlie Hayes
RF Dante Bichette
1B Andres Galarraga
C Joe Girardi
2B Nelson Liriano
P David Nied

On the surface of it, this seemed like a strange way for a spanking new ballclub—especially this particular new club—to draft its first droves of building-block talent. The Rockies had already sold 24,000 full-season tickets, after all, and certainly they didn't need to lure fans with established if fading big league faces during their maiden season. Yet when all was said and done the Colorado field generals had selected ballplayers as if 1992 ticket sales and not 1996 pennant hopes were the key franchise motives. The order of the day in Denver, from round one on, was obviously familiar big league names. This did not mean going for those high-priced available stars which both teams shunned with equal wisdom, but it did mean taking players like Hayes, Cole, Girardi, and Aldred in the first round, then younger veterans like Junior Felix and Fred Benavides in later rounds. It seemed as though GM Bob Gebhard, player development director Dick Balderson, scouting director Pat Daugherty, and chief scout Larry Bearnarth universally preferred ballplayers they had all personally seen in big league settings as they crisscrossed the majors during the previous summer. One had to grant that these Rockies would now be able to field an opening day line-up that had anything but a "minor league" look, especially when one added to the draft roster the free-agent signings of such veterans as slick gloveman

Andres Galarraga and former Blue Jays, Twins and Royals infielder Nelson Liriano.

Colorado front office braintrust also demonstrated an acute awareness of the thin mountain air that would be flowing through their home field when they stocked up on a small truckload of draft-day long-ball hitters. From the inventory of major league veterans were plucked Charlie Hayes (18 dingers in 1992 with the Yankees), Jerald Clark (whose occasional righthanded power produced a career-high 22 1992 doubles in San Diego), and Kevin Reimer (traded for equal-potential powerman Dante Bichette); from the minors would come Jim Tatum, already a popular Denver hero after his league-leading .329 BA, 19 HRs and 101 RBI for the American Association Zephyrs. But pitching was not entirely ignored in the process either. And here again the accent was on those players with previous proven big league experience. A long list of journeymen hurlers tabbed by the Rockies included Willie Blair (Houston, 5–7, 4.00 ERA), Scott Aldred (Detroit, 3–8, 6.78 ERA), Darren Holmes (Milwaukee, 4–4, 2.55 ERA), and Calvin Jones (Seattle, 3–5, 5.69 ERA). And these trusted and partially proven arms were joined by prospects like Andy Ashby (Philadelphia, 1–3, 7.54 ERA) Denis Boucher (Cleveland, 2–2, 6.37 ERA), Lance Painter (AA Wichita, 10–5, 3.53 ERA), and Keith Shepherd (Philadelphia, 1–1, 327 ERA), all also boasting at least a brief taste of the big league mound. The Rockies also apparently liked catchers, employing four of their first 27 selections to tab potential starting backstops.

That the Rockies would depart radically from standard approaches to earlier expansion drafts was not altogether surprising in light of the inaugural activities of this latest of baseball expansion ballclubs. A somewhat different way of thinking was best showcased when it came to selection of a field manager. It was indeed a bold and popular step after all to tab former big-league slugger Don Baylor for the top bench post, especially against the present backdrop of baseball's highly checkered record of sporadic minority hiring. A true skeptic might claim that again the neophyte club seemed to have the issue of ticket sales foremost in mind. Baylor was, after all, a familiar and much-loved big league name, but a man whose reputation had been earned on the playing field (338 career homers over 19 seasons) and not from the manager's benchwarming seat. Baylor had enjoyed only five games as an interim skipper for Milwaukee in 1991 while Brewers boss Tom Trebelhorn had served out a brief suspension, but the bulk of Baylor's limited bench experience had come in the 1992 campaign as a hitting instructor with the St. Louis Cardinals. Now he would not only have to occupy the hot spot as an expansion manager faced with lengthy droughts of inevitable losing, but also as one of the game's few black-skinned skippers as well. Nonetheless, it was somehow ironically appropriate that an expansion ballclub would tab a black manager to launch the 1993 campaign. Only days before Baylor had been appointed to join the ranks of pioneers like Frank Robinson, Larry Doby, Maury Wills, Felipe Alou and Hal McRae, Toronto's Cito Gaston (himself once a starting outfielder for the expansion San Diego Padres) had become the first man of his race to pilot a ballclub in the Fall Classic. Now even expansion baseball would have a minority manager assigned to the game's most thankless and arduous job of surviving at the big league level with a roster of strictly minor league talent.

Other building blocks of the organization also seemed sound enough and held considerable promise for a winning baseball future. Colorado had mirrored the activities of their expansion rivals in Miami by raiding one of baseball's most respected front offices— that of the Montreal Expos—for the backbone of their executive and front office personnel. John McHale, Jr.—no stranger to expansion headaches as son of the first chief executive in Montreal—was lured from a successful Colorado law practice to become the new club's first Executive Vice-President for Baseball Operations. General manager and Senior VP Bob Gebhard had himself spent thirteen seasons with the Expos front office before enjoying four summers as player personnel director with the Minnesota Twins. Even Scouting Director Pat Daugherty had once cut his baseball teeth in a similar position with the Montreal front office for a full half dozen seasons.

All this painstaking construction of a major league franchise had indeed been launched well over a year and a half earlier. And it had begun against a considerable backdrop of negativism and doubt surrounding the area's true baseball viability. Colorado's mountain capital had actually been something of a surprise selection for baseball expansion when it had won out over Buffalo and Washington, as well as over a second Florida site in either St. Petersburg, Tampa or even Orlando. Yet the reason for Denver's first-place finish in the June 1991 expansion sweepstakes was not altogether inexplicable, given today's reigning baseball orientations. Here was a huge untapped television market spreading throughout the Rocky Mountain time zone and stretching across the southwest desert states of Arizona and New Mexico as well. Such a TV factor would itself be sufficient to override Denver's often spotty record in past ventures at supporting high-level minor league baseball.

Certainly it was true that Denver had been a minor league hotbed way back in the baseball golden years of the fifties. As home site for Yankees Triple-A talent farm, Denver's Bears nursed big league talents like Tony Kubek, Bobby Richardson, Johnny Blanchard, Ryne Duren, Ralph Terry and Don Larsen—soon enough World Series heroes all. And the largest minor league crowd (65,666 on July 3, 1982) had been once drawn to Mile High Stadium for patriotic fireworks and the American Association's Denver Bears. But Denver's minor league attendance track record of late, perhaps hampered by affiliation with the Milwaukee Brewers, was poor indeed when compared with rival expansion sites and minor-league hotbeds like Buffalo and Louisville. Denver was pro football country after all. The sale of 20,000-plus season tickets for a much-hyped opening campaign itself couldn't cool the skepticism of many veteran baseball watchers, especially concerning this mountain city's prospects for supporting an expansion team at today's needed attendance levels and over the long haul of almost certain losing seasons.

Baseball fever and Rockies fever, nonetheless, seemed to be reaching epidemic pitch in the weeks just before and after Expansion Draft Day 1992. Attracted as much by "hip" fashion statement as by any legitimate baseball interest, youngsters around the country were now found sporting the sleek raven-colored Rockies cap with its attractive white double-strike "CR" logo. The Colorado Rockies were apparently already an overnight merchandizing success in this bottom-line era of promotions and glitzy product marketing. Now it only remained to be seen if interest would remain at the same frenzied peak once the April cry of "play ball!" was heard throughout the nation's ballparks. Would it again be the all-too-typical scenario of first-year Mudville blues? Or would an aura of "Rocky Mountain High" soon spur a legitimate challenge to the existing expansion record of 70 victories by baseball's very first "new kid on the block"—the 1961 Los Angeles Angels?

In baseball, Opening Day is indeed always a time for renewed hope and for the joyful if always somewhat naive shout of "Wait until this year!" And why after all should it be any different in an interloper city without any past pennant disasters that yet cry out for the constant balm of springtime renewal!

Rockies Front-Office Lineup

Chairman, Chief Executive Officer
Jerry McMorris
President and CEO, NW Transport Service

Chief Executive Officer, President
John Antonucci
Owner and CEO, Superior Beverage Company

Executive Vice-President, Baseball Operations
John McHale, Jr.
Member, Denver Baseball Commission and practicing Denver attorney-at-law

Senior Vice-President, Chief Financial Officer
Kevin Jordan
Chief Financial Officer for several multinational companies (with Denver-based CONCORD Group)

Senior Vice-President, Baseball Operations
Bernie Mullen
Senior Vice-President for Baseball Operations, Pittsburgh Pirates (1986–1990)

Vice-President, Sales
Dave Glazier
Manager of Sports Sales for WLWT-TV, Cincinnati (1990–1991)

Senior Vice-President, Public Affairs
Dean Peeler
Public Affairs Manager, Exxon Corporation (1981–1991)

Senior Vice-President, General Manager
Bob Gebhard
13 seasons in Montreal Expos organization and 4 years as Minnesota Twins Vice President

Assistant General Manager
Randy Smith
Director of Scouting, San Diego Padres (1988–1991)

Director of Player Development
Dick Balderson
Director of Scouting, Chicago Cubs (1989–1991)

Director of Scouting
Pat Daugherty
Scouting Supervisor for 6 seasons with Montreal Expos

Field Manager
Don Baylor
Batting Instructor and Coach, St. Louis Cardinals (1992)

Colorado Rockies Expansion Draft Selections

First Round (*Experienced major league player)

Pick	Name	Position (Age)	1992 Franchise	1992 Ballclub (Highest)
1	David Nied	RHP (24)	Atlanta Braves	Atlanta Braves
2	Charlie Hayes	3B (27)*	New York Yankees	New York Yankees
3	Darren Holmes	RHP (26)*	Milwaukee Brewers	Milwaukee Brewers
4	Jerald Clark	LF (26)*	San Diego Padres	San Diego Padres
5	Kevin Reimer#	LF (28)	Texas Rangers	Texas Rangers
6	Eric Young	2B (25)	Los Angeles Dodgers	Los Angeles Dodgers
7	Jody Reed##	2B (30)*	Boston Red Sox	Boston Red Sox
8	Scott Aldred	LHP (24)*	Detroit Tigers	Detroit Tigers
9	Alex Cole	RF (27)*	Pittsburgh Pirates	Pittsburgh Pirates
10	Joe Girardi	C (28)*	Chicago Cubs	Chicago Cubs
11	Willie Blair	RHP (26)*	Houston Astros	Houston Astros
12	Claude "J" Owens	C (23)	Minnesota Twins	Orlando (AA)
13	Andy Ashby	RHP (25)*	Philadelphia Phillies	Philadelphia Phillies

#Traded to Milwaukee Brewers for outfielder Dante Bichette
##Traded to Los Angeles Dodgers for RHP Rudy Seanez

Second Round (*Experienced major league player)

Pick	Name	Position (Age)	1992 Franchise	1992Ballclub (Highest)
14	Fred Benavides	SS (26)*	Cincinnati Reds	Cincinnati Reds
15	Roberto Mejia	2B (20)	Los Angeles Dodgers	Vero Beach (A)
16	Doug Bochtler	RHP (22)	Montreal Expos	Harrisburg (AA)
17	Lance Painter	LHP (25)	San Diego Padres	Wichita (AA)
18	Butch Henry	LHP (24)*	Houston Astros	Houston Astros
19	Ryan Hawblitzel	RHP (21)	Chicago Cubs	Charlotte (AA)
20	Vinnie Castilla	SS (25)*	Atlanta Braves	Atlanta Braves
21	Brett Merriman	RHP (26)	California Angels	Edmonton (AAA)
22	Jim Tatum	3B (25)	Milwaukee Brewers	Denver (AAA)
23	Kevin Ritz	RHP (27)*	Detroit Tigers	Detroit Tigers
24	Eric Wedge	C (24)*	Boston Red Sox	Boston Red Sox
25	Keith Shepherd	RHP (24)	Philadelphia Phillies	Philadelphia Phillies
26	Calvin Jones	RHP (29)*	Seattle Mariners	Seattle Mariners

Third Round (*Experienced major league player)

Pick	Name	Position (Age)	1992 Franchise	1992 Ballclub (Highest)
27	Brad Ausmus	C (23)	New York Yankees	Columbus (AAA)
28	Marcus Moore	RHP (21)	Toronto Blue Jays	Knoxville (AA)
29	Armando Reynoso	RHP (26)*	Atlanta Braves	Richmond (AAA)
30	Steve Reed	(RHP (26)	San Francisco Giants	San Francisco Giants
31	Mo Sanford	RHP (25)	Cincinnati Reds	Nashville (AAA)
32	Pedro Castellano	3B (22)	Chicago Cubs	Iowa (AAA)
33	Curtis Leskanic	RHP (24)	Minnesota Twins	Portland (AAA)
34	Scott Fredrickson	RHP (25)	San Diego Padres	Wichita (AA)
35	Braulio Castillo	OF (24)*	Philadelphia Phillies	Philadelphia Phillies
36	Denis Boucher	LHP (24)*	Cleveland Indians	Cleveland Indians

Rockies Memorable Franchise "Firsts"

First Scheduled Game: April 5, 1993 versus New York Mets at Shea Stadium (New York)

First Scheduled Home Game: April 9, 1993 versus Montreal Expos at Mile High Stadium (Denver)

First Manager: Don Baylor (no previous major league managerial experience)

First General Manager: Bob Gehhard (former VP for Player Personnel with Minnesota Twins)

First Owner: Colorado Baseball Partnership, headed by John Antonucci (CEO for the Superior Beverage Group)

First Coaches: Ron Hassey (1st Base), Jerry Royster (3rd Base), Amos Otis (Hitting Instructor)

First AAA Minor League Affiliate: Colorado Springs Sky Sox, Pacific Coast League

First Player on 40-Man Roster: Travis Buckley, RHP

First Trade: Acquired Travis Buckley (RHP) from Montreal Expos for player to be named later (November 9, 1992)

First Household-Name Roster Player: Andres Galarraga, 1B (signed as free agent on November 16, 1992)

First Player Selected in Expansion Draft: David Nied, RHP from Atlanta Braves

First Uniform: Black, Silver and White pinstripped, with "CR" logo on black cap and "Rockies" in block letters on uniform front

First Ballpark: Mile High Stadium (home of NFL Denver Broncos); 75,000 seating capacity; Baseball Dimensions: LF–335 Ft.; CF–420Ft., RF–345 Ft.

First Play-by-Play Announcer: Jeff Kingery (Radio)

Colorado Rockies First 40-Man Roster (Spring 1993)

Position	Name	Bats/ Throws	Age	1992 Big League Experience
Pitcher	David Nied	R/R	23	Atlanta Braves
Pitcher	Darren Holmes	R/R	26	Milwaukee Brewers
Pitcher	Scott Aldred	L/L	24	Detroit Tigers
Pitcher	Willie Blair	R/R	29	California Angels
Pitcher	Andy Ashby	R/R	26	Houston Astros
Pitcher	Doug Bouchtler	R/R	22	None
Pitcher	Lance Painter	L/L	25	None
Pitcher	Butch Henry	L/L	24	Houston Astros
Pitcher	Ryan Hawblitzel	R/R	21	None
Pitcher	Brett Merriman	R/R	26	None
Pitcher	Kevin Ritz	R/R	27	Detroit Tigers
Pitcher	Keith Shepherd	R/R	24	Philadelphia Phillies
Pitcher	Calvin Jones	R/R	29	Seattle Mariners
Pitcher	Marcus Moore	B/R	22	None
Pitcher	Armando Reynoso	R/R	26	Atlanta Braves
Pitcher	Steve Reed	R/R	26	San Francisco Giants

Colorado Rockies First 40-Man Roster (Spring 1993) *(continued)*

Position	Name	Bats/ Throws	Age	1992 Big League Experience
Pitcher	Mo Sanford	R/R	25	None
Pitcher	Curtis Leskanic	R/R	24	None
Pitcher	Scott Fredrickson	R/R	25	None
Pitcher	Denis Boucher	R/L	24	Cleveland Indians
Pitcher	Rudy Seanez	R/R	24	Los Angeles Dodgers
Catcher	Joe Girardi	R/R	28	Chicago Cubs
Catcher	Claude "J" Owens	R/R	23	None
Catcher	Brad Ausmus	R/R	23	None
Infielder (3B)	Charlie Hayes	R/R	27	New York Yankees
Infielder (2B)	Eric Young	R/R	25	Los Angeles Dodgers
Infielder (SS)	Fred Benavides	R/R	26	Cincinnati Reds
Infielder (2B)	Roberto Mejia	R/R	20	None
Infielder (SS)	Vinny Castilla	R/R	25	Atlanta Braves
Infielder (1B)	Jim Tatum	R/R	25	Milwaukee Brewers
Infielder (1B)	Eric Wedge	R/R	24	Boston Red Sox
Infielder (3B)	Pedro Castellano	R/R	22	None
Outfielder	Jerald Clark	R/R	29	San Diego Padres
Outfielder	Alex Cole	L/L	27	Pittsburgh Pirates
Outfielder	Braulio Castillo	R/R	24	Philadelphia Phillies
Outfielder	Dante Bichette	R/R	29	Milwaukee Brewers

36 players on roster as of December 1, 1992

Comparisons With the Past

Previous Major League Expansion Team Records and Statistics (#)

Team	Year	Record (Place)	Avg.	Runs	Hits	HRs	ERA	Shutouts
Los Angeles Angels	1961	70–91 (8th)	.245	744	1331	189	4.31	5
Washington Senators	1961	61–100 (10th)	.244	618	1307	119	4.23	8
Houston Colt 45's	1962	64–96 (8th)	.246	592	1370	105	3.83	9
New York Mets	1962	40–120 (10th)	.240	617	1318	139	5.04	4
Kansas City Royals	1969	69–93 (4th)	.240	586	1311	98	3.72	10
Seattle Pilots	1969	64–98 (6th)	.234	639	1276	125	4.35	6
Montreal Expos	1969	51–110 (6th)	.240	582	1300	125	4.33	8
San Diego Padres	1969	52–110 (6th)	.225	468	1203	99	4.24	9
Seattle Mariners	1977	64–98 (6th)	.256	624	1398	133	4.83	1
Toronto Blue Jays	1977	54–107 (7th)	.252	605	1367	100	4.57	3

#Records and Statistics courtesy of the Florida Marlins and *USA Today Baseball Weekly*

Previous Expansion No. 1 Draft Picks

Ballclub	Year	No. 1 Pick	Expansion Year Performance
Los Angeles Angels (AL)	1961	Eli Grba (RHP)	11–13, 4.25 ERA
Washington Senators (AL)	1961	Bobby Shantz (LHP)	Traded for 3 minor leaguers
Houston Colt 45's (NL)	1962	Eddie Bressoud (SS)	Traded for Don Buddin (SS)
New York Mets (NL)	1962	Hobie Landrith (C)	Traded for Marv Throneberry (1B)
Kansas City Royals (AL)	1969	Roger Nelson (RHP)	7–13, 3.31 ERA
Seattle Pilots (AL)	1969	Don Mincher (1B)	.246 BA, 24 HRs, 78 RBI
Montreal Expos (NL)	1969	Manny Mota (IF)	Traded for Ron Fairly (OF)
San Diego Padres (NL)	1969	Ollie Brown (OF)	.264 BA, 20 HRs, 61 RBI
Seattle Mariners (AL)	1977	Ruppert Jones (OF)	.263 BA, 24 HRS, 76 RBI
Toronto Blue Jays (AL)	1977	Bob Bailor (SS)	.310 BA, 5 HRs, 32 RBI

14

Florida Marlins
Baseball's Big Splash in the Caribbean
PETER C. BJARKMAN

Florida Marlins Pre-History

It of course wouldn't be the Detroit Tigers or Boston Red Sox or Chicago Cubs—proud century-old ballclubs sporting ancient venerable playing grounds and steeped in eons of sustaining diamond tradition. Yet a National League ballclub playing in the palm-lined city of Miami and named Marlins somehow seemed like a natural phenomenon which should already have happened years, even decades ago. Southern Florida had long been ready for big-time baseball, and baseball couldn't be more ready for a home within southern Florida. After all, this had been the resting place of the national pastime's favorite renewal ritual—spring training—for almost the entire century. And it is cradle as well to the nation's bulging and baseball-crazy population of recent Hispanic and Caribbean immigrants, many of them transplanted from the island nations of Cuba and Puerto Rico where baseball is as indigenous as it is anywhere in rural Missouri or sunny California. More pragmatically—in this age of multi-million-dollar salaries and big-business promotion—there is the matter of a massive untapped Florida public and cable television market. America's favored pastime just doesn't seem like it can fail to be a summer-long hit within the fan-rich Sunshine State.

Dedicated "ney-sayers" have for some time dismissed Miami and touted rival expansion sites like Buffalo, Memphis and Washington by claiming that mid-summer rain showers will likely wash out a third of the big league contests scheduled from June through late August. But nature's wrath and daily thunder clouds hadn't ever dampened the enthusiasm of south Florida fans who had flocked to Miami Stadium in the mid-fifties to witness ageless pitching legend Satchel Paige (he was at least 55 at the time) dazzle International League opponents for the proud Miami Marlins of an earlier epoch. And it was clear from the start that those running the new Florida franchise, from the highest level of management on down to the public relations staffers, were well aware of the multitude of factors sustaining the idea of Florida big league baseball. They were thus primed to market their product on an extensive statewide basis. This regional effort was most evident in the choice of franchise name— a merging of the familiar "Marlins" moniker, offering its invocation of a rich minor league tradition, with the place-name of the entire state, an appeal to fan-support stretching from Biscayne Bay to west coast Tampa, inland Orlando and Jacksonville of the far north.

Yet the statewide appeal of this new Florida big league franchise would unfortunately suffer a severe blow before the Marlins ever even played their first official senior circuit game. Potential disaster arose with the parallel efforts of rival forces in the Tampa Bay region, themselves bent on securing a big league club of their very own. Citizens in the twin cities of Tampa and St. Petersburg were much embittered by the awarding of an expansion team to rival Miami in early summer 1991. After all, it had been almost a forgone conclusion when expansion plans had been first announced several seasons earlier that a new ballclub would be placed somewhere within the population-rich state of Florida. But residents of the central regions were not the least bit thrilled that Miami won and they had lost. Local merchants and politicians saw only one scenario in the birth of the big league Marlins—millions of dollars in anticipated commerce and tourism escaping southward toward Dade County. West coast state residents were hardly to be pacified by the promise of televised coverage of a team that was theirs in name only and that resided several hundred miles outside their backyard community.

And then there were still further cracks in the marriage of east and west coast Florida baseball interests. A futile effort by St. Petersburg city fathers to attract either the Seattle Mariners (spring 1992) or later the San Francisco Giants (summer 1992) to take up residence in the vacant Suncoast Dome (which already failed in 1989 to lure the escape-minded White Sox out of their American League roost in the Windy City) would only further alienate mid-state fans from the Miami club and its wealthy owner, Wayne Huizenga. Huizenga was blamed by enraged Tampa fans and media as the villain who had lured baseball out from under them during expansion competition, and then (so the belief stood) lobbyed behind the scenes with other National League owners to eventually block a possible Giants franchise shift as well. As the first exciting season of play approached for the Marlins, many embittered residents of the Tampa area threatened to withhold both their TV-viewing support and their ticket-buying dollars from the state's new showcase big league club. Only time would tell if the boycott might amount to much, or if it would have any real impact on the Marlins' future box office fortunes.

If Marlins ownership couldn't win over hardened Tampa Bay fans seemingly far more concerned with regional pride than with any prospect of big league baseball in their own backyard, they could indeed take steps to cement a following among the majority of the region's hardcore baseball fans. And those first tentative steps were boldly taken on the afternoon of the 1992 major league expansion draft. For it was in that draft lottery that the new Miami ballclub dramatically demonstrated its apparent commitment to stock the organization with a healthy supply of exciting young prospects boasting genuine long-term potential. The Marlins shunned high-priced free agents who might have added some name recognition but offered little in the way of overnight on-field success. Instead of George Bell or Jack Morris or Kelly Gruber, it would be Bret Barbarie and Trevor Hoffman and Jose Martinez and Nigel Wilson to fire up the local fandom.

The Florida Marlins brass indeed handed their fans and their franchise a promising future on Draft Day. While Colorado seemed preoccupied with a successful Opening Day lineup geared to April 5, 1993, the Sunshine Staters remained determined to worry about the present later and thus to concentrate on the future now. Marlins headman Wayne Huizenga was quick to point out that there was still plenty of time between mid-November and the first flurries of spring training to fill out a 40-man roster through trades and free agent deals. The Marlins, moreso than the Rockies, would obviously be looking to free agents (albeit moderate free agents like Orestes Destrade or Scott Fletcher and not bank-breaking mercenaries like Bobby Bonds or Joe Carter) over the coming winter months.

But the news on Draft Day was a full stable of promising young prospects. Heading the list were Nigel Wilson in the outfield, Bret Barbarie and Jeff Conine in the infield, and a lengthy "wish list" of young pitchers to flesh out a rotation and staff a bullpen. Wilson, a native of Canadian soil who belted 26 homers with AA Knoxville, is an unquestioned prospect, yet the 6–1, 185-pound all-lefty slugger will most likely require another full season of ripening somewhere within the high minors. There are questions about Wilson's defense for one thing, and his arm is at best average after suffering a separated shoulder three seasons back. Barbarie struggled early in 1992 after much buildup and after being handed the third base job in Montreal, but by late season he was again demonstrating that he could play everyday in the big leagues. Conine has overcome a serious 1991 wrist injury and now seems ready after batting at a .302 clip for AAA Omaha. And among the pitchers the three standouts seemed to be Trevor Hoffman (7–6 between AAA and AA in the Cincinnati organization), Jose Martinez (the Mets top pitching prospect who was the only 20-game winner in the minors during 1991) and Pat Rapp (earlier projected as a starter for San Francisco in 1993). Yet the starting rotation (likely to be Scott Chiamparino, David Weathers, Pat Rapp, Ryan Bowen and Jack Armstrong) will be a huge question mark going into the first months of the new season. This is clearly the immediate weak point of the ballclub and one can't feel too good about the chances of a team that may have to tap Jack Armstrong (2–13 with Cleveland in 1992) as its most likely Opening Day moundsman.

Projected Draft-Day Florida Marlins Starting Lineup

CF Chuck Carr
LF Monty Fariss
2B Bret Barbarie
1B Jeff Conine
RF Junior Felix
C Rob Natal
SS Walt Weiss
3B Gary Scott
P Jack Armstrong

The Marlins demonstrated a noteworthy fascination with right-handed pitchers as the November 17th draft rapidly unfolded. In the second round they would grab eight of these orthodox mounds-men in a row: viz., Cris Carpenter, Jack Armstrong, Scott Chiampar-ino, Tom Edens, Andres Berumen, Robert Person, Jim Corsi, and Richie Lewis. And then Dombrowski pulled off three big trades to close out the draft festivities. In the most spectacular move, White Sox lefthander Greg Hibbard departed immediately after his first round selection (Florida's sixth pick) to the Chicago Cubs in exchange for promising but unfulfilled infielders Gay Scott and Alex Arias. Catcher Eric Helfand (first round, ninth pick) was a prospect Tony LaRussa and Oakland had not truly wanted to relinquish, and Helfand was soon enough shipped back to the Bay Area for the A's player Miami really wanted, game-wise if unspectacular shortstop Walt Weiss. Finally, lefty hurler Danny Jackson (3rd round, 27th pick) went to Philadelphia and righty Tom Edens (2nd round, 22nd pick) to Houston, both moves bringing two valued young pitching prospects (Joel Adamson and Matt Whisenant from the Phillies and Hector Carrasco and Brian Griffiths via the Astros).

One thing clearly ironic about this Miami franchise from its earliest days was the degree to which the ballclub seemed linked by fate and planning to the far north county of baseball's hinterland—Canada. Two of the first three ballplayers taken in the expansion draft, of course, had noteworthy Canadian connections. Nigel Wilson had been plucked from the Toronto roster and was in fact himself a Toronto native (his father had been a cricket star in Trinidad who later emigrated to Ontario). Bret Barbarie, though California-born, was nonetheless a cherished prospect out of the Montreal Expos organization. But all this was not after all inexplicable. Much of the front office staff—starting with GM Dombrowski and his assistant Frank Wren, and including Scouting Director Gary Hughes and Player Development Director John Boles as well—had been assembled overnight by raiding the self-same Montreal organization. And now it was clear with the youth-movement draft that the same philosophy would be employed here by the very people who had quickly built Montreal into one of the finest top-to-bottom organizations in all baseball. They had done it on the baseball frontier in Montreal with very little available cash. Perhaps here the same daring approach, backed by Huizenga's large pocketbook, would bring even more startling results. Miami fans could reasonably nurse fond dreams that it would be so.

Of course all the emphasis wasn't entirely on the new and the novel with this expansion Florida ballclub. When it came to selecting a field manager, for example, it would be an often-recycled name, culled from baseball's timeworn old-boy network, and not a fresh face at all that would eventually come to the fore. Rene Lachemann can boast of little previous big league success (207–274, no finish higher than 4th and three last-place prizes) with managing winning baseball. Fired from his last post after losing 94 games for Milwaukee in 1984, Lachemann has been biding his time for six seasons as a bench assistant and third base coach under Tony LaRussa in Oakland. But perhaps this two-time loser (also fired by Seattle's Mariners after three earlier losing campaigns) would possess just the necessary patient personality and mandatory sense of humor required to steer a youth-glutted expansion ballclub.

Lachemann also filled out his staff with other altogether familiar big league faces—Marcel Lachemann, Cookie Rojas, Doug Rader and Vada Pinson. Pitching coach Marcel Lachemann (7–4, 3.45 ERA in three abbreviated big league seasons with Oakland) was brother to the manager and had teamed with his younger sibling once before on a major league bench. Hitting instructor Doug Rader once held a reputation as one of the game's biggest flakes during his own lengthy playing days. Yet as a manager himself, Rader had indeed known a measure of success in the not-too-distant past over a five-year span (1983–1986, 1989) as head man with the Rangers, White Sox and Angels. Vada Pinson was a one-time Cincinnati hitting legend (four-time .300-plus hitter) who had already put in several seasons as a base coach under Sparky Anderson in Detroit. And third base signal-caller Cookie Rojas, a native Cuban, seemed something of a concession to the Latin population to which the team would apparently have to appeal for hometown support. While available Latinos like Rojas, Manny Mota and Tony Perez had been passed over for the Miami managerial slot, the presence of Rojas on the bench was more than just a ceremonial token. Cookie had been one of the few previous Latin skippers in the big leagues (as California Angels boss in 1988), and his baseball know-how had consistently received the highest technical marks among his contemporaries.

It might also be noted in profiling Florida's expansion ballclub that the much-discussed Marlins' Montreal front office bloodlines not only trumpet bright prospects for a winning baseball organization, but may well also echo some of the zaniness and a touch of the bizarre that has always shadowed Canada's own first expansion franchise. The Marlins' inaugural uniforms, for example, seem to challenge those once worn in Montreal (the tri-colored beanies sported from 1969 through 1991) as the most garish and silly flannels ever donned by a National League ballclub. And uniforms are not the only potential embarrassment for the fledgling Marlins. An inaugural home playing grounds within the NFL venue of the Miami Dolphins is filled with every bit the same potential for disaster as the ill-starred Olympic Stadium in Montreal. A March 1992 trial spring training contest between the Yankees and Braves, for example, had almost been cancelled within an hour of game time when rival managers were horrified to discover that the untutored Miami grounds crew had neglected to install pitching mounds within the two bullpens. And constant rainouts in Miami during July pose the same ominous threat in the tropics that frigid early and late season snowfalls have long offered for Quebec.

But none of this could dim the euphoria of southern Florida fans who were now exulting in the fact that long overdue major league baseball had finally been dropped into their very own backyard. And what a season, indeed, to start up an expansion saga— the first new season after baseball's most recent expansion ballclub (and the only one since the Cinderella New York Mets) had just become the sport's reigning World Series champions. Would Miami boast the next Blue Jays or the next Mets? Or were tropical baseball fans about to be saddled with a resurrected version of the moribund Seattle Pilots? The safest bet, of course, was that any answer was at least several pennant races down the road.

Marlins Front-Office Lineup

Owner
H. Wayne Huizenga
Owner, Blockbuster Entertainment Corporation

President, Chief Operating Officer
Carl Barger
Chief Operating Officer, Pittsburgh Pirates (1988–1991)

Vice-President, Finance
Jonathan Mariner
Vice-President of Finance and Administration, Greater Miami Convention and Visitors Bureau

Vice-President, Communications
Dean Jordan
Director of Broadcasting and Advertising, Pittsburgh Pirates (1987–1990)

Vice-President, Business Operations
Richard Andersen
Vice-President of Administration and Operations, Pittsburgh Pirates (1987–1991)

Vice-President, Sales
Don Smiley
Various administrative posts with Huizenga Holdings and Blockbuster Entertainment Corporation

Executive Vice-President, General Manager
Dave Dombrowski
General Manager, Montreal Expos (1990–1991)

Assistant General Manager
Frank Wren
Assistant Scouting Director, Montreal Expos (1986–1991)

Director of Scouting
Gary Hughes
Director of Scouting, Montreal Expos (1986–1991)

Director of Player Development
John Boles
Director of Player Development, Montreal Expos (1990–1991)

Field Manager
Rene Lachemann
Former manager of Seattle Mariners and Milwaukee Brewers

Florida Marlins Expansion Draft Selections

First Round (*Experienced major league player)

Pick	Name	Position (Age)	1992 Franchise	1992 Ballclub (Highest)
1	Nigel Wilson	OF (22)	Toronto Blue Jays	Knoxville (AA)
2	Jose Martinez	RHP (21)	New York Mets	Binghamton (AA)
3	Bret Barbarie	IF (25)*	Montreal Expos	Montreal Expos
4	Trevor Hoffman	RHP (25)	Cincinnati Reds	Nashville (AAA)
5	Pat Rapp	RHP (25)	San Francisco Giants	San Francisco Giants
6	Greg Hibbard#	LHP (28)*	Chicago White Sox	Chicago White Sox
7	Chuck Carr	CF (24)	St. Louis Cardinals	St. Louis Cardinals
8	Darrell Whitmore	RF (24)	Cleveland Indians	Kingston (A)
9	Eric Helfand##	C (23)	Oakland Athletics	Oakland Athletics
10	Bryan Harvey	RHP (29)*	California Angels	California Angels
11	Jeff Conine	1B (26)*	Kansas City Royals	Kansas City Royals
12	Kip Yaughn	RHP (23)	Baltimore Orioles	Hagerstown (AA)
13	Jesus Tavares	CF (21)	Seattle Mariners	Jacksonville (AA)

#Traded to Chicago Cubs for infielders Alex Aries and Gary Scott
##Traded back to Oakland Athletics for shortstop Walt Weiss

Second Round (*Experienced major league player)

Pick	Name	Position (Age)	1992 Franchise	1992 Ballclub (Highest)
14	Carl Everett	OF (22)	New York Yankees	Ft. Lauderdale (A)
15	Dave Weathers	RHP (23)*	Toronto Blue Jays	Syracuse (AAA)
16	John Johnstone	RHP (23)	New York Mets	Binghamton (AA)
17	Ramon Martinez	SS (23)	Pittsburgh Pirates	Salem (A)
18	Steve Decker	C (27)*	San Francisco Giants	San Francisco Giants
19	Cris Carpenter	RHP (27)*	St. Louis Cardinals	St. Louis Cardinals
20	Jack Armstrong	RHP (27)*	Cleveland Indians	Cleveland Indians
21	Scott Chiamparino	RHP (26)*	Texas Rangers	Texas Rangers
22	Tom Edens#	RHP (31)*	Minnesota Twins	Minnesota Twins
23	Andres Berumen	RHP (21)	Kansas City Royals	Appleton (A)
24	Robert Person	RHP (23)	Chicago White Sox	Sarasota (A)
25	Jim Corsi	RHP (31)*	Oakland Athletics	Oakland Athletics
26	Richie Lewis	RHP (26)	Baltimore Orioles	Baltimore Orioles

#Traded to Houston Astros for righthanded pitchers Brian Griffiths and Hector Carrasco

Third Round (*Experienced major league player)

Pick	Name	Position (Age)	1992 Franchise	1992 Ballclub (Highest)
27	Danny Jackson#	LHP (30)*	Pittsburgh Pirates	Pittsburgh Pirates
28	Rob Natal	C (27)*	Montreal Expos	(Indianapolis (AAA)
29	Jamie McAndrew	RHP (25)	Los Angeles Dodgers	Albuquerque (AAA)
30	Junior Felix	OF (25)*	California Angels	California Angels
31	Kerwin Moore	OF (22)	Kansas City Royals	Memphis (AA)
32	Ryan Bowen	RHP (24)	Houston Astros	Houston Astros
33	Scott Baker	LHP (22)	St. Louis Cardinals	St. Petersburg (A)
34	Chris Donnels	3B (26)	New York Mets	New York Mets
35	Monty Farris	OF (25)*	Texas Rangers	Texas Rangers
36	Jeff Tabaka	LHP (28)	Milwaukee Brewers	El Paso (AA)

#Traded to Philadelphia Phillies for lefthanded pitchers Joel Adamson and Matt Whisenant

Marlins Memorable Franchise "Firsts"

First Scheduled Game: April 5, 1993 versus Los Angeles Dodgers at Joe Robbie Stadium (Miami)

First Scheduled Road Game: April 12, 1993 versus San Francisco Giants at Candlestick Park

First Manager: Rene Lachemann (former manager for Seattle Mariners and Milwaukee Brewers)

First General Manager: Dave Dombrowski (former GM of Montreal Expos)

First Owner: Wayne Huizenga (video rental tycoon, Blockbuster Videos)

First Coaches: Marcel Lachemann (Pitching Coach), Cookie Rojas (3rd Base, Infield Instructor), Vada Pinson (1st Base), Doug Rader (Hitting), Frank Reberger (Bullpen)

First AAA Minor League Affiliate: Edmonton (Canada) Trappers, Pacific Coast League

First Player on 40-Man Roster: Nigel Wilson OF (from Toronto Blue Jays)

First Trade: Acquired Alex Arias (SS) and Gary Scott (3B) from Chicago Cubs for Greg Hibbard (LHP) on November 17, 1992

First Household-Name Roster Player: Bryan Harvey (RHP and relief ace with California Angels, taken as 10th pick in first round of Expansion Draft)

First Player Selected in Expansion Draft: Nigel Wilson, OF prospect from Toronto Blue Jays

First Uniform: Teal, Black and White pinstripped, with "F" encircled by jumping marlin on teal cap and "Marlins" in block letters on uniform front

First Ballpark: Joe Robbie Stadium (home of NFL Miami Dolphins); 67,500 seating capacity; Baseball Dimensions: LF–335 Ft.; CF–410 Ft.; RF–345 Ft.

First Play-by-Play Announcers: Joe Angel (Radio, English) Dave O'Brien (Radio, English), Jay Randolph (TV, English), Gary Carter (TV, English), Selo Ramirez (Radio, Spanish), Manolo Alvarez (Radio, Spanish)

Florida Marlins First 40-Man Roster (Spring 1993)

Position	Name	Bats/ Throws	Age	1992 Big League Experience
Pitcher	Jose Martinez	R/R	22	None
Pitcher	Trevor Hoffman	R/R	25	None
Pitcher	Pat Rapp	R/R	25	San Francisco Giants
Pitcher	Bryan Harvey	R/R	29	California Angels
Pitcher	Kip Yaughn	R/R	23	None
Pitcher	David Weathers	R/R	23	None
Pitcher	John Johnstone	R/R	23	None
Pitcher	Cris Carpenter	R/R	27	St. Louis Cardinals
Pitcher	Jack Armstrong	R/R	27	Cleveland Indians
Pitcher	Scott Chiamparino	L/R	26	Texas Rangers
Pitcher	Andres Berumen	R/R	21	None
Pitcher	Robert Person	R/R	23	None
Pitcher	Jim Corsi	R/R	31	Oakland Athletics
Pitcher	Richie Lewis	R/R	26	Baltimore Orioles
Pitcher	Jamie McAndrew	R/R	25	None
Pitcher	Ryne Bowen	R/R	24	Houston Astros
Pitcher	Scott Baker	L/L	22	None
Pitcher	Jeff Tabaka	R/L	28	None
Pitcher	Hector Carrasco	R/R	23	None
Pitcher	Brian Griffiths	R/R	24	None
Pitcher	Joel Adamson	L/L	21	None

Florida Marlins First 40-Man Roster (Spring 1993) *(continued)*

Position	Name	Bats/ Throws	Age	1992 Big League Experience
Pitcher	Matt Whisenant	R/L	21	None
Catcher	Steve Decker	R/R	26	San Francisco Giants
Catcher	Rob Natal	R/R	27	Montreal Expos
Infielder (2B)	Bret Barbarie	B/R	25	Montreal Expos
Infielder (1B)	Jeff Conine	R/R	26	Kansas City Royals
Infielder (SS)	Ramon Martinez	R/R	24	None
Infielder (3B)	Chris Donnels	L/R	26	New York Mets
Infielder (3B)	Gary Scott	R/R	24	Chicago Cubs
Infielder (SS)	Alex Arias	R/R	24	Chicago Cubs
Infielder (SS)	Walt Weiss	B/R	28	Oakland Athletics
Outfielder	Nigel Wilson	L/L	22	None
Outfielder	Chuck Carr	B/R	24	St. Louis Cardinals
Outfielder	Darrell Whitmore	L/R	24	None
Outfielder	Jesus Tavarez	R/R	21	None
Outfielder	Carl Everett	B/R	22	None
Outfielder	Junior Felix	B/R	25	California Angels
Outfielder	Kerwin Moore	R/R	22	None
Outfielder	Monty Fariss	R/R	25	Texas Rangers

39 players on roster as of December 1, 1992

Comparisons With the Past

Individual Player Expansion Team Records (#)
Individual Hitting

Batting Average	.310	Bob Bailor	Toronto Blue Jays	1977
At-Bats	597	Ruppert Jones	Seattle Mariners	1977
Runs Scored	92	Albie Pearson	Los Angeles Angels	1961
Hits	166	Rusty Staub	Montreal Expos	1969
Doubles	30	Danny O'Connell	Washington Senators	1961
Triples	9	Marty Keough	Washington Senators	1961
	9	Charlie Neal	New York Mets	1962
	9	Al Spangler	Houston Colt 45's	1962
	9	Nate Colbert	San Diego Padres	1969
Home Runs	34	Frank Thomas	New York Mets	1962
Runs Batted In	94	Frank Thomas	New York Mets	1962
Stolen Bases	73	Tommy Harper	Seattle Pilots	1969

Individual Pitching

Wins	13	Gene Brabender	Seattle Pilots	1969
	13	Dave Lemanczyk	Toronto Blue Jays	1977
Losses	24	Roger Craig	New York Mets	1962
ERA	3.01	Dick Farrell	Houston Colt 45's	1962
Games	74	Dan McGinn	Montreal Expos	1969
Innings Pitched	252	Dave Lemanczyk	Toronto Blue Jays	1977
Games Started	36	Ken McBride	Los Angeles Angels	1961
Complete Games	13	Roger Craig	New York Mets	1962
	13	Jay Hook	New York Mets	1962
Shutouts	5	Bill Stoneman	Montreal Expos	1969
No-Hitters*	1	Bill Stoneman	Montreal Expos	1969
Saves	16	Vincente Romo	Seattle Mariners	1977
Walks	123	Bill Stoneman	Montreal Expos	1969
Strikeouts	203	Dick Farrell	Houston Colt 45's	1962

*No-Hitters during expansion season only
#Records and Statistics courtesy of Florida Marlins and *USA Today Baseball Weekly*

Contributors

Paul D. Adomites (Pittsburgh Pirates). A resident of Pittsburgh, Adomites is former publications director for the Society for American Baseball Research and editor of *The SABR Review of Books,* an annual discussion of baseball's numerous books and rich literature. Freelance writer and editor, author of *The Bridges of Pittsburgh* and numerous articles on topics as diverse as ethnic cooking and the history of technology.

Art Ahrens (Chicago Cubs). Co-author (with Eddie Gold) of several volumes on Chicago Cubs history, including *Day by Day in Chicago Cubs History* (Leisure Press, 1982) and *The Golden Era Cubs, 1876–1940* (Bonus Books, 1985). Graduate of the University of Illinois, Chicago Circle, a lifelong Chicago resident, and active contributing member of the Society for American Baseball Research.

Peter C. Bjarkman (a.k.a. "Doctor Baseball") (Introduction, Cincinnati Reds, Brooklyn-Los Angeles Dodgers, Montreal Expos, Philadelphia Phillies, Colorado Rockies, Florida Marlins). Freelance author and baseball historian who has published coffee-table histories of the Los Angeles Dodgers, Brooklyn Dodgers, Cincinnati Reds and Toronto Blue Jays, written several inspirational biographies (Roberto Clemente, Duke Snider, Ernie Banks) for juvenile readers, and is presently completing books on baseball's role in American literature and on Latin American baseball history and Latin American big-league players.

Stan W. Carlson (St. Louis Cardinals). Member of the Society for American Baseball Research and longtime Minneapolis resident. Freelance writer as well as owner and publisher of Olympic Press, and author of several baseball titles, including *The Wind-Up Baseball Annual* (1939, 1940) and *Lou Gehrig, Baseball's Ironman* (Garrard, 1940).

John M. Carroll (Houston Colt .45s-Astros). Professor of American History at Lamar University and resident of Beaumont, Texas. Author of numerous professional articles in the field of diplomatic history and member of the Society for American Baseball Research. Recently published an article on the origins of Texas baseball in *Southwestern Historical Quarterly* and is author of *Fritz Pollard: An American Pioneer* (University of Illinois Press, 1990).

Pete Cava (New York Mets). Press Information Director of the Athletics Congress for the United States, America's governing body for track and field. Author of numerous baseball book reviews, a longtime active member of the Society for American Baseball Research, and currently a resident of Indianapolis, Indiana.

Morris Eckhouse (Boston-Milwaukee-Atlanta Braves). Freelance author of baseball books and articles and executive director of the Society for American Baseball Research. Co-author of *This Date in Pittsburgh Pirates History* (Stein and Day, 1980) and of a juvenile biography of Bob Feller. Currently a resident of South Euclid, Ohio, Eckhouse served as chairman of SABR's 1990 20th Annual National Convention in Cleveland, Ohio.

David L. Porter (San Diego Padres). Louis Tuttle Shangle Professor of History and Political Science at William Penn College in Oskaloosa, Iowa, and member of both the Society of American Baseball Research and the Sports History Society of North America, as well as other professional and academic historical societies. Editor of the massive five-volume *Biographical Dictionary of American Sports* (Greenwood, 1987–1990) and author of several books on congressional history and the New Deal era.

Fred Stein (New York-San Francisco Giants). Lifetime Giants fan who first discovered the Polo Grounds in the 1930s and has since written prolifically on Giants history in *Under Coogan's Bluff: A Fan's Recollection of the New York Giants Under Terry and Ott* (Chapter and Cask, 1978) and *Giants Diary: A Century of Giants Baseball in New York and San Francisco* (with Nick Peters). Longstanding member of the Society for American Baseball Research and 35-year resident of Northern Virginia suburbs of Washington, D.C.